The Lotus Guide tc

LOTUS BOOKS Pathways to Mastery Series

Who Should Read This Book

For novice to advanced-intermediate users. This book helps you quickly master 1-2-3 Release 2.3's spreadsheet tools and find the answers, reminders, and pointers you need to be productive with 1-2-3 in new ways.

What's Inside

- Accessible, incisive tutorials covering all the new features in Release 2.3 and a wealth of shortcuts, good ideas, and tips to extend your spreadsheet skills
- Special techniques for printing presentation-quality reports with Wysiwyg, the new spreadsheet publishing add-in
- In-depth coverage of business math—shows you how to do *more* with @functions
- Convenient tear-out command guide (at the back of the book) and a handy cheat sheet (between pages 7 and 8) for easy reference while you work

About *LOTUS BOOKS*

LOTUS BOOKS, written in collaboration with Lotus Development Corporation, help you derive the most from Lotus software. There are four series within Lotus Books:

Start Here books introduce beginning users to Lotus software with simple step-by-step instructions.

Pathways to Mastery titles provide the authoritative perspective and expertise from Lotus. Each book is a fast-paced, clear, and concise guide that helps you build on what you know and teaches new product features quickly.

Business Solutions books concentrate on using software to meet your specific business and professional needs; they provide essential tools for working faster and smarter.

Technical Reference titles provide advanced information for experts, programmers, and applications developers.

The Lotus Guide to 1-2-3 Release 2.3

Daniel Gasteiger
Nicholas Delonas

BRADY
LOTUS BOOKS

New York London Toronto Sydney Tokyo Singapore

LOTUS BOOKS

Published by Brady
A division of Simon & Schuster, Inc.
in association with Lotus Publishing

Manufactured in the United States of America

10 9 8 7 6 5 4 3 2 1

ISBN: 0-13-529371-5

Acknowledgments

The authors extend thanks to Susan Hunt for initiating this project; to Ellie McCarthy for her edit of the original manuscript; to Steve Ormsby for his technical review of the manuscript; to Betsy Staples for her copy edit of the manuscript; to Julie O'Leary for her administrative help; to Penny Gibson for keeping things on track; and to Sharon Lee for her management of an often grueling production schedule. Special thanks to Stacy Gasteiger without whom this book wouldn't yet be a completed manuscript.

Dedication

The authors dedicate this book to their respective parents: Edgar and Charlotte Gasteiger, and John and Nadia Delonas.

Limits of Liability and Disclaimer of Warranty

Trademarks

Contents

Introduction

If you understand the fundamentals of working with 1-2-3, then this book is for you. It takes you beyond the basics and teaches what you need to know to apply 1-2-3 to all your business problems. The text strives to explain topics so that even novice users can understand and apply the concepts.

By working through the book, you'll gain a thorough understanding of 1-2-3's features. You'll see how to lay out spreadsheets and how to manipulate and analyze data. You'll also learn how to clarify and enhance information in the sheet, how to emphasize data by graphing it, and how to prepare printed output that catches the reader's attention. The information this book offers can turn 1-2-3 into your most powerful tool for business.

The book contains six sections, each divided into chapters. The sections focus on specific aspects of using the spreadsheet—general spreadsheet tasks, creating formulas and applying @functions, using the data analysis features, creating reports based on the sheet, and writing macros. Chapters focus on specific tasks and tools. For example, within the Formulas section a chapter explains how to create string formulas and how to use string-related @functions.

The material late in the book builds on information in earlier chapters. However, you shouldn't have too much trouble if you prefer to skip around among the chapters. Each one pretty much stands on its own.

And, if you don't want to read so much, don't worry. We've highlighted key points and other amusing tidbits throughout the book. You're bound to find something of interest even if you just flip pages. The discussions in this book provide enough detail to allow novice spreadsheet users to follow along. However, if the material moves a little quickly for you, consider reading one of the texts aimed at beginning spreadsheet users.

One appropriate source for review is the Start Here series published beginning March 1989 in *LOTUS* magazine. That material forms the basis of an upcoming Lotus Book, *Start Here With 1-2-3*—an ideal text to prepare new spreadsheet users for the material in this book. Look for it in autumn of 1991.

The big news about 1-2-3 Release 2.3 is Wysiwyg (pronounced wizzy-wig). Wysiwyg is an add-in that provides 1-2-3 with a graphical user interface (GUI) and spreadsheet publishing features. With Wysiwyg active you can create boxes around spreadsheet cells and ranges; apply shading to spreadsheet ranges; alter fonts, font styles, and font sizes; insert graphs into the spreadsheet; and customize graphs to the smallest detail. With 1-2-3 and Wysiwyg you can produce slick reports that rival those produced by dedicated desktop publishing systems.

Even without Wysiwyg attached, Release 2.3 has a new mouse-driven user interface that mimics a GUI. This means that you can issue commands and perform procedures as you always have in 1-2-3, or you can apply a mouse during your work sessions. The spreadsheet's mouse-driven interface is quite similar to Wysiwyg's, so you can use the mouse in either environment.

The first chapter of the book explores the use of the mouse interface with the old, familiar spreadsheet—without Wysiwyg attached. It should help you decide whether to use a mouse. Other chapters explore keystroke commands and techniques that, when mastered, let you perform certain spreadsheet tasks more quickly than you could with a mouse. The subsequent material shows no preference for the keyboard or a mouse. Throughout we report appropriate command sequences and leave it to you to use the mouse or the keyboard as you desire.

Should you start reading with the first chapter? That depends. There are plenty of features in Release 2.3 that didn't exist in Lotus Development Corporation's 2.x spreadsheet line. The Prologue offers an overview of those new features for people who are upgrading or who are considering the upgrade from Release 2.01 or 2.2. The information in the Prologue won't necessarily get you using 1-2-3's latest features, but it will give you a good idea of what this new release has to offer.

Preface: What's New in 2.3

Should you use 1-2-3 Release 2.3? You may feel that you already get just about everything you need from Release 2.2 or Release 2.01. On the other hand, Lotus may have added enough nifty stuff to their premier spreadsheet product to make the upgrade worthwhile. You be the judge.

If you're considering an upgrade, an abbreviated overview of Release 2.3's new features might help you make up your mind. If you have already upgraded, you can use the overview to help spot the new features you've been anticipating. But first, there are two points that you might be pleased to know.

Keep Your Computer

Lotus 1-2-3 Release 2.3 runs in 320K of RAM on an IBM or compatible computer. Most other full-featured computer spreadsheets, including 1-2-3 Releases 3 and 3.1, require at least a megabyte of RAM and an 80286-based (AT class) machine. It's very unlikely you'll need to upgrade your hardware to run Release 2.3.

Remain Compatible

Release 2.3 creates files with .WK1 extensions. These files differ slightly from the Release 2.2 worksheet files, but not enough to be incompatible. Release 2.3 files are downwardly compatible with Releases 2.2 and 2.01. 1-2-3 Release 2.3 can read files that have .WKS, WK1, .WRK and .WR1 worksheet formats.

Variations on Old Themes

One Key Cell Erasure

Users have carped for years about the /Range Erase command. Four keystrokes to erase a single cell is excessive. In Release 2.3, pressing the Delete key while 1-2-3 is in Ready mode blanks the current cell.

Use Wildcards to Search Spreadsheet Ranges

You can use the wildcard characters ? and * in your search string when you issue the /Range Search command. The wildcard characters work here as they do in DOS and in database querying operations.

Added Confirmation Steps

When you select /Worksheet Erase Yes or you select /File Retrieve and specify a filename, Release 2.3 alerts you if you haven't saved since last modifying the sheet. You have the option of proceeding or terminating the command.

Fast Directory Changes

In Release 2.3 when you select /File Directory, you can edit the existing directory path. In earlier releases of 1-2-3, you had to type over the existing directory setting.

Efficient Memory Use with LIM 4.0

If you have expanded memory that conforms to the Lotus/Intel/Microsoft memory specification version 4.0, you can create larger spreadsheets than ever before. A user-selectable option lets you trade off speed and compatibility with add-ins designed for earlier releases of 1-2-3 in exchange for more RAM storage.

Drive with a Mouse

With or without Wysiwyg, 1-2-3 lets you use a mouse to issue commands to get around in the spreadsheet. For many tasks, working with a mouse is quicker than working with only the keyboard.

Dialog with the Sheet

In keeping with the mouse interface, in Release 2.3, dialog boxes replace settings sheets. You can still select such settings as global cell formats and recalculation order via menus. However, if you prefer you can activate dialog boxes and simply click the settings you want. The first few chapters of the book tell you more about dialog boxes.

Indicate Ranges in Advance

Also to complement the mouse interface, Release 2.3 lets you select a range before you issue a command that affects that range. If you press the ABS key (F4) while 1-2-3 is in Ready mode, you can highlight a range, but dragging the mouse also preselects a range. Such commands as /Range Erase, /Range Format, and so on, automatically use the highlighted range at the point where you normally indicate a range.

New Graph Options

Release 2.3 offers several new graph options. For example, you can have Release 2.3 fill in the area under a line graph, display bar graphs vertically or horizontally, and even create three-dimensional bar graphs. We explore the graphing options of 1-2-3 in depth in the Spreadsheet Output section.

More Efficient Printing

With a little advanced preparation, you can enable Release 2.3 to print in the background, thus freeing you to work in the sheet while your printer is running. A new printing option lets you create encoded print files that contain whatever printer codes 1-2-3 normally uses to control the printer. When you print encoded files from DOS, any special formatting and text attributes established within the sheet emerge on the printed page. We expand on this a bit in the section on spreadsheet output.

Altered Database

Release 2.3's data query commands and @D functions ignore blank rows in a criterion range if any row contains a criterion. Earlier releases of 1-2-3 assume that extra blank rows mean "select all records." Also, criteria entered as labels can begin with the operators <, >, =, <>, >=, and <=. 1-2-3 assumes that such a criterion refers to the database field identified by the field header above the criterion. This simplifies criteria for database querying operations.

New Macro Features

Learn Mode Abbreviates Macros

The Macro Learn mode you know (and love?) stores a macro command for each keystroke it records—even when those strokes are sequences of LeftArrow or RightArrow key presses. Release 2.3's Learn mode abbreviates sequences of cursor movement key presses. For example, the old Learn mode commands {D}{D} become {D 2} in 1-2-3 Release 2.3.

Further Macro Enhancements

Four new macro commands in Release 2.3 provide the ability to create slick fill-in-the-blank data entry forms under macro control. The {FORM} command is similar to the Range Input command, but it lets you redefine the meanings of selected keystrokes. The {FORMBREAK} command terminates operations started by a {FORM} command. The {APPENDBELOW} command copies data from a source location to the row beneath a target location. Then it expands existing range name definitions downward to incorporate the copied data. The {APPENDRIGHT} command copies data to the right of a target location and expands range name definitions to the right.

Add-Ins

What-You-See-Is-What-You-Get Spreadsheet Publishing

The Wysiwyg add-in lets you apply lines and shading to spreadsheet ranges. With it you can alter the fonts and fonts styles of spreadsheet entries. You can place graphs in the sheet and soup up the graphs with arrows, boxes, and text labels. In contrast to work with Allways, the spreadsheet publishing add-in included with Release 2.2 of 1-2-3, you can do all of this directly in the spreadsheet and still have access to all the standard 1-2-3 commands. There's more about Wysiwyg in later sections.

Ride the Audit Trail

A new add-in that comes with 1-2-3 Release 2.3 helps you to follow a spreadsheet's audit trail. Borrowing technology from Lotus's HAL add-in, the Auditor quickly finds and reveals all formulas in the sheet, all the cells involved in circular references, all the cells that contribute to calculations in the current cell, and all the cells whose calculations depend in any way on a selected cell.

Magellanesque File Viewing

Release 2.3 includes an add-in called Viewer. Drawing on technology from Lotus's Magellan, Viewer lets you examine the contents of spreadsheet files before you retrieve them. This can save a lot of time when you're searching for a spreadsheet whose name you can't remember. Viewer also helps you establish file-linking formulas.

More New Features of Release 2.3

We haven't listed all of the new features of 1-2-3 Release 2.3. The latest version of the program includes new printer drivers, a new user-controllable display color scheme, a modified Help facility, modified error handling, and more. While we explore some of the new features in the remainder of this book, we do not delve into them specifically. Where appropriate we point out ways that Release 2.3 performs differently from earlier releases of the spreadsheet software.

Foreword

We at Lotus are pleased to present to you the latest in a line of classic spreadsheets: 1-2-3 Release 2.3, the fastest graphical spreadsheet yet developed.

Our vision in developing 1-2-3 Release 2.3 is to enhance vastly the spreadsheet's ease of use and graphical attractiveness. At the same time, we desire to maintain the speed and compact size of the product, which enable it to run swiftly on all generations of PCs. This is the most popular spreadsheet in the world, and we aim to keep it that way.

You will find the product more visually appealing, with colorful screens and mouse support built into the product. The Wysiwyg functions enable you to apply fonts, bolding, color—all while your spreadsheet is active. Your spreadsheet background colors can also be configured with Wysiwyg. Graphic editing has been vastly enhanced. In addition, 1-2-3 Release 2.3 now supports new chart types (horizontal, mixed, frame on/off and 3D effects) to improve your capability to analyze and present your data.

A major stride forward in useability is presented with on line tutorials, a very helpful help system, improved error handling, and interactive dialog boxes to quicken the pace with which you can accomplish your spreadsheet tasks. With the interactive dialog boxes, you can now set up the graphs or print jobs without long strings of menu commands.

One of the major aids to useability will certainly be the Viewer. Accessed from the /Add-In Attach menu, the Viewer incorporates Lotus Magellan technology, which enables a spreadsheet user to see the contents of a file on disk before it is retrieved. This will save many minutes of looking for just the right file and make file linking much easier.

Printing is also much easier and of much higher quality with the Wysiwyg function. And you will love being able to automatically compress your work to fit on a single page!

Other new features include the Auditor, an add-in which enables you to trace the logic in your spreadsheet. It is especially helpful in checking that your model is sound or in decoding someone else's work.

My personal vision for 1-2-3 Release 2.3 is that it will make spreadsheet users much more productive by reducing the time it takes to accomplish a task. I believe it will also make 1-2-3 much more accessible to people who use numbers or data but who, up to now, found the spreadsheet too difficult to learn or use. And for those of you already knowledgeable in 1-2-3 but who want to enhance your ability to use it to solve your business problems, I hope you find this new version not only more capable, but easier to learn.

Eileen M. Rudden
General Manager, DOS Spreadsheets
Lotus Development Corporation

Section 1
Life in the Sheet

It's possible that you use computers and, consequently, 1-2-3 because you have to, not because you want to. Perhaps someone gave you a computer and software and simply left you to struggle along on your own. On the other hand, you might have been handed a collection of spreadsheets that someone else assembled to simplify your involvement with 1-2-3. Whatever the case, by the time you buy a book about how to use 1-2-3, you've probably decided that knowing more about the product can help with your work.

Lotus 1-2-3 can help with your work—quite often in direct proportion to how well you understand and can apply the software. With a solid grounding in the spreadsheet's capabilities, you can analyze the health of your business, project next year's earnings, prepare slick reports on your department's progress, and maintain large customer databases. This book gives you that grounding.

Part of your success with 1-2-3 will grow from the perspective that you bring to it. To its early adopters, the electronic spreadsheet was like a scratch pad. Accomplished users treat the spreadsheet as a large piece of blank paper. They drop in numbers, labels, and formulas to create rough representations of the problems the spreadsheet can solve. Then they move things around, apply cell formatting, alter column widths, superimpose more numbers, labels, and formulas, and so on. Eventually, they produce worksheets that can accept new data, perform complex calculations, and print reports far more quickly than they could without the software.

The point is, work from the moment you decide to build a model until you produce a finished product is freeform. Within 1-2-3's rules you can fiddle all you want and eventually produce a handy business model. To some degree, working in a spreadsheet is computer doodling. That's the inspiration for this section.

Believe it or not, there are few computing tasks that 1-2-3 can't handle when you apply the right commands. This section explores procedures and tasks that should become second nature as you increase your spreadsheet proficiency. It also introduces some commands that solve common spreadsheet problems.

The section begins by exploring the mouse interface. It moves from there into keyboard techniques for navigating in the spreadsheet. Then it discusses ways to customize the spreadsheet. It includes an in-depth exploration of the Copy and the Move commands, an overview of how the function keys work, and a look at a potpourri of features that don't fit into a specific category but can be very useful. The section continues with a discussion of commands that let you work with data from many files and closes with an explanation of add-ins—particularly the three that come with 1-2-3: Viewer, Auditor, and Wysiwyg.

By the time you work through this section of the book, you will be well on your way to being a proficient spreadsheet doodler.

1

A Rodent on Your Desk: Work in a GUI

Being able to use a mouse could dramatically affect your approach to working with 1-2-3. A mouse can replace the arrow keys for navigation in the sheet. It can also eliminate your involvement with the slash key to access the menus. Because of its global usefulness, you should become familiar with the capabilities of the mouse. If you don't yet own a mouse, you may decide to buy one when you see how it works.

The new mouse interface is available to you if you have a mouse properly installed on your computer and you selected a mouse driver when you installed 1-2-3. There is no need to install or attach an add-in. The mouse interface mimics a classic GUI—Graphical User Interface.

One striking characteristic of a GUI is the way that it empowers a mouse. Rather than pressing the slash key to produce a menu, you can activate menus simply by moving the mouse around on your desk. In a spreadsheet, you can select ranges in the same manner. You make selections from menus by pressing the mouse button.

There are some advantages to working with a mouse. For example, most GUIs are easier to learn than their textual counterparts. On the other hand, if you're proficient with the keyboard, you may resist adopting a mouse.

Like them or not, GUIs and mice are here to stay, and some of the tasks you'll do in Release 2.3 are far easier if you use a mouse. Once you understand how the

In this chapter you will:

- *Learn how a graphical user interface (GUI) differs from a textual interface*
- *Learn what an icon is*
- *Use a mouse (if you have one) to build a small spreadsheet model*
- *Use the navigation icons*
- *Learn how a mouse accesses the Help facility*
- *Learn what a dialog box is*
- *Use a mouse to work with dialog boxes*
- *Use the keyboard to modify settings in a dialog box*

mouse works in 1-2-3, you'll be able to decide for yourself whether to add one to your system.

What Is This Graphical Stuff Anyway?

Perhaps you've heard the term GUI bandied about, but you're not sure you know what it means. Understanding GUIs can help you make up your mind about using a mouse.

The classic 1-2-3 display is textual; the individual elements on the display consist of text characters. Typically, there is room on such a display for 80 characters across and 25 characters down.

Each of the allowable textual display characters corresponds to a numeric code—a number from 0 to 255. Most of the allowable characters are letters of the alphabet and numbers; others are punctuation marks and arithmetic operators such as plus and equal signs. A few more of the textual display characters are geometric shapes, such as vertical and horizontal lines, which when grouped properly make up boxes and borders to enhance the presentation of the more common textual elements.

Each character is made up of an array of points (pixels), but your software doesn't need to know that to make the characters appear. Rather, 1-2-3 simply directs numeric codes to your computer's display adapter (the plug-in card that determines what type of monitor your computer can use). The adapter activates groups of pixels in specific character positions as directed by the software.

Since there are only 2,000 character positions on the display, very little information must pass from 1-2-3 to the display adapter to alter what you see. Little or no time elapses between the moment you issue a command that alters the display and the moment the display actually changes. That's the benefit of textual displays and interfaces—even on the slowest computers they respond very quickly.

In contrast, drawing a graphical display is quite time-consuming. To create a graphical display, software must activate each of the pixels in the display one-by-one. The lowest-resolution business machines (the ones having the grainiest and therefore poorest graphics) have 320 pixels across and 200 down. That's 64,000 positions that the software must activate to complete a display. Chances are, your monitor is better than the worst, so you're looking at at least 128,000 pixels whenever you start up 1-2-3.

The advantage of a graphical display is that it can hold any design you are patient enough to create. This lets you mix fonts and font styles, illustrations, moving pictures, and so on to create pages and pictures that you simply can't make on a textual display. For example, when you plot a graph in 1-2-3, the display switches from textual to graphical so that the software can use lines and fonts that aren't available in Text mode.

A graphical user interface takes advantage of the graphical display by showing pictures, or icons, that represent the tasks you might wish to perform. For example, in a GUI spreadsheet, the image of an arrow pointing to the right might represent the task of moving the cell pointer to the right.

While graphical displays are more sluggish than textual displays, they also require more RAM than their textual counterparts. True GUI interfaces are so slow and so RAM hungry that their proponents recommend running them on computers that have high-speed 80386 microprocessors. The popular Microsoft Windows provides DOS users with a GUI in which they can run both text-based and specially designed GUI programs.

As stated earlier, Release 2.3's mouse-driven interface is not a true GUI. That is, the display still runs in text mode, so there is no degradation in performance over earlier releases of the spreadsheet. However, Release 2.3 lets you use an installed mouse to move the cell pointer, highlight ranges, and issue commands.

Mousing Around

If you have a mouse or are considering getting one, follow along with the remainder of this chapter. You'll gain a solid understanding of how the mouse works in 1-2-3. If you've already decided against a mouse, at least read the section about dialog boxes near the end of the chapter; it includes information about dialog boxes that is important whether or not you use a mouse. Later sections of this book highlight features of Release 2.3 that could influence your decision.

Assuming you have installed your mouse correctly, a rectangular pointer appears on the spreadsheet when you start 1-2-3 Release 2.3. The pointer occupies the space of a single character position on the monitor. When you move the mouse on your desk, the rectangular pointer moves on the display.

The following exercise will give you a feel for work with a mouse in the spreadsheet. It explains all procedures in terms of movements of the mouse, the rectangular mouse pointer, and the mouse buttons. You can perform the tasks as well by issuing commands at the keyboard, of course, but if you're new to mice, stick with the text and you'll be up to speed by the end of the chapter.

Build a Small Model

The worksheet in the illustration shows a month of production output for a small leather shop that specializes in hand-crafted items. The exercise is simply to build the model in Figure 1.1 by using the mouse in several common tasks. If some of the tasks are unfamiliar, follow along anyway; we explore the tasks in depth at other points in this book.

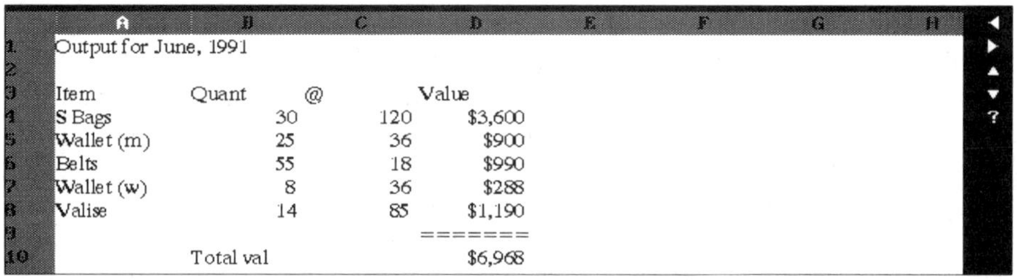

FIGURE 1.1. A worksheet with which to practice using the mouse.

Start in a blank worksheet with the cell pointer in cell A1. Type the label *Output for June, 1991* and press Return. Now leave the keyboard for a moment and grasp the mouse. Hold it gently down on your desk and slide it around until you identify the rectangle whose movements on your display coincide with movements of the mouse. The moving rectangle is the mouse pointer.

Move the mouse around until the mouse pointer falls on cell A3, and then quickly press and release the left mouse button. Pressing and releasing the mouse button very rapidly is called *clicking.* You just clicked cell A3, and the cell pointer should have jumped directly to that cell. If the cell pointer hasn't jumped to A3, try clicking with the right mouse button. Whichever button gets a reaction out of the cell pointer is the one you should use when the text says to click something. You empowered the button when you first installed 1-2-3.

Enter the label *Item* in cell A3. Click cell A4, and enter *S Bags.* Click A5, and enter *Wallet (m).* Actually, for these one-cell-at-a-time movements, the mouse can be a hindrance. If you prefer, use the cursor-control keys on the keyboard to complete the entries shown in row 3 and range B3..C8. You will have to begin the entry in cell C3 by typing an apostrophe label prefix ('@), but other than that there shouldn't be any surprises with these entries. See the box titled A Prefix Makes a Label Entry for more about label prefixes.

To enter the label *Total value:*, click cell B10. Press the Spacebar four times to space the words properly in the cell, and then type *Total value:*. To

A Prefix Makes a Label Entry

There is a small group of characters that you can use to begin formulas in 1-2-3. The plus and minus signs, an opening parenthesis, and an at sign (@) are all valid formula starters. If you type any of these as the first character of a cell entry, 1-2-3 expects the balance of your entry to constitute a valid formula. If the entry doesn't turn out to be a formula, 1-2-3 won't let you enter it into the cell.

When you want a nonformulaic entry to begin with one of the formula starters, the first character you must type is a label prefix character. The example worksheet in this chapter has a lone @ sign in cell B3. If you were to type @ and press Return, 1-2-3 would reject the entry, because a single @ sign isn't a formula. Instead, type an apostrophe and then the @ sign.

The chapter titled Lessons With Labels in this section explains more about formulas, labels, and label prefix characters.

enter the dividing line in cell D9, click that cell and then enter \= . So far, the performance of the mouse has been pedestrian at best. It gets better.

For example, the mouse can speed entering and copying formulas. The entries in column D are formulas that multiply values from the Quant column (column B) times values from the @ column (column C). To create them, first enter the one that goes in cell D4. Get to D4 by clicking it. Type a plus sign to begin the formula. Click cell B4, the first cell you will include in your formula. *B4* appears on the edit line adjacent to the plus sign. Type an asterisk—the multiplication sign in 1-2-3—and then click cell C4. The first formula is finished. Click anywhere on the display to enter it into cell D4.

The next step is to copy the formula from cell D4 to range D5..D8. Roll the mouse away from you on your desk until the mouse pointer passes above the top frame of the sheet. This activates the main menu.

You can select Copy by clicking the word Copy in the menu . . . but don't do it. Instead, press and hold the left mouse button. Drag slowly back and forth across the menu making sure that the mouse pointer remains within the row of menu options. As you drag, the menu pointer follows the mouse pointer. Should you decide not to make a menu selection, simply drag down onto the worksheet and release the mouse button. However, you're about to copy a formula, so bring the mouse pointer (and consequently the menu pointer) to rest on the word Copy. Release the mouse button.

Double click cell D4 to select it as the range to copy from. To double click a cell, place the mouse pointer on it, and press and release the mouse button twice in rapid succession. Indicate the range to copy to by moving the mouse pointer to cell D5 and then dragging from D5 to cell D8. To drag, hold down the mouse button, roll the mouse until you have highlighted the target range,

A Caution About Dragging

The mouse in 1-2-3 is just a little unresponsive; you can move the mouse more quickly than your software can react. This unresponsiveness crops up most often when you need to drag within the spreadsheet. If you're quick, you might depress the mouse button and start dragging before 1-2-3 is ready. Rather than stretching a highlight over the sheet, you may end up just dragging the cell pointer around.

When you need to drag, pause for a moment after depressing the mouse button. You'll know that 1-2-3 is ready to drag when a range reference appears in the control panel.

and then release the button. Click anywhere on the spreadsheet to complete the copy procedure.

Ok, copying the formula might have seemed involved, but don't let the directions fool you. With very little practice you'll be able to repeat these procedures in seconds—far more quickly than we can explain them. The key is to master clicking, double clicking, and dragging. Those three procedures can activate any of 1-2-3's commands. Try another task to improve your proficiency with the mouse.

The total value formula in cell D10 is an @SUM function. Use the mouse to enter it. First, click cell D10 and type *@SUM(*. Drag from cell D4 to cell D8, and then type a closing parenthesis. Click anywhere on the sheet to enter the formula.

The final step in making your practice worksheet match ours is to assign a currency numeric display format. Again, we use the mouse to do this, but this time we add a new twist. You'll assign the currency format to range D4..D10. With earlier versions of the software, you would do this by selecting the Range Format command and then indicating the target range to format. In 1-2-3 Release 2.3, you can select the target range and then issue the command. Try it.

Drag from cell D4 to cell D10. Activate the menu by moving the mouse pointer into the menu area, and then click Range on the menu. Click Format on the resulting menu, and then click Currency. Type 0 to tell 1-2-3 that you don't want decimal places to show in the formatted cells, and, without pressing Return, click anywhere on the display.

Lotus 1-2-3 applies the currency format to the selected range. What's more, the range remains selected. If you don't like the result of your formatting procedure, you can reactivate the menu and try an alternative format without having to reselect the range.

Lotus Guide to 1-2-3 Release 2.3
Cheat Sheet

Keyboard Navigation Commands

RightArrow	move right
LeftArrow	move left
UpArrow	move up
DownArrow	move down

Home	jump to top-left of sheet
PgUp (BigUp)	jump up one screen
PgDown (BigDown)	jump down one screen
Tab (BigRight)	jump right one screen
Shift-Tab (BigLeft)	jump left one screen
End then RightArrow	slide right
End then LeftArrow	slide left
End then DownArrow	slide down
End then UpArrow	slide up
End then Home	jump to bottom-right of active area

Function Key Names

F1: HELP	F6: WINDOW
F2: EDIT	F7: QUERY
F3: NAME	F8: TABLE
F4: ABS	F9: CALC
F5: GOTO	F10: GRAPH
Alt-F1: COMPOSE	Alt-F4: UNDO
Alt-F2: STEP	Alt-F5: LEARN
Alt-F3: RUN	

The Movement Icons and Help

A few features in Release 2.3 of 1-2-3 were added especially for mouse enthusiasts. One of those features is evident to anyone who has a mouse installed: there are four triangles and a question mark next to the spreadsheet directly beneath the mode indicator. See Figure 1.2.

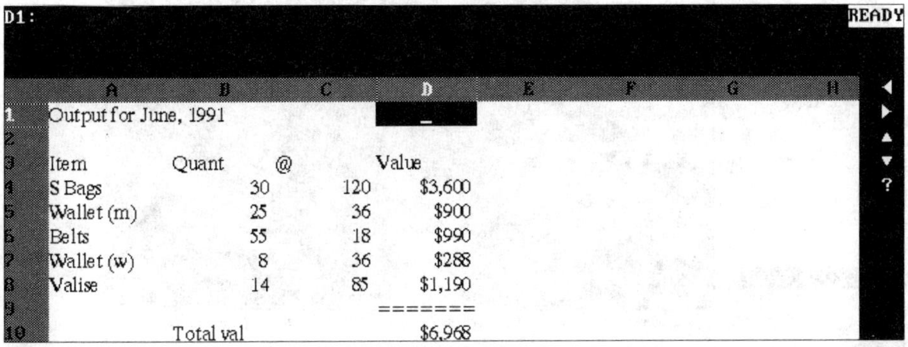

FIGURE 1.2. The navigation icons appear to the right of the spreadsheet.

The triangles are navigation icons that work just like cursor-movement keys. When you press the RightArrow cursor key, the cell pointer moves to the right. When you click the navigation icon that points to the right, the cell pointer also moves to the right. The icons provide added mouse control so that you don't have to resort to the keyboard for certain navigation tasks.

Exercise the Icons

Try it. Move the mouse pointer until it falls on the triangle that points to the right. Watch the cell pointer as you click the icon. Click several more times until the cell pointer hits the edge of the display and the worksheet scrolls to the left. Click the other navigation icons to move the cell pointer around the sheet. Use the navigation icons when you want to move the cell pointer beyond the currently visible area of the spreadsheet.

Do you want to get back to cell A1 in a hurry? Click the top-left corner of the worksheet frame—the square to the left of the first visible column letter and above the first row number.

Clicking the question mark that appears beneath the navigation icons activates 1-2-3's on-line Help facility. Go ahead and click the help icon. A box like the one shown in Figure 1.3 pops up on the display and hides much of the underlying spreadsheet.

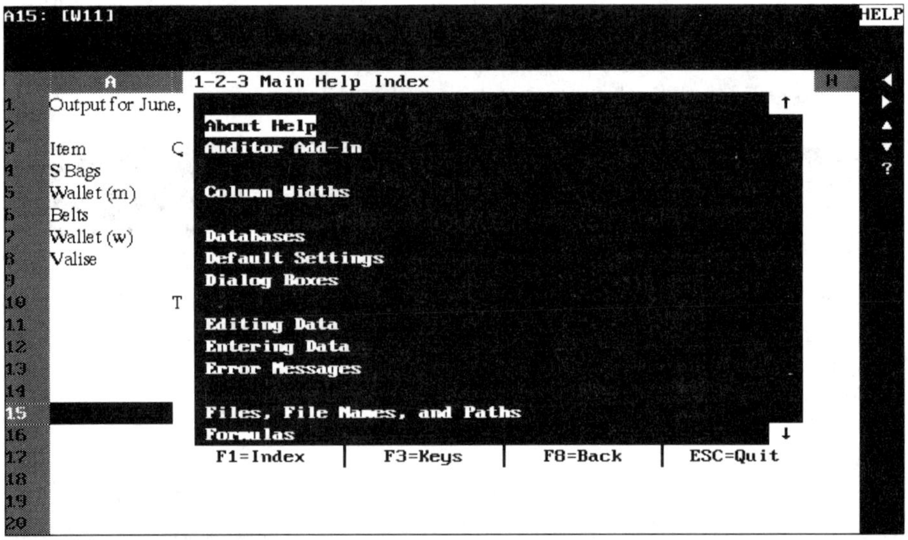

FIGURE 1.3. The help index appears superimposed on the spreadsheet.

Don't worry, the box will go away when you finish with the Help facility.

The 1-2-3 Help facility is context-sensitive. That means that it presents information pertinent to whatever procedure you are involved in when you call for help. The spreadsheet was in Ready mode when you clicked the help icon, so 1-2-3 presented the help index.

The help index is a list of topics about which more information is available. You can select any topic simply by clicking. If you don't see a topic that interests you, click the arrow in the bottom right corner of the box until new topics scroll onto the list. To scroll quickly, hold down the mouse button while the mouse pointer rests on the arrow.

Scroll down until the option Ranges is visible in the index, then click that option. 1-2-3 presents a body of text that teaches you about worksheet ranges. There is more text than can fit in the help box, so scroll down through it by clicking the arrow in the bottom right corner of the box. At the end of the discussion about ranges, there is a list of related topics. Click any one of them to learn more.

In the bottom border of the help box is a list of options that apply while you're using the Help facility. Click the box labeled Index to view the help index. Click the Keys box to see a list of the keystrokes you can use to work

Icons for File Commands

With the File Save, File Retrieve, and other file-related commands, 1-2-3 presents a set of icons to help you mouse around with the directory paths. Clicking the List icon is equivalent to pressing the NAME key (F3). The left- and right-facing triangles duplicate the LeftArrow and RightArrow keys, and the up- and down-facing triangles duplicate the PageUp and PageDown keys. Clicking the question mark icon activates the Help facility.

Click the double period icon (..) to move up one directory level. Click any directory name in the file listing to make that directory active. Likewise, click the appropriate drive letter to switch disk drives for your file operations. With a little fiddling, you'll see that the icons are natural expressions of the more familiar file-handling keystrokes.

in the Help facility. Click the box labeled Back to work your way back through the topics you've already examined, and click the Escape box to return to the worksheet.

You don't need to click the Escape box to exit from the Help facility. Instead, switch mouse buttons and simply click anywhere on the display. Almost every procedure that you can undo in 1-2-3 by pressing the Escape key (building formulas, making menu selections, highlighting ranges, and activating help) you can also undo by switching mouse buttons and clicking. So, if you use the left mouse button to issue commands, the right mouse button serves as an Escape key, and vice versa.

Dialog Boxes: The New Settings Sheets

It used to be that a settings sheet would appear superimposed on the spreadsheet when you selected /Worksheet Global. The settings sheet revealed whatever selections you had already made to affect global settings. The settings sheet remained visible as you made selections from the menu, or you could hide the settings sheet by pressing the WINDOW key (F6) and continue to work with the menu options.

Lotus 1-2-3 Release 2.3 replaces settings sheets with dialog boxes. A dialog box is nothing more than a settings sheet with which you interact directly—as though having a dialog.

The idea of a settings sheet is that it reveals at a glance the settings you have established in the worksheet. What is the global display format? What is the default column width—that is, the width of each column when you start the software? Is recalculation set to automatic or manual? Without a settings sheet, you would have to issue several commands to learn these things. In a dialog box, you not only see the current settings, you can alter them easily.

The down side of a dialog box is that generally it provides little information about how each of its options affects the spreadsheet. Using the menus, you can highlight an option and immediately view an extended prompt that reveals something about what the option will do. This isn't the case with a dialog box.

While the dialog boxes in Release 2.3 are better than most in helping you to understand the meanings of their options, they are more terse than the menus. If you're accustomed to reading the menus for guidance as you work, you might find dialog boxes a little frustrating.

The instructions we give throughout this book are expressed primarily in terms of standard 1-2-3 menu sequences. This is only to maintain consistency and not to advocate the use of menus over dialog boxes. In almost all cases you'll see how to translate menu sequence instructions into dialog box selections if you give the matter a little thought.

Whatever the case, don't completely disregard dialog boxes. The overview of established settings they provide can save a lot of poking around as you decide how to modify the sheet. In addition, as you become more familiar with the options 1-2-3 offers, you will be able to get to them much more quickly via dialog boxes than you will via the menus.

In the Dialog Box with a Mouse

The dialog box goes hand-in-hand (foot-in-foot?) with the mouse. You can point to specific check boxes in a dialog box and click to make selections quite rapidly. The dialog box reveals at a glance the options you have selected and lets you change selections without wading through complex sequences of menu commands.

Try It

Use the mouse to activate the menu. Click Worksheet and then Global. The global settings dialog box appears superimposed on the spreadsheet (Figure 1.4).

You can see immediately what settings are established. For example, the check box preceding the label Protection on is empty. That means that the Protection on option isn't selected. If protection were activated, the check

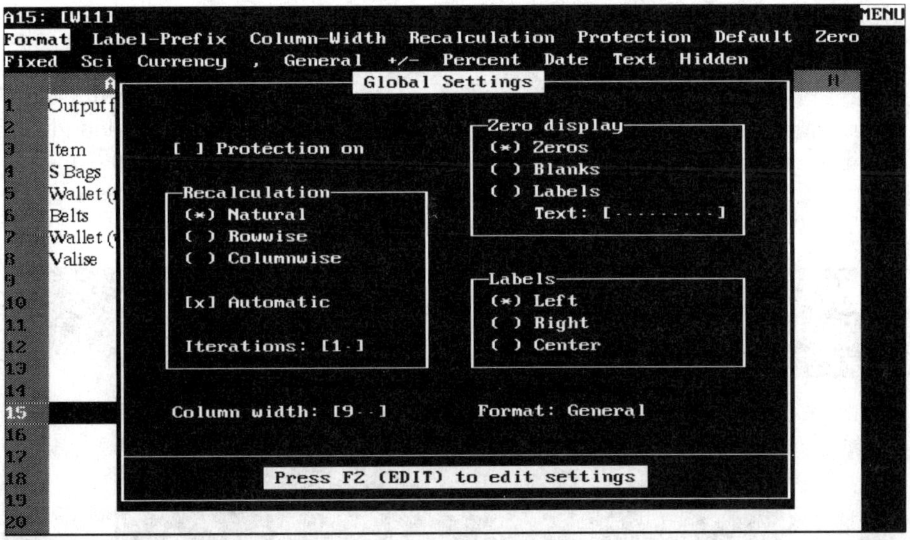

FIGURE 1.4. A spreadsheet with the global settings dialog box displayed.

box would contain an x. Below that, an asterisk appears next to the Natural Recalculation option. This means that Natural is the option selected from among the three available.

At the moment, the dialog box isn't active—you can't have a dialog with it because the standard 1-2-3 menu is still in control. Activate the dialog box by clicking anywhere within it.

Now, do you want to alter a setting? Change the worksheet's Recalculation order from Natural to Columnwise. To do this, simply click the check box next to the Columnwise option. Change the Column width setting by clicking it and changing the value from 9 to 11—use the Delete or Backspace key to remove the 9, and then type *11*. Press Return to lock in the new setting.

When you finish conversing with the dialog box, click OK to preserve the new settings, or click Cancel to be rid of them and return to the previous settings. In either case, press the Escape button on the mouse several times to return to Ready mode.

From time to time throughout the remainder of this book we'll point out procedural differences for mouse users when we give keystroke-by-keystroke instructions. Where we omit such information, it is because the menu sequences are identical with or without a mouse. You should be able to apply your mousing experience whether or not we explain the specific mouse strokes involved. We'll alert you when the mouse is more useful for a task than the keyboard is.

Explore a Dialog Box Rodent-Free

As stated earlier, you can use dialog boxes without a mouse. When you select /Worksheet Global, a dialog box appears on the sheet, revealing which global options are already established. You can continue to work with the menus and ignore the dialog box, or you can activate the dialog box by pressing the EDIT key (F2). See Figure 1.5.

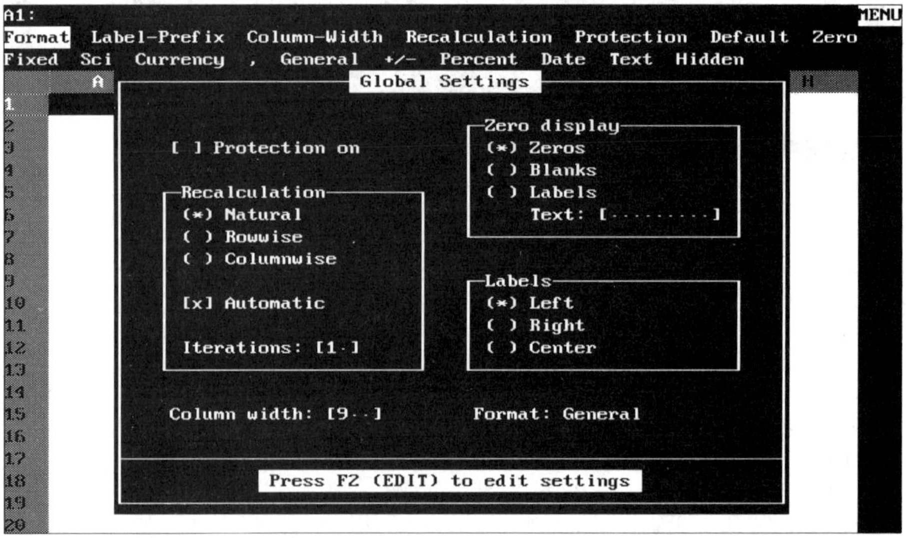

FIGURE 1.5. The Worksheet Global settings sheet reveals the options that are currently selected. New settings don't take effect unless you finish your dialog by choosing OK.

Get Some Practice

Select /Worksheet Global to produce the dialog box, and then press the EDIT key. 1-2-3's traditional menu drops away, and the mode indicator in the top-right of the display reads *Settings*.

A highlight appears on the OK button near the bottom-right corner of the box. Use the arrow keys to move the highlight among the selections listed in the box as you would to move among items on a menu.

Press Return when you have highlighted the Recalculation option. Notice that the Natural option under Recalculation has an asterisk next to it identifying it as the current setting. Use the arrow keys to move the highlight down to the Rowwise option.

Keyboard Users Shouldn't Dialog
The keyboard procedures for working with dialog boxes are a bit clumsy when compared to working with a mouse, so if you're mouse-free, consider working only with the menus. Look at the dialog boxes when you want to know which settings are established, but don't activate the dialog box to make changes.

Press the Spacebar, and the asterisk shifts from the check box next to the Natural option to the one next to the highlighted option; the highlight remains in place, even though you've altered the Recalculation order. When there are several options under a single heading in a dialog box and one of them is marked by an asterisk, you select the one you want by highlighting it and pressing the Spacebar.

You can also select one of the options by highlighting it and pressing Return or by typing the off-colored letter in the option's name. However, when you use either of these alternate selection methods, the highlight jumps back to the OK button in the bottom-right corner of the dialog box. Try it. Move the highlight back to the Natural option, and press Return.

If you wish to change other settings, use the arrow keys once again to navigate in the dialog box. Alternatively, type any of the off-colored letters to make selections. Make a few selections of your own in this dialog box, and experiment until you understand the various ways that highlighting options, pressing the Spacebar, and pressing Return can alter established settings.

When you finish experimenting, highlight the OK button and press Return to preserve your changes, or highlight the Cancel button and press Return to abandon your changes. In either case, press Escape several times to return to Ready mode.

Having completed this chapter, you should:

- *Be able to hold your own when the topic turns to textual interfaces and GUIs*
- *Understand the advantages of graphical interfaces*
- *Recognize opportunities in 1-2-3 to apply a mouse*
- *Know that you can extrapolate your experience with a mouse to work in almost any GUI software*

2

Keyboard Navigation Aids

Perhaps the first lesson you learn after you realize that a spreadsheet has row numbers and column letters is how to move the cell pointer. Moving from one cell to the next in a column or row becomes second nature in a trice. However, even after years of spreadsheet computing, many users can't get around the spreadsheet as quickly as 1-2-3 allows. Knowing all of your navigation options can speed you through any spreadsheet task.

An accomplished spreadsheet keyboard jockey can do magic with 1-2-3. With a little practice, you can run the cell pointer ragged. Many of the 1-2-3 keyboard navigation aids can eliminate hundreds of keystrokes from a typical work session.

In this chapter you will learn how to:

- *Use the PageUp and PageDown keys*
- *Use the BigRight and BigLeft keys*
- *Use the Home key*
- *Use the End key in conjunction with other cursor-movement keys*
- *Use the GOTO function key (F5)*
- *Use the cursor keys to select cells and ranges*
- *Anchor and unanchor the range highlight*
- *Preselect a range before issuing commands*
- *Ride the range to expand the highlight in a new direction*

Cruise with the Cursor Keys

To fully understand the nuances of spreadsheet navigation, it's best to work in a spreadsheet that contains data. If you're not already facing the 1-2-3 display, get there, and build a simple worksheet.

A Sample Worksheet

Enter the label *Test* into cell B1 of an otherwise blank worksheet. Copy the label to range B1..D10 by selecting Copy, indicating cell B1 as the range to copy from, and indicating range B1..D10 as the range to copy to. Use the Copy command a second time to copy from cell B1 to range B12..D20. The spreadsheet should appear as in Figure 2.1.

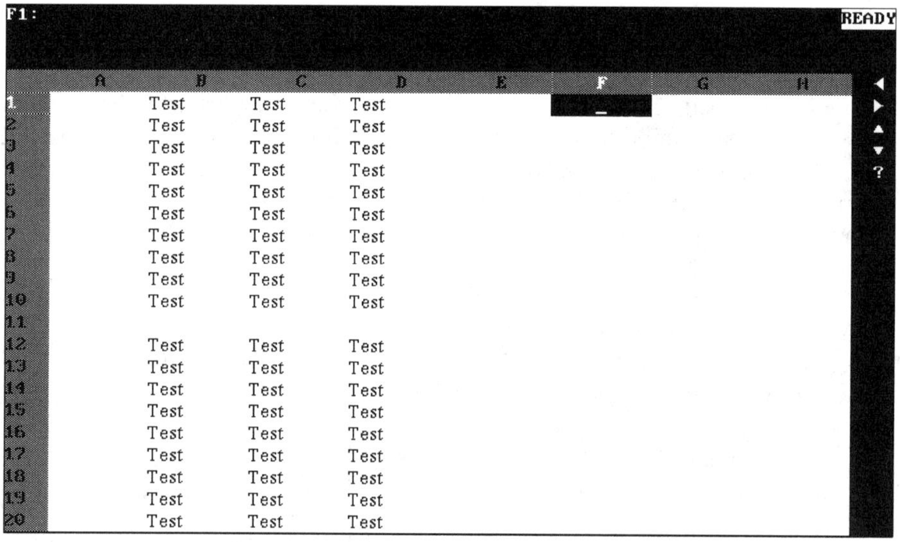

FIGURE 2.1. Recreate this worksheet for some practice using 1-2-3's navigation tools.

It's not a thrilling sample worksheet, but taking it for a spin will reveal some useful keystrokes.

Simply preparing the sample worksheet for this exercise, you have probably already used the arrow keys on the cursor keypad. Pressing RightArrow moves the cell pointer to the right, and pressing LeftArrow moves it to the left. Likewise, pressing UpArrow and DownArrow moves the cell pointer up and down, respectively. All of this and the tasks that follow assume that 1-2-3 is in Ready mode (*Ready* appears in the indicator at the top-right of the display) and that no titles are set (via the Worksheet Titles command) in the spreadsheet. We'll see how titles affect worksheet navigation when we discuss them in a later chapter.

Take Giant Leaps: PgUp and PgDn

For big jumps, other cursor keys come into play. If you think of the spreadsheet as stationary, then pressing the PgDn key shifts the display window down one screen. Therefore, if your display shows 20 rows of the spreadsheet and row 1 is the top visible row, pressing PgDn shifts the display so that row 21 becomes the top row. The position of the cell pointer on the display doesn't change, but a new cell moves in under it.

Try it. With the cell pointer in cell B1, press PgDn. Depending on the display drivers installed on your system (consult the Display Drivers box), the display shifts over the spreadsheet and a new row appears below the top border. Press PgDn once more, and you jump farther down into the worksheet. It should look like Figure 2.2.

FIGURE 2.2. The display shown in Figure 2.1 after you press PgDn.

The PgUp key does just the opposite of the PgDn key. When you press it, the display window shifts up one screen in the display. Press PgUp once to see it in action.

The behavior of the PgDn and PgUp keys may seem unimportant, but knowing how these keys work could affect the way you design spreadsheets.

Display Drivers

The number of rows and columns that appear on your monitor depends on the display driver you select when you install the software. Historically, it wasn't practical to display more than 20 spreadsheet rows and about 8 spreadsheet columns, so that has become the standard to which most of us are accustomed.

Today's monitors have such sharp resolution that you can squeeze 45 rows (and quite possibly more if you have the right display drivers) on the display and still read the data clearly. Drivers that come with 1-2-3 let you display up to 50 lines (45 spreadsheet rows).

Drivers reside in a file on disk, and 1-2-3 automatically draws information from that file when you start the program. You use the Install program to alter the drivers in the driver file. For instructions on how to do this, see Appendix A. Be aware that this book describes the worksheet and offers instructions assuming that you've selected an 80 x 25 screen display. If you are using a different size screen display, you may wish to change the driver now.

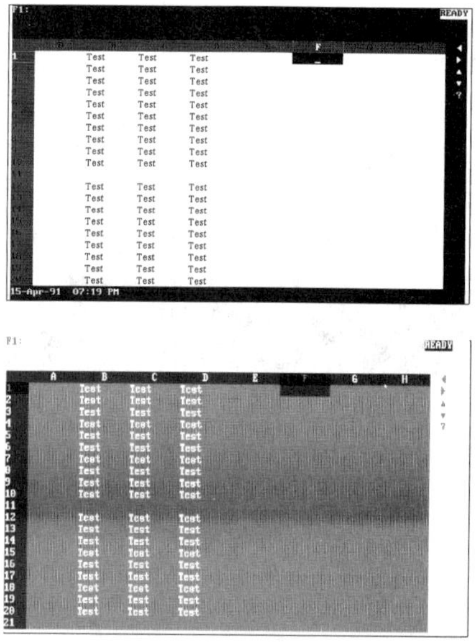

FIGURE 2.3. 1-2-3 displayed with 80 x 25 and with 80 x 50.

Suppose that the information you need to store in the sheet falls into several categories. It might, for example, represent five or six products that your company sells. If you can group all the information from a single product onto one screen of the spreadsheet, you can *stack* the product information as shown in Figure 2.4. That way, each press of the PgDn key takes you to the data about a specific product.

Even when the information about each product doesn't fill the display, you might opt to arrange it all in a stack. The first screen would start in row 1, the next in row 21, and so on, with blank rows between the last row of data for one product and the first row for the next.

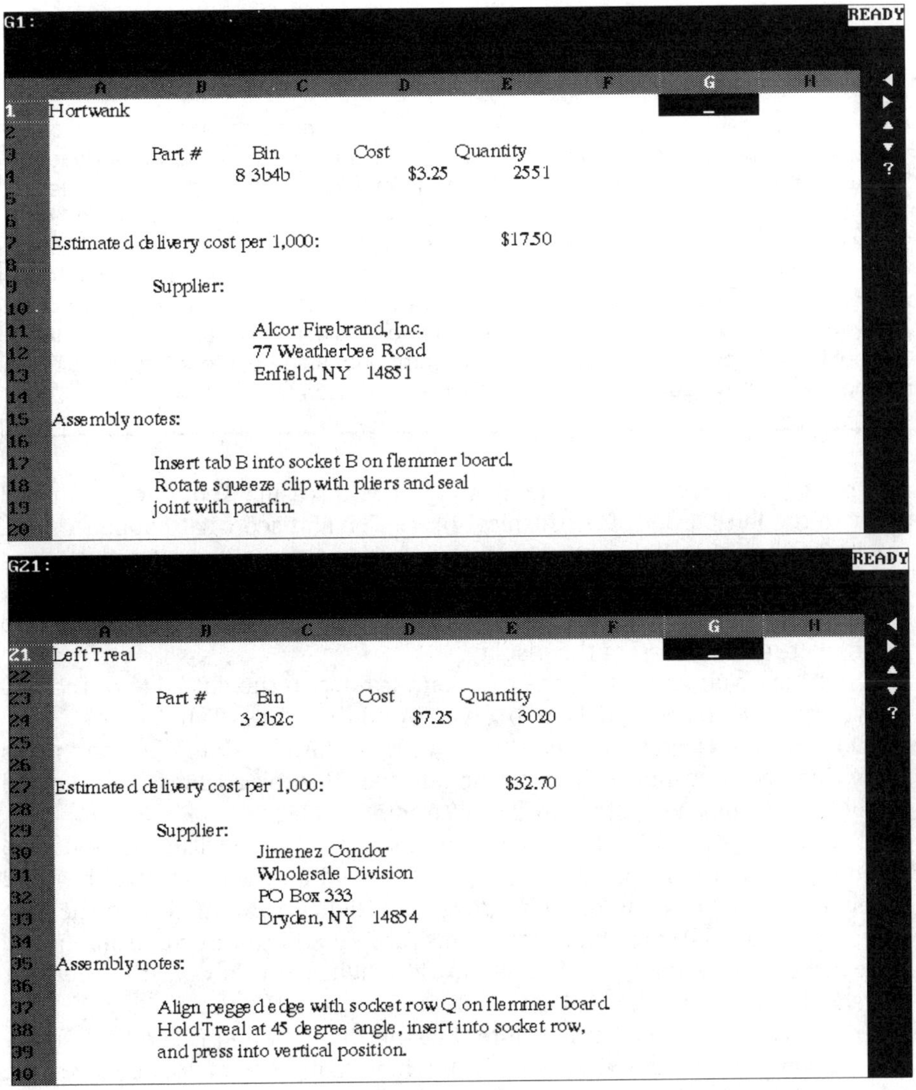

FIGURE 2.4. Stacking the data allows you to put all information about a specific product on a single page.

From Side-to-Side: The Tab Key

For left-to-right movement, the Tab key is analogous to the PgDn key. It lets you move quickly among columns of data in the sheet. Pressing Tab shifts the display window one screen to the right on the spreadsheet. If you haven't

Move the Sheet, Not the Cell Pointer: ScrollLock

When you press the ScrollLock key, the Scroll indicator appears at the bottom of the display. From then until you press ScrollLock again, the arrow keys move the worksheet within the display window.

Suppose that the cell pointer is in the middle of the display and you press ScrollLock. Now pressing DownArrow moves the worksheet up behind the window—as if the DownArrow key were moving the window down. The cell pointer doesn't move to a new cell until it hits the frame. Then the spreadsheet continues to move up beneath the cell pointer.

Pressing ScrollLock lets you change the part of the sheet that is visible without having to move the cell pointer to a particular edge of the display. This can save time when you're making minor adjustments and moving the pointer from one side to the other requires repetitive keystrokes.

altered column widths and column A is visible, pressing Tab moves column I over to the left border of the display. Press Tab and see what happens.

Oops! The worksheet shifted as predicted, but the cell pointer did something screwy. Instead of maintaining its position relative to the spreadsheet frame as it did when you pressed PgDn and PgUp, the cell pointer ended up in the left-most column of the display.

. Each time you press Tab, the cell pointer hops to the left edge of the display. Try it again. Press RightArrow twice, and then press Tab.

Do you want to go back the other way? Hold down the Shift key and press Tab. The display window shifts to the left over the spreadsheet, and the cell pointer slams up against the worksheet frame.

There is a variation on this theme. Rather than pressing Tab and Shift-Tab to jump left and right on the sheet, you can hold down the Control key and press either RightArrow or LeftArrow. Ctrl-RightArrow duplicates the Tab key, and Ctrl-LeftArrow duplicates Shift-Tab. To add to the confusion, many spreadsheet users refer to the Tab and Ctrl-RightArrow keys as the BigRight keys and to the Shift-Tab and Ctrl-LeftArrow keys as the BigLeft keys.

In any case, it's important to note that the BigRight and BigLeft keys shift the display one screen width, no matter how many columns appear on the screen. With all column widths at nine characters (the default), the display shifts exactly eight columns. However, with column widths at 36, for example, the display shifts only two columns at a time. All of this becomes second nature as you bounce around your spreadsheet applications.

From Beginning to End and Back

A lot of work in the spreadsheet begins near cell A1. Perhaps that's why there is a key reserved to take you there quickly. You can use it to reorient yourself rapidly or to find the origin of your spreadsheet, should you lose sight of it as you cruise among your entries. The key that gets you quickly to cell A1 is the Home key. Press it now, and the cell pointer jumps to the top-left corner of the spreadsheet; cell A1 appears in the display.

Plan spreadsheets with the Home key in mind. Store data that you need to access often—variables, perhaps—in the top-left of the work area, and you will be able to get there quickly via a single keystroke.

The keystroke opposite of the Home key involves two key presses. When you press the End key followed by the Home key, the cell pointer jumps directly to the last cell in the active area of the spreadsheet.

The active area comprises a rectangle defined by the right-most column that contains data or has a unique numeric display format and the bottom-most row. In your practice worksheet, the active area is range A1..D20. Prove it by pressing End and then Home. The cell pointer jumps to cell D20. These two keystrokes can save a lot of poking when you need to examine the lowest extremes of your worksheet calculations, and you should remember them as you lay out a model.

Variations on the Arrow Keys

Another useful spreadsheet navigation tool is the End key used in conjunction with the arrow keys. The End-Arrow key combinations let you scurry about among tables of entries, sliding from one end of a range to the other instantaneously. You can make these rapid jumps even when the destination cells aren't visible on the display.

To understand the effects of the End-Arrow key combinations, first get the cell pointer to cell B1. Do this quickly by pressing Home and then Right-Arrow. Now press the End key followed by the DownArrow key. The cell pointer skates down column B to cell B10, coming to rest in the last contiguous data cell.

There are several scenarios to consider when you press End and an Arrow key:

1. If the cell pointer is in a blank cell, it races in the direction of the arrow key until it encounters a nonblank cell or the edge of the worksheet.
2. If the cell pointer is in a nonblank cell and the adjacent cell in the direction of the arrow key is also nonblank, the pointer zips to the last contiguous nonblank cell.
3. If the cell pointer is in a nonblank cell and the adjacent cell in the direction of the arrow key is blank, the pointer zooms in that direction to the next nonblank cell or to the edge of the worksheet.

So far, you have demonstrated scenario number 2. The pointer zipped from data cell B1 to the last contiguous data cell in column B. Press End and then DownArrow a second time to demonstrate scenario number 3. The pointer zooms to cell B12.

Press End DownArrow again to repeat scenario number 2. The pointer zips to cell B20. Press DownArrow once, and then press End RightArrow to demonstrate scenario number 1. The cell pointer races from cell B21 to cell IV21—the edge of the worksheet in the direction of the arrow key you pressed.

Race, zip, and zoom a little more until you get a good sense of how the End key works. Press End UpArrow to race to cell IV1, then press End LeftArrow to race to D1. Press End LeftArrow once more to zip to cell B1.

Notice that each time you press End, an indicator appears in the bottom-right corner of the display. Should you decide after pressing End that you don't want to make a quick hop with the cell pointer, press End a second time to extinguish the End indicator. Pressing the End key is one of the few things that you can't undo by pressing Escape.

Use End to Tour the Sheet

One way to take advantage of the End key, is to design spreadsheets that include *navigation markers*. Such markers might be single-cell entries that reside at various intervals in otherwise empty columns. To view various portions of the spreadsheet, you would position the cell pointer in the navigation column and then press End DownArrow or End UpArrow to move from one section of the sheet to another. Likewise, you can prepare navigation rows to allow quick hops across the spreadsheet.

When you want to scan the perimeter of a table of data, such as a lookup table, a data table, or a database, apply the End key to hop quickly from one corner to another.

All of the navigation techniques we have explored so far work as well when 1-2-3 is in Point mode as they do when it is in Ready mode. (We get to Point mode in a moment.) While you're highlighting cells and ranges for formulas or as you issue menu commands, you can press the PgDn, PgUp, BigRight, BigLeft, Home, End Home, and End Arrow keys as needed. One of the most powerful applications of this technique arises when you must highlight ranges that are adjacent to established data sets.

Try it in your practice worksheet. Move the cell pointer to cell A1, and enter the label *Trial.* Now use the End key to copy the label down column A. With the cell pointer in A1, select Copy and press Return. Press RightArrow to highlight range A1..B1. Press End DownArrow and expand the highlight to range A1..B10. Press LeftArrow and shrink the highlight so that it covers only column A. Finally, press Return. You highlighted a 10-cell range by substituting four cursor-control keystrokes for the more obvious nine. Better yet, if the entries in column B had extended contiguously down several hundred rows, the same four keystrokes would have highlighted all of them.

Highlighting a range this way isn't intuitive. You extend the highlight over cells whose contents you don't want to alter and then reduce the highlight to encompass the appropriate cells. In spite of that weirdness and the involved explanation of the procedure, after a few practice runs you'll be able to do it without thinking.

Try a few more for practice. Enter a label in cell A12, and copy it to range A12..A20 using the same End DownArrow key sequence. Then enter another label in cell E1, and copy it to range E1..E10.

Direct Access

One more navigation aid worth learning about early in your spreadsheeting career is the GOTO function key (F5). It lets you move the cell pointer directly to a cell anywhere in the spreadsheet—regardless of the spreadsheet layout. When you press F5, 1-2-3 displays the prompt *Enter address to go to:* You simply type a cell address and press Return. The cell pointer jumps directly to the destination cell.

The GOTO key has no effect while 1-2-3 is in Point mode. You can use it to hop around the sheet only in Ready mode. On the other hand, coupled with mnemonic range names that identify significant worksheet ranges, the GOTO key conquers even the largest spreadsheets.

You can enter a range name rather than a cell address in response to the GOTO prompt. Hence, should you wish to examine a database named *maindb* at the far end of your spreadsheet, you have only to press the GOTO

Quick Round Trips for Macro Enthusiasts

Quite often in large spreadsheets you want to examine data or formulas stored in one area while you're working in another area. Moving the cell pointer can mean losing track of what you were doing. It would be nice to be able to jump off for a moment and then return directly to the cell from which you came. The two macros in the following illustration can help:

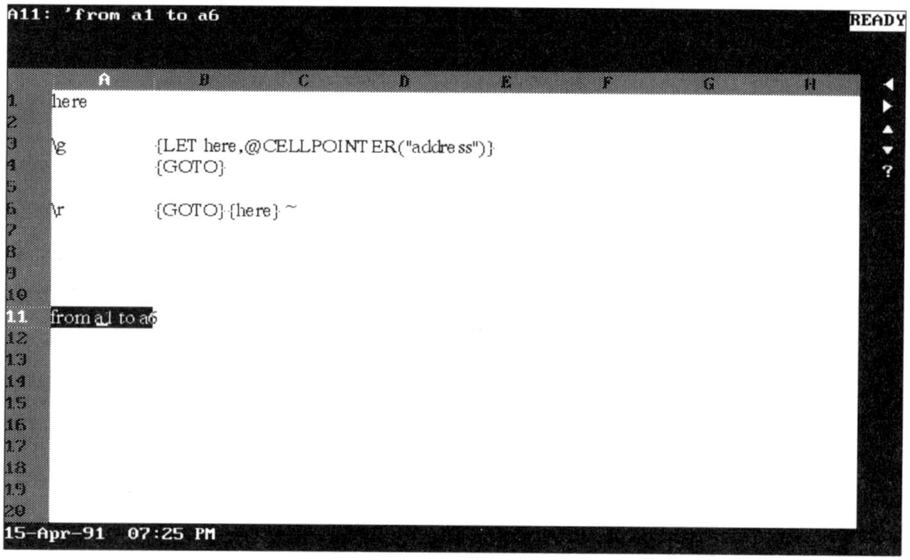

FIGURE 2.5. The boomerang GOTO macros.

The first macro, named *\g*, stores the address of the current cell in a cell named *here*. Then the macro presses the GOTO key and stops. You enter a target address as you would using the GOTO key alone and press Return. The cell pointer jumps to the target cell.

The second macro presses the GOTO key and calls the cell named *here* as the target address. The cell pointer returns to the cell it was in when you last ran the first macro.

To create the macros, enter labels as shown. Start with a label prefix when you enter the label for cell A3 and for cell A6. Assign the labels in column A as names for the adjacent cells of column B: Select Range Name Labels Right, and indicate range A1..A6.

Run the first macro by holding down the MACRO key (Alt) and pressing G. Enter your target address at the resulting prompt. Return to your starting point by holding down the MACRO key and pressing R.

A slight problem with the way these macros work arises when the cell you want to examine isn't on the display when you run the first macro. The macro that returns the cell pointer to its starting point doesn't restore the spreadsheet's position in the display window. Rather, the starting cell and the cell pointer end up in the top-left corner of the display. It's a little disorienting, but at least you return to your starting cell without too much poking around the keyboard.

key and enter *maindb*. The box titled Quick Round Trips describes some simple macros that use the GOTO key to let you examine any part of the spreadsheet and then return to your starting point.

If your target cell isn't on the display, 1-2-3 delivers the cell pointer and the target cell positioned in the top-left corner of the display. To see how this works, press GOTO and enter G120 as the target address. The display shifts, and cell G120 appears in the top-left corner.

When the target cell is already visible, the GOTO key simply moves the pointer to it. Press GOTO, and enter H123 to prove it.

Here's a bit of trivia: You can use the GOTO key to have 1-2-3 display a single cell within the spreadsheet frame. Press GOTO and enter the cell address IV8192. That's the cell at the bottom-right corner of the spreadsheet. The resulting display isn't very useful, but it is amusing. Press Home to return to the action.

Keyboard Navigation in Point Mode

Frequently, while issuing spreadsheet commands or creating formulas, you must somehow tell 1-2-3 what cells or ranges to act upon. When you want to copy or move cells, format them, establish database ranges, or enter @functions, you can indicate the requisite cells by typing the addresses of the cells, by highlighting the cells with the cell pointer, or by clicking and dragging with a mouse. When you highlight cells with the cell pointer you work in Point mode.

Some of us are visually oriented. This means that we prefer to see the action as it unfolds. Using Point mode lets you do exactly that. You know what range is involved in an operation because you see it highlighted on the display as you work.

Some users think Point mode is overrated. They wonder why you would want to scramble around the spreadsheet highlighting ranges when you could simply type cell and range addresses. There's only one valid way to find out: try it and see if you like it. The exercises that follow give you some experience. You may discover that some tasks go much more quickly when you use the arrow keys exclusively than they do when you type cell and range addresses.

Lotus 1-2-3 goes into Point mode automatically when you issue commands from the menus. For example, when you select Range Erase before erasing a cell or a range of cells, 1-2-3 prompts you to indicate a range. At that moment, the spreadsheet is in Point mode.

	A	B	C	D
1	Cage	Animal	Feed	Extension
2	36C	Jerboa	Kibbles	9786
3	33C	Wombat	Kibbles	9788
4	32C	Red Fox	Roger's	9756
5	38C	Lemur	Veg + fruit	9747

FIGURE 2.6. Create this worksheet with which to practice pointing in 1-2-3.

Practice in Point Mode

Create the simple spreadsheet shown in Figure 2.6 so you can work through a few quick examples. You'll pick up some skills that you can apply during any spreadsheet work session. The techniques that you'll use work with almost all of 1-2-3's commands.

Begin each of the entries in ranges A2..A5 and D2..D5 with an apostrophe label prefix so that your worksheet will match ours. This worksheet is a subset of a larger one that contains information about the animals in a zoo.

To see Point mode at work, erase the entry for the Red Fox from row 4. Begin by placing the cell pointer in cell A4. Then select Range Erase. The resulting prompt in the control panel reads *Enter range to erase: A4..A4*. The reference to A4..A4 is a range reference. That means that you can expand the reference to include more cells simply by pressing an arrow key.

Press the RightArrow key three times to highlight range A4..D4. Press Return to tell 1-2-3 that that is the range you want to erase. The data disappears instantly.

Start Anywhere: Anchoring the Cell Pointer

Point mode has many subtleties, and understanding those subtleties can save time. Consider that when you issued the Range Erase command, 1-2-3 entered Point mode with the cell pointer *anchored* in the current cell—cell A4. You could tell that the pointer was anchored because the default target for erasure appeared as a range reference rather than as a single-cell reference.

Some of 1-2-3's commands offer a single-cell reference as the default rather than a range reference. For example, when you select Copy, the default range to copy from appears as a range reference, but the default range to copy to appears as a single-cell reference.

For many tasks, you may want the cell pointer anchored. But suppose that you've issued a command and you don't want it to act on the currently offered cell? Then you need to unanchor the pointer. Erase the Feed and Extension entries for the Jerboa to see how this works. Proceed as follows:

Anchored—Sometimes Yes, Sometimes No

There's really no rhyme nor reason to the way 1-2-3 offers a highlight when you issue a command. If you select Copy, the range to copy from appears as a range reference. If you select Data Fill, the range to fill appears as a single-cell reference.

You might think that the designers of 1-2-3 put a lot of thought into which commands should offer range highlights versus single-cell highlights, but that's not the case. Many years ago we asked a 1-2-3 developer why some commands work one way and other commands work the other way. The answer: Those decisions were made arbitrarily.

Leave the pointer in cell A4, and select /Range Erase. The default range to erase appears as A4..A4. If you pressed an arrow key now, the cell pointer would expand rather than move to the range you wanted to erase. To free the pointer, press either Escape or Backspace. Now you can use any of the navigation techniques that you learned earlier in the chapter to move the cell pointer to cell C2. Press RightArrow twice and UpArrow twice.

The pointer now highlights cell C2, but your intent is to erase cells C2 and D2. To erase both cells in a single operation, you must re-anchor the cell pointer. Press the period key, and a range definition appears in the control panel. This time, the cell pointer is anchored in cell C2, so you can press RightArrow to highlight the entire range to erase. Press Return to complete the erasure.

Notice that after erasing the highlighted range, 1-2-3 returns the cell pointer to the cell from which you initiated the operation. Except in a few cases, such as when you issue the Range Search command, the pointer always returns to its starting cell after you complete a menu sequence.

Select First, Issue Commands Later

A debate over how command sequences ought to be structured rages among computerists. Should you issue a command (the verb) and then indicate an item on which the command should work (the object), or should you select an object and then select a verb?

If you're speaking English and you don't want your conversational style to stand out, you probably compose sentences in the verb-object sequence: Move the chair, copy the report, and eat the pie.

At some point in the recent past, some clever computer programmer decided that normal English wasn't appropriate for issuing software commands and offered the object-verb alternative that was popularized by Apple Macintosh computers. 1-2-3 Release 2.3 lets you phrase commands in this inverted syntax: The chair, move it; the report, copy it; the pie, eat it. Of course, in the spreadsheet you're more likely to be referring to spreadsheet ranges than to chairs and pies.

Object-verb syntax advocates will tell you that their approach is more intuitive. That is, if you were to stumble by accident upon a way to issue commands, you would naturally choose an object followed by a verb—particularly when you use a mouse. Mouse or no mouse, the approach is contrary to the way most of us speak. In fact, the object-verb syntax is a work-around for problems that arise when pull-down menus and dialog boxes appear superimposed on the work environment: How can you select ranges when the sheet is buried under menus and dialog boxes? If you have already selected the object, however, it won't bother you to lose sight of it as you work through menus that represent the verbs.

In any case, the object-verb approach is here to stay. When using almost any GUI product, expect to select objects before issuing commands.

Let's see how it works when you issue commands via the keyboard only. With the cell pointer in A4, press the ABS key (F4). 1-2-3 offers a range highlight anchored in the current cell. You could expand the highlight as usual, but press Escape to unanchor it instead.

Move the unanchored pointer to cell D1, and press the period to re-anchor it. Press DownArrow four times to highlight all the entries in column D, and press Return. This locks in the selection so that you can issue a menu command.

Select /Range Erase. 1-2-3 automatically erases the preselected range. The range remains selected even as 1-2-3 returns to Ready mode. This way, you can select a range once and issue more than one menu sequence to affect the range. You might, for example, assign several display formats in sequence until you come upon the one you like.

Working with a mouse, you can use either the verb-object or the object-verb approach. In either case, to highlight a range, move the mouse pointer to the top-left corner cell of the range. Drag to the bottom-right corner cell. When you release the pointer, the range is selected. Note that when you use the mouse to override a default range reference, you needn't press Escape or Backspace first, as you do when you use the keyboard. Any selection with the mouse automatically overrides an established default option.

Ride the Range When You're Highlighting in the Wrong Direction

One more tidbit that is useful to know when you use the keyboard to highlight ranges is how to change the anchor cell without collapsing the range reference. It wouldn't do to highlight several rows and columns and then realize that you started highlighting one row too far down in the sheet. It would be a pain to escape from what you were doing and reissue the commands so you could begin highlighting in the correct row.

Typically, you learn to indicate a range by stretching the highlight from the top-left corner cell downward and to the right. Actually, you can stretch the highlight in any direction. Just keep in mind that the cell that contains the centered flashing cursor is always diagonally opposite the anchor cell. Do one more operation to understand how this works: erase all the records from the animal database.

Again, start with the pointer in cell A4. This time, press the ABS key (F4) and press RightArrow twice to extend the highlight over range A4..C4. Press DownArrow to highlight row 5 as well as row 4. Ok, that's two rows of the database. But how to highlight the other two rows?

While you're highlighting a range, pressing the period key moves the anchor from one corner of the highlight to another. This movement, sometimes called *riding the range*, goes from corner-to-corner, usually clockwise around the range.

You have already highlighted two rows of the desired range, but the anchor is in cell A4. If the anchor were in cell A5 or C5, you could extend the highlight upward to include rows 3 and 2 of the database. Move the anchor by pressing the period key twice. Whether the anchor moves clockwise or counterclockwise, it ends up in cell C5; the flashing cursor ends up in A4. Press UpArrow twice to highlight the two additional rows, and then press Return to lock in the highlight. Finally, select /Range Erase, and press Return to blank out the database.

Having completed this chapter you should:

- *Understand the advantages of working with the keyboard*
- *Be capable of getting around in—and therefore be more able to create—large spreadsheets*
- *Know the subtleties of Point mode and be able to apply your knowledge when working with any spreadsheet commands*
- *Be prepared to work with object-verb command syntaxes in GUI software products*

3

Lessons with Labels

A spreadsheet is useful only if you understand what its numbers and calculations represent. That's why 1-2-3 lets you label the worksheet. You have probably already used labels extensively in your own worksheets. This quick review looks at some labeling tidbits that might help you work more quickly as you lay out new spreadsheet models.

The Nature of a Label

Lotus 1-2-3 recognizes three types of cell entries: numbers, formulas, and labels. Numbers are the basic building blocks for describing business problems. They are easy to work with: type a number and press Return, and 1-2-3 enters exactly what you typed into the current cell.

Formulas are the tools with which you manipulate the numbers. Formulas can show the relationships between numbers. They make predictions and show how the numbers change when conditions change. Using numbers and formulas, your spreadsheets let you do what-if analyses of your business. Formulas can be very involved, so we devote an entire section to them later in this book.

Labels are the tools we use to describe the spreadsheet. A label can specify the meaning of a number or of a formula. It can separate data items from the formulas that sum the items. A label might even serve as a title for a spreadsheet, revealing at a glance what problem the spreadsheet handles. Working with labels is only a little more involved than working with numbers.

In this chapter you will:

- *Review the differences between labels and values*
- *Learn how to enter labels that look like numbers*
- *Use label prefix characters to alter the alignment of labels*
- *Use menu commands to realign entire ranges of labels*

Automatic Labels: When You Make a Cell Entry

The first key that you press when you begin a cell entry determines what type of entry 1-2-3 expects you to make. If the first character you type is a number, 1-2-3 expects your entire entry to be a number; the Value indicator appears in the top-right corner of the display.

If the first character you type is an arithmetic operator or an @ sign, 1-2-3 expects your entry to be a valid formula. Again, the Value indicator appears. When the first character you type to make a cell entry is a letter or one of several punctuation characters, 1-2-3 displays the Label indicator and automatically inserts a label prefix in the cell ahead of your entry. The prefix character makes the label.

Try a few. Start in a blank worksheet with the cell pointer in A1 and type the letter *T*. Notice the label indicator. Finish your entry by typing *est*, and press Return. The word *Test* appears in cell A1.

Look at the current cell indicator in the control panel. It reveals that cell A1 contains the entry *'Test.* (Figure 3.1) The apostrophe is the label prefix that 1-2-3 inserted automatically.

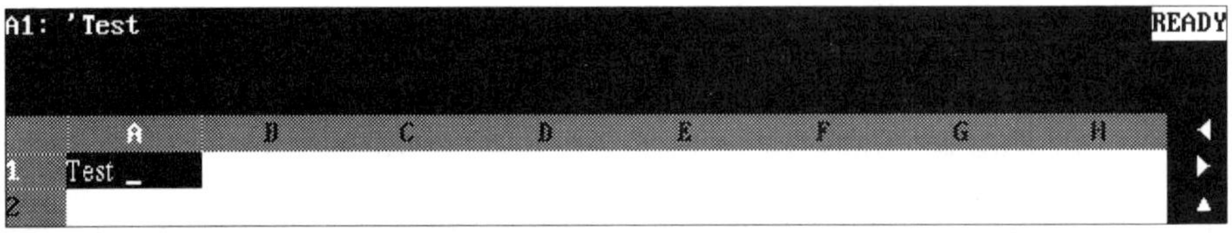

FIGURE 3.1. Notice the label prefix visible in the control panel.

While the label prefix character is part of the cell's contents, 1-2-3 knows not to display it along with the label that you typed.

A label entry is very different from a numeric entry. In a sense, a label is an arbitrary string of characters that has no mathematical relationship to other labels. In other words, you can't solve mathematical equations with labels as you do with numbers. Therefore, you might think that labels lack numeric value. Rationally, they have no value. However, in 1-2-3 a label has the numeric value of 0. This is important to understand because it lets you create labels that look like numbers.

Do-It-Yourself Labels That Look Like Numbers

You might want to use the spreadsheet to keep track of people's mailing addresses or telephone numbers. Entering a phone number, a street address, or a zip code into a cell offers a challenge: how do you get 1-2-3 to recognize that your entry isn't a value? Try one. Move the cell pointer to cell A2 and enter the phone number *212-555-3377*.

Did the number –3720 appear in the cell? If not, then you already know what we're getting at. If so, it's because the first character you typed was a number; 1-2-3 assumed you were making a numeric or a formulaic entry and treated your entry as a subtraction problem—212 minus 555 minus 3377 equals –3720.

To prevent this type of confusion, begin with a label prefix when you need to store numbers as labels. Move to cell A3 and type an apostrophe. 1-2-3 displays the label indicator. Now type the phone number *212-555-3377*. When you press Return, the number appears in the cell as you typed it. Remember: the entry is a label; to 1-2-3 it now has the numeric value of 0.

You can type a label prefix character to begin any label entry. Try another one in cell A4. Type *'Another test*, and press Return. 1-2-3 recognizes that you have begun the entry with a label prefix. The apostrophe becomes part of the entry, but 1-2-3 displays only the characters that follow it. While you can start every label by typing a prefix, save some effort. Let 1-2-3 recognize your standard label entries and insert the label prefixes automatically. Start with apostrophes only when you need to tell 1-2-3 that an entry beginning with a number isn't, in fact, a number or a formula.

Those Labels Seem Rather Wide

You might have noticed that two of the labels you have entered are longer than column A is wide; the labels seem to spill over into column B.

No matter how long the label you enter (a cell can hold no more than 240 characters), all of its characters reside in a single cell. 1-2-3 allows extra characters to extend over adjacent cells unless something is stored in one of them. Confirm this by entering an even longer label into cell A5. Try, *This is a very long label.*

The entry extends out over column C, but when you look at the current cell indicator in the control panel, you see that cell A5 contains the entire label. Move the cell pointer to cell B5 and check out the current cell indicator. There is nothing in cell B5.

Now enter the number *8* into cell B5. 1-2-3 cuts off the label in cell A5 so the display isn't too confusing. The entire label still resides in cell A5, but it no longer displays at its full length. Move the cell pointer to A5, and check the current cell indicator once more to see that the original label is intact.

Align the Short Labels

While many of the labels you'll use to describe the entries in your spreadsheets will be long, many others will be short. If a label is shorter in length than the cell holding it is wide, you can select how 1-2-3 aligns the label in the cell.

One place to take advantage of the label alignment options is in tables of information. Let's enter the labels for a small table and see how adjusting the label alignments can help to clarify the worksheet.

Start by issuing the Worksheet Erase Yes command to dispose of the work you have already done. The first labels you'll enter are column headers that identify the months for data that you might record. Use the months in shown Figure 3.2.

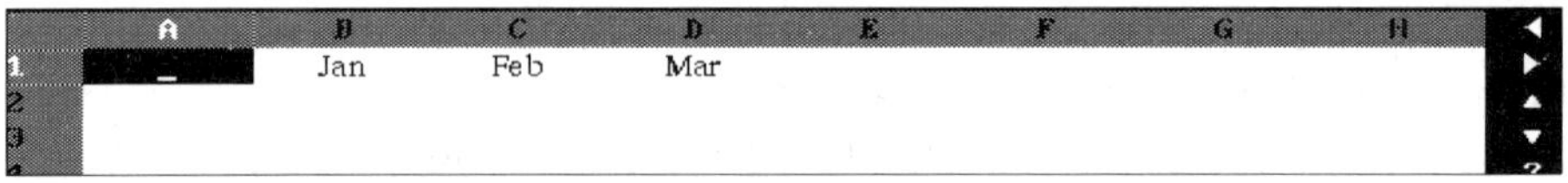

FIGURE 3.2. You can use the caret (^) label prefix to center labels.

Notice that each of the headers in Figure 3.2 is centered in the column containing it. We accomplished this by starting each of the entries with a caret (^) label prefix. Move the cell pointer to cell B1 in your worksheet and type a caret. 1-2-3 displays the label indicator. Finish the entry by typing *Jan* and pressing Return. The result is a centered label.

A centered label is no different from one that begins with an apostrophe prefix; only its position in the cell is different. For that reason, you might think of the label prefix as a *label display format*, similar in function to a numeric display format.

Perhaps the worksheet you're building tracks the revenue generated by the sale of various wholesale items. Enter a few of those items in column A, but first widen the column so that the label entries won't spill over into column B.

Move the cell pointer to cell A2. Select Worksheet Column Set-Width, and increase the column width to 13 characters. Now type a quotation mark to begin your entry. Finish the entry by typing *Radio*, and pressing Return. This time, the label aligns with the right end of the cell.

Enter "*Speakers* in cell A3 and "*Amplifier* in cell A4. As you've guessed, the quotation mark label prefix marks a right-aligned label.

One other label prefix you're likely to use often as you design your own spreadsheets is the *repeat* prefix. When an entry begins with a backslash (\), 1-2-3 displays the label's characters repeatedly across the width of the cell. The label itself may have only one character, but no matter what the width of the cell, it will appear filled. Try some to see how this works.

Move the cell pointer to cell B5. Chances are that you would calculate the total sales for each month by entering formulas at the ends of the columns. To help distinguish totals from the other numbers, you might enter a dividing line in row 5. The backslash label prefix simplifies the job.

Underlines for Wysiwyg Users
If you're working with Wysiwyg attached, you may forgo dividing lines created by the repeat label prefix. The Wysiwyg menu sequence :Format Lines Double Bottom, for example, creates double underlines within selected cells. The last chapter in this section provides an overview of Wysiwyg's capabilities, and we explore those capabilities in depth in the section devoted to spreadsheet output.

Type \= , and press Return. 1-2-3 repeats the equal sign across the width of cell B5, though you can see in the control panel that the label in B5 consists of only one character (remember that the label prefix isn't part of the label). Enter \= into cells C5 and D5 to complete the dividing line. Your finished worksheet should look like Figure 3.3.

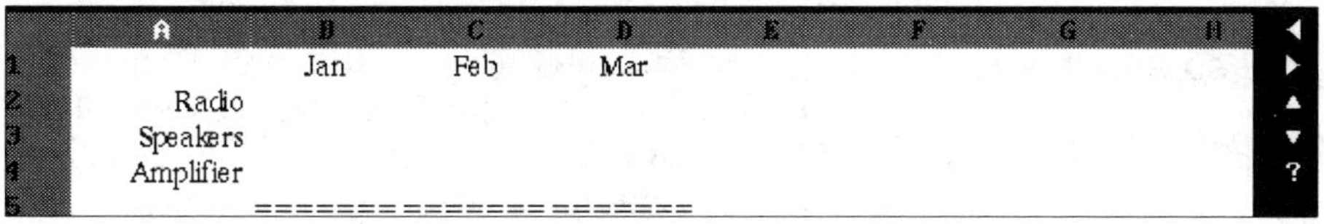

FIGURE 3.3. Worksheet using a combination of label prefixes.

Quick Realignments: The Range Label Commands

Typing a label prefix character for each label you enter can be tedious. Fortunately, you don't have to do this often. But what if you need to enter 30 or 40 right-aligned labels consecutively down a column or 12 centered labels across a row? Don't bother at all with alignment prefixes until you finish the entries.

Once you have stored a label with any type of label prefix, you can use a short menu sequence to alter the alignment. Realign the labels in row 1 to see how this works. If you prefer, start by moving the cell pointer to cell B1. In any case, select Range Label Left, and indicate range B1..D1 as the range of labels to align. 1-2-3 replaces the caret label prefix in each cell with an apostrophe prefix, and the labels shift to the left in their cells. Use the Range Label Center command to reestablish the caret prefixes.

Label Prefixes Override Special Characters

Just one more tidbit about labels for now. Sometimes you want a label entry to begin with a label prefix character, an @ sign, an arithmetic operator (+ or –), or even a slash. If you start by typing a label prefix, 1-2-3 absorbs the character and doesn't display it in the cell. Likewise, if you start with other operators or an @ sign, 1-2-3 thinks you're typing a formula. Most puzzling, when the first key you press to make an entry is a slash, you activate 1-2-3's menu.

The way to deal with all of these problems is to begin by typing a label prefix. So, to enter a quotation as a label, you would type '"*Four score and seven years...*" . To start a label with an @ sign, type '@, and so on.

All in all, there's really nothing tricky about using labels in your worksheets. 1-2-3 looks after you as you enter labels that begin with letters. If that's not enough, you can easily establish any entry as a label by starting the entry with a label prefix character. Your choice of prefix determines how 1-2-3 displays the label in the cell. And even if you have entered a bunch of labels with one type of prefix, you can change alignments quickly by applying the Range Label commands.

The chapter titled Math With Labels in the Formulas section of this book takes a closer look at ways to use labels in the spreadsheet.

Having completed this chapter you should:

- *Have a clear sense of the differences between labels and values*
- *Know how to realign labels so they augment understanding of the values in your spreadsheets*
- *Be able to create labels using any characters*
- *Know the basics that will help you to understand more complex label-related topics that arise in the Formulas section of this book*

4

Customize the Environment

If you're going to learn to use the 1-2-3 spreadsheet as a giant sheet of doodling paper, you should be familiar with the tools that will make each doodle uniquely yours. The 1-2-3 environment is quite rigid—when you've seen 100 or so spreadsheets, they start to look pretty much the same. However, within the rules of the environment are hundreds of elements that you can manipulate to suit your needs. These include the widths of columns, the numeric display formats of cells, and the alignment of labels.

We have already discussed how labels work in the spreadsheet. Reviewing some of the other fundamentals of spreadsheet customization gives us a chance to answer some important questions about the spreadsheet environment—for example, what is the difference between a global and a local setting? Even if your worksheets contain no more than numbers and labels, certain of 1-2-3's features can help you to emphasize your entries or clarify their meanings. Along the way we'll look at some useful customization tools that are easy to overlook.

The commands and techniques in this chapter are so useful that you will probably apply some of them in every spreadsheet you create. And even if you are familiar with some of the commands, you might discover variations on them that can speed you through a session with 1-2-3.

In this chapter you'll learn how to:

- *Use the cursor keys to set and reset individual column widths*
- *Set and reset the widths of several columns at once*
- *Hide and redisplay columns*
- *Select options for the entire worksheet (Global options)*
- *Assign numeric display formats*
- *Display formulas in the spreadsheet*
- *Create simple bar charts in the sheet*

Column Widths to Fit

Learning to set the widths of individual columns comes early in a spreadsheeting career: Move the cell pointer to the column in question, select Worksheet Column Set-Width, and enter a value to indicate the number of characters that should fit across the column. If the resulting column width isn't appropriate, you reissue the Worksheet Column Set-Width command, and enter a new value. Eventually, you come up with an appropriate width setting. That's how many of us have done it for years, but there's a little-known variation to this approach that can save a lot of guess work.

To appreciate the alternate method, start with a blank worksheet and enter an 11-digit number into cell A1—*11111111111* would be appropriate. The number appears in scientific notation as *1.1E+10*. To view the entry as you typed it, you must widen the column.

Set Widths in Wysiwyg

If you are working with Wysiwyg attached, you can use either the arrow keys or the mouse to adjust column widths. Simply drag the line to the left of the column letter in the spreadsheet frame. When you depress the mouse button to drag, a dotted line extends down the display to reveal the width of the column relative to entries in the sheet. Dragging right expands the column; dragging left narrows it. When you release the mouse button, the column assumes the width represented by the position of the dotted line.

With the pointer in cell A1, select Worksheet Column Set-Width. Then, rather than enter a number, press the RightArrow key. With each press of RightArrow, the column expands. You must press it three times before the 11 digits supersede the entry in cell A1, but you know instantly that the column is a satisfactory width before you press Return and leave the menus. Whenever you adjust a column width to fit existing entries, use the Right- and Left-Arrow keys in response to the *Enter column width* prompt.

Back to Nine

Once you have set a column width, it's easy to lose sight of the original default width of that column. Unless you have fiddled with the global defaults (check out the box titled Change the Default Width), columns in your

Change the Default Width

The commands on the Worksheet Column menu have local effects; they alter the width of selected columns. To change the widths of all columns at once, select Worksheet Global Column Width.

Any columns whose widths you have set using Worksheet Column commands will retain their settings. All other column widths will adjust to the new default. The Worksheet Column Reset-Width command will return any column to the new default width.

spreadsheet start out at nine characters wide. Sometimes, in a width-setting frenzy, you might be tempted to use the Worksheet Column Set-Width command to set a column width back to 9.

Instead, use the Worksheet Column Reset-Width command. It automatically removes all effects of the Worksheet Column Set-Width command. This puts the column in synchrony with any columns whose widths you haven't set.

Column Ranges

The Worksheet Column Set-Width command affects the width of one column at a time. Another command, which sets the widths of several contiguous columns at once, is particularly handy when preparing a worksheet that will contain several columns of similarly formatted data, such as the sales figures for several months or monthly production figures. Try it. Select /Worksheet Column Column-Range Set-Width. 1-2-3 prompts you to indicate a range of columns whose widths you wish to alter.

For now, indicate columns A, B, and C by typing A1..C1 or by highlighting the three-cell range. There is no need to include cells to the bottom of the worksheet. The Column-Range command alters the widths of all columns within a range, no matter how many rows the range spans.

When 1-2-3 prompts you to enter a column width, press the RightArrow or LeftArrow key until the column reaches the desired width. You can return the widths of several columns to the default of 9 by selecting Worksheet Column Column-Range Reset-Width and indicating the desired range of columns.

Hidden Columns

Some of the information in your spreadsheets—constants used in calculating the mix for certain chemicals used in manufacturing, for example—may not be important to a reviewer's understanding of the model. There may be formulas whose results feed into other formulas but that are not relevant in and of themselves. Occasionally, you have data that you simply don't want other people to see. Perhaps most often, you have several columns that you would like to print or view side-by-side that are separated by intervening data and formulas. All of these are reasons to hide columns.

Before you try hiding columns, enter a few numbers and labels in columns C, D, and E—what you enter isn't important. When you have finished, place the cell pointer in cell C1, and select Worksheet Column Hide. 1-2-3 prompts you to indicate which columns to hide. Press RightArrow twice to indicate range C1..E1, and press Return. The columns vanish from the display; column B appears snuggled up against column F. It should look like Figure 4.1.

FIGURE 4.1. A worksheet with columns C through E hidden.

Hidden columns behave in strange ways. They don't appear on the display while 1-2-3 is in Ready mode. They do, however, appear in Point mode—sometimes. Try copying a cell and see how this works. No matter where the

> **Local Versus Global**
>
> Most of the formatting options in 1-2-3 can have either a global or a local effect. A local effect changes selected cells, columns, or rows. A global effect changes all the cells of the worksheet except those already altered by a local effect.
>
> When you apply a global formatting option, such as Worksheet Global Format or Worksheet Global Label-Prefix, your selection becomes the default for the current worksheet. A default setting is one that applies automatically unless you change it deliberately. Resetting a local formatting option returns selected cells, columns, and rows to the default.
>
> Global formatting options are saved along with the worksheet. If you save and retrieve at a later time, your selected defaults remain in place.

cell pointer is, select Copy. The hidden columns instantly appear on the display, their column letters marked with asterisks.

You can point to cells in these columns to use them as sources or destinations for the Copy command, for the Move command, for Range naming commands, and so on. When you issue one of these commands, the columns vanish as the command takes effect.

Hidden columns don't appear on the display, however, when you set a print range. This lets you highlight columns that appear adjacent so that they come out adjacent on the printout.

When you wish to restore hidden columns, select Worksheet Column Display and indicate the columns that have asterisks adjacent to the column letters in the spreadsheet frame.

Numbers with Meaning

You probably already know about 1-2-3's numeric display format feature, a capability that lets you determine what type of notation the software uses on each of the numbers entered in the sheet. Does an entry represent dollars and cents? Is it really a percentage? Would it be clearer in scientific notation? As long as an entry has a numeric value, you can assign it a numeric display format.

Fiddle with Formats

By way of review, build the small spreadsheet shown in Figure 4.2.

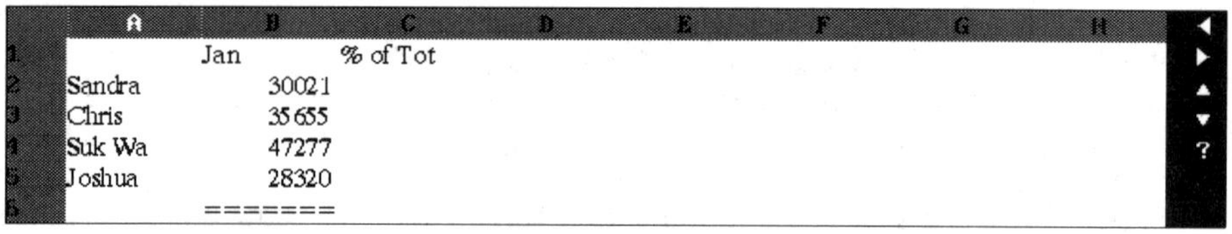

FIGURE 4.2. Worksheet with which to practice formatting numbers.

First enter labels in column A and cells B1 and C1. Enter the values in range B2..B5, enter \= in cell B6 to create the dividing line, and enter the following formulas:

B7: @SUM(B2...B5)
C1: +B2/$B$7

Copy the formula from cell C2 to range C3..C5.

As entered, what the values in this spreadsheet represent is not clear. The numbers in column B could be dollars, units sold, or even accumulated test scores. Are the values in column C percentages or simply relatively small numbers?

Before you get confused, assign some cell formats to reveal the missing information. Select Range Format Currency, and enter 0. This tells 1-2-3 not to show decimal places in the formatted numbers. Indicate B2..B7 as the range to format.

> **Text Formatting**
> The Text formatting option causes 1-2-3 to display actual formulas, rather than formula results, in the sheet. 1-2-3 still calculates the formulas, but all you see in a cell formatted with the Text option are the characters that represent the underlying calculations.

The entries in column C are percentages. Each shows what percent of the total in cell B7 is represented by the corresponding value in column B. Use the Range Format command to make the values in column C appear as percentages without decimal places.

As you apply the Range Format command, pause for a moment to appreciate the available formatting options. There are ten. Figure 4.3 shows the value 33,333 as it appears with several of the available formats.

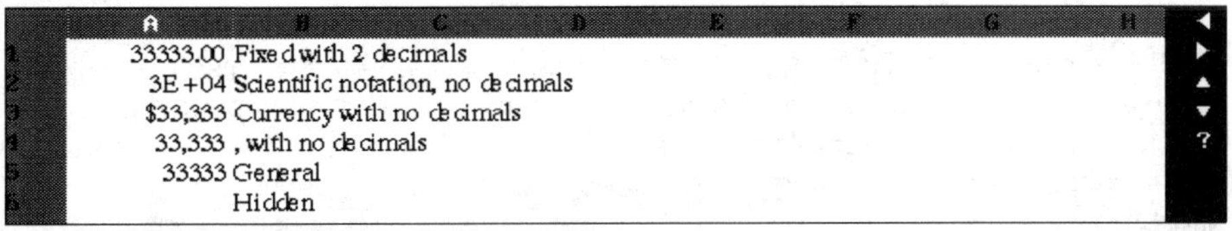

FIGURE 4.3. Examples of the numerical formats available in 1-2-3.

We take a close look at date formats in Chapter 16 in the Formulas section of the book. In the meantime, check out the boxes on +/– Graphs and Text Formatting for explanations of those options.

The Default Cell Format

In many spreadsheets, almost every cell represents a particular type of information. A balance sheet, for example, is filled with dollar amounts. This being the case, assigning cell formats to selected cells and ranges is a waste of effort. If most numeric entries in a sheet will have the same numeric display format, set that format as the default for the worksheet.

In your practice worksheet, select Worksheet Global Format Currency. Enter *2* to indicate that you want two decimal places to show on every entry. The worksheet appears unchanged. But notice what happens when you enter a value in a blank cell: enter *7* in cell D2. 1-2-3 displays the entry in the new default format.

The default display format is General. Knowing this, you can use the Worksheet Global Format command to change back at any time. Any numeric entries that haven't been formatted via the Range Format command reflect the Global Format.

Save RAM
Using the Range Format command to assign numeric display formats consumes a small amount of RAM for each formatted cell. If most of your spreadsheet cells will have a format other than the default General, save RAM by using the Worksheet Global Format command to change the default.

+/– Graphs

Before Lotus included Allways and then Wysiwyg with 1-2-3, you couldn't display graphs along with the spreadsheet. To compensate, the company offered a +/– option on the Range Format menu. You may stumble across this format in older worksheets, and you may even find opportunities to apply it in some of your own sheets.

A cell that has the +/– format shows values as a series of plus or minus signs. If the value of the cell is positive, the cell shows plus signs. If the value is negative, it shows minus signs. A zero displays as a single decimal point. For example, cells B1, B2, and B3 in the following worksheet contain the values 7, 0, and -3, respectively.

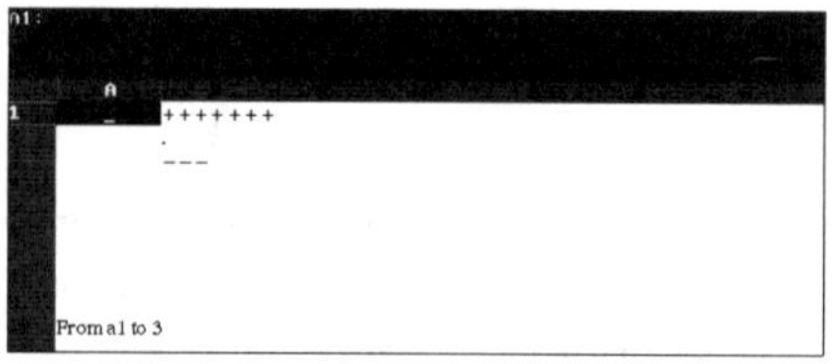

Make simple graphs of your data by reducing them to small numbers and assigning them the +/– format. Adjust column widths as needed to accommodate this unusual display.

Clock or Not

The date and time display in the bottom-left corner of your screen offers one more opportunity to customize your spreadsheet environment. When you first start 1-2-3, the date and time appear as DD-MMM-YY HH:MM AM/PM. So, on July 27, 1992 at 12:35 in the afternoon you would see 27-Jul-92 12:35 PM.

To alter the date and time display, select Worksheet Global Default Other Clock. The resulting menu offers several options. The first option, Standard, is what already appears on the display. The second option, International, switches the date display to match whatever is currently set as the D4 format. It switches the time display to match the current D9 format. We'll see how to change the D4 and D9 formats in a moment.

But do you really need a clock on the display while you work? You might find it more useful to exchange the date and time display for the name of the current file. Selecting Filename from the Worksheet Global Default Other Clock menu substitutes the name of the current file at the bottom-left of your display.

Go International: Calendars, Clocks, Currencies, and Negatives

Some of 1-2-3's customization features let you adapt the spreadsheet to standards used outside of your native country. A case in point: in the United States classic date notation is MM/DD/YY, while in Europe the format is DD/MM/YY. The difference is minor, but it is easy to make mistakes in dates that fall before the 13th of a month. Does 3/12/91 represent March 12 or December 3?

Depending on who you do business with, you may want to alter some of the international settings. To do this, select Worksheet Global Default Other International. The resulting dialog box lists the available options.

Suppose that you want to change the international date format. Select Date and choose one of the listed options: MM/DD/YY, DD/MM/YY, DD.MM.YY, or MM-DD-YY. The one you choose becomes the D4 format mentioned earlier. Likewise, to alter the international time format, select Time. Whichever format you choose from among the four offered becomes the D9 format mentioned earlier.

The Global Default Other International menu lets you select the way 1-2-3 punctuates values. By default, 1-2-3 uses periods as decimal points and commas to separate the thousands places from the hundreds. It requires that you use commas to separate the arguments in @functions and macro commands. You can, however, select from among eight punctuation options. You might prefer to use a period as the thousands separator and a comma to mark the decimal point. Two of the choices offer this arrangement—one that requires you to use the period also as the argument separator and one that requires you to use the semicolon.

Semicolons for All Occasions

If you need to alter the international punctuation options quite often, use the semicolon (;) to separate arguments in @ functions and macro commands. No matter which punctuation option you select, 1-2-3 understands the semicolon as an argument separator.

Don't expect to be able to use all of your old worksheets if you change the international punctuation option. Numbers in older worksheets automatically reflect alterations to the international punctuation option, but punctuation in your macros might not be compatible from one international format to the next.

Compose a Currency Symbol

Lotus 1-2-3 lets you build unusual characters that you can't normally type from your keyboard. Among the most useful of these characters are the symbols that represent currencies in various countries. In the United States the currency symbols are the dollar sign ($) and the cent sign (¢). In Japan, the yen sign (¥) comes in handy, while in England you might prefer the pound sign (£).

You create these symbols by issuing a compose sequence. Start the sequence by pressing the COMPOSE key (hold down Alt and press F1). The next two keys you press define the character you compose. Type *c/* to create a cent sign. The following table lists some other useful compose sequences (currency-related and otherwise):

To create this character:	Press:
£	COMPOSE L-
f	COMPOSE ff
¥	COMPOSE y-
₧	COMPOSE pt
π	COMPOSE pi
¡	COMPOSE !!
¿	COMPOSE ??

One of the more interesting international options lets you establish a custom currency symbol. Select Currency from the Worksheet Global Default Other International menu. 1-2-3 prompts you to enter a currency sign. You can enter any string of up to 15 characters. Use a compose sequence (see the box titled Compose a Currency Symbol) to create one of the common currency signs (£, *f*, ¥, ₧), or choose a word or character sequence that suits you.

After you enter a symbol or a string, 1-2-3 asks whether to insert the symbol before or after a formatted number. Whichever you select, your entries replace the original currency formatting symbols that 1-2-3 displays when you issue the Range Format Currency and the Worksheet Global Format Currency commands.

The currency symbol customization feature lets you engage in some amusing pranks. (Please don't do this to someone else's copy of 1-2-3 and then tell them that we said it was a good idea.) Suppose that you enter a zero as the currency symbol and tell 1-2-3 to use the symbol as a suffix. Any numeric

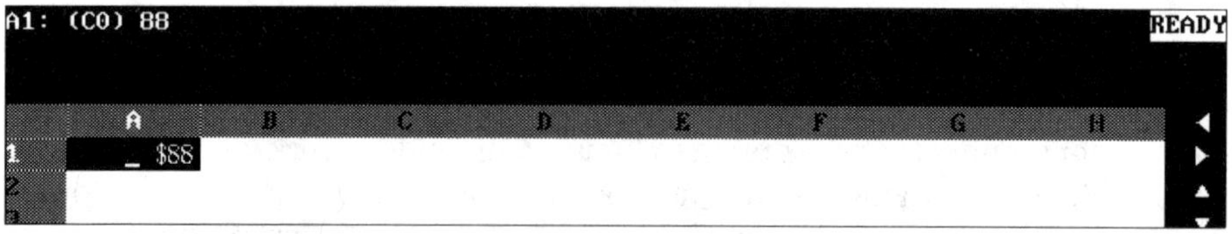

FIGURE 4.4. By customizing your currency symbol to be a 0, you can make any number look bigger.

entries assigned a currency format would then appear with an extra zero, as shown in Figure 4.4.

You can see in the control panel that the entry in cell A1 is 88, but it appears in the cell as 880. The added 0 doesn't enter into any of the spreadsheet calculations, but it sure makes the spreadsheet nonsensical. You can return the sheet to a more sensible condition by using the Worksheet Global Default Other International Currency command. Replace the 0 currency symbol suffix with a more conventional dollar sign prefix.

Make Some of Your Changes Permanent

Individual column width settings and range formats become part of the worksheet in which you assign them. 1-2-3 saves these settings to disk along with the spreadsheet. Other settings, including the date and time display and the international currency format, are universal and apply to all the spreadsheets you retrieve or create during the current work session.

In fact, the settings you establish under the /Worksheet Global Default menu disappear when you exit 1-2-3. They disappear, that is, unless you make a point of saving them. To save changes made on the Global Default menu so they take effect every time you start 1-2-3, select Update from that menu. 1-2-3 stores the settings on disk in a file named 123.CNF. Later chapters explore other options that you can change on the Global Default menu.

Having completed this chapter you should:

- *Know how to hide nonessential information to reduce clutter on your spreadsheet and simplify some printing tasks*
- *Understand the nature of global versus local spreadsheet settings*
- *Be capable of customizing your spreadsheets with a look all your own*
- *Know how to modify spreadsheets for international business*
- *Have a solid grounding in the customization features that you will need as you develop complex spreadsheet models*

5

Fiddle with Function Keys

You probably have at least ten function keys, numbered F1 through F10, somewhere on your keyboard. If this isn't the case, your fingers have been doing gymnastics to apply some of the more useful tools in 1-2-3. Your software has its own names for the F keys, and as you'll see, each of those keys can help as you create complex spreadsheets.

Lotus provides some plastic peel-and-press templates that you can use to label your computer's function keys and make 1-2-3 easier to use. If you have lost your template, or haven't gotten around to putting it on your keyboard, see the list of F keys paired with the names 1-2-3 assigns at the beginning of the chapter.

In this chapter you will:

- *Learn the uses of the 1-2-3 function keys:*

F1: HELP	*F2: EDIT*
F3: NAME	*F4: ABS*
F5: GOTO	*F6: WINDOW*
F7: QUERY	*F8: TABLE*
F9: CALC	*F10: GRAPH*
Alt-F1: COMPOSE	*Alt-F2: STEP*
Alt-F3: RUN	*Alt-F4: UNDO*
Alt-F5: LEARN	

The notation Alt-F1 means, while holding down the Alt key, press F1.

Lost? Confused? In a Panic? Press HELP (F1)

When you press the HELP key, a dialog box pops up over the worksheet. The box usually contains information that relates to whatever you were doing in the spreadsheet at the moment you pressed HELP. In other words, the help that 1-2-3 offers is context-sensitive.

Use the arrow keys or mouse to scroll the text in the help box up or down as needed. Many of the topics discussed in help suggest other topics you can consult. You can jump directly to one of those topics by highlighting with the cursor keys and pressing Return or by clicking with the mouse.

Instant Help with @Functions and Macro Commands
Release 2.3's Help facility is far more helpful than the help in earlier releases of 1-2-3. For example, if you're not sure of the syntax of a formula or a macro command, type the @function or command, and then press HELP. The resulting dialog box gives information related to what you just typed.

You can activate an index to the help system by pressing F1 while the help dialog box is visible or by clicking the index button in the bottom-left corner of the box. Once in the index, select any topic about which you want further information by highlighting it and pressing Return or by clicking it with a mouse. When you have finished with the Help facility, press Escape to return to the spreadsheet.

Don't Retype to Fix Mistakes; Use the EDIT Key (F2)

As you first type a cell entry, it appears on the edit line in the control panel. As long as it is on the edit line, you can modify it by pressing the Backspace key to remove the unwanted characters and typing the new ones in.

After you complete an entry, it no longer appears on the edit line. However, you can bring an entry back to the edit line by putting the cell pointer on the cell and pressing EDIT.

Try It

In a blank worksheet, enter the label *Edit test* into cell A1. Move the cell pointer off of A1 and back, and then press EDIT.

With 1-2-3 in Edit mode, use the arrow keys to move the edit cursor back and forth on the edit line. Any characters that you type in Edit mode appear at the location of the edit cursor. When you press Delete, the character at the cursor vanishes. Pressing Backspace removes the character to the left of the cursor.

When you finish editing, you can either press Return to commit your changes to the spreadsheet or press Escape to abort the edit. The changes you make on the edit line don't take effect until you press Return.

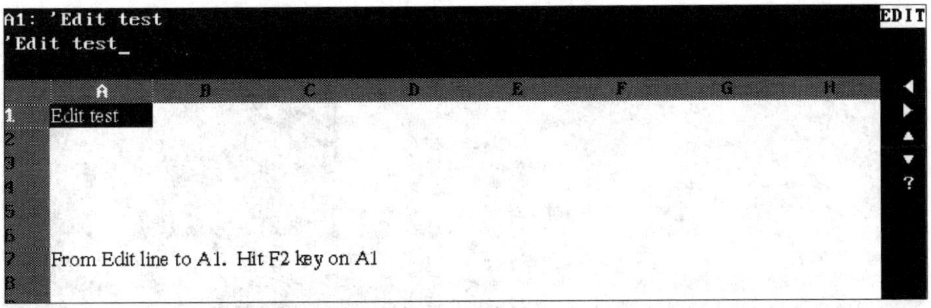

FIGURE 5.1. Pressing the EDIT key (F2) brings the contents of a cell onto the edit line of the control panel. When you make changes and press Return, you replace the original entry.

You don't always have to press the EDIT key to activate Edit mode. 1-2-3 automatically goes into Edit mode when you try to make a cell entry that doesn't make sense. Such an entry might be a formula that has unmatched parentheses or includes references to nonexistent cell addresses. Also, if you begin an entry by typing a number and then mix in letters, 1-2-3 rejects the entry and enters Edit mode. This might happen when you enter a street address such as *11 Westford Avenue* without first typing a label prefix.

Expanded Menus Speed Selections: NAME (F3)

You may face menus that vary in length at any of several points in a 1-2-3 work session. Usually, you encounter such menus when you save and retrieve files. When you select File Retrieve, for example, 1-2-3 lists in the control panel several files that are available in the current directory. If you have more file names than can fit across the display, you must use the arrow keys to make a second set of names visible, and then a third set, and so on. To retrieve a file, you highlight one of the names and press Return.

If you prefer to see all of the available file names at once, press the NAME key. 1-2-3 expands the menu of file names to use as much of the display as is necessary. If there are still too many names to list at once, the arrow keys will scroll new ones onto the display. Even with the menu expanded, you highlight a file name and press Return to retrieve the file.

The NAME key actually exists for a use other than the one just described. Its real purpose is to help you work in a spreadsheet that contains a great many range names (see the box titled Names Instead of Addresses for an explanation of range names).

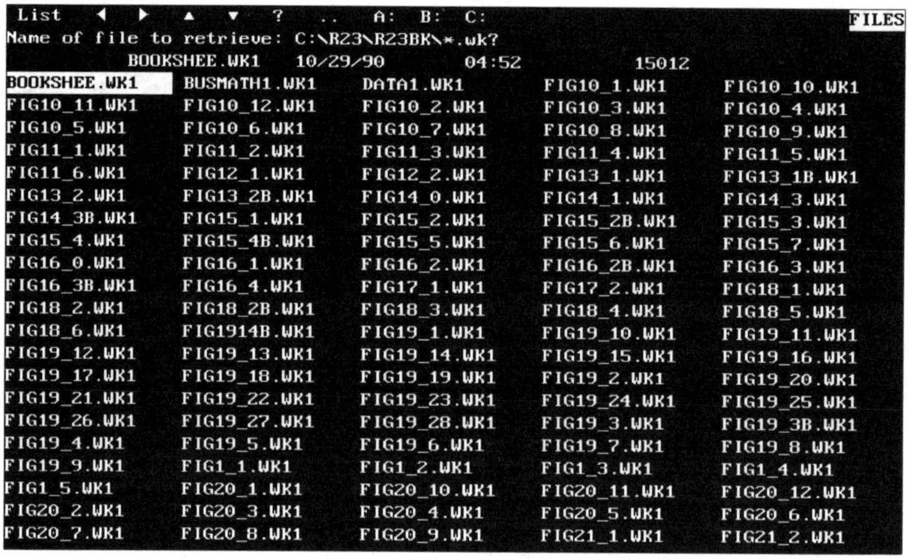

FIGURE 5.2. Your computer will show a listing of files similar to this one when you use the NAME key (F3) in conjunction with the File Retrieve command.

Try the Name Key

Try a little experiment to see how the NAME key can help you work with named cells and ranges. Use the Range Name Create command to establish two range names in the sheet. Assign the name *first* to cell A3 and the name *second* to cell A4. Enter the value *8* into A3 and *3* into A4. Now move the pointer to cell A5, and type a plus sign.

The plus sign tells 1-2-3 that what follows is a formula. It will be a simple formula that adds the value in *first* to the value in *second*. Rather than type out the range names, use the NAME key to insert them. Press NAME, and a menu that offers the two names you just created appears. Highlight the name *first*, and press Return. Now the formula you are creating reads *+FIRST*.

Type a second plus sign, and press NAME. Select *second* from the resulting menu and your formula reads *+FIRST+SECOND*. Press Return to enter the formula into cell A5. If the process of creating a formula is new to you, jump ahead to the Formulas section of this book for more information about it.

The point of this exercise is to show that whenever you would normally point to indicate a range, you can just as well press the NAME key and choose a range name from the resulting menu. Of course, using the NAME key this way makes sense only if you have created range names in your spreadsheet.

Names Instead of Addresses

While cell addresses uniquely identify each entry in a spreadsheet, they can be pretty meaningless to someone trying to interpret a collection of spreadsheet calculations. The expression @SUM(B2..B4) obviously totals some numbers, but what do those numbers represent? If the expression read @SUM(jansales), its meaning would be much more clear. Your formulas can be this clear if you create range names in the spreadsheet.

You can name any cell or rectangular range of cells. To assign a name, select Range Name Create, enter a name that describes the purpose of the range, and indicate the range to name. From then on you can refer to the range by its name, rather than by its range address.

To assign a currency format to every cell in a range named jansales, select Range Format Currency, enter *0*, and then enter *jansales*. Do you want to sum the entries in *jansales*? Place the cell pointer in the cell that will receive the sum. Then type *@SUM(jansales)*, and press Return.

Make Formulaic References Stick: ABS (F4)

The ABS key has several functions. We explored one of them in Chapter 2. There we explained how the ABS key lets you highlight a range before you issue a command.

To do this, press the ABS key. 1-2-3 prompts *Range:*, offering an anchored range reference in the current cell. Use the arrow keys to expand the highlight until it covers whatever range you want to use in the command you are about to issue. When you issue a command, Range Erase, for example, 1-2-3 automatically applies the command to the pre-selected range. Simply press Return to complete the command sequence.

Another of the ABS key's uses is a little harder to explain, and it won't make much sense if you don't already understand the difference between

NAME Simplifies Dialogs

When you hit a point in a dialog box at which you need to identify a range, pressing the NAME key produces a menu of established range names. For example, suppose you select Graph and then activate the X range check box in the dialog box. When you press NAME, another box, listing named ranges, appears. You can select from this list to establish the graph's X range.

ABS Lets You Point in a Dialog

When you want to establish a range setting in a dialog box, the ABS key can save a lot of effort. Pressing ABS temporarily suppresses the dialog box and lets you use Point mode to establish the reference.

For example, suppose that you have selected Graph and activated the X range check box. Press ABS, and you can use the arrow keys or the mouse to highlight a range in the spreadsheet. When you press Return or click the mouse to lock in the selected range, the dialog box reappears with the range reference entered in the X range check box.

relative and absolute cell references. Chapter 13 in the Formulas section explains those differences.

You use the ABS key to establish absolute references as you create and edit formulas. To see how this works, place the cell pointer in any blank cell in the worksheet and type *+A1*. Before you press Return to complete the entry, press the ABS key. 1-2-3 inserts dollar signs before the column letter and the row number in the cell reference you have just typed. Press the ABS key a second time and see what happens.

Each time you press the ABS key, 1-2-3 offers a different configuration of absolute references within the reference you have just established in a formula. The first time you press ABS, the reference becomes $A$1. The second time you press ABS, the reference becomes A$1; the third time it becomes $A1; and the fourth time it reverts back to A1. Once you have established the appropriate type of reference, you can continue building the formula.

The ABS key inserts absolute reference symbols, whether you're typing a formula or entering the formula in Point mode. What's more, the ABS key will alter the reference types within an established formula when 1-2-3 is in edit mode. Pressing ABS inserts absolute signs into the reference nearest the edit line cursor.

Get There in a Hurry: GOTO (F5)

When you know the address or the range name of a cell that you want to examine, and the cell isn't already on the display, the GOTO key will get you to it in a hurry. To view any cell, press the GOTO key and enter the cell's address. Alternatively, press GOTO, and enter a range name.

In worksheets that contain many range names, you might try using the GOTO key in conjunction with the NAME key. Pressing GOTO followed by NAME produces a menu of range names from which you can select a destination range. Pressing the NAME key a second time expands the range name menu to use as much of the display as it needs to reveal all the established names.

When Your Worksheet Does Windows: WINDOW (F6)

The WINDOW key lets you jump from one window to another and back when you have the display split into two windows on the worksheet. If you are not familiar with windows in the spreadsheet (this has nothing to do with the product called Microsoft Windows), you might want to read the next chapter titled Some Handy Tools. One of the subsections of that chapter talks briefly about worksheet windows.

Please Repeat the Answer: The QUERY Key (F7)

The use of the QUERY key won't make sense unless you are familiar with 1-2-3's database features. The Data Analysis and Statistics section explains these in depth.

If you are using the Data Query commands, you may benefit from using the QUERY key. The QUERY key repeats whichever Data Query operation you last performed, without resorting to the menus. For example, you might select Data Query Extract and then quit back to Ready mode. After examining the extracted records, you can change the criteria and press QUERY to perform a new extract operation. This saves wading through the Data Query menus each time you want to examine a collection of selected records.

If you want to use the Query Find command rather than Data Query, you must once again resort to the Data Query menus. However, after you issue the Data Query Find command, pressing QUERY will result in a repeat of the Find command, not Extract.

Set the Table Once: TABLE (F8)

F8 is another key whose purpose won't make much sense until you've logged some hours with the Data commands. Pressing TABLE recalculates whatever data table you last defined via the Data Table menus.

You might select Data Table 1, indicate a table range, and then indicate an input cell. After the calculation, you can alter some of the values in the left column of the table or alter one of the table's formulas and then press TABLE without resorting to the menus. 1-2-3 calculates new table values based on the changes you have made to the table. This saves walking through the Data Table menus repeatedly to see the results of changes you make in the structure of a data table.

Update Formulaic Calculations: CALC (F9)

CALC is one of the more versatile function keys. You use it both to force recalculation of all the formulas in the worksheet and to convert individual formulas into the values that they currently calculate.

You use the CALC key to update the worksheet only under certain circumstances. Normally, 1-2-3 updates the worksheet automatically whenever you enter something into a cell, copy or move ranges, or otherwise alter the spreadsheet layout. This way, formulas always return results based on the data currently in the spreadsheet. When a worksheet grows very large, recalculation can become time-consuming. You might wait several seconds after each change to the sheet before 1-2-3 returns to Ready mode.

If your worksheet model is getting sluggish, you can deactivate automatic recalculation. Do this by selecting Worksheet Global Recalculation Manual. You'll eliminate the lag time after altering the worksheet, at a cost: formulaic calculations won't necessarily reflect the currently entered values. A formula that reads +A1+A2 won't respond to a change in a value in cell A1.

In manual Recalc mode, when there is any chance that the worksheet's calculations aren't current, the calc indicator appears at the bottom of the display. This is a reminder to you to press CALC before drawing conclusions from your worksheet. Pressing CALC forces the formulas to recalculate, taking into account all the changes made to the sheet since the previous recalculation.

Do you want to convert a formula into its current value? One way is to apply the CALC key. After you create a formula by typing operators, cell addresses, and @functions, you can press CALC before pressing Return. 1-2-3 resolves the formula you have typed, and its result appears on the edit line in the control panel. Likewise, after you have entered a formula, you can return it to the edit line by pressing the EDIT key and then press CALC to convert it to its current value. CALC won't evaluate a formula if 1-2-3 is in Point mode.

Try it in any worksheet. Move the cell pointer to a blank cell and type *+8+12* without pressing Return. The addition formula appears on the edit line in the control panel. Press CALC, and the result, 20, replaces the formula on the edit line.

Review the Current Graph: GRAPH (F10)

Here's yet another function key whose purpose might have little meaning early in your spreadsheeting career. The GRAPH key gives you instant access to the current graph. When you press GRAPH, 1-2-3 displays either the graph you last defined via the Graph menu or the named graph that you last made current by selecting Graph Name Use. Pressing GRAPH will produce the graph display no matter what else you were doing in the spreadsheet. 1-2-3 needn't be in Ready mode as was necessary with earlier releases of the program. Consult Section 4 for information on creating and naming graphs in 1-2-3.

Type Unusual Characters: COMPOSE (Alt-F1)

Your spreadsheet can display far more characters than there are keys on your keyboard. Of course, the Shift key alone adds some 40 characters beyond the lowercase letters, the ten digits, and the basic punctuation set. However, the COMPOSE key lets you create many more characters.

In Chapter 4, Customize the Environment, we looked at a few of the characters that you can create using COMPOSE. Those were primarily currency symbols such as, £, ¥, and ₧, which you might use if you are doing business internationally. Those characters were just the tip of the iceberg, however.

Many of the special characters are needed when you are writing text in a language other than English. You might need an accent on a letter or a common symbol that isn't otherwise represented on the keyboard. You create such characters by pressing COMPOSE and then typing two characters.

Be a Composer

Try a few. To press COMPOSE, hold down the Alt key and press F1. Release the Alt key, and then type a colon followed by a minus sign. A division sign (÷) appears on the edit line. Press COMPOSE again, and type a plus sign followed by a minus sign. A plus/minus sign (±) appears after the slash. Do you speak Spanish? Press COMPOSE, and type n~.

You'll find a complete list of compose sequences in the 1-2-3 documentation. In the meantime, here are a few more sequences to whet your appetite:

To create this character:	Press:
≥	COMPOSE >=
°	COMPOSE ^0
Pr	COMPOSE ^p
•	COMPOSE ^.
¼	COMPOSE 14
½	COMPOSE 12
ô	COMPOSE ^o
è	COMPOSE e'

Before you fill your spreadsheets with all of these fancy characters, you should be aware of limitations you may encounter when you try to print them. While 1-2-3 will display the composed characters, many printers won't be able to reproduce them.

The only way to be sure that your printer can recreate a composed character is to try printing it. In some cases, you will get the character as it looks on your monitor. Other times, your printer may substitute a less attractive character in place of the one you composed. The best way to get around these problems is to print from within the Wysiwyg add-in that we explore a bit at the end of this section.

In any case, experiment in advance before you rely on the COMPOSE key to spruce up your spreadsheets. It might be a waste of effort if you can't print the characters that lend extra meaning to your models.

Slow Motion Macros: STEP (Alt-F2)

Are you writing macros yet? If not, you have no use for the STEP key. However, as you begin to write macros, you will find the STEP key indispensable when you want to track down errors in your macro code. The section titled Macros gives you a solid introduction to the topic.

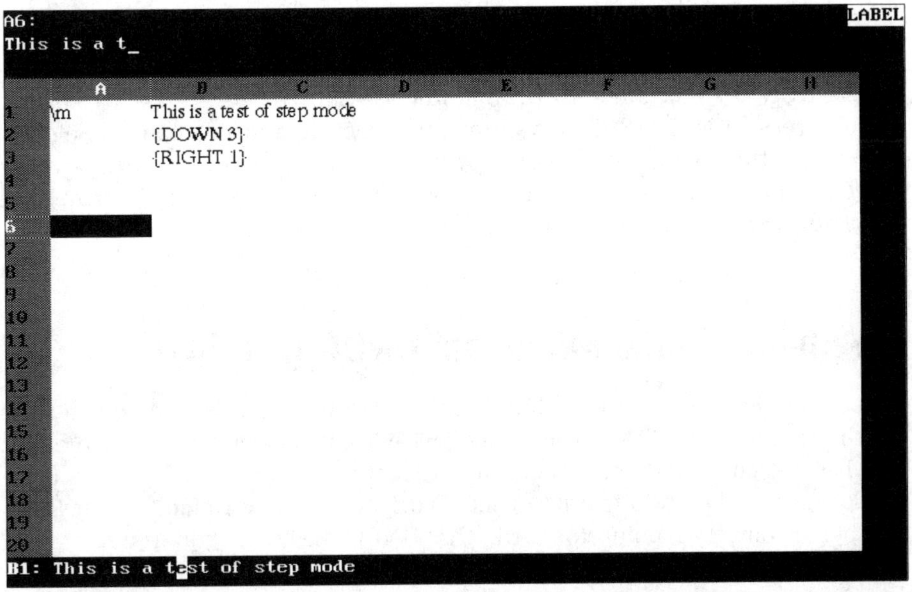

FIGURE 5.3. 1-2-3 displays the currently active macro code when you activate Step mode before starting the macro.

Pressing the STEP key activates the step indicator at the bottom of the display. While the step indicator is visible, 1-2-3 processes macros keystroke-by-keystroke, command-by-command, but only one at a time. You must press a key after each command is processed to get 1-2-3 to proceed to the next command.

As an added bonus, while in Step mode, 1-2-3 displays whatever line of code it is currently processing. A highlight appears on the keystroke or macro command that 1-2-3 will process with your next keypress. It should look something like Figure 5.3.

The purpose of Step mode is to let you observe the macro's progress while you also see the macro's effects in the worksheet. If there is an error in the macro, you can usually isolate it easily when it occurs in step mode.

A Macro of Any Name: RUN (Alt-F3)

Another macro-related function key, the RUN key lets you activate a macro no matter what range name you've assigned it. The classic macro name consists of a backslash followed by a single letter, such as *\m*, or *\s*. To start such a macro running, you hold down the MACRO key (Alt), and press the letter of the macro's name.

The RUN key was added to 1-2-3 in Release 2.2. To activate a macro of any name, press RUN. 1-2-3 displays a menu of available macro names. Select a name from the menu, enter a name by typing it and pressing Return, or enter the cell address of a macro to run. If you don't see on the menu a name that you know exists in the worksheet, press the NAME key to expand the menu.

Go Ahead, Make Mistakes: UNDO (Alt-F4)

Lotus 1-2-3 has a feature called undo that is normally inactive when you start up the spreadsheet. The feature does just what it says: it removes the effect of whatever command you issued most recently.

To activate the undo feature, select Worksheet Global Default Other Undo Enable. From that point forward, the UNDO key lets you recover from mistakes.

Try It

See how it works. Get to a blank worksheet (select Worksheet Erase Yes and Yes a second time if 1-2-3 warns you that you haven't saved), and enable the undo feature. Enter some data in the worksheet.

Place the cell pointer in A1 and enter *test*. Select Copy, and indicate cell A1 as the range to copy from. Then indicate range B2..C5 as the range to copy to. Your worksheet should match Figure 5.4.

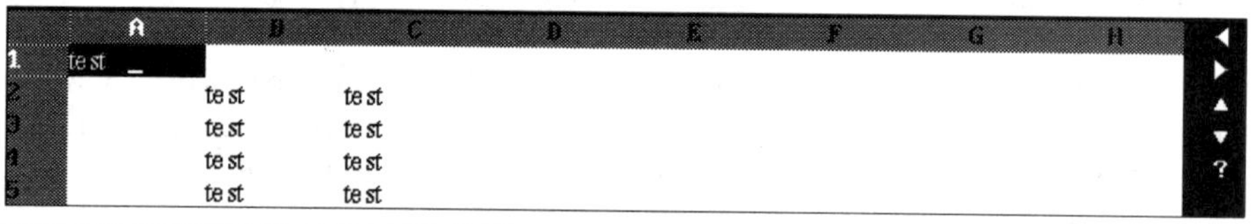

FIGURE 5.4. Create this uninspiring worksheet to test the UNDO function key.

Pretend that this is very important data, that it took you three hours to enter it, and that you haven't yet saved the worksheet. (Heaven forbid that this situation should ever occur.)

That's the scenario. Now you're about to make a big mistake. Select Range Erase, and indicate range C2..D4 as the range to erase. Oops! Some of the

Quick Spreadsheet Comparisons

Lotus 1-2-3 Release 2.3's UNDO key offers a handy way to compare the contents of two spreadsheets. Suppose that you want to flip from one sheet to another and back so that you can compare some sales projections, year-end results, or even some of the formulas used to describe a business problem.

Start by making sure you have saved both worksheets. With the undo feature enabled, retrieve one of the worksheets, and then retrieve the other one. When you retrieve the second worksheet, the first one seems to go away, but it doesn't really. Until you alter something in the second worksheet, you can flip back to the earlier one by pressing the UNDO key.

Navigate in either worksheet by pressing the arrow keys. Examine the underlying contents of formula cells by moving the cell pointer to them and looking at the current cell indicator in the control panel. As long as you don't make any entries or issue any commands, you can flip from one sheet to the other indefinitely.

precious data vanished—you meant to indicate range D2..E4 as the range to erase. Don't panic. Instead, hold down the Alt key and press F4. 1-2-3 instantly cancels your last command—the Range Erase command—and your data returns.

The UNDO key can reverse the effects of almost any command that you issue in 1-2-3. It can even unretrieve a file and return you to the spreadsheet that was current before you issued the File Retrieve command.

There are times that 1-2-3 won't be able to undo things. They arise when the worksheet you're working in is very large. There may not be enough space in RAM for the software to keep track both of what you just did and what the sheet was like before you did it. 1-2-3 flashes a warning on the display when it won't be able to undo a command. If the warning appears often in a given spreadsheet, you're better off selecting /Worksheet Global Default Other Undo Disable to deactivate the undo feature.

Record Keystrokes to Use as Macro Instructions: LEARN

Oh, boy. Another function key that matters only if you're already familiar with macros. You know where to look if you haven't used them yet. On the other hand, if you have worked with macros in 1-2-3 at all, you might be interested in the LEARN key.

Before you can use the LEARN key, you must establish a *learn range* in the spreadsheet. The learn range acts as a recording area in which 1-2-3 can keep track of the keys you press during the work session. To establish a learn range, select Worksheet Learn Range and highlight a range. The range need fall in only one column of the sheet because 1-2-3 uses just the left-most column for its recording.

After establishing a learn range, press the LEARN key to activate learn mode. 1-2-3 displays an indicator at the bottom of the display, and while the indicator is present, 1-2-3 records label representations of every keystroke you make. Stop keystroke recording by pressing the LEARN key a second time. If the learn range becomes full of recorded keystrokes before you stop recording, 1-2-3 alerts you with an error message.

Typically, you use Learn mode to record the keystrokes that perform a procedure you want to include in a macro. Then you copy the labels from the learn range into your macro.

Having completed this chapter you should:

- *Be better able to identify function keys by name as well as number*
- *Have a sense of the ways in which function keys extend the capabilities of 1-2-3*
- *Recognize opportunities to speed your work by applying function keys*
- *Be able to work more efficiently as you create bigger and more complex spreadsheets*

6

Copy and Move—A Quick Review and Then Some

The Copy and Move commands are fundamental tools of any spreadsheet. The Copy command saves hundreds of keystrokes by letting you enter labels and formulas once and copy them as needed. The Move command lets you rearrange a spreadsheet to make way for data as you doodle with your creation and shape it into a viable model.

We refer to the Copy command repeatedly throughout this book, making the assumption that you have used it often in your own spreadsheets. If our assumption is wrong, you might want a little refresher. We don't cover all of it in this chapter, but if you read ahead you will gain a solid understanding of how to apply the Copy command. You might even learn some things you don't already know about this versatile command. In the meantime, we'll contrast the functionality of the Copy command with that of the Move command and offer a way to think of these commands that helps in understanding why they work as they do.

In this chapter, you will:

- *Review how the Copy command duplicates cells*
- *Copy patterns of cell entries*
- *Explore the effects of the Move command*

The Basic Copy: Copy One Cell

Start in a blank worksheet. To get there, select /Worksheet Erase Yes Yes. Of course, before you can try out the Copy command, you must have something to copy. Enter your name into cell A1.

There are several ways to copy a single cell to another cell. Try this one: If you're using the keyboard, start with the cell pointer in the cell that you plan to copy—in this case, cell A1. With the pointer there, select Copy from the main menu. Notice that 1-2-3 offers a range reference as the default range to copy from. For the moment, that isn't important; press Return to accept cell A1 as the range to copy from.

Lotus 1-2-3 offers a single-cell reference as the range to copy to. Press DownArrow to highlight cell A2, and press Return to indicate that this is the target range. Your name appears in cell A2, and the cell pointer returns to cell A1.

Copy with a Mouse
To copy your name from cell A1 to cell A2, select Copy from the menu. Double click cell A1, and then double click cell A2.

With what you know about working in Point mode, it should be a snap to copy your name from cell A1 to cell A3, starting with the cell pointer in cell A3. Move the cell pointer to cell A3, and try to copy your name before you read the text that describes the procedure.

How'd you do? Did you select Copy, press Escape to unanchor the range reference, press UpArrow twice, and then press Return twice? That would work. You also could select Copy, type *A1*, and press Return twice. In either case, the cell pointer would end up in cell A3 where it began.

One Begets Many

Often in 1-2-3 you need to repeat a cell's contents in several other cells. If those cells constitute a range, a single Copy command will serve.

For example, copy your name from cell A1 to range B1..E1. With the cell pointer in A1, select Copy and press Return. Then press RightArrow so that the cell pointer is in cell B1. Press the period key to anchor the pointer, and press RightArrow three times to extend the highlight. Finally, press Return.

The Mouse Begets Many
Use the mouse to copy your name from cell A1 to range B1..E1 as follows: Select Copy from the menu and double click cell A1. Drag from cell B1 to cell E1, and then click anywhere on the spreadsheet.

Sometimes the cell you want to copy resides in the top-left corner of the range to which you want to copy it. If that's the case, don't hesitate to include the From cell as part of the To range. Enter your name into cell C3 to see how this works.

Copy your name from cell C3 to range C3..D5. If you didn't include cell C3 in the To range, you would have to perform two copy procedures. Instead, select Copy and indicate cell C3 as the range to copy from. Indicate range C3..D5 as the range to copy to. You can copy any cell onto itself without harming its contents—even if the cell contains a formula.

When you copy a single cell to a range, 1-2-3 places a copy in each cell of the target range. We use this feature repeatedly throughout this book.

From Many to One?

Lotus 1-2-3 lets you abbreviate commands when you want to copy a range of cells to another area of the spreadsheet. Let's copy the block of entries from range C3..D5 to range C7..D9. Select Copy and indicate range C3..D5 as the range to copy from. Indicate only cell C7 as the destination range. 1-2-3 assumes that you want to copy the entire From range and uses whatever space it needs—even when you indicate just a single-cell target range.

Copy Preselected Ranges

When you preselect a range and then issue the Copy command, 1-2-3 doesn't prompt you to indicate a range to copy from. Rather, it uses the preselected range as the range to copy from and prompts you to indicate a target cell or range for the copy operation. This is particularly slick when you're using a mouse.

For example, to copy from range C3..D5 to range C7..D9, drag with the mouse from C3 to D5. Then select Copy. Finally, double click cell C7.

There are also shortcuts for replicating a row or a column. For example, you might wish to copy a single column into several adjacent columns. To see the allowable shortcut, enter the number *1* into cell A11. Enter *2* into A12, and enter *3* into cell A13. To copy these entries to columns B, C, and D, select Copy and indicate range A11..A13 as the range to copy from. Indicate range B11..D11 as the range to copy to.

Copy Patterns

The Copy command has an interesting property that lets you use it to establish patterns of entries in the spreadsheet. The simplest application of this feature is to copy an entry to every other cell in a column. By applying the Copy command once in just the right way, you can avoid having to issue it repeatedly.

Suppose you want to copy the label in cell A1 to cells A3, A5, and A7. Select Copy, indicate range A1..A6 as the range to copy from, and indicate cell A3 as the range to copy to.

Lotus 1-2-3 copies the range row-by-row. In this case, it starts by copying cell A1 to cell A3. Then it copies cell A2 to cell A4. When it copies cell A3 to cell A5, it finds the newly established label in A3, and replicates it in cell A5. It copies the blank cell A4 to cell A6 and the new label from cell A5 to A7. This happens very quickly, so normally you wouldn't be aware of the sequence. However, when you copy a large range into itself, you expose the Copy command's functionality.

Here's a more realistic example: Suppose that you have made some entries, as shown in Figure 6.1, that you want to repeat six times at regular intervals —perhaps with two rows separating each copy from the preceding one— down the sheet.

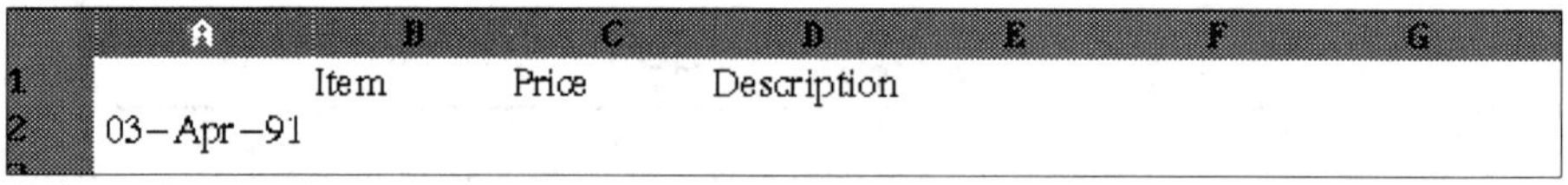

FIGURE 6.1. This simple spreadsheet shows a collection of entries that you might need to repeat six times down columns A through D of the spreadsheet.

Rather than make the entries six times—a time-consuming procedure— use the Copy command to create all of them at once. Select Copy, and indicate range A1..D20 as the range to copy from. Then indicate cell A5 as the range to copy to.

Using the Copy command you can repeat any pattern of entries by indicating a large range to copy from and a range to copy to that falls somewhere within the From range. Experiment on your own to develop a knack for selecting the appropriate ranges.

Move Versus Copy

The Copy command replicates everything about a cell—its contents, its format, and its protection status (explained in the next chapter). We have used the command here to copy labels and values, but it works as well in copying formulas. Actually, the Copy command has extra utility in copying formulas. Explore that utility in depth by working through the Formulas section of this book.

In the meantime, here's a way to think about the Copy command that might help you to understand the Move command. The Copy command leaves the contents of the From cell intact. It erases whatever is in the target cell and builds a copy of the From cell. The existing target cell remains intact; only its contents and attributes change.

The Move command works much like the Copy command. However, the Move command rips cells out of the worksheet and drops them back in, obliterating any cells at the target location. The newly located cells take on new cell addresses, and the area from which the moved cells were ripped heals over with fresh, unused cells.

While the Copy command leaves all formulaic references and range settings intact, the Move command can seriously alter such settings. Let's look at the Move command more closely.

When It Just Doesn't Belong Where It Is, Move It

The obvious first exercise for the Move command is to move one cell to a new location. Try it. Move cell A1 to cell A11. Select Move from the main menu, and indicate cell A1 as the range to move. Indicate cell A11 as the target cell. No tricks yet, your name vanishes from cell A1 and replaces the entry in cell A11.

Copy And Move Wysiwyg Formats

Wysiwyg formatting acts like numeric display formatting when you issue Copy and Move commands. 1-2-3 copies lines, shading, font types, and font styles along with cells and ranges and replicates them in the destination cells.

When you move cells and ranges in Wysiwyg, you rip everything about the cells and ranges out of the sheet. For example, if you move a cell out of a shaded range, the shading goes along with the cell—1-2-3 leaves a normal blank cell within the range.

You'll see in later discussions about Wysiwyg that the add-in offers menu options that copy and move formatting options without disturbing the contents of the cells and ranges involved.

To appreciate the Move command, you'll have to prepare a scenario that involves formulas. Here's a simple one: enter the formula @SUM(B11..B13) into cell B15. Use the Copy command to copy the formula to range C15..D15. There are now three formulas in the worksheet that you can use to test the Move command.

For the first test, move cell A13 onto cell B13. Select Move, indicate A13 as the range to copy from, and indicate cell B13 as the range to copy to. The formula in cell B15 returns ERR. This is because moving data onto one of the formula's referenced cells destroyed the cell, along with all references to it. If you had copied from cell A13 onto cell B13, the formula's referenced cell would have remained intact, and the formula would still return a sum.

The lesson, then, is to be cautious about where you move cells and ranges. If you obliterate cells that are crucial to your formulas' calculations, it could take hours to track down the problem and rebuild your spreadsheet.

For the second test, move cell C11 to cell B11. But before you do, check out the formula in cell C15. It currently reads @SUM(C11..C13), which refers to the cell you're about to move. Select Move, indicate cell C11 as the From range, and indicate cell B11 as the To range. Once again check out the formula in C15. It now refers to range B11..C13.

The Move command ripped cell C11 out of the sheet and dropped it in a new location. The formulaic reference to cell C11 went along for the ride. The lesson here is to be cautious when you move things. During a move operation, formulas try to keep track of the specific data to which they already refer. Try another test to illustrate the point.

The third test involves moving a cell that contains a formula. We might as well make it the formula in cell C15. Select Move, and indicate cell C15 as the range to move. Then indicate cell C17 as the target range. When it reaches its destination, the formula still refers to range B11..C13. Once again, during a move operation, formulas try to keep track of the specific data to which they already refer. Given this fact, you can plan moves to include formulas along with all the cells to which they refer. You can also move formulas away from the cells they reference to make way for new data. The following illustration shows a situation in which you might try the latter type of move. (Don't actually create the worksheet shown in Figure 6.2; we have one more task to perform in your current practice sheet).

	A	B	C	D	E	F	G
1		Product	Revenue				
2	Stacy	Boots	$27,889		04–Jul		
3	Cindy	Pumps	$26,675		05–Jul		
4	Cindy	Boots	$22,997		06–Jul		
5	Stacy	Pumps	$21,189		07–Jul		
6		=======	=======		08–Jul		
7			$98,750		09–Jul		

FIGURE 6.2. A worksheet in which you might want to move formulas away from the cells they reference to make room for more data.

The spreadsheet contains a small table in range A1..C7 and another table beginning in column E. You want to add two rows of data to the first table, and inserting rows in the sheet is out of the question; it would mess up the table to the right. (The next chapter includes an explanation of how to insert rows.) If you move the bottom two or three rows of the table downward, adding rows is a snap.

To do this, you would select Move from the menu, indicate range A4..C7 as the range to move, and indicate cell A6 as the target cell. The formula that started out in cell C7 would end up in cell C9. It would then refer to range C2..C7; the formula's reference to cell C5 would move along with cell C5. The formula would reflect entries made to the new rows within the table.

The final experiment we suggest is to move a formula along with all the cells to which it refers. You'll see that the formula continues to refer to its data, no matter where it ends up in the sheet. Select Move, and indicate range D11..D15 as the range to move. Indicate cell D14 as the target cell.

After the move, check out the @SUM formula in column D. It now refers to a new range, but still to the data that you moved along with it.

A Quick Recap

This chapter has led you through several applications of both the Copy command and the Move command. While our intent was to give you a grounding in how to use the commands, perhaps the most important tidbit is the fundamental difference in the way the commands treat cells in the target ranges.

The Copy command leaves cells in both the source range and the target range intact. It erases data in the target cells and applies the display formats and the protection statuses of the cells it is copying. Formulas and settings that refer to the target cells accept the new information copied to those cells.

The Move command rips cells out of the spreadsheet and drops them back into it, completely obliterating any data existing in the target range. Formulas and settings that refer specifically to cells in the target range of a Move command are invalidated when the target cells are obliterated.

Having completed this chapter you should:

- *Understand the subtleties of copying and moving cells and ranges*
- *Have a sense of what to suspect when ERRs arise in the spreadsheet*
- *Know how to save time by applying the Copy command in clever ways*

7

Handy Tools

By now it should be apparent that 1-2-3 has a wealth of useful features. Any one of them could be the focus of an entire chapter in a book and some provide fodder for several chapters. Fortunately, you can learn a small percentage of 1-2-3's features and still become very proficient with the spreadsheet. Equally fortunate, the more you master the fundamentals, the easier it is to understand and apply some of the more esoteric features.

Rather than spend several chapters delving into those esoteric features, we've rounded several of them up here. Normally, you might overlook these gems. However, some day you'll ask, How can I do that in 1-2-3?, and the answer will be here in this chapter. These commands let you work efficiently with 1-2-3. They help you to save RAM, to speed recalculation, and to enter data rapidly.

In this chapter you will learn about the following commands:

- *System—access DOS without unloading 1-2-3*
- *Range Value—convert formulas to their current values*
- *Range Transpose—flip ranges of cells 90 degrees*
- *Worksheet Titles—clarify entries in the sheet*
- *Range Protect and Range Unprotect—stave off unwanted meddling*
- *Worksheet Windows—work at opposite ends of the sheet*
- *Range Justify—square off a range of long labels*
- *Worksheet Insert—place blank rows or columns in the sheet*
- *Worksheet Delete—remove rows or columns from the sheet*
- *Data Fill—create number series*

Quick Access to DOS: The System Command

The more familiar you become with your computer, the more likely you are to be working in DOS. Activities such as copying and renaming files go quite quickly in DOS, and others, such as creating and deleting directories, you can't do at all from within 1-2-3. If you work much in DOS, you will find many opportunities to use the System command.

When you select System from 1-2-3's main menu, 1-2-3 itself slides out of the way, and DOS loads on top of it. The DOS prompt appears, and you can issue DOS commands and even start up other programs. You might capitalize on the System command when you need to back up a spreadsheet to a floppy disk, but you must first format the disk. Or, save some time copying spreadsheet files by using DOS's COPY command rather than loading each file into 1-2-3 and saving in a new directory or on a new disk.

When you want to return to 1-2-3, enter *exit* at the DOS prompt. You return to 1-2-3 where you left off; the spreadsheet you were working on is still loaded and ready for action.

Using the System command is not the same as selecting Quit from the 1-2-3 menu. When you select Quit, the current spreadsheet and all of the 1-2-3 program code vanish from RAM. When you select System, the spreadsheet and program code remain in RAM; they simply become inactive.

One cautionary note about the System command: it is possible (though it happens rarely) that other programs you run in DOS might try to use parts of RAM that contain the inactive 1-2-3 program code. This could make it impossible to reenter 1-2-3 from DOS, and it could even force you to restart your computer. To protect your data, be sure you have saved your work before you issue the System command. And don't forget how you got into DOS in the first place. You might accidentally start up 1-2-3 a second time, when you should really issue the DOS exit command.

Convert Formulas to Values: The Range Value Command

Sometimes you no longer need the formulas in your worksheet. You are still interested in the results of the formulas, but the formulas themselves are just slowing you down. Formulas use up more memory than numbers and labels do, and spreadsheets that contain a lot of formulas tend to respond more slowly than those with only a few formulas. The Range Value command can clean things up for you.

The Range Value command replaces formulas with the current values of the formulas. To see how it works, start in a blank worksheet and enter the formula *@RAND* into cell A1. The @RAND function returns a random number between zero and 1 (see the Formulas section for more information on @RAND). Use the Copy command to copy from cell A1 to range A1..C10. Now each cell in A1..C10 contains an @RAND formula.

Each time you alter the spreadsheet, the values of the @RAND functions change. The Range Value command can record a snapshot of the current values. One way to use the command is to copy just the values of the formulas to a new location. This doesn't remove the original formulas from the sheet, but it lets you preserve the results of a set of calculations, alter some variables, and compare the new calculations with the old. A second way to use the Range Value command is to copy the formulas' values so that they actually replace the original formulas. This increases the speed, and decreases the RAM requirement of a spreadsheet. Try the first method first.

With the cell pointer in cell A1, select Range Value, indicate range A1..C10 as the range to convert, and indicate cell A12 as the target range. 1-2-3 records the values of the formulas in the target range and simultaneously updates the worksheet so that the @RAND functions return new values. The entries in range A12..C21 show the values the @RAND functions were showing before you issued the Range Value command.

Now try Range Value the other way by converting all of the @RAND formulas into values in the cells that they now occupy. Select Range Value and indicate range A1..C10 as the range to convert. Indicate cell A1 as the target range. The formulas are gone, and only their values remain.

Flip 90 Degrees: Range Transpose

Here's a situation that arises from time to time when you're laying out a spreadsheet: you enter a series of labels across a row and then realize that the labels would be better listed down a column. Alternatively, you might enter a list of numbers down a column and then wish you had entered them across a row. In either situation, help is only three keystrokes away.

The Range Transpose command copies a range of cells, flipping the copied entries 90 degrees. To see how this works, enter labels and values as shown in Figure 7.1.

	A	B	C	D	E	F	G	H
1		Eric	Kirstin	Kris	Alyson			
2		25000	22000	27000	21000			

FIGURE 7.1. Set up your worksheet like this to try out the Range Transpose command.

Select Range Transpose, and indicate range B1..E2 as the range to transpose. Indicate cell A4 as the target range. The worksheet ends up like Figure 7.2.

	A	B	C	D	E	F	G	H
1		Eric	Kirstin	Kris	Alyson			
2		25000	22000	27000	21000			
3								
4	Eric	25000						
5	Kirstin	22000						
6	Kris	27000						
7	Alyson	21000						

FIGURE 7.2. We transposed the entries in range B1..E2 to produce the listing in range A4..B7 of this worksheet.

If you were to transpose range A4..B7, the resultant entries would match those from which you originally transposed the range. 1-2-3 transposes only labels and values. If there are formulas in the source range, 1-2-3 places the current values of the formulas in the transposed target range. The conversion is necessary to prevent confusion that would arise from adjusting transposed formulaic references—to what cells should transposed formulas refer?

Lock Information on the Display as Worksheet Titles

When you start compiling data, you might enter a header at the top of each column to identify the type of information the column contains. Then, as you enter data down the columns, those headers scroll off the display. When you have made the 21st entry (depending on your display driver), the headers no longer show as you work your way through the sheet.

The Worksheet Titles command lets you lock rows and columns onto the display. After you set horizontal titles, you can scroll to the end of the spreadsheet and your column heads will remain visible. Give it a shot.

Enter labels as shown in Figure 7.3.

	A	B	C	D	E	F	G	H
1	Employee phone list							
2								
3	First	Last	Extension					

FIGURE 7.3. Create this worksheet to experiment with locking titles.

Now move the cell pointer to row 4 of the spreadsheet—anywhere in the row is fine—and select Worksheet Titles Horizontal. 1-2-3 returns to Ready mode, and the display appears unchanged. However, you can no longer move the cell pointer above row 4. For that matter, rows 1, 2, and 3 can no longer scroll off of the display.

Press PageDown several times, and you see that the column headers and the spreadsheet title in cell A1 remain visible no matter how far down the sheet you travel. You could be entering data in row 8000 and still see that column A is for first names, column B for last names, and column C for extensions.

Press the Home key, and the cell pointer jumps to cell A4, the cursor keys don't allow access to the titles area of the sheet. However, if you need to work in the titles area, press the GOTO key (F5) and enter a target address within the titles—cell A1 would do in this example. The cell pointer jumps to A1. The titles appear to double on the screen. You can navigate as needed within the titles rows until you scroll the second set of titles upward and off the display.

To clear the titles, select Worksheet Titles Clear. Should you wish to lock a column or columns on the display, use the Worksheet Titles Vertical command. The Worksheet Titles Both command establishes as titles both the rows visible above the cell pointer and the columns visible to the left of the pointer.

Lock in a Cell's Contents: Range Protect

Lotus 1-2-3 can keep you and other users from changing the contents of a cell. When you create complex formulas or build tables of vital data, for example, you might want to lock in the entries so that no one can accidentally alter them or remove them from the spreadsheet. The Range Protect and the Worksheet Global Protection commands work together to guard your entries.

To explore these commands, select Worksheet Erase Yes Yes to prepare the sheet for this discussion. Then enter your name into cell A1.

Every cell in the spreadsheet starts out with an electronic security system built-in. These security systems aren't activated, but they are in place and ready for use. A simple menu sequence activates all the security systems. Give it a try: select Worksheet Global Protection Enable. Now all the cells in the worksheet are protected from change.

Try to replace your name in cell A1. Type someone else's name and press Return. 1-2-3 flashes the error indicator, and a dialog box appears to tell you that cell A1 is protected. When worksheet protection is on, you can't alter a protected cell. The cell's security system prevents you from entering data, copying data into the cell, or affecting the cell's contents in any way. Because all cells start out with protection installed, activating protection makes it so that the worksheet won't allow any changes.

When you build spreadsheet models, you might want to be able to establish protection on some cells and leave other cells unprotected. This lets you alter the sheet without risk to formulas and data that you have already entered. Protection lets you do this. Because all cells start out with protection on, you selectively remove protection from the cells that you want to be able to change. Then, when you activate protection, only the unprotected cells allow changes.

Try it. Select Range Unprotect, and indicate range B1..B4. You can make all the changes you want to the contents of these unprotected cells. Try entering your name into cell B2. 1-2-3 accepts the name without a hitch. When you move the cell pointer, however, you will notice that the color of B1's entry is different from that of cell A1. The alternate coloration identifies cells from which you have removed the electronic protection. Unprotected cells display in an alternate color (or intensity) whether or not you have activated global protection.

Should you want to reestablish protection on a range of cells, select Range Protect, and indicate the range. To deactivate protection on all protected cells, select Worksheet Global Protection Disable.

Two points clarify how protection works:

1. The Range Unprotect command removes the electronic security systems from cells in a range. This is equivalent to removing a security alarm system from a house. Using the Range Protect command reinstalls a security system in each cell in a range.
2. The Worksheet Protection Enable command activates all the existing security systems. If a cell has had its security system removed via the Range Unprotect command, then there is nothing for the Worksheet Protection Enable command to activate in that cell—you can still alter the cell's contents.

1-2-3 copies the protection status (protected or unprotected) of a cell along with the cell's contents when you issue the Copy command.

One note of caution: each cell unprotected by the Range Unprotect command eats up a little more RAM than a protected cell. If you are working under RAM constraints, avoid unprotecting large numbers of cells unnecessarily.

One Sheet, Two Views: Worksheet Windows

When a worksheet gets very large, you might have trouble keeping track of what you've done in one part of it while working in another part. Building formulas in row 700 that depend on entries in and around row 200 can be pretty tricky—unless you use windows.

Windows in the worksheet have nothing to do with the product called Microsoft Windows. Think of the visible area of the spreadsheet as showing through a window. The worksheet itself is too large to show all at once on the display; that's why you look through a window at only a part of it. When you move the cell pointer and scroll the worksheet, you cause the worksheet to move behind the window.

The Worksheet Windows command splits the display into two windows onto the worksheet. Each window can look onto a different part of the sheet, and each can have its own global cell format and individual column widths.

An Exercise with Windows

Create a window as follows: Move the cell pointer to about the middle of the screen, and select Worksheet Window Horizontal. A row of column letters slices the display in half—1-2-3 has created a second worksheet frame. This frame marks the boundaries of the second window, as shown in Figure 7.4.

FIGURE 7.4. A 1-2-3 display with windows established.

You are looking at two windows on a single spreadsheet. Data that you enter through either window ends up in the sheet. Also, any commands that you issue in either window affect the sheet identically—with a few exceptions.

Make the Mouse Do Windows in Wysiwyg

If you typically work with Wysiwyg active, your mouse can make windows in a flash. To split the windows horizontally, drag the line immediately above the upper-most number visible in the spreadsheet frame. When you start dragging, a dotted line extends across the sheet; the window splits wherever that line is when you release the mouse button. Likewise, to split the window vertically, drag the line immediately to the left of the first letter visible in the spreadsheet frame.

Select Worksheet Global Format Currency, and enter *0*. Now enter numbers in a few cells of the upper window. The numbers appear with a currency format. The newly entered numbers appear in the lower window too, but without the currency format. Press the WINDOW key (F6) to move the cell pointer into the lower window, and enter numbers in a few cells there. These values appear in the general format in the current window, and as currency in the upper one. The Global format that you established in the upper window has no effect on the lower window. Any cells formatted via the Range Format command have the same display format in both windows.

With the cell pointer still in the lower window, use the Worksheet Column Set-Width command to change the widths of several columns. Column widths in the upper window are unaffected by the Set-Width commands issued in the lower window, and vice versa. You can set unique worksheet titles in each window as well, but we'll leave you to explore that on your own.

Windows give you two perspectives on one set of data, but that's not all they offer. With the cell pointer somewhere below row 100 in the sheet, let's create a formula that refers to some cells around row 30.

Start by pressing the WINDOW key (F6) and moving the cell pointer in the upper window down to cell A30. Press WINDOW again, and use the GOTO key (F5) to get the cell pointer to cell A110. Type a plus sign to begin the formula.

If you are working without a mouse, press the WINDOW key, and the cell pointer jumps to cell A30 in the upper window. That's the first cell we will include in the formula, so type a second plus sign. Press WINDOW again, and then press RightArrow so the cell pointer moves to cell B30. Press Return to complete the formula.

Hopping from window-to-window to create formulas this way is much more efficient than poking around with the cursor-movement keys to locate cells at opposite ends of the sheet. If you customarily enter formulas by exploiting Point mode, then doing so across windows will simplify the procedure in large spreadsheets.

Build Formulas with a Mouse in Windows

If you are working with a mouse, hop from one window to the other simply by clicking the target window. To build a formula containing cells in both windows, click anywhere in the upper window, and get the cell pointer to cell A30. Click in the lower window, and get the cell pointer to A110. Type a plus sign to begin the formula, and then click cell A30 in the upper window. Type a second plus sign, and place the mouse pointer on cell B30 in the upper window. Press and hold the mouse button until 1-2-3 highlights cell B30, then change mouse buttons and click to collapse the range reference, B30..B30, on the edit line to a single-cell reference. Change mouse buttons again, and click anywhere to enter the formula.

If you simply type a plus sign in one window and click a cell in the other window, 1-2-3 doesn't include the clicked cell's reference in the formula you are creating. Instead, it activates the window that you clicked and offers whatever cell was current in that window before you started typing the formula. Holding down the mouse button is the only way to establish a formulaic reference across windows using the mouse exclusively.

Normally, the worksheet behind the windows remains in synchrony with itself when you scroll the cell pointer to one side. This means that if you move the cell pointer to cell D110 and then switch windows, the pointer jumps to cell D30 in the other window. Likewise, if you move the pointer to cell K30 in the upper window, it jumps to cell K110 when you switch to the lower window.

Working with windows synchronized lets you easily examine information within columns (or rows) at opposite ends of the spreadsheet. With unsynchronized windows, hopping from one to the other doesn't cause the readjustment. You can examine entirely unrelated areas of the spreadsheet and jump quickly from one to the other when the windows aren't synchronized.

The Worksheet Window Unsynch command overrides synchronization. After you issue this command, cell pointer movements in the lower window have no relationship to those in the upper window, and vice versa. To resume synchronized window scrolling, select Worksheet Window Synch.

When you finish working with two windows, select Worksheet Window Clear. 1-2-3 retains the global cell format, column widths, and titles that you set in the upper window.

The Worksheet Window Vertical command creates two windows by establishing a second vertical frame containing row numbers. The rules described for work in horizontal windows apply as well to work in vertical windows. When you clear vertical windows, 1-2-3 retains column widths set in the left window. You can't establish both horizontal and vertical windows at the same time.

Rudimentary Text Processing: Range Justify

When your business's data and calculations reside in a spreadsheet, you are often tempted to create elaborate documents such as memos and letters that include paragraphs of text to accompany the other spreadsheet structures. The Range Justify command helps accomplish this.

The Range Justify command fits long labels into a prescribed width. Create a sample paragraph to see how this works. Start in cell A1 of a blank worksheet (select Worksheet Erase Yes Yes), and type the following sentence, attributed to Abraham Lincoln. (Don't press Return when you are finished.):

> Four score and seven years ago our fathers brought forth on this continent a new nation, conceived in liberty, and dedicated to the proposition that all men are created equal.

You'll notice that when the cursor on the edit line hits the right edge of the display, the entire entry scrolls to the left across the control panel. Finally, when you have typed all the characters, press Return to enter the label. It stretches beyond the right edge of the worksheet window.

With the cell pointer still in A1, select Range Justify. Expand the highlight to cover range A1..D6. When your worksheet matches Figure 7.5, press Return.

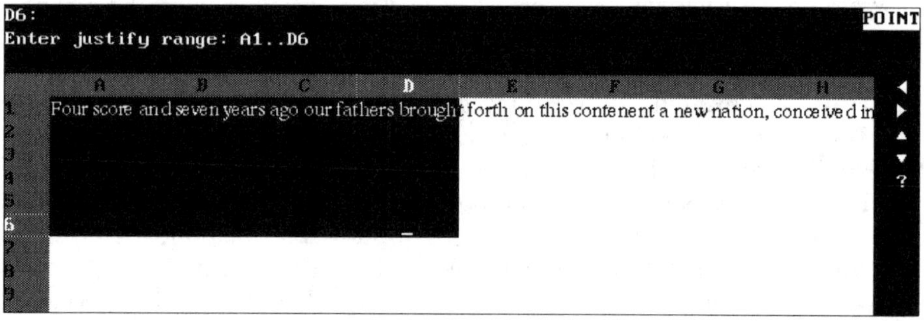

FIGURE 7.5. 1-2-3 during the Range Justify highlighting.

Lotus 1-2-3 splits the long label into six new labels, each in its own row. None of the new labels stretches past column D. 1-2-3 has justified the sentence into a block whose width was defined by the width of the range that you indicated.

The Range Justify command will rearrange all of the labels within the designated range. Reapply the command. Select Range Justify, and indicate

Text Processing for Wysiwyg Users

If you always work with Wysiwyg active, the :Text Edit command obviates the need for the Range Justify command. When you select :Text Edit, Wysiwyg prompts you to highlight a range that will receive text. Then an edit cursor appears at the beginning of the selected range. The spreadsheet acts as a very limited word processor until you have filled the edit range or until you press Escape. Find more about the Text Edit command in Section 4 of this book.

range A1..F6 as the range to justify. 1-2-3 rearranges the labels to fit in a block the width of the justify range.

When you indicate a multi-row range to the Range Justify command, you limit the justification effects to the entries, and the rows, within that range. In other words, if you select Range Justify and indicate range A1..C2, 1-2-3 tries to fit the labels that are in A1..A2 into the width of three columns. Try it.

Because the labels won't fit in the space indicated, an error condition arises. When you press Escape to clear the error, you find that most of the words ended up in the last row of the justify range—row 2. The labels below row 2 weren't affected because they were outside the justify range.

If you indicate a one-row justify range, 1-2-3 justifies all contiguous labels below and including the one in the indicated row. To see how this works, select Range Justify, and indicate range A1..D1. 1-2-3 justifies all contiguous labels in column A.

It is prudent to indicate a multi-row range when you use Range Justify. When you use a single-row justify range, 1-2-3 moves cells that have nothing to do with the labels being justified. This can destroy the alignment of information stored in tables below the text you are entering.

Make Way for More Stuff: The Worksheet Insert Commands

You have just entered 10 rows of sales data, and you realize that you left out one of your salespeople. To make matters worse, you forgot to reserve a column in which to enter descriptions of the items that the sales team sells. No problem. 1-2-3 can easily insert rows and columns just about anywhere you need them.

Practice Inserting Rows and Columns

To practice inserting rows and columns, you don't need to enter 10 rows of data; just recreate the small worksheet shown in Figure 7.6.

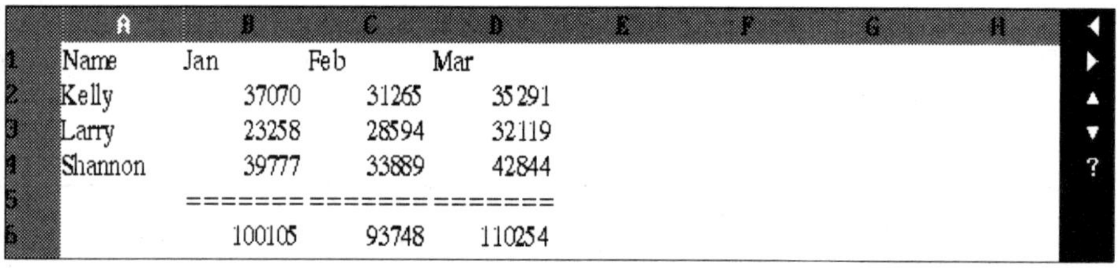

	A	B	C	D	E	F	G	H
1	Name	Jan	Feb	Mar				
2	Kelly	37070	31265	35291				
3	Larry	23258	28594	32119				
4	Shannon	39777	33889	42844				
5		=======	=======	=======				
6		100105	93748	110254				

FIGURE 7.6. Create this worksheet with which to practice inserting rows and columns.

Enter the labels and values shown in range A1..D4. Enter \= into cells B5, C5, and D5 to create the dividing line in row 5. In cell B6 enter the formula *@SUM(B2..B4)*. (You'll find more about the @SUM function in the Formulas section of this book.) Select Copy, indicate cell B6 as the range to copy from and range C6..D6 as the range to copy to.

You have entered sales figures for Kelly, Larry, and Shannon, but how are you going to fit Jim's efforts into the model? He should have been first on the list (it's alphabetized), so you'll have to make space between the column headers and Kelly's record.

Move the cell pointer to any cell in row 2 and select Worksheet Insert Row. Press Return to indicate that a single row should be inserted at the cell pointer. Everything in the sheet at and below the cell pointer moves down, and a blank row—the new row 2—appears.

Enter Jim's record in the new row. Enter *Jim* in cell A2, *41500* into cell B2, *43889* into C2, and *44110* into cell D2. But wait. What about those formulas? The row you inserted isn't included in the ranges that the formulas sum. You must manually adjust the formulas to account for the new data.

Place the cell pointer in cell B7, and press the EDIT key (F2). Change the first reference in the formula to B2 rather than B3, so that the new formula reads @SUM(B2..B5), and then copy the formula to range C7..D7.

This is an important lesson. When you use the Insert Row command to alter the worksheet, don't assume that existing formulas are aware of the alterations. If you insert a row above a referenced range or just below a referenced range, the formulas containing the references won't have a clue about the new rows. Likewise, a range name or a range setting in a settings dialog box won't detect inserted rows if the rows don't fall between the top-left and bottom-right corner cells of the range.

In this case, you inserted a row above the ranges that the @SUM formulas referenced. If the row had been within the referenced ranges, the formulas would have adjusted to include the new row in their calculations. Isn't it convenient that you omitted Patty's record from the worksheet? Entering her sales information will reveal how the formulas can adjust automatically to accommodate a new row.

Select Worksheet Insert Row, and indicate row 5—any range of cells in that row will do—as the range of rows to insert. Enter *Patty* in the new cell A5, *36991* in cell B5, *37777* in C5, and *36363* in cell D5. As you make each of the numeric entries, notice that the formulas account for them automatically.

The underlying rule is that when you insert a row or rows within an established worksheet range, the range definition expands to include the added cells, as shown in Figure 7.7.

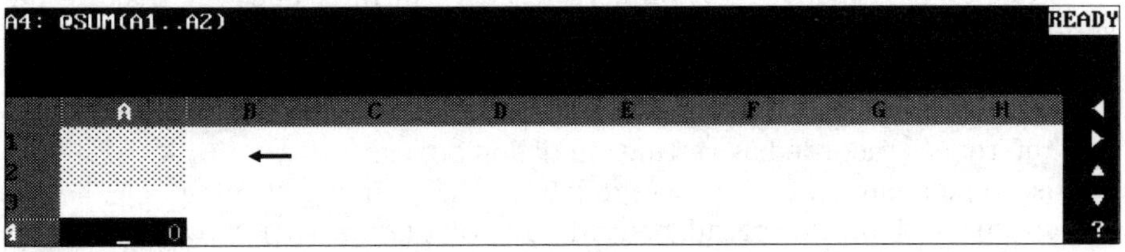

FIGURE 7.7. When you insert rows between the top-left and the bottom-right cells in a range, the range's reference expands to include the new rows. Inserting a single row at the arrow would alter the formula to read @SUM(A1..A3).

The Worksheet Insert Column command differs from Worksheet Insert Row only in the obvious way: it inserts columns rather than rows. If you decide to use either of these commands, be cautious. When you insert a row, you insert a row across the entire spreadsheet. You might disrupt tables of data stored to one side or another of the data with which you are currently working. Likewise, when you insert a column, you insert that column to the full depth of the sheet.

Trash Data: The Worksheet Delete Commands

If you can insert rows and columns into the sheet, you must be able to delete rows and columns from the sheet. Indeed, you can. But do so cautiously. When you delete a row or a column, you essentially rip cells right out of the fabric of the sheet. This can seriously upset formulas and settings that refer to those cells.

Consider the worksheet with which you've been fiddling. Larry doesn't work out of your office; his data slipped into your spreadsheet by accident. You can get him out of your worksheet in a flash as follows: place the cell pointer on his name, select Worksheet Delete Row, and press Return to delete the current row. Larry's data vanish, along with the row that contained them. The summary formulas reflect the change.

The @SUM formulas still work because the row you deleted didn't include the top-left or bottom-right corner of the ranges they reference. However, check out what happens when you delete a row that contains one of those cells.

Select Worksheet Delete Row, and indicate row 5—any number of cells in the row will do. 1-2-3 removes the row from the worksheet, and the summary formulas return ERR. Watch what you delete!

Lotus 1-2-3 keeps track of range references in the same way that we describe them; it records only the top-left and the bottom-right corner cells. You can remove any of the cells between those two, but deleting one of the key corner cells invalidates any reference to the range—both formulaic reference and references recorded as settings in dialog boxes.

Also remember that when you delete a row, you are deleting cells across the entire width of the spreadsheet. If you don't know what is over to the left or the right, find out before you issue the Delete Rows command.

Of course, the Worksheet Delete Column command takes out columns. Treat it with the same respect you afford the Worksheet Delete Row command.

Enter Number Sequences: The Data Fill Command

Whether the universe was created this way or we decided that it must be so, things have sequences. And, especially when we work in spreadsheets, it seems that we need to number those sequences. The Data Fill command makes numbering easy.

Try the Data Fill Command

To try out the Data Fill command, first use the Worksheet Erase command to clear out the spreadsheet you've been using. The task is to number the first 20 cells of column A from 1 to 20—perhaps to mark a series of transactions that you will be recording in columns B, C, and D.

With the cell pointer in A1, select Data Fill. 1-2-3 prompts for a range to fill; indicate range A1..A20. 1-2-3 prompts you to enter a Start value. The

Start value is the number that 1-2-3 will enter in the first cell of the target range. Enter *1*. 1-2-3 prompts for a Step value. This is the interval by which 1-2-3 will count for each successive entry in the target range. You are numbering the range 1 through 20, so you're counting by intervals of 1; enter *1* as the Step value. Finally, 1-2-3 prompts for a Stop value. This is the highest value 1-2-3 will enter in the target range.

The default Stop value that 1-2-3 offers is 8191. Because you are filling only a 20-cell range, you don't need to change the default; the size of the range limits how high the numeric sequence goes. Simply press Return, and 1-2-3 fills the range with sequential values.

You probably have the idea, but fill one more range just for practice. Select Data Fill. 1-2-3 offers the previous fill range as the one to fill; override the range definition, and set B1..B20 as the new range to fill. Enter *5* as the Start value and *5* as the Step value. This time, enter *30* as the Stop value—30 is the highest number 1-2-3 should place in the fill range.

The resulting numbers are in sequence, starting with 5 and increasing by 5 with each successive cell. Despite the 20-cell fill range, 1-2-3 enters only six values in the sheet. The last entry is 30, matching the Stop value that you stipulated.

Use the Data Fill command to generate any sequence of numbers having a regular interval. For example, you might generate a sequence of weekly dates by entering *@DATE(91,6,6)* as the Start value (see the Formulas section for information about the @DATE function), *7* as the Step value and *@DATE(91,10,6)* as the Stop value.

Having completed this chapter you should:

- *Be familiar with some of the more esoteric features of 1-2-3*
- *Know various shortcuts for re-arranging data in the sheet*
- *Have a sense of how to work efficiently in large spreadsheets*
- *Understand how to make way for new information in the sheet*
- *Be able to alter the sheet without invalidating formulas and settings that involve range references*
- *Know how to enumerate rows and columns and generate number series efficiently*

8

From Sheet-to-Sheet: File Commands

Eventually in your work with spreadsheets, it may strike you that some of the data you entered in one sheet would be really useful in another sheet. You might, for example, want to use a tax or commission table in several spreadsheets. Or, you might simply want to consolidate totals from several quarterly spreadsheets into a single annual summary sheet.

Fortunately, 1-2-3 lets you move data easily from one sheet to another. You might choose to copy information as it appears in a worksheet on disk to one in RAM. If that's too drastic, you can just as well write formulas in one spreadsheet that return values from other spreadsheet files on disk—that is, you can link spreadsheets.

Save a File to Disk: A Quick Review

If you have come this far without saving a file on disks, you are a very patient person. Disk files are recordings of what you have created in the spreadsheet. If you don't save a spreadsheet on disk, you lose your work when you shut off the computer. When you save a file, you can retrieve it as needed in future work sessions.

In this chapter, you will learn how to:

- *Manage your file directories*
- *Combine different files*
- *Link information from different spreadsheets*

To save a file in 1-2-3, select File Save. There are two scenarios:

1. If you are saving the spreadsheet for the first time, 1-2-3 prompts you to enter a file name and offers a menu listing of the files already created on disk. You can select an existing file name (if you want to replace the

Password-Protect Files

By assigning a password as you save a file, you can prevent anyone who doesn't know the password from retrieving the file. This lets you store confidential information in spreadsheets without concern that unauthorized people might view the information. To assign a password, select File Save, and type the desired file name, but don't press Return. Rather, press the Spacebar, type *P*, and then press Return. 1-2-3 prompts you to enter a password. Enter up to 15 upper- and lowercase characters (the characters won't appear on the display as you type them). 1-2-3 prompts you to confirm the password—that means you must enter it a second time, exactly as you did the first time.

When you try to retrieve a password-protected worksheet, 1-2-3 prompts you to enter the password that you assigned when you saved the file. Your entry must match the original password exactly (including upper- and lowercase letters), or 1-2-3 won't bring the file into RAM. If you forget the password, you won't be able to retrieve the file.

A note of caution: password protection can't prevent someone from erasing a file from a disk. Keep backup copies of all files whose contents are important to you.

existing file with the new one you have just created) or enter a unique name for the file you are saving.

2. If you have already saved the current file at least once, 1-2-3 offers to save the file under the name you last used. Either press Return to erase the earlier version of the file and reuse the file name or enter an alternate file name.

Whatever the case, after saving a copy of the current worksheet in a disk file, 1-2-3 returns to Ready mode. You can continue working in the sheet, erase it, or retrieve a different sheet.

Where the Files Go: File Directories

DOS and, consequently, 1-2-3 save files in *directories*. A directory is a subdivision of the disk, like a filing drawer in a file room. A hard disk can be divided into many directories, while each floppy disk typically contains a single directory, though you can divide a floppy disk if you wish.

All disks have a *root* directory. Every other directory on the disk must be contained in the root. Continuing the file room analogy, the root directory is the file room itself. Its full name depends on the letter of the disk drive that contains it. So, the root directory of the C drive is called C:\, and the root of the A drive is A:\.

A directory within the root directory can have any name made up of eight or fewer alphanumeric characters. Your root directory may contain a subdirectory called 123 that holds the 1-2-3 program files. Alternatively, your 1-2-3 directory might be called LOTUS. Whatever it is, you established it when you first installed 1-2-3 on the disk. The *full path name* to a directory named 123 on the C drive is C:\123.

There may be many directories within the root directory of your drive, and each of those directories can have further directories within it. So, for example, the C:\123 directory might contain a directory called DATA whose full path name would be C:\123\DATA. The arrangements of directories on a disk is the disk's *directory tree*. See Figure 8.1.

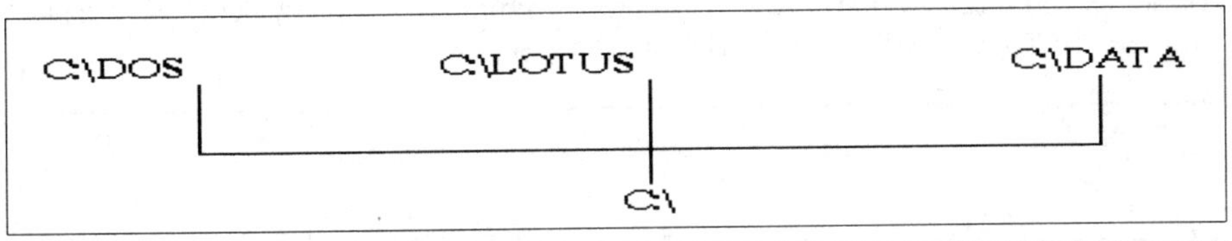

FIGURE 8.1. The simple directory tree of a disk that contains three directories off the root directory.

The important thing to know about any directory is that it can hold files. When you first install it, 1-2-3 automatically saves files in the directory that holds the 1-2-3 program files. You or someone else might have changed this at some point. If you haven't, it's a good idea to do so. The files installed in your 1-2-3 program directory are merely clutter around your data files when you store them all in one directory.

It is good practice to put all the program files associated with a particular software package in a single directory. Place data files in directories of their own; spreadsheet files might go in one directory, word processing files in another, and so on. See the box titled Create Directories on Your Disks for help in creating data directories.

To change the directory that 1-2-3 uses to save files, select /Worksheet Global Default Directory, and enter the full path name to the desired directory. Select Update from the resulting menu, and then select Quit.

Create Directories on Your Disks

If you are storing data of many types on a single disk, it can be helpful to divide the disk into directories whose names bring to mind the types of data they contain. For example, you might name a directory BUDGET to receive spreadsheet files in which you create budgets for your business. A directory named SALES might contain your company's accumulated sales records.

You must work within DOS to create disk directories. Get to DOS either by quitting 1-2-3 or by selecting System from 1-2-3's main menu. Make a directory current in DOS by entering the command *CD dirpath* where dirpath is the full path name to the desired directory. For example, to get to the root directory on the C drive (assuming C is the current drive), enter *CD C:*. To get to the directory named C:\BUDGET, enter *CD C:\BUDGET*.

Use DOS's MD command to create new directories. To create a directory named SALES in the root directory, make the root current, and then enter *MD SALES*. To create a directory named C:\123\DATA, make the C:\123 directory current, and issue the command *MD DATA*. Consult the DOS manual for more information about working with disk directories.

Redirect File Commands on the Fly

When you select File Retrieve, 1-2-3 offers a menu of the files available to retrieve from the current directory. You can select any file by highlighting it with the menu pointer and pressing Return. What if you know, however, that the file you want to retrieve isn't in the current directory but resides, instead, in the root directory?

Many users back out of the File Retrieve menus and use the File Directory command to tell 1-2-3 to look for files in a directory other than the current data directory. This is wasted effort. You can select any directory (and any disk, for that matter) by altering the path name specified on the command line in the control panel when you are saving files, retrieving them, or otherwise working with file-related commands.

While the menu of available files is visible, 1-2-3 also displays the prompt, *Name of file to retrieve.* Following the prompt is the path name to the current directory. By pressing Escape once or twice, you can clear the path and make room to enter an alternate. If you enter *C:\BUDGET*, 1-2-3 makes a menu of the spreadsheet files stored in the BUDGET directory. If you enter *C:*, 1-2-3 lists any spreadsheet files stored in the root directory, along with the names of directories created there. You can activate any listed directory by selecting its name from the menu listing. 1-2-3 then lists any spreadsheet files available in the newly selected directory.

Use the Mouse to Redirect

If you are using the mouse, a collection of icons appears in the control panel when you select File Retrieve—or any of the other file-handling commands. To have 1-2-3 list files in the directory above the current directory, click the double period icon (..). To list files in any listed directory, simply click the directory name in the listing. Click one of the disk drive names (A, B, or C) to view a listing of files on that drive. When you click a worksheet file name, 1-2-3 retrieves the selected file.

Because every hard disk layout is unique, it is impossible to provide an example that you can follow to try out these features with predictable results. We suggest instead that you use the File Retrieve command to experiment with changing directories as you issue file-related commands. If you stick with the File Retrieve command, you needn't be concerned about accidentally erasing a disk file. As you master the subtleties of retrieving files from any directory or disk in your system, you'll be able to extrapolate the experience to saving and listing files as well.

Four Consolidation Methods: File Combine

File basics out of the way, we can explore techniques for working with data stored in several files, both on disk and in RAM. Various consolidation techniques let you bring data from many files into one, laying the data out side-by-side, and even adding up values in a summary spreadsheet. You might use such techniques to consolidate sales information submitted by different sales centers, to add up quarterly or monthly production results recorded in their own spreadsheets, and so on. To see these techniques at work, create sample worksheets as explained in the setup box.

How to Set Up the Worksheets

	A	B	C	D	E	F
1		First Quarter Sales				
2		Sully's Billiard Supply				
3						
4		East	West			
5	19 oz cues	$142,000	$113,900			
6	20 oz cues	$99,300	$75,500			
7	21 oz cues	$133,000	$88,700			
8	cust. cues	$77,900	$66,700			
9		=======	=======			
10		$452,200	$344,800			

1. Column Widths

Set the widths of columns as follows: A, 13; B, 10; C, 10.

2. Labels

Enter labels as shown. Start with an apostrophe label prefix when you make the entries in cells A5, A6, and A7. Create the dividing line in cells B9 and C9 by entering \= into each of those cells.

3. Values and Formulas

Enter the values in range B5..C8, and enter the formula *@SUM(B5..B8)* into cell B10. Copy the formula to cell C10.

4. Numeric Display Formats

Select Range Format Currency, enter *0*, and indicate range B5..C10 as the range to format.

5. Save the File

Select File Save, and enter the name *CUE1ST*.

6. Modify the Sheet

Change the label in cell B1 to read *Second Quarter Sales.* Replace values in the sheet as follows: B5, *127900*; C5, *105800*; B6, *87300*; C6, *69500*; B7, *122700*; C7, *89300*; B8, *76200*; C8, *79500.*

7. Save Under a New Name

Select File Save, and enter *CUE2ND*. The new file name that you type automatically replaces the earlier name in the control panel. 1-2-3 creates a new file named CUE2ND on disk, leaving the CUE1ST file intact.

8. Erase the Sheet

Select File Erase Yes to clear the CUE2ND worksheet from RAM.

If you have completed the setup instructions, you have two worksheets on disk that represent the first and second quarter sales of Sully's Billiard Supply. It's a bit into the third quarter, and Sully has asked you to give him a worksheet that summarizes sales for the first half of the year. We'll look at several ways to create such a consolidation.

Stick It All Together with Brute Force

One way to consolidate worksheets is to place the information from each worksheet into its own area of one worksheet. This way you can see the information from several worksheets laid out side-by-side. Of course, if the spreadsheets you want to consolidate are very large, you might not be able to fit them into a single sheet, then you might resort to other consolidation methods discussed later.

Try it. Enter the label *First Half Sales* into cell B1 and the label *Sully's Billiard Supply* into cell B2. This will form the basis of your first consolidation.

Move the cell pointer to cell A4, and select File Combine. There are three options on the resulting menu: Copy, Add, and Subtract. For this consolidation, select Copy. Select Entire-File, and 1-2-3 prompts for the name of the file to combine. Select CUE1ST. The data from the first file you saved appears in the sheet, beginning at the location of the cell pointer.

Actually, you just combined more information than you really need in this sheet. The label in row 5 is superfluous. Use the Worksheet Delete Rows command to remove it, but remove only the one row. Then move the cell pointer to cell A15 and use the File Combine Copy command to bring in the data from the file named CUE2ND. Once again, use the Worksheet Delete Rows command to eliminate the redundant label that appears in row 16.

All of the data from the first half of the year is now in the consolidation spreadsheet. It is a simple matter to enter the label *Total* in cell A26 and enter an addition formula in cell B26 that sums the first and second quarter totals. That formula would be +B12+B23, and you would copy it to cell C26 to sum the western region's sales alongside those of the eastern region.

This isn't the slickest consolidation on the planet. The truth is, Sully isn't interested in what happened each quarter. He wants a summary of regional sales for each product for the entire first half of the year. Using this consolidation, he would have to add up first and second quarter figures to see the data that interests him.

Having used the File Combine Copy command to bring the data together, you could write and copy a formula to add up the quarterly results. However, by using a different File Combine command, you might have avoided all that trouble in the first place.

The File Combine Copy command brings information from a disk file into the current sheet in a manner similar to the way the Copy command recreates information in the sheet. Any incoming cell that contains data supercedes the corresponding cell of the current worksheet. Consider a simple scenario.

The current worksheet contains entries in cells A1 and B1, as shown in Figure 8.2.

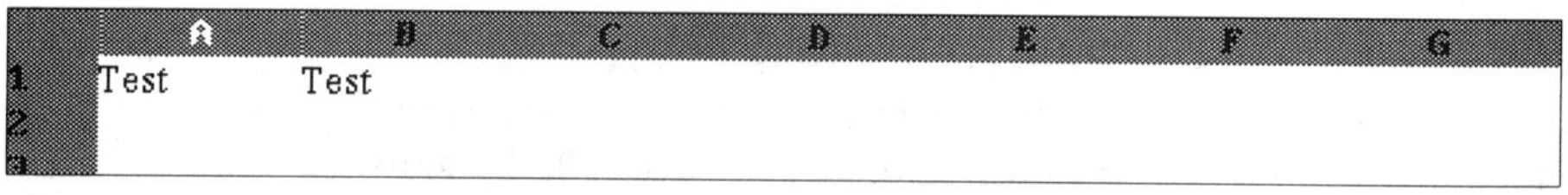

FIGURE 8.2. A simple worksheet that helps to clarify the File Combine command.

The incoming worksheet contains entries in cells A1 and A2, as shown in Figure 8.3.

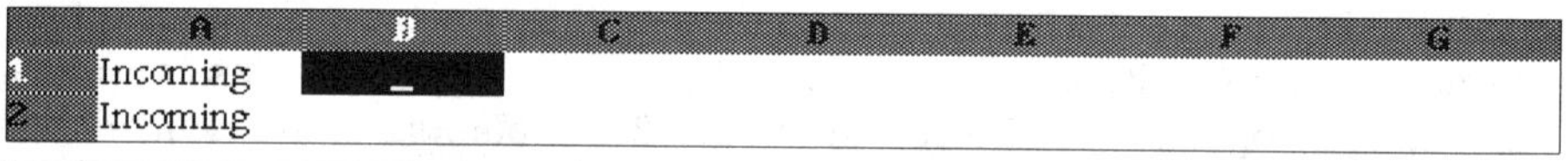

FIGURE 8.3. Worksheet to combine with the worksheet in Figure 8.2.

When you use the File Combine Copy command, the entries from the incoming worksheet—cells A1 and A2—replace any entries in the current sheet. When incoming cells are blank, cells in the current sheet retain their status. The current sheet appears as Figure 8.4 after the Combine Copy operation.

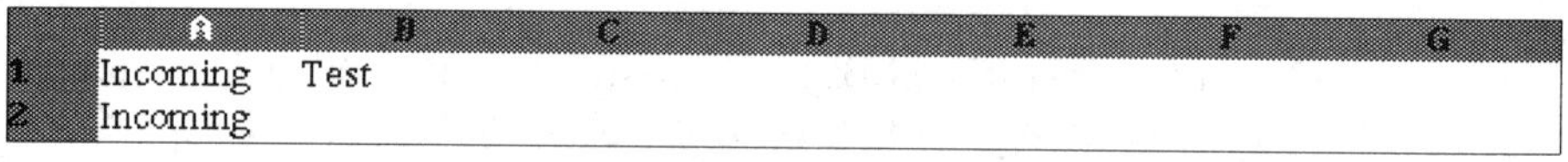

FIGURE 8.4. Worksheet combining the worksheets in Figures 8.2 and 8.3.

Let's do a consolidation that uses a File Combine option to add up values brought into the current spreadsheet from several other sheets.

Insta-Consolidations: File Combine Add

As long as the layout of data is identical from one worksheet to another, you can have 1-2-3 add incoming values to corresponding values in the current sheet. Combining files of several months' data in this way lets you quickly calculate a summation of results for a quarter or for a year. Start fresh to see how this works. Select File Retrieve Yes, and retrieve the file named CUE1ST. You'll use this as the basis for the consolidation.

With the cell pointer still in cell A1, select File Combine Add Entire-File, and then select CUE2ND as the file to combine. The values in columns B and C increase to reflect the totals of the sales figures from the first and the second quarters. Now you can edit the label in cell B1 to read *First Half Sales* and save the consolidated sheet under a unique file name.

The File Combine Add command brings only values (both raw numbers and the current values of formulas) from the disk file into the current sheet. If an incoming value corresponds to a blank cell, the cell receives the value. If an incoming value corresponds to a numeric cell, 1-2-3 adds the values in the two cells. If an incoming value corresponds to a label or a formula entry, 1-2-3 abandons the incoming value.

Here's a simple scenario to clarify the command's operation:

The current worksheet contains a label in cell A1, a value in cell B1, and a formula (+B1+2) in cell C1. See Figure 8.5.

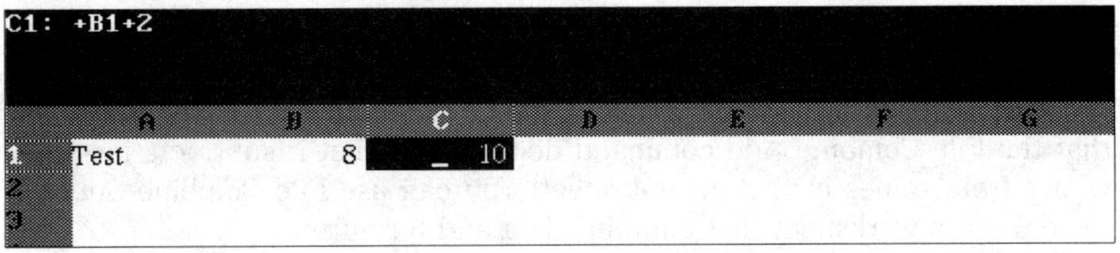

FIGURE 8.5. Entries in the current worksheet.

The incoming worksheet contains labels in cells A1 and A2, values in cells B1 and B2, and formulas (+B1+2 and +C1+2, respectively) in cells C1 and C2, as shown in Figure 8.6.

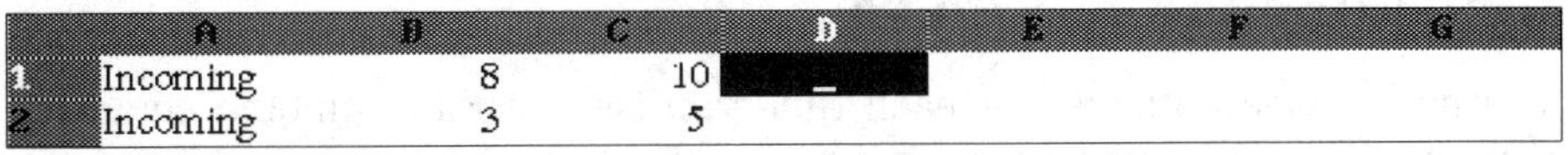

FIGURE 8.6. Contents of the incoming worksheet.

The worksheet that results when you place the cell pointer in A1 and select File Combine Add Entire-File, looks like Figure 8.7.

	A	B	C	D	E	F	G
1	Test	16	18				
2		3	5				

FIGURE 8.7. Results of using the Combine Add command.

The Combine Add command ignores the labels from the incoming sheet. It adds the incoming value 8 from cell B1 of the disk file to the value in cell B1 of the current sheet. The result is 16. The entries that result in cells B2 and C2 are both values from the incoming sheet. The formula from cell C2 doesn't make the trip; only its current value does. Cell C1 in the final sheet still contains the formula +B1+2. 1-2-3 doesn't disturb formulas in the current sheet when you use the File Combine Add command to bring in data.

You used the File Combine Add command to consolidate one worksheet into another. There is no limit to the number of worksheets you combine in your own applications. You might need to consolidate four quarterly worksheets at the end of a year or even 12 monthly worksheets. As long as the worksheets are laid out identically, the consolidation is a snap.

Go Negative: File Combine Subtract

The File Combine Subtract command treats incoming data in the same way that the File Combine Add command does except that it subtracts incoming values from values in the current sheet. You can use File Combine Subtract to zero out a worksheet that contains data and formulas.

To do this, make sure you have saved the worksheet and keep a copy of the sheet in RAM. Then use the File Combine Subtract command to superimpose the worksheet on itself. The formulas and labels remain intact, but the values all revert to zero.

Consolidation in Pieces

You might have noticed that each time you issue a File Combine command you must choose between combining an entire worksheet and combining only a part of a worksheet. When your worksheets have a common structure, com-

Save Only Pieces: The File Xtract Command

The File Combine commands let you bring entire spreadsheets or pieces of spreadsheet files from disk into the current sheet. It is also possible to save entire spreadsheets or just pieces of spreadsheets. You might choose to do this to isolate a table that you will be combining into several other sheets. Save only the table to disk, and you don't have to specify a range each time you issue the File Combine command. Alternatively, a block of data and formulas in an existing spreadsheet might be the perfect beginning for a new spreadsheet.

To save a portion of the current sheet, select File Xtract. You can elect to create a file that includes whatever formulas are in the range that you plan to extract or one that contains only the current values of formulas. Whichever you select, 1-2-3 prompts you to enter a file name and then prompts you to identify the range to extract. The top-left corner cell of the range you specify becomes cell A1 in the new worksheet.

Be aware when you extract a range to a disk file that you are creating a new spreadsheet on the disk. Formulas included in the extract range will refer to new cells in the new spreadsheet. If you extract formulas without extracting the cells to which they refer, the formulas will return different values in the new sheet.

bining them with the Combine Add command is simple. However, when your worksheets aren't of identical dimensions, you may need to pull pieces of one off the disk into the current sheet.

This will be the case when you create tables, such as tax tables or commission schedules, in one sheet that you need to use in several others. After you save the worksheet containing the table, you retrieve another sheet, move the cell pointer to an area that can hold the table, and use the File Combine Copy command to bring the table into the sheet. Use the current practice worksheet to simulate this situation.

For the sake of this discussion, we'll say that the worksheet named CUE1ST on disk contains a commission table in range E5..D8. Because Sully uses the table to calculate the sales commission pools for each of his sales offices, he wants that table to appear somewhere in the worksheet that you're preparing for him. Let's put the commission table off to the right of the consolidated sales figures.

Move the cell pointer to cell I1; the location of the cell pointer determines where the top-left corner cell of an incoming file or range will end up during any File Combine operation. Select File Combine Copy Name/Specified-Range. 1-2-3 prompts for the range to combine. You can enter a range name or a cell or range specification. Enter E5..D8, and then select CUE1ST as the file to combine.

Being able to combine pieces of disk files in the current sheet lets you consolidate files of dissimilar layouts. Knowing the layout of each file, you might combine a row of 19-ounce billiard cue sales from row 5 of one file, from row 22 of another file, and from row 10 of yet another file.

Then Again, Why Combine When You Can Link?

The data that you combine become part of the file into which you combine them. They have no physical connection to the files from which they come. This means that your consolidation files won't reflect changes made in the files that make up the consolidation.

In other words, right now your consolidation worksheet shows the combined sales from the first and second quarter worksheets stored on disk. Sometime after creating the consolidation and saving it under a unique file name, you might receive further information about second quarter sales. You would then retrieve the CUE2ND worksheet and update it to reflect the new sales data.

When you retrieve the consolidation worksheet after making changes in CUE2ND, the consolidation isn't aware that you have made the changes. You would have to repeat the entire consolidation procedure from step 1 to produce an accurate first half report. Depending on the detail you are trying to achieve, you might prefer to use file linking formulas to perform worksheet consolidations.

Before you try linking formulas, be sure that you understand how to create basic mathematical formulas to perform addition, subtraction, multiplication, and division in the worksheet. The section on formulas later in this book explains spreadsheet math.

A linking formula is just like a basic addition formula. Try one in your practice sheet. Move the cell pointer to cell B15 and enter *+<<CUE1ST>>B10*. The formula returns 452200, the summary value in cell B10 of the worksheet named CUE1ST. Move the cell pointer to cell B16, and enter *+<<CUE2ND>>B10*. It returns the summary value from cell B10 of the worksheet named CUE2ND.

Select Copy, indicate range B15..B16 as the range to copy from and cell C15 as the range to copy to. The copied formulas return summary values from the two cells C10 of the disk-based worksheet files. To complete the formulaic consolidation, enter \= into cells B17 and C17. Then enter the formula *+B15+B16* into B18, and copy it to cell C18.

Recalculate Linking Formulas

Lotus 1-2-3 automatically updates file linking formulas when you retrieve a worksheet that contains them. However, you might be working on a network where other people are altering the contents of files to which your file is currently linked. Or you might be working in a multitasking environment like Windows and changing values in several worksheets through several sessions with 1-2-3.

If you suspect that the values in a linked spreadsheet might have changed, but the changes aren't reflected in the linking formulas, select File Administration Link-Refresh. This forces 1-2-3 to check the disk and update the linking formulas.

If you were to save this worksheet, you could retrieve either of the quarterly sales sheets (CUE1ST or CUE2ND), make changes to it, and resave it under its original file name. When you retrieved the consolidation worksheet, the file linking formulas would reflect the changes to the quarterly sheet.

The file references you used to create the file linking formulas included only file names. The first formula, for example, was +<<CUE1ST>>B10. When the link reference is to a file name only, 1-2-3 looks for the named file in the current data directory (established by the File Directory command).

Were you to alter the data directory specification by selecting File Directory and entering a new path, the linking formulas would return ERR; they wouldn't be able to find the linked files in the new directory. Actually, if different files existed in the new directory but had the same file names as those referenced by the linking formulas, 1-2-3 would link the formulas to the new files. Changing the data directory setting back to the directory that contained the true CUE1ST and CUE2ND files would reestablish the original links.

If you tend to alter the data directory specification from time to time during a work session, you might prefer to lock a file link into a particular file and directory. To do this, enter the file's full path name rather than just its file name.

For example, if 1-2-3 saves files in a directory named C:\123DATA, you could create the linking formula in cell B15 to read +<<C:\123DATA\CUE1ST>>B10. No matter what directory you set as the data directory, this formula will always look for a value in cell B10 of the file named CUE1ST in the directory named C:\123DATA.

1-2-3 can link only one cell per formula. What's more, a linking formula can't involve any operations beyond the link itself. You must create a separate formula for each value that you want to bring into a sheet from another worksheet. A formula such as +<<CUE1ST>>B10+<<CUE2ND>>B10 or even one as simple as +<<CUE1ST>>B10+8 simply isn't valid in Release 2.3.

Combine, Link, Consolidate

Working with 1-2-3's File Combine commands gives you access in any worksheet to the data stored in all of your worksheets. You can use the commands to bring tables from one sheet to another and to consolidate data from several sheets into one. But the File Combine commands don't serve all your consolidation needs. When your consolidation worksheets must be aware of changes made to sheets they consolidate, use file linking formulas.

Having completed this chapter you should:

- *Know some shortcuts for locating files to retrieve or combine*
- *Understand the various strategies for consolidating data from several files*
- *Be capable of planning spreadsheets of periodic data—monthly, quarterly, and so on—that you can consolidate easily*
- *Have a handle on linking spreadsheets so that changes made in one sheet are reflected in the formulas of others*

9

Beyond the Spreadsheet: Add-Ins Enhance 1-2-3

Electronic spreadsheets aren't the only things for which people buy computers. You can, however, do so much with a spreadsheet that you may never look for another type of software—especially when you start to use spreadsheet add-ins.

Add-ins are programs that attach to 1-2-3 in such a way that they seem to be part of the spreadsheet software. Once attached, an add-in provides features that 1-2-3 itself lacks. The add-in capability lets corporations create customized software applications that run in the familiar spreadsheet; users throughout the corporation adjust quickly to programs that build on their existing knowledge of 1-2-3. Such add-ins might manage inventories, schedule shipping, or perform quality control analyses.

The add-in feature also lets independent software programmers create tools that they can sell to any spreadsheet user who wants to buy them. Some of these commercially available add-ins simply put more @functions at your disposal, allowing you to handle a wider range of calculations than you can with the @functions built into the spreadsheet. Other add-ins offer the ability to do word processing, to print spreadsheets sideways on a page, and to work with database files as you would with stand-alone database management software such as Ashton Tate's dBase III. There is really no limit to the ways add-ins can enhance 1-2-3.

In this chapter, you'll learn:

- *What add-ins are*
- *How to attach add-ins to 1-2-3*
- *How the Viewer add-in helps with file retrieval and linking*
- *How to check out formulas and assumptions with the Auditor*

Add-Ins That Come in the Box

One of the best things about add-ins is that Lotus includes several of them in the package with 1-2-3. Those add-ins are probably already on your hard disk if you are currently using the spreadsheet software. However, it is possible that you or whoever installed 1-2-3 for you chose not to install any or all of them when 1-2-3 was first set up. Five add-ins come in the package:

- 1-2-3 Go
- The Auditor
- The Viewer
- Macro Library Manager
- Wysiwyg

1-2-3 Go is a series of computer-based lessons that teach how to use 1-2-3. It is somewhat unusual in that you can run it either as an add-in in 1-2-3 or as a stand-alone program from within DOS. When you run it as an add-in, you can go directly from the lessons to the worksheet and try out the commands you have learned.

The Auditor add-in helps you to decipher the relationships between the formulas in a spreadsheet. For the small spreadsheets we use in most of our examples, you would never need anything like the Auditor. However, when your spreadsheets grow very large, you might have difficulty identifying which formulas depend on certain cells for their calculations or which cells play into the calculations of certain formulas. The Auditor tracks these relationships and highlights them for you in the sheet. It also lets you list the interdependencies of cells and formulas.

The Viewer add-in lets you review the contents of worksheet files without actually retrieving the files. When you activate the Viewer, you can highlight file names on a list, as you do when you retrieve files. When you highlight a name, the contents of that file appear in a window to the right of the list of names. File contents appear as quickly as you highlight names, so you can rapidly scroll through the names until you see the file you want to retrieve. The Viewer's features are a subset of the features of Lotus's Magellan disk management software.

The Macro Library Manager add-in lets you keep macros in RAM, but not as part of the current spreadsheet. This makes your macros available in every spreadsheet, without taking up space in any of them. Unlike worksheet-based macros, macros loaded into the Macro Library Manager can erase the current worksheet and retrieve files without disabling themselves. Find more about the Macro Library Manager add-in in the Macros section of this book.

Wysiwyg is by far the most impressive of the add-ins Lotus includes with the spreadsheet software. It turns 1-2-3 into a graphical spreadsheet publishing environment in which you can make cell entries using special fonts and font styles, put boxes around cells, apply shading to the sheet, and even perform rudimentary word processing. Wysiwyg lets you place graphs directly into the sheet alongside spreadsheet data and customize those graphs by superimposing text, lines, arrows, circles, and more. In fact, Wysiwyg is so rich in useful features that we devote several chapters to it. The next chapter in this section provides a sweeping overview of its capabilities, and Chapter 25 in Section 4 explores the add-in in depth. If you are a veteran 1-2-3 user, Wysiwyg may change the way you work with spreadsheets.

A Closer Look at an Add-In: The Viewer

Before you can take advantage of the benefits of an add-in, you must attach it to 1-2-3. A commercially available add-in will include instructions that explain how to make it work. And, as stated earlier, the add-ins that come with 1-2-3 are probably already available on your hard disk.

Assuming you can find the Viewer on your disk, we'll use it to explore the fundamentals of working with add-ins. Along the way, you will see how the Viewer helps you to locate files in crowded disk directories.

Just to be safe, start this excursion with a blank worksheet. Make sure you have saved if you mean to, and then select Worksheet Erase Yes.

To attach an add-in to 1-2-3, select Add-In Attach and choose the name of the add-in from the resulting menu. In this case, select VIEWER.ADN. The resulting menu lets you elect to attach the add-in to a particular function key. You activate an add-in that is attached to a function key by holding down the Alt key and pressing the function key. If you choose not to attach to a function key, you can activate the add-in by selecting Add-In Invoke from the main menu. For this exercise, attach the Viewer to function key F7. Finally, select Quit from the resulting menu; 1-2-3 returns to Ready mode.

So, you may ask, what's the point? There's nothing at all different about the worksheet. Where's the add-in? It's attached, but it's not doing anything at the moment. Let's put it to work retrieving a file.

To activate the add-in, hold down the Alt key and press F7. Alternatively, you can activate the Viewer by selecting File View from 1-2-3's menus. A small menu appears, offering three choices, as seen in Figure 9.1.

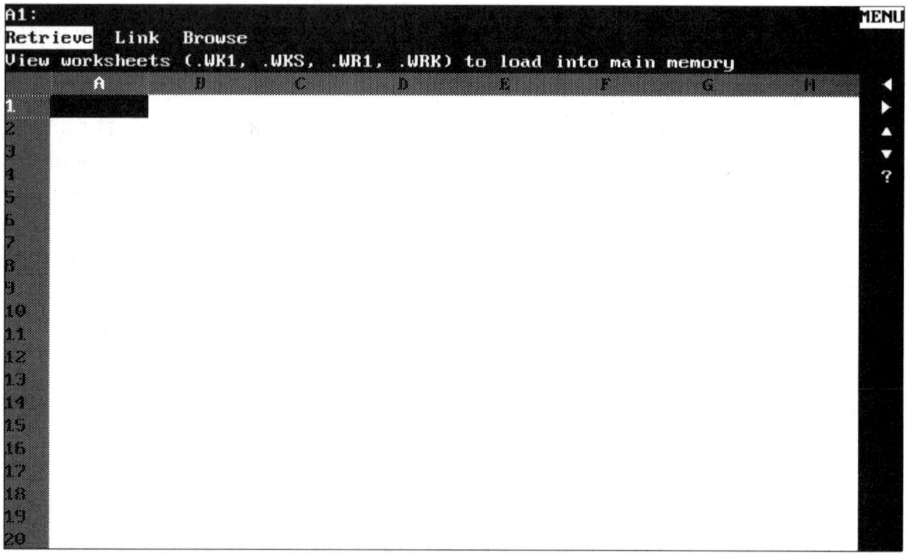

FIGURE 9.1. A blank sheet with the Viewer menu active.

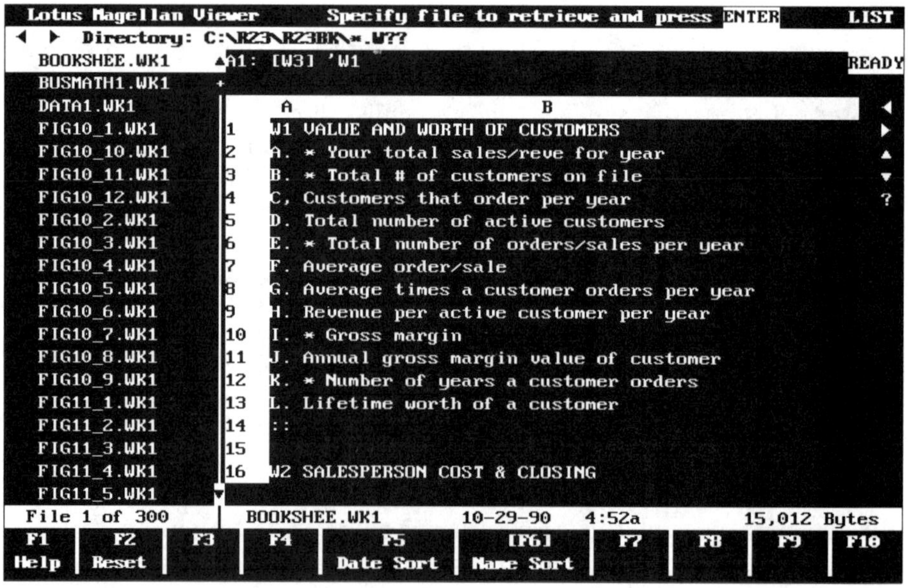

FIGURE 9.2. Viewer display of files.

If you plan to retrieve a file with Viewer's help, select Retrieve. If you plan to use Viewer to establish a spreadsheet linking formula, select Link. If your only interest is to take a look at information stored in other files, select Browse. We'll use Viewer to retrieve a spreadsheet from disk, so select Retrieve. The Viewer display replaces 1-2-3's spreadsheet display as shown in Figure 9.2.

Your display won't match ours exactly; the names of your files and directories will be different. What's important is to understand the elements of the display.

The box on the left side of the display lists the files that are available in the current directory. A menu pointer rests on the first file name in the list. The window on the right side of the display shows what seems to be a 1-2-3 spreadsheet. It isn't a real spreadsheet in that you can't simply hop over to it and start entering values and formulas. However, it represents the top-left corner of the sheet whose name is highlighted. If no spreadsheet appears in the window, there are no spreadsheets stored in the current directory.

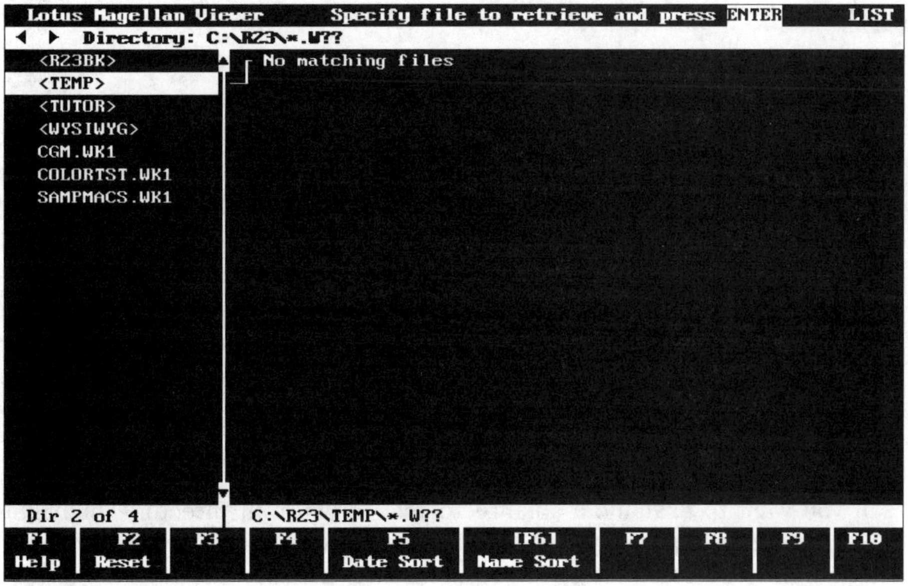

FIGURE 9.3. The Viewer display when there are no spreadsheet files in the current directory.

If Viewer isn't offering you a list of spreadsheet files, this exercise may not be terribly meaningful to you. The purpose of the add-in is to help you examine files stored on disk without having to retrieve them. You'll need to begin building and saving your own spreadsheets before you'll get any use out of the Viewer add-in.

If there is a listing of spreadsheet files, press the DownArrow key to highlight the second file name in the list. Immediately, an image of the new file appears in the viewing window. Press DownArrow and UpArrow to scroll through the list of file names. Each time you highlight a new file name, the top-left corner of the file appears in the window.

Should you wish to examine more of the selected file than appears in the viewing window, press the RightArrow key. The pointer jumps to the window and lets you navigate in the spreadsheet as you would if it were active in 1-2-3. You can't view a spreadsheet's formulas in the viewing window, but you can explore extensively to examine data and the current values of the formulas.

When you have found the sheet that you want to retrieve, simply press Return. Whether the pointer is in the viewing window or active in the file name list, 1-2-3 retrieves the selected spreadsheet and returns to Ready mode. Go ahead and retrieve whatever file is currently highlighted; then we'll work with another of the add-in's viewing modes.

Search Through Any Directory

When you activate the Viewer add-in with the Retrieve, Link, or Browse option, you get a listing of the files and directories in the current directory. The Viewer isn't limited to this directory, it lets you search through any directory on any disk in your system. Press F7, and select Browse to see how you can examine all the files on your disks.

At first, the Viewer offers a listing of the directories and files in 1-2-3's current default data directory. While in Browse mode, the Viewer reveals the contents of many files other than spreadsheets. You can't retrieve these files into 1-2-3, but you might want to review notes in a word processing file without having to exit 1-2-3 and load up your word processor.

If you want to examine a subdirectory of the current directory, highlight the directory name and press the RightArrow key. To examine the directory in which the current directory resides, press the LeftArrow key.

You are probably viewing a subdirectory at this point, so press the LeftArrow key. In fact, press the LeftArrow key repeatedly until the Viewer lists only the disk drives available on your system. It will look something like Figure 9.4.

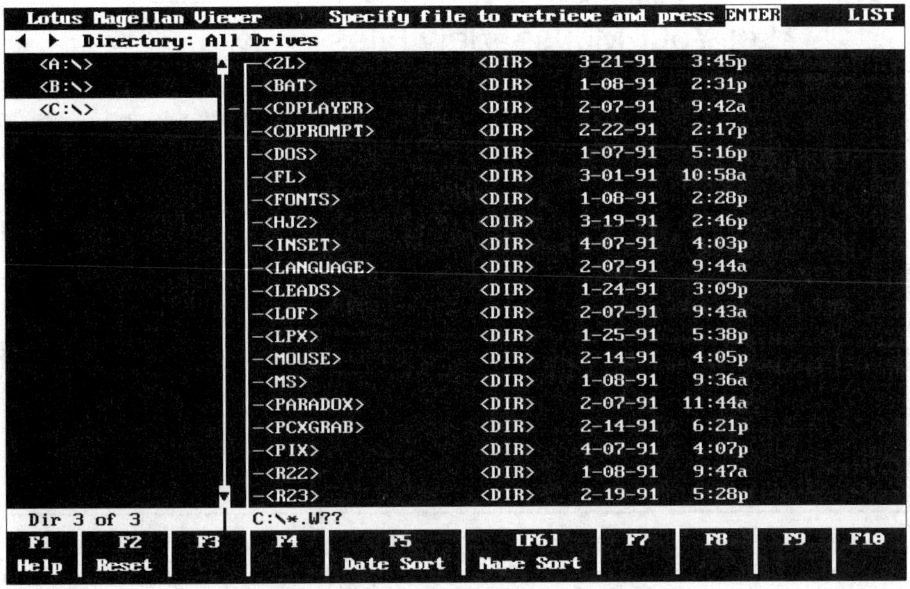

FIGURE 9.4. The Viewer display when you have backed out to the disk drive selection level.

The viewing window shows the subdirectories and files stored in the root directory of whichever disk drive is highlighted in the listing window. When you press UpArrow to highlight one of the floppy drive names, the Viewer prompts you to insert a disk and press RightArrow to list the contents of the disk. To select a directory on the hard disk, highlight the name of the hard disk and press RightArrow. Scroll to the name of the desired directory and press RightArrow again.

Unfortunately, we can't provide step-by-step instructions for examining the contents of the directories on your disks, because your computer's directory structure is undoubtedly different from the structure we would describe. You will have to explore the Viewer's directory navigation abilities on your own.

The UpArrow and DownArrow keys let you navigate within file name listings and within the images of files that appear in the viewing window. The LeftArrow and RightArrow keys let you move into and out of the viewing window, and up and down the directory tree. At any point during a session with the Viewer, the display tells you the name of the current directory and the name of the file visible in the viewing window.

Let Your Mouse View Files

Nowhere is the mouse easier to use than in the Viewer add-in. If you have the hang of mousing around the spreadsheet, menus, and dialog boxes, then you probably won't need any guidance to work with the Viewer.

For example, you need only click a file name in the name list to produce an image of that file's contents in the viewing window. Click in the viewing window, and the highlight is there. To move the worksheet around in the viewing window, start on the sheet and drag off the edge of the sheet in the direction you want to explore.

Two triangles appear at the left end of the top frame of the Viewer. Clicking the triangle that points to the left is equivalent to pressing the LeftArrow key. Clicking the right-facing triangle duplicates pressing the RightArrow key. The buttons along the bottom of the display are labeled clearly to identify their functions, and clicking the Enter button at the top of the display doubles for pressing the Return key. Click around the Viewer display for a bit, and you'll be as comfortable with it as you are with the spreadsheet.

Other options you can choose from the display include the ability to alphabetize the file listing or arrange files in order of their creation dates. A short help dialog box is available to remind you of the Viewer's fundamentals—press the HELP key (F1) while Viewer is active to see the help box. Fiddle with the Viewer add-in to retrieve, link, and browse files until you have a good idea of how it works. You may decide to work always with the Viewer add-in attached and to give up 1-2-3's File Retrieve command.

An Overview of the Auditor Add-In

The Auditor add-in is a little easier to explore in print than the Viewer is. As explained earlier, this add-in can reveal the audit trail of values calculated in your spreadsheets. Which cells play in a formula's calculations? Which calculations does a particular cell affect? In what order does 1-2-3 calculate the formulas in a given range? The Auditor can answer these questions easily.

You might ask such questions when you return to a large spreadsheet after several days or weeks. You might ask the same questions when someone hands you a spreadsheet on disk and asks you to look it over.

Attach the Auditor

Before we explore the Auditor, you should create the simple practice worksheet shown on page 112. The worksheet includes several simple formulas, so you may choose to work through the Formulas section of the book before you continue with this discussion. See the setup box for instructions on creating the practice worksheet.

Granted, the worksheet you just created is so simple that identifying how the formulas and values interrelate isn't a challenge. But even a simple sheet will serve to demonstrate the Auditor in action. Start by attaching the Auditor to function key F8. Here's a memory refresher: Select Add-In Attach, choose AUDITOR.ADN from the menu of available add-ins, and select 8 from the resulting menu. Select Quit to return to spreadsheet Ready mode.

The Auditor at Work

One question you might have when you examine a spreadsheet for the first time—or even after a few weeks have passed since you last worked with it—is, where does that number come from? In this particular sheet, you might look at the formula in cell B14 and ask this question. Better still, you might ask it of the Auditor.

Try it. Move the cell pointer to cell B14 and activate the Auditor add-in by holding down the Alt key and pressing F8. A dialog box pops up on the sheet, and a menu appears in the control panel. You can use the menus to alter the dialog box settings, use a mouse in the dialog box, or activate the box by pressing the EDIT key (F2). At this point, the relevant setting is Highlight, which you can see is already selected. Press the WINDOW key (F6), if you wish to hide the dialog box.

The Auditor menu lists quite a few options. The first selection, Precedents, reveals which cells in the spreadsheet are involved in any way in a formula's calculations. That sounds like what we're looking for, so select Precedents. The Auditor prompts you to indicate a cell. The cell pointer is already on the desired cell, so simply press Return.

The Auditor highlights all of the numeric entries in column B. This means that all of those entries play into the calculation in cell B14 in some way. (Press F6 if Auditor's dialog box obstructs your view of the sheet.) With the cells highlighted, you know which ones to examine in determining how the cells and formulas interrelate. If you need to know more about these relationships, the Auditor can help again.

How to Set Up the Auditor Practice Sheet

If you worked through the last chapter, you saved a file named CUE1ST. Retrieve that file as the basis for this new example, and skip down to step 5. If you didn't save that worksheet, create the worksheet beginning with step 1:

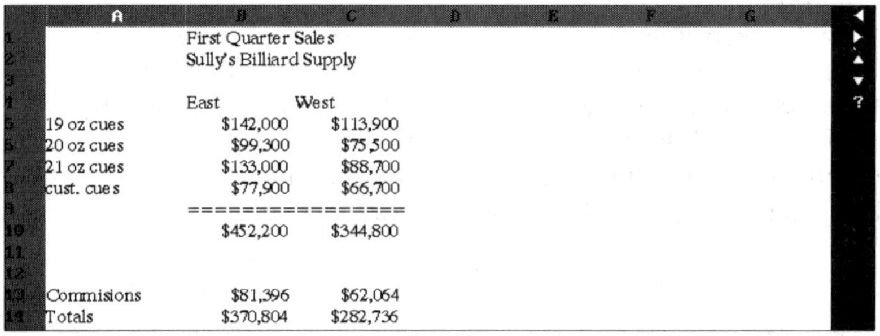

	A	B	C
1		First Quarter Sales	
2		Sully's Billiard Supply	
3			
4		East	West
5	19 oz cues	$142,000	$113,900
6	20 oz cues	$99,300	$75,500
7	21 oz cues	$133,000	$88,700
8	cust. cues	$77,900	$66,700
9		==========	==========
10		$452,200	$344,800
11			
12			
13	Commisions	$81,396	$62,064
14	Totals	$370,804	$282,736

1. Column Widths

Set the widths of columns as follows: A, 13; B, 10; C, 10.

2. Labels

Enter labels as shown. Start with an apostrophe label prefix when you make the entries in cells A5, A6, and A7. Create the dividing line in cells B9 and C9 by entering \= into each of those cells.

3. Values and Formulas

Enter the values in range B5..C8, and enter the formula *@SUM(B5..B8)* into cell B10. Copy the formula to cell C10.

4. Numeric Display Formats

Select Range Format Currency, enter *0*, and indicate range B5..C10 as the range to format.

5. Additional Formulas, Labels, and Formats

Enter the label *Commissions* in cell A13 and the label *Totals* in cell A14. Then enter the formula *+B10*.18* into cell B13, and enter *+B10-B13* into cell B14. Assign the currency format with no decimal places to the new formula cells and copy them to the adjacent cells of column C.

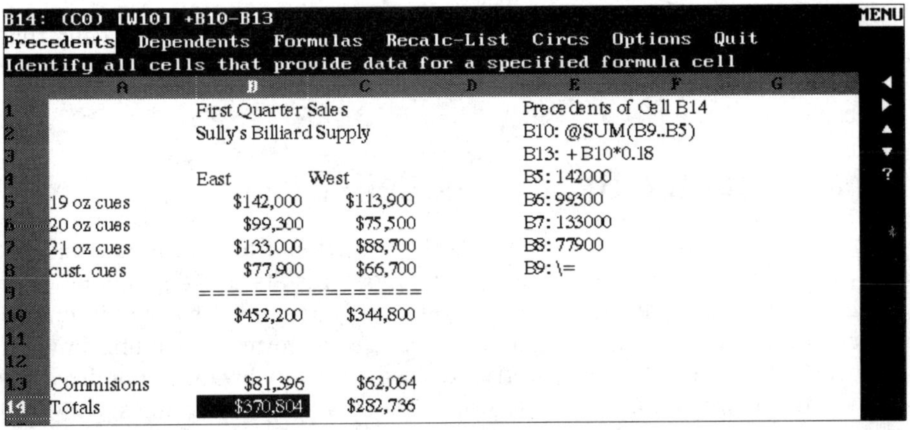

FIGURE 9.5. Auditor after the List Precedents procedure.

Reapply the Precedents command, but first change the settings so that Auditor works in Trace mode rather than Highlight mode. Do this via the menus by selecting Options Trace Quit. Alternatively, press Window to bring up the dialog box, and select Trace in the dialog box using either the mouse or the keyboard.

Select Precedents, and once again indicate cell B14 as the precedent source cell. The Auditor highlights cell B10—the first of the cells referenced in cell B14's formula. Select Forward or Backward to navigate among the cells that contribute to cell B14's result. Look in the control panel to see the contents of each cell as it is highlighted. When you have finished examining the interrelated cells, press Return.

The Trace option still might not satisfy your need to understand the interdependencies of the formulas in your spreadsheets. Even in this simple example it is difficult to recognize one formula's reliance on another as the Auditor traces the precedents. In a larger model, tracing a formula's precedent relationships might send the highlight all over the worksheet without clarifying anything. If that is the case, you might prefer to use the Auditor's List option.

Select Options List Quit, or select List in the dialog box, and then select Precedents one more time. Indicate cell B14 as the source cell, and notice that the Auditor prompts for one more piece of information—a target range in which to create a list.

You don't have to be too careful when you indicate the list range; Auditor won't overwrite existing spreadsheet data. For this exercise, indicate cell E1. The Auditor creates a list of labels that reveal the cells and cell contents of every cell contributing to the calculation in B14. You may need to press the WINDOW key (F6) to clear the dialog box from in front of the list. (Figure 9.5).

The listing makes it easy to trace the relationships among the cells that Auditor has highlighted in the sheet.

What About the Dependent Cells?

Just as Auditor can illuminate the cells that contribute to a formula's calculation, it can also point out the formulas whose results are dependent on a selected cell. You might wish to check on a cell's dependents if you intend to alter a value in the cell. Sometimes the string of formulas leading onward from a single cell can become pretty involved, and you'll want to confirm that the value you are about to change will affect only specific formulas.

Before you exercise the Auditor's Dependents option, you must reset the worksheet to remove highlights from the cells that Auditor identified as precedent to cell B14. To do this, select Options Reset Highlight Quit.

In practice, you select one of Auditor's three operating modes—Highlight, Trace, or List. For this example, select Highlight. Then select Dependents from Auditor's main menu. When prompted to identify a cell, indicate cell C6. Auditor highlights cells C10, C13, and C14. The calculations in these three cells rely in some way on the entry in cell C6.

The Other Audits: Formulas, Recalc-List, Circs

One of the simplest operations that Auditor performs is to identify which cells in the worksheet contain formulas. This can help you to track down data entry areas in the sheet. To find all the formulas, start by issuing the Options Reset Highlight command to clear the highlights that resulted from your last command. Then select Formulas. Auditor reveals formulas in cells B10 and C10 and in range B13..C14.

The Recalc-List option identifies the order in which 1-2-3 calculates a spreadsheet's formulas. This is especially useful when the calculation order is set to Natural. (See the box titled Calculate Row-by-Row, Column-by-Column, or Au Naturel for information about the calculation order.) While this command works in Highlight, Trace, and List mode, it isn't particularly meaningful when applied in Highlight mode. Its effect in that mode is only to highlight cells that contain formulas. However, in Trace mode the Recalc-List option lets you move the cell pointer from one formula cell to the next in the recalc order. In List mode, the Recalc-List option lists the formula cells in the spreadsheet in the order in which they are calculated.

Calculate Row-by-Row, Column-by-Column, or Au Naturel

When you first install 1-2-3 on your computer, it automatically calculates spreadsheets in *natural order*. This means that no matter how you lay out your formulas, 1-2-3 figures out which formulas must be calculated first so that they return proper results before formulas that depend on them are calculated, and so on. In other words, 1-2-3 calculates the least dependent formulas first and works its way up to the most dependent formulas—the ones that rely on results from the most other formulas.

If you prefer, you can set 1-2-3 to calculate formulas in the worksheet row-by-row or column-by-column. You make the setting by selecting Worksheet Global Recalculation and then Natural, Rowwise, or Columnwise.

The Rowwise and Columnwise options allow 1-2-3 to remain compatible with ancient spreadsheet products that couldn't perform calculations in natural order. They also let you control the progression of calculations in worksheets in which you have deliberately created circular references to solve reiterative calculations. We look a little more at circular references in the next section in this chapter. We also look closer at the Rowwise and Columnwise recalculation options in the Formulas section of this book.

Auditor's Circs option identifies all the cells involved in circular references. (See the box titled Going Nowhere Fast: Circular References for a definition of the term.) This feature works a little differently from the other selections on Auditor's main menu. When you select Circs, if there are any circular references in your model, the spreadsheet display falls away, and a full-screen menu listing of cell addresses appears. Each address listed identifies a cell whose formula contains a circular reference.

Going Nowhere Fast: Circular References

It is possible to create a formula in your spreadsheet that somehow includes itself in its own calculations. For example, the formula +A1+1 stored in cell A1 refers to itself, and the formula +B1+2 stored in cell A1 refers to itself if the formula in cell B1 is +A1+3. Such a formula is said to be a circular reference—a formula whose results are based on its own results. We look at circular references in depth in the Formulas section of this book.

You can move a menu highlight within the listing (or click with the mouse) to select a cell. If the selected cell's formula refers to more than one other cell, the Auditor lists the references on a new menu. However, if the selected cell's formula has only one reference to another cell, you get bumped back to Auditor's main menu.

The Circ option's greatest utility is in obtaining the original list of all cells that contain circular references. Rather than discover only one such cell at a time, as 1-2-3's Worksheet Status command allows, you can quickly get an overview of all the circular references established in the sheet.

Add-In Maintenance Basics

You'll use some add-ins so much that you may choose to leave them attached at all times. In fact, you can set 1-2-3 to attach the add-ins of your choice automatically whenever you start up the spreadsheet. To do this, select Worksheet Global Default Other Add-In Set, and select a number that isn't already in use (as revealed by the list in the dialog box).

Lotus 1-2-3 presents a menu listing of the available add-ins. Select one from the list, and if you wish, select a function key to which 1-2-3 should attach the add-in. 1-2-3 asks whether you want an add-in to start running automatically after it is loaded. You probably won't want an add-in to be activated, only ready for use when you press the appropriate Alt-function key combination. Select Quit to return to the default settings menu, and select Other Add-In if you wish to establish a second auto-attach add-in. When you finish setting auto-attach add-ins, select Update from the Worksheet Global Default menu. This records your settings in a disk file that 1-2-3 consults each time you start up.

No matter how much you like the add-ins, there are times when you are better off not having them attached. There are two ways to clear them from

If You Prefer the Dialog Box...

When you select Worksheet Global Default, 1-2-3 superimposes a dialog box on the display. Set add-ins to attach automatically when you load the spreadsheet software by activating the dialog box (press F2 or click anywhere in the box with the mouse). Then select one of the numbered options within the selection box titled Auto-attach Add-ins. Enter the name of an add-in that you want to have available in every work session. Alternatively, press the NAME key (F3), and select the name of the add-in from the list box that appears.

To associate an add-in with a specific function key, select the function key name in the selection box titled Add-in Keys. A box pops up listing the add-ins that you have set to attach automatically. Click the name of the add-in that should be associated with the selected key.

To make permanent the settings you established in the dialog box, select Update. This records your changes in the configuration file on disk and drops you out of the dialog box back to the menus. Select Quit (and maybe Quit again) to return to Ready mode.

RAM. One way is to select Add-In Detach and indicate the name of the add-in that you want to be rid of. The other way is to select Add-In Clear, and detach all current add-ins in one operation.

Some Cautions About Add-Ins

By now it should be apparent that add-ins can add significant features to the spreadsheet software. Unfortunately, add-ins do suffer from a few limitations. The biggest problem is the amount of RAM they occupy when they are attached to the spreadsheet. If you are running on a computer that has 640K of RAM, loading 1-2-3 with several add-ins significantly limits the size of your spreadsheets. If a spreadsheet barely fits in RAM without an add-in attached, you may not be able to run that particular sheet and an add-in simultaneously.

A second limitation arises only with certain add-ins. It is easy to come to rely on add-ins in your own work. However, when you pass spreadsheet files along to co-workers who don't have the same add-ins, those co-workers may not be able to use the spreadsheets as you intended. A worksheet customized with the Wysiwyg add-in, for example, reverts to the standard 1-2-3 appearance when used without Wysiwyg. While such a worksheet might be a work of art on your system using Wysiwyg, it could be rather drab and cryptic to someone who doesn't use the add-in.

Whatever you do, don't let the shortcomings of add-ins deter you from using them. The Viewer add-in alone can save lots of aggravation when your disk becomes crowded with files and you can't remember what any of them contain. Also, don't limit your acquaintance with add-ins to the ones that come packaged with 1-2-3. Check with a local software vendor, or browse through some computer magazines to see what add-ins are available commercially.

Having completed this chapter you should:

- *Understand what add-ins are*
- *Have a good idea of how add-ins extend the capabilities of your spreadsheet*
- *Be able to apply the Viewer to simplify work with files as your disk becomes more and more cluttered*
- *Know how to apply the Auditor to identify relationships among formulas in your spreadsheets*
- *Be prepared to seek out commercially available add-ins that can solve specific business problems, or simplify common spreadsheet tasks*

10

Desktop Publishing from Your Spreadsheet: Wysiwyg

In the preceding chapters, you have seen references to an add-in called Wysiwyg (pronounced wizzy-wig). Wysiwyg takes 1-2-3 from the realm of the familiar and ordinary into the realm of the new and exciting by adding powerful spreadsheet publishing features to your box of tools. These features let you apply unique fonts and font styles to spreadsheet entries. They let you establish shading in cells and ranges and place boxes around ranges. Wysiwyg also lets you place graphs and graphic images into the spreadsheet alongside data and formulas. Such features let you create professional quality reports and presentations based on your own data.

Earlier releases of 1-2-3 included an add-in called Allways that offers many of the features of Wysiwyg, but the new add-in relegates Allways to the status of a mere step in the right direction. Wysiwyg makes the whole trip into spreadsheet publishing, working so closely with 1-2-3 that once it's attached you might not think of it as an add-in at all. This chapter offers an overview of Wysiwyg's features. Section 4 of the book covers several of those features in much greater detail.

Wysiwyg's forte is that whatever you see on the display as you spruce up a worksheet is exactly what comes out of your printer when you produce hard copy. Of course, black and white printers can't reproduce the colors that you incorporate into the display, but all other design elements come through cleanly. The add-in lives up to the industry acronym from which it gets its name—What-You-See-Is-What-You-Get. That is, what you see on the display is what you get from your printer.

In this chapter, you will:

- *Gain a general understanding of Wysiwyg's features*
- *Explore reasons to work with and without Wysiwyg*

Wysiwyg Attached

Attaching Wysiwyg to 1-2-3 transforms the spreadsheet display. The transformation is subtle: lines that separate the column letters and row numbers in the spreadsheet frame appear, and the mouse pointer changes from a rectangle into an arrow head. A much greater transformation takes place "under the hood."

Leave your computer alone for now, and explore with us some of the capabilities that Wysiwyg adds to 1-2-3.

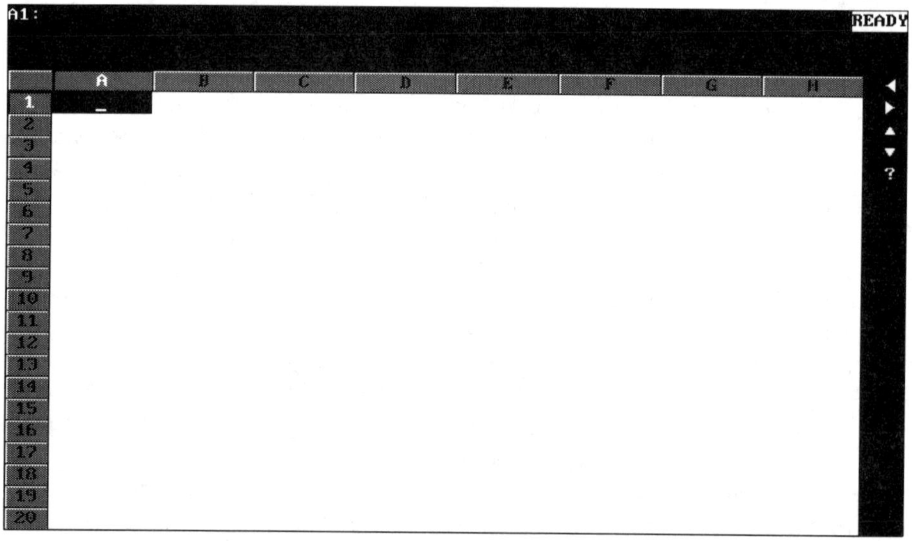

FIGURE 10.1. The 1-2-3 display transformed by the Wysiwyg add-in.

The first thing to notice about Wysiwyg is that entries in the spreadsheet look different from those made without the add-in attached. This is because Wysiwyg uses a proportionally spaced font for all of your entries. A proportionally spaced font is one in which a character takes up more or less space in a line depending on the character's width. The letter *i*, for example, is narrower than the letter *m*. Your computer's standard monospaced font reserves a set amount of space for each character.

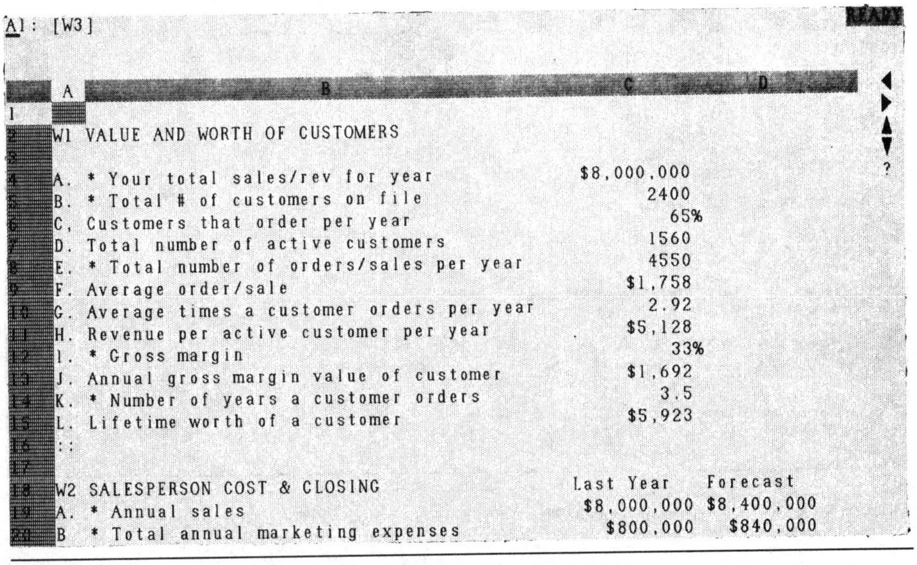

FIGURE 10.2. A 1-2-3 worksheet "straight up" without Wysiwyg attached.

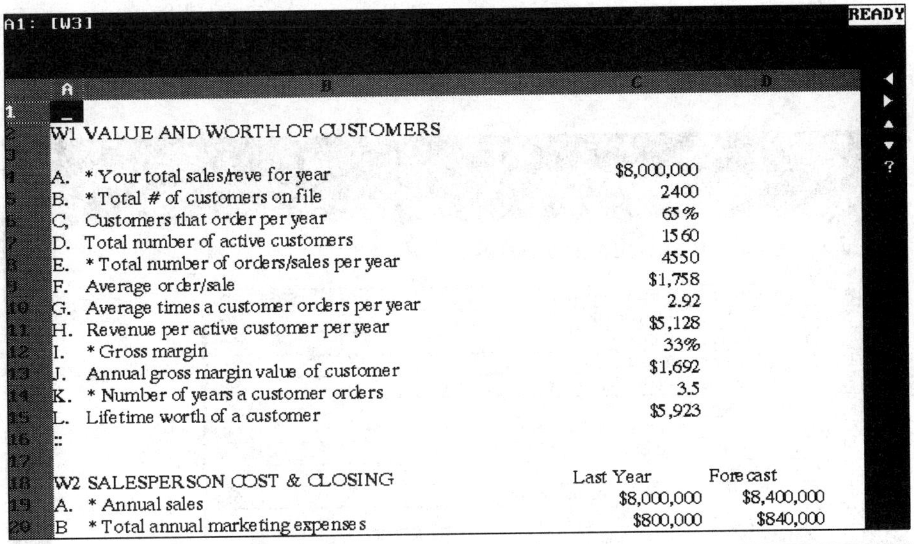

FIGURE 10.3. The same 1-2-3 worksheet with Wysiwyg attached.

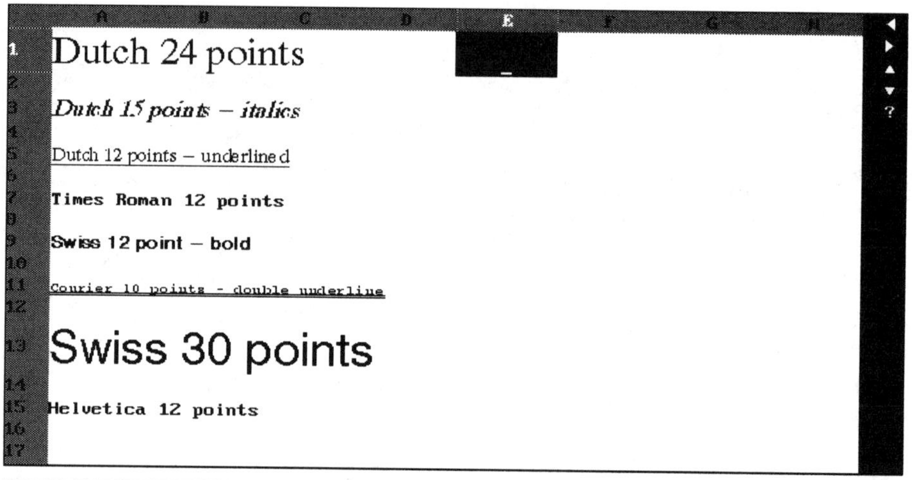

FIGURE 10.4. Wysiwyg allows up to eight fonts, in a wide variety of sizes and styles, in a sheet.

Going one better, Wysiwyg lets you alter the font to suit your tastes. You can apply any of the fonts packaged with the software or select from fonts available on your own printer. You can use as many as eight different fonts in a single spreadsheet, and you can apply special attributes such as boldface, italics, and underlines. See Figure 10.4.

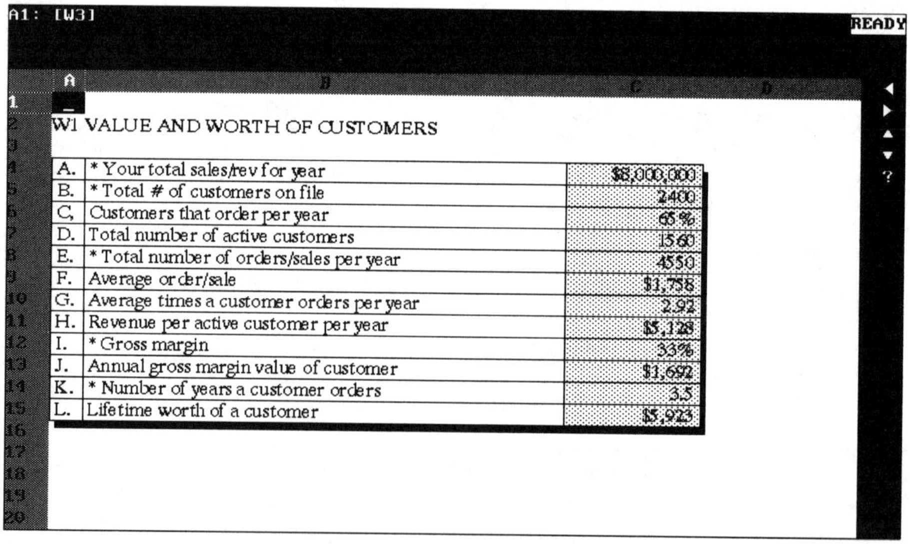

FIGURE 10.5. Wysiwyg lets you add special effects to spreadsheet ranges.

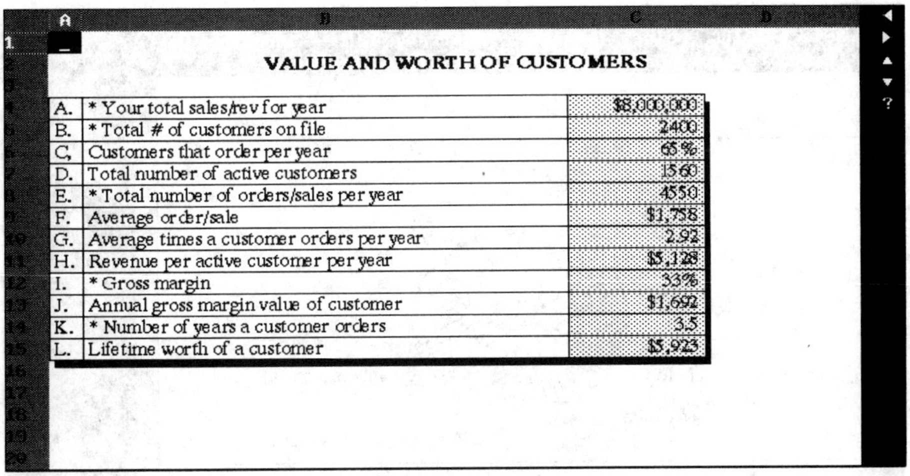

VALUE AND WORTH OF CUSTOMERS

A.	* Your total sales/rev for year	$8,000,000
B.	* Total # of customers on file	2400
C.	Customers that order per year	65%
D.	Total number of active customers	1560
E.	* Total number of orders/sales per year	4550
F.	Average order/sale	$1,758
G.	Average times a customer orders per year	2.92
H.	Revenue per active customer per year	$5,128
I.	* Gross margin	33%
J.	Annual gross margin value of customer	$1,692
K.	* Number of years a customer orders	3.5
L.	Lifetime worth of a customer	$5,923

FIGURE 10.6. Wysiwyg centered the title in this sheet so we didn't have to.

Wysiwyg lets you put lines around cells and ranges, and apply special shading to the worksheet. One option even creates a three-dimensional shadow effect so that your entries seem to jump out from the sheet, as shown in Figure 10.5.

Text handling commands built into Wysiwyg let you align text across a range of columns rather than just within individual cells. Wysiwyg will center a title over any range you select, as shown in Figure 10.6.

Snazzy Graphs Come with the Territory

Wysiwyg's graph editing capabilities let you dramatically alter the graphs that you create from data in your spreadsheet (we explore the graphing features of 1-2-3 in the section titled Present Your Data). In fact, some of the graph tools let you draw pictures much as you would with a stand-alone paint package. The graph in Figure 10.7 is a pie graph ready for editing in Wysiwyg's graph editor.

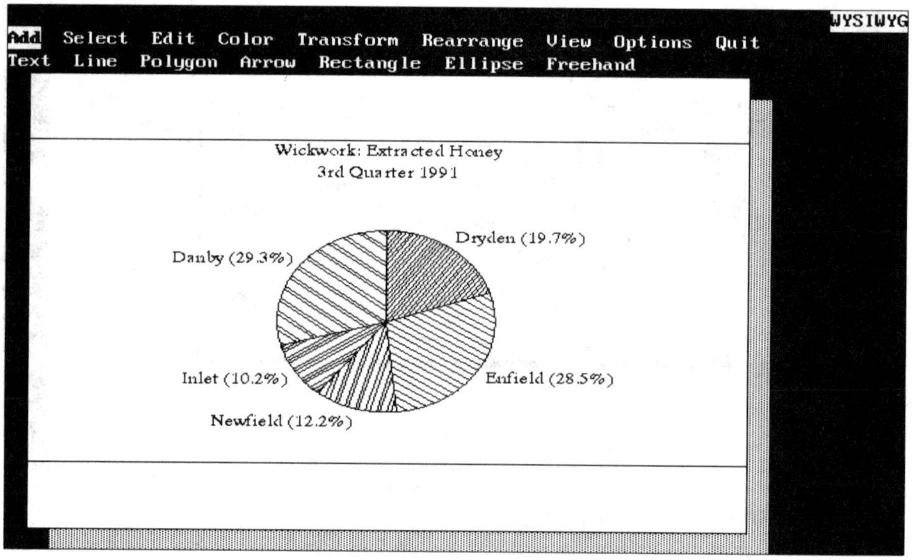

FIGURE 10.7. This is how your screen appears as you work with Wysiwyg's graph editing tools to jazz up a standard pie chart.

If you go in for serious self-expression, or you simply want some custom artwork to spiff up a page, you will appreciate Wysiwyg's freehand drawing feature. We used the drawing tools to work up the city on a flower shown in Figure 10.8.

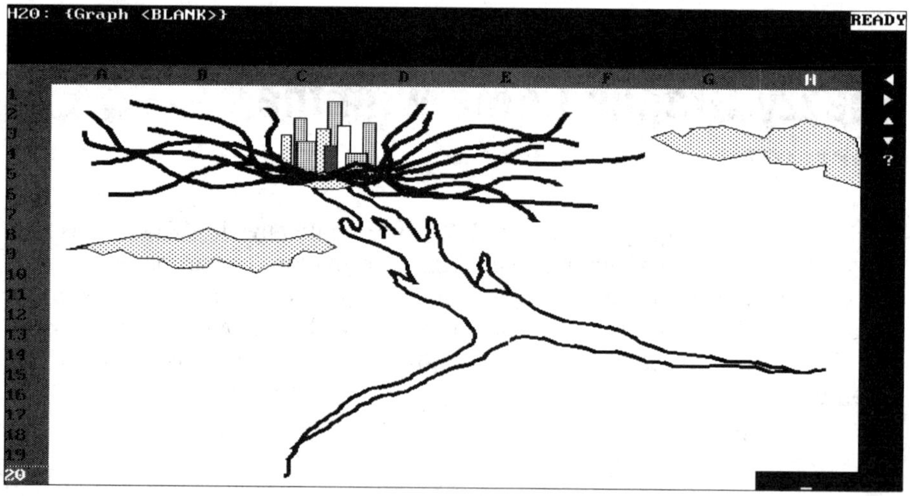

FIGURE 10.8. You can get carried away with Wysiwyg's freehand drawing capabilities.

What makes these graph-enhancing capabilities so stellar is the ability that Wysiwyg has to display graphics directly on the worksheet. You can place graphic images alongside text and data right on the display, as shown in Figure 10.9.

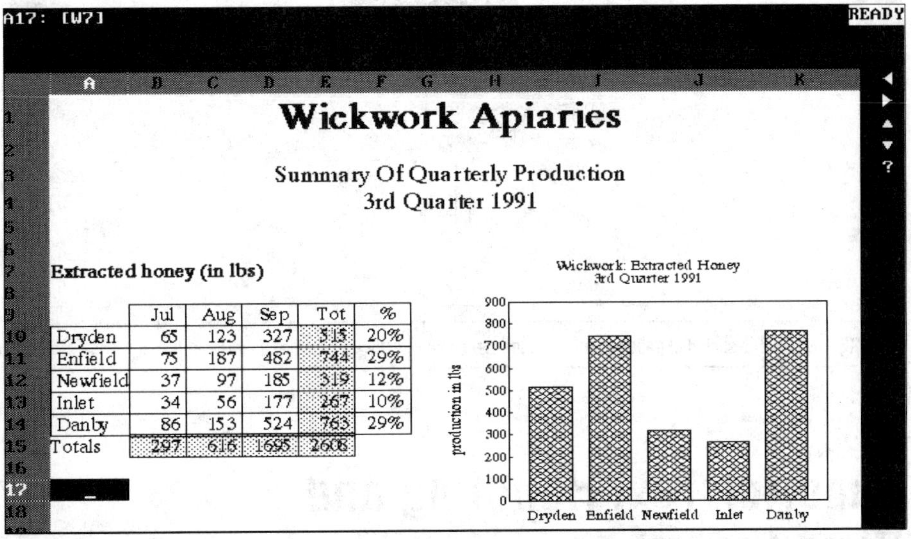

FIGURE 10.9. A spreadsheet with graphs alongside the data gets your message across very clearly.

If Wysiwyg limited you to using graphs created and enhanced in 1-2-3, it would be a very powerful tool. But with Wysiwyg you can incorporate into a spreadsheet any graphic image or clip art available in .CGM format, like the image that appears in Figure 10.10.

FIGURE 10.10. The slick illustration in this spreadsheet came directly from Lotus's Freelance Plus.

Superior Text Handling and Page Layout

Working with blocks of text in 1-2-3 is, at best, a bother. The Range Justify command helps you to lay out paragraphs, but other than that, you face a lot of busy work when you write memos, letters, and reports inside the spreadsheet.

Wysiwyg changes that. In its text-editing mode, Wysiwyg provides an automatic wordwrap feature and left, right, and full-justification for paragraphs. Wysiwyg fits text automatically around graphics displayed on the worksheet and even lets you alter the fonts and font styles of individual characters within a single worksheet cell. See Figure 10.11.

Because the normal spreadsheet display shows only about a third of an actual printed page, Wysiwyg includes a print preview capability that lets you review the full pages of a document before you send them to the printer. You have full control over margins, headers, and footers. If your printer allows it, you can even print the page rotated 90 degrees into landscape mode.

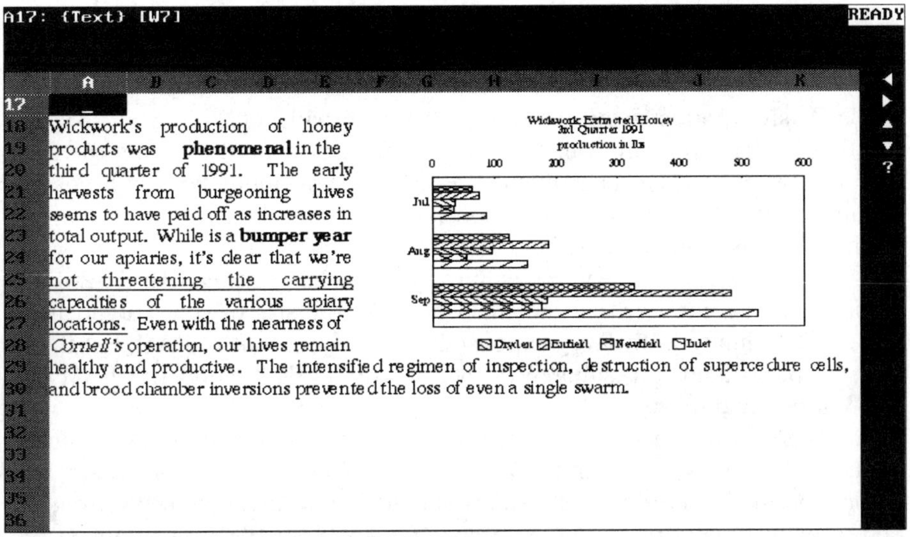

FIGURE 10.11. We entered the text in this worksheet using Wysiwyg's text editing and alignment features.

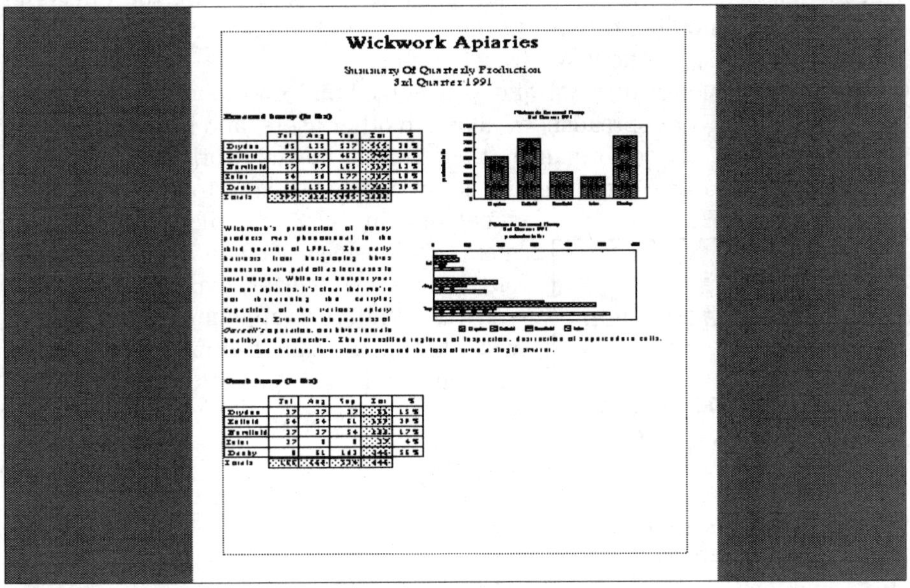

FIGURE 10.12. A screen preview of a document enhanced in Wysiwyg.

Forever Wysiwyg?

While Wysiwyg adds many features to your spreadsheet, all of 1-2-3's preexisting features remain available with Wysiwyg attached. Pressing the slash key still produces the main menu; the cursor-movement keys still get you around in the sheet; and the function keys still function. If this is true, you might ask, why ever work without Wysiwyg attached?

Like all add-ins, Wysiwyg consumes RAM. While you can run 1-2-3 and Wysiwyg on a computer that has 512K of RAM, the size of your spreadsheets will be quite limited. Wysiwyg supposedly uses about 90K of RAM, but in one test we performed, attaching Wysiwyg ate up 114K beyond the RAM that 1-2-3 normally requires.

Another reason not to use Wysiwyg in all your spreadsheets is to maintain compatibility between your files and those of coworkers and others with whom you might share worksheets. A spreadsheet enhanced in Wysiwyg can be pretty disappointing—even unintelligible—without Wysiwyg attached.

A final reason not to work with Wysiwyg concerns speed. A graphical user interface is necessarily less responsive than a textual interface. You will notice considerable lag time between issuing commands and seeing the effects of those commands on the display, particularly on XT class machines. 1-2-3 performs more quickly without Wysiwyg attached.

If you have plenty of RAM and you don't build enormous spreadsheets, if you don't pass your spreadsheets along to other users, and if you don't mind the degradation in performance, then by all means work with Wysiwyg attached. It is natural for experienced spreadsheet users to build a spreadsheet first in 1-2-3 and then add enhancements in Wysiwyg (hence the organization of this book). However, experienced or not, you may find that applying enhancements while laying out data, formulas, and labels is efficient and can lead to more polished spreadsheet designs.

Having completed this chapter you should:

- *Have a good sense of the spreadsheet publishing options available with Wysiwyg*
- *Understand the tradeoffs of working with Wysiwyg attached*
- *Be prepared to explore the Wysiwyg spreadsheet publishing features in depth*

Section 2
Formulas

The heart of spreadsheet computing is the ease with which you can build reusable formulas. The formulas you create show results almost instantly, but more important, once you have entered formulas in the sheet, you don't have to retype them each time you want to do identical calculations using a new set of values.

Your formulas can sum columns of numbers, calculate statistics, and even manipulate the characters in labels. As your familiarity with 1-2-3 grows, you will learn to develop complex formulas to solve many of your business problems. There are few calculations you can't perform using formulas in 1-2-3.

This section explores 1-2-3's abilities to do calculations. It begins by reviewing the fundamentals of doing math in the spreadsheet. Then it introduces @functions—some of the greatest time-savers that 1-2-3 offers. The discussion covers several types of @functions—some to help with mathematics, others to help with financial calculations, and yet others to help you manipulate labels much as you do numbers.

The section also explains how absolute and relative references work in formulas, and it delves into the intricacies of conditional math—that is, formulas whose calculations change as information in the spreadsheet changes.

When you complete this section, you will have a firm grasp of the tools available to solve complex business problems—from summarizing monthly transactions, to calculating sales commissions, to determining the depreciation on an asset for a given month.

11

Math in the Sheet

The most powerful weapon in your spreadsheet computing arsenal should be a firm grasp of 1-2-3's mathematics capabilities. Performing operations of addition, subtraction, multiplication, division, and equality should be second nature; these five basic operations can combine to describe all of the others.

Many spreadsheet enthusiasts barely go beyond these calculation fundamentals, yet they create elaborate models that describe all of their companies' business. This refresher explains how to use arithmetic operators to make 1-2-3 calculate exactly what you have in mind. It also explores the order of precedence that 1-2-3 uses when it evaluates formulas. The information in this chapter is the foundation for all the calculations you will ever do with a spreadsheet—calculating sales summaries and commissions, projecting revenue, analyzing your company's financial health, determining loan payments, and so on.

The Front Four: Addition, Subtraction, Multiplication, and Division

In this chapter, you will learn how to:

- *Do addition, multiplication, subtraction, and division*
- *Use other mathematical operators*
- *Set up formulas, keeping track of order of precedence*
- *Do quick calculations without entering anything into the spreadsheet*

Math begins with addition. Many problems involve the question, "How many do I get when I add up these values?" Addition, then, is a good place to begin understanding how to do math in 1-2-3.

Suppose that you want to add the values 177 and 136. If you read the box titled Quick Calculations, you will see that you can type *177+136* and press CALC. 1-2-3 returns the result of the addition, but the addition formula itself is lost.

Quick Calculations

Sometimes, as you are laying out the sheet, you need to know the result of a simple calculation. Don't resort to a hand-held calculator or pencil and paper. Instead, type the calculation as you would into a calculator, and then press the CALC key (F9).

Try it. No matter where the cell pointer resides at the moment, type the expression *24*2.5.* DON'T PRESS RETURN!

Because you haven't pressed Return, the expression remains on the edit line in the control panel. Press the CALC key. The formula vanishes, and its result, 60, appears in its place.

Do you want to enter the value in the current cell? Press Return. To dispose of the value without altering the worksheet, press Escape. To use the value in further calculations, type more mathematical expressions, and press CALC. You can perform these quick calculations as long as 1-2-3 is in Ready mode.

A second way to do the addition is to start with the pointer in a blank cell —use A1 of a blank worksheet. Type the expression *+177+136*, and press Return. 1-2-3 enters the formula into A1 and displays the result, 313. We'll explore in a moment why you should begin a formula by typing a plus sign.

When you look at the worksheet, you see 313. However, because the pointer is in cell A1, the underlying formula of that cell appears in the control panel, as shown in Figure 11.1.

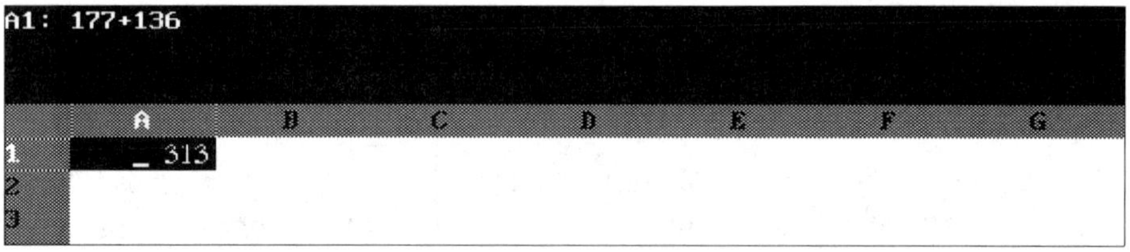

FIGURE 11.1. A simple formula in cell A1 performs addition.

The formula does addition, but it is not very useful. It occupies a single cell and calculates a single result. To reuse the formula, you would have to rewrite it. Move the cell pointer to cell B1, and we'll prepare a more versatile addition formula. In fact, we'll create a small spreadsheet, Figure 11.2, to highlight the four basic math operations and help you understand reusable formulas.

	A	B	C	D	E	F	G
1	313	Add	Sub	Mult	Div		
2		177	169	23	1440		
3		136	174	72	12		
4		313	−5	1656	120		

FIGURE 11.2. Follow the instructions to duplicate this worksheet demonstrating basic mathematical operations.

Develop a Worksheet for Basic Math

Enter the labels shown in row 1 of Figure 11.2. Begin each by typing a caret so that the labels will be centered in their cells. Put the first value for your addition formula, 177, into cell B2. Enter *136* into cell B3. Finally, with the pointer in cell B4, type *+b2+b3*, and press Return.

The formula in cell B4 returns the same result as the one in cell A1. However, to change the result in B4, you need only change the entry in cell B2 or cell B3.

For example, to determine the sum of 177 and 298, move the pointer to cell B3 and enter *298*. Sum 19 and 67 by entering *19* in cell B3 and *67* in cell B2. That's how easy it is to reuse formulas that refer to spreadsheet cells.

Try a few more formulas. Move the pointer to cell C4, and enter *+C2–C3*. This means, "subtract the value in cell C3 from the value in C2, and show the result." Enter in cells C2 and C3 the values that appear in the illustration

Next, enter *+D2*D3* into cell D4. The asterisk represents multiplication, so this formula returns the product of the values in cells D2 and D3. Again, enter the values shown to see the formula work. Finally, enter the formula +E2/E3 into cell E4. The entry returns ERR to indicate that something isn't right.

The slash symbol means divide, so the expression +E2/E3 means, "divide the value in cell E2 by the value in cell E3." Blank cells have the numeric value of 0, and division by zero isn't allowed (it is mathematically impossible). Hence the ERR result. However, enter any value in cell E2, and a non-zero value in cell E3, and the formula in E4 performs the division.

A formula you create in 1-2-3 can contain references to as many cells as you wish as long as the total number of characters in the formula is fewer than 240. You could enter in cell A7 the expression +A1+A2+A3+A4+A5 to sum the values in range A1..A5. Or, you might enter the formula +B1*B1*B1 in cell B2 to calculate the cube of a value in cell B1.

A formula returns its result based on the values currently stored in the cells the formula references. This means that you can lay out a series of formulas that perform investment analyses, calculate loan schedules, and so on, based on cells gathered in a reserved area of the spreadsheet. When you want to analyze a particular investment or loan scenario, you simply enter new values into the referenced cells.

Why Start Formulas with +?

When you begin a cell entry by typing a plus sign, 1-2-3 anticipates that you will be entering a formula and displays the Value indicator at the top-right of your monitor. You have ready access to Point mode as long as the plus sign is the only thing you have typed. Using Point mode lets you establish a formula's references to other cells without actually typing those references.

Give it a try. Move the pointer to cell B6 and type +. Then press the UpArrow key. The pointer moves, and the address of the currently highlighted cell (B5) appears on the edit line adjacent to the plus sign you typed. See Figure 11.3.

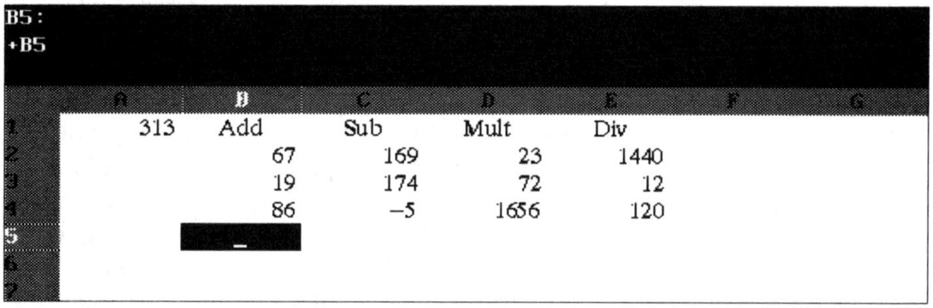

FIGURE 11.3. Using Point mode to create formulas.

Press UpArrow three more times until the pointer rests in cell B2. This is the first cell your new formula will reference. To build in the next cell reference, type an arithmetic operator. In this case, type a plus sign.

Formulas Don't Have to Start with +
Many spreadsheet users come to believe that all formulas must begin with a plus sign. This is not the case. A formula can begin with a value, with a plus or minus sign, with an opening parenthesis, with the pound sign (#) as part of one of the operators #NOT#, #AND#, and #OR#, or with an at sign (@) that begins one of the built-in @functions. The next chapter introduces @functions.

The cell pointer jumps back to cell B6, and the first reference—to cell B2—is locked into the edit line. Press UpArrow three times until the pointer highlights cell B3. The edit line in the control panel should contain the characters +B2+B3. If that were the formula you wished to create, you would press Return. But let's make the formula a little more complex.

Type an asterisk, and once more the pointer jumps to cell B6. Press UpArrow twice to highlight cell B4. Now the edit line shows +B2+B3*B4. Press Return to complete the formula. 1-2-3 enters it into the starting cell, cell B6.

Some people think of their spreadsheet entries in terms of cell and range addresses. Others pay more attention to the cell entries and tend to ignore specific addresses. You may be most comfortable typing cell addresses as you build formulas in the sheet. However, if you think about formulas more in terms of their relationships to other information in the sheet, you may prefer to point as you enter calculations. When you highlight a cell or a range to include in a formula, you leave little room for doubt as to which references the formula will include.

A Few More Operators

Lotus 1-2-3 provides several arithmetic operators beyond the front four. The caret is the operator of exponentiation. To raise a number to a power, enter the number followed by a caret followed by the power. To see this work, move the cell pointer to cell B5 and enter *+5^3*. The result is 125—five cubed.

You use plus and minus signs to establish negativity or positivity of values that you enter in 1-2-3. If a value is negative, precede it with a minus sign. If it is positive, you can precede it with a plus sign. However, if you omit the sign, 1-2-3 assumes that the value is positive.

The remaining arithmetic operators express equality and inequality. These consist of the equal sign, the greater than and less than signs, and combinations of these three signs. You have probably seen them in such statements as 4>3, 7<12, and 8>=6. These expressions don't seem to have much meaning in and of themselves, but as we'll see later on, they are extremely useful in spreadsheet calculations.

There are three more operators that play an important role in expressing equality and inequality, but again, their uses may not be clear at this juncture. Those operators are #NOT#, #AND#, and #OR#. You will find more detail about them in the chapter on conditional math and extended Boolean Expressions. We mention them here because it's important to understand how the arithmetic operators are interrelated.

To ERR Is Spreadsheet

Lotus 1-2-3 lets you know when you ask it to perform a calculation that is somehow invalid. If your formula includes elements that don't make any sense at all, such as numbers followed by letters (55j, for example) or mismatched parentheses, 1-2-3 won't let you enter it into a cell. Rather, your computer beeps, 1-2-3 goes into Edit mode, and you have an opportunity to fix your mistake and try entering it again.

If a formula's syntax is valid, but you have asked it to perform an impossible calculation, such as dividing by zero, 1-2-3 displays ERR in the cell. Usually, ERRs don't crop up in cells unless the cells have at one time held viable formulas. Fiddling around in the worksheet and destroying cells referenced in existing formulas is the easiest way to generate ERRs.

For example, if a formula in cell A3 reads +A1+A2 and you delete row 1 of the worksheet, you destroy one of the formula's references. The formula will contain an ERR that you will have to replace with a new reference before you can expect a useful calculation. ERR, then, is 1-2-3's way of telling you that something about your spreadsheet may be very wrong.

What the Formula Does: Order of Precedence

We interpret written words by scanning from left to right and processing each word or phrase sequentially. This is not the way we interpret mathematical expressions. Some of the arithmetic operators demand to be interpreted before others, regardless of their sequence in a formula. The priority status of the operators is called their *order of precedence.*

The table lists arithmetic operators in their order of precedence from highest to lowest priority.

Doing Math: Order of Precedence

Operator	Operation	Precedence
^	Exponentiation	1
+ and –	Positivity and Negativity	2
* and /	Multiplication and Division	3
+ and –	Addition and Subtraction	4
= and <>	Equal and Not Equal	
>=	Greater Than or Equal To	
<=	Less Than or Equal To	5
#NOT#	Logical Test: Not	6
#AND#	Logical Test: And	
#OR#	Logical Test: Or	7

The formula you created a few moments ago in cell B6 uses two types of arithmetic operators—the plus sign and the multiplication sign. It reads +B2+B3*B4 and returns 313. How does 1-2-3 interpret the formula to return this value?

The formula interpreter scans to find the operator of highest precedence. It finds the multiplication sign and multiplies the value in cell A2 times the value in cell A3. These cells are empty, so the result is zero. 1-2-3 then performs the operation of next lowest precedence. In this case that is to add the value in cell A1 to the product of the multiplication—313+0 is 313. When 1-2-3 finds two or more operations of the same precedence in a formula, it processes the left-most operation first and works from left to right through the operations with that precedence.

As you can see, it is important to have a firm grasp of the order of precedence. If 1-2-3 had interpreted the formula simply by reading from left to right, the result would be 0: cell A1 (313) plus A2 (0) equals 313; 313 times cell A3 (0) is zero.

More Precedence Practice

If you are comfortable in your understanding of the order of precedence, skip ahead to the subsection titled Precedence Preference. If you would like some further practice with the precedence concept, try the following exercise.

The spreadsheet in Figure 11.4 shows several rows of values. Following the spreadsheet is a list of formulas that refer to the spreadsheet cells, preceded by addresses of the cells in which you will eventually enter the formulas.

	A	B	C	D	E	F	G
1	2	4	6	4			
2	8	1	0	2			
3	9	8	7	2			
4	4	4	2	5			
5	2	6	3	8			
6	4	2	8	7			

FIGURE 11.4. This worksheet is full of data with which you can practice creating formulas with the right order of precedence.

F1: +A1*B1+B1^A1*D1+C1*D1*B1
F2: +A2–B2/C2+2
F3: +A3+B3–C3*D3
F4: +A3+B3^C3/D3
F5: –A5+B5*C5–D5*C5^A5
F6: +A6^B6/C6+D6+A6*B6/C6

For practice in mastering the order of precedence of the mathematical operators, analyze the formulas on paper and write down your results. To follow the logic of the formula listed for cell F1, substitute the values from the spreadsheet:

+2*4+4^2*4+6*4*4

Scan for the operation of highest precedence—exponentiation (^):

4^2 = 16

Substitute the result:

+2*4+*16**4+6*4*4

Scan for the operations of second highest precedence—multiplication and division (* and /). There are four, so you must resolve them one by one from left to right:

2*4 = 8, *16**4 = 64, 6*4*4 becomes 6*4 = 24 and *24**4 = 96

Make substitutions:

8+64+96

Scan for operations of next level of precedence—addition and subtraction. There are two, so resolve them from left to right:

8+64 = 72, and *72+96* = 168

When you have worked out the other formulas on paper, start in a blank worksheet (select Worksheet Erase Yes), enter the values shown in Figure 11.4, and build the formulas in column F to check your answers.

Precedence Preference: Control the Operator Precedence

Sometimes it is impossible to write a formula that expresses your calculation needs if you use only the arithmetic operators. How, for example, can you get 1-2-3 to sum the values from two cells and multiply the result times 3 or raise the result to a power? You use parentheses. Expressions enclosed in parentheses are solved first as 1-2-3 calculates a formula.

The expression +A1+A2*A3 means, "multiply the value from cell A2 times the value from cell A3 and add the value from cell A1." By adding parentheses, you can completely alter the meaning. The formula +(A1+A2)*A3 means, "sum the values from A1 and A2, and multiply the result times the value from A3."

Parentheses can combine in almost any arrangement to define a calculation. They can set apart discrete sequences of calculations or prioritize expressions embedded within other expressions. The following formula contains calculations nested within other calculations:

+((A1+B1)*C1)/(D1–B1)+A1

Let's see the formula at work when it resides in cell F1 of a worksheet with entries as shown in Figure 11.5.

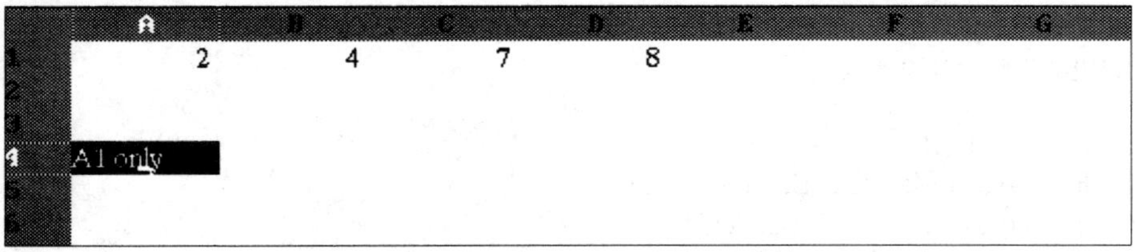

FIGURE 11.5. Enter these values in the worksheet.

First, substitute the values:

+((2+4)*7)/(8–4)+2

1-2-3 solves the expression in the innermost set of parentheses first. So, resolve the expression (2+4) and substitute:

+(6*7)/(8–4)+2

Work through the formula from left to right and resolve all expressions within parentheses:

(6*7) = 42 and (8–4) = 4, so the formula becomes *+42/4+2*

Resolve the highest priority expression (division in this case):

42/4 = 10.5, so the formula becomes *+10.5+2*

Resolve the lower priority operation:

+10.5+2 = 12.5

	A	B	C	D	E	F	G
1	2	3	5	7			
2	2	4	6	8			
3	8	4	9	3			
4	7	2	1	4			

FIGURE 11.6. Enter these numbers in a worksheet to practice using parentheses in formulas.

Figure 11.6 shows a list of values that you can use should you want further practice with the calculation precedences. Analyze each of the following formulas using the values shown in the figure. Work the formulas out on paper, and then enter the values and formulas in an otherwise blank worksheet to gauge your success:

F1: +(A1+B1)*(D1–C1)
F2: +A2+(A2–(C2–B2+D2)*A2)
F3: +(A3–B3)*(D3–(C3/D3))*B3
F4: +A4+A4^(D4–C4*B4)/(B4*D4)

Math on Your Own

This chapter may have felt a bit like remedial math. While none of the problems it has presented apply directly to your business chores, they all come into play as you increase your spreadsheet skills. Calculating price increases, discounts, commissions, taxes, and financial ratios all require an understanding of basic mathematics. Only continued practice will prepare you to face the challenges a spreadsheet can conquer.

Having completed this chapter you should:

- *Understand the basics of writing mathematical formulas in the spreadsheet*
- *Know how to use the spreadsheet as a desktop calculator*
- *Be familiar with all of the arithmetic operators*
- *Understand the calculation order of precedence, and be able to control the order*
- *Be able to create spreadsheets that represent simple business problems such as sales and production summaries and revenue projections*
- *Be prepared to explore more complex and more useful concepts in spreadsheet math*

12

An Introduction to @Functions

If you worked through the last chapter, you now remember how to do math the hard way. By combining series of arithmetic operators and cell references, you can express just about any mathematical problem. However, such endeavors can lead to ridiculously involved formulas—especially when you need to calculate statistics such as sums, averages, and standard deviations.

Doubling the indemnity, you would have to know, or have a good source book of the myriad calculations that are common in business. For most of us, calculating straight-line depreciation, mortgage payments, and internal rates of return isn't second nature. For 1-2-3's @functions, it is. This chapter is a brief review for readers who already use @functions and a solid introduction for those who don't.

In this chapter you will:

- *Learn what @functions are*
- *Learn terms associated with @functions*
- *Apply the @SUM function using Point mode*
- *Review a few common math-related @functions: @ROUND, @INT, @SQRT, @PI, @SIN, @RAND*
- *Learn about spreadsheet ERRs*

What Are @Functions?

@Functions are formulas that are built into 1-2-3. They provide shortcuts to performing many common calculations. The typical @function has three major components—an @ sign, a function name, and an argument or a list of arguments enclosed in parentheses.

@AVG(A1..B4)

This function has the three basic components: an @ sign, a function name (AVG), and a single argument that is a reference to spreadsheet range. It calculates the average of the values stored in range A1..B4.

Some of the calculations that @functions perform include the operations typically found on scientific pocket calculators such as sine, cosine, tangent, arcsine, arccosine, arctangent, and square root.

Other @functions calculate the sums, averages, and standard deviations of lists of values. Still other functions, described in the chapter called Do Business Math, perform the involved business-related calculations mentioned earlier. The logical @functions (explored in depth in the Conditional Math and the Extended Boolean Expressions chapters) let you build intelligence into your spreadsheets.

Some @functions perform calculations that have meaning only in a spreadsheet environment. They return such information as row numbers of specific cells and widths of selected columns. See the chapter called @Functions for the Spreadsheet Environment for more about these gems.

Date- and time-related @functions help you to establish and to keep track of dates important to the information in your worksheets. You can learn more about them by reading the chapter called Date a Spreadsheet. A handful of functions, called the @D functions (pronounced "at dee") perform statistical analysis of information stored in databases. You will find much more about the @D functions in the Data Analysis and Statistics section. Finally, 1-2-3 contains a collection of functions that let you do "math" with strings of alphanumeric characters. The chapter Math with Labels explains how to use these functions to selectively cut character strings into pieces and reassemble them as needed.

This chapter looks at a few of the functions most closely tied to basic arithmetic calculations. Working with these functions will give you a good foundation from which to further your exploration of the spreadsheet's most powerful tools.

Sum Many Values: @SUM

There is no function in 1-2-3 used more than @SUM. It saves oodles of keystrokes when you want to total the values in a range. The function's syntax is @SUM(*list*) where *list* is a description of the values to sum.

The items in *list* must be separated by commas, and they can consist of values, cell references, range references, formulas, and even @functions. The following are examples of valid @SUM functions:

@SUM(2,4,1,6,9)
@SUM(A1..A4)
@SUM(A1..A4,9,B1..B7)
@SUM(@AVG(A1..A4),B1,C3,C4+8)

Practice with @SUM

You probably already use the @SUM function to return subtotals at the ends of columns of data as shown in Figure 12.1. There are several ways to create such functions.

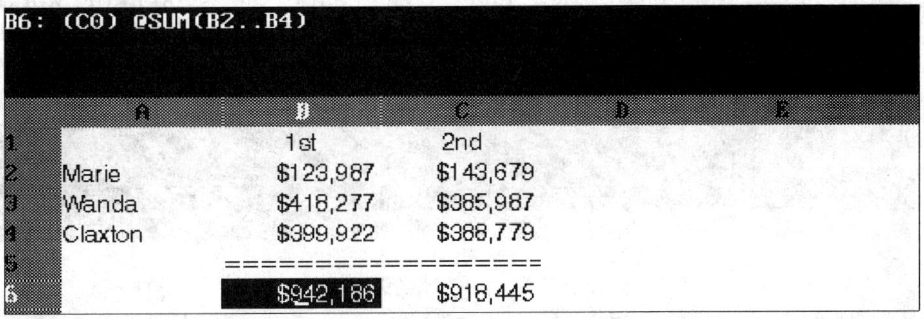

FIGURE 12.1. Build this worksheet to see how the @SUM function works.

Suppose you wanted to enter the @SUM function shown in cell B6. One way would be to place the cell pointer in B6 and simply type the function, @SUM(B2..B4). Another way would be to use Point mode as you do when entering cell references that follow arithmetic operators (explained in the chapter titled Math in the Sheet). Build the simple worksheet to see how this works.

Begin with the caret label prefix to enter the labels in cells B1 and C1. Enter the labels in column A, and create the dividing line in row 5 by entering \= in cells B5 and C5. Omit the punctuation—the dollar signs and commas—when you enter the values in range B2..C4. Then use the Range Format Currency command and indicate no decimal places to format range B2..C6.

A Reminder About Dividing Lines for Wysiwyg Users

Wysiwyg obviates the need to use an entire row for a dividing line as we do in so many of our figures. If you are working with Wysiwyg activated, create underlines within cells by selecting :Format Lines Double Bottom and highlighting the cells.

Don't use this technique while you are following our discussions, or your practice spreadsheets may end up with spacings that don't match ours. For now, work with the dividing lines that we suggest. We'll explore Wysiwyg in great detail in Section 4.

To enter the first @SUM formula, move the cell pointer to B6 and type *@SUM(*. Press the UpArrow key, and the cell pointer moves up in the worksheet. The edit line of the control panel offers the newly highlighted cell as an argument for the @SUM function as in Figure 12.2.

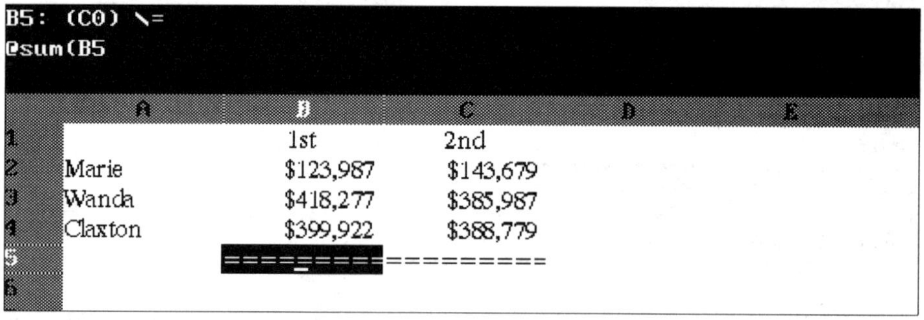

FIGURE 12.2. Entering an @SUM function in cell B6.

You aren't going to include cell B5 in the sum. So, press UpArrow three more times until the cell pointer highlights cell B2. This is the first cell of the range you're going to highlight. To turn the cell reference into a range reference, press the period key. The cell pointer becomes anchored in cell B2 so that when you press DownArrow, the pointer expands into a highlight.

Press DownArrow twice to stretch the highlight over cells B2, B3, and B4. Type a closing parenthesis, and press Return to enter the completed @SUM formula in cell B6. The procedure takes much longer to explain than it does to perform. With a little practice you'll be able to use Point mode very efficiently as you enter formulas. See Chapter 1 for a thorough discussion of Point mode.

Sum with a Mouse

To create an @SUM function using the mouse, start by clicking the cell that will receive the formula. Type *@SUM(*, then drag from the first summary cell to the last. Finally, type a closing parenthesis, and press return—or click anywhere on the worksheet.

Try it in this practice worksheet. Click cell C6 and type *@SUM(*. Move the mouse pointer to cell C2, press and hold the left mouse button, and drag to cell C4. Release the mouse button, and type a closing parenthesis. Then click anywhere.

However you create an @SUM function, it is clearly more efficient than entering an addition formula that uses a plus sign and a reference to each cell in the range to sum. That's the whole point of spreadsheet @functions. Use whatever method you prefer to establish a second @SUM function in cell C6 of the practice worksheet.

A Few Math-Related Functions: @ROUND, @INT, @SQRT, @PI, @SIN, @RAND

Any single @function lends itself to pages of discussion. It is not enough to know what an @function does, you must also understand when to use it. As stated earlier, the purpose of this chapter isn't to provide the exhaustive education you would need to make use of all of the @functions. Rather, it highlights a few of the more generally applicable functions. Some of these functions—@INT, @SQRT, @PI, and @SIN—duplicate ones that you find on scientific calculators. The others—@ROUND, and @RAND—are a bit more esoteric. The @ROUND function is important in correcting rounding errors—a common spreadsheet problem—and the @RAND function is useful in creating spreadsheet models that reflect elements of chance that arise in many business scenarios. Understanding these basics will get you started with @functions so that you can select and apply the functions appropriate to your own needs.

Formatting Changes Appearances, @ROUND Changes Values

Many of the numeric display formats require that you decide how many decimal places should show for each formatted value. A currency format with two decimal places always shows two digits after the decimal point. Likewise, a fixed format with five decimal places shows five digits after the decimal point. A numeric display format doesn't alter the value in a cell. The value 3.447 displayed with two decimal places appears as 3.45, but the underlying value remains 3.447. Any formulas that include this formatted value will use 3.447 to calculate their results.

The @ROUND function literally changes the value of a number that it rounds off. The expression @ROUND(3.447,2) returns 3.45; formulas that refer to this rounded value use 3.45 to determine their results.

@ROUND

Lotus 1-2-3 performs its calculations to 15 decimal places. Sometimes the decimal places in your calculations proliferate as a result of successive subtractions, multiplications, and divisions. At any point you can round off some of those decimal places by applying the @ROUND function.

This function has the syntax @ROUND(*value,places*). The *value* argument represents a number, a cell reference, or a formula that resolves to a number. The *places* argument represents the number of decimal places to which 1-2-3 should round the *value* argument.

The formula @ROUND(3.1416,2) returns the value 3.14. The expression @ROUND(A1,1) returns 7.5 if cell A1 contains the entry 7.48.

Use a negative *places* argument if you want to round into the integer portion of a value. For example, the expression @ROUND(1473.21,–2) returns 1500—the value 1473.21 rounded to the nearest hundreds.

@INT

Related to the @ROUND function, is @INT. You may use the @INT function extensively if your financial calculations deal with very large numbers and it is your policy to disregard fractions of dollars.

The function has the syntax @INT(*value*) where *value* is any number, cell reference, or formula that returns a number. The @INT function simply strips any decimal portion from *value*. Hence, @INT(27.3) returns 27.

Use the @INT function in conjunction with simple subtraction when you want to know the decimal portion of a value. For example, the expression +A1–@INT(A1) returns .12 when cell A1 contains the value 857.12.

@SQRT

The @SQRT function calculates the square root of a number. Its syntax is, guess what, @SQRT(*value*). Once again, *value* can be any number, cell address, or formula.

@PI

The @PI function calculates nothing but pi (π). Of course, it doesn't calculate pi exactly, only an abbreviation of pi. But for any trigonometric calculations, this @function is a handy approximation. Note that the @PI function is one of a few @functions that don't accept arguments.

@SIN

Speaking of trigonometry, the @SIN function fits right in. It has the syntax @SIN(*value*) and returns the sine of *value*. Other functions to help with trigonometry include @COS, and @TAN, which calculate the cosines and tangents of values, respectively.

@RAND

Building financial scenarios, projections, simulations, and the like is the forte of spreadsheet computing. Sometimes, however, projecting the outcomes of events isn't meaningful when you omit an element of chance from your basic assumptions. That's where the @RAND function comes in.

ERRs with @Functions

ERRs can arise in your spreadsheets when you accidentally wipe out cells referenced by established formulas. You might do this by carelessly deleting rows or columns or by haphazardly moving ranges around in the sheet. ERRs also arise when you supply inappropriate arguments for your @functions.

Some @functions allow any type of argument—numbers, labels, cell addresses, formulas. Other @functions are limited in the types of arguments that they accept or, more important, that make sense to them. When you supply an invalid argument, the @function returns ERR. This way, you know instantly that something about the formula is wrong and must be corrected.

For example, 1-2-3 has no way to express imaginary numbers. Consequently, it can't calculate the square root of a negative value. The formula @SQRT(–4) returns ERR. Many of the @functions we'll explore in later chapters are finicky about the arguments they accept and will return ERR when you violate their conventions.

For example, you might estimate a projection of next year's revenues by entering a series of hard numbers in the sheet. Factors that contribute to the projection might include the cost of materials, the cost of labor, distribution expenses, and so on. While the hard numbers represent your best guesses at these expenses, reality is fraught with unpredictable events. Your predictions would be more realistic if you introduced a random element into your guesses. The cost of materials might become a random number between $12,000 and $23,000; the cost of labor might run between $567,000 and $789,000.

The @RAND function returns a value between 0 and 1. The value returned is unpredictable enough that you can consider it random. If your application needs a random value that falls within a specified interval, the @RAND function can generate the value.

Suppose that *highest* represents the largest value in the allowable interval, and *lowest* represents the lowest value in the interval. The following formula should return a random number within the interval:

@RAND*(*highest –lowest*)+*lowest*

To see the formula at work, use it to generate random numbers between 50 and 75. Find a blank cell in your spreadsheet, and enter the statement *@RAND*(75–50)+50.* There is no telling what value you will get, but it will be within the interval.

What formula would you use to return an integer value between 50 and 75? Try to figure it out before you read the rest of this paragraph. The answer is to enclose the preceding formula within the parentheses of an @INT function. The modified formula would be @INT(@RAND*(75–50)+50).

An important point to understand about the @RAND function is that its result changes every time the worksheet is recalculated. This means that as long as the spreadsheet is in automatic recalculation mode, any changes you make to the spreadsheet can alter the results of formulas that use @RAND.

Try it. Move the cell pointer to a blank cell, but make sure the @RAND formula you have entered is still visible in the sheet. Notice the current value of your @RAND formula, and then enter any label into the blank cell. Your formula's result probably changed. If the result didn't change, well, that's the nature of probability. Enter a new label into the current cell, and perhaps the formula will change this time.

If after you have made 30 or 40 entries, the formula's value still hasn't changed, you're cheating. Is the Calc indicator visible at the bottom of your display? Then the worksheet isn't in automatic recalc mode. If the Calc indicator isn't visible, then you have witnessed a statistically improbable event.

Having completed this chapter you should:

- *Have a basic understanding of what @functions are*
- *Know how @functions can significantly simplify your formulas*
- *Be prepared to explore and apply even more useful, albeit esoteric, @functions*

13

One Handles Many: Relative Versus Absolute References

A spreadsheet formula is dynamic. You can enter it once and then copy it to reuse it throughout a spreadsheet. You probably already know how to sum a column of values and then copy the summary formula to successive columns. In each column the formula adjusts to sum entries in that column. You can copy a formula entered in column A to sum the same number of cells in column B, C, D, and so on out to column IV.

This characteristic of formulas—the fact that their references are relative to their positions in the spreadsheet (we'll explain this further in a moment) —is very important. Being able to reuse a single entry repeatedly can save hours of typing. But not all formulas work this way. It is possible to write formulas whose references never change, no matter where you copy them in the sheet. These references—absolute references—can be as powerful as relative references, and it is important to understand how to apply them.

This chapter explains the differences between relative and absolute references. It reviews how relative references make your formulas reusable, and it shows how absolute references can calculate percentages and running totals of values in the spreadsheet.

In this chapter you will learn:

- *The nature of relative references in formulas*
- *The difference between absolute and relative references*
- *How to create absolute references*
- *How to combine absolute and relative references to calculate percentages*

Build a Practice Worksheet

You might recognize part of the spreadsheet in Figure 13.1. We have simply reproduced a worksheet from the previous chapter and added two more columns of data. You will use the worksheet to create summary formulas and to calculate percentages in ways that demonstrate the differences between absolute and relative cell references.

	A	B	C	D	E	F
1		1st	2nd	3rd	4th	
2	Marie	$123,987	$143,679	$137,849	$140,999	
3	Wanda	$418,277	$385,987	$377,744	$344,772	
4	Claxton	$399,922	$388,779	$391,121	$411,987	
5		==========	==========	==========	==========	
6						
7						

FIGURE 13.1. Build this sample worksheet from a previous chapter with the additional data in columns D and E.

To follow this discussion, build the sample worksheet. Begin each of the column headers in row 1 with a caret label prefix. Enter the values in range B2..E4, and use the Worksheet Global Format command to assign a currency with no decimal places display format. Enter \= into cell B5, and copy it to range C5..E5 to create the dividing line in row 5.

Enter the formula *+B2+B3+B4* into cell B6. (Yes, the @SUM function would serve, but this simple addition formula better illustrates the concept we're exploring.) Quite clearly the formula adds up the values in cells B2, B3, and B4. To sum the values in columns C, D, and E, copy the formula across row 6. With the cell pointer in B6, select Copy and press Return. Press RightArrow, period, RightArrow two more times, and press Return. If you prefer the mouse, select Copy from the main menu. Double click cell B6, then drag from cell C6 to cell E6. Finally, click anywhere in the sheet.

However you copied the formula, the column totals now appear across row 6 of the sheet. Check out the formula in cell C6. It reads +C2+C3+C4. The formula in cell D6 reads +D2+D3+D4. How could this happen when the formula you entered was +B2+B3+B4? It happened because your original formula contained relative references.

What Is a Relative Reference?

To you, the formula in cell B6 reads +B2+B3+B4. To 1-2-3 it reads, "add the value that is four cells up to the value that is three cells up and also to the value that is two cells up." 1-2-3 shows you the cell addresses in the formula so that you can see what is going on (not to mention that cell addresses provide a convenient way of describing your spreadsheet calculations).

To 1-2-3, the meaning of the copied formula in cell C6 doesn't change. It still means, "add the value that is four cells up to the value that is three cells up and also to the value that is two cells up." The cells that are four, three, and two cells up relative to cell C6 are different from those relative to cell B6. Consequently, the formula in cell C6 returns a different total.

The emphasis here is relativity. The addition formula you have created finds values to add up relative to its position in the worksheet. The cell addresses that appear in copies of the original formula reflect this.

As you can see with this simple addition formula, relative cell references can significantly reduce the busywork involved in laying out a spreadsheet. When you need totals at the ends of several columns, you write one formula and copy it. If you need to know the sines of a long list of numbers, enter one formula and copy it. Need to round off a bunch of values? You have the idea. Save the worksheet at this point under the name PRACTICE. You will be making significant changes to it, but we will need to retrieve it in its current condition for an exercise that comes near the end of this chapter.

Try one more formula with relative references. Enter @SUM formulas in column F to calculate totals for the entries in rows 2, 3, and 4. Start by entering *@SUM(B2..E2)* into cell F2. Then use the Copy command to replicate the formula in range F3..F4. If asterisks appear in cells F3 and F4, check out the box titled When Asterisks Appear—A Reminder.

When Asterisks Appear—A Reminder
When a cell that contains a value displays asterisks, the value, together with the assigned numeric display format, is too wide to fit in the column. If this happens in your worksheet, use the Worksheet Column Set-Width command to widen the column until the underlying value appears as it should.

Unless you take special action when you create a formula, all of its references are relative. Any copy you make of the formula will adjust automatically to its new location in the sheet. So, what steps can you take to override this feature?

How Would You Sum It Up?

How many ways can you think of to establish a total in cell F6 of your practice worksheet? The total should reveal the revenue generated by all three sales reps for the entire year. Don't peek. Make a list that includes only spreadsheet techniques (using a pocket calculator or a scratch pad isn't a valid way to sum numbers, considering what you already know about 1-2-3), and then compare your list to ours. We have listed five of the simplest approaches, though there are quite a few other possibilities:

- Create a formula that sums the entries in range F2..F4.
- Create a formula that sums the entries in range B6..E6.
- Copy the formula from cell F4 to cell F6. In F6 it sums the column totals from cells B6, C6, and D6.
- Copy the formula from cell E6 to F6. The copied formula sums the individual annual sales totals.
- Create a formula that sums the values in range B2..E4.

You might have come up with other ways to produce the total in cell F6. Any approach that works is valid, but you should try to use the easiest method for solving a spreadsheet problem in most instances.

Make Identical Copies: Absolute References

There are times when you need a formula that you can copy about the spreadsheet without having new cell references crop up in every copy. Actually, it is more likely that you will need formulas in which some of the cell references change when they are copied, and other references don't change. One application where such references are useful is in calculating percentages; another is in calculating running totals. In any case, formulaic references that are fixed to a specific cell or range are called *absolute references.*

The model you have created so far shows the sales revenue generated by three employees in four quarters. Row 6 of the model shows the sales team's quarterly sales totals, and column F shows each salesperson's annual total. Two pieces of information will make the model more complete.

First, what is the total sales revenue for the year? The obvious place for that amount to appear is cell F6. There are at least five ways to get it there using procedures that we have already explored in this section of the book. For this exercise, enter the formula *@SUM(B2..E4)* into cell F6.

Or, Do You Prefer Cross-Foot Totals?

You can't be too careful about the accuracy of your spreadsheets. When formulas are interrelated from one end of the sheet to the other, a single incorrect entry can throw off all of your calculations. One way to keep a lookout for mistakes is to create cross-foot totals.

Before you add the percentage calculations, the practice worksheet in this chapter appears as follows:

	A	B	C	D	E	F
1		1st	2nd	3rd	4th	
2	Marie	$123,987	$143,679	$137,849	$140,999	$546,514
3	Wanda	$418,277	$385,987	$377,744	$344,772	$1,526,780
4	Claxton	$399,922	$388,779	$391,121	$411,987	$1,591,809
5		==========	==========	==========	==========	
6		$942,186	$918,445	$906,714	$897,758	$3,665,103

The practice worksheet before you calculate percentages.

Formulas in row 6 calculate quarterly totals for each column, and formulas in column F calculate annual totals for each salesperson. A formula in cell F6 calculates the sum of all the values in range B2..E4.

Suppose that you incorrectly enter the formula in cell B6 so that it sums only cells B3 and B4. In a small model you will see such a mistake easily, but in a larger model you might miss it. Cross-foot totals reveal the error in a flash.

In cell F7, enter *@SUM(F2..F4)*. In cell G6 enter *@SUM(B6..E6)*. The formulas' results should be equal—one sums the quarterly totals to return a total for all the data, the other sums the totals for each salesperson and returns a total for all the data. These sums should match the value that appears in cell F6. After confirming the accuracy of your formulas you may wish to remove the cross-foot totals.

The information that will complete the sales data table is a list that shows what percent of sales each person generated. You will use an absolute reference in column G to perform that calculation.

A percentage is a fraction of a total. In this case, we are calculating the fraction of total sales each rep generated. You express the percentage mathematically as *repsales/totsales* where *repsales* is the total sales of a particular sales rep, and *totsales* is the total sales of all the reps.

The formula +F2/F6 entered into cell G2 certainly calculates Marie's percentage of sales. But if you copy it down column G, the formula returns ERR for Wanda and Claxton. That's because in cell G3, the formula's second reference is to cell F7, and in G4 that reference is to F8, another blank cell. Division by 0 doesn't work, so 1-2-3 displays ERR.

If the reference to cell F6 in this formula were absolute, it wouldn't change when copied down the column. In cell G3 the formula would read +F3/$F$6, and in cell G4 it would read +F4/$F$6. In each case it would calculate the proper sales percentage.

Let's create the percentage formula to see an absolute reference in action. Move the cell pointer to cell G2 and type +. Depending on your preference, type F2, use the cursor keys to highlight F2, or use the mouse to click that cell. Type a slash (for division), and then type the reference (omitting the dollar signs for the moment), highlight, or click cell F6. Whichever technique you use, press the ABS key (F4) once the cell address appears on the edit line in the control panel. 1-2-3 inserts the absolute reference symbols for you. Press Return to enter the formula into cell G2.

Oops. The resulting calculation appears in the cell as 0 dollars. What gives? With the global numeric display format set at currency with no decimal places, a percentage—which is a fraction of 1—appears as 0 dollars. Select Range Format Percent, enter *2* for two decimal places, and indicate cell G2. It is a simple matter to copy the formula down column G and see that it does calculate the desired percentages.

Mix Absolutes with Relatives

The example we have presented to explain absolute and relative references is straightforward. You might use the technique repeatedly and never encounter other uses for absolute references. On the other hand, absolute references can help solve some rather complex spreadsheet problems.

You see, it is possible to mix absolutes and relatives within a single cell reference or even within a range reference. The formula +B$2 contains a *mixed reference.* The reference to column B is relative, but the reference to row 2 is absolute. Enter the formula into cell B9 to see how it works.

As you would expect, the formula returns the value stored in cell B2. Predict what will happen when you copy the formula down a row. OK, now copy the formula to cell B10. Were you right? The formula still returns the value from cell B2.

Now predict what the formula will do when copied to cell C10. Copy it. Were you right this time? In cell C10 the formula returns the value from cell C2. No matter where you copy this mixed reference formula in the worksheet, it returns the value from row 2 of the column it occupies. You could use such a formula to calculate several columns of sales percentages.

	A	B	C	D	E	F
1		1st	2nd	3rd	4th	
2	Marie	$123,987	$143,679	$137,849	$140,999	
3	Wanda	$418,277	$385,987	$377,744	$344,772	
4	Claxton	$399,922	$388,779	$391,121	$411,987	
5		=========	=========	=========	=========	
6		$942,186	$918,445	$906,714	$897,758	

FIGURE 13.2. The PRACTICE worksheet.

Remember the file named PRACTICE that you saved a few pages back? Retrieve it so you can follow this discussion. The practice worksheet looks like Figure 13.2.

What formula can you create in cell F2 to calculate first quarter sales percentages for Marie? More to the point, what formula can you create in F2 that

Mixed References Calculate Running Totals

Here's an amusing exercise: start in a blank worksheet and rapidly enter a series of arbitrary numbers in column A starting in cell A1. These numbers represent any type of sequential transaction that you might record in the sheet.

Your mission is to create a formula that when entered in cell B1 and copied down column B will return a running total of the values in column A. The figure below will give you an idea of how your finished spreadsheet might look:

	A	B	C	D	E	F	G
1	8	8					
2	3	11					
3	5	16					
4	2	18					
5	7	25					

What your worksheet should look like if you create running totals in column B.

How'd you do? The solution is quite simple when you employ the @SUM function and a mixed relative and absolute range reference. Place the cell pointer in B1 and type *@SUM($A$1..A1)*. Enter the formula and then copy it down column B as needed. In each successive copy of the formula the first part of the range reference remains $A$1. The second part of the reference adjusts to match the current row. In cell B2, the formula reads @SUM($A$1..A2), in cell B3 it reads @SUM($A$1..A3), and so on.

will calculate quarterly sales percentages for each rep in each quarter when copied to range F2..I4? Puzzle it out before you read ahead.

The formula is +B2/B$6. It divides the value in cell B2 by the total in cell B6. Both references to column B in the formula are relative; they will adjust when copied to the right across the sheet. The reference to row 2 in the formula is also relative, so it will adjust when you copy the formula down the sheet. The reference to row 6 is absolute; no matter where you copy the formula, it will refer to row 6.

Enter the formula into cell F2, and then use the Range Format command to assign cell F2 a percentage format. Use the Copy command to copy cell F2 to range F2..I4. The resulting formulas reveal, for example, that Wanda generated 42% of sales in the third quarter.

Having completed this chapter you should:

- *Understand how relative cell references let you reuse formulas efficiently*
- *Know the difference between relative and absolute references*
- *Recognize opportunities to mix relative and absolute references to calculate percentages and running totals*

14

Formulas That Make Decisions: Conditional Math

Many of the calculations that describe a business depend on conditions that can change from one day to the next: Projected growth in sales may be affected by seasons. Increasing interest rates may require alternative investment strategies. Changing stock prices may demand changing treatment of a stock portfolio, and so on.

You can always keep track of changing variables by reading through a spreadsheet, noting changes in your data and altering formulas to reflect new conditions. However, it is more efficient to have 1-2-3 monitor changing conditions and update the formulas for you. All of this may sound a little complicated, but it is quite easy when you understand how to apply conditional math.

We deal with conditional math almost constantly: If it's cold outside, wear an overcoat; if it's warm, wear a windbreaker. If the water is boiling, add the noodles; otherwise, wait for the water to boil. If the stock price goes above $25 a share, sell; otherwise, hold. All of these are conditional statements.

The element that makes a statement conditional is the equation it draws. In the spreadsheet, a conditional equation can have only one of two solutions—true or false. To illustrate, the statement, *the stock price goes above $25 a share* can be true or false.

> *In this chapter you will:*
>
> - *Learn what a conditional statement is*
> - *Apply the @IF function*
> - *Explore the logical operators*
> - *Review several logical functions: @FALSE, @TRUE, @ISERR*
> - *Revisit ERR and apply the @ERR function*
> - *Delve into the intricacies of Boolean (true-false) math*
> - *Write compact conditional statements*

Coupled with each solution to a conditional statement is an action. When the stock does go above $25 a share, you sell. If it remains below $25 a share, you hold.

Conditional Math in the Sheet: The @IF Function

You use the @IF function in 1-2-3 to express a conditional statement and to define the actions that should result when the conditions of the statement are met. The function has the syntax @IF(*condition,true_action, false_action*). Both the *true_action* and the *false_action* arguments can be values, strings (explored in depth in the next chapter), cell references, or formulaic expressions.

The *condition* argument in the @IF function must be a statement that is either true or false (see the box titled The Truth, Numerically Speaking for a more complete explanation). The expression +A1>7 is such a statement. It means, "the value in cell A1 is greater than 7."

You might use an @IF function to determine the commission percentage due a sales person when there is an earnings threshold in the commission scale. The commission is 10% when sales are $70,000 or less, but it moves to 12% when sales exceed $70,000. A very simple @IF formula returns the correct percentage. It reads @IF(A1>70000,.12,.1). Entered in a cell other than A1, this formula returns 12% if the value in A1 is greater than 70,000. If the value of A1 is 70,000 or less, the formula returns 10%.

Build an @IF formula to gain an understanding of how the function works. In cell D1 of an otherwise blank worksheet, enter the expression @IF(A1>=B1,100,–100). This means, "if the value in cell A1 is greater than or equal to the value in B1, return 100. Otherwise, return –100."

When you first enter the formula, it returns 100 because two blank cells are equal in value. Enter any positive value in cell B1, and the formula returns –100. Enter a greater value in cell A1, and the @IF formula returns 100.

Complex Logical Statements

Conditional statements express the logic of relationships between variables. To that end, there are several *logical operators* that help to describe those relationships. It is quite simple to express equality and inequality using

The Truth, Numerically Speaking

In 1-2-3, conditional statements can be either true or false; they can have one of only two results. To simplify the mathematics of conditional statements, a true result has the value of 1 and a false result has the value of 0. This system of math that involves only two possible values was conceived originally by a mathematician named George Boole and so has the name Boolean Algebra.

When an expression, such as +A1=B1 is true, the result is 1. It follows then that when such an expression is false, its result is 0. Test this for yourself. In a blank worksheet, enter *3* in cell A1 and *4* in cell B1. Then enter *+A1=B1* in cell B3. The formula returns 0 because the statement A1=B1 is false.

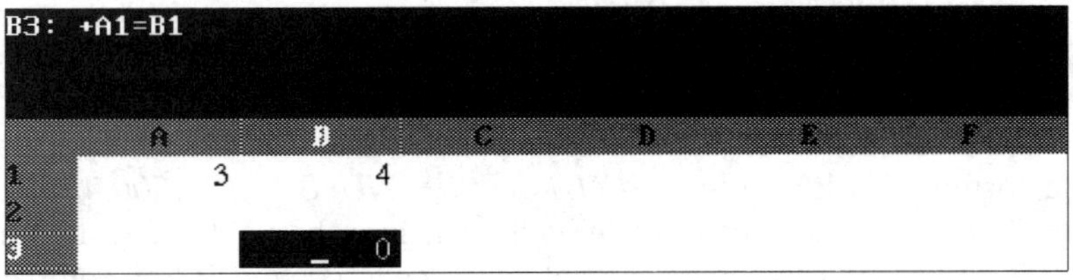

Using Boolean arithmetic to compare cell A1 with cell B1.

Change the entry in cell B1 to *3*. Instantly, the Boolean formula in cell B3 returns 1, because its equation A1=B1 is now true.

equals, greater than, and less than signs. Sometimes, however, you need to combine a list of conditions that together express a complex set of circumstances.

You might want to sell your stock only when its price passes $25 a share and the prime interest rate is less than 7%. Or, perhaps you want to price a task in a project proposal at $3,500 if the cost of materials is less than $1,200 or if the interest rate on a related construction loan is less than 12%. If neither of these conditions is met, you will price the task at $4,200. These are complex conditions.

Explore the second scenario by building a small model to match the worksheet in Figure 14.1.

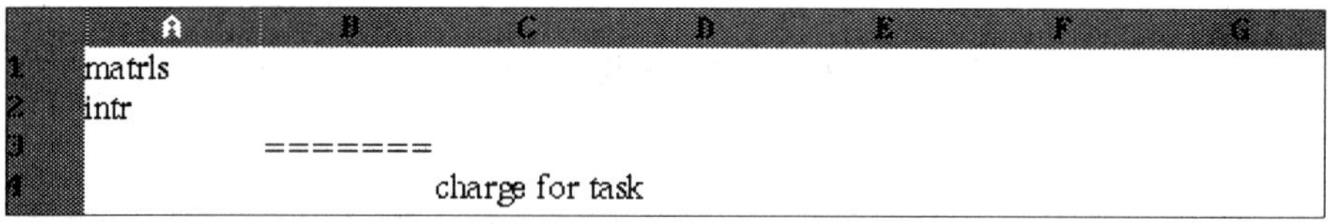

FIGURE 14.1. Create a worksheet to match this one and try out a complex conditional statement.

Enter the few labels as shown. Then, in cell B4, enter the formula *@IF(B1<1200#OR#B2<.12,3500,4200).*

At first, the formula returns 3500 because both conditional expressions, B1<1200 and B2<.12, are true. If either of them is true, the expression returns 3500. Prove it by entering the number *1* into cell B2. This makes the expression B2<.12 false, but the @IF formula still returns 3500.

Now enter *1300* into cell B1. The @IF formula returns 4200. Its result changes because neither of the expressions in the logical or statement is true.

Would you quote the lower price only if both conditions were met? Then you would resort to the logical #AND# operator. Try the #AND# operator in a second formula. In B5, enter *@IF(B1<1200#AND#B2<.12,3500,4200).* This returns 3500 only when the entry in cell B1 is less than 1200 and the entry in cell B2 is less than 12%. Vary the values in cells B1 and B2 to compare the behaviors of formulas written with #OR# and #AND# operators.

Perhaps It's #NOT# Logical

It can be useful to have an action take place only when a certain condition isn't met. For example, if two summary formulas should return identical values, you might want a formula to warn you when the results are not equal. The following @IF formula expresses the problem one way, assuming the summary formulas are in cells D10 and F9: @IF(D10<>F9,0,1). It means, "if the value in cell D10 doesn't equal the value in F9, return 0, otherwise return 1."

You can express the same idea by applying the logical #NOT# operator. Using #NOT#, the formula becomes @IF(#NOT#D10=F9,0,1).

You can combine the logical operators as needed to express complex relationships among variables in your worksheets. The expression @IF(A1=B1#AND##NOT#B1>30,A1,0) combines the #AND# and #NOT# operators to mean, "if the value in cell A1 equals the value in cell B1, but B1 is not greater than 30, return the value from cell A1. Otherwise return 0."

Two Logical @Functions: @TRUE and @FALSE

As you work more with conditional formulas in 1-2-3, you may come to express many outcomes of your calculations in terms of Boolean math. Resorting to 1-2-3's way of reporting on the spreadsheet's condition—with ones and zeros—might start to feel natural to you. For example, you might create a simple conditional formula that alerts you when a value you have plugged in at the top of a worksheet has produced a desired target value on the bottom line. The formula could return 1 when the target is met, and 0 until then.

Lotus 1-2-3 includes two simple @functions that can help to clarify conditional statements of this type. Those functions are @TRUE and @FALSE. As you might guess, the @TRUE function has the Boolean value of 1, and @FALSE has the value of 0. You can use them interchangeably with their corresponding values when it is important to be able to decipher conditional statements at a glance.

The worksheet in Figure 14.2 shows the first few rows of a budget projection model. The cells of column B are data entry cells for expenditures. That is, you use them to enter budget line items. The cells of column E are entry cells for income revenue projections. Cell E1 contains an @IF formula that compares the total revenues bottom line with the total expenditures bottom line.

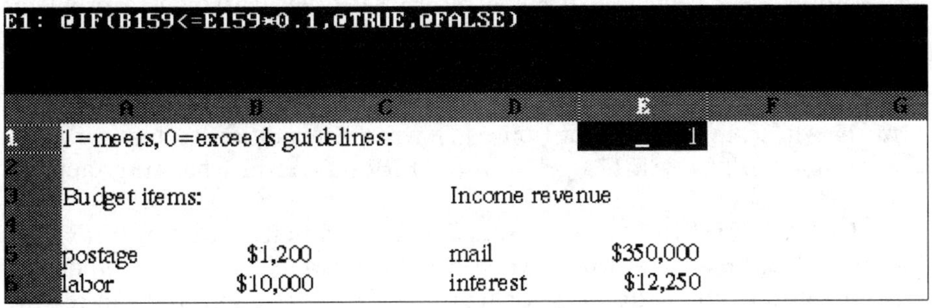

FIGURE 14.2. This worksheet will return 1 if the budget items are less than the income revenue and a 0 if they exceed income revenue.

The formula returns 1, or true, when the total of the budget items is less than or equal to 10% of the revenue. It returns 0 if the budget items exceed 10% of revenue.

Conditions That Involve ERR

When a spreadsheet calculation returns ERR, just about any formula referring to that calculation also returns ERR. Your calculations may need to be aware when such ERRs arise—perhaps one of the values involved in division is 0 or a cell entry isn't appropriate for an @function that refers to the cell. If a formula can detect the ERR condition, its result won't also have to be ERR. Figure 14.3 shows a spreadsheet in which you can explore this phenomenon.

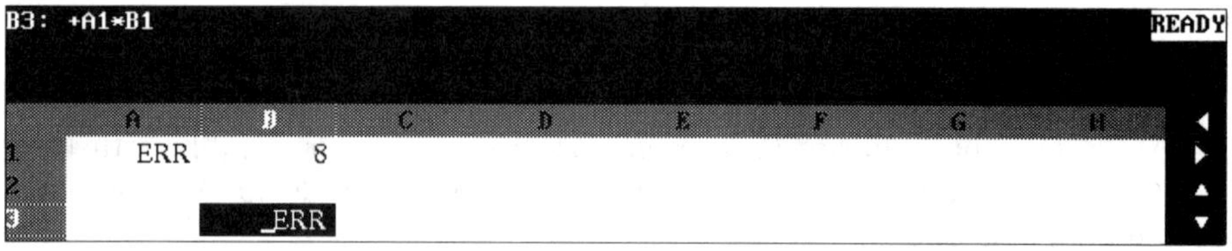

FIGURE 14.3. The ERR in cell B3 lets you know there is something wrong with the formula or with one of the cells to which it refers.

Create the spreadsheet by entering @ERR into cell A1. (See the box for information about the @ERR function.) Enter *8* in cell B1, and enter *+A1*B1* in cell B3. Because the formula refers to a cell that contains ERR, the formula also returns ERR. Having a formula return ERR can alert you to problems elsewhere in the spreadsheet.

When a conditional statement refers to an ERR cell, the statement returns ERR just like any other formula. Enter *@IF(A1>B1,10,100)* in cell C3 to confirm this. It seems, then, that you can't write a condition to test for ERR; the formula @IF(A1=@ERR,0,A1) returns ERR no matter what entry appears in cell A1.

In fact, the @ISERR function tests for ERR without returning ERR. The formula @ISERR(A1) returns 1 when cell A1 contains ERR and 0 when cell A1 contains any non-ERR entry. Using the @ISERR function, you can rewrite the conditional statement that tests cell A1. The new formula would read @IF(@ISERR(A1),0,A1).

A Function to Return ERR?

The @ERR function may seem a little silly. Why would you deliberately create an ERR in your spreadsheet? There are times when it is useful.

Suppose that your model calculates quantities that must fall within specified limits. Budget categories, production quotas, and staffing ceilings are examples of such calculations. You can include the @ERR function in a conditional statement to alert you when an amount exceeds a limit. The following worksheet illustrates such a formula:

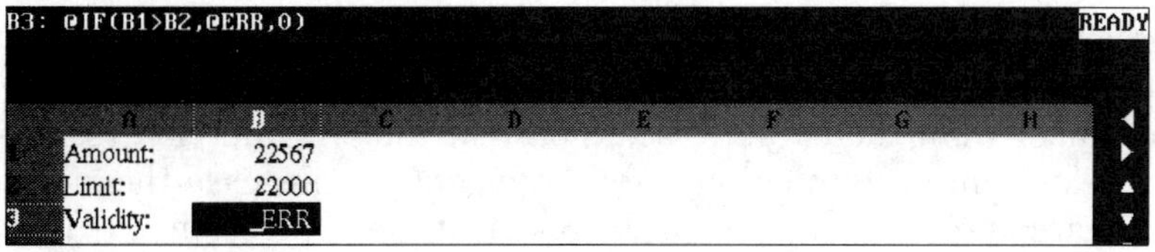

The ERR in cell B3 lets you know that you have exceeded your limit.

The ERR result stands out so you know immediately that something isn't right.

Extended Boolean Expressions

As you create larger and more complex applications, you are likely to discover more and more uses for conditional statements. You will probably apply the @IF function liberally. However, as your skill at describing conditions mathematically increases, so will the complexity of your @IF formulas. In time you may be nesting one @IF function inside another.

In the typical worksheet, this shouldn't be a problem. In larger worksheets, there is a danger that complex formulas could become too involved. The size of formulas is an issue because long formulas use up more RAM than short ones do. The most useful way to cut the size of your formulas is to learn to replace @IF statements with Boolean expressions. Even if you never use these techniques in your own worksheets, they are useful to know in case you inherit worksheets from co-workers who do apply Boolean expressions in place of the @IF function.

The Classic Boolean Shrink

As you know, the @IF function determines its result based on the outcome of a conditional statement. If the conditional statement is true, the formula returns one result. If the conditional statement is false, the formula returns a different result. Here is an example of an @IF formula that contains a classic conditional statement:

@IF(A1=1,1,0)

The expression means, "if the value in cell A1 is 1, then return 1. Otherwise, return 0."

Remember from the earlier discussion that the @IF function resolves the equation built into the function's first argument. In this case the equation is A1=1. That expression has a numeric result. If the expression is true, its numeric result is 1. If the expression is false, its numeric result is 0. In other words, were you to enter the expression +A1=1 into cell B1 the result would be either 1 or 0, depending on whether cell A1 contained the value 1 or not.

Try it, so that you understand what we're expressing. Start in a blank worksheet and enter the formula *+A1=1* into cell B1. The formula returns 0 because cell A1 is blank. Enter *1* into cell A1, and the formula in cell B1 returns 1. Finally, enter *2* into cell A1, and the formula in B1 once again returns 0.

Perhaps you have figured out where this is leading: the conditional formula @IF(A1=1,1,0) returns the same results as the shorter expression +A1=1. Compare the two. Enter *@IF(A1=1,1,0)* into cell B2. Then vary the value stored in cell A1 and observe the formulas in cells B1 and B2. Both formulas return 1 when there is a 1 in cell A1; they return 0 for any other value stored in A1. The Boolean expression is shorter than the @IF formula, so at least for this very simple example, you are already saving RAM when you compose conditional statements.

The Extended Boolean Shrink

So what? How often do you write a conditional statement that returns 1 or 0 depending on the value stored in another cell? Perhaps never. On the other hand, it is quite common to write conditional statements that return a non-zero value when the condition is met and 0 when the condition is not met. A Boolean expression can serve in this situation as well.

Suppose that your @IF formula reads @IF(A4>20,.12,0). Such a formula might calculate a commission if a sales amount exceeds a minimum target. In this case, the commission will be 12% if the sales amount exceeds a target of 20 units. Otherwise, there will be no commission.

The conditional statement in the @IF formula is A4>20. It returns 1 or 0. When it returns 1, the @IF formula returns .12. When the conditional statement returns 0, the formula returns 0. 1 times .12 is .12. 0 times .12 is 0. This suggests a formula to replace the @IF formula: (A4>20)*.12

Check it out to be sure we're not kidding. Enter the formula *@IF(A4>20,.12,0)* into cell B4. Enter *(A4>20)*.12* into cell B5. At this point, cell A4 is empty and so has the value 0. Both of the new formulas also return 0. Test them by entering *21* into cell A4. Immediately the formulas in cells B4 and B5 return .12—the proper commission percentage. But the formula in cell B5 performed with five fewer characters than the one in cell B4. You have saved RAM by using a Boolean expression in place of an @IF formula.

Learn to Recognize Boolean Opportunities

While the concept of Boolean math is no more difficult to understand than that of @IF formulas, sometimes it is more difficult to recognize opportunities in which to apply these RAM savers. The only way to learn is to practice. Here are a few problems to try. What formulas can you create using Boolean expressions in place of the @IF functions in the following formulas?

```
@IF(A1>=10,A1,0)
@IF(A1>=100,A1+10,A1)
```

For the first formula, try (A1>=10)*A1. For the second formula use (A1>=100)*10+A1.

There isn't always a Boolean substitute for an @IF function, and even when there is, the Boolean expression won't necessarily be shorter than the @IF formula. Also, the meaning of a Boolean statement is rarely as easy to recognize as that of an @IF formula. Experiment on your own to increase your proficiency with these mathematical oddities. And watch out as you continue reading this book. We have sprinkled a few uses of Boolean math throughout the remaining chapters.

Think Conditionally

The few examples in this chapter barely reveal the power of conditional math. The @IF function and the logical operators become the heart of many worksheets that predict trends in business, budgets, payroll, investment, and more. If you can ask a question about your business beginning with "What if?" then you can probably build conditional formulas to help find answers.

While conditional math is powerful for solving business problems that involve numerical calculations, it is even more powerful for work with databases. Several chapters in Section 3 include discussions that relate conditional math to database operations.

To this point, we have used conditional math only with numbers. It is possible to combine these mathematical concepts with strings of alphanumeric characters so that your formulas provide English-language clues as to the conditions in your spreadsheets. The following chapter discusses 1-2-3's ability to manipulate character strings and shows some examples that capitalize on conditional math.

Having completed this chapter you should:

- *Know how to express business problems whose outcomes depend on variables in the worksheet*
- *Understand the concept of Boolean operations*
- *Be able to apply the logical operators*
- *Be able to apply Boolean expressions to reduce the size of your conditional formulas and the RAM requirements of your spreadsheets*

15

Math with Labels

Here's an odd concept: You can do arithmetic with labels. We're not talking about doing algebra where letters represent numbers. We're talking about manipulating labels, or character strings, by combining several into one, extracting pieces from one into another, and substituting pieces of one string for pieces of another. All of these operations fall under the heading of *string manipulation*.

String Arithmetic Is Useful

There are many reasons to do string manipulation in the spreadsheet. Most of them are a bit esoteric. At times, for example, your macros will be most efficient when you use string arithmetic to create the macro commands. A macro that relies on string arithmetic appears in the chapter titled Simulate a Horse Race in the Applications section. You might use string arithmetic to pull information out of a database and format it as mailing labels. We look at databases in Section 3, and we present a macro for printing mailing labels in the Advanced Applications section at the end of the book.

Sometimes it is useful to have formulas that chop the first letters off labels and create abbreviations of people's names. Other times you might create conditional formulas that return numbers under some circumstances and labels under others. You might even create a conditional formula that would return a string to alert you that a value in the spreadsheet had reached

In this chapter you will:

- *Combine strings of alphabetic characters formulaically*
- *Learn about literal strings*
- *Apply string functions: @LEFT, @RIGHT, @MID, @UPPER, @LOWER, @STRING, @VALUE, @LENGTH . . . .*
- *Learn the relationships between numbers and character strings*
- *Explore the process of developing complex formulas*

certain thresholds. All of these calculations are possible with string arithmetic.

Even if you don't anticipate a need to use string calculations in your spreadsheets, this section has a lot to offer. Understanding the relationships between strings and numbers could help you out of a jam when your spreadsheet calculations don't behave as expected. Moreover, the discussions in this section lead you through the development of a complex string formula. You can apply the step-wise procedure when you develop complex formulas of any type.

Concatenation: Label Addition

There is one operator to perform label arithmetic. It is the operator of string addition, which computerists call *concatenation.* The concatenation operator is the ampersand (&). When you want to combine two labels into one—to combine two columns of labels into a single column, for example—use the ampersand. The following simple exercise shows how this works.

Start in a blank worksheet, and enter your first name into cell A1. Enter your last name in cell A2. In cell A4, enter the formula *+A1&A2.* If you were the authors of this book, your worksheet might look like the one shown in Figure 15.1.

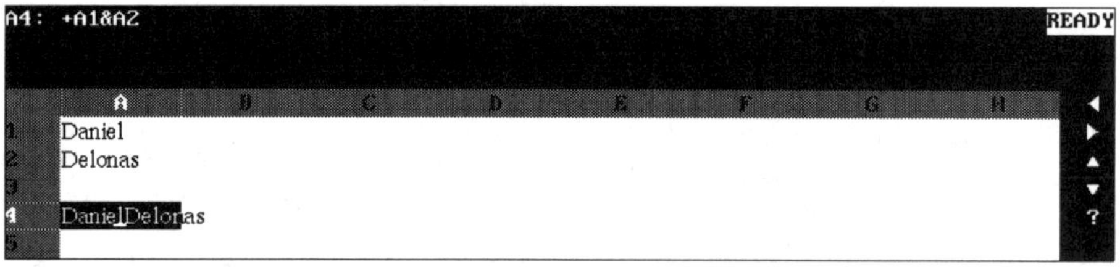

FIGURE 15.1. The formula in cell A4 combines the labels from cells A1 and A2.

In many cases, you will want the concatenated character strings to butt up against each other as they do in this worksheet. In other instances you will want space between the strings to make them more readable. To do this, you must include a *literal string* in your concatenation formula.

A literal string is the label arithmetic equivalent of a number. Think about it this way: in the numeric formula +A1+8+A2, cells A1 and A2 formula act as variables. The number 8 is a constant; it appears literally in the formula. That is the nature of a literal string: it appears literally within a formula.

To put a space between strings, use a string that consists of a single space character. (A space is just as much a character as a letter or a digit.) Any literal string that you include in a formula must be enclosed in quotation marks. The modified formula is +A1&" "&A2. Enter it in place of the formula in cell A4. Be sure to press the Spacebar to create the gap that falls between the quotation marks.

You might use concatenation when you have entered labels of varying lengths and want to pair the labels in preparation for printing. This situation arises often when you are dealing with databases that contain people's names. If one column contains first names and another column contains last names, a simple concatenation formula can combine the names easily.

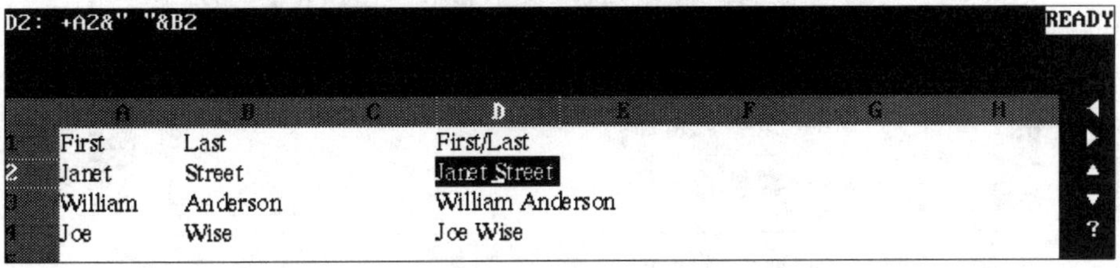

FIGURE 15.2. The concatenation formulas in column D let you combine the names from columns A and B.

Figure 15.2 shows the results of several identical concatenation formulas. The formula in cell D2 is +A2&" "&B2— quite similar to the last formula we looked at. Copied down the column, the formula concatenates each name pair from columns A and B. Cell D1 of the worksheet also contains a concatenation formula, as you can see on the edit line of the control panel. The literal string in D1's formula is "/".

Conditional Math with Strings

If you read the box titled Strings Aren't Numbers, or Are They?, you understand that all strings have the numeric value of zero. This should make it difficult to compare two labels. Is the label in cell A1 identical to the label in cell B1? This type of label comparison might not seem important now, but should you wish to create worksheets that communicate in English with their users or should you write macro applications for others to use, label comparing formulas will be indispensable. Create a simple worksheet to see how they work.

Strings Aren't Numbers, or Are They?

In real life, character strings have no numeric meaning. Theoretically, the expression +8+"word" doesn't make sense. In 1-2-3, however, a character string has the numeric value of 0. This means that you can include in numeric formulas references to cells that contain strings, and those references won't cause problems with your calculations.

This feature is particularly useful when you build @SUM formulas that refer to ranges whose dimensions change from time to time. The following worksheet shows a common scenario:

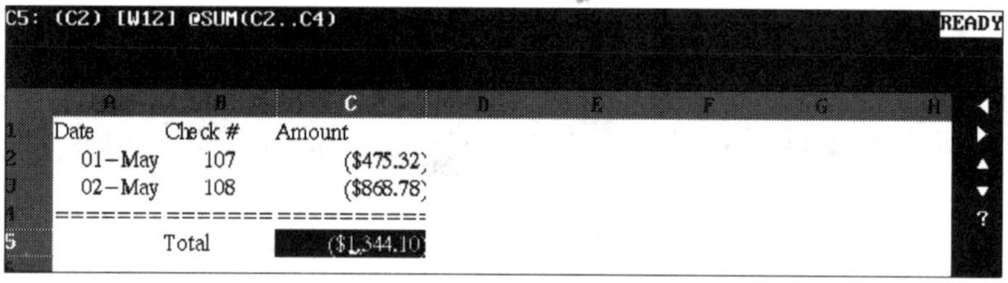

You can use string characters to set up @SUM formulas that will easily accommodate data when you insert rows.

To enter a checking account transaction in this worksheet, you must make way for the new entry. As you can see in the control panel, the summary formula in cell C5 encompasses the range C2..C4. Cell C4 contains a dividing line label, but it does not affect the summation.

Because of the way the formula is designed, you can use either of two techniques to make way for new entries. If there is nothing in your worksheet that will be damaged by inserting a row, place the cell pointer in row 4, select /Worksheet Insert Row, and press Return. If you prefer not to insert an entire row, select /Move, indicate range A4..C5 as the range to move, and indicate cell A5 as the target range. In either case, when you make an entry in the new row 4, it will be reflected in the summation formula.

Start in a blank sheet, and enter the formula *+A1=B1* into cell B3. Because cells A1 and B1 are blank, the formula returns 1, the Boolean value for true. Now enter your first name in cell A1 and your last name in cell B1. Unless your parents had a warped sense of humor, the labels in A1 and B1 don't match. Lo and behold, the Boolean formula in cell B3 returns 0. See Figure 15.3.

If the labels are numerically zero, why doesn't the formula return 1? After all, 0=0. The reason is that when your formulas compare character strings

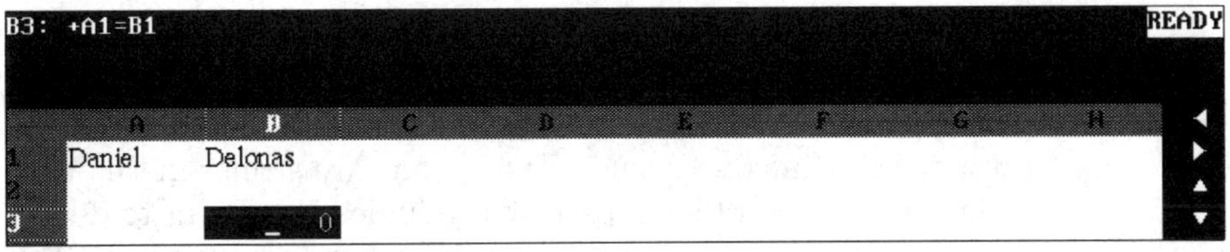

FIGURE 15.3. The string formula in cell B3 proves that you don't have the same first and last name.

with each other, 1-2-3 disregards the numeric component; it compares strings as strings. As strings, the entries in cells A1 and B1 are not the same. Hence the 0 result.

Enter your first name in cell B1 to match the entry in cell A1; the entry in B3 returns 1. Do one more test. Reenter your first name in cell B1, but this time use all capital letters. The comparison formula will probably still return 1. Except under certain circumstances, 1-2-3 is case-insensitive when comparing strings in conditional statements. See the box called How 1-2-3 Compares Strings for more information on case sensitivity.

How 1-2-3 Compares Strings

By default (that is, unless you specify differently), 1-2-3 doesn't recognize a difference between upper- and lowercase letters when comparing strings. An uppercase A is the same as a lowercase a. This behavior is controlled by something called the collating driver.

There are three collating sequences. The default sequence is Numbers First. With this selected, the Data Sort command (explained in the Data Analysis and Statistics section) places numeric entries above alphabetic ones when you use it to alphabetize lists of entries. The Numbers Last option causes numeric entries to come after alphabetic ones when you sort lists. The ASCII option is a bit harder to explain.

Each character that your monitor displays has a numeric ASCII code between 0 and 255. A lowercase a has the code 97, while an uppercase A has ASCII code 65. With the ASCII collating sequence, 1-2-3's Data Sort command alphabetizes entries based on the ASCII code values of the characters in the entries. An ASCII comparison of the strings Name and name reveals that the strings aren't identical. Unless you are creating highly specialized spreadsheet applications, you should stick with the Numbers First or Numbers Last collating driver. Instructions for selecting an alternative collating driver appear in Appendix A.

So, how can a formula tell when two strings are identical? The simplest way is to use the @EXACT function. This function has the syntax, @EXACT(*"string1"*, *"string2"*). It performs a character-by-character comparison of the two strings, considering only the ASCII codes that make up the strings. When the strings match, the function returns 1 for true. When the strings don't match, the @EXACT function returns 0.

You might wonder why anyone would want to compare strings in this way. In truth, you might never need to compare strings unless you want to design spreadsheets with which users interact in words rather than numbers. You are most likely to do this with spreadsheets that are macro-driven, so learning the basic techniques could prove useful down the road. Section 6 at the end of this book contains a few worksheet models that rely on string arithmetic.

Some Practice with String Comparisons

Figure 15.4 shows a simple "English-speaking" model.

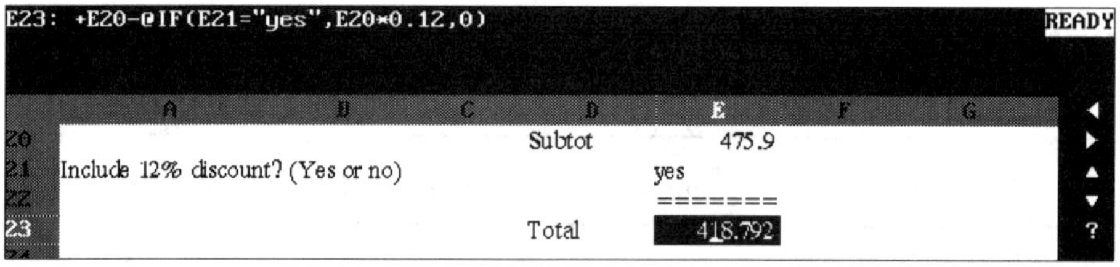

FIGURE 15.4. Build this worksheet to help you learn how string comparisons can be used.

We will use the sheet in Figure 15.4 to explore two important aspects of string arithmetic—what happens when strings sneak into numerical calculations and what happens when numbers sneak into string calculations. Build the model now if you want to follow along; it simulates a worksheet used in a retail store to record customer purchases. The checkout clerk enters *yes* or *no* in the sheet depending on whether a customer presents a special discount coupon.

First, erase the sheet you have been using. To do that, select Worksheet Erase Yes (and probably Yes a second time since there is no reason to have saved what you have been doing). Enter the labels shown in cells D20, A21, and D23. We have padded some entries with leading spaces to make them align flush right. Enter \= in cell E22 to create the dividing line, and then enter the following formula into cell E23:

```
+E20–@IF(E21=“yes”,E20*0.12,0)
```

Enter *475.9* into cell E20 and *yes* into cell E21. Your spreadsheet should match ours.

The formula in cell E23 calculates the charge for items sold in the store. As a result of a promotional mailing, many customers have the 12% discount coupons. A salesperson enters the prices of purchased items in rows 1 through 18 of column E. In reality a formula in cell E20 sums the entries. We have simulated the data entry part by substituting a value as the subtotal in E20.

The final total formula in cell E23 contains a conditional statement that reads @IF(E21="yes",E20*0.12,0). The meaning is, "if the entry in cell E21 is yes, return the product of cell E20 times .12. Otherwise return 0."

Whatever the result of the conditional statement, the formula subtracts it from the value in cell E20. So, if cell E21 contains yes, the formula subtracts 12 percent from the purchase subtotal. If cell E21 contains no (or some other non-yes entry), the formula subtracts 0 from the purchase subtotal.

An @Function Solves a Problem: @S

So far, you know that labels have the numeric value of 0. You have also seen that when 1-2-3 compares two strings, it ignores the numeric values of the strings and focuses on the characters in the strings instead. What happens when 1-2-3 compares strings with numbers? Understanding this can affect the way you write string formulas and plan your spreadsheet models.

You can see how 1-2-3 mixes strings with numbers very quickly by changing the entry in cell E21 of your model. Replace whatever label is in that cell with the number 8. The summation formula returns 475.9; it doesn't calculate the 12% discount.

For the most part, if any element of a formula is numeric, 1-2-3 performs arithmetic operations as if all the elements of the formula are numeric. Consequently, the comparison E21=yes translates to E21=0 when cell E21 contains a number; the literal string yes assumes the value 0; any string would assume the 0 value. Eight doesn't equal 0, so the formula doesn't calculate the discount. So far, this isn't a problem. But what do you think will happen if cell E21 is left blank or contains a zero?

Enter 0 into E21 to confirm your suspicion. The summation formula in cell E23 includes the 12% discount. The formula's true condition is, E21=yes, yet E21=0 is also true. In other words, if a conditional formula compares a string with a number and the number is zero, 1-2-3 doesn't distinguish between the zero value and the string.

The zero value of strings can really mess up a worksheet. What is the point of writing a conditional statement if it confuses labels with values and returns incorrect calculations? Don't worry, you can work around the problem by employing the @S function.

The @S function has the syntax @S(*range*) where *range* is any cell or range in the spreadsheet. If you use a multi-cell reference as *range*, the function considers only the top-left corner cell of the range. It seems silly, but that's the way the function works. If *range* contains a label or a formula with a string result, the @S function returns the string. If *range* contains a number or a numeric calculation, @S returns a null string. See the box titled Strings That Aren't: The Null String, for an explanation.

Strings That Aren't: The Null String

One of the hardest string arithmetic concepts to grasp is that of a null string. A null string is a character string that has no characters. The literal representation of a null string is a pair of quotation marks with nothing between them (""). See the main text for an explanation of literal strings.

To enter a null string in the worksheet, type a label prefix character (', ", or ^), and press Return. The label prefix appears adjacent to the current cell indicator in the control panel, but nothing appears in the spreadsheet as revealed in cell A1 below:

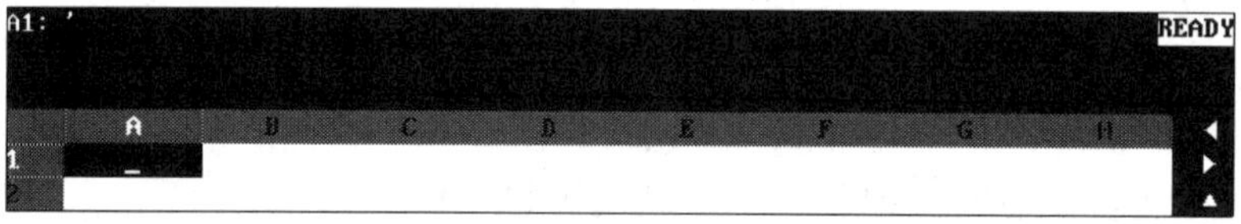

A label prefix by itself acts as a null string.

A null string may not contain characters, but 1-2-3 treats it like any other string. It is particularly useful in conditional statements when you wish to display a certain label or value under some circumstances, and a blank cell under other circumstances. For example, the expression @IF(A1>90,A1,"") entered in cell A3 of a worksheet returns the value from cell A1 if that value is greater than 90. Otherwise it returns a null string so that cell A3 appears to be blank.

Modify the formula in cell E23 to read as follows:

+E20–@IF(@S(E21)="yes",E20*0.12,0)

By incorporating the @S function in the conditional statement, the modified formula never compares the string yes with a numeric entry. The final total formula calculates the 12% discount only if cell E21 contains the string yes and not if it contains the value 0 or is blank. That's what it seemed the original @IF formula was supposed to calculate.

String Operations with Numbers Involved

If it seems difficult already to keep track of what happens when your formulas try to intermix strings with numbers, hold onto your hat. As you have seen, 1-2-3 is forgiving when strings sneak into numeric mathematical operations. It isn't so accommodating when numbers sneak into string operations.

Still, you can imagine instances in which it would be nice to incorporate numbers within strings. It's easy enough to look at the bottom line of your spreadsheet's calculations and include the numbers there in labels that you type. If the bottom line is $12,000, you might enter a label that reads *The crew generated $12,000 in revenue on Thursday.* It is quite another task to write a formula that returns this string.

The problem in question sounds quite simple: write a string formula that combines strings and numbers to produce a simple sentence. Solving this problem is very involved. On the other hand, working it through is a good exercise with which to introduce several string-handling @functions. Also, coming up with a solution will help to develop an understanding of how to approach problem-solving with spreadsheet formulas.

Concatenation is one operation in which strings and numbers commonly clash. Enter a simple formula to see how. Blank the worksheet, and enter the formula *+A1&A2* into cell A4. 1-2-3 coughs up an ERR. You tried this same formula a few minutes ago and it didn't return ERR, so what's the problem?

The problem is rooted in the observation made at the beginning of the chapter: numbers are fundamentally different from strings. While 1-2-3 can overlook the difference in doing numerical arithmetic and pretend that strings equal 0, it can't overlook the difference while doing string arithmetic. How do you concatenate (which means, "link or chain together") numbers?

Cells A1 and A2 are blank, so the formula in cell A4 is trying to concatenate two zero values. Enter your first name into cell A1, and the ERR remains in A4. You simply can't concatenate a numeric value and a string.

Conversely, @VALUE

It would be unfair to give the @STRING function so much coverage without at least mentioning @VALUE. The @VALUE function returns a number based on the appearance of a character string. Its syntax is @VALUE(string). String can be any character string that looks like a number, or a reference to a cell that holds such a string. In addition, the @VALUE function can refer to any numeric entry or formula.

The expression @VALUE("88") returns the value 88. @VALUE(A1) returns the value 9 when cell A1 contains the characters '9. Conveniently, the @VALUE function ignores leading and trailing space characters when it evaluates a numeric string. Consequently, the expression @VALUE("   88   ") also returns the value 88.

Using @S functions in your formula will eliminate the ERR by automatically converting any numeric entries in the referenced cells into null strings. Go ahead and change it to read @S(A1)&@S(A2). With a label in cell A1 and A2 blank, the formula returns the label from cell A1 concatenated to a null string; the result of the formula equals the label in A1.

Practice Combining Text and Numbers

The first @function you will need to combine numbers into strings is the @STRING function. The @STRING function converts a value into a string whose characters match those of the original value. The function has the syntax @STRING(*value,places*) where *value* is any number, a formula, or a reference to a cell and *places* is the number of decimal places you want to include in the function's result. @STRING(8,0) returns the literal string 8 and @STRING(777,2) returns the string "777.00".

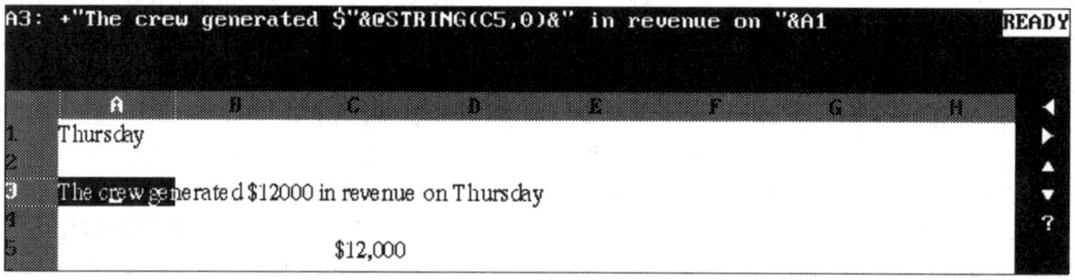

FIGURE 15.5. Build this worksheet for practice concatenating text with numbers.

Figure 15.5 simulates the problem in question. It contains a string formula that combines a number from a spreadsheet's bottom line into a sentence that explains what the spreadsheet calculates. Create the worksheet to see how the @STRING function lets you concatenate numbers with strings.

To simplify the discussion, we have omitted calculations that contribute to the spreadsheet's bottom line, and we have entered the bottom line in cell C5. That cell has a currency with no decimal places numeric display format.

Cell A1 contains the label *Thursday*. It identifies the weekday on which this spreadsheet was created. At the end of the day shift, a manager retrieves this sheet, enters the day in cell A1, and enters the day's business transactions elsewhere in the sheet. The formula in cell A3 draws from the bottom line in C5 and from the header in A1 to report the revenue generated and the current weekday. That formula reads:

```
+"The crew generated $"&@STRING(C5,0)&" in revenue on "&A1
```

You can see that the formula contains two literal strings. The first is "The crew generated $", and the second is " in revenue on ". Note the leading and trailing spaces in the second literal string. They ensure proper spacing in the string result of the formula.

Concatenated between the two literal strings is the expression @STRING(C5,0). Also concatenated, at the end of the formula, is the string in cell A1.

So, you might ask, where's the comma in $12000? It's there in cell C5, but not in the string formula. The @STRING function returns a string representation of a value only. The dollar sign and comma that appear in cell C5 are superimposed on the value by the numeric display format to make the value look like a dollar amount.

The formula you entered in cell A3 includes a dollar sign in the first literal string. You need to get pretty fancy to include the comma as well. Other @functions can help with the problem, but it's not going to be easy.

Hard Core String Manipulation: @RIGHT and @LEFT

To simplify the discussion of how to rewrite our formula so that it places a comma in the number 12000, we will focus only on the 12000. Remember, by the time it appears on the display as a result of the formula's calculations, the 12000 is a character string, not a number.

As a character string, "12000" is subject to manipulation by any number of string functions. One of the available functions, @LEFT, can return a string that consists of characters removed from the left end of another string. Another function, @RIGHT, returns a string taken from the right end of a target string.

The @LEFT and @RIGHT functions are quite similar. Their syntaxes are @LEFT(*string,n*), and @RIGHT(*string,n*). In each case, *string* is a literal string, a string formula, or a reference to a cell that contains a string, and *n* is the number of characters to return. If either of these functions refers to a numeric entry, it will return ERR.

The expression @LEFT("Spooner",5) returns Spoon—the five left-most characters of Spooner. @RIGHT("Killjoy",3) returns joy—the three right-most characters of Killjoy. Enter these functions in cells A7 and A8 of your worksheet to be sure that you understand how they work.

Using the @LEFT and @RIGHT functions, you can extract pieces from the string "12000" and concatenate those pieces with a comma. The formula might look like this:

@LEFT("12000",2)&","&@RIGHT("12000",3)

Again, enter it in the worksheet, in cell A9, so you can see it in action.

Remember that the formula we are trying to create must return a string based on a value in cell C5. To achieve this, you must substitute the @STRING function in place of the literal strings in this new formula. The resulting formula is:

@LEFT(@STRING(C5,0),2)&","&@RIGHT(@STRING(C5,0),3)

Go ahead and enter this in cell A10. When you are done, your worksheet should match the one in Figure 15.6.

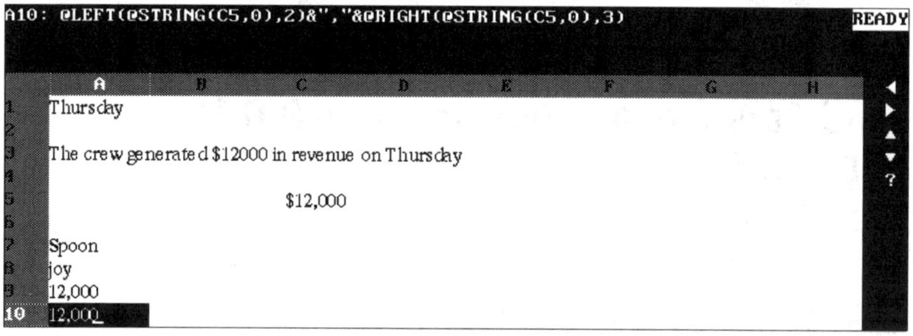

FIGURE 15.6. Your worksheet should look like this after you apply all the string formulas we have discussed so far.

It's getting pretty complex. If the formula in cell A10 solves the original problem—inserting a comma in a string in just the right place—then we have solved the problem. We need only replace the @STRING expression in cell A3 with the expression from cell A10.

Not so fast. How careful was our work with that formula? It handles the value 12000, but what if the work crew only generates $9,000 in revenue? Or better, what if they generate $109,000 in a day? Will the expression in cell A10 put the comma in the right place?

First make a prediction, and then fiddle a little to find out if you are correct. What will appear in cell A10 when you enter 9000 into cell C5? Make the entry. Were you right? Did you think that the formula in A10 would return "90,000"? Well, something is obviously wrong with the formula. Predict what happens if the day's revenue is $109,000 then change the entry in cell C5. If you predicted that the formula in A10 would return "10,000", you can start shopping for a cap and gown.

It is clear that the formula isn't entirely reliable; its reliability depends on your situation. Is it reasonable to expect that a day's revenue will ever exceed $99,999 or drop below $10,000? If not, don't make a formula better than it needs to be—that's a waste of time.

The expression you have created in cell A10 places a comma correctly for any value between $10,000 and $99,000. But what if you need a formula that works for values ranging from $1,000 to $999,999?

Introducing @LENGTH

The problem is that the numeric string with which you are dealing changes in length as it changes in value. When the value in cell C5 is less than 10,000, @STRING(C5,0) returns a string of four or fewer characters. When the value in C5 is greater than 99,999, @STRING(C5,0) returns a string of at least six characters.

The function @RIGHT(C5,3) will always return the last three characters that constitute the numeric string. It's the @LEFT function that's causing trouble. Somehow our formula must tell the @LEFT function how many characters are left after the last three are removed. For this we employ the @LENGTH function.

The @LENGTH function returns a number that represents the number of characters in a string. The expression @LENGTH("elephant") returns 8, and @LENGTH(A1) returns 6 when cell A1 contains the label *quotas*. If @LENGTH refers to a numeric entry, the function returns ERR. To help solve our larger formula problem, we will use the expression

@LENGTH(@STRING(C5,0)). It returns the length of the numeric string no matter what its underlying value.

By subtracting 3 from the total length of @STRING(C5,0), our formula can determine how many characters stand to the left of the comma that it inserts. With that information, we can get the desired results from the @LEFT function:

```
@LEFT(@STRINGS(C5,0),@LENGTH(@STRING(C5,0))–3)
```

Enter this into cell A11. With the value 109,000 in cell C5, the formula returns the literal string "109". Change the value in C5 to 9,000, and the new formula returns "9". Change the entry in C5 to its original value of 12,000, and the formula in cell A11 returns the string "12". You are almost home.

Use the concatenation operator to combine this expression with the literal string ",", and the @RIGHT expression. That formula becomes:

```
@LEFT(@STRING(C5,0),@LENGTH(@STRING(C5,0))–3)&","&
  @RIGHT(@STRING(C5,0),3)
```

Enter it into cell A12. Test the expression by varying the value in cell C5. That value is currently 12000. Change it to 9000, and your latest string formula returns the character string "9,000". Enter 109000 into cell C5. You have it!

What a chore. But the work is not finished. You still need to insert the entire expression between the ampersands in that original string formula:

```
+"The crew generated $"&@LEFT(@STRING(C5,0),
  @LENGTH(@STRING(C5,0))–3)&","&@RIGHT(@STRING(C5,0),3)&
  " in revenue on "&A1
```

Don't worry, not all formula development is this involved, though some is much worse. With a little practice you will be able to work out just about any calculation. But remember this exercise when you're feeling stumped. A complex problem becomes quite easy to solve when you break it down into small steps.

Cosmetic String Manipulation: @LOWER, @UPPER, and @PROPER

Enough of this grueling string manipulation. Several other string @functions can help with the type of formulaic surgery you have just performed. Check out your spreadsheet's documentation for information on the @MID, @FIND, and @REPLACE functions. In the meantime, let's look at a few simple string functions that can help you clean up messy label entries.

Often as you work in the spreadsheet you find entries whose appearances aren't entirely pleasing. Perhaps you once entered a column of people's names in uppercase, or someone handed you a spreadsheet file that interspersed company names in uppercase with initial-capped entries. You might prefer all the entries to appear in uppercase or in lowercase. Or perhaps, as you might with a list of people's names, you prefer that only the first character of each word in a label be capitalized.

Several @functions let you alter the appearance of a string. The @LOWER function returns a string whose characters are all lowercase. Its syntax is simply @LOWER(*string*) where *string* is a literal string, a string formula, or a reference to a cell that contains a string. As with most other string functions, when the @LOWER function refers to a numeric value, the function returns ERR.

The @UPPER function has the opposite effect. It returns a string whose characters are all uppercase. Related to the @LOWER and @UPPER functions is @PROPER. It uppercases every letter in a string that follows a space character and lowercases all the other characters. For example, the expression @PROPER("this is a test") returns the string "This Is A Test".

All of these functions seem rather impotent; by the time you enter the function, you might as well retype the label on which the function acts. You might as well retype the label, that is, if you are dealing with only one. But recall that the original concept was to convert columns of labels. How would you handle that?

Figure 15.7 shows the first six entries in a column of names that someone has entered entirely in uppercase.

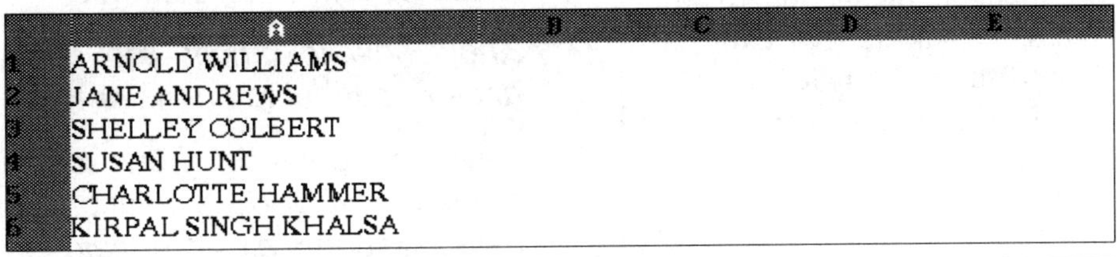

	A	B	C	D	E
1	ARNOLD WILLIAMS				
2	JANE ANDREWS				
3	SHELLEY COLBERT				
4	SUSAN HUNT				
5	CHARLOTTE HAMMER				
6	KIRPAL SINGH KHALSA				

FIGURE 15.7. You can convert all these uppercase labels to lowercase or mixed case with simple string functions.

Using the @PROPER function together with the Copy, Range Value, and Range Erase commands, you can convert these entries—even several hundred such entries—in a few moments. Here's how to proceed:

Enter the formula *@PROPER(A1)* into cell C1. With the cell pointer still in C1, select /Copy, and press LeftArrow twice, End, DownArrow, RightArrow twice, and Return. This copies the formula down column C as far as there are names in column A. Now select /Range Value, and press End DownArrow, Return, LeftArrow twice, and Return. Finally, select /Range Erase, and press End DownArrow, and Return.

These instructions may be familiar. They are a variation of a technique presented in Chapter 2. While the technique requires a great many keystrokes, with a little practice you will be able to rattle them off in seconds.

More String Functions

Don't let the subhead fool you, we are no longer discussing string arithmetic. We are pointing out that more string functions exist and that you should look into them. You may never need these functions beyond our little exercise. But, if you understand how to use string functions and know what they offer, you might unexpectedly discover the perfect uses for them.

Understanding strings and string arithmetic prepares you to work with databases. You can use string formulas to help locate specific information stored in a database. You can also use string formulas, as we have done in this section, to design spreadsheets that express their results in English rather than just numbers.

Having completed this chapter you should:

- *Be able to create spreadsheets that interact with users in English*
- *Understand how to trouble-shoot formulas that involve strings*
- *Know how to modify the appearance of a label to suit your taste*
- *Have a sense of how to think through involved calculations and develop complex formulaic solutions by breaking problems down into small pieces*
- *Be ready to tackle the concepts presented in the upcoming Section 3*

16

Dates in a Spreadsheet

Much of the work you do in a spreadsheet involves time. You deal with fiscal years, quarters, and months. You record the dates of bank transactions, the start dates and termination dates of employees, and the purchase dates of capital equipment. You need a way to keep track of time in the worksheet.

Many users think they have this date stuff licked, but many of them are fooling themselves. They might, for example, enter the date July 4, 1991 as a label by typing an apostrophe followed by the characters 7/4/91. The entry looks convincingly like a date, but looks are deceiving. An important step in developing your spreadsheet expertise is to learn how 1-2-3 really handles dates.

If a date is a label, how do you calculate the number of days that fall between two calendar dates? How can your formulas determine the number of working days required to complete a project? In short, if dates in the spreadsheet aren't numeric, you can't easily use them in time-related calculations.

> *In this chapter you will:*
>
> - *Learn how 1-2-3 handles dates*
> - *Explore the date-related @functions: @DATE, @NOW, @DAY, @MONTH, @YEAR*
> - *Apply date-related numeric display formats*
> - *Perform arithmetic calculations with dates*
> - *Convert labels that look like dates into date serial numbers*
> - *Use the @CHOOSE function to determine the weekday of a given date*
> - *Get an overview of the time-related functions*

How Does 1-2-3 Handle Dates?

To 1-2-3, time began on January 1, 1900. That was day 1. The spreadsheet software itself didn't exist before the 1980s, but the designers of 1-2-3 built it to consider January 1, 1900 as day 1.

Lotus 1-2-3 assigns each day a serial number that represents the number of days that have passed since the turn of the century. Therefore, January 1, 1900 is day 1, January 2, 1900 is day 2, and so on. More than 33,000 days have passed since 1899, so dates in our time have fairly large serial numbers. 1-2-3 can handle 200 years' worth of serial numbers—through December 31, 2099.

By using this date serial number scheme, 1-2-3 can calculate the number of days between two dates. In fact, 1-2-3 lets you perform many calculations that involve dates. Your spreadsheets can help you to keep track of accounts receivable and automatically watch for overdue payments. They can help with project scheduling, schedule the payments of loans, and even track time-related production and research data.

Fortunately, 1-2-3's designers don't expect us to keep track of date serial numbers. They have equipped 1-2-3 with tools that translate serial numbers into recognizable dates and convert dates from a format we recognize into the serial numbers that 1-2-3 can manipulate.

Some of the tools you use to work with dates are @functions; others are numeric display formats. Most important to 1-2-3 are the @functions, and the @function with which you should be most familiar is @DATE.

Enter Dates Rather Than Labels

The @DATE function creates date serial numbers. Its syntax is @DATE(*yy,mm,dd*) where *yy* represents a year, *mm* represents a month, and *dd* represents a day. The expression @DATE(91,7,4) returns 33423—the serial number of July 4, 1991. Try entering it into cell A1 of an otherwise blank worksheet.

While 1-2-3 knows that the number in cell A1 is a date, there is little about it that would convince a casual observer. Assigning an appropriate numeric display format will clarify things. With the cell pointer still in cell A1, select Range Format Date. There are quite a few date formats available. For now, select the first format, 1, and then press Return to format the current cell. Oops! The cell fills with asterisks.

Don't worry, you already know what causes the asterisks—entering a formatted entry that is too wide to fit in a cell. So, select Worksheet Global Column Set-width, and expand the column width to 10. The date finally appears.

@DATE Is a PAIN. Why Bother?

The @DATE function certainly doesn't improve your ability to enter dates in the sheet. Not only do you have to enter the year, the month, and the day in a mixed-up order (compared to the standard MM/DD/YY), you have to assign a numeric display format before the resulting serial numbers appear as dates. Why go to all the trouble when *'7/4/91* is a perfectly recognizable date entry? Actually, there are quite a few reasons.

As stated earlier, 1-2-3 can perform calculations with date serial numbers. The formula @DATE(91,7,4)+7 returns a serial number for the date that

A Macro Eases Date Entries

It's a pain to have to type @DATE(91,7,7) to enter the date 7/7/91 into the worksheet. Because the function requires the year number before the month number, it is easy to complete the entry incorrectly and then have to edit it. The macro in the following worksheet lets you enter dates in the more familiar MM/DD/YY format:

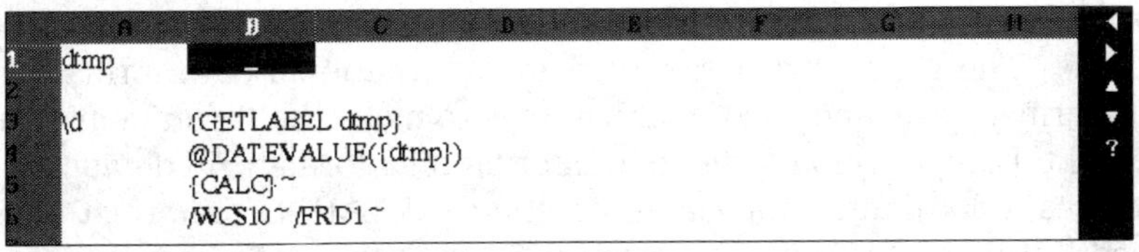

Copy these entries to create a simple date entry macro.

Create the macro by entering labels as they appear in the illustration. Start each of the labels in cells A3, B4, and B6 by typing an apostrophe label prefix character. Note that while the entry in cell B4 looks like a formula, it is a label—the cell entry must begin with an apostrophe. Use the Range Name Labels Right command to assign the labels in column A as names for the adjacent cells of column B. Cell B1 should be named *dtmp*, and cell B3 should be named *\d*.

Use the macro by positioning the cell pointer in the cell that will receive the date you plan to enter. Hold down the MACRO key (Alt), and press D. Now type a date in the MM/DD/YY format, and press Return. The macro enters a serial number for the date you typed, sets the column to a width of 10 characters, and assigns the cell a Date 1 format.

Find more about macros in Section 5 of this book. We talk a bit about the @DATEVALUE function at the end of this chapter.

comes seven days after the fourth of July. The entry *'7/4/91* is a label. Its numeric value is 0, so 1-2-3 can't use it to perform date-related calculations.

Perhaps more important, using the @DATE function makes your entries more useful to 1-2-3's database facility. The database query commands and database @functions can easily find information based on the dates associated with that information as long as you have recorded the dates as serial numbers. When you record dates in a database as labels, tracking down specific information can become a complex problem. This will make much more sense after you have worked through Section 3 of this book.

Practice with Dates and Formats

For practice, use the @DATE function to enter dates into cells A2 and A3. Enter @DATE(91,8,8) into cell A2 and @DATE(91,12,1) into cell A3. Assign the Date 2 format to cell A2 and the Date 3 format to cell A3. Cell A2 shows just a day and a month—August 8. Cell A3 shows a month and year—December, '91. While all three cells contain full date serial numbers, the selected display formats determine what information about the recorded dates 1-2-3 will reveal.

So far, you have used three of the five date formatting options in your worksheet. The remaining options are for international date formats. Select Range Format Date, and use the arrow keys to move the menu pointer until it falls on the Date 4 option—the long international format. By default, this option makes a date entry appear in the standard MM/DD/YY format (don't be alarmed if it doesn't). Move the menu pointer to the Date 5 option. This, the short international format, makes a date entry appear as MM/DD.

These last two date format options are modifiable, so they may not offer the display formats we have cited. Check out Chapter 4 for information on how to alter the international Date 4 and Date 5 options. In the meantime, press Escape several times and return the spreadsheet to Ready mode.

To generate serial numbers for dates in the 1900s, use year values from 0 to 99. For dates in the 2000s, use year values from 100 to 199. For example, @DATE(101,1,1) returns the serial number for January 1, 2001.

Practice: How Many Days Between Dates?

It might not be clear at first why you would want to do arithmetic with dates. Perhaps you will never have the need. On the other hand, once you are familiar with the tools that can help with date arithmetic, you may find many ways to use them.

We have already suggested one of the simplest calculations that you might perform: determining the number of days between two dates. Subtract the earlier date from the later, and 1-2-3 provides an answer. See Figure 16.1.

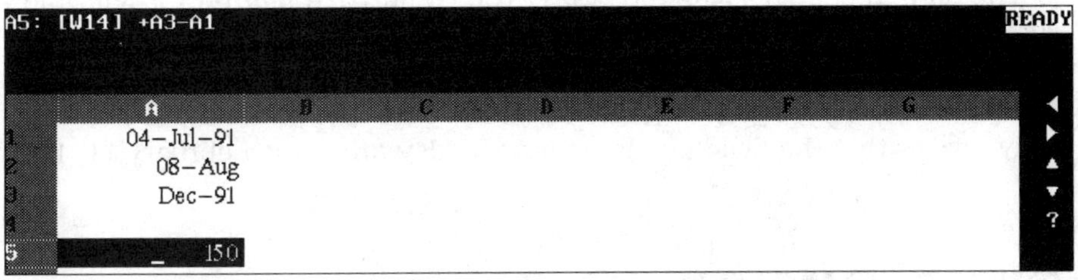

FIGURE 16.1. Because you used the @DATE function to enter your dates, you can easily calculate the number of days between them. The highlighted formula calculates that there are 150 days between July 1 and December 1, 1991.

To see 1-2-3 perform this calculation, enter the formula *+A3–A1* into cell A5 of your practice worksheet. 1-2-3 reveals that 150 days fall between July 4 and December 1. This is a convenient calculation for people facing deadlines. They can quickly determine how many days are available in which to complete a project.

Suppose that you need to establish a deadline based on your estimate of how long it will take to complete a project? Then you need to know what the date will be some number of days in the future. In other words, what will the date be 7, 20, or 50 days from now?

To have 1-2-3 figure it out, enter the formula *@DATE(91,6,6)* into cell B1, assign it a Date 1 format, and increase the width of column B to 10 characters. Enter *7* into cell B2, and enter the formula *+B1+B2* into cell B3. Assign the Date 1 format to cell B3. Your worksheet should look like the one in Figure 16.2.

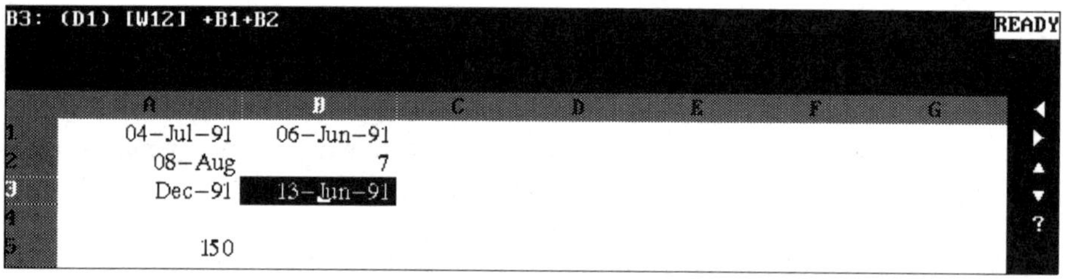

FIGURE 16.2. You can use date mathematics to simplify project scheduling.

The date in cell B1 is June 6, 1991. You could have figured that out more quickly on your fingers, but what date will it be 20 days after the 6th of June? Enter 20 into cell B2 to find out. What day is 250 days from June 6th? Now the questions are getting tougher. Enter 250 into cell B2, and 1-2-3 immediately reveals that the deadline date for a 250-day project is February 11, 1992.

@YEAR, @MONTH, @DAY

Some of your calculations could require knowledge of the year, the month, or even the day of a particular date. Does the date fall in '91 or 92? Is it in June or July? Is it before the 15th of a month or after the 15th? Many of your financial transactions depend on this type of information. For example, it is usually best to close on the purchase of a house near the end of a month. And knowing what month, quarter, or year a loan is due can affect your investment plans for that period.

You can tell at a glance when a particular date falls within your fiscal calendar, but your formulas need a little help to deduce the information. Three @functions provide that help.

The @YEAR function returns a number that represents the year of a specified date. The @MONTH function returns the number of a date's month, and the @DAY function returns a date's day number within the month. Take these functions for a spin.

Enter the formula *@YEAR(B3)* into cell C1 of your practice worksheet. Enter *@MONTH(B3)* into cell C2 and *@DAY(B3)* into cell C3. Assuming you have left the value 250 in cell B2, these three formulas return 92, 2, and 11, respectively. Let's look at some circumstances in which you might apply these functions.

Many business transactions require activity on a yearly basis. If you make a loan on June 8, 1991, you might need to report on the status of that loan on June 8, 1992. In fact, you might want to generate a list of dates on which to

What About Leap Years?

The 1-2-3 date features are aware of leap years. The expression @DATE(91,2,29) isn't valid (it returns ERR), because there is no February 29th in 1991. The formula @DATE(92,2,29) is valid; there is a leap day in 1992.

Unfortunately, 1-2-3's designers built an extra leap day into the spreadsheet's 200 year calendar. The extra day is February 29, 1900. Many users over the years have pointed out that the first year of a century is a leap year only when it is evenly divisible by 400; 1900 was not a leap year. The error shouldn't affect your calculations unless some of your business transactions span the first year of this century.

prepare annual reports. The problem is more difficult than it sounds. Clear the worksheet you have been using (select Worksheet Erase Yes Yes), and we'll build a formula that calculates the serial number for "same day next year."

Because of leap years, it is not enough to add 365 days to the current date and expect to end up with the same month and day in the next calendar year. Instead, use the @YEAR, @MONTH, and @DAY functions to extract the year, month, and day numbers from this year's day. Build the results of these functions into an @DATE formula that calculates next year's date.

Practice: Same Day Next Year

Enter the formula *@DATE(91,6,8)* into cell A1, and assign the Date 1 format to cells A1 and A2. Widen the column to 12 characters to reveal the date (10 will do until the end of the century, but dates in the next century will require a column width of 12), and then see if you can create a formula in cell A2 that calculates the date a year later. Devise the formula so that when you copy it down column A it will calculate the date for each successive year. Don't read ahead if you don't want to know the answer yet.

Any luck? If you have written a formula to do the job, use the Copy command to copy it from cell A2 to range A3..A10. Do the copies return June 8 for each year following 1991? Here is the formula we would use in cell A2:

```
@DATE(@YEAR(A1)+1,@MONTH(A1),@DAY(A1))
```

Our formula is a simple @DATE function. Its first argument is *@YEAR(A1)+1*. The @YEAR function returns the year number of the previous year, and adding 1 returns the next year number. The @DATE function's second argument is *@MONTH(A1)*. It returns the month number from the previous year—which will be the same month number in each successive year. The @DATE function's third argument is *@DAY(A1),* and it returns the same day number each year.

Did we cheat with our formula? Yes. Copied down column A, each copy returns the same day next year, unless the original date in cell A1 is a leap day. What can you do about it? How about, never do business on a leap day? That's probably the easiest answer. After all, there is no same date next year on a leap day. You will have to decide as you work more with date arithmetic how important leap days are in your own calculations. You might simply ignore them if you find they complicate matters too much. In this case, if you pretend that February 28 is the same day next year when the first day is a leap day, you can create a formula that always calculates the same day next year. Here is one such formula:

```
@DATE(@YEAR(A1)=1,@MONTH(A1),@CHOOSE(@DAY($A$1)=29#AND#
  @MONTH($A$1)=2,@DAY(A1),@IF(@MOD(@COUNT($A$1..A1),4)
  =0,29,28),@DAY(A1)))
```

To see the formula in action, enter it into cell A2 in place of whatever you have entered there. We have shown the formula on several lines so that it fits across the page. You should enter all of it into cell A2. Don't include spaces or any other extra characters where the lines break in the book.

Copy the completed formula down the column. You see that it does return the same day in each successive year. Now change the entry in cell A1 to @DATE(92,2,29)—that's the upcoming leap day. The formulas return the date of February 28 in non-leap years, and February 29 in leap years. We will leave it to you to puzzle out how the formula works and to come up with shorter solutions, if you desire them. In the meantime, if you think you will use this formula, save the worksheet in which you created it. You will be able to combine the formula into other worksheets as needed.

Know the Day of the Week

You will notice, if you peruse a listing of date-related @functions, that none of them have anything to do with weekdays. Knowing a date is nice, but knowing the day of the week on which a date falls is even nicer. It wouldn't do to schedule an important project to end on a Friday when everyone will want to get out of the office as early as possible—or worse, to accidentally schedule a business meeting for a weekend.

What Are Those Functions: @CHOOSE, @MOD, and @COUNT?

The "same day next year" formula that we have presented to handle leap days is rather complex. It uses three @functions that might be new to you: @CHOOSE, @MOD, and @COUNT.

The syntax of the @MOD function is @MOD(*value1,value2*). The function determines how many times *value2* can be divided into *value1* without resorting to fractions, and it returns the remainder. If *value1* is evenly divisible by *value2*, the remainder is 0.

The @CHOOSE function is a kind of extended @IF function. Its syntax is @CHOOSE(*value,result0,result1,result2...*). The function returns a result selected by *value*. If *value* is 0, the function returns *result0*. If *value* is 1, the function returns *result1*, and so on. The *value* argument can be a number, a cell reference, or a formula that results in a value. The *result* arguments can be numbers, literal strings, cell references, or formulas.

The @COUNT function simply counts the number of items in a list. The function's syntax is @COUNT(*list*), and *list* can include numbers, literal strings, range references, and single cell references separated by commas. Each number, literal string, or single cell reference in *list* counts as one item. A reference to a single cell counts as one even when the cell is blank. Within referenced multi-cell ranges, only cells that contain entries are counted. The formula @COUNT(A1..B2,C1) would return 4 in the worksheet shown below. There are three entries in the range A1..B2, and the reference to cell C1 counts as 1, even though cell C1 is blank:

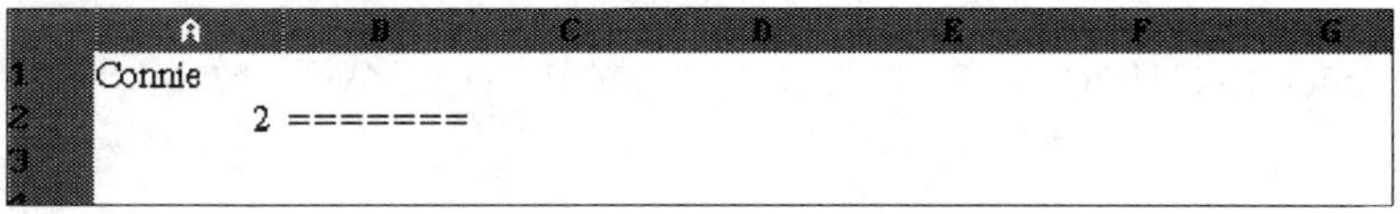

Try out the @COUNT function on this worksheet.

If you want to know the weekdays of 1-2-3's date calculations, don't turn to your desk calendar. Instead, use a handy formula that relies on the @MOD and the @CHOOSE functions (the box titled What Are Those @Functions...? explains how these functions work).

There are seven weekdays. If you divide all positive integers by 7, there are exactly 7 possible remainders—0, 1, 2, 3, 4, 5, and 6. Date serial numbers are positive integers, so dividing any one of them by 7 will leave at least one of these remainders. Figure 16.3 illustrates how this works.

	A	B	C	D	E	F	G
1	07–Jul–91	1 Sun					
2	08–Jul–91	2 Mon					
3	09–Jul–91	3 Tue					
4	10–Jul–91	4 Wed					
5	11–Jul–91	5 Thu					
6	12–Jul–91	6 Fri					
7	13–Jul–91	0 Sat					
8	14–Jul–91	1 Sun					

FIGURE 16.3. Build this worksheet to see how 1-2-3 can figure out what day of the week any date is or was.

Cell A1 contains the formula @DATE(91,7,7). July 7, 1991 is a Sunday. Cell B1 contains the formula @MOD(A1,7). Dividing the serial number for July 7, 1991 by 7 leaves a remainder of 1.

The formula in cell A2 is +A1+1, and as you can see, it returns the serial number for July 7, 1991—Monday. The corresponding @MOD formula in cell B2, @MOD(A2,7) returns 2. With each successive date, the @MOD function returns a remainder that is greater by 1 than that of the previous date. Of course, when you get through a week, the sequence repeats itself. All that remains to be established is which of the remainders calculated by the @MOD functions represents each weekday.

We have done that work for you. As a result of the extra leap day in February 1900 (see the box titled What About Leap Years? earlier in this chapter), the first day of the week, Sunday, is identified by the remainder 1. Monday is 2, Tuesday is 3, and so on. Saturday, unfortunately, is 0.

Understanding all this, you might create the following formula to return the weekday of a date stored in cell A1:

```
@CHOOSE(@MOD(A1,7),"Sat","Sun","Mon","Tue","Wed","Thu","Fri")
```

Live for the Moment: @TODAY and @NOW

You don't always have to type the @DATE function to enter dates in the spreadsheet (see the box titled A Macro Eases Date Entries for one alternative). There is a shortcut for entering today's date. Actually, there are two shortcuts. One is the @TODAY function, and the other is @NOW.

The @TODAY and @NOW functions are quite similar. @TODAY returns the serial number of the current date as represented by your computer's built-in clock. If the clock display in the bottom-left corner of the display shows the wrong date, then the @TODAY function will return an incorrect date. Assuming your computer's clock is correct, the @NOW function provides a mechanism to let printouts from your spreadsheet reflect the date on which

If Your Clock Is Off

Most computers today have built-in battery powered clocks that keep the correct time even when you turn off the power. Early computers and some of the slower models don't have batteries, so you must set their clocks at the beginning of each work session.

If your clock shows the wrong date or time, you can set it during the current work session by leaving 1-2-3 and issuing the DOS DATE and TIME commands. At the DOS prompt, enter *DATE.* DOS shows you the current date setting and prompts you for a new one. Enter the current date. Then enter *TIME* at the DOS prompt, and replace the incorrect time with the current time. On most new computers, the new date and time settings remain in effect even after you shut off and restart your computer.

If your computer clock is battery powered, but it doesn't retain the correct date and time when you restart the computer, you may need to run special setup software to set the clock. Consult your computer documentation or the documentation that accompanied any plug-in memory or utility boards you may have installed for instructions on setting the clock. Of course, it is always possible that the clock battery is dead. Replacing it could eliminate all problems with maintaining the correct date and time.

they are made. Also, by equating project or payment due dates to the @NOW function, your spreadsheets can keep track of whether the projects or payments are late.

To use the @TODAY function, simply enter it into any cell. Don't expect the function itself to appear in the cell—1-2-3 converts it automatically into the formula @INT(@NOW). You are allowed to enter @TODAY because early releases of 1-2-3 had the @TODAY function but no @NOW function. By converting @TODAY into the alternative formula, Release 2.3 maintains formulaic compatibility with other Lotus spreadsheet products. If you prefer to look at date displays rather than date serial numbers, assign a cell in which you have entered @TODAY a date format and set the column width to fit.

The @TODAY function is particularly useful in worksheets from which you regularly print reports. If you want the day's date to appear on each printout, establish a date cell with the @TODAY function and include that cell in the range to print. The @TODAY function is updated automatically whenever 1-2-3 recalculates the spreadsheet, so with worksheet recalculation set to automatic, your reports will always include a date stamp.

The @NOW function works like the @TODAY function with a twist. It includes a decimal component that represents the amount of the day that has passed since midnight. On June 1, 1991 at 3:00 P.M., the @TODAY function returns 33390. The @NOW function returns 33390.625. It reveals that 62.5% of the current day has passed at 3:00 P.M.

Date-Stamp Your Spreadsheet File

You use some worksheets day after day, week after week. For many applications, it can be important to know when you last used a particular spreadsheet. Because the @TODAY and the @NOW functions are updated automatically to reveal the current date, entering one of them into the sheet won't necessarily shed light on when you last used it.

The simple macro in the following illustration records the current date as a value, eliminating the @NOW function from which the value is derived:

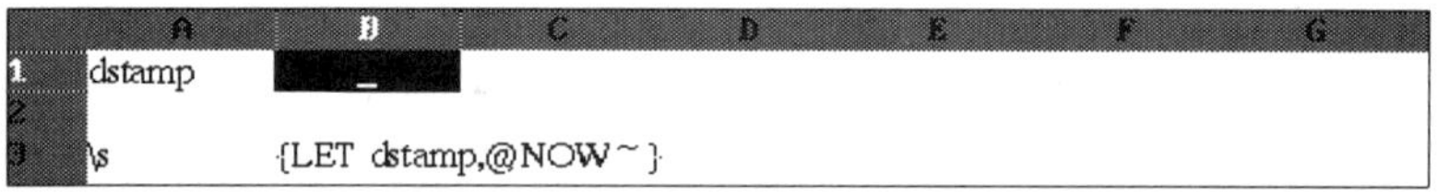

This simple macro can date-stamp your worksheets.

To create the macro, enter labels as shown. Start the label in cell A3 by typing an apostrophe label prefix. Use the Range Name Labels Right command to assign the labels in column A as names for the adjacent cells of column B. Finally, set the width of column B to 10 or more characters, and assign a Date 1 format to cell B1.

To date-stamp the worksheet, hold down the MACRO key (Alt), and press S. Date-stamp the worksheet after each use, and make sure you save after you date-stamp. Next time you retrieve the sheet, you will know when you last modified it.

A Brief Overview of Math in Time

Yes, 1-2-3 uses serial numbers to keep track of hours, minutes, and seconds, just as it uses serial numbers to keep track of days. As with dates, there are numeric display formats and @functions to help you interact with 1-2-3's unusual time-keeping scheme.

A time serial number represents that percentage of the day that has passed since midnight. The serial number .25 represents 8:00 A.M., .5 represents noon, and .75 represents 8:00 P.M. A combined date and time serial number represents a certain hour, minute, and second of a specific calendar date. For example, the serial number 33582.5 represents noon on December 10, 1991.

The @HOUR function returns the hour represented by a time serial number; @MINUTE returns the minute within an hour; and @SECOND returns the second within a minute.

To help you interpret time serial numbers, 1-2-3 offers four time display formats. You assign one of these formats by selecting Range Format Date Time. You will probably have to adjust column widths to accommodate the time formats, just as you must to accommodate some of the date formats. You should be able to apply your knowledge of dates and date formats as you work on your own to solve time management problems.

If You Have Already Entered Dates as Labels

Is there anything you can do if you have already entered a number of dates as labels? Don't worry, you probably won't have to reenter them to convert them to serial numbers. Suppose that your worksheet contains a column of date labels like the one shown in Figure 16.4.

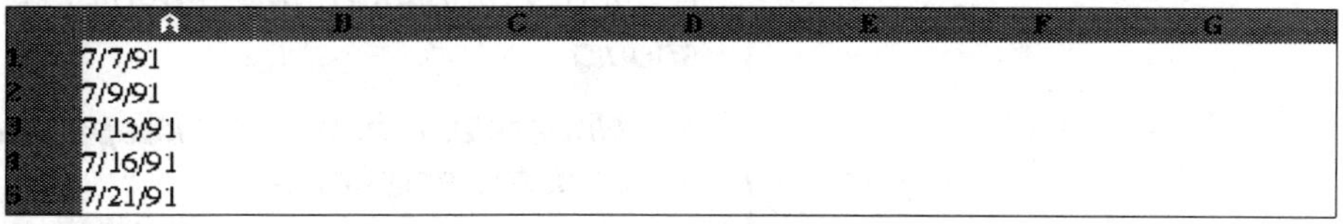

FIGURE 16.4. If you have already entered your dates as labels as in this worksheet, use the @DATEVALUE function to convert them to date serial numbers.

The @DATEVALUE function can convert these to date serial numbers in seconds.

The syntax of the @DATEVALUE function is @DATEVALUE(*datelabel*) where *datelabel* can be a literal string that looks like a date or a reference to a cell that contains such a string. To see the function in action, enter the list of labels shown in column A of an otherwise blank worksheet. Start each of the entries by typing an apostrophe label prefix.

Place the cell pointer in cell B1, and enter the formula *@DATEVALUE(A1)*. It returns a date serial number. Use the Copy command to replicate the formula down column B as needed. Use the Range Value command to copy the results back into column A. To do this, select Range Value and indicate range B1..B5 as the range of formulas to convert. Indicate cell A1 as the target range. Finally, use the Range Erase command to remove the formulas from column B.

The @DATEVALUE function can convert any label whose appearance matches a currently valid date format. If you were to alter the international date format as explained in Chapter 4, the @DATEVALUE function would be unable to convert labels stored in the MM/DD/YY format. Experiment with the features until you understand how they work.

The @TIMEVALUE function converts labels that match a valid time format into time serial numbers. Check out the Range Format Date Time menu to determine which time formats are valid.

Having completed this chapter you should:

- *Understand how 1-2-3 keeps track of dates and times*
- *Know which display formats clarify dates in the sheet*
- *Have a sense of how 1-2-3 uses your computer's built-in clock*
- *Know how to build date-related formulas for such applications as loan calculations, project scheduling, and accounts receivable*
- *Know how to have 1-2-3 calculate the weekday*
- *Be able to apply the @NOW function to date-stamp printed reports and the spreadsheet*
- *Understand how to convert dates that you have already entered as labels into date serial numbers*

17

Again and Again: Circular References and Worksheet Recalculation

With all the formulas you write, you are bound to stumble across a Circ indicator some day in your spreadsheeting career. To many users the Circ indicator is an error flag; they take it to mean that they have made a mistake somewhere in the worksheet. In reality, it is no more than an alert signal. A circular reference is a mistake only if you didn't intend to create it.

There are reasons to establish circular references. When you understand what circular references are and how they work, you may find uses for them in your own worksheets. They have the greatest utility in scientific calculations where the results of a process feed back into the process and thereby affect the outcome of the process itself. In business, there are a few calculations that benefit from circular references. One that we will explore in this chapter is a commission payment made against net revenue generated by a sales agent.

Whether or not you find uses for them, it is important for you to understand circular references so that you know how to react when they arise in your spreadsheets. As an added bonus, working through this chapter

In this chapter, you will learn how to:

- *Create a circular reference*
- *Control the behavior of a circular reference to calculate the number of times you have recalculated the sheet*
- *Selectively recalculate spreadsheet ranges to speed work in the sheet*
- *See a reiterative calculation at work to calculate a commission payment*
- *Set 1-2-3 to reiterate automatically*

exposes you to many tidbits about spreadsheet recalculation techniques. You won't necessarily be able to apply everything that you learn here, but you might feel gratified to have a better understanding of what goes on under the hood when 1-2-3 recalculates the spreadsheet.

What Is a Circular Reference?

A circular reference is a formula that somehow includes itself in its own calculations. For example, the formula +A1+1 stored in cell A1 refers to itself. Enter it into cell A1 of an otherwise blank worksheet. Notice after you enter the formula that the Circ indicator appears at the bottom of the display. The indicator doesn't tell you which cell contains the circular reference, only that such a reference exists in the worksheet.

The result of the circular formula is 1. That is because 1-2-3 evaluated the formula as you entered it. At that moment, cell A1 was blank and so had the value of 0. The expression +A1+1 was equivalent to the expression +0+1, and that is what the formula reveals.

Now, however, the meaning of the circular formula is +1+1. It adds 1 to the value in cell A1. It seems that the formula in cell A1 ought to return 2. If the value in cell A1 were 2, the meaning of the formula would be "add 1 to 2," and it should return 3. This line of reasoning could continue indefinitely.

So why has 1-2-3 settled on the value 1 for the circular formula? It is because the software is designed to calculate each formula once whenever you make a change to the worksheet. If you change the worksheet again, you will see that 1-2-3 hasn't actually settled on a value for the formula in cell A1. Move to cell B1, and enter the number 7. The formula in cell A1 returns 2. With the cell pointer still in B1, press the Delete key. This erases the entry from B1 and causes 1-2-3 to recalculate the sheet, so the formula in cell A1 returns 3. Every time 1-2-3 recalculates the worksheet, the formula in cell A1 adds 1 to itself. There is little practical use for the formula with the spreadsheet in Automatic Recalc mode, but it clearly illustrates the nature of a circular reference.

Control a Circular Recalculation

The simplest way to limit the recalculation of a circular reference is to limit recalculation of the entire worksheet. Rather than run 1-2-3 in automatic recalc mode, change the setting to Manual mode. Do this now by selecting Worksheet Global Recalculation Manual.

Now when you make changes in the worksheet, the formula in cell A1 retains its current value. You can work throughout the sheet indefinitely, and 1-2-3 will never update the circular formula.

On the other hand, when you work in Manual Recalculation mode, the formulas in your worksheet don't necessarily reflect up-to-the-minute entries. To see what this means, reenter the value 7 in cell B1, and enter the formula *+B1*2* in cell B2. The formula returns a correct result because 1-2-3 evaluates it "on the fly" before storing it in the cell.

However, what happens when you alter the value in cell B1? Try it. Enter *20* into cell B1. The formula in cell B2 still returns 14. If you didn't know that B2's formula refered to cell B1, you wouldn't know at a glance the current result was incorrect. You might notice at a glance that the calc indicator was illuminated at the bottom of your display. This is 1-2-3's alert that you have altered the worksheet and that your formulas might not be aware of the updates.

You could update cell B2's formula by pressing the CALC key (F9), but the CALC key causes 1-2-3 to recalculate everything in the spreadsheet; the circular formula in cell A1 would also be recalculated. Press CALC to see this happen.

Now the formula in cell B2 returns 40, and the formula in cell A1 returns 4. Apparently, using Manual Recalculation mode provides only limited control over the calculation of circular references.

Selective Recalculations

There are several methods by which you can recalculate selected areas of a spreadsheet in Manual Recalc mode—cell-by-cell or entire ranges at once. The simplest is to use the EDIT key (F2) to recalculate individual cells. Remember that when you enter a formula, 1-2-3 calculates the formula's result on the fly. The result is based on current values in the sheet. In Manual Recalc mode that calculation may not be reliable if you haven't updated the entire spreadsheet recently. On the other hand, if you are sure that the values in a formula's dependent cells are current, you might want to recalculate only the formula. In especially large sheets, this can save a lot of waiting for a more global spreadsheet recalculation.

Change the value in cell B1 to 4 so you can see the effects of a single-cell recalculation. Then move the pointer to cell B2. Press the EDIT key (F2), and press Return. The formula returns 8, reflecting the altered value in cell B1. In the meantime, the circular formula in cell A1 still returns 4.

This technique works because editing a formula is equivalent to entering a new formula. 1-2-3 doesn't know when you press Return to finish the edit whether you have altered the formula, so it recalculates on the fly to ensure the formula's result.

Recalculate Ranges of Cells

If you could recalculate cells only one at a time, you might choose never to do selective recalculations. Fortunately, the Copy command lets you recalculate an entire range of cells in a single operation. When you copy a range directly onto itself, 1-2-3 recalculates every formula in the range on the fly without updating other areas of the spreadsheet. Do a little experiment to see how this works.

Enter the value 1 into cell A4, and enter the formula *+A4+1* into cell A5. Copy the formula from cell A5 to range A6..A9. If you have followed along with every step of this exercise, your worksheet should match the one in Figure 17.1.

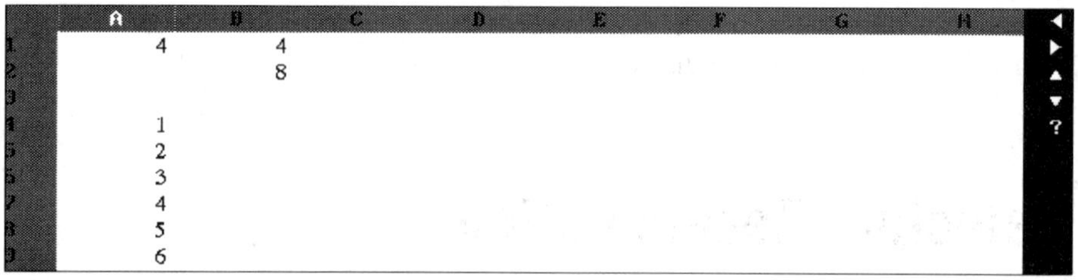

FIGURE 17.1. Copy this worksheet to experiment with range recalculation.

Each formula in range A5..A9 relies for its result on the result of the formula preceding it. The formula in cell A5 relies on the entry in cell A4; the one in A6 relies on the result of the formula in cell A5; and so on. The formula in cell A9 can't return an accurate result unless all the formulas above it to cell A5 are calculated first. Enter *2* into cell A4 to prove this.

Because the worksheet is in Manual Recalc mode, none of the formulas reflect the change in cell A4. Move the cell pointer to cell A9, and press EDIT Return. The formula continues to return 6. It can't reflect the change to cell A4 because none of the preceding formulas do.

Now apply the Copy command. Select Copy, and indicate range A4..A9 as the range to copy from. Indicate cell A4 as the range to copy to. When the dust settles, all of the formulas in the copied range return accurate results. The circular formula in cell A1 still returns 4.

A Caution on Copy Command Recalculations

The Copy command performed handily in the scenario we just created. We made it easy. However, there are times when this type of localized recalculation can give misleading results. It is possible, for example, to write a sequence of formulas that won't all update properly with a single issuance of the Copy command.

The Copy command replicates a range one cell at a time, working from the top of a range to the bottom. This means that in our example, the Copy command updates the formula in cell A4, then the one in cell A5, then the one in cell A6, and so on. It all happens very quickly, but this row-by-row calculation order can cause a problem. Set up a new scenario to illuminate the situation.

Enter the value 1 into cell B9, and enter the formula *+B9+1* into cell B8. Copy the formula from cell B8 to range B4..B7. Each of the formulas in range B4..B8 adds 1 to the value in the cell below it. This sequence of formulas works just like the sequence in column A—until you use the Copy command to perform a local recalculation.

Enter the value 2 into cell B9. As you would expect, the formulas' values don't change. Now select Copy, indicate range A4..A9 as the range to copy from, and indicate cell A4 as the range to copy to. 1-2-3 updates only one formula in the range!

Remember, the Copy command updates cell B4's formula, then cell B5's formula, then cell B6's, and so on. None of the earlier formulas can be aware of the change to cell B9 before the formula in cell B8 recognizes it. Therefore, only cell B8 reflects the new value in cell B9.

Once again select Copy, indicate range A4..A9 as the From range and cell A4 as the To range. This time 1-2-3 updates the formula in cell B7. Issue the Copy command three more times to update the remaining formulas in column B. This repeated copying of the range results in what is called a *reiterative calculation* of the formulas. Each iteration brings the formulas one step closer to revealing their true values based on the data supplied.

When a Circular Reference Is a Mistake

Quite often the circular references that arise in your spreadsheets aren't intentional. For example, you might accidentally write an @SUM formula that includes itself in the range to sum. Any number of errors in logic or even in typing can result in the Circ indicator appearing at the bottom of the display.

When the Circ indicator appears, and you know it indicates a mistake, first select Worksheet Status. The dialog box that appears reveals one of the cells involved in the circular reference. You might be able to trace the logic of the formula in the identified cell and recreate the formula to eliminate its circularity.

If the information from the Worksheet Status dialog box isn't enough to let you resolve the problem, consider attaching and using the Auditor add-in. That add-in can list all of the circular references in the sheet and even trace the sequence of formulas involved in such references. Instructions for using the add-in appear in Chapter 9.

What About the Circular Reference?

So far you have entered a formula with circular references in the sheet, and you have learned a few ways to keep that formula from doing anything. What's the point? The only apparent use of a circular reference is to keep track of how many times you press the CALC key while worksheet recalculation is set to manual. There's more.

Most spreadsheet documentation suggests another use for circular references, but stops short of presenting specific examples. A circular reference describes a problem in which the calculation depends in part on the result of the calculation. Complex financial and engineering problems might calculate circular references reiteratively to arrive at an approximate solution.

Fine, but how does this look in practice? The truth is, if you think you need to use circular references, you probably already know how they apply in practice. We argue that anything you can do with a circular reference you can do more cleanly with a macro, and we encourage you to dive into Section 5 of this book. Before you go, work through a hypothetical circular reference scenario that illustrates these arcane calculations.

The Circular Scenario: A Practice Worksheet

You are a salesperson (don't panic, it is just a scenario). You sell for a stingy boss who pays your commission on net revenue rather than on gross sales. To calculate net, your boss feels he must subtract your commission before he knows the proper amount on which to base the commission. Not only does this sound impossible, it's a bummer.

Unfortunately for you, it is not impossible for 1-2-3 using a circular reference. Set up the formulas as follows:

Start by erasing the current practice worksheet. Do this by selecting Worksheet Erase Yes Yes. Be aware that erasing the sheet reactivates Automatic Recalculation mode. Enter labels in column A of the resulting blank sheet as shown in Figure 17.2.

A	B
Gross	
Net	0
percent	0.14
commis	0

FIGURE 17.2. Copy this worksheet to see a circular reference at work.

The labels represent the entries and the calculations that will appear in column A. For now, leave cell B1 blank, but enter the percentage into cell B3. Enter either *.14* or *14%*, and use the Range Format Percent command to assign it a format with no decimal places.

Your boss's net calculation is quite simple: subtract your commission from your gross. The formula to do this is +B1–B4. Enter it into cell B2.

The commission calculation, as irksome as it may be, is also simple: multiply the commission rate times the net amount. The formula to do this is +B2*B3. Enter it into cell B4. Notice that the Circ indicator appears when you enter the commission formula.

With the formulas in place, it is quite easy to calculate your commission. Just enter your sales gross into cell B1. For this exercise, enter *4000*. 1-2-3 reports that your commission is $560.

Hold on a minute. The net amount in the spreadsheet shows as $4,000. This can't be right because it matches the gross amount. The net is the gross minus the commission. Time for a reiterative calculation. Press the CALC key (F9), to perform the first iteration.

Rats! As you should have guessed, your commission decreased and your boss's net increased. Now you are getting only $481.60, and he is getting $3,440. But you are not finished yet; things are not as bad as they look. Press the CALC key again and see what happens to your commission. This time it increases! 1-2-3 is zeroing in on the best estimate of your commission.

Press the CALC key repeatedly until the commission and net amounts stabilize. Your commission is about $491, and your boss's net is $3,509.

More About Reiterative Calculations

The circular reference in our commission scenario is quite simple. 1-2-3 resolves it in only a few calculations of the worksheet. The worksheet might require many more calculation iterations to solve complex circular models, but you don't have to sit around pressing the CALC key to make this happen.

Lotus 1-2-3 lets you dictate how many iterative calculations of the sheet should take place with each recalc. As simple as our little worksheet is, it requires 13 recalculations to stabilize the circular reference. If you knew this in advance, you could set 1-2-3 to perform those calculations automatically when you entered the gross amount in cell B1.

To set recalculation iterations, select Worksheet Global Recalculation Iteration. You can enter any number from 1 to 50. Enter 15 to cinch the circular calculation. When 1-2-3 returns to Ready mode, the circular formulas will instantly calculate commission and net on any value you enter in cell B1.

When you set the recalculation iteration count, 1-2-3 ignores it unless there is at least one circular reference in the spreadsheet. Actually, 1-2-3 uses the iteration count under other circumstances as well.

Who Goes First: The Calculation Order

When you first install 1-2-3 on your computer, it automatically calculates spreadsheets in *natural order.* No matter how you lay out formulas in the sheet, 1-2-3 determines which formulas need to be calculated first so that they return proper results before formulas that depend on them are calculated, and so on.

Our exercise with the Copy command illustrated what happens when you override the natural recalculation order. Rather than calculating the first formula in sequence stored in cell B9, the Copy command calculated the formulas row-by-row down the column—exactly opposite to the natural order established by the formula's own references.

You don't need to use the Copy command to have 1-2-3 calculate formulas row-by-row. In fact, the Worksheet Global Recalculation menu lets you select Automatic, Rowwise, or Columnwise.

The Rowwise and Columnwise options control the progression of calculations in worksheets designed to work against the natural order. As you learned from the Copy command exercise, when 1-2-3 recalculates formulas in a Rowwise manner, formulas toward the top of the sheet that refer to entries lower in the sheet may not reflect current entries. This also applies when you select the Columnwise recalculation option; formulas at the left end of the sheet may not reflect that status of cells at the right end of the sheet. Setting a high calculation iteration count overcomes the problem. 1-2-3 always obeys the iteration count when the calculation order isn't set to Natural.

Having completed this chapter you should:

- *Understand what a circular reference is*
- *Be able to control recalculation of the spreadsheet in Manual Recalc mode*
- *Recognize opportunities to apply circular references in your own models*
- *Know how to locate erroneous circular references in your spreadsheets*
- *Be familiar with formulas whose results rely in part on their own results*

18

@Functions for the Spreadsheet Environment

Lotus 1-2-3 offers far more @functions than the typical user ever uses. If you are in business, you probably rarely if ever put together trigonometric equations. Likewise, if you are involved in clinical drug testing, you are not likely to give the financial @functions much exercise.

One collection of @functions is relevant to almost everyone who builds spreadsheet models, however. These @functions grew naturally out of the spreadsheet's structure—without a spreadsheet, it would be hard to conceive of such calculations. This collection of @functions is so hard to categorize that Lotus has traditionally referred to them simply as the "special" functions. Anyone who uses a spreadsheet can use it more effectively with a solid grasp of the special functions.

The special functions do such things as identify the types of entries contained in cells, the formatting of cells, the name of the current file, and the number of columns or rows in a range. You might never need such functions until you begin writing macros that must be aware of myriad conditions in the sheet. For example, you might write a macro to erase any labels from within a column of spreadsheet data. That macro would have to be able to identify which cells contained labels. Some of the special @functions give your macros information that you can see perfectly well.

In this chapter, you will learn how to:

- *Learn about @functions tailor-made for work in the spreadsheet:*

  @VLOOKUP, @HLOOKUP, and @INDEX find entries stored in tables

  @@ redirects the operations of table-related formulas

  @COLS and @ROWS count the numbers of cols or rows in a range

  @CELL and @CELLPOINTER return specific information about cells

Other special functions find values stored in tables by looking for related values. You might use such functions to look up tax rates based on known income levels. Another function finds values based on their locations relative to the top-left corner of a specified range. These @functions can serve you whatever your profession. Let's look first at the most generally useful of these special functions.

Data in Tables: @VLOOKUP

The use of tables of data was epidemic even before computers became so much a part of business. Tax tables, commission tables, tables of postal rates —we have all encountered tables on the job and in our personal lives. It is fortunate, then, that the spreadsheet lends itself so well to the use of information stored in tables.

Properly designed tables make such information easy to access, especially in 1-2-3. If you arrange table entries in ascending order of value, the @VLOOKUP function can return entries from anywhere in the table. Consider the simple commission table shown in Figure 18.1.

	A	B	C	D	E	F	G
1	Monthly	0–2 yrs	3–5 yrs	6+ yrs			
2	0	9%	10%	11%			
3	3000	11%	12%	13%			
4	4500	15%	16%	18%			
5	6000	17%	18%	20%			

FIGURE 18.1. You can easily find data in this table using the @VLOOKUP function.

The table lists revenue thresholds in column A and corresponding percentages in columns B, C, and D. Column B lists the percentages of gross earned by salespeople in their first and second years with the company. Column C shows percentages earned by sales people in their third, fourth, and fifth years of service. Column D reveals percentages for people who have been with the company for more than five years.

As a sales rep in your first year with the company, if you generate between $45,000 and $60,000 in revenue during a given month, you earn 15% of your gross for that month. If you generate more than $60,000 in a month, you earn 17% of your gross. Likewise, in your fourth year, generating between $30,000 and $45,000 of revenue in a month earns you 12% of your gross for that month.

Visually scanning a table of this size reveals answers to questions about sales commissions quite easily. However, for very large tables, eyeing the data is inefficient. And even if you are a speed reader, why look things up in a table when an @VLOOKUP function can do it for you?

Practice with @VLOOKUP

To see the @VLOOKUP function in action, create the small sales commission worksheet shown in Figure 18.1. Enter labels as shown in row 1—start with a caret label prefix for the labels in cells B1, C1, and D1. To enter a percentage, either type the actual percentage (9%, for example) or type the decimal equivalent of the percentage (.09). Finally, use the Range Format Percent command and assign a format with no decimal places. Let's calculate a sales commission.

The question: What is the commission percentage for Ruth who made $45,000 in sales for March of her third year? Enter the following formula into cell A7 for an answer:

```
@VLOOKUP(45000,A2..D5,2)
```

It returns .16; Ruth has earned 16% of her gross for the month.

The @VLOOKUP formula has three arguments. The first argument is an amount (or a label) that the function should find in the left-most column of a table. The second argument is a worksheet range that contains the target lookup table. The third argument identifies a column of the table.

Our @VLOOKUP formula uses 45,000 as the value to find in the table. The table range, A2..D5, includes the lookup column and the related values. The column identifier is 2. It means, "find an entry in the column that is 2 columns from the table's left-most column." That's column C in this example.

It was convenient that Ruth brought in exactly $45,000, but how can you look up Bud's commission? He generated $33,000 in revenue during March of his eighth year with the company. Try entering *@VLOOKUP(33000,A2..D5,3)* into cell A8. It returns .13, revealing that Bud should receive a 13% commission for March.

The @VLOOKUP function searches a table's lookup column for the lookup value. Failing to find the lookup value, it locates the first amount in the table that is greater than the lookup value and returns an entry from the preceding row.

Simplify Table Lookups

If your only use for the @VLOOKUP function is to find information quickly in a large table, try setting up a worksheet as follows:

After creating the table, enter some labels as suggested by the ones in column E of this illustration:

	A	B	C	D	E	F	G
1	Extension		Name:				
2	7960		Office:				
3	2828		Ext:				

You can simplify your table lookup function.

These match the column headers of the table shown in Figure 18.2. To be able to look up information quickly, you would enter the formula *@VLOOKUP(F1,A2..C5,1)* into cell F2 and the formula *@VLOOKUP(F1,A2..C5,2)* into cell F3. When you want information about Larry, you enter *Larry* in cell F1; the formulas look up his office and extension. For information about Bobbi, enter her name in cell F1.

In other words, Bud's @VLOOKUP formula doesn't find 33,000 in the lookup column. The first value that it finds greater than 33,000 is 45,000 in cell A4. Therefore, it returns an entry from the row above—row 3 of the sheet. Bud's column identifier is 3, so the formula returns .13 from column D.

Look Up a Label

The @VLOOKUP function can find strings as well as values in the lookup column. Suppose, for example, that a table contained a listing of employee names in its left-most column and related information in other columns, as shown in Figure 18.2.

As long as each label in the lookup column is unique, you can apply the @VLOOKUP function. Do you want to know Bud's extension? Enter the formula *@VLOOKUP("Bud",A2..C5,2)*. To find Bobbi's office number, enter *@VLOOKUP("Bobbi",A2..C5,1)*.

If the label that you are looking up doesn't exist in the lookup column or if two or more labels match, the @VLOOKUP function returns ERR. Whether you are looking up labels or values, if the column identifier refers to a column outside the lookup range, the @VLOOKUP function also returns ERR.

Name	Office	Extension
Ruth	A-7	7960
Bud	C-10	2828
Larry	A-9	7962
Bobbi	C-11	2829

FIGURE 18.2. You can use the @VLOOKUP function to look up labels as well as numbers.

And the @HLOOKUP Function?

The @HLOOKUP function is the @VLOOKUP function flipped on its side. It looks in the first row of a table for the lookup value and returns an entry whose location is determined by a row identifier. Given the table shown in Figure 18.2, the formula @HLOOKUP("Office",A1..C5,3) would return A-9—the office number that is three rows down from the first row in the table range. See Figure 18.3.

Name	Office	Extension
Ruth	A-7	7960
Bud	C-10	2828
Larry	A-9	7962
Bobbi	C-11	2829

FIGURE 18.3. You can use the @HLOOKUP function to search through tables horizontally.

Another Table-Related Function: @INDEX

Lotus 1-2-3 offers other functions specifically designed to help you work with tables. Once collection of such functions, the @D (pronounced "at-dee") functions, falls in the category of *database functions*. We cover them in-depth in the Data Analysis and Statistics section of this book.

Another table-related function that falls within the special category is the @INDEX function, which finds a table entry based on the entry's location relative to the top-left corner cell of a range. For example, the formula @INDEX(A1..D12,2,3) returns the table entry that is two columns to the right and three rows down from cell A1. The function is particularly useful in macros that must modify every value in a range, because it can pull values from the range without knowing the specific addresses of the values.

Given the sample worksheet in Figure 18.4, predict what values some @INDEX functions will return.

	A	B	C	D	E	F	G
1	54	22	26	52			
2	83	54	37	74			
3	79	97	18	95			
4	58	77	49	82			
5	77	21	47	87			

FIGURE 18.4. The @INDEX function pulls entries from tables of values and numbers.

What result would you get from the formula @INDEX(A1..D5,1,4)? How about from the formula @INDEX(A1..D5,0,0)? What value would the formula @INDEX(A1..D5,3,3) return? Finally, what about the formula @INDEX(A1..D5,4,4)?

The first formula returns 21—the value that is one column to the right and four rows down from the top-left cell of the indexed range. The second formula returns 54; that is the cell zero columns to the left and zero rows down from cell A1. The third formula returns 82. The fourth formula returns ERR because the column identifier, 4, is outside the specified range.

The @INDEX function may not seem particularly useful right now. But it can solve some complex problems when you apply it in certain macros. The @INDEX function can return a value from anywhere within a range without knowing specific cell addresses, and a macro using the @INDEX function may not need to move the cell pointer, thus improving the macro's processing speed. The whole topic of the @INDEX function in macros is beyond the scope of this book. However, you can see the @INDEX function at work in the Advanced Applications section.

The Indirect Reference: @@

Another @function that helps in your work with tables of data is particularly difficult to describe. In fact, it is easiest to describe if we start out by explaining how it works with tables that consist of only one cell.

The @@ function has the syntax @@(*target*). Target can be a string or string formula or a cell reference. The @@ function looks at *target* to find the address or name of a cell. It returns the value found in the named cell. You might use the @@ function to redirect a set of calculations to use one table of data or another, depending on which table you feel applies to the calculations you want to do.

Our best effort to explain the @@ function in words can't approach the quality of hands-on experience. Do a little experiment. In a blank worksheet (erase whatever exercise you have been following), enter the list of values that appears in Figure 18.5.

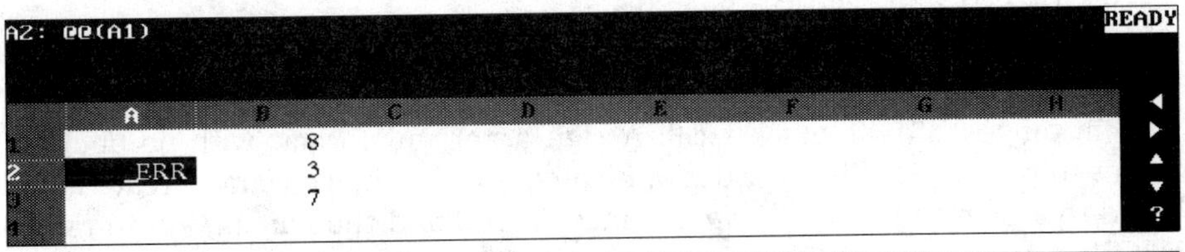

FIGURE 18.5. Copy this worksheet with which to experiment with the @@ function.

In cell A2, enter @@(A1). It should return ERR because the @@ function's argument must be a literal string or a reference to a cell that contains a label. What is more, the string referenced by the formula must represent a valid cell or range address or a range name established in the sheet.

To see how an indirect reference works, enter the label *B1* into cell A1. This tells the @@ function to return the value found in cell B1; the result in cell A2 is 8. Change the label in cell A1 to read *B2*. The @@ function in cell A2 returns 3. Change the label to *B3*, and the function returns 7.

As we implied earlier, the @@ function can refer to entire tables of data as opposed to the single-cell references you are creating here. One benefit of the function comes when you look up entries made in several tables in a single worksheet. For example, the worksheet in Figure 18.6 shows two small commission tables.

In a month when the company sales are not good, the sales manager calculates commissions based on the table labeled *Lousy*. As an incentive for the sales team to work together, in banner sales months the sales manager

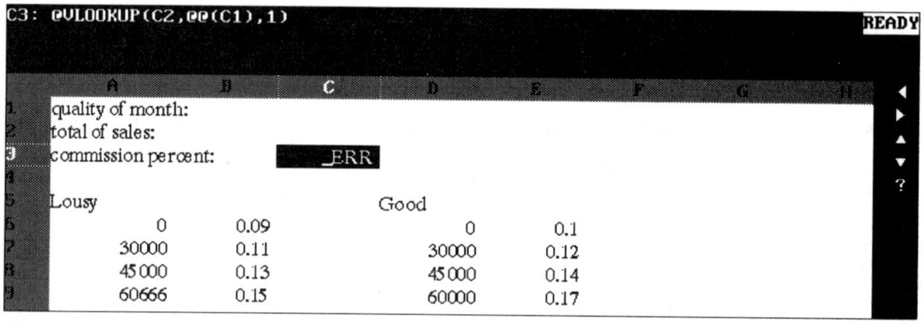

FIGURE 18.6. Use this worksheet to further test the @@ function.

calculates commissions based on the table labeled *Good*. There is also a table labeled *Stellar* (omitted from the illustration) used in the rare months in which sales exceed even the most optimistic projections. Coinciding with the tables are the range names, *lousy*, *good*, and *stellar*, assigned to ranges A6..B9, D6..E9, and G6..H9, respectively.

If you wish to create the worksheet, enter labels as shown in cells A1, A2, A3, A5, and D5. Enter values in ranges A6..A9 and D6..D9, and enter percentages in ranges B6..B9 and E6..E9. Assign a percent format with no decimal places to ranges B6..B9 and E6..E9. Finally, use the Range Name Create command to assign the name *lousy* to range A6..B9 and the name *good* to range D6..E9.

Cell C3 contains the formula @VLOOKUP(C2,@@(C1),1). Right now it returns ERR because the @@ function it contains refers to an empty cell. However, suppose it has been a good month. You would enter the label *good* in cell C1. In cell C2, you would enter the total revenue generated by one of the sales reps. The @VLOOKUP formula in cell C3 would return the applicable sales percentage from the table named *good*. In a not so good month, the label *lousy* in cell C1 would return sales percentages from the table named *lousy*. Enter the formula in C3, and fiddle with entries in cells C1 and C2 until you get a good sense of how the @@ function works in conjunction with the @VLOOKUP function.

Short-Cut Percentages

You can enter a percentage either by typing the desired percentage complete with a percent sign (9%, for example) or by entering the decimal equivalent of the percentage (.09). If you enter a number followed by a percent sign, 1-2-3 automatically divides the number by 100 before entering it into the current cell.

The Dimensions of a Range: @COLS And @ROWS

Here are some more @functions that come in handy particularly when you write macros. Quite simply, the @COLS function returns a value that represents the number of columns a range traverses. The @ROWS function counts the number of rows a range spans. The functions have the syntaxes, @COLS(*range*) and @ROWS(*range*).

Uses for the @COLS and @ROWS functions sometimes arise in a macro when it is important for the macro to determine the size of a range. For example, the macro might need to know that a range spans 40 rows, and therefore 40 possible entries, so that it knows to perform exactly 40 operations—one on each entry.

Information, Please: @CELL and @CELLPOINTER

There are times when it is useful to know something about a cell other than its contents. What is the cell's current display format? What width is the column that contains the cell? What is the cell's address? Of course, you can learn most of these things simply by looking at the cell, but your formulas and macros need a different way to learn them. The @CELL and @CELLPOINTER functions are their teachers.

The @CELL function returns specific information about a preset cell. The @CELLPOINTER function can return the same type of information about the cell that currently holds the cell pointer.

The @CELL function has the syntax @CELL*("attrib",cell),* where *attrib* is one of several words that describes the information you want to know. *Cell* identifies the cell whose characteristics you want to learn. The following is a

@CELL Tells You the File's Name

One of the most asked questions about 1-2-3 is, "How can I get the file name to appear automatically in the worksheet?" You can give up the clock display in the bottom-left of the display in exchange for the file name by selecting Worksheet Global Default Other Clock Filename and Quit. This doesn't get the file name into the worksheet, however; it only makes the name visible on the display. The @CELL function can place the file name into the sheet.

Select a cell in which you want the file name to appear. In that cell, enter *@CELL("filename",address),* but substitute the address of an adjacent cell for *address.* So, if you enter the formula into cell A1, you might enter it as *@CELL("filename",B1).*

list of allowable words to use as the *attrib* argument. Adjacent to each word is a description of the information that the @CELL function returns when you apply the particular word:

Attrib Word	Result
"address"	The absolute address of the referenced cell. For example, $A$1.
"col"	The column number (from 1 to 256) of the referenced cell.
"contents"	The current value or label value in the referenced cell.
"filename"	The full path name of the current file or a null string if you haven't yet saved the file at least once.
"format"	A code that represents the numeric display format of the referenced cell. The code matches the one that 1-2-3 displays alongside he current cell indicator when you place the cell pointer in the referenced cell. For example, if the cell has a Date 1 format, the result of the @CELL function is D1, and if the cell has a percent format with two decimal places, the result is P2.
"prefix"	The label prefix of the referenced cell (if the cell contains a label).
"protect"	The protection status of the referenced cell. The formula @CELL("protect",B4) returns 1 if cell B4 is protected, and 0 if protection has been removed via the Range Unprotect command.
"row"	The row number (from 1 to 8192) of the referenced cell.
"type"	The type of entry in the referenced cell. returns l if cell B8 contains a label, b if cell B8 is blank, and v if cell B8 contains a number or a formula.
"width"	A number that represents the width of the column in which the referenced cell resides.

We apply a few @CELL functions using various attribute words in the Macros and the Sample Applications sections of this book.

The @CELLPOINTER function accepts the same attribute words as the @CELL function. But because @CELLPOINTER reveals the attributes of the current cell, there is no need for a cell reference in this @function. Its syntax is simply @CELLPOINTER("*attrib*").

A Word of Caution

Lotus 1-2-3 updates the @CELL and the @CELLPOINTER functions along with other formulas in the sheet during normal recalculations. It is possible, however, to alter the attributes of a cell without causing a recalc. This means that the @CELL and @CELLPOINTER functions may not necessarily return correct results even when the worksheet is in Automatic Recalculation mode; formulas that rely on these functions may simply give the wrong answers.

To see how this can be, start in a blank worksheet and enter the formula *@CELLPOINTER("width")* into cell A1. Enter *@CELLPOINTER("prefix")* into cell A2. Now move the cell pointer to cell B1, and press the CALC key (F9). For most readers, the formulas return 9 and a null string—there should be a 9 in cell A1, and cell A2 should appear blank.

Now enter the label *test* into cell B1. An apostrophe appears in cell A2 to reveal that the current cell's label prefix is now an apostrophe. Select Worksheet Column Set-Width, press the RightArrow key several times, and press Return. Immediately select Range Label Center, and press Return. You have both altered the width of the current column and changed the prefix of the label in the current cell, but the formulas in column A don't reveal the changes. Only when you force recalculation will the formulas be correct.

The @CELLPOINTER function is even less reliable than the @CELL function in that any movement of the cell pointer may produce a new result in the @CELLPOINTER function. At least the @CELL function's reference is fixed to a particular cell. Make sure that you (or your macros) recalculate the worksheet before accepting as correct any calculation that relies on these two unusual functions.

Having completed this chapter you should:

- *Have a sense of the diversity of spreadsheet-specific @functions*
- *Understand how formulas simplify the use of tax tables, commission tables, tables of interest rates, and so on*
- *Be able to apply @functions that return information about the spreadsheet such as the dimensions of ranges, the formatting of cells, and the name of the current file*
- *Be prepared to use the special @functions when you start to work with macros*

19

Business Mathematics

You probably wouldn't be using 1-2-3 if you weren't involved in business. It stands to reason, then, that you will apply your spreadsheet to some of the more common business problems. You may already be a financial wizard who understands why and how to calculate such numbers as the present value, the internal rate of return, the periodic payment on a loan, and the depreciation allowance for a capital investment. On the other hand, these calculations and their uses may be unfamiliar to you.

Whatever your savvy in the area of business math, this chapter should be useful to you. If you are well versed in business math, this chapter will help you to understand how each of 1-2-3's tools solves a familiar business problem. If you aren't familiar with the calculations that are considered important to business, this chapter will define those problems and show you how to apply the spreadsheet to solve them. Using 1-2-3's built-in @functions and the techniques presented here, you can handle virtually any business problem you are likely to encounter.

In this chapter you will learn how to calculate:

- *Present value of a future amount*
- *Net present value of a series of cash flows*
- *Internal rate of return on a series of cash flows*
- *Effective interest rate on a deposit*
- *Present and future values of an annuity*
- *Future value of a deposit*
- *Rates and terms on an investment*
- *Payments on a loan*
- *Eight different types of depreciation*

Calculating Present and Future Values of Investments

Businesses invest in all manner of assets. These assets can be the tangible possessions of the firm, such as buildings, desks, phones, land, computers, cash, and so on.

They also can be intangible properties such as employee expertise and the goodwill of long-term customers.

For a business to be successful, it must invest in assets that are worth more than they cost. The difference between the value and the cost of a firm's assets is the profit by which the business flourishes.

Estimating the value of assets isn't always easy. Even if you are pretty sure how much money each asset will generate, inflation and the missed opportunity of alternate investments complicate business decisions. Businesses and individuals must understand the underlying issues involved before they can even begin to make intelligent investment choices.

Probably the most critical concept in finance is that a dollar today is worth more than a dollar tomorrow. For example, suppose you have $100,000 and your uncle offers to sell you a condominium for that amount. You happen to have a crystal ball and know that you can sell the condo in a year. You will net $106,000 after commissions and closing costs. Is it a good deal?

Property taxes, condo fees, rental income, and other considerations aside (this is a fantasy scenario), the answer depends entirely on the other investment opportunities you have open to you. If the annual yield on government securities is 7%, your uncle's condominium is clearly not a good deal. That is because investing the $100,000 in the securities pays back $107,000 a year from now. So, if you invested in the condominium, you would be out $1,000 next year.

If all investment choices were this clear cut, there would be little need for the business functions in 1-2-3. But most investment decisions are complex, so investors need a way to make comparisons easier.

Apples and Oranges: Compare Two Investments

Companies commonly use several methods or measures to evaluate investments. We'll consider two of them:

- Internal rate of return (IRR)
- Net present value (NPV)

The best and most accurate of the methods is NPV, though the reasons for this go beyond the scope of this book. Here, we will simply examine and compare NPV with the ever-popular IRR method.

NPV is the result of converting all dollar values projected over the life of an investment into present value (PV) amounts, adding them up, and seeing if you come out ahead. This means discounting future values by the rate of return on a comparable investment. Many corporations establish such discount rates. Some call this rate the *hurdle rate* or the *cost of capital*.

In the real estate example, we assumed that both the condominium and the securities were risk free and thus comparable. To figure out the PV of next year's $106,000 condominium revenue, you can use the securities rate of 7% to discount the future value (FV) of $106,000 into today's dollars. To do that you simply divide $106,000 by 1.07. The resulting $99,065.42 gives the value of next year's $106,000 in today's dollars. So the decision is easy. You're not going to exchange $100,000 for $99,065.42.

Another way to look at this is to discount the FV (return) of the condominium investment to its PV and then subtract the investment amount. This gives the Net Present Value (NPV) of the investment. Here $99,065.42 – $100,000 yields ($934.58). Since the NPV is less than zero, this is a bad investment. Given only the choice between the securities and the condominium, you would invest your money in the securities, because they have an NPV of 0 (the PV of an investment is the investment amount—$100,000 subtracted from itself is 0), which is better than the loss on the condominium.

There is no @function in 1-2-3 to calculate the PV of a future amount for a given discount rate. But it is easy enough to create a formula. The basic equation for PV is:

PV = FV / (1 + *i*)^*n*

where FV is future value, i is the discount rate per period, and n is the number of compounding periods between the present and future values. Typically, financial calculations use a month as the length of a period, but a period could be a day, a week, or even a year. The period in this particular calculation is a year—that is, the bond pays off exactly 7% at the end of a year.

An Exercise on Present Value

Figure 19.1 shows a PV worksheet. You can create it and save it to call upon when you want to compare investments of your own. To create the worksheet, enter labels and values as shown, omitting for now the value in B4. That value is a formula that you will enter in a moment.

	A	B	C	D	E
1		$106,000.00			
2	rate	7.00%			
3	periods	1			
4	PV				

FIGURE 19.1. Create this simple worksheet to calculate the present value of a future amount.

The value in cell B1 represents the FV of the condo investment. To compare that with the FV of the bond investment, you enter the bond's interest rate in cell B2 and the number of periods of the investment (1 year) in cell B3.

Select Range Format Currency 2, and indicate cell B1. Assign the same display format to cell B4. Then select Range Format Percent 2, and indicate cell B2. Note that B2 contains the value .07 not 7.

Now enter *+B1/(1+B2)^B3* into cell B4. This formula determines the PV of a future dollar amount given the variables in range B1..B3. You can see that it is the same PV equation shown earlier.

Save this worksheet by selecting File Save and entering *PV_CALC*.

Use @IRR to Compare Investments

Now suppose you have a niece who would like to buy the condominium in 12 months when she receives money from an inheritance trust. Until then she offers to pay you $700 per month rent. To figure out whether this makes the condominium a good investment, create a worksheet to analyze the problem. In this worksheet, you will use the @IRR and @NPV functions to evaluate the attractiveness of the investment.

The @IRR formula determines the Internal Rate of Return (IRR) on a series of cash flows. It assumes that the cash flows are periodic—they occur at regular intervals over the life of the investment—and that you have included all the cash flows related to the investment. The syntax for the formula is @IRR(*estimate,range of cash flows*).

The @IRR formula requires you to estimate the rate of return. This helps narrow the calculations required. If your guess is far from the actual IRR (if an IRR even exists), the function returns ERR. Once you determine the IRR of one investment, you can compare it with the rate of return on a similar investment. If it is higher, then you should go ahead with the investment. If it is lower, you should forgo the investment. We'll see how this works in a moment when we create the model that evaluates the condo investment.

@NPV

The @NPV formula determines the Net Present Value (NPV) of a series of cash flows. It also assumes that the cash flows are periodic and that you have included all the cash flows related to the investment. The syntax for the formula is @NPV(*hurdle rate,range of cash flows*).

The NPV tells you what an investment is worth in today's dollars. If NPV is greater than zero, you should go ahead with the investment. Otherwise, forget it.

Consider the Condo with @IRR and @NPV

To see how @NPV and @IRR work, start with a blank worksheet and select Worksheet Global Column-Width 14. Then select Range Format Currency 2, and indicate range B2..D17. Select Range Format Percent 2, and indicate range D15..D16. Enter the labels and values shown in Figure 19.2, but omit the values in column D. Those are formulas that you will enter in a moment.

D15: (P2) @IRR(0.07/12,D2..D13) READY

	A	B	C	D	E
1	Month	In	Out	Nat	
2	0		$100,000.00	($100,000.00)	
3	1	$700.00		$700.00	
4	2	$700.00		$700.00	
5	3	$700.00		$700.00	
6	4	$700.00		$700.00	
7	5	$700.00		$700.00	
8	6	$700.00		$700.00	
9	7	$700.00		$700.00	
10	8	$700.00		$700.00	
11	9	$700.00		$700.00	
12	10	$700.00		$700.00	
13	11	$100,000.00		$100,000.00	
14					
15			Monthly IRR	0.64%	
16			Annual IRR	7.66%	
17			NPV	$582.91	

FIGURE 19.2. To decide whether to invest in your uncle's condominium, set up a worksheet that shows all cash inflows and outflows. Column C lists the money you use to buy the condo. Column B lists the monthly rent you will receive and the amount you will get when you sell. Column D shows the net cash flow for each month. With a hurdle rate of 7%, the @IRR and @NPV functions tell you that this is a good investment.

Enter the formula *+B2–C2* in cell D2, and copy it to range D3..D13. Make sure that your formulas return results that match ours.

This simple worksheet analyzes the cash flows for the condominium investment with your niece involved. Column A identifies the months (periods) for each cash flow. Column B lists all cash that comes in, and column C lists all cash that goes out. Column D is simply the net cash flow that results when you subtract the cash flows in column C from those in column B. Note that in column D cash outflows are negative and cash inflows are positive—cash that goes out of your pocket is always negative, and cash that comes into your pocket is always positive.

Before you can figure out the IRR of the cash flows in column D, you need to take a guess at the rate. Since you want to compare this investment with the securities investment, use 7% as a hurdle rate. But remember 7% is an annual rate and the periods shown here are months. So you need to divide the 7% by 12. Fortunately, you can do that as you enter the formula.

Enter *@IRR(0.07/12,D2..D13)* in cell D15 to determine the IRR on this investment. Now enter *+D15*12* in cell D16 to give the annual IRR. This is simply the monthly IRR times 12. The result is 7.66%. So the IRR tells us that the condo beats out the securities investment.

To calculate the NPV, again use the 7% hurdle rate. Enter *+D2+@NPV(0.07/12,D3..D13)* in cell D17. The result is $582.91. Since the NPV is greater than zero, you should go ahead with the investment. Note that the @NPV function assumes cash flows occur at the end of each period. Therefore, you must add the cash flow from period zero to the result of the NPV calculation on the subsequent cash flows.

The two results say the same thing. This is a good investment—as long as all else is equal. In real life, that will probably never be the case. There is, for example, more chance of your niece defaulting on the rental agreement than there is of the U.S. government defaulting on the securities. That makes the condominium investment riskier, but we have ignored risk in this comparison.

When using IRR and NPV, try to compare investments of comparable risk —otherwise the results will be questionable.

NPV Is Better Than IRR

The concept of the IRR is fairly easy to grasp. Most of us get the gist of it, because we grew up collecting interest on savings accounts. But IRR is much less useful and reliable than NPV.

Consider the condominium example. What if the cash flows were reversed? Figure 19.3 shows that scenario.

Here instead of investing $100,000, you are borrowing it and paying back a monthly fee and the full amount next year as you would a mortgage with a

Month	In	Out	Nat
0	$100,000.00		$100,000.00
1		$700.00	($700.00)
2		$700.00	($700.00)
3		$700.00	($700.00)
4		$700.00	($700.00)
5		$700.00	($700.00)
6		$700.00	($700.00)
7		$700.00	($700.00)
8		$700.00	($700.00)
9		$700.00	($700.00)
10		$700.00	($700.00)
11		$100,000.00	($100,000.00)
		Monthly IRR	0.64%
		Annual IRR	7.66%
		NPV	($582.91)

FIGURE 19.3. Here you can see the advantage of NPV over IRR. The cash flows are reversed so that you are borrowing money rather than investing it. Still IRR tells you it is a good investment because it returns a higher rate than your hurdle rate of 7%. But NPV tells the real story with a net present value loss.

balloon payment. Clearly, this is not a good investment. But you wouldn't know that from the IRR. The annual IRR is still 7.66%. That's because IRR doesn't distinguish between investing and borrowing.

NPV gives the real picture. This investment results in a net loss in today's dollars.

Would renting to your niece be taking advantage of her? Not necessarily. She gets an additional intangible asset: she *wants* to live in the condominium.

IRR has other problems. For example, sometimes a series of cash flows can have more than one IRR or no IRR at all. These situations arise when the sign of the cash flow changes several times. With the condominium, for example, you might show positive cash flow in some months from incoming rent and negative cash flow in other months if you need to invest heavily in repairs to appliances and what not. As a rule of thumb, don't use IRR if there is more than one change in the sign of your cash flow. For IRR to be useful, the first cash flow in your investment scenario should be negative (a cash outflow) and all subsequent cash flow should be positive (cash inflow).

Even when the IRR is accurate, NPV is still more useful when considering more than one investment. You can't sum or average IRRs to evaluate several investments. You can, however, sum NPVs and get meaningful results.

The point to remember is that NPV is as reliable as the projected cash flow and hurdle rate you feed it. This is not the case with any of the other investment methodologies, including IRR. So, whenever possible, use NPV to evaluate investments.

Which Bank's Rate Is Better?

Suppose Jeepers Greeprags wants to deposit $10 million in a savings account. Bank 1 offers Mr. Greeprags an annual rate of 7.11%, compounded monthly. Bank 2 offers him an annual rate of 7.15%, compounded quarterly. Which bank offers the better rate?

To figure it out, enter labels and values as shown in the figure.

The first step is to figure out the FV of the deposit. The basic equation is:

FV = PV * (1 + i) ^ n

So enter the formula *+B3*(1+B5/B4)^B4* in cell B7, and copy it to cell C7. These formulas return the amount of money Jeepers could have next year in each of the banks. It is easy to see that Bank 1 is a better deal—by $233.06.

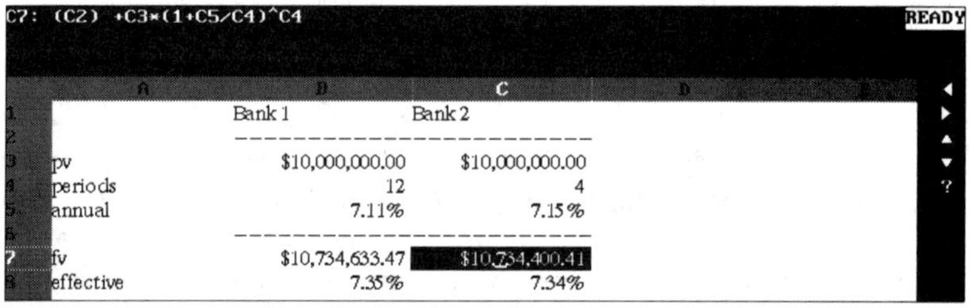

C7: (C2) +C3*(1+C5/C4)^C4 READY

	A	B	C	D
1		Bank 1	Bank 2	
2		------------	------------	
3	pv	$10,000,000.00	$10,000,000.00	
4	periods	12	4	
5	annual	7.11%	7.15%	
6		------------	------------	
7	fv	$10,734,633.47	$10,734,400.41	
8	effective	7.35%	7.34%	

Use the values in this worksheet to calculate future values.

If you want to see the effective yield for each of the banks, you can enter the formula *(B7–B3)/B3* in cell B8. Copy that formula to cell C8 to compare the yields.

Loans and Annuities

Lotus 1-2-3 includes six @functions for examining annuities and loans—@CTERM, @FV, @PMT, @PV, @RATE, and @TERM. An annuity is usually an asset that pays a series of equal payments over a specified period. Fixed-rate mortgages and installment loans are examples of annuities. You might need to calculate the periodic payment on a loan given the principal amount, an interest rate, and the number of periods in the life of the loan. Or, in considering an investment fund, you might want to calculate the future value of an investment if you make regular payments into the fund.

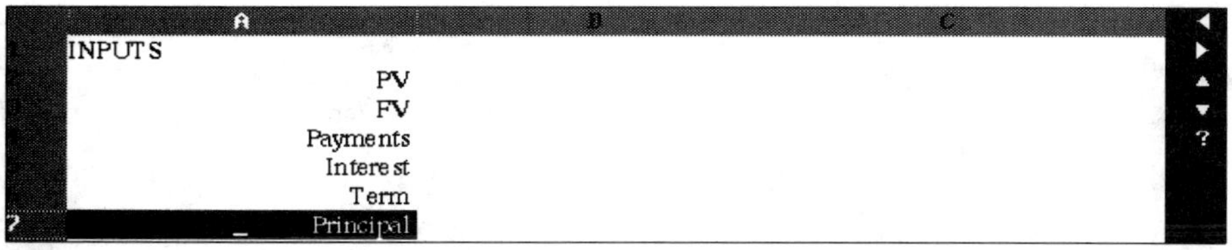

FIGURE 19.4. These labels reveal what data you must supply to make use of 1-2-3's annuity and loan analysis functions.

Figure 19.4 shows the components of a loan or annuity that might interest you. To see how the loan/annuity @functions work, create a worksheet that uses them all. We will use the worksheet as we explore the calculations you often do in business when considering periodic loans and investments. When we have finished, you should be able to apply the financial @functions in your own financial models.

Practice Calculating Loans and Annuities

Start in a blank worksheet. Select Worksheet Global Column-Width and enter 23. Move the cell pointer to cell B1, select Worksheet Column Set-Width and enter 12. Set the column width of column C to 1.

Select Worksheet Global Format Currency 2. Enter the labels as shown in Figure 19.4. Use the Range Label Right command to realign the labels in range A2..A7. Finally, select Range Name Labels Right, and indicate range A2..A7 to assign the labels in that range as range names for the adjacent cells in column B.

Save the worksheet as LOANS.WK1.

Now continue building the worksheet by entering labels as shown in Figure 19.5. Use the Range Label Right command to right-align the labels in range A10..A20.

Select Range Format Percent 2, and indicate cell B5. Similarly format ranges as follows:

Cell	**Format**
B6	General
B12..B13	Percent 2
B14..B17	General

When you are finished building this worksheet, you will have an easy way to figure out any of the loan/annuity parameters labeled in range A10..A20. The labels in range D10..D20 reveal what information is required for each

	A	C
9	FORMULAS	REQUIRED INPUTS
10	PV (annuity)	Payments, Interest, Term
11	FV (annuity)	Payments, Interest, Term
12	Rate	FV, PV, Term
13	Rate * 12	FV, PV, Term
14	Compounding term	Interest, FV, PV
15	Compounding term / 12	Interest, FV, PV
16	Term	Payments, Interest, FV
17	Term / 12	Payments, Interest, FV
18	PV (annuity & prin.)	Payments, Interest, Term, Principal
19	FV (annuity & prin.)	Payments, Interest, Term, Principal
20	Payments on principal	Pricipal, Interest, Term

FIGURE 19.5. Build this worksheet to find out almost anything you could want to know about a loan or annuity. The labels in column C tell you the entries required by the various @functions and formulas you will create.

formula that you will enter. So that we can more clearly explain the @functions, we'll take each in turn.

Present and Future Values of an Annuity: @PV and @FV

If you are used to a business calculator, you might find the @PV and @FV functions in 1-2-3 a little confusing. The @PV function doesn't let you calculate the PV of a future amount. The @FV function doesn't take the PV (principal) into account. Both calculations apply only to the payments of an annuity. They calculate the future and present values of those payments only.

Both @functions use the same arguments. The syntax is @PV(*payments, interest, term*) for the PV function and @FV(*payments, interest, term*) for the FV function. To see how they work, consider the following problem.

Suppose you want to buy an electric guitar and amplifier. You figure you will need a little more than $1,000 for the setup, and you can save that much in a year. Your question is, "Will depositing $100 a month in a regular savings account yield enough cash to buy the equipment in 12 months?"

See How It Works

To solve this kind of problem enter values as shown in Figure 19.6. The savings account has a nominal annual interest rate of 5.25%, compounded monthly. That means the monthly interest rate is 5.25% divided by 12. So enter the formula *.0525/12* in cell B5. The entry 5.25%/12 will yield the same result.

	A	B	C	D
1	INPUTS			
2	PV			
3	FV			
4	Payments	$100.00		
5	Interest	0.44%		
6	Term	12		
7	Principal			

FIGURE 19.6. To determine either the present or the future value of an annuity, you simply enter the periodic payments, the interest rate, and the term.

Now enter the formula *@FV(payments,interest,term)* into cell B11. If you have a problem entering the formula, check that you created all the range names correctly or reenter the formula as *@FV(B4,B5,B6)*. The name *payments* should be assigned to cell B3, *interest* to cell B4, and *term* to B5.

The formula tells you that the FV of your monthly deposits is $1,229.30. So if your projection on the future cost of the equipment is correct, the $100 deposited each month is enough.

What lump sum could you deposit today so that its value would match your $100 monthly deposits at the end of the year? To find out, use the @PV function.

Enter *@PV(payments,interest,term)* in cell B10. The result is $1,166.56. It tells you that if you deposit $1,166.56 in your savings account today, it will yield the same return in one year as depositing $100 each month for a year.

Figure 19.7 shows the results of the @PV and @FV formulas in the worksheet.

	A	B	C	D
9	FORMULAS		REQUIRED INPUTS	
10	PV (annuity)	$1,166.56	Payments, Interest, Term	
11	FV (annuity)	$1,229.30	Payments, Interest, Term	
12	Rate		FV, PV, Term	
13	Rate * 12		FV, PV, Term	
14	Compounding term		Interest, FV, PV	
15	Compounding term / 12		Interest, FV, PV	
16	Term		Payments, Interest, FV	
17	Term / 12		Payments, Interest, FV	
18	PV (annuity & prin.)		Payments, Interest, Term, Principal	
19	FV (annuity & prin.)		Payments, Interest, Term, Principal	
20	Payments on principal		Pricipal, Interest, Term	

FIGURE 19.7. Given the entries shown in Figure 19.6, 1-2-3's @PV and @FV formulas tell you the present and future values of the annuity.

@PV and @FV assume that you make your deposits at the end of each month. If you want to make deposits at the beginning of each month, you must use the formulas @PV(*payments,interest,term*)*(1+*interest*) and @FV(*payments,interest,term*)*(1+*interest*).

Before continuing, use the File Save command to save the worksheet to disk.

Calculating Rates and Terms on an Investment: @RATE, @CTERM, and @TERM

Sometimes you need to consider several one-shot investment opportunities; you have a fixed amount to invest, and you need to know how long the money will be tied up at a given interest rate. Alternatively, you might need access to the money at a certain time, so you want to know what interest rate is necessary to reach an investment target.

Consider saving for the guitar. Suppose that instead of depositing monthly amounts, you would rather just transfer some money into savings and let it accrue interest. You want to know the interest rate required to buy the guitar in 12 months if you deposit $900 today. To calculate this, use the @RATE function.

Practice with @RATE

Erase range B4..B5. The @PV and @FV formulas in range B10..B11 will return ERR after you do this. Don't worry about that. In this model, most of the unused formulas return ERR when one of their required arguments refers to a blank cell. When you enter values in the referenced cells, the formulas will work.

Now enter the desired FV of $1,000 in cell B3 and the PV of $900 in cell B2 as shown in Figure 19.8.

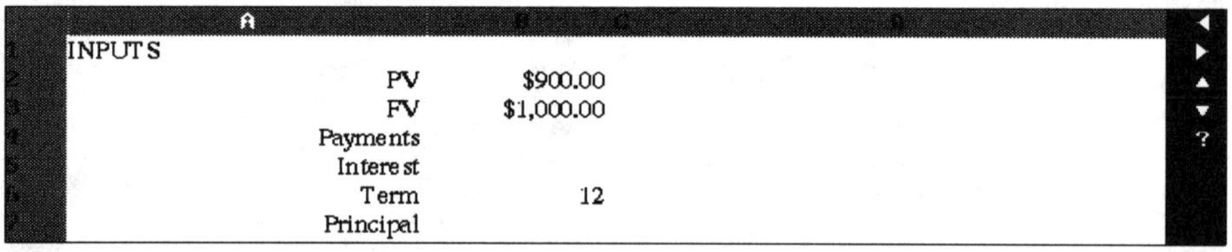

FIGURE 19.8. Simply enter the present and future values and the term to find out the interest rate.

To figure out the rate, enter *@RATE(fv,pv,term)* in cell B12. The formula returns 0.88%. But remember, this is the monthly rate. To figure out the annual rate, you must multiply this amount by 12. So, enter the formula *+B12*12* in cell B13.

The result is 10.58% as shown in Figure 19.9.

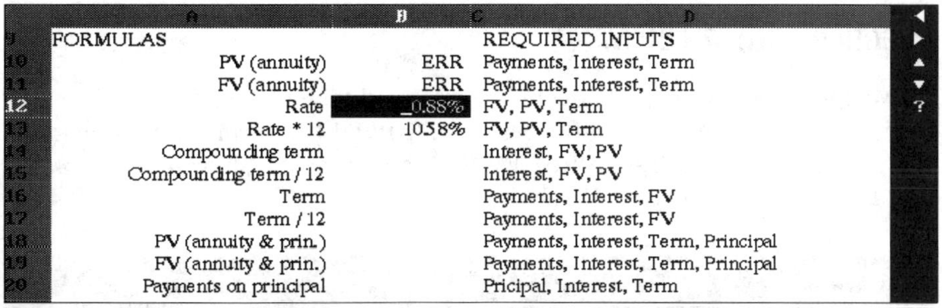

	A	B	C	D
9	FORMULAS		REQUIRED INPUTS	
10	PV (annuity)	ERR	Payments, Interest, Term	
11	FV (annuity)	ERR	Payments, Interest, Term	
12	Rate	0.88%	FV, PV, Term	
13	Rate * 12	10.58%	FV, PV, Term	
14	Compounding term		Interest, FV, PV	
15	Compounding term / 12		Interest, FV, PV	
16	Term		Payments, Interest, FV	
17	Term / 12		Payments, Interest, FV	
18	PV (annuity & prin.)		Payments, Interest, Term, Principal	
19	FV (annuity & prin.)		Payments, Interest, Term, Principal	
20	Payments on principal		Pricipal, Interest, Term	

FIGURE 19.9. The @RATE function tells you the interest rate required to accumulate a future value given a present value and term.

Practice with @CTERM

That's a pretty high rate; it will be hard to find a bank that generous. Suppose the best annual rate you can find is 8%. Now you wonder how long it will take your $900 deposit to yield $1000 at 8%. To figure that out, erase cell B6 and enter the monthly rate as +0.08/12 in cell B5.

Now enter the formula *@CTERM(interest,fv,pv)* in cell B14. It returns 15.85669926, telling you that you have about 16 months to wait for that $1,000. For many calculations, you will want to know the term in years, so enter the formula *+B14/12* in cell B15. Your screen should look like Figure 19.10.

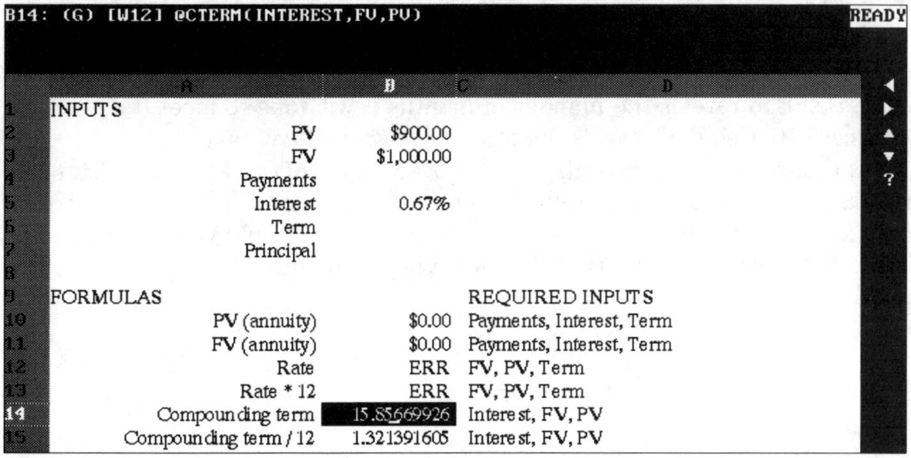

B14: (G) [W12] @CTERM(INTEREST,FV,PV) READY

	A	B	C	D
1	INPUTS			
2	PV	$900.00		
3	FV	$1,000.00		
4	Payments			
5	Interest	0.67%		
6	Term			
7	Principal			
8				
9	FORMULAS		REQUIRED INPUTS	
10	PV (annuity)	$0.00	Payments, Interest, Term	
11	FV (annuity)	$0.00	Payments, Interest, Term	
12	Rate	ERR	FV, PV, Term	
13	Rate * 12	ERR	FV, PV, Term	
14	Compounding term	15.85669926	Interest, FV, PV	
15	Compounding term / 12	1.321391605	Interest, FV, PV	

FIGURE 19.10. The @CTERM function tells you how many periods it will take an investment to reach a future value given the present value and the interest rate.

Practice with @TERM

Now suppose you want to know how long it will take to save $1,000 if you deposit $100 per month in the 8% account. To find the term given a payment, the interest rate, and the desired FV, first enter those values in cells B3, B4, and B5 as shown in Figure 19.11.

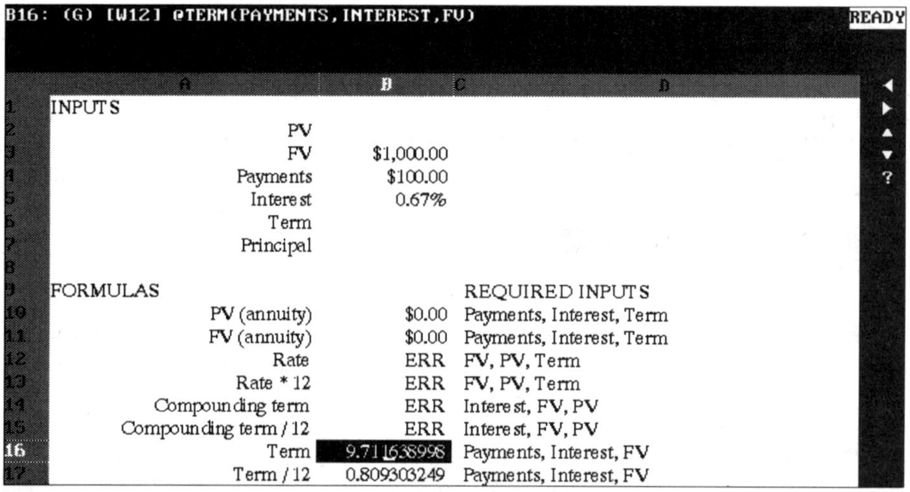

FIGURE 19.11. The @TERM function tells you how many deposits you will have to make to reach an investment goal given the target amount (future value), the interest rate, and a monthly deposit amount.

Then enter *@TERM(payments,interest,fv)* in cell B16 and *+B16/12* in cell B17. Cell B16 reveals the number of months it will take to meet the goal—in this case 10. Cell B16 reveals the number of years it will take.

Appropriate use of the @RATE, @CTERM, and @TERM functions can give you a quick overview of your investment options. Can you dump a lump sum into an account and wait for the interest to accrue? Should you make periodic deposits? How long will it take to reach a target amount?

Realistic Present and Future Values

Most of the time, you will probably want a principal amount factored into present and future value calculations of annuities. Remember that 1-2-3's @PV and @FV functions don't automatically do this for you. You can do it by adding the principal amount to the @PV formula and the FV of the principal amount to the @FV formula.

Say you put $20,000 down on a house. You get a fixed rate mortgage of 9.75%, and must pay $975 per month for 15 years. Set this problem up by entering values in range B4..B7 as shown in Figure 19.12.

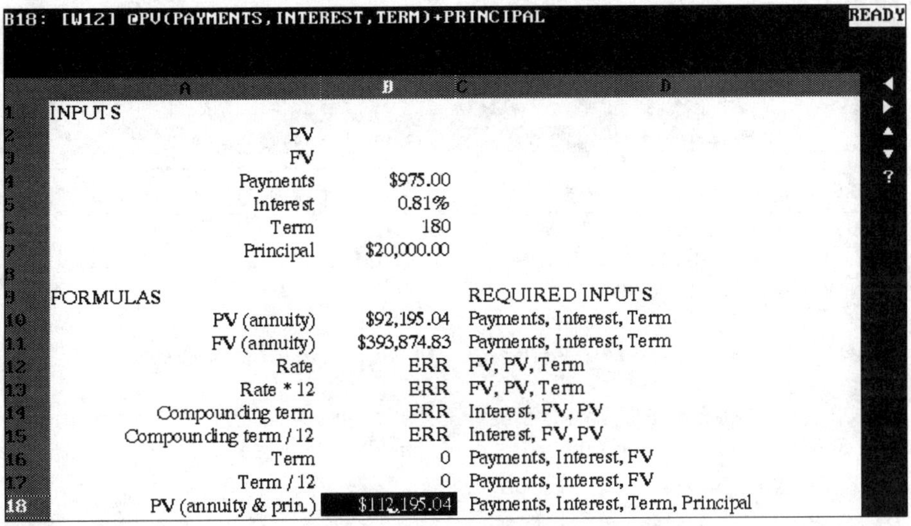

FIGURE 19.12. It is easy to create a formula that returns the present value of an annuity and principal given the principal or down payment, the term, the interest rate, and the payment amount.

Figuring the PV of the money you are putting out is easy. You just add the PV of the payments to the principal. Enter *@PV(payments, interest, term)+principal* in cell B18. The formula returns $112,036.47—the purchase price of the house. Calculating FV is almost as easy.

Suppose you want to know the amount of money you will have next year if you start with $500 and deposit $100 each month in a passbook savings account. Assume the account pays 5.25% annual interest.

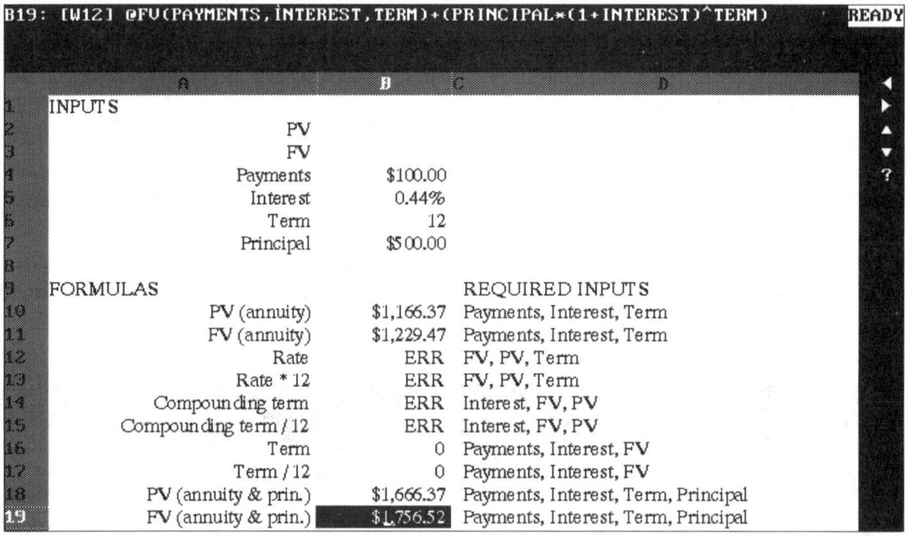

FIGURE 19.13. The formula in cell B14 returns the future amount of an annuity and a principal.

Change the values in range B4..B7 to match the ones shown in Figure 19.13. Now to find the FV, enter

@FV(payments,interest,term)+(principal(1+interest)^term)*

in cell B19. The formula returns $1,756.19, telling you the amount of money you will have in your account in 12 months. That is more than enough for the electric guitar setup.

@PMT

Sometimes you just have to borrow money, or, if you are in the business, you have to lend it. 1-2-3 can calculate loan payments, taking into account the interest rate of the loan, the compounding period (compounded monthly, yearly, etc.), and the principal.

Suppose, for example, that you just can't wait for the guitar; you want to know how much you would have to pay per month to buy it on credit at an annual rate of 19%. Continue with the spreadsheet you have been building. Erase range B4..B7, and enter new values as shown in Figure 19.14.

Enter *0.19/12* as the interest rate in cell B5. Then enter the formula *@PMT(principal,interest,term)* in cell B20. The formula returns $92.16—your monthly payment. Can you afford it?

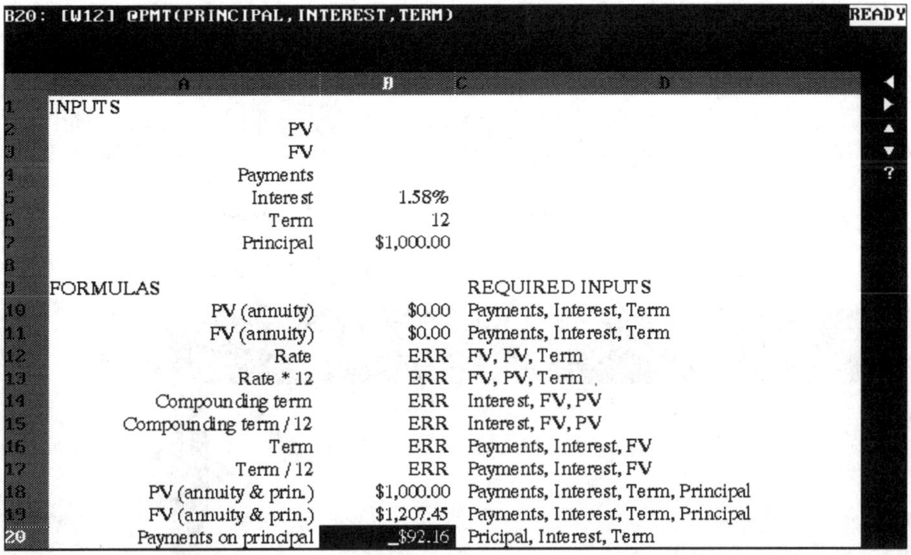

	A	B	C D
1	INPUTS		
2	PV		
3	FV		
4	Payments		
5	Interest	1.58%	
6	Term	12	
7	Principal	$1,000.00	
8			
9	FORMULAS		REQUIRED INPUTS
10	PV (annuity)	$0.00	Payments, Interest, Term
11	FV (annuity)	$0.00	Payments, Interest, Term
12	Rate	ERR	FV, PV, Term
13	Rate * 12	ERR	FV, PV, Term
14	Compounding term	ERR	Interest, FV, PV
15	Compounding term / 12	ERR	Interest, FV, PV
16	Term	ERR	Payments, Interest, FV
17	Term / 12	ERR	Payments, Interest, FV
18	PV (annuity & prin.)	$1,000.00	Payments, Interest, Term, Principal
19	FV (annuity & prin.)	$1,207.45	Payments, Interest, Term, Principal
20	Payments on principal	_$92.16	Pricipal, Interest, Term

FIGURE 19.14. The @PMT function quickly calculates your monthly payments on a loan.

Save this worksheet so you have it available in the future should you want to perform any of the calculations it contains. After saving, you might as well select Worksheet Erase Yes to clear the sheet from RAM. You will need a blank sheet for further discussions in this chapter.

You should now be familiar with the functions that 1-2-3 offers to help you perform common calculations related to analyzing investments and loans. That's one side of the business @functions. Another important category of business calculations includes those that determine depreciation on an asset.

Depreciation

Depreciation is a difficult concept, but it is an important one to any company that owns property and equipment. The concept of depreciation is complicated by the fact that various professions use the word differently. In the business world, depreciation is a way to allocate the cost of an asset over time. By doing this, a company spreads out over several years the tax savings associated with the purchase of capital equipment. Also, by depreciating assets over time, the company's financial reports give a more accurate picture of the company's value. The way a business allocates the cost of an asset has

Figuring Amortization

Pamela Hamel is buying a farm in Littybitty, Arkansas. She is buying it for $145,000 with a down payment of $21,000. The First National Bank of Littybitty gives her a fixed-rate mortgage at 9.875%.

Pamela wants to keep track of the principal she owes and plans to pay additional principal when she can. How does she keep track of the money she owes the bank?

Well, clever as she is, Pamela sets up a worksheet in 1-2-3. Take a look at her model.

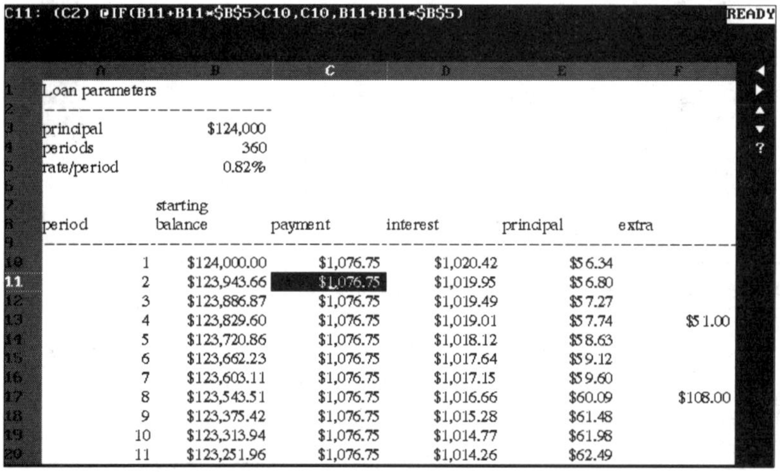

C11: (C2) @IF(B11+B11*$B$5>C10,C10,B11+B11*$B$5) READY

Loan parameters

principal	$124,000
periods	360
rate/period	0.82%

period	starting balance	payment	interest	principal	extra
1	$124,000.00	$1,076.75	$1,020.42	$56.34	
2	$123,943.66	$1,076.75	$1,019.95	$56.80	
3	$123,886.87	$1,076.75	$1,019.49	$57.27	
4	$123,829.60	$1,076.75	$1,019.01	$57.74	$51.00
5	$123,720.86	$1,076.75	$1,018.12	$58.63	
6	$123,662.23	$1,076.75	$1,017.64	$59.12	
7	$123,603.11	$1,076.75	$1,017.15	$59.60	
8	$123,543.51	$1,076.75	$1,016.66	$60.09	$108.00
9	$123,375.42	$1,076.75	$1,015.28	$61.48	
10	$123,313.94	$1,076.75	$1,014.77	$61.98	
11	$123,251.96	$1,076.75	$1,014.26	$62.49	

This worksheet model calculates amortization.

To see how Pamela's model works, enter labels and values as shown. Select Data Fill, and indicate A10..A369 as the range to fill. Enter *1* as the Start value, *1* as the Step value, and *360* as the Stop value. Then enter the following formulas:

B3: 145000–21000
B4: 30*12
B5: 0.09875/12
B10: +B3
C10: +B3*B5/(1–(1+B5)^–B4)
D10: +$B$5*B10
E10: +C10–D10
B11: +B10–E10–F10
C11: @IF(B11+B11*$B$5>C10,C10,B11+B11*$B$5)
D11: +$B$5*B11
E11: +C11–D11
Copy range B11..E11 to range B12..B369.

Whenever Pamela pays more than the amount required by the bank, she enters the extra amount in the appropriate row of column F. The worksheet automatically subtracts this amount from the principal.

nothing to do with the market value of the asset; it has to do only with spreading the cost over the useful life of the asset.

For example, say your business buys a $100,000 Automated Donut Maker that you expect to have in useful service for seven years. If you write off the whole cost of the machine now, profits on this year's books will be somewhat lower than profits in the following years that the Donut Maker is in service. To avoid this, you can spread the cost over the full seven years. Each year's books will include a depreciation expense for the asset, and that expense will be charged against that asset's book value.

Book Depreciation Methods for Financial Reporting

There are several accepted depreciation methods. Of these, the *straight-line* method is the most widely used. Other popular methods include *decreasing charge* (accelerated) methods and the *activity* method.

The reason for the popularity of the straight-line method is its simplicity. You have to determine only three values to calculate a depreciation charge for each period. These three values are:

- Cost of the asset
- Estimated service life
- Salvage value

Finding the cost of the asset is easy; that's what you paid for it. But determining the other two values is a little tougher. Most companies have their own guidelines, which vary from business to business. If you are calculating depreciation on your company's assets, find out what the established guidelines are. There are few hard and fast rules, however, and we will proceed under the assumption that you can eventually develop a fair estimate of an asset's useful life and salvage value.

The service life of a product is rarely the same as the physical life of that product. For example, there are ancient machines in museums that are still in good working order, but few would argue that the machines should still be in service. So the service life of an asset ends when the asset is no longer useful or profitable to the company.

The salvage value of the asset is the estimated amount of money that the company can expect to receive when the asset is sold or removed. Again, these estimates can vary from company to company on identical assets.

After you determine the cost, the salvage value, and the service life of an asset, you simply subtract the salvage value from the cost and divide by the service life to get the depreciation charge. You might think that such a simple calculation hardly warrants an @function, but 1-2-3 gives you one anyway. The @SLN function has the syntax @SLN(*cost,salvage,life*).

An @SLN Practice Scenario

Suppose you buy a Donut Maker II at a cost of $100,000. Based on experience, you think it will be in productive service for 10 years and have a salvage value of $2,000. It is easy then to set up a straight-line depreciation schedule in 1-2-3 as shown in Figure 19.15.

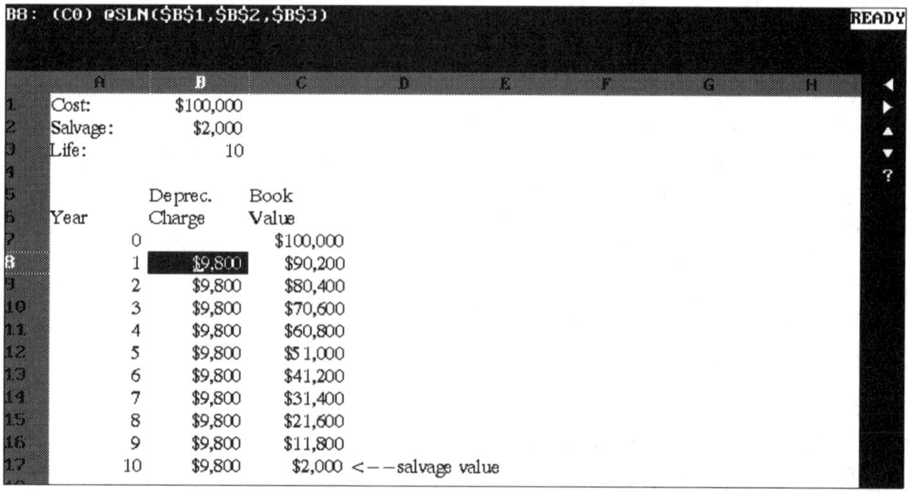

B8: (C0) @SLN($B$1,$B$2,$B$3) READY

	A	B	C
1	Cost:	$100,000	
2	Salvage:	$2,000	
3	Life:	10	
4			
5		Deprec.	Book
6	Year	Charge	Value
7	0		$100,000
8	1	$9,800	$90,200
9	2	$9,800	$80,400
10	3	$9,800	$70,600
11	4	$9,800	$60,800
12	5	$9,800	$51,000
13	6	$9,800	$41,200
14	7	$9,800	$31,400
15	8	$9,800	$21,600
16	9	$9,800	$11,800
17	10	$9,800	$2,000 <--salvage value

FIGURE 19.15. 1-2-3 makes it easy to set up a straight-line depreciation schedule with the @SLN function.

To create this worksheet, enter labels and values as shown in ranges A1..C6 and A7..A17. Enter the following formulas:

C7:	+B1
B8:	@SLN($B$1,$B$2,$B$3)
C8:	+C7–B8

Copy the formulas in range B8..C8 to range B9..B17. Select Worksheet Global Format Currency and enter 0. Assign the General format to cell B3 and to range A7..A17. Then save the worksheet under the name DEPRTION.

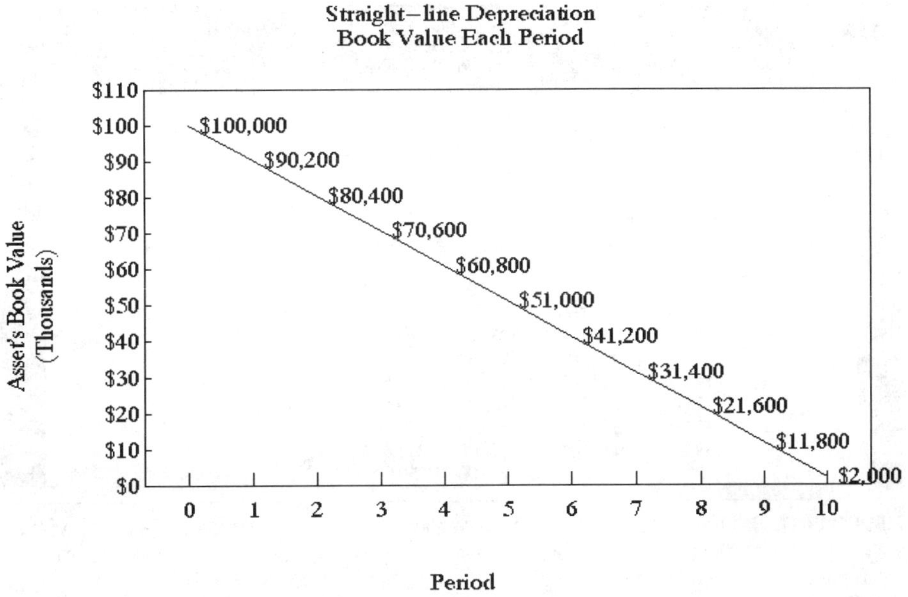

FIGURE 19.16. It is easy to see where the straight-line depreciation method gets its name. This graph shows an asset's book value over its useful life as it is depreciated using the @SLN function.

Your worksheet reveals that the book value of the Donut Maker II declines uniformly each month. Figure 19.16 shows a graph of the book value per period when depreciating using the SLN method. You can see where this depreciation method gets its name. (The Spreadsheet Output section of this book explains how to create graphs in 1-2-3.)

The simplicity and intuitiveness of straight-line depreciation are great. So what's the catch? Straight-line depreciation raises several objections. First, you have to assume that an asset's economic usefulness is the same every year. This is rarely the case. Second, you must assume that maintenance costs on your assets are essentially the same each year. This, too, seems unlikely. Finally, straight-line depreciation distorts the rate-of-return analysis on an asset.

Let's say that the Donut Maker II brings in a constant revenue stream of $25,000 per year. Figure 19.17 shows a rate-of-return analysis on the machine.

As you can see, the rate of return climbs rapidly as the value of the asset depreciates. Except for a little-used compound interest method, all the popular depreciation methods distort rate-of-return analyses. So the simplicity of the straight-line method is an excellent argument for its use.

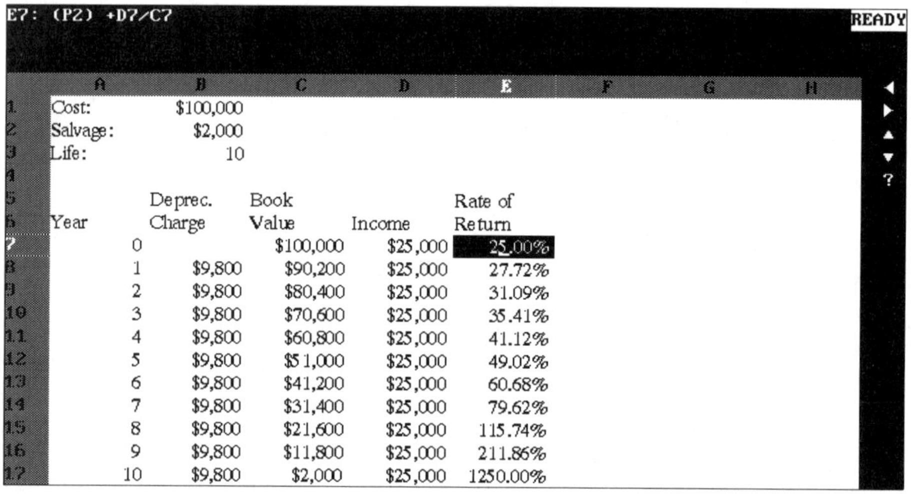

E7: (P2) +D7/C7 READY

Cost:	$100,000			
Salvage:	$2,000			
Life:	10			
	Deprec.	Book		Rate of
Year	Charge	Value	Income	Return
0		$100,000	$25,000	25.00%
1	$9,800	$90,200	$25,000	27.72%
2	$9,800	$80,400	$25,000	31.09%
3	$9,800	$70,600	$25,000	35.41%
4	$9,800	$60,800	$25,000	41.12%
5	$9,800	$51,000	$25,000	49.02%
6	$9,800	$41,200	$25,000	60.68%
7	$9,800	$31,400	$25,000	79.62%
8	$9,800	$21,600	$25,000	115.74%
9	$9,800	$11,800	$25,000	211.86%
10	$9,800	$2,000	$25,000	1250.00%

FIGURE 19.17. One major objection to the SLN depreciation method is that it distorts the return-on-investment analysis. Here you can see how the rate of return soars as this asset is depreciated. But most depreciation methods suffer with this flaw.

Accelerated Depreciation Methods

Some accountants contend that, because an asset is generally more productive early in its life and requires more maintenance late in its life, more of the depreciation should be charged earlier. This line of reasoning resulted in the wide acceptance of two decreasing charge methods—*sum-of-the-year's-digits* and *declining balance*.

Sum-of-the-Year's-Digits

The sum-of-the-year's-digits (SYD) method calculates each period's depreciation charge separately. You calculate the depreciation for each period by subtracting the salvage value of the asset from the original cost of the asset. You multiply the result times the years remaining in the asset's useful life, and you divide by the sum of the years. The sum of years is 1 + 2 + 3 + ... 10. But an easier way to calculate the sum of the years is with the formula:

n * [(n + 1) / 2]

where n is the number of years in the life of the asset. For the Donut Maker II, the formula is n * [(n + 1) / 2] = 10 * (11/2) = 55. Under the SYD depreciation method, you use the number of years remaining in any given year as a numerator and the sum of years as a denominator. Then you multiply the quotient by the depreciation base (cost less salvage—here, $98,000).

The following table shows the calculation required to determine the depreciation charge for each period for the Donut Maker II.

Period	Calculation	Result (rounded)
1	98,000 * 10 / 55	$17,818
2	98,000 * 9 / 55	$16,036
3	98,000 * 8 / 55	$14,255
4	98,000 * 7 / 55	$12,473
5	98,000 * 6 / 55	$10,691
6	98,000 * 5 / 55	$8,909
7	98,000 * 4 / 55	$7,127
8	98,000 * 3 / 55	$5,345
9	98,000 * 2 / 55	$3,564
10	98,000 * 1 / 55	$1,782

1-2-3 makes calculating SYD much easier than this. You just use the @SYD function. This function has the syntax @SYD(*cost,salvage,life,period*), where *cost, salvage,* and *life* have the obvious meanings, and *period* represents the particular year for which you are calculating a depreciation charge.

Practice with @SYD

To apply the @SYD function, modify the DEPRTION.WK1 file as shown in Figure 19.18. Enter new labels as shown in range D4..E6. Then enter the following formulas:

```
D8: @SYD($B$1,$B$2,$B$3,A8)
E8: +E7–D8
```

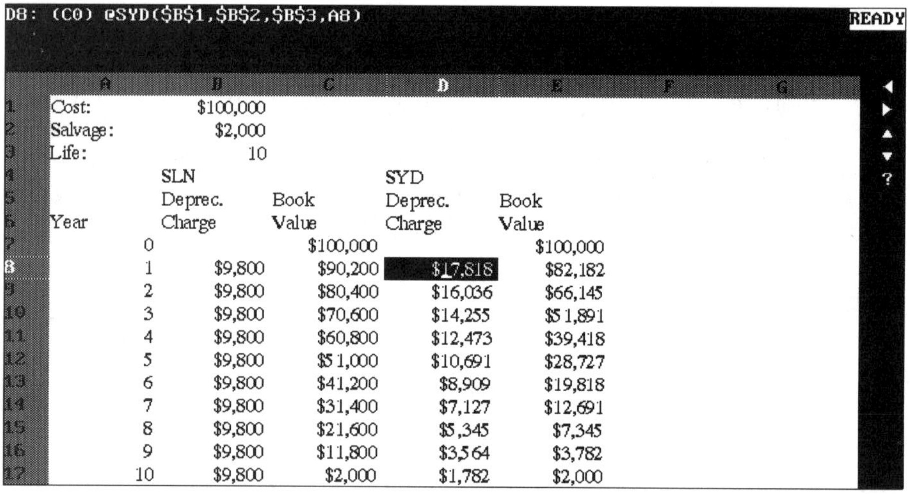

D8: (C0) @SYD($B$1,$B$2,$B$3,A8) READY

Cost:	$100,000			
Salvage:	$2,000			
Life:	10			
	SLN		SYD	
	Deprec.	Book	Deprec.	Book
Year	Charge	Value	Charge	Value
0		$100,000		$100,000
1	$9,800	$90,200	$17,818	$82,182
2	$9,800	$80,400	$16,036	$66,145
3	$9,800	$70,600	$14,255	$51,891
4	$9,800	$60,800	$12,473	$39,418
5	$9,800	$51,000	$10,691	$28,727
6	$9,800	$41,200	$8,909	$19,818
7	$9,800	$31,400	$7,127	$12,691
8	$9,800	$21,600	$5,345	$7,345
9	$9,800	$11,800	$3,564	$3,782
10	$9,800	$2,000	$1,782	$2,000

FIGURE 19.18. Here is a side-by-side look at the charges and resulting book values using the SLN and the sum-of-the-year's-digits (SYD) depreciation methods.

Copy the formula (+$B$1) from cell C7 to cell E7. Copy the formulas in range D8..E8 to range D9..D17. Then save the file.

Figure 19.19 shows a graph that compares the effect on the book value of the SYD method with that of the SLN method.

Declining Balance

The declining balance (DB) method simply increases the rate of depreciation calculated by the SLN method by some percentage. If you have a 10-year life on an asset, the SLN method uses a depreciation rate of 10% per year. The DB method for an asset with a 10-year life span might use a rate of 20% (this is the *double declining balance* method or DDB) which is twice the rate of the SLN method. The only difference is that you apply the percentage to the book value of the asset in each period so that depreciation expense for each period is different. For the Donut Maker II, the formula for DDB is *book value* * 2 / 10.

Unlike other depreciation methods, the DB method doesn't take the salvage value of an asset into account. Figure 19.20 shows the DEPRTION file modified to include the DDB method.

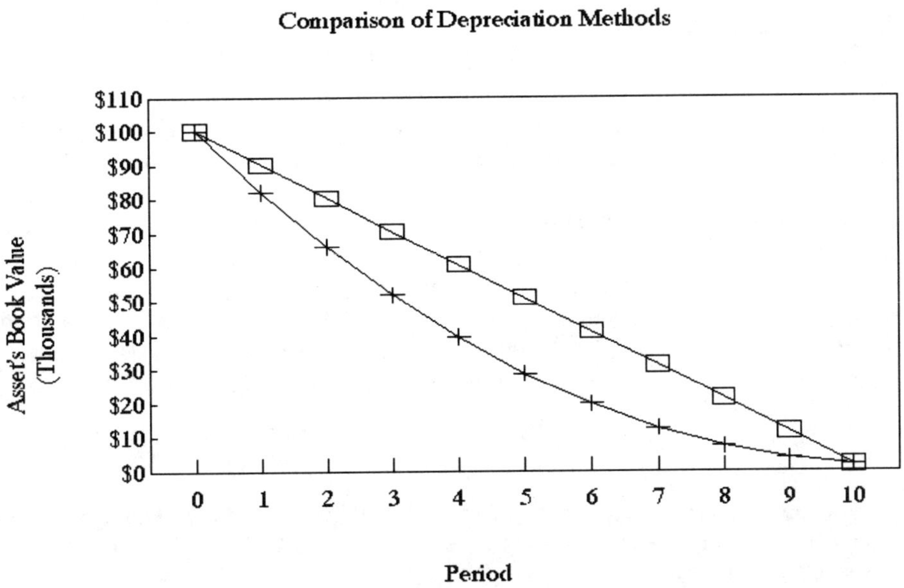

FIGURE 19.19. This is a graphical representation of the effect on book value of SLN and SYD depreciation. Note that more of the depreciation charge occurs earlier in the life of the asset under SYD depreciation.

	A	B	C	D	E	F	G
1	Cost:	$100,000					
2	Salvage:	$2,000					
3	Life:	10					
4		SLN		SYD		DDB	
5		Deprec.	Book	Deprec.	Book	Deprec.	Book
6	Year	Charge	Value	Charge	Value	Charge	Value
7	0		$100,000		$100,000		$100,000
8	1	$9,800	$90,200	$17,818	$82,182	$20,000	$80,000
9	2	$9,800	$80,400	$16,036	$66,145	$16,000	$64,000
10	3	$9,800	$70,600	$14,255	$51,891	$12,800	$51,200
11	4	$9,800	$60,800	$12,473	$39,418	$10,240	$40,960
12	5	$9,800	$51,000	$10,691	$28,727	$8,192	$32,768
13	6	$9,800	$41,200	$8,909	$19,818	$6,554	$26,214
14	7	$9,800	$31,400	$7,127	$12,691	$5,243	$20,972
15	8	$9,800	$21,600	$5,345	$7,345	$4,194	$16,777
16	9	$9,800	$11,800	$3,564	$3,782	$3,355	$13,422
17	10	$9,800	$2,000	$1,782	$2,000	$2,684	$10,737

FIGURE 19.20. The @DDB function makes it easy to calculate double declining balance depreciation. Here, you can compare the effect with the SLN and SYD methods.

Practice with @DDB

To update your practice sheet, enter the new labels as shown in range F4..G6. Copy the formulas from range E7..E17 to cell G7. Then enter the formula *@DDB($B$1,$B$2,$B$3,A8)* in cell F8, and copy it to range F9..F17. You can see that the syntax for 1-2-3's @DDB formula is, oddly, @DDB(*cost,salvage,life,period*). Though the DDB calculation doesn't use the salvage value, 1-2-3 wants you to enter one anyway. That is because sometimes the DDB formula would yield a depreciation charge in the last period that is larger than salvage value. Since book value cannot be less than the salvage value, the @DDB function automatically reduces the depreciation charge so that the ending book value is the salvage amount.

Write Your Own DDB Formula
Here's a challenge. Given your understanding of @functions and depreciation, can you write an alternate formula in cell F8 of Figure 19.20 to yield the same result as the @DDB function?
One formula would be: @IF(G7–G7*2/$B$3>$B$2,G7*2/$B$3,G7–$B$2)

Note that in the last period, the Donut Maker II isn't fully depreciated. Businesses that use a DB method often switch to the SLN or SYD method near the end of an asset's life so they can depreciate the asset to its salvage value.

Pure Declining Balance

The most "pure," though rather rare, form of DB is called the *fixed-percentage-of-book-value* method. This method finds a rate that depreciates an asset exactly to its salvage value. It will work only if the asset has a salvage value. To calculate depreciation expense under this method, use the formula (1–(*salvage/cost*)^(1/*life*))***period*.

To see how the fixed-percentage-of-book-value method works, modify the DEPRTION file as shown in Figure 19.21. Enter new labels in range H3..I6, and then copy the formulas from range G7..G17 to cell I7. Enter the formula *(1–($B$2/$B$1)^(1/$B$3))*I7* in cell H8, and copy it to range H9..H17.

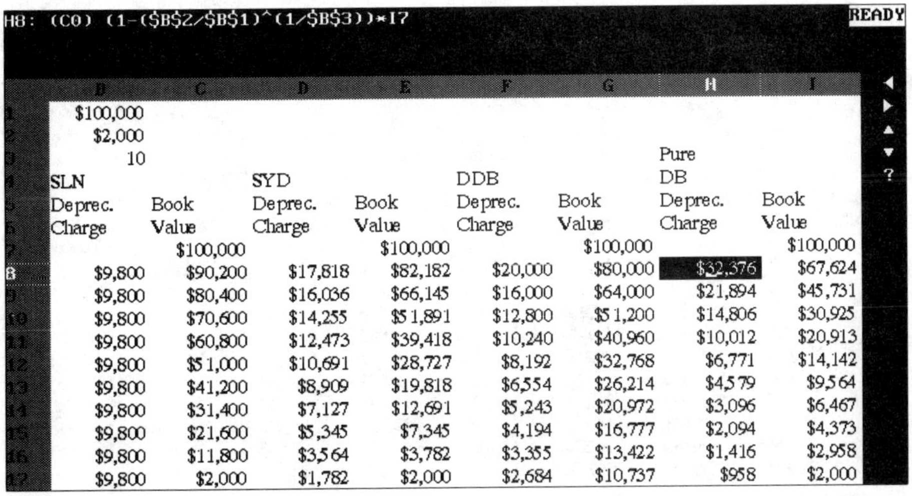

H8: (C0) (1-($B$2/$B$1)^(1/$B$3))*I7 READY

	B	C	D	E	F	G	H	I
1	$100,000							
2	$2,000							
3	10						Pure	
4	SLN		SYD		DDB		DB	
5	Deprec.	Book	Deprec.	Book	Deprec.	Book	Deprec.	Book
6	Charge	Value	Charge	Value	Charge	Value	Charge	Value
7		$100,000		$100,000		$100,000		$100,000
8	$9,800	$90,200	$17,818	$82,182	$20,000	$80,000	$32,376	$67,624
9	$9,800	$80,400	$16,036	$66,145	$16,000	$64,000	$21,894	$45,731
10	$9,800	$70,600	$14,255	$51,891	$12,800	$51,200	$14,806	$30,925
11	$9,800	$60,800	$12,473	$39,418	$10,240	$40,960	$10,012	$20,913
12	$9,800	$51,000	$10,691	$28,727	$8,192	$32,768	$6,771	$14,142
13	$9,800	$41,200	$8,909	$19,818	$6,554	$26,214	$4,579	$9,564
14	$9,800	$31,400	$7,127	$12,691	$5,243	$20,972	$3,096	$6,467
15	$9,800	$21,600	$5,345	$7,345	$4,194	$16,777	$2,094	$4,373
16	$9,800	$11,800	$3,564	$3,782	$3,355	$13,422	$1,416	$2,958
17	$9,800	$2,000	$1,782	$2,000	$2,684	$10,737	$958	$2,000

FIGURE 19.21. In this case, the @DDB function doesn't depreciate to salvage value. A few accountants use a form of DDB called the fixed-percentage-of-book-value method. Once you know the logic, 1-2-3 makes it easy to create a formula as shown here.

150% Declining Balance

Lotus 1-2-3 Release 2.3 includes only the @DDB function, which is a 200% DB method to calculate declining balance depreciation expense. In other words, the @DDB function uses a depreciation rate that is twice the rate of the @SLN function. But many businesses use other percentages for their DB calculations. A common alternate percentage is 150%.

You can create your own formula for calculating depreciation expense using DB at 150% of the SLN method with the following formula:

```
@IF(book–book/life*1.5>salvage,book/life*1.5,book–salvage)
```

where *book* is the book value, *life* is the useful life of the asset, and *salvage* is the expected salvage value. To change the formula so that it yields other percentages for DB calculations, simply replace the value 1.5 wherever it appears. For example, if you change the two instances of 1.5 to 2, the formula yields the same results as the @DDB function.

Figure 19.22 shows the DEPRTION file modified to include 150% DB calculations. To change your file, enter labels as shown in range J4..K6.

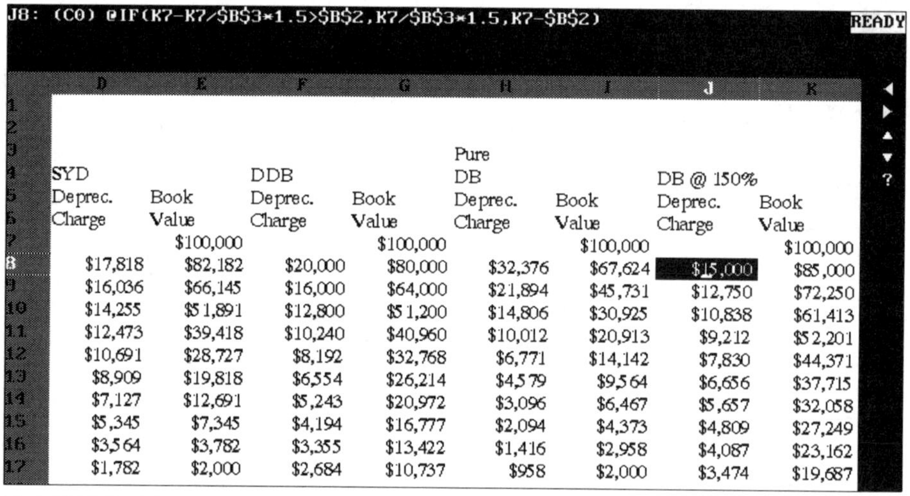

J8: (C0) @IF(K7-K7/$B$3*1.5>$B$2,K7/$B$3*1.5,K7-$B$2) READY

	D	E	F	G	H	I	J	K
1								
2								
3					Pure			
4	SYD		DDB		DB		DB @ 150%	
5	Deprec.	Book	Deprec.	Book	Deprec.	Book	Deprec.	Book
6	Charge	Value	Charge	Value	Charge	Value	Charge	Value
7		$100,000		$100,000		$100,000		$100,000
8	$17,818	$82,182	$20,000	$80,000	$32,376	$67,624	$15,000	$85,000
9	$16,036	$66,145	$16,000	$64,000	$21,894	$45,731	$12,750	$72,250
10	$14,255	$51,891	$12,800	$51,200	$14,806	$30,925	$10,838	$61,413
11	$12,473	$39,418	$10,240	$40,960	$10,012	$20,913	$9,212	$52,201
12	$10,691	$28,727	$8,192	$32,768	$6,771	$14,142	$7,830	$44,371
13	$8,909	$19,818	$6,554	$26,214	$4,579	$9,564	$6,656	$37,715
14	$7,127	$12,691	$5,243	$20,972	$3,096	$6,467	$5,657	$32,058
15	$5,345	$7,345	$4,194	$16,777	$2,094	$4,373	$4,809	$27,249
16	$3,564	$3,782	$3,355	$13,422	$1,416	$2,958	$4,087	$23,162
17	$1,782	$2,000	$2,684	$10,737	$958	$2,000	$3,474	$19,687

FIGURE 19.22. Though 1-2-3 doesn't include a declining balance method using a rate of 150%, it is easy enough to create your own as shown here in cell J8.

Copy the formulas from range I7..I17 to cell K7. Then enter the formula *@IF(K7–K7/$B$3*1.5>$B$2,K7/$B$3*1.5,K7–$B$2)* into cell J8, and copy it to range J9..J17. Save the file.

Figure 19.23 shows a graph of the declining book values of Donut Maker II under all the depreciation methods we have discussed so far.

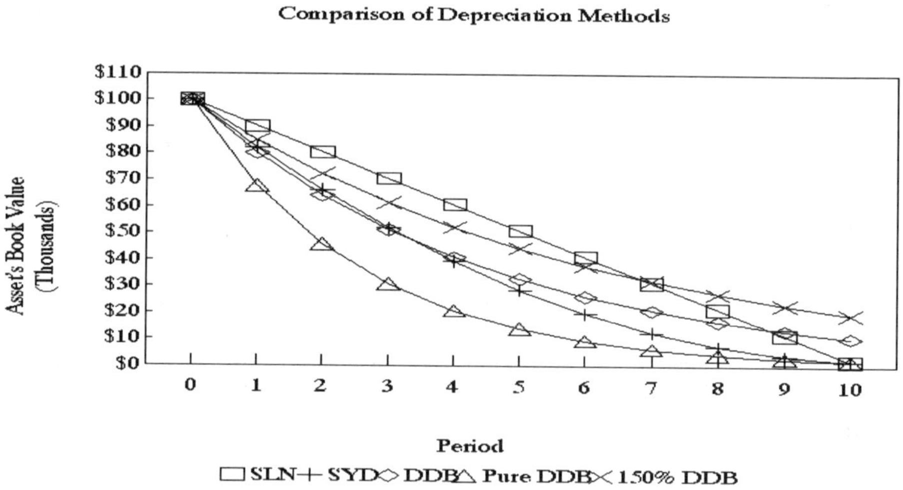

FIGURE 19.23. This graph shows the effect on book value of all the depreciation methods we have discussed so far.

The Activity or Variable Charge Method

Under the activity depreciation method, you depreciate an asset based on how much you use it rather than on how long you have owned it. For example, you might depreciate a truck according to its mileage. Or you might use hours in service to depreciate the Donut Maker II.

C8: (C0) ($B$1-$B$2)*B8/$B$3 READY

	A	B	C	D
1	Cost:	$100,000		
2	Salvage:	$2,000		
3	Life:	100,000		
4				
5			Depr.	Book
6	Year	Hours	Exp	Value
7	0			$100,000
8	1	12,000	$11,760	$88,240
9	2	14,000	$13,720	$74,520
10	3	8,000	$7,840	$66,680
11	4	13,000	$12,740	$53,940
12	5	7,000	$6,860	$47,080
13	6	14,000	$13,720	$33,360
14	7	12,000	$11,760	$21,600
15	8	14,000	$13,720	$7,880
16	9	9,000	$5,880	$2,000
17	10	6,000	$0	$2,000

FIGURE 19.24. If your company uses the Activity method to depreciate assets, you should have no trouble modifying this worksheet to suit your needs.

Figure 19.24 shows a worksheet using the activity method. The mathematics are conceptually simple. In range B1..B3 you enter the cost, salvage value, and useful life (in hours) of the asset. The table lists years in column A and the hours used each year in column B. You enter the hours as each year passes.

As before, column D lists the book value of the asset after depreciation. Cell D7 contains the formula +B1. Cell D8 contains the formula +D7–C8, and we have copied the formula to range D9..D17.

The following equation represents the logic of the depreciation formula we have to create:

(cost less salvage) * *(hours this year)* divided by
(the total estimated hours)

Therefore, the formula in cell C8 is ($B$1–$B$2)*B8/$B$3.

We could just copy the formula down the column, but that creates a problem: We must watch to make sure that the book value of the asset doesn't drop below the salvage value. A more complex formula in cell C9 can monitor itself for that possibility:

```
@IF(@SUM($C$8..C8)+($B$1–$B$2)*B9/$B$3>($B$1–$B$2),($B$1–
$B$2)–@SUM($C$8..C8),($B$1–$B$2)*B9/$B$3)
```

We have entered this formula in cell C9 and copied it to range C10..C17. The formula determines if the depreciation amounts to date plus what would normally be the current year's depreciation amount, exceed the depreciable base (cost less salvage) of the asset. If they do, the formula returns the depreciable base less the depreciation expense to date. That leaves the book value at the salvage amount. Otherwise, the formula calculates the expense amount using the simple logic of the formula in cell D8.

The placement of $ signs in the formula is important here. If the use of mixed absolute and relative references is confusing, please refer to Chapter 13 earlier in this section.

The Modified Accelerated Cost Recovery System (MACRS)

The U.S. government requires companies to use the *modified accelerated cost recovery system* (MACRS) for tax depreciation. The MACRS replaces the ACRS which covers properties placed in service after 1980 and before 1987.

Congress enacted MACRS to provide rapid depreciation and to eliminate disputes over useful life, salvage value, and depreciation methods for tax purposes. The faster write-off means a larger deduction and, theoretically, stimulates capital investment.

Explaining the complexities of IRS rules governing depreciation goes beyond the scope of this book. However, once you understand what you are trying to do, 1-2-3 can help you construct a useful depreciation worksheet.

Under MACRS, the IRS assigns each depreciable asset a useful life of 3, 5, 7, 10, 15, or 20 years. You depreciate property in the 3-, 5-, 7-, and 10-year classes using a 200% declining balance method with a switch to SLN at the point where the SLN method yields a higher depreciation expense.

That sounds simple enough, but MACRS complicates the calculations with half-year and mid-quarter conventions. Under the half-year convention, you treat all property acquired during a year as if you acquired it mid year. This

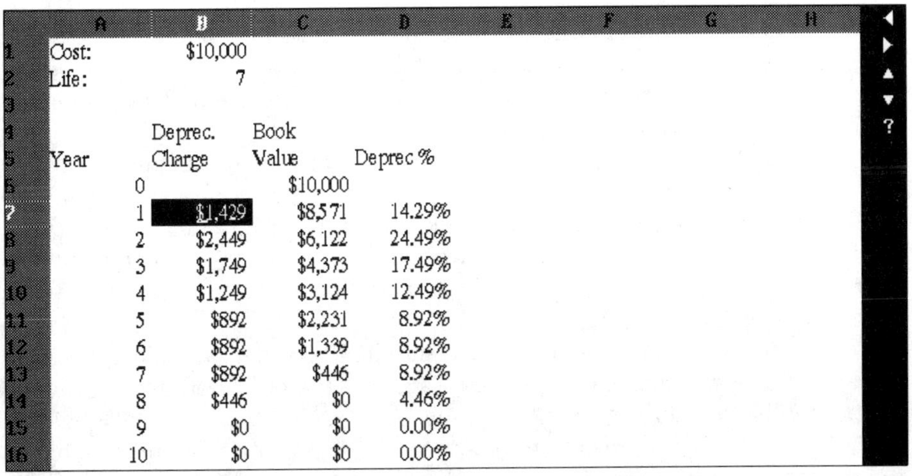

	A	B	C	D
1	Cost:	$10,000		
2	Life:	7		
3				
4		Deprec.	Book	
5	Year	Charge	Value	Deprec %
6	0		$10,000	
7	1	$1,429	$8,571	14.29%
8	2	$2,449	$6,122	24.49%
9	3	$1,749	$4,373	17.49%
10	4	$1,249	$3,124	12.49%
11	5	$892	$2,231	8.92%
12	6	$892	$1,339	8.92%
13	7	$892	$446	8.92%
14	8	$446	$0	4.46%
15	9	$0	$0	0.00%
16	10	$0	$0	0.00%

FIGURE 19.25. It is complex, but you can set up a worksheet to calculate tax depreciation using the MACRS mid-year convention.

mid-year convention applies only if the depreciable assets placed in service in the last three months of the taxable year comprise 40% or less of the total assets you acquired that year. Otherwise, you must depreciate all assets individually under the more complex mid-quarter rule.

Practice with MACRS

Figure 19.25 shows a worksheet that calculates depreciation under the mid-year rule. To see it in action, start in a blank worksheet, and enter the labels shown in range A1..D5. Also, enter the numbers shown in column A.

Assign the General format to cell B2, and assign the Percent format with two decimal places to cell D7. Then enter formulas in the cells indicated:

```
C6:   +B1
B7:   @DDB(B1,0,B2,1)*0.5
C7:   +C6–B7
D7:   +B7/$B$1
B8:   @IF(A8>$B$2,C7,@IF(2/$B$2*C7>C7/($B$2–A8+1.5),2/$B$2*C7,
      C7/($B$2–A8+1.5)))
```

Copy range C7..D7 to range C8..C16. Copy cell B8 to range C8..C16.

To calculate the depreciation on any 3-, 5-, or 7-year asset, simply enter the cost in B1 and the IRS-defined life in cell B2. The formulas calculate the depreciation schedule.

As you can see, the formulas to determine the depreciation amount under the mid-year convention are complex. While it is possible to set up a similar worksheet for assets using the mid-quarter convention, the added complexity of the required formulas may make the effort required outweigh the benefit derived. A better approach is to enter the IRS tables into a worksheet and then use a formula to look up the appropriate depreciation rate for your situation.

If you learn how to get 1-2-3 to look up a rate in a table, you will have no trouble managing depreciation worksheets, no matter how Congress changes the rules. Your first step is to decide how to set the tax table up in the worksheet.

Under the mid-quarter convention, the IRS provides a table for assets placed in service during each quarter. Each asset is classified not only by its life but by the quarter it goes into service.

To figure out the depreciation for any asset, you must know three things—the asset's property class (3-year, 5-year, etc.), the quarter the asset went into service, and the current year. Figures 19.26 and 19.27 show how to get these parameters into a single (two-dimensional) table.

A	B	C	D	E	F	G	H
Year	Q1–3yr	Q1–5yr	Q1–7yr	Q2–3yr	Q2–5yr	Q2–7yr	Q3–3yr
1	58.33%	35.00%	25.00%	41.67%	25.00%	17.85%	25.00%
2	27.78%	26.00%	21.43%	38.89%	30.00%	23.47%	50.00%
3	12.35%	15.60%	15.31%	14.14%	18.00%	16.76%	16.67%
4	1.54%	11.01%	10.93%	5.30%	11.37%	11.97%	
5		11.01%	8.75%		11.37%	8.87%	
6		1.38%	8.74%		4.26%	8.87%	
7			8.75%			8.87%	
8			1.09%			3.33%	

FIGURE 19.26. For the MACRS mid-quarter convention, it is easier to set up a tax table than to create a mathematical formula. In this table, each column shows the depreciation rates for 3-, 5-, and 7-year properties purchased in each quarter.

I	J	K	L	M	N	O	P
Q3–5yr	Q3–7yr	Q4–3yr	Q4–5yr	Q4–7yr			
15.00%	10.71%	8.33%	5.00%	3.57%			
34.00%	25.51%	61.11%	38.00%	27.55%			
20.40%	18.22%	20.37%	22.80%	19.68%			
12.24%	13.02%	10.19%	13.68%	14.06%			
11.30%	9.30%		10.94%	10.04%			
7.06%	88.50%		9.58%	8.73%			
	88.60%			8.73%			
	5.53%						

FIGURE 19.27. This is the remainder of the MACRS tax table started in Figure 19.26.

Here, row A identifies the four quarters for 3-, 5-, and 7-year class properties. To set this table up, start in a blank worksheet and issue the Worksheet Global Format command. Set the global format to Percent with two decimal places. Use the Range Format General command to format range A2..A9. Then enter labels and values as shown. Remember that percents must be entered as 1/100th of the value displayed. To enter a percent, enter the decimal equivalent of the percentage. For example, .5 equals 50%. Alternatively, enter the percentage amount followed by a percent sign. For example, 1-2-3 converts the entry 50% to the value .5.

Since you have to depreciate assets individually under the mid-quarter convention, you might want to create a table that calculates depreciation for the current year only. Figure 19.28 shows such a table.

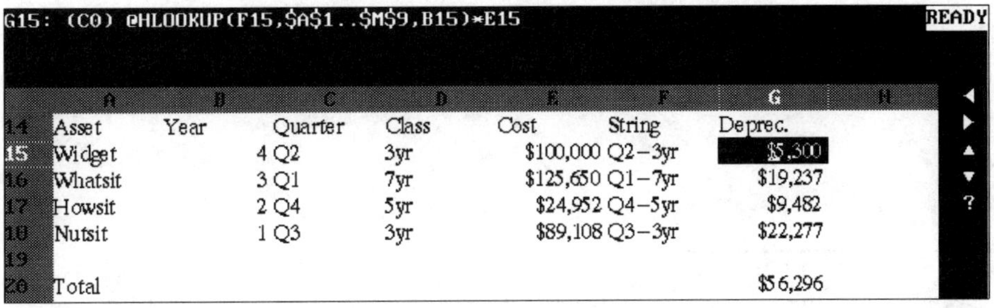

G15: (C0) @HLOOKUP(F15,$A$1..$M$9,B15)*E15 READY

	A	B	C	D	E	F	G	H
14	Asset	Year	Quarter	Class	Cost	String	Deprec.	
15	Widget	4	Q2	3yr	$100,000	Q2–3yr	$5,300	
16	Whatsit	3	Q1	7yr	$125,650	Q1–7yr	$19,237	
17	Howsit	2	Q4	5yr	$24,952	Q4–5yr	$9,482	
18	Nutsit	1	Q3	3yr	$89,108	Q3–3yr	$22,277	
19								
20	Total						$56,296	

FIGURE 19.28. After you enter the tax table, the @HLOOKUP function makes it easy to calculate the depreciation expense for your assets.

This table resides in the same sheet as the IRS's depreciation just entered. To incorporate this new table, format range B15..B18 as General and range E15..G20 as Currency with no decimal places. Enter labels and values as shown. Preface the labels in range D15..D18 with apostrophes. Enter the following formulas in the cells indicated:

F15: +C15&"–"&D15
G15: @HLOOKUP(F15,$A$1..$M$9,B15)*E15

Copy the formulas from range F15..G15 to range F16..F18. Enter the formula *@SUM(G15..G18)* into cell G20.

The formula in cell F15 returns a string that identifies the quarter purchased and the year-class for an asset named in cell A15. The formula in cell G15 uses this string to look up the appropriate percentage by which to multiply the asset's cost. The formula in cell G15 uses an @HLOOKUP function.

The @HLOOKUP function has the syntax @HLOOKUP(*item,range,row offset*). Here, the string formulas in column F supply the *item* argument. The @HLOOKUP formula searches for a match in the first row of the table you created in range A1..M9. When it finds that match, it returns the value that is as many rows down as the value in the third argument, *row number*. Chapter 18 looks more closely at @functions that look up items in tables.

Having completed this section you should:

- *Understand the options 1-2-3 offers for analyzing investments*
- *Know how to calculate the periodic interest and principal payments on a loan*
- *Have a sense of how businesses depreciate assets*
- *Be able to apply several depreciation methods*
- *Be able to talk intelligently about investment and depreciation with an accountant or financial consultant*

Section 3 Data Analysis and Statistics

Analysis. That's what the spreadsheet is about. Do your data follow a trend? Can you project next year's earnings? Is there a relationship between the mix of chemicals and the hardness of the finished material? All the labels, display formats, and calculations in the world are meaningless without some type of analysis.

So far, we have explored the tools that you use as you lay out and customize worksheets. We have also worked with formulas—the mechanisms by which you define relationships among the pieces of data in a sheet. This section goes deeper. In it we explore 1-2-3's functionality as a database management tool. We see how to manipulate lists of information, and we bring 1-2-3's extensive analytical capabilities to bear on large amounts of data.

As a database manager, 1-2-3 lets you store thousands of entries in the sheet in such a way that you can alphabetize the entries and arrange them in ascending or descending numerical order. You can easily locate any piece of information stored in a database, no matter how large the database. And your searches can return information that fits complex profiles such as "What is the average of sales in the fourth quarter for reps in the Eastern Division who have been with the company for five years or longer?"

Lotus 1-2-3 helps you to perform statistical analyses of your data. On the low end, you can calculate simple averages and standard deviations. On the high end, you can perform regression analyses that reveal whether and how much certain variables influence your business. In either case, the tools that 1-2-3 provides for the task at hand make such analyses accessible even to people who have little background in statistics.

Even if you have no interest in database management or statistical analysis, don't pass up this section of the book. You might discover, as your understanding of these tools increases, that there are many ways you can apply them to your own business needs. Your skill with 1-2-3 should be pretty well developed by this point, so expect things to move along more quickly in this section.

20

Introduction to 1-2-3 Databases

A database is a collection of information. Usually, the information in a database has a special format that makes it easy to review. For example, consider the entries in a telephone book or a newspaper listing of stock prices. You can find entries in either of these databases quite easily. That is one of the great powers of a computer-based database: it lets you sort through enormous amounts of data and find specific items almost effortlessly. You might use a database to store customer names and addresses, employment records, inventory lists, listings of experimental results, sales data, delivery records, and so on. There is really no limit to the possibilities.

A database in 1-2-3 is little different from any other database. The structure of the spreadsheet helps to define the arrangement of information in the database. However, in 1-2-3, the layout of the information isn't the only aspect of a database that makes the information it contains accessible. 1-2-3 has many commands and @functions that are designed specifically for work with databases. 1-2-3's database facility gives you a powerful tool with which to manage data storage.

If you want to maintain a customer tracking list that requires hundreds of thousands of entries, then 1-2-3 is not a suitable choice. For that kind of job, you need a software package specifically designed to handle very large data files. On the other hand, you may have just a few hundred or even a couple thousand entries. If you need to find information quickly and easily, or you are more interested in analyzing data than in creating complex reports from a variety of data sources, then 1-2-3 is well suited to your needs.

In this chapter you will learn how to:

- *Set up a database in 1-2-3*
- *Arrange data alphabetically or numerically*
- *Find information in a database*
- *Extract information from a database*
- *Delete records from a database*
- *Use the QUERY key (F7) for fast data queries*
- *Import data from other programs*
- *Parse text files*

Databasics: Coming to Terms with Database Terms

Before learning the tools and techniques for working in a database, you should know what elements make up a database in 1-2-3.

Figure 20.1 shows a typical worksheet database. The database itself consists of the entries in range A4..E11. It is simply a table that lists employees' numbers, their first and last names, their dates of hire, and their current hourly wages.

	A	B	C	D	E	F	G
1							
2							
3							
4	Emp. #	Fname	Lname	Hired	Wage		
5	154	Pedro	Jones	18-Mar-80	$12.59		
6	175	Auo	Reed	09-Dec-80	$10.88		
7	295	Reisha	Cosmo	02-Oct-81	$9.98		
8	446	Raul	Jones	25-Jun-82	$9.85		
9	547	Grumph	Pontiac	22-Apr-83	$9.51		
10	585	Sallis	Aphrus	19-Jun-89	$6.86		
11	734	Gertrude	Woko	20-Jan-90	$5.70		

FIGURE 20.1. A simple 1-2-3 database that stores employee information. 1-2-3's database tools let you sort, analyze, and manipulate such databases in a variety of ways.

The information about each employee resides in a single row called a *record*. As you can see, each record stores the employee information in the same way. Column A holds the employee number, column B holds the employee's first name, and so on.

Each column in a 1-2-3 database is called a *field*, and the first row of a database contains the *field names*. Here, the labels *Emp. #, Fname, Lname, Hired,* and *Wage* in row 4 are field names.

Create this sample database; we will use it to explore the data-handling features of 1-2-3. Start in a blank worksheet and enter labels as shown in Figure 20.1. Use the Range Name Create command to assign the name *database* to range A4..E11. Then save the file as DATABASE.WK1.

Sorting Data

Sorting is to databases what summing is to spreadsheets. Arranging the records in your database in some logical order is one of 1-2-3's most useful capabilities. Right now, the records are sorted according to employee number.

That also happens to be in ascending order of date of hire—either key will help you to locate records. However, it might be even more useful to alphabetize the list of employees by name. With such a small database, it would be easy enough to use the Move command and rearrange the records. But what if this table contained hundreds of employee records?

Sort Some Database Records

To sort a database in 1-2-3, you use the Data Sort command. See how that works by selecting Data Sort. 1-2-3 displays the sort settings dialog box as shown in Figure 20.2. You must identify to 1-2-3 which data you wish to sort and which field should determine the order of the database records.

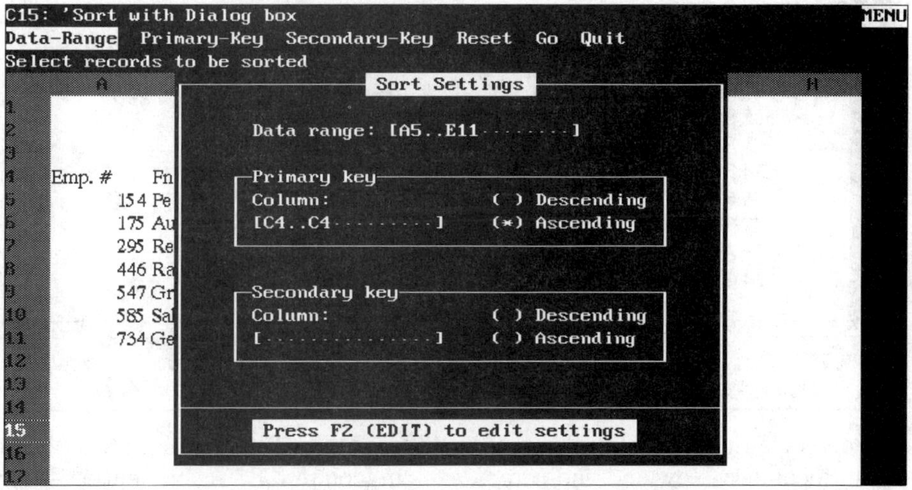

FIGURE 20.2. At first glance, the Data Sort menu and dialog box can be intimidating. But just take one step at a time, and you will find that sorting data in 1-2-3 is very easy.

Select Data-Range, and indicate range A5..E11. Setting up the data range correctly is crucial. Note that the range does not include the field names in row 4. Also note that the range includes all the columns of the database. This is very important. If you were to sort without including all the columns, you would corrupt the database; entries in the excluded columns would no longer coincide with entries in the sorted columns.

Now that 1-2-3 knows the range you want to sort, you must tell it *how* to sort that data. You do this by specifying one or two *key* fields.

Say you want to sort these employee records by last name. To do that, select Primary-Key and indicate cell C4. Actually, you can select any cell in column C to identify the last name (Lname) field; the row number doesn't matter.

Lotus 1-2-3 asks how you want to arrange the database. Enter *A* to specify ascending order. That tells 1-2-3 to sort the records according to last name, alphabetically from A to Z. Selecting descending order would sort from Z to A.

Now select Go. 1-2-3 arranges the database as shown in figure 20.3. Do you see a problem? Raul and Pedro Jones are in the wrong order. That is because 1-2-3 based the sort on last names only. Raul and Pedro have the same last name, so 1-2-3 treated the two records as equivalent and "guessed" where they should fall in the sort order.

	A	B	C	D	E	F	G
1	Emp. #	Fname	Lname	Hired	Wage		
2							
3							
4	Emp. #	Fname	Lname	Hired	Wage		
5	585	Sallis	Aphrus	06/19/89	$6.86		
6	295	Reisha	Cosmo	10/02/81	$9.98		
7	154	Pedro	Jones	03/18/80	$12.59		
8	446	Raul	Jones	06/25/82	$9.85		
9	547	Grumph	Pontiac	04/22/83	$9.51		
10	175	Auo	Reed	12/09/80	$10.88		
11	734	Gertrude	Woko	01/20/90	$5.70		
12							

FIGURE 20.3. The Data Sort command easily alphabetized this database. But sorting by last name left Pedro and Raul Jones in the wrong places. To sort by first and last name you must specify both a primary and a secondary key.

You solve this kind of problem by specifying a *secondary key*. Select Data Sort Secondary-Key and indicate a cell in column B. Again, enter *A* for ascending, and then select Go.

This time Pedro and Raul are both in the right places. Setting a secondary sort key tells 1-2-3 how to sort records when entries in the primary key field match.

Find Records

Lotus 1-2-3 sorts a small database like the one in our example very quickly. Of course, a database containing 2,000 records takes somewhat longer to sort. If you just want to find a particular record, then sorting the whole database to help with your search is impractical.

Fortunately, 1-2-3 provides another way to look for records in a database. You can simply ask to see a record that meets a specific criterion. For example, you might ask to see any record that contains the name Reed in the Lname field or all records in which the Wage field entry is greater than $9. To do this, you must first set up a *Criteria range* in your worksheet. A Criteria range consists of a row containing some or all of the field names used in your database. It also contains at least one row below those field names in which you can enter the criterion or criteria that identify the records you want to find.

This may sound complicated, but it is not that hard once you get the hang of it. Figure 20.4 shows the employee database with a Criteria range added. The most important thing to remember is that the field names in the Criteria range must exactly match the field names in the database. If the field names in the ranges don't match, 1-2-3 won't know which database fields to search while looking for records that match the established criteria. To avoid making small mistakes, your best bet is simply to copy the database field names into the Criteria range. In the following exercise you build a Criteria range and use it to locate records in the small database you have already created.

	A	B	C	D	E	F	G
1	Emp. #	Fname	Lname	Hired	Wage		
2							
3							
4	Emp. #	Fname	Lname	Hired	Wage		
5	585	Sallis	Aphrus	06/19/89	$6.86		
6	295	Reisha	Cosmo	10/02/81	$9.98		
7	154	Pedro	Jones	03/18/80	$12.59		
8	446	Raul	Jones	06/25/82	$9.85		
9	547	Grumph	Pontiac	04/22/83	$9.51		
10	175	Auo	Reed	12/09/80	$10.88		
11	734	Gertrude	Woko	01/20/90	$5.70		
12							

FIGURE 20.4. To set up a Criteria range in row 1, copy the field names from row 4. Next assign the name *crit* to range A1..E2. Finally, select Data Query Criteria and enter *crit.*

A First Database Query

Once you have created a database, you must execute 4 steps to perform a simple database find operation—the simplest of the queries:

1. Establish a Criteria range
2. Enter a criterion

3. Set the database Input and Criteria ranges on the Data Query menus
4. Select Find from the Data Query menu

The order of these events isn't so important as long as you complete steps 1 through 3 before you do step 4. Proceed as follows: Use the Copy command to copy range A4..E4 to cell A1. Then use the Range Name Create command to assign the name *crit* to range A1..E2. This isn't necessary, but using range names will clarify your activity with the database commands.

Now select Data Query to bring up the Query menu. Before you can use the Find command, you must tell 1-2-3 where the database is in the worksheet. You also must specify the location of the Criteria range. The database, including the field names, is called the Input range. Select Input, and enter *database* to establish the named range as the database. Then select Criteria and enter *crit*.

You are almost ready to search for a record. There is one last thing: you must specify a criterion for the database search. The criterion is an entry that uniquely identifies the database record or records that you want to find. You must enter the criterion in a cell of the Criteria range, so select Quit to get back to Ready mode. Then move the cell pointer to cell A2, and enter the value 175. This tells 1-2-3 to locate records with an employee number of 175.

Select Data Query Find. 1-2-3 highlights the record for Auo Reed.

Note that you can't move the highlight up or down by pressing an arrow key. That is because the spreadsheet is now in Find mode, as the mode indicator in the top-right corner of the display shows. If there were more records that matched the criterion, you could move the highlight down to the next matching record. To see how that works, get out of Find mode and change the criterion. Exit Find mode by pressing Return. Then select Quit.

Erase cell A2 and enter *Jones* in cell C2. This tells 1-2-3 to search for all records that contain the label *Jones* in the Lname field. Notice how easy it is to query the database once you have established the Input and Criteria range settings. You need only alter the criteria to select a completely different set of records.

Select Data Query Find. 1-2-3 highlights the Pedro Jones record as shown in Figure 20.5. This time you can move the highlight, because another record matches the criterion. Press DownArrow, and 1-2-3 highlights Raul Jones's record. The Find command lets you quickly review all the records in a database that match the specified criterion.

Locating records isn't the only thing you can do with the Find command. Suppose Raul Jones just got a 5% raise. You can use the Find command to

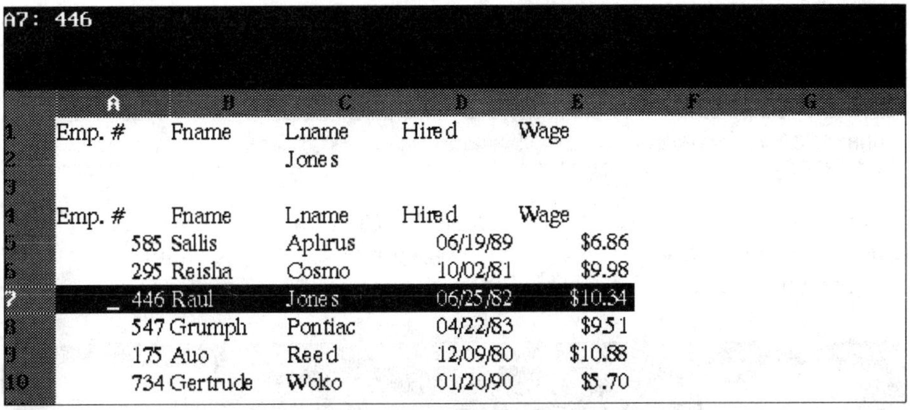

FIGURE 20.5. The Data Query Find command locates records in a database quickly and easily.

locate Raul's record, and then you can edit that record. To see how, press the RightArrow key four times. Press the EDIT key (F2), type **1.05*, press the CALC key (F9), press the Backspace key twice, and then press Enter.

Exit Find mode by pressing Return and then selecting Quit. Then save the worksheet.

Extract Records

Though editing data in Find mode is handy, it is often not enough. Suppose you need to analyze a subset of database records using all the analytical tools available in 1-2-3. You might, for example, want to graph the salaries of all employees hired before 1982.

There are a couple of ways to do such analyses. One method is to use the Data Query Extract command to copy all records that match a criterion from the database to an output range. Then you can examine, manipulate, and analyze the subset of records without disturbing the main database.

An Extraction Exercise

To extract records, you must first establish an output range in much the way that you create a Criteria range. First copy the labels from range A1..E1 to cell I1 in the DATABASE worksheet, as shown in Figure 20.6. Use the Range Name Create command to assign the name *out* to range I1..M1.

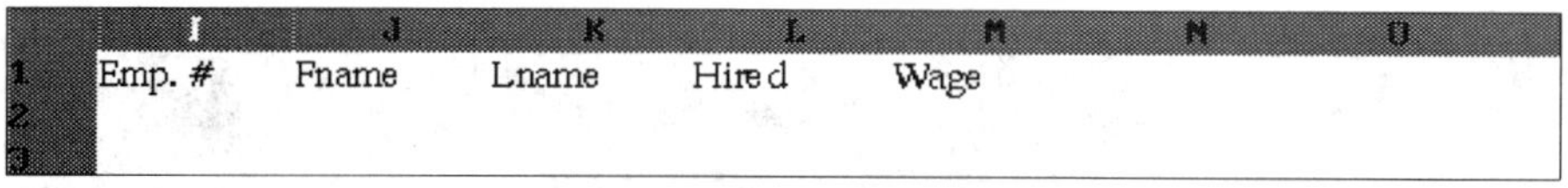

FIGURE 20.6. Copy the field names from the Criteria range to create an Extract range.

Leave the label *Jones* in cell C2 of the Criteria range. Now select Data Query Output, and enter *out*. Your Data Query dialog box should match the one shown in Figure 20.7. Select Extract.

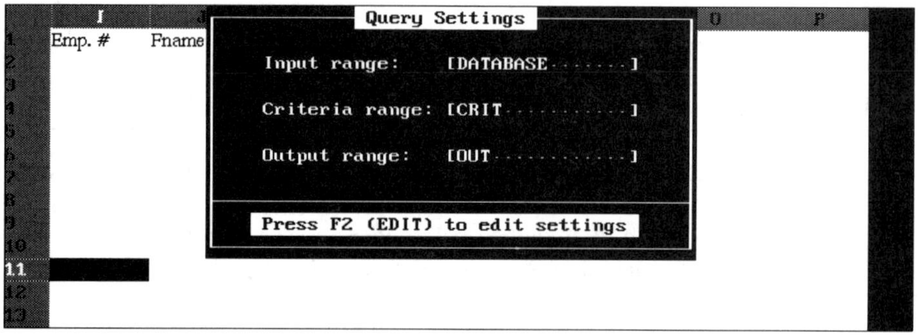

FIGURE 20.7. Before you can extract records from the database, you must specify all three Query Ranges—Input, Criteria, and Output.

When you select Quit, you see that 1-2-3 has copied Pedro and Raul's records to the rows beneath the Extract range. 1-2-3 extracted all the records that had *Jones* as a last name. Note that these are copies of the records in the database, not the records themselves. You can change or even erase the records in the Extract range without affecting the records in the database.

If you were to change the criteria and then reissue the Data Query Extract command, 1-2-3 would write over the previously extracted records. To see how this works, narrow the criteria by entering *12.59* in cell E2, but leave the label *Jones* in cell C2.

Select Data Query Extract Quit. Now look at the entries beneath the Extract range. 1-2-3 erased the old extract records and copied the new one in their stead. This time, only one record matched the criteria—Pedro Jones's record.

Data Query Extract Kills

When you set a one-row Output range as we did in the accompanying exercise, be sure there is nothing of value in the worksheet below that output range. 1-2-3 automatically erases every cell in the output columns beneath a one-row Output range whenever you issue the Query Extract command—no matter how many matching records there are in the database.

To limit the scope of this erasure, use multi-row Output ranges for extract operations. Anticipate the largest number of records you will extract at one time, and include as many rows in the Output range. For example, if you thought you might extract three records from the database in our example, you would set range I1..M4 as the Output range. Before copying selected records from the database in response to an Extract command, 1-2-3 erases only cells within the Output range beneath the field names.

Extract Selected Fields

The Data Query Extract command needn't pull all the information in each matching record form the database. Why extract all the information about a customer from a mailing list database when you are looking only for the customer's phone number? The field headers you use in the Output range actually determine what is extracted and what isn't.

So, for example, if you want only an employee's number and hire date to appear in the Output range, use only the field names *Emp. #* and *Hired* as headers in that range. Also, be sure that the dimensions of the Output range coincide with the number of field names you use.

Try another data extract to confirm this. Copy the field name from cell I1 to cell O1, and copy a second field name from L1 to P1. Select Data Query Output, and indicate range O1..P1 as the new Output range. Finally, select Extract and Quit. 1-2-3 copies entries from only the employee number and the date hired fields of database.

Select Data Query Output, and re-enter *out* as the Output range. Then return to Ready mode and save the DATABASE file.

A Note on Matching Criteria

We go more into database matching criteria in greater detail in Chapter 21. In the meantime, it is important that you understand how a criterion match works.

When you issue a Database Query (Find, Extract, or Delete), 1-2-3 compares the entries in the Criteria range with the first record in the database. If the entries match, the first record is *found*. If the entries don't match, the record is *ignored*. 1-2-3 then compares the Criteria range entries with the second database record, with the third, and so on, marking each as found or ignored, as appropriate.

In making the record comparisons, 1-2-3 assumes a blank cell in the criterion to mean, "match any entry." That is why you don't need an entry in every criterion cell to perform a database search. There is a catch, however. If you leave all the criterion cells blank, the criterion matches all database records. With no entries beneath the field names in a Criteria range, a Query Extract copies all the database records, and a Query Delete erases all of them.

Delete Records

Deleting records is as easy as extracting them. You just use the Data Query Delete command to remove records that match the established criteria. Use the Delete command with caution or you might trash records you would rather preserve. If, for example, you use the Delete command when the second row of the Criteria range is blank, you will erase the entire database. So, it is a good idea to extract records before deleting them. That way you can look them over and make sure they are the ones you want to eliminate.

Delete Some Records for Practice

To see how the Data Query Delete command works, continue using the DATABASE worksheet. Leave the criteria as they were with *Jones* in cell C2 and *12.59* in cell E2. These criteria identify Pedro Jones.

Select Data Query Delete. 1-2-3 prompts you to confirm that you really want to delete the matching records. Select Delete, and 1-2-3 removes Pedro Jones from the employee database.

Rapid-Fire Queries

Once you get used to 1-2-3's Data Query commands, there is almost no end to the ways you can look at data. But going back and forth between changing criteria and running through the Data Query menus (or dialog box) can get tedious. Fortunately, 1-2-3 provides a handy short-cut in the QUERY key (F7). The QUERY key repeats the last Data Query command you issued.

Try the QUERY Key (F7)

To see how the QUERY key works, create a worksheet of the final grades for a college class, as shown in Figure 20.8.

	A	B	C	D	E	F	G	H
1	Major	Numeric				Name	Major	Letter
2								
3								
4								
5	Name	Major	Letter	Numeric				
6	Allen	PYS	B+	3.33				
7	Blake	PHI	A	4.00				
8	Brown	CS	C–	1.67				
9	Casner	PHI	D+	1.33				
10	De Cocker	CS	A	4.00				
11	Kirby	CS	B	3.00				
12	Oakley	BUS	C–	1.67				
13	Peterson	MUS	B–	2.67				
14	Scott	PHI	C–	1.67				
15	Smith	MUS	C+	2.33				
16	Su	CS	B–	2.67				
17	Warner	PHI	C	2.00				
18	Wolosen	CS	A	4.00				
19	Yeats	PYS	B+	3.33				

FIGURE 20.8. 1-2-3 lets you look at a database of final grades for a college class in a variety of ways.

After entering the labels and values, use the Range Name create command to assign range names as follows:

Name	**Range**
crit	A1..B3
input	A5..D19
output	F1..H1

Before you can use the QUERY key for rapid-fire queries, you must use the Data Query commands to establish the requisite settings. Select Data Query to bring up the Query menu. Establish the Input, Criteria, and Output ranges as shown in Figure 20.9. Finally, select Extract to specify a query action for the QUERY key to repeat.

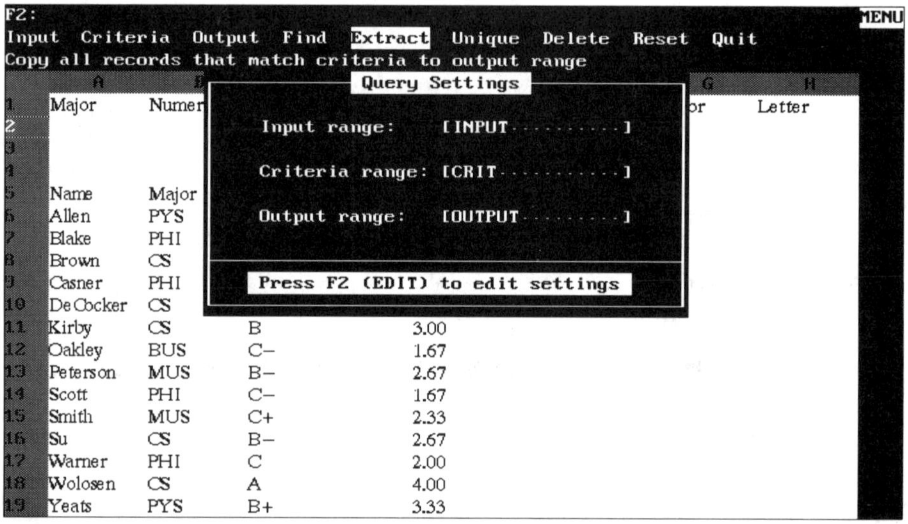

FIGURE 20.9. Use the Data Query menu to prepare for working with the QUERY key (F7). Perform the query you wish to repeat once, and then return to Ready mode. After that, you can repeat the query operation simply by pressing the QUERY key.

Now you can quickly perform a series of extracts without ever again accessing the Query menus. Say you want to know which students had numeric grades higher than 3. Enter *'>3* under the *numeric* field name in the Criteria range, and press QUERY. 1-2-3 does a fast extract, as shown in Figure 20.10.

Experiment with changing criteria and pressing the QUERY key. Almost as quickly as you can enter labels in the Criteria range, you can extract matching records to the Output range. If you use the Data Query Find command, the QUERY key lets you search for records in the database as quickly as you can create criteria.

Exercise caution when using the QUERY key to delete records. 1-2-3 does prompt you to confirm your intent before deleting matching records, but, there is no way to preview the records that will be deleted without going back into the Data Query menus.

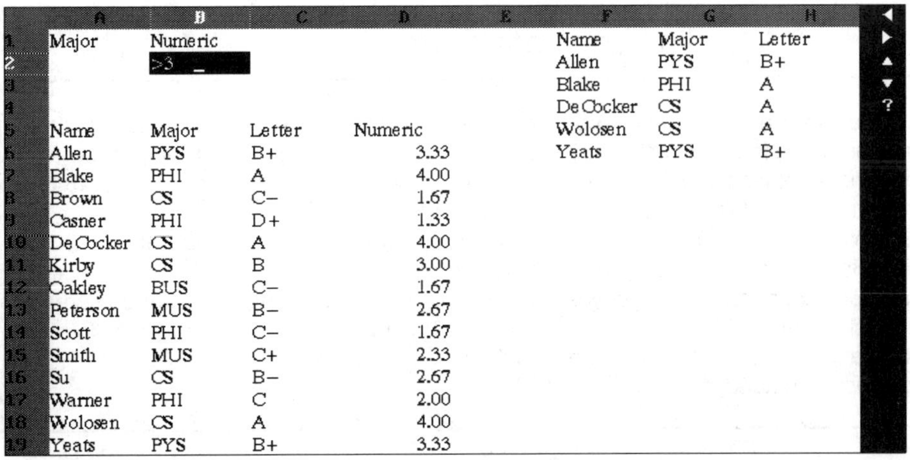

	A	B	C	D	E	F	G	H
1	Major	Numeric				Name	Major	Letter
2		>3				Allen	PYS	B+
3						Blake	PHI	A
4						De Cocker	CS	A
5	Name	Major	Letter	Numeric		Wolosen	CS	A
6	Allen	PYS	B+	3.33		Yeats	PYS	B+
7	Blake	PHI	A	4.00				
8	Brown	CS	C–	1.67				
9	Casner	PHI	D+	1.33				
10	De Cocker	CS	A	4.00				
11	Kirby	CS	B	3.00				
12	Oakley	BUS	C–	1.67				
13	Peterson	MUS	B–	2.67				
14	Scott	PHI	C–	1.67				
15	Smith	MUS	C+	2.33				
16	Su	CS	B–	2.67				
17	Warner	PHI	C	2.00				
18	Wolosen	CS	A	4.00				
19	Yeats	PYS	B+	3.33				

FIGURE 20.10. Entering criteria and pressing the QUERY key yields an instantaneous extract of matching records. You can repeat the Query Find and Query Delete commands just as easily.

Managing Data from Mainframes and Other Programs

Once you master the basics of 1-2-3, you may want to use it to work with data from other programs or data that you download from your company's mainframe or minicomputer. This is usually fairly easy. For example, you can use 1-2-3's translate utility to translate data from 1-2-3 Releases 1A, 2, 2.01 and 2.2; dBase II and III; DIF files; Enable 2.0; Multiplan (SYLK); SuperCalc 4; Symphony Releases 1.0 to 2.0; or VisiCalc. That might be all the translating power you need. But often, data downloaded from mainframes and other programs is in simple text (ASCII) files.

To 1-2-3, a text file is simply a list of labels, though those labels might appear as sequences of numbers interspersed with spaces so that they appear to be columns of data. 1-2-3 can't simply retrieve data from a text file, but bringing such data into the sheet is not hard to do.

To analyze the data in a text file, you first import the file into 1-2-3. Then, depending on the layout of that file, you must separate the text into discrete cells. Sometimes this is easy to do; sometimes it is very difficult. If the text file consists of columns of numbers, the job is fairly elementary.

To Translate Files

Lotus 1-2-3 comes with a stand-alone program that translates files from Release 2.3 spreadsheet file format to other popular formats and from other formats into the Release 2.3 format. The file formats that the translate utility handles include dBase II and III, DIF files, Enable, Multiplan, and Supercalc 4 spreadsheets, and even Visicalc files.

Unless you indicate otherwise, the translate program is automatically placed on your hard disk when you install 1-2-3. To find out whether the program is there, quit 1-2-3 and make the 1-2-3 program directory current in DOS. Enter the command TRANS.

If DOS reports File not found, rerun 1-2-3's install program to make the translate facility available. Otherwise, follow the on-screen prompts to translate files from one format to another.

Import an ASCII File

To learn how to handle a text file, first create one. To do that, enter labels and values in a blank worksheet as shown in Figure 20.11.

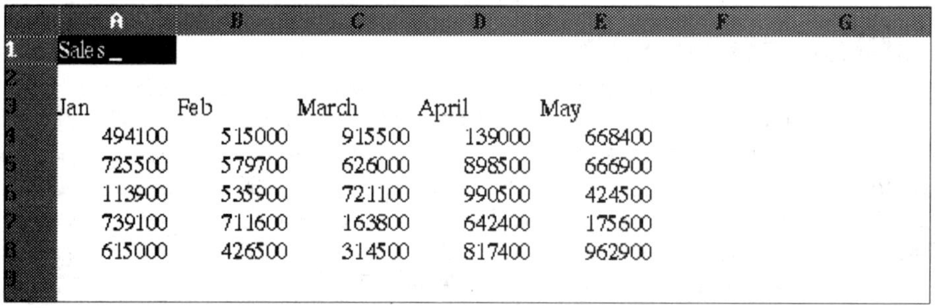

FIGURE 20.11. Create this simple worksheet. Then use the Print File command to save this data as a text file.

Use the worksheet data to create a text file. Select Print File, and enter *temp.prn*. Select Range from the print menu, and indicate range A1..E8. Select Options Margins None Quit Go, and finally select Quit. 1-2-3 makes an image of the file on disk as it would print the image on paper.

To examine the results of your handiwork, select Worksheet Erase Yes Yes. Then, without moving the cell pointer (keep it at A1), select File Import Text and indicate TEMP.PRN as the file to import.

Delimited ASCII Files

An ASCII file is simply a listing of long labels on disk. 1-2-3 can read such a file into the sheet when you issue the File Import Text command. A delimited file is a bit more complex than a straight ASCII file.

A delimited file contains commas that separate one discrete bit of data from the next. A single line of such a file might read 8,108,21,7. Delimited strings must be literal (enclosed in quotes), so a single line that contains text and numbers might read:

"Doug",77,"Knives",2100,10

1-2-3's File Import Numbers command reads each datum from a delimited file into its own cell.

1-2-3 brings in the print file, TEMP.PRN, as a set of seven long labels. Move the cell pointer down to cell A4 to see that the appearance of distinct columns of numbers is deceptive. A4 contains all the numbers in row 4 as a single long label. This is the nature of an ASCII file—to 1-2-3 it appears to be a series of long labels.

Now move the cell pointer back to A1 by pressing the Home key. Select File Import Numbers, and indicate TEMP.PRN. Though the spreadsheet appears unchanged, new data have replaced the labels starting in row 4. Move the cell pointer down to cell A4.

You can see that the numbers are now in distinct cells and only the label in cell A3 needs separation. That is because the File Import Numbers command assumes that the file you are importing is a *delimited* file. The TEMP.PRN file, strictly speaking, is not a delimited file. But since the numbers are in columns separated by spaces, 1-2-3 treats it as if it were.

Even using the File Import Numbers command, you are stuck with the column labels all strung together as a long label in cell A3. Since the File Import Numbers command ignores labels unless they are delimited with quotation marks, the long label from the previous File Import Labels command is still there. In this case, it is easy enough just to re-enter those labels. But sometimes you are left with hundreds of long labels that you have to separate into columns. In such cases, the Data Parse command can often do the job.

Parse Some Data

To see how Data Parse works, use it to separate the long label in row 3. Move the cell pointer to A3, and select Data Parse. Select Format-Line Create Input-Column, and indicate range A3..A4. Then select Output-Range, and indicate A4. Finally, select Go.

Where Do ASCII Files Come From?

Any serious program that produces text can produce ASCII files. Word processors, database managers, and spreadsheets fall into this category with few exceptions. Because ASCII files are relatively simple and universal, they make for easy exchange of information between programs.

You might also encounter ASCII files if your company has a mainframe or a minicomputer. Those machines generally let you download data to your own computer in ASCII format.

Finally, on-line information services most often supply data in ASCII format. You might, for example, download a daily or weekly stock quotation as a collection of long labels. Applying 1-2-3's Data Parse command can quickly convert such data into numbers that you can manipulate in the spreadsheet.

Move the cell pointer to cell A4, and you will see that the Data Parse command has separated the long label. Now each column identifier is a short label in the appropriate column.

You have probably also noticed the odd line of characters in row 3. That is called a *format line*. 1-2-3 separates long labels according to the format line you create with the Format-Line Create command. The format line starts with a split-vertical-bar label prefix followed by symbols that show the expected structure of the long labels you want to split up. Letters show the type of data the Parse command expects to find. The other symbols simply indicate the width that each block of data encompasses. Here, *L>>****** tells the Parse command to treat the characters in the first portion of the long labels as labels and to include up to nine characters from each label as part of the first column. There is no functional difference between the >s and the *s. The > characters simply show the number of characters that were present in the long label on which the format line is based.

In this example, you are breaking a long label into shorter labels, so all the data-type symbols are Ls. But the Data Parse command recognizes other data types as well. Figure 20.12 shows an example of another format line.

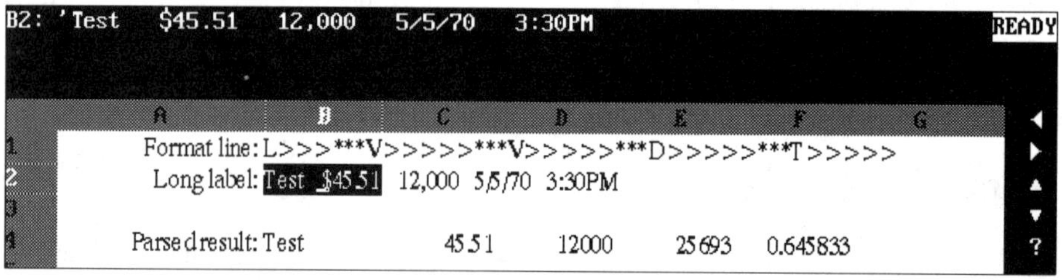

FIGURE 20.12. This illustration shows a format line above a long label in cell B2. The resulting, unformatted, parsed data is in range B4..F4.

Here the format line shows most of the data-type symbols—L for labels, V for values, D for date values, and T for time values. Data Parse also allows the S data-type symbol, which tells 1-2-3's parser to skip that block of characters. You can edit a format line to contain this data type to throw out columns of data you don't want.

There is nothing really tricky about parsing long labels into individual cells. Always start with the Data Parse Format-Line Create command to generate a model format line based on the first long label to parse. Edit the resulting format line if necessary, and then establish the input range to include all the records as well as the format line. Finally, establish an output range to hold the parsed data, and select Go. The whole process becomes easy when you try it a few times on your own data.

Having completed this chapter you should:

- *Know what a database is, and recognize opportunities to organize your information into databases*
- *Understand the terms related to working with databases*
- *Be able to alphabetize lists of information or arrange them in numerical order*
- *Know how to locate specific information stored within a database*
- *Be able to bring data from external programs into the spreadsheet and work with them as a 1-2-3 database*

21

Data Analysis with Statistical @Functions and Creative Criteria

How many employees earn over $50,000 a year, and what is the sum of their salaries? What was the lowest unit sales amount for a selected product? What was the average revenue generated by reps in the quarter? These are typical of the questions you might want to answer with information stored in a database. You answer such questions by applying statistical @functions.

Statistical @functions fall into two categories. The first category includes @functions that evaluate all the values in a range. The @SUM function falls into this group. The other category includes @functions that evaluate a subset of the values in a database based on records that meet specified criteria.

In this chapter you will learn how to:

- *Find the largest value in a range*
- *Find the smallest value in a range*
- *Find the average or mean value of a range*
- *Find the standard deviation of values in a range*
- *Find the variance of values in a range*
- *Determine all the above measures for values in a database in records that match a criterion*
- *Create complex database matching criteria*
- *Use wild card characters in criteria*
- *Use logical operators in criteria*
- *Use formulas as criteria*
- *Match records by searching for strings in a field*

Try Out the Statistical @Functions

To see how these @functions work, start by creating some sample data as shown in Figure 21.1. Set the width of column E to 21 and the width of column F to 11. Use the Worksheet Global Format command to assign the Currency format with 0 decimal places to the entire worksheet. Use the Range Name Create command to assign the name *crit* to range A1..C2. Name range A4..C4, *database*, and name range C5..C14, *column*. Select Range Name Labels Down, and indicate range A4..C4. Then save the file as STATFUNC.WK1 so you can keep it for future reference.

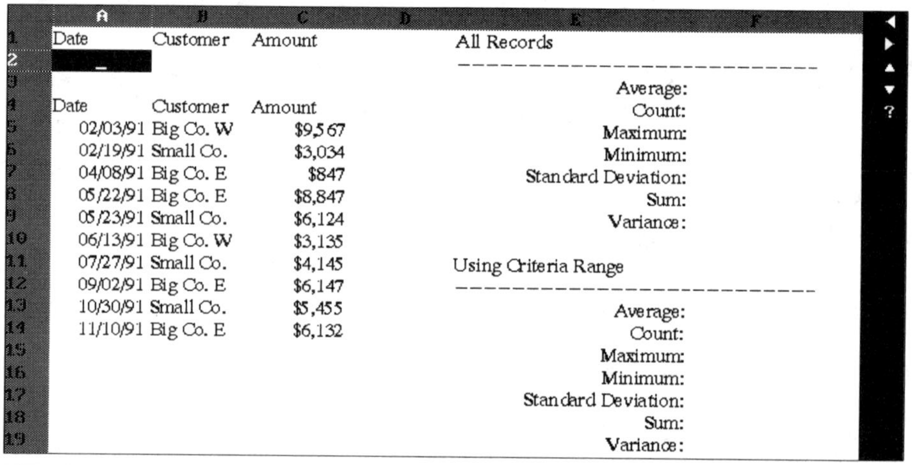

FIGURE 21.1. Create this sample database to test some of 1-2-3's statistical @functions.

Column E contains labels showing the type of information you can glean using 1-2-3's built-in @functions. The labels serve to organize the formulas you will enter according to the two categories of statistical @functions. You have probably already applied at least one of these functions in other exercises. So go ahead and enter *@SUM(column)* into cell F8.

If you feel comfortable with the @SUM function, using the other @functions in the first category is a piece of cake. To calculate the average (mean) purchase amount for entries in the database, enter *@AVG(column)* in cell F3. If you want to know how many non-blank cells there are in *column*, enter *@COUNT(column)* in cell F4. Use the Range Format command to assign the General display format to this cell.

If you want to know the largest and smallest amounts in *column*, enter *@MAX(column)* and *@MIN(column)* into cells F5 and F6 respectively. Determining the standard deviation (s) is just as easy. Enter *@STD(column)* in cell F7. For the variance (s2) enter *@VAR(column)* in cell F9.

As you can see, calculating statistical measures for all the values in a given range is very easy. Doing the same calculations for a subset of records in a database is only a little more difficult.

The database statistical or @D functions all use the same syntax. They each take three arguments—*input, offset*, and *criteria*. So, for example, the @DSUM function is @DSUM(*input, offset, criteria*). The first and last of these arguments should be familiar since they identify the Input and Criteria ranges you have used for the Data Query operations. Here the Input range is *database*, and the Criteria range is *crit*.

The offset argument tells the @function which column you want to evaluate in the database. The offset identifies a column by how many columns it is to the right of the first column in the database. In this case, you are analyzing the data in column C. That column is two columns to the right of the first column in the *database* range. Column A would be offset 0 (0 columns to the right), and column B would be offset 1.

Enter *@DAVG(database,2,crit)* in cell F13. Right now it returns the same value as the @AVG formula in cell F3. Do you know why? If your answer is, "It returns the average of all the values in column C of *database* because there is no criterion in the Criteria range, *crit*," fix yourself an ice cream sundae.

Don't enter a criterion just yet. This way you can check as you enter the rest of the @D functions, that they return the same answers as the corresponding @functions in range F3..F9. Enter the following:

```
F14:   @DCOUNT(database,2,crit)
F15:   @DMAX(database,2,crit)
F16:   @DMIN(database,2,crit)
F17:   @DSTD(database,2,crit)
F18:   @DSUM(database,2,crit)
F19:   @DVAR(database,2,crit)
```

Assign the General format to cell F14.

Now you are ready to experience the convenience of the @D functions. Move the cell pointer to cell B2, and enter *Small Co.* as shown in Figure 21.2. Note that the values returned by the @D functions change. They return results only for records of the Small Company. You can see at a glance that there are four such records in the database, that the average of sales to the Small Company is $4,690, that total sales were $18,758, and so on.

The @D functions intimidate many 1-2-3 users, but as you can see, they are really not difficult to use. You have to understand how to set up a Criteria

	A	B	C	D	E	F
1	Date	Customer	Amount		All Records	
2		Small Co.			----------------------------	
3					Average:	$5,343
4	Date	Customer	Amount		Count:	10
5	02/03/91	Big Co. W	$9,567		Maximum:	$9,567
6	02/19/91	Small Co.	$3,034		Minimum:	$847
7	04/08/91	Big Co. E	$847		Standard Deviation:	$2,527
8	05/22/91	Big Co. E	$8,847		Sum:	$53,433
9	05/23/91	Small Co.	$6,124		Variance:	$6,386,760
10	06/13/91	Big Co. W	$3,135			
11	07/27/91	Small Co.	$4,145		Using Criteria Range	
12	09/02/91	Big Co. E	$6,147		----------------------------	
13	10/30/91	Small Co.	$5,455		Average:	$4,690
14	11/10/91	Big Co. E	$6,132		Count:	4
15					Maximum:	$6,124
16					Minimum:	$3,034
17					Standard Deviation:	$1,192
18					Sum:	$18,758
19					Variance:	$1,420,235

FIGURE 21.2. The @D functions let you glean statistical information about a subset of records in a database. You need only enter the criterion for the records you want to analyze.

range, and you must grasp the meaning of the three arguments. After that, statistical analysis is a snap. Save this worksheet, and refer to it later if you forget how the @D functions work.

The @D functions are particularly useful in large databases. But before you apply them to your own spreadsheets, be sure you understand how they work in this one. Change the selection criterion a few times and observe the results of the @D formulas until you are sure you have the hang of it.

Also, add another column of values to the database in column D. Then write some new @D formulas that sum and average entries from the new column.

Creative Criteria Pinpoint Database Records

Whether querying a database or applying @D functions, only your ability to create meaningful criteria limits what you can learn. Until now, we have used only simple criteria in our work with databases; we have asked such questions as Where are the Jones's records? and What's the scoop on the Small Company? What if the questions you have are more complex?

For example, what if you want stats on all of Big Company—east and west? You can't enter a single label that matches both entries in the customer field—or can you? Actually, you can.

Create Criteria Wild Cards

Enter the label *B** into cell B2. This tells 1-2-3 that you want to look at all records whose customer fields start with the letter B. That works here, because you know that only Big Co. E and Big Co. W start with B. If you didn't know that, you could narrow the search by using the criterion *Big Co. ?*.

Both of these criteria make use of *wild card characters*. The asterisk (*) at the end of a string tells 1-2-3 to match all remaining characters. So, the string *B** means, "match all entries that start with B without regard to subsequent characters, if any." The criterion B without the asterisk selects only entries that contain the letter B by itself in the customer field.

The question mark wild card (?) tells 1-2-3 to match any single character at its location in the label. The criteria *Big Co. ?* selects any records that start with *Big Co.* followed by a space and any character. This criterion would not find records that read *Big Co.* without a following letter. Similarly, it wouldn't match records that read such things as *Big Co. West*. If you wanted to find such records, you would use the asterisk wild card, i.e. *Big Co. **.

Logical Operators Help to Narrow a Search

Wild card characters aren't the only tools that can help you to define matching criteria. Sometimes you need to draw on mathematical relationships to describe the entries you want to find in a database. For example, you might want to find all records whose sales in March were between $850,000 and $950,000. Or, you might want to find any salaries above $8 an hour. To that end, you can create criteria for database queries and @D functions using the following logical operators in labels:

Operator	Matches fields that are:
<*string*	Less than *string*
<=*string*	Less than or equal to *string*
<>*string*	Not equal to string
=*string*	Equal to *string*
>*string*	Greater than *string*
>=*string*	Greater than or equal to string
~*string*	Not *string*

You can use the operators on fields that contain either values or labels. For example, entering '>*C* in cell B2 of the STATFUNC worksheet matches all the Small Co. records. That is because those are the only records that are *greater than* the label C. In other words, these are records that 1-2-3 would sort after the label C.

You use an operator for a value field the same way. For example, erase the criterion in cell B2 and enter '>*6000* in cell C2. This selects the database records whose *amount* field entries are greater than $6,000.

Experiment using the operators to see how each works. Remember to start each of your criterion entries with an apostrophe or other label prefix ("" or ^) followed by the operator and, finally, the string.

Multiple Conditions

There are times when a single condition is not enough. Say, for example, that you don't want to take the exceptional records into account. Here, you might want to examine all records with sales less than 8,000 and more than 1,000. To set up that kind of criterion you create a logical formula in the Criteria range.

A logical criterion formula uses the first record in the database as a representative record. Use the fields in that record to create logical formulas in the Criteria range. To see how this works, enter the formula *+C5<8000#AND#C5>1000* in cell C2 as shown in Figure 21.3. This formula matches all records whose *amount* entry is less than 8000 and greater than 1000. 1-2-3 matches a record for a *condition1#* AND#*condition2* criterion, when both *condition1* and *condition2* are true.

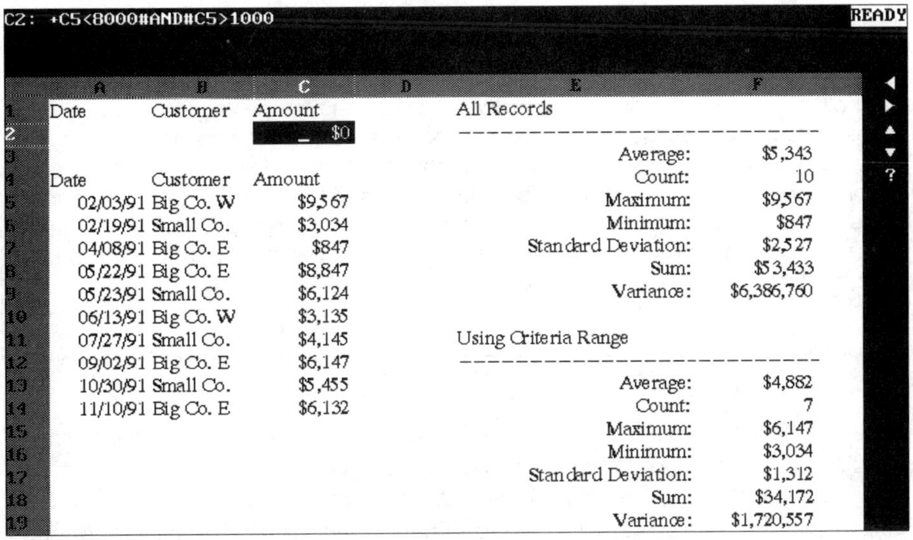

FIGURE 21.3. Use a logical formula that refers to the first record for the field you want to match. Here, the formula +C5<8000#AND#C5>1000 tells 1-2-3 to match all records that have a value in the *amount* field that is less than 8000 and greater than 1000.

A logical criteria formula should refer only to the database field that corresponds to the Criteria field in which the formula resides. While 1-2-3 lets you create a formula such as +B5="Small Co."#AND#C5<8000, it is better to enter '=*Small Co.* in cell B2 and '<*8000* in cell C2. Such constructs are clearer and easier to modify.

Some 1-2-3 professionals like to name the cells in the first record of a database with the field names for the database. If you created this worksheet according to the directions given earlier, you have already assigned those range names, and they appear in the criterion formula that you just entered. If the names don't appear there, you can assign them now. Just move the cell pointer to the first field name in cell A4, select Range Name Labels Down, and indicate all the field names in range A4..C4. 1-2-3 displays the range names in the criterion formula when you return the cell pointer to cell C2.

What if you want to select records that meet either one condition or another condition? To do this, you must add rows to the Criteria range. In the STATFUNC worksheet, adding rows to the Criteria range means replacing the

Reassign Range References

In the main text we explain how the Range Search command's Replace option can alter the range references used in established formulas. There is another way to reassign range references—both the ones used in formulas and the ones established as settings in 1-2-3's various dialog boxes.

In our main worksheet, the formulas in range F3..F9 all refer to range C5..C14. Suppose that you add another data record, and you want to expand the formulaic references? Use a range name.

Proceed as follows: Select Range Name Create, and enter the name *test.* Indicate range C5..C14 as the range to name. Now select Range Name Create a second time. Indicate *test* as the range to name, but indicate a new, expanded range for the name to encompass—say, range C5..C15. All of the formulas in range F3..F9 reflect the new range reference. Use the Range Name Create command again to reduce the reference back to C5..C14.

criteria reference in each of the @D functions in range F13..F19. One way to do that is to apply the Range Search command.

First select Range Search and enter A1..C2 as the string to search for. Indicate F13..F19 as the Search range. Then select Both Replace and enter A1..C3 as the replacement string. Finally, select All when 1-2-3 highlights the first replacement incidence in cell F13. 1-2-3 edits all the formulas to use A1..C3 as their Criteria range.

Now that you have two rows for entering criteria, enter any #OR# condition in the second row. For example, you can enter *'B** in cell B2 and *'>5000* in cell C3. The compound criterion matches all records that have a customer name beginning with the letter B *or* that have an amount greater than 5000.

Formulas in the Criteria Range

The number of ways you can use the Criteria range to match records in a database is limited only by your imagination. If you understand how 1-2-3 uses formulas in the criteria, it is easy to find a formula to fit your particular needs.

Remember that a criterion formula should refer to the first record in the database. That first record acts as a reference record. 1-2-3 examines all records one-by-one, replacing the cell references to the first record with references to each subsequent one. When a record's entries make the criterion formula resolve to True, the record is a match. Actually, any record that resolves the criterion formula to a value other than 0 or ERR is considered a match.

We are going to look at two criterion formulas that solve common data query problems—finding specific strings anywhere within a field and locating specific dates. First, re-establish the range references in your @D formulas so that they refer to range A1..C2. Select Range Name Create, enter *crit*, and press DownArrow Return. Then select Range Name Create, enter *crit*, and press UpArrow Return.

Find a Specific String

How would you write a criterion formula to match records that contain a specific string anywhere within a label in a given field? In other words, your formula should find all records that contain "red" in a selected field, whether "red" appears alone in the field or embedded in a longer string such as "Fred," "redress," or "cornered."

Hint: the solution uses an @FIND function.

To see how it works, clear the criteria from in the STATFUNC worksheet and enter *@FIND("mall",B5,0)+1* into cell B2. With that criterion, the @D functions find all the records that have *Small Co.* in the customer field—only those entries contain the string "mall."

You may wonder why we have added 1 to the result of the @FIND formula. Why not simply use @FIND("mall",B5,0) as the criterion formula? If you don't add 1, the function misses records that start with the letters mall. For example, if the customer were Mallwart, the @FIND formula alone would return 0, because the string "mall" starts at offset 0. And, since the @FIND function returns ERR if the search string isn't present, we can safely add to the @FIND function without causing the formula to match unwanted records. If the record doesn't contain the string, the formula returns ERR and 1-2-3 doesn't match it. If the record does contain the string, *@FIND("mall",B5,0)+1* returns a non-zero value.

You are not limited to entering all the conditions of a formula in the Criteria range itself. For example, you could enter *@FIND($D$1,B5,0)+1* in the customer field of the Criteria range and then enter the strings you want found in cell D1. Any formula criterion can refer to a cell or cells in the worksheet, but references to cells outside the database should typically be absolute.

A criterion formula can compare fields. For example, you might want to compare one quarter's results with another's as shown in Figure 21.4.

To match all records in which the Q2 amount is greater than the Q1 amount, you just enter *+B6<C6* anywhere in the Criteria range. Note that

Why Absolute?

When 1-2-3 evaluates a criterion formula, it shifts the formulaic references from one cell to the next down the spreadsheet. It does this until it has examined every record in the database. Even references to cells outside the database adjust downward in preparation for evaluation of each record. They adjust downward, that is, if the references aren't absolute.

If a criterion formula compares database entries with cells outside the database, use absolute references to the external cells.

both of the formula's references are relative. If you enter *+B6<$C$6,* 1-2-3 matches all records in which the Q1 amount is smaller than the East Division's Q2 amount.

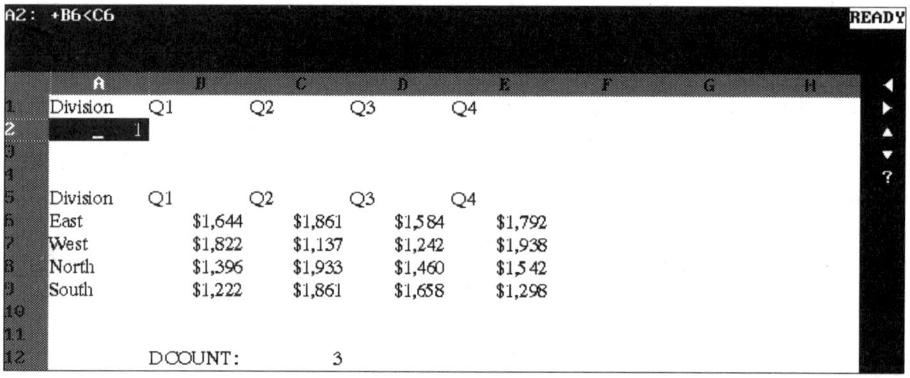

FIGURE 21.4. To match records by comparing one field to another, enter a representative formula for the first record anywhere in the Criteria range. Here, the @DCOUNT formula in cell C12 matches all records in which the Q2 amount is greater than the Q1 amount. The formula that expresses this condition is in cell A2 but could be anywhere in the Criteria range.

Find Specific Dates

How would you go about finding records that contain specific dates?

There are many ways to do this. One method is to create a logical formula that references a date field in the database. For example, consider the database in Figure 21.5. The criterion formula +A5>@DATE(91,5,24) in cell A2 selects all records containing a date value greater than that returned by @DATE(91,5,24).

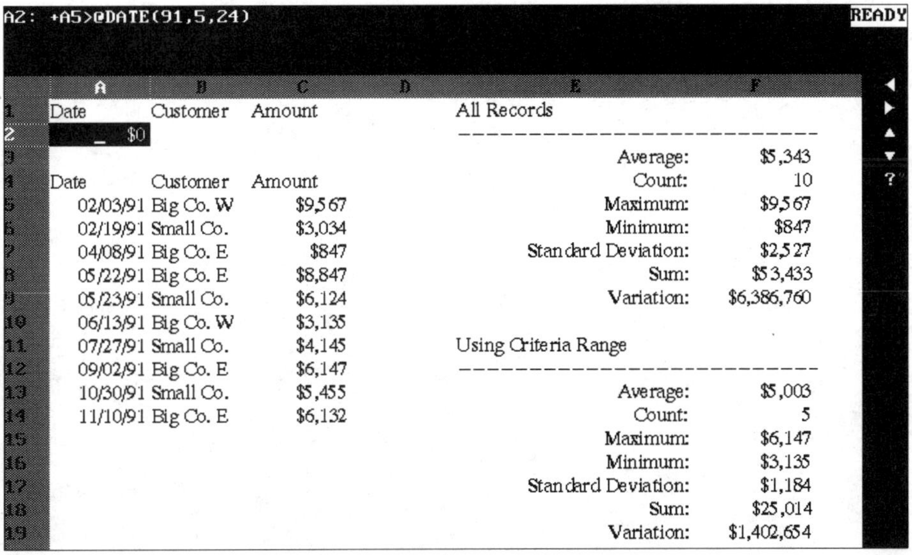

FIGURE 21.5. Use dates as criteria by applying the @DATE function in logical formulas.

You can use any time-related @functions in a Criteria range. For example, the criterion formula @DAY(A5)=3 matches all records whose dates fall on the third day of the month. @MONTH(A5)=2 matches all records whose dates are in February. @YEAR(A5)=91 matches records with dates in 1991.

In some databases, you may have entered dates using the value of the @NOW function. That would make comparisons to @DATE formulas more complex, because the @NOW function generates a value that includes a decimal portion to represent the time of day. When you want to make comparisons in such databases, use the @INT function to trim the fractional portion from the stored date values. For example the formula +@INT(A5)=@DATE(91,5,22) will find any record whose date is May 22, 1991, regardless of whether the date serial number in the database includes a decimal component.

Having completed this chapter you should:

- *Understand how to perform statistical calculations on ranges of values*
- *Be able to perform statistical calculations on database records that fall within specific categories*
- *Know how to narrow down a database search to find only the records of specific interest*
- *Be well-versed in spreadsheet database techniques and see opportunities to apply databases in your own work*

22

In-Depth Data Analysis

What if you spend $50,000 on advertising in the next quarter? Or $45,000? Or $60,000? What happens if you increase the percentage of potassium in the fertilizer mix by 5%? What if the increase is 7% or 8%? Is there a relationship between the color of a product and how well the product sells? Does the amount spent on advertising in a particular market actually affect sales, and if so, by how much?

There is no end to the questions you might ask when analyzing your business. When you understand the tools that let you perform what-if analyses, frequency distributions, and regression analyses, you will be able to have 1-2-3 answer these questions for you. Even if you don't know what a frequency distribution or a regression analysis is, follow along. You will gain some insights that will let you begin doing your own in-depth data analyses.

In this chapter you will learn how to:

- *Perform what-if analyses with one- and two-way data tables*
- *Cross tabulate data in a database*
- *Calculate frequency distributions and plot them as histograms*
- *Use the Matrix Multiply command to solve simultaneous equations*
- *Perform a regression analysis to make predictions based on historical data*
- *Plot a regression analysis and a demand curve to evaluate the results of test marketing*

Data Tables for What-If Modeling

It's easy to set up financial analyses in 1-2-3. You can happily plug in numbers until the worksheet tells you what you want to know. But what if the numbers aren't accurate? Projections are especially prone to error, and that can mean disaster.

To help you deal with an uncertain world, 1-2-3 includes commands that let you conduct what-if and sensitivity analyses. Applied properly, these commands can reveal how the bottom line varies as your assumptions change. This chapter explores some of the tools and techniques you can use in 1-2-3 to analyze your business.

Re-Use a Business Calculation: Data Tables

Imagine that your company is considering the purchase of a wax injector that has a useful life of just 12 months. The machine costs $100,000, and you believe it will have a salvage value of about $95,000, because its parts are quite valuable. While you have it, you think the wax injector will generate about $1,200 of profit per month. To clarify the situation, you produce the worksheet shown in Figure 22.1.

Create the worksheet by entering the labels and values in column A. Enter *.58%* into cell B1 and *1200* into cell B2. Assign the percent format with two decimal places to cells B1 and B4. Assign the currency format with no decimal places to cells B2..B3 and B7..B19. Then enter formulas in the cells indicated:

```
B3: +B7+@NPV(B1,B8..B19)
B4: @IRR(B1,B7..B19)
B8: +$B$2
B19: 95000
```

Copy the formula from cell B8 to range B9..B18.

The @NPV and @IRR formulas in cells B3 and B4 tell you that the purchase is a go. (The chapter on business math in the previous section explains these functions in depth.) But you wonder about the risk involved. The biggest question in your mind concerns the reliability of the $1,200 profit per month. What if the machine is more costly to operate than expected? How bad would it be if the profit per month were $1,175? $1,150? $1,000?

You could try to plug in different values and see how each affects the NPV, but that is time consuming and hard to document. Fortunately, there is an easier way; you can use the Data Table command.

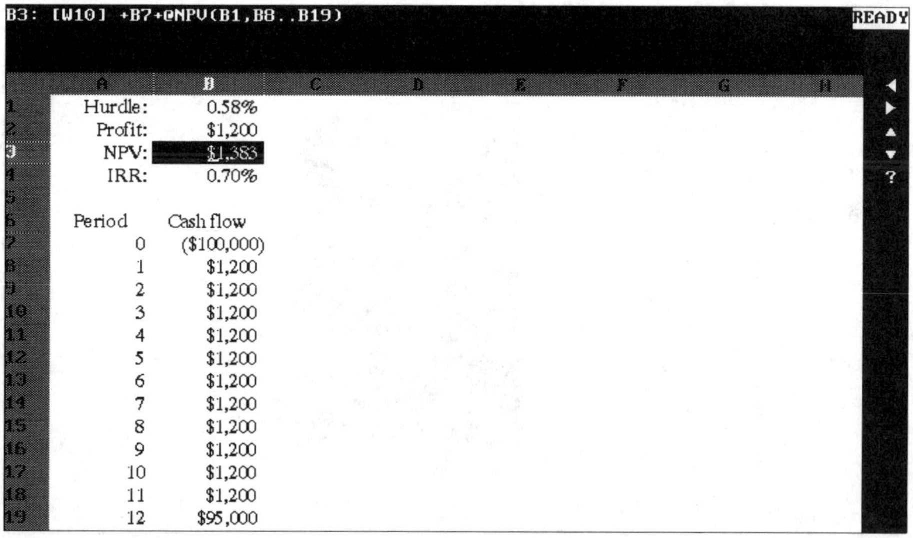

B3: [W10] +B7+@NPV(B1,B8..B19) READY

	A	B
1	Hurdle:	0.58%
2	Profit:	$1,200
3	NPV:	$1,383
4	IRR:	0.70%
5		
6	Period	Cash flow
7	0	($100,000)
8	1	$1,200
9	2	$1,200
10	3	$1,200
11	4	$1,200
12	5	$1,200
13	6	$1,200
14	7	$1,200
15	8	$1,200
16	9	$1,200
17	10	$1,200
18	11	$1,200
19	12	$95,000

FIGURE 22.1. A quick analysis based on projections shows that the machine purchase is worthwhile. The NPV is positive, and the IRR is higher than the hurdle rate. But are the projections accurate?

The Data Table command can create a range of cells that shows what happens when you change one or two variables in a specified calculation. Build one to see how this works.

Generate a Data Table

You want to see how changing the projected monthly profit affects the NPV. Enter a column of possible monthly profits. Then enter a reference formula as a header in the next column as shown in Figure 22.2. For this exercise, the formula is +B3. Assign the text format to the formula in cell E2 so you can easily see what the formula does. Then select Data Table 1, and indicate range D2..E16 as the Table range. Indicate cell B2 as Input cell 1. 1-2-3 generates the table shown in Figure 22.3.

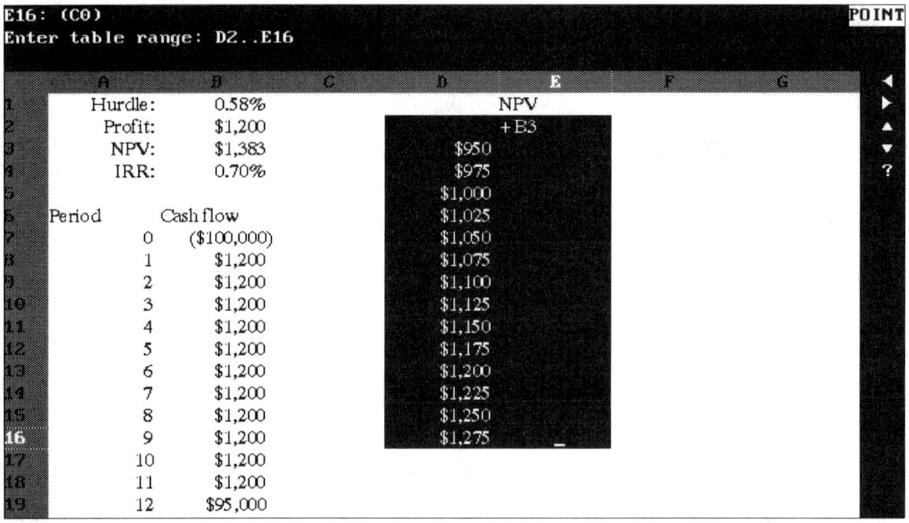

FIGURE 22.2. You set up for the Data Table command by creating a column of values that represent alternate projections.

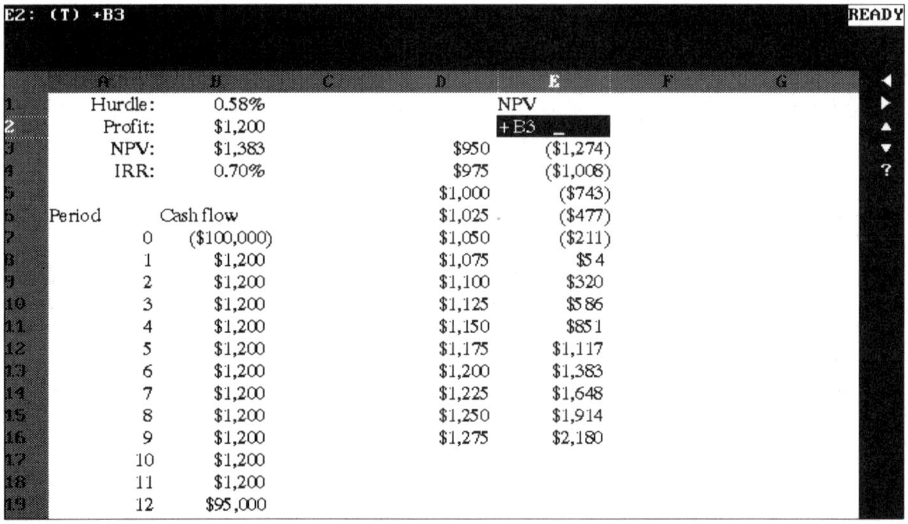

FIGURE 22.3. The Data Table command reveals how NPV varies with the profit per month. Buying the wax injector is profitable as long as the profit per month doesn't drop much below $1,075.

How to Fill a Data Table

When you issue the Data Table command, 1-2-3 prompts you to indicate a Table range and an Input cell. It copies the first value from the left column of the table into the Input cell. Then it calculates the values in the worksheet based on the copied value and enters the result of the table's formula into the appropriate row of the table.

1-2-3 repeats this copying, calculation, and recording of results for each value in the left column of the table until the table is full. The Data Table command leaves the original contents of the Input cell intact.

When you change just one variable, such as monthly profit, you produce a *one-way* Data Table. One-way Data Tables let you examine the effect of one variable on one or more formulas. In this example, IRR also depends on the profit per month. You don't have to create another Data Table to see how variations in the profit variable affect that formula. You can simply add more columns to the current Data Table. Just create more formulas as column headers, and then reissue the Data Table 1 command and expand the Table range to include the new columns. Here you can enter *+B4* in cell F2 and *+B4*12* in cell G2. Select Data Table 1, enter D2..G16, and then enter *B2* as the Input cell 1. Figure 22.4 shows the resulting table.

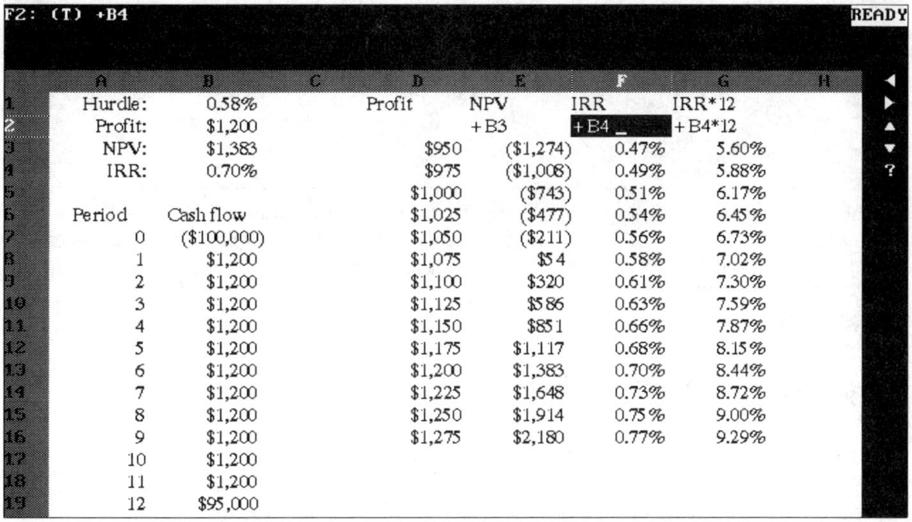
F2: (T) +B4 READY

	A	B	C	D	E	F	G	H
1	Hurdle:	0.58%		Profit	NPV	IRR	IRR*12	
2	Profit:	$1,200			+B3	+B4	+B4*12	
3	NPV:	$1,383		$950	($1,274)	0.47%	5.60%	
4	IRR:	0.70%		$975	($1,008)	0.49%	5.88%	
5				$1,000	($743)	0.51%	6.17%	
6	Period	Cash flow		$1,025	($477)	0.54%	6.45%	
7	0	($100,000)		$1,050	($211)	0.56%	6.73%	
8	1	$1,200		$1,075	$54	0.58%	7.02%	
9	2	$1,200		$1,100	$320	0.61%	7.30%	
10	3	$1,200		$1,125	$586	0.63%	7.59%	
11	4	$1,200		$1,150	$851	0.66%	7.87%	
12	5	$1,200		$1,175	$1,117	0.68%	8.15%	
13	6	$1,200		$1,200	$1,383	0.70%	8.44%	
14	7	$1,200		$1,225	$1,648	0.73%	8.72%	
15	8	$1,200		$1,250	$1,914	0.75%	9.00%	
16	9	$1,200		$1,275	$2,180	0.77%	9.29%	
17	10	$1,200						
18	11	$1,200						
19	12	$95,000						

FIGURE 22.4. By adding more variable-dependent formulas at the top of the Data Table range, you can see the effect of varying one value on several formulas.

Two-Way Data Tables

You also can analyze data using a *two-way* Data Table. This works the same way as the one-way table except that you vary values in two input cells rather than one. Unlike a one-way Data Table, a two-way Data Table shows the results for only one formula at a time.

Consider the wax injector example. You might wonder not just about the profit per month projection but also about the projected salvage value. You can set up a two-way Data Table that varies both of these values and see the effect on NPV. Figure 22.5 shows such a table.

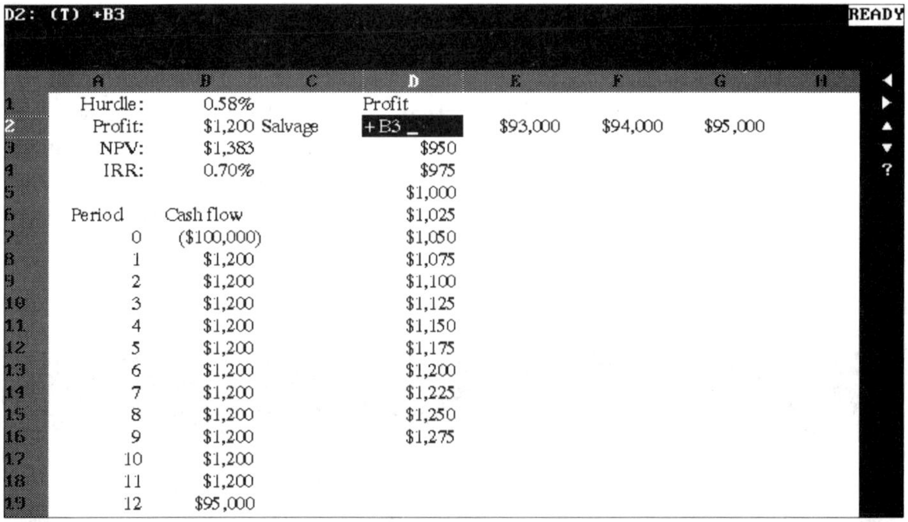

D2: (T) +B3 READY

	A	B	C	D	E	F	G	H
1	Hurdle:	0.58%		Profit				
2	Profit:	$1,200	Salvage	+B3 _	$93,000	$94,000	$95,000	
3	NPV:	$1,383		$950				
4	IRR:	0.70%		$975				
5				$1,000				
6	Period	Cash flow		$1,025				
7	0	($100,000)		$1,050				
8	1	$1,200		$1,075				
9	2	$1,200		$1,100				
10	3	$1,200		$1,125				
11	4	$1,200		$1,150				
12	5	$1,200		$1,175				
13	6	$1,200		$1,200				
14	7	$1,200		$1,225				
15	8	$1,200		$1,250				
16	9	$1,200		$1,275				
17	10	$1,200						
18	11	$1,200						
19	12	$95,000						

FIGURE 22.5. A two-way Data Table can evaluate only one formula. You enter the formula in the top-left corner of the table—here, in cell D2. The left column of the table contains the values for the first Input cell as in the one-way Data Table. The top row of the table contains the values for the second Input cell.

Generate a Two-Way Table

To try out the two-way table, first erase the one-way table from your worksheet. Do this by selecting Range Erase and indicating range F1..G16. Leave the entries in column D to serve as the basis for the two-way table.

Enter the formula *+B3* into cell D2, and enter the values shown in range E2..G2. Format the cells, if you wish, to match our illustration. Once you've

Repeat Performance With The TABLE Key (F8)

The values that 1-2-3 enters in a Data Table are static. That is, they don't reflect changes made to the worksheet. So, if you were to generate a table and then modify the formulas on which the table was based, the results might no longer be correct. Alternatively, you might calculate a table and then decide that the Input values from the left column of the table were not appropriate to the problem you were trying to solve.

In either case, if you have changed the sheet and you want to recalculate an established Data Table, simply press the TABLE key (F8). There is no need to access the menus when you want to recalculate a table.

prepared the range for the Data Table command, select Data Table 2, indicate D2..G16 as the Table range, *B2* as Input cell 1, and *B19* as Input cell 2. Figure 22.6 shows the result.

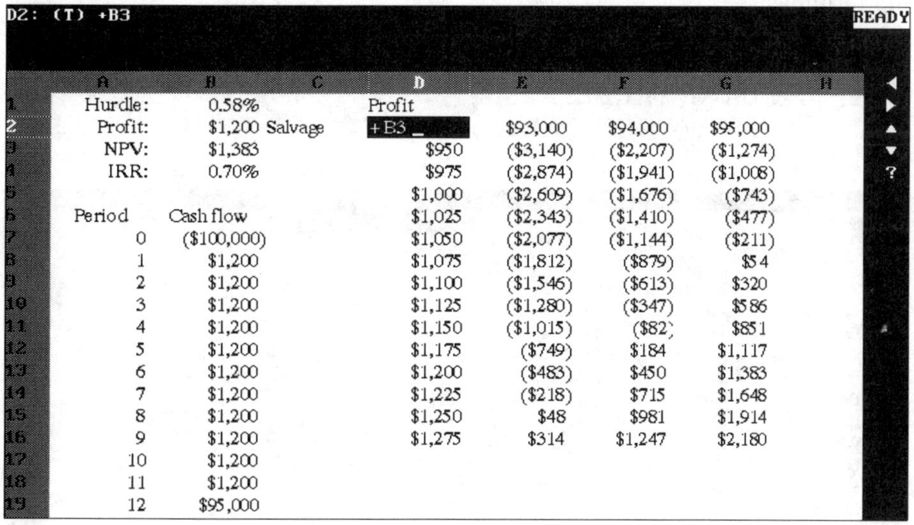

D2: (T) +B3 READY

	A	B	C	D	E	F	G	H
1	Hurdle:	0.58%		Profit				
2	Profit:	$1,200	Salvage	+B3	$93,000	$94,000	$95,000	
3	NPV:	$1,383		$950	($3,140)	($2,207)	($1,274)	
4	IRR:	0.70%		$975	($2,874)	($1,941)	($1,008)	
5				$1,000	($2,609)	($1,676)	($743)	
6	Period	Cash flow		$1,025	($2,343)	($1,410)	($477)	
7	0	($100,000)		$1,050	($2,077)	($1,144)	($211)	
8	1	$1,200		$1,075	($1,812)	($879)	$54	
9	2	$1,200		$1,100	($1,546)	($613)	$320	
10	3	$1,200		$1,125	($1,280)	($347)	$586	
11	4	$1,200		$1,150	($1,015)	($82)	$851	
12	5	$1,200		$1,175	($749)	$184	$1,117	
13	6	$1,200		$1,200	($483)	$450	$1,383	
14	7	$1,200		$1,225	($218)	$715	$1,648	
15	8	$1,200		$1,250	$48	$981	$1,914	
16	9	$1,200		$1,275	$314	$1,247	$2,180	
17	10	$1,200						
18	11	$1,200						
19	12	$95,000						

FIGURE 22.6. The two-way Data Table shows you that the profitability of the purchase is somewhat sensitive to fluctuations in the salvage value of the machine. If the salvage value drops to $93,000, then the table doesn't show a positive NPV until the profit per month reaches $1,250, which is above the current projection.

Cross Tabulating Data

The Data Table command also provides a handy way to analyze information in a database. You can use it to cross tabulate data according to varying criteria. For example, the database in Figure 22.7 shows data on sales for four retail stores. Suppose you wanted to know the total sales, the average sales per month, and the standard deviation on sales for each store.

A Data Table Tabulation

The easiest way to tabulate database information is with the Data Table command. To see it in action, enter the labels and values shown in Figure 22.7. Assign the Currency format with no decimal places to range C5..C20, and then set up a Data Table as shown in Figure 22.8. Row 2 contains the following formulas:

E2:	@DSUM(A4..C20,2,A1..A2)
F2:	@DAVG(A4..C20,2,A1..A2)
G2:	@DSTD(A4..C20,2,A1..A2)

	A	B	C	D	E	F	G
1	Store						
2							
3							
4	Store	Month	Sales				
5	Boston	Jan	$528,697				
6	Brockton	Jan	$581,211				
7	Weymouth	Jan	$627,803				
8	Barnstable	Jan	$596,968				
9	Boston	Feb	$620,246				
10	Brockton	Feb	$542,197				
11	Weymouth	Feb	$623,504				
12	Barnstable	Feb	$729,228				
13	Boston	Mar	$725,774				
14	Brockton	Mar	$509,634				
15	Weymouth	Mar	$557,183				
16	Barnstable	Mar	$571,500				
17	Boston	Apr	$671,297				
18	Brockton	Apr	$595,720				
19	Weymouth	Apr	$575,656				
20	Barnstable	Apr	$633,848				

FIGURE 22.7. This worksheet shows a database of sales for four retail stores during the first four months of the year.

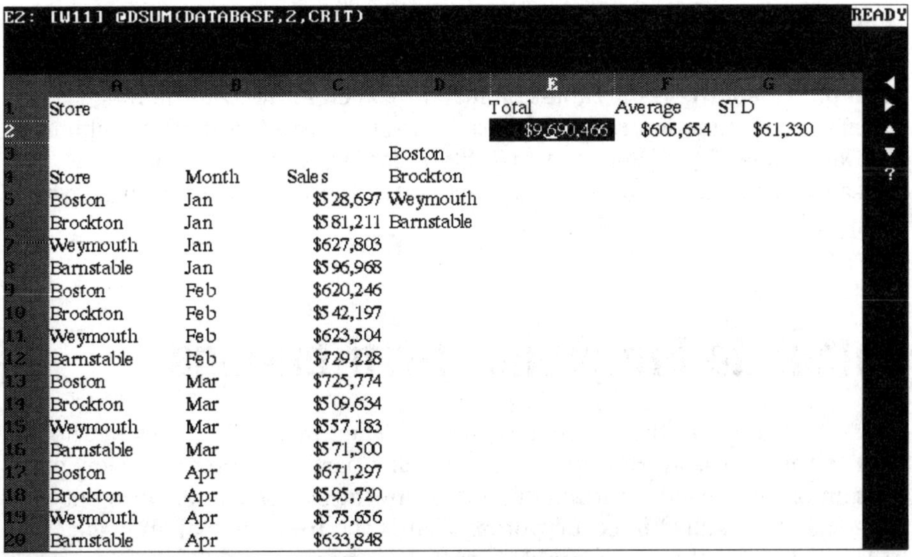

E2: [W11] @DSUM(DATABASE,2,CRIT) READY

	A	B	C	D	E	F	G
1	Store				Total	Average	STD
2					$9,690,466	$605,654	$61,330
3				Boston			
4	Store	Month	Sales	Brockton			
5	Boston	Jan	$528,697	Weymouth			
6	Brockton	Jan	$581,211	Barnstable			
7	Weymouth	Jan	$627,803				
8	Barnstable	Jan	$596,968				
9	Boston	Feb	$620,246				
10	Brockton	Feb	$542,197				
11	Weymouth	Feb	$623,504				
12	Barnstable	Feb	$729,228				
13	Boston	Mar	$725,774				
14	Brockton	Mar	$509,634				
15	Weymouth	Mar	$557,183				
16	Barnstable	Mar	$571,500				
17	Boston	Apr	$671,297				
18	Brockton	Apr	$595,720				
19	Weymouth	Apr	$575,656				
20	Barnstable	Apr	$633,848				

FIGURE 22.8. Set up a one-way Data Table using @D functions as the Data Table formulas.

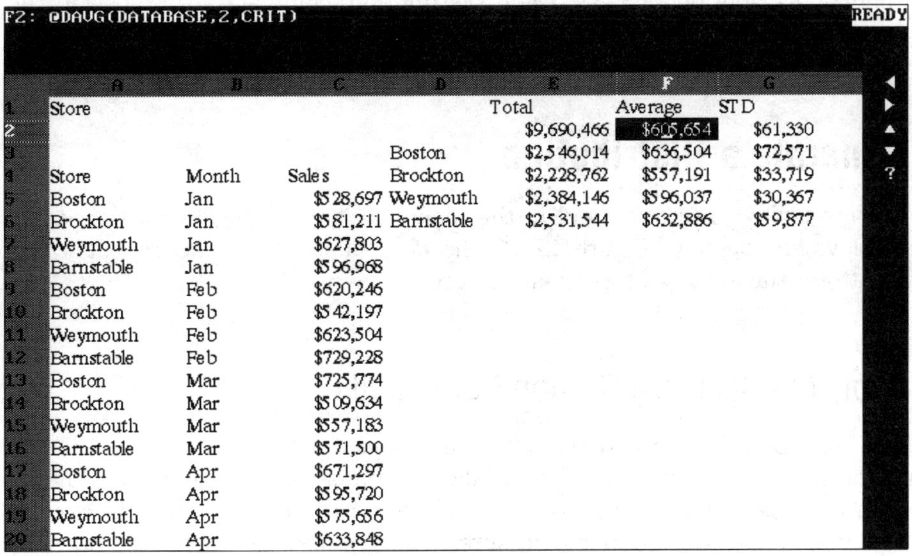

F2: @DAVG(DATABASE,2,CRIT) READY

	A	B	C	D	E	F	G
1	Store				Total	Average	STD
2					$9,690,466	$605,654	$61,330
3				Boston	$2,546,014	$636,504	$72,571
4	Store	Month	Sales	Brockton	$2,228,762	$557,191	$33,719
5	Boston	Jan	$528,697	Weymouth	$2,384,146	$596,037	$30,367
6	Brockton	Jan	$581,211	Barnstable	$2,531,544	$632,886	$59,877
7	Weymouth	Jan	$627,803				
8	Barnstable	Jan	$596,968				
9	Boston	Feb	$620,246				
10	Brockton	Feb	$542,197				
11	Weymouth	Feb	$623,504				
12	Barnstable	Feb	$729,228				
13	Boston	Mar	$725,774				
14	Brockton	Mar	$509,634				
15	Weymouth	Mar	$557,183				
16	Barnstable	Mar	$571,500				
17	Boston	Apr	$671,297				
18	Brockton	Apr	$595,720				
19	Weymouth	Apr	$575,656				
20	Barnstable	Apr	$633,848				

FIGURE 22.9. The Data Table command quickly generates a cross tabulation of the information in the database. This feature is especially useful for large databases.

There is no trick to using @D functions in a Data Table. The @D functions change their values according to the entries in the Criteria range. If you set the Input cell of the Data Table command to a cell in the Criteria range, 1-2-3 calculates @D function results for each criterion listed in the left column of the Data Table. Try it. Select Data Table 1, set D2..G6 as the Table range, and indicate A2 as the Input cell. 1-2-3 generates the cross tabulation shown in Figure 22.9.

Calculate Frequency Distributions

How often? You can frequently measure the success of a business by the answer to this question. How often do you sell a particular product? How often does an order exceed a certain quantity? How often does an experiment produce specific results? In other words, what is the frequency of an event?

More importantly, how often does any of the possible outcomes of an event occur? How often are sales between 0 and $1,000; how often are they between $1,000 and $2,000; and so on? The answer to this question is a frequency distribution. 1-2-3's Data Distribution command can answer the question easily.

Generate a Distribution

You are trying to find a trend in the highly variable billings for a temporary employment agency. Figure 22.10 shows a table of the hours billed per month for the agency's top 10 customers.

Apply the Data Distribution Command

The Data Distribution command can help reveal a trend. For example, you might like to know how often you billed a company some number of hours during the period the data covers. Before you can find out, you will have to duplicate our model in your own spreadsheet. Enter the labels as shown in rows 1 and 3 and in range A14..A16. Enter the values (sorry there are so many) in range A4..H13, and then enter formulas as listed:

	A	B	C	D	E	F	G	H
1			Temporary Contractor – Hours Billed					
2								
3	Customer	Jan	Feb	Mar	Apr	May	Jun	Total
4	1	323.4	192.5	333.0	267.6	241.3	140.0	1497.8
5	2	579.6	95.2	461.1	218.9	462.9	583.1	2400.8
6	3	305.9	237.3	324.3	290.0	219.6	96.6	1473.7
7	4	286.3	588.7	314.5	465.7	493.3	644.0	2792.5
8	5	592.2	539.0	467.4	440.8	226.3	109.9	2375.6
9	6	252.0	558.6	297.3	450.6	338.6	334.6	2231.8
10	7	138.6	385.7	240.6	364.2	395.3	448.0	1972.4
11	8	641.2	208.6	491.9	275.6	245.9	149.1	2012.3
12	9	420.0	398.3	381.3	370.5	447.5	552.3	2569.9
13	10	69.3	252.0	206.0	297.3	250.1	157.5	1232.2
14	Total	3608.5	3455.9	3517.5	3441.2	3320.8	3215.1	20559.0
15	Average	360.9	345.6	351.8	344.1	332.1	321.5	2055.9
16	St. Dev.	184.3	164.8	92.2	82.4	103.3	206.6	

FIGURE 22.10. The @SUM, @AVG, and @STD functions can help clarify this data. But the distribution of the data is not readily apparent. What percentage of the time does the company bill between 400 and 480 hours? The Data Distribution command can answer this question.

B14: @SUM(B4..B13)
B15: @AVG(B4..B13)
B16: @STD(B4..B13)
H4: @SUM(B4..G4)

Copy range B14..B16 to range C14..H14. Copy cell H4 to range H5..H13. Then erase cell H16.

To prepare the data distribution, select Data Fill and indicate I1..I10 as the range to fill. Enter *80* as the Start value, enter *80* as the Step value, and accept *8191* as the Stop value. Now select Data Distribution, indicate B4..G13 as the Values range, and specify I1..I10 as the Bin range. The Data Distribution command enters values in column J as shown in Figure 22.11.

	I	J	K	L	M	N	O
1	80	1.0					
2	160	7.0					
3	240	7.0					
4	320	14.0					
5	400	11.0					
6	480	9.0					
7	560	5.0					
8	640	4.0					
9	720	2.0					
10	800	0.0					
11		0.0					

FIGURE 22.11. The Data Distribution command examines a range of values and tells you how many of those values fall within each bin in the Bin range.

The values in column J are the distribution of the values in range B4..G13. Reading from the top of the column, you see that one value was 80 or less, seven values were between 80 and 110, seven were between 160 and 240, and so on. Each of the numerical intervals defined by the values in column I is called a *bin.* The Data Distribution command counts the values that fit into each bin and enters the results in the column adjacent to the Bin range.

Note that the Data Distribution command entered the value 0 in cell J11—below the last row of the Bin range. The Data Distribution command always enters a value beyond the last bin. That represents the number of values that didn't fall into any bin. Here, all the values had bins so 0 appears in cell J11.

The whole point of the frequency distribution is that it illuminates a trend in your billing. The tendency is toward bills of $320 to $400. Such information might lead you to emphasize efforts to find more long-term, higher-yield contracts. Frequency distributions can alert you to seasonal trends and to downturns and up-turns in sales. Generating a frequency distribution for a year's data can help you to decide whether an exceptional month is truly exceptional or merely part of a consistent ebb and flow in your business.

Generate a Histogram

The Data Distribution command is useful for creating what statisticians call a *histogram.* A histogram is simply a bar graph of a data distribution. To create a histogram, plot the results of the Data Distribution command as a bar graph. Using the Drop-Shadow feature on the bar graph makes an effective histogram. The section of this book titled Spreadsheet Output explains how to create graphs of spreadsheet data. The box titled Plot the Histogram gives brief instructions.

Plot the Histogram
To chart the frequency distribution, select Graph Type Bar. Then select Type Features Drop-Shadow Yes Quit. Set I1..I10 as the X data range and J1..J10 as the A data range. Enter titles and legends to match the ones in the illustration.

The histogram makes any trends in your data jump right off the display.

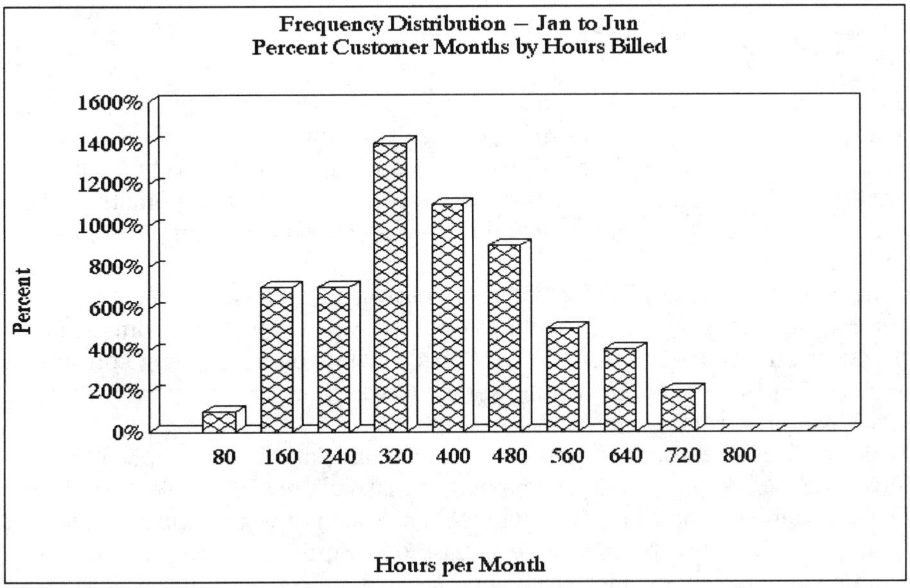

FIGURE 22.12. A bar graph using the 3D-Effect option makes an effective histogram.

Matrix Multiplication Solves Advanced Problems

Invert matrixes, matrix multiplication, simultaneous equations—these sound like good chapters to skip. None of these terms sounds as though it relates in any way to solving business problems. Well, stick around. You may find some uses for 1-2-3's data matrix operations.

The Matrix Multiply command lets you quickly increase or decrease a column of numbers by a percentage—to calculate price increases or discounts across an entire line of merchandise, for example. The Matrix commands also help you to solve simultaneous equations so that you can determine which process or machine among several is the most, or the least, efficient. Before we look at applications of the Matrix commands, we'll risk boring you a bit with an explanation of what the commands do.

What Is a Matrix?

In the spreadsheet world, a matrix is simply a range of contiguous numbers. Mathematicians use *matrix multiplication* to solve systems of linear equations. If that sounds complex, there is a good reason for it: it is complex. But that doesn't mean that mortal businesspeople can't make use of matrix mathematics to deal with such real world issues as cost allocation and productivity evaluation.

Mathematicians talk about matrices in terms of their dimensions. A 5 by 7 matrix is a matrix with 5 rows and 7 columns. A 1 by 1 matrix is a matrix with 1 row and 1 column, or a single cell. This row-by-column naming convention is important when you are trying to decide whether you can perform matrix math on a particular range of cells.

Lotus 1-2-3 handles two kinds of matrix calculations—multiplication and inversion. Multiplying a matrix by another matrix is not as simple as multiplying one value by another, but a detailed discussion of what happens in matrix multiplication is beyond the scope of this book. Suffice it to say that when you multiply one matrix by another, you get a third matrix.

Not all matrices can be multiplied, and multiplying matrix A by matrix B doesn't yield the same result as multiplying matrix B by matrix A. In other words, unlike normal multiplication, matrix multiplication is not commutative, just as subtraction isn't commutative (12 – 4 isn't the same as 4 – 12.)

Before you can multiply two matrices, the number of columns in the first matrix must match the number of rows in the second. So, if matrix A is 2 rows by 5 columns and matrix B is 5 rows by 7 columns, the two can be multiplied. The resulting matrix is 2 by 7.

This is all rather abstract, but there is an easy way to remember the rule. Always refer to matrices in terms of the row dimension by the column dimension. Place the two matrix definitions side-by-side, and a simple rule tells you whether they can be multiplied. For example, matrix A is (6 by 7) and matrix B is (7 by 1). Place them together, and they appear as (6 by 7)(7 by 1).

The rule is, when the inside numbers of a pair of matrices are equal, the matrices can be multiplied; the resulting matrix will have the dimensions of the two outside numbers. Hence, matrix A and matrix B can be multiplied, and the result will be a (6 by 1) matrix. You can't multiply matrix B times matrix A because their inside numbers (1 and 6) don't match.

The inverse of a matrix is another matrix such that matrix A multiplied with its inverse and its inverse multiplied with matrix A both yield an *identity matrix*. An identity matrix is a special matrix made up of 0s and 1s. It has 1s in the upper-left and lower-right corners and 0s in the other two corners.

Well, so what? You can forget a lot of this information and still get some use from the Data Matrix commands. Before you skip ahead to the next chapter, look at some uses of matrix operations.

Change Column by a Percentage

The easiest thing to do with matrix math is to change a column of numbers by some percentage. This technique uses less memory than entering a column full of formulas to make the conversions. It comes in handy in very large worksheets where memory is limited. To see how it works, create the worksheet shown in Figure 22.13.

	A	B	C	D	E	F	G
1	Item	Price		Factor			
2	0	$682		0.8			
3	1	$660					
4	2	$711					
5	3	$57					
6	4	$112					
7	5	$574					
8	6	$229					
9	7	$681					
10	8	$871					
11	9	$532					

FIGURE 22.13. Create this worksheet to see how the Data Matrix Multiply command can change a column of numbers by a specific percentage.

Here, we are going to reduce all the values in range B2..B11 by 20%. That is the same as multiplying each value by .8 or 80%—the value stored in cell D2.

Range B2..B11 is a 10 by 1 matrix (rows by columns) and range D2..D2 is a 1 by 1 matrix. You can multiply them because the first matrix has the same number of columns as the second matrix has rows—the interior numbers match.

To multiply the matrices, select Data Matrix Multiply, indicate range B2..B11 as the First range, cell D2 as the Second range, and cell C2 as the Output range. As you can see, 1-2-3 enters a column of values that are 20% less than the original values.

Here, you specified C2 as the Output range so you could compare the results of the matrix multiplication with the original values. When you want to save memory, you can specify the first cell of the original matrix as the

Output range. In this case, you would select B2 as the Output range, and the Matrix Multiply command would overwrite the original values in column B.

Suppose you want to change two columns by a percentage. The easiest way is simply to issue the Matrix Multiply command once for each column. In other words, multiply the first column by the 1 by 1 matrix and then multiply the second column by the 1 by 1 matrix. You can also solve the problem with a single matrix multiplication, but you will have to be creative.

	A	B	C	D	E	F	G
1	Item	Price	Price 2	Factor			
2	0	$682	$100	0.8	0		
3	1	$660	$100	0	0.8		
4	2	$711	$100				
5	3	$57	$100				
6	4	$112	$100				
7	5	$574	$100				
8	6	$229	$100				
9	7	$681	$100				
10	8	$871	$100				
11	9	$532	$100				

FIGURE 22.14. To change two columns by a percentage, you must set up a 2 by 2 matrix as shown here in range D2..E3.

Try one. Enter *100* in cell C2, and copy it to range C3..C11. Those entries and the ones in column B will decrease by 20%.

Now create a 2 by 2 matrix as shown in range D2..E3 of Figure 29.2. The top-left and bottom-right values are the amounts by which to multiply entries in columns B and C. The top-right and bottom-left values must be zero. Select Data Matrix Multiply. Indicate B2..C11 as the First range, and D2..E3 as the Second range. Indicate cell B2 as the Output range.

Solve Simultaneous Equations

When two or more polynomials express relationships of the same variables, the polynomials are called simultaneous equations. As unlikely as it seems, such equations describe many business problems. For example, the waste output of a group of piece workers should be related to their output of finished product. But does each worker waste the same amount?

Waste and product numbers from several days of work by three laborers might combine into the following formulas:

day 1: 10 worker X + 13 worker Y + 11 worker Z = 10 lbs waste
day 2: 12 worker X + 10 worker Y + 11 worker Z = 11 lbs waste
day 3: 12 worker X + 12 worker Y + 12 worker Z = 11 lbs waste

Solving these simultaneous equations should reveal how much material each worker generated per finished product in the three-day period.

The Matrix commands in 1-2-3 let you solve simultaneous equations easily. In fact, you can solve for up to 256 variables in 256 equations. To see how, consider a more modest example:

Solve for x and y where

$7x + 11y = 108$ and
$3x - 11y = 33$

This example is a set of two simultaneous equations with two variables. In general, to solve a set of *n* simultaneous equations with *n* variables using matrix math, follow these steps:

1. Create an *n* by *n* matrix (A) of the equation coefficients
2. Create an *n* by 1 matrix (B) of the equation constants
3. Use the Data Matrix Inverse command to create the inverse matrix (C) of matrix A
4. Multiply matrix C by matrix B to yield the solution in matrix D.

Solve a Simultaneous Equation

In this example, you must first create a 2 by 2 matrix of the equation coefficients and a 2 by 1 matrix of the equation constants, as shown in Figure 22.15.

	A	B	C	D	E	F	G
1	x	y		constants			
2	7	11		108			
3	3	−11		33			

FIGURE 22.15. To solve for two variables given two simultaneous equations, start by setting up a 2 by 2 matrix of the variable coefficients and a 2 by 1 matrix of the equation constants.

The next step is to create the inverse matrix of the coefficient matrix. To do this, select Data Matrix Invert. Indicate A2..B3 as the range to invert. Then indicate cell A5 as the Output range.

The last step is to multiply the inverted matrix by the matrix of constants to yield a solution. Select Data Matrix Multiply, and indicate A5..B6 as the First range to multiply. Then indicate D2..D3 as the Second range to multiply. Finally, indicate B8 as the Output range.

Lotus 1-2-3 lists the answers in the order in which the variables appear in the original equations. Clarify the answers by entering x into cell A8 and y into A9. Your worksheet should match the one in Figure 22.16.

	A	B	C	D	E	F	G
1	x	y		constants			
2	7	11		108			
3	3	-11		33			
4							
5	0.1	0.1					
6	0.027272	-0.06363					
7							
8	x	14.1					
9	y	0.845454					

FIGURE 22.16. 1-2-3 lists the solution as a matrix in range B8..B9. Enter labels in range A8..A9 to clarify the answer.

A quick verification shows that the matrix procedures really did solve the equations:

7*14.1 + 11*0.845454 = 108 and
3*14.1 − 11*0.845454 = 33

You can follow the same steps to solve any collection of simultaneous equations. The trick, then, is to recognize business problems for which simultaneous equations can provide solutions.

Business Applications of Matrix Math

Matrix math is particularly helpful in answering cost allocation, efficiency, and productivity questions. Suppose you own a materials processing plant, for example, and you want to know how efficient each of your three conveyor belts are. You would start by entering data on the amount of material processed by each belt during the last three months. You would then enter the amount of diesel fuel used by all the belts during those months. Figure 22.17 shows the worksheet.

	A	B	C	D	E	F	G
1		Tonnage Processed					
2		Belt1	Belt2	Belt3			
3	Jan	1,170.6	1,174.3	1,129.8			
4	Feb	1,142.2	1,114.4	1,074.2			
5	Mar	1,191.7	1,128.8	1,191.1			
6							
7		Gallons of Diesel					
8	Jan	4,771.4					
9	Feb	4,566.9					
10	Mar	4,890.8					

FIGURE 22.17. The data on the tonnage processed by each belt and the total fuel consumed form two matrices. The first is a 3 by 3 matrix; the second is a 3 by 1 matrix.

Solve the Problem: Are the Machines Equal?

To create this worksheet, set the global format to punctuated (,) 1, and then enter labels and values as shown.

Solving this problem is just a matter of solving three simultaneous equations. Range B3..D5 is a 3 by 3 matrix (A) of the equation coefficients. Range B8..B10 is a 3 by 1 matrix (B) of the equation constants. Following the steps explained in the previous section, the next step is to use the Data Matrix Inverse command and create the inverse matrix (C) of matrix A. Select Data Matrix Invert, indicate B3..D5 as the range to invert, and then indicate cell B12 as the Output range.

1-2-3 creates the inverse of the matrix as shown in Figure 22.18.

B12: -0.0309857711 READY

	A	B	C	D	E	F	G	H
12		(0.0)	0.0	(0.0)				
13		0.0	(0.0)	(0.0)				
14		0.0	(0.0)	0.0				
15								

FIGURE 22.18. The inverse matrix of range B3..D5 presents no apparently meaningful numbers. It simply represents an intermediate step toward an answer.

The last step in solving this problem is to multiply matrix C by matrix B to yield the solution in matrix D. Select Data Matrix Multiply, and indicate B12..D14 as the First range. Indicate B8..B10 as the Second range, and then indicate B17 as the Output range.

Enter labels to clarify the results, as shown in Figure 22.19.

B17: 1.099206053 READY

	A	B	C	D
16		Gallons Used per Ton Processed		
17	Belt1	1.1		
18	Belt2	0.9		
19	Belt3	2.2		

FIGURE 22.19. Enter labels next to the resulting matrix to clarify the results of the matrix multiplication. Here you can see that belt 2 is the most efficient of the conveyors and that belt 3 may need servicing or replacement.

Perform Regression Analyses

Suppose you work in a company that administers an aptitude test to all engineers who apply for employment. The company uses the test as one of several factors in deciding whether to hire the applicant, and your boss asks you to find out how well the aptitude tests predict job performance. This type of problem is ideally suited to *regression analysis.*

Regression analysis isn't something you go through on a psychiatrist's couch. Rather, it is a statistical technique that lets you make predictions based on accumulated data. You can use 1-2-3's ability to perform a regression even if you are unfamiliar with the statistical theory behind the analysis.

	A	B	C
1		Aptitude	Manager's
2	Employee	Test	Rating
3	1	91	4.3
4	2	78	3.1
5	3	86	3.7
6	4	79	2.9
7	5	98	4.2
8	6	98	5.0
9	7	69	2.5
10	8	69	2.2
11	9	71	1.9
12	10	81	3.2
13	11	84	3.5
14	12	81	3.1
15	13	54	1.2
16	14	100	4.0

FIGURE 22.20. The worksheet identifies each randomly chosen engineer with a number in column A. Column B shows each engineer's aptitude test score, and column C shows his or her performance rating.

Set Up the Analysis

The first step in trying to answer the question about test scores involves selecting a *sample* group. If your company is small enough, you could study data on all the engineers employed. But if the company is large, you need to come up with a representative sample. This sample should be *randomly* selected from the entire pool of engineers employed. Also, the size of the sample group should be large enough to yield meaningful results. The larger your sample, the more accurate your analysis will be.

Using a pair of dice, you select 14 engineers at random from an employee list. Then you gather information on those engineers and set up a worksheet as shown in Figure 22.20 with each employee's aptitude test score in one column and his or her most recent performance review rating in the next. A perfect score on the aptitude test is 100, and the managers rate the engineers from 0 to 5. A score of 5 means that the employee far exceeds expectations. A score of less than 2 means that the employee needs to improve.

The XY graph shown in Figure 22.21 shows the relationship between the aptitude scores and the performance ratings. This graph reveals that there is, in fact, a relationship between the two. Regression analysis simply refines this visual assessment and lets you make predictions based on future test scores.

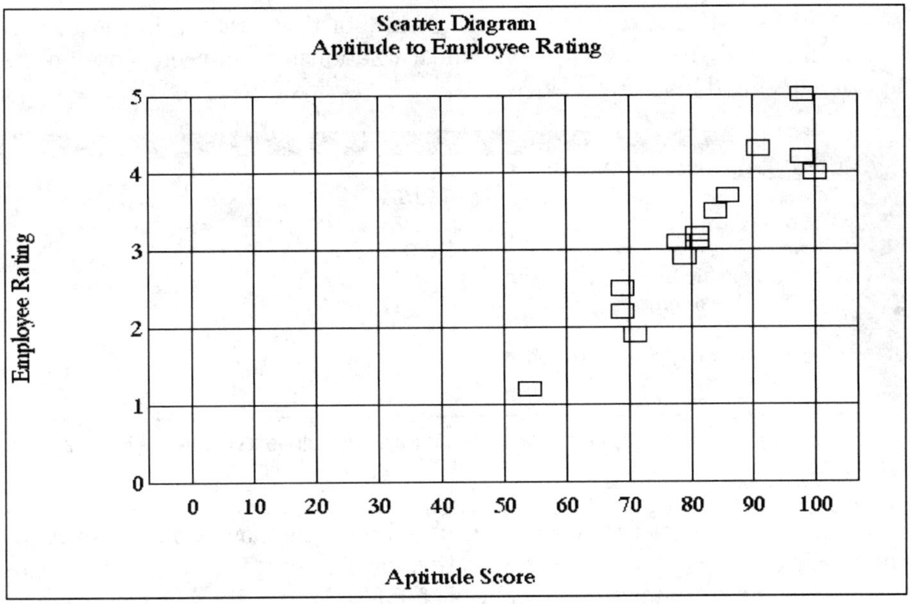

FIGURE 22.21. A graph shows you that there is indeed a relationship between aptitude scores and performance. To refine your understanding of this relationship, use 1-2-3's built-in regression analysis capabilities.

Do the Analysis

To perform a regression analysis you must identify two sets of variables—independent and dependent. The goal of regression analysis is to develop a model by which you can predict dependent values based on changing independent variables. Here, you want to know if you can predict an employee's performance based on an aptitude score. The performance rating is the dependent variable. You want to know how reliably it can be predicted based on the aptitude test score—the independent variable.

To see how this works, enter labels and values as shown in Figure 22.20. Select Data Regression X-Range, and indicate B3..B16 as the Independent Variables range. Select Y-Range, and indicate C3..C16 as the Dependent Variables range. Select Output-Range, and indicate cell A21. Finally, select Go to generate a regression analysis.

Move your cell pointer to cell A21 so you can review the regression results. They should match the results shown in Figure 22.22. At first glance, a regression analysis can seem intimidating. But it is easy to use the analysis to answer basic business questions once you know what to look for. For example, this analysis yields the answer to your boss's question. The value next to the label *R Squared* tells you what proportion of variation in the dependent variable the independent variable explains. Here, *R Squared* reveals that the score on the aptitude test explains 90.6942% of the variation in the performance rating; there is a very strong linear relationship between score on the aptitude test and job performance.

	A	B	C	D	E	F	G
21		Regression Output:					
22	Constant			-2.91689			
23	Std Err of Y Est			0.326184			
24	R Squared			0.906942			
25	No. of Observations			14			
26	Degrees of Freedom			12			
27							
28	X Coefficient(s)		0.075185				
29	Std Err of Coef.		0.006952				

FIGURE 22.22. The Data Regression Go command generates the results of the regression analysis in the designated Output range.

If your boss is statistically sophisticated, he or she may also want to know the *adjusted* r^2. 1-2-3 doesn't provide this figure, but it is not difficult to calculate. The equation for adjusted r^2 is as follows:

$$r^2_{adj} = 1 - [\ (1 - r^2)\ *(n - 1)\ /\ (n - 2)\ ]$$

where n is the value next to the label *No. of observations*. The adjusted r^2 takes into account both the sample size and the number of independent variables that affect the dependent variable. It may provide a better measure of reliability when your data include multiple columns of independent variables. In this example, you can calculate the adjusted r^2 by entering *1–(1–D24)*(D25–1)/(D25–2)* into cell D31. The resulting 89.9187% again shows a strong relationship between the aptitude score and job performance. Enter *Adj. R Squared* in cell A31 to remind you what the value is. Save the worksheet, calling it STATS.WK1.

Predicting Results: The Regression Formula

Of course, determining that a relationship exists between variables is not really useful unless you can come up with some kind of model for predicting future results. To do that, you must create an equation into which you can plug any independent variable to predict a dependent variable. Here, you want an equation that predicts a future managerial rating based on an applicant's aptitude score.

The general form of the equation is:

y = constant + (x coefficient * x)

where y represents the dependent variable (future performance), and x represents the independent variable (aptitude score). You can plug any aptitude score into this equation along with the constant and the x coefficient to get a prediction of the managerial rating.

In this case the constant is in cell D22, and the x coefficient is in cell C28. It is not important to understand how the regression formula was derived or what the constant and the x coefficient represent. Knowing the formula and how to apply it gives you enough to work with a regression analysis. Prove it. Enter the formula *+$D$22+$C$28*B3* into cell D3. Copy that formula to range D4..D17 as shown in Figure 22.23.

D3: (F1) +$D$22+$C$28*B3 READY

Employee	Aptitude Test	Manager's Rating	Predicted
1	91	4.3	3.9
2	78	3.1	2.9
3	86	3.7	3.5
4	79	2.9	3.0
5	98	4.2	4.5
6	98	5.0	4.5
7	69	2.5	2.3
8	69	2.2	2.3
9	71	1.9	2.4
10	81	3.2	3.2
11	84	3.5	3.4
12	81	3.1	3.2
13	54	1.2	1.1
14	100	4.0	4.6

FIGURE 22.23. After generating a regression analysis, you can create formulas that predict a dependent value based on an independent value. Here, the predicted values are next to the actual values.

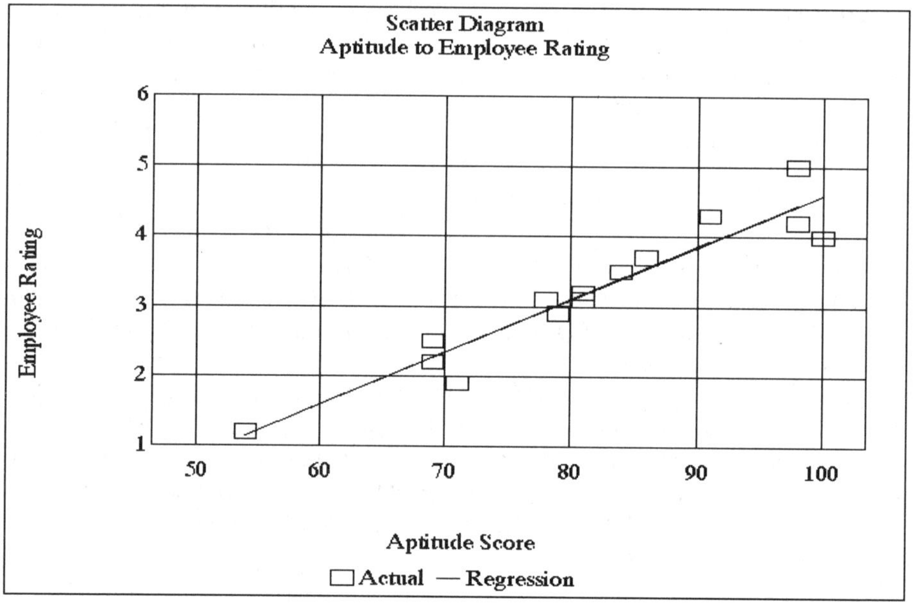

FIGURE 22.24. The regression values plot a line that best fits the actual data. You can look at such a graph to get an understanding of how well the regression equation predicts results. Here, the correlation between aptitude test scores and performance results is very high.

Employee	Aptitude Test	Manager's Rating	Predicted
1	91	4.3	3.9
2	78	3.1	2.9
3	86	3.7	3.5
4	79	2.9	3.0
5	98	4.2	4.5
6	98	5.0	4.5
7	69	2.5	2.3
8	69	2.2	2.3
9	71	1.9	2.4
10	81	3.2	3.2
11	84	3.5	3.4
12	81	3.1	3.2
13	54	1.2	1.1
14	100	4.0	4.6
New	89		3.8

FIGURE 22.25. Now that you have a column of regression-based formulas, you can enter an aptitude test score and see the predicted managerial rating for a new employee.

By placing predicted results next to actual results, you can plot a graph that compares actual data with predicted results, as shown in Figure 22.24. You should generally plot regression equations against the actual data to get a clear sense of how well the regression equation predicts the dependent variable.

Now that you have the regression equation formulas, it is easy to make a prediction for a new employee. Say you want to predict the managerial rating for a new engineer who scored 89 on his aptitude test. Enter the test score into cell B17 as shown in Figure 22.25. Cell D17 returns the predicted rating of 3.8.

Multiple Regression Models

Suppose you want to examine several independent variables to learn their influence on the dependent variable of job performance. In Figure 22.26, there are three independent variables—aptitude test score, college grade point average, and sex. You have already seen the results of a regression analysis on the independent variables in column B (aptitude test scores) in Figure 22.22. Figure 22.27 shows the results for simple linear regression analyses on the independent variables in columns C and D.

Employee	Aptitude Test	College GPA	Sex Male?	Manager's Rating
1	91	3.69	1	4.3
2	78	3.28	0	3.1
3	86	3.37	1	3.7
4	79	3.00	1	2.9
5	98	3.39	1	4.2
6	98	4.00	0	5.0
7	69	2.85	0	2.5
8	69	2.57	0	2.2
9	71	2.23	1	1.9
10	81	3.19	0	3.2
11	84	3.51	0	3.5
12	81	3.20	1	3.1
13	54	1.76	1	1.2
14	100	3.23	0	4.0

FIGURE 22.26. You can enter more than one column of independent variables.

College GPA			
	Regression Output:		
	Constant		−1.96056
	Std Err of Y Est		0.329027
	R Squared		0.905312
	No. of Observations		14
	Degrees of Freedom		12
	X Coefficient(s)	1.669699	
	Std Err of Coef.	0.155881	
Sex Male?			
	Regression Output:		
	Constant		3.357142
	Std Err of Y Est		1.055710
	R Squared		0.025197
	No. of Observations		14
	Degrees of Freedom		12
	X Coefficient(s)	−0.31428	
	Std Err of Coef.	0.564300	

FIGURE 22.27. By entering alternate Output ranges, you can compare the results of simple linear regressions using different independent variables.

The regression analysis on the college GPA shows a significant correlation between grade point average and future performance. The r^2 is over 90%. The r^2 for the regression analysis done on the applicants' gender shows no significant correlation between the sex of the applicant and future job performance. The r^2 is barely 3%.

Regress Yes/No Data

Sometimes the data you use for a regression analysis consists of yes/no or true/false information. For example, you can express a person's sex in terms of female or not female (or male and not male). In either case, let one condition be the "true" condition, and give it the value 1. The other condition should receive the value 0.

So far, the best correlation is between the aptitude test score and the managerial rating. That has an r^2 of about 90.7%, while the r^2 for the GPA regression was about 90.5%. You can do an even more reliable regression if you use both independent variables. This is called *multiple regression analysis.*

Before you try a multiple regression analysis, erase the regression formulas from column D of your practice worksheet. Insert two new columns at column D, and enter the new data shown in Figure 22.26. Finally, erase the output from the previous regression analysis.

Now, select Data Regression X-Range, and indicate range *B3..C16* as the independent variables. Select Y-Range, and indicate *E3..E16* as the dependent variables. Select Output-Range, and indicate *A21*. Select Go, and 1-2-3 generates the regression analysis shown in Figure 22.28.

	A	B	C	D	E	F	G
21		Regression Output:					
22	Constant			-2.86728			
23	Std Err of Y Est			0.178186			
24	R Squared			0.974544			
25	No. of Observations			14			
26	Degrees of Freedom			11			
27							
28	X Coefficient(s)		0.040653	0.892938			
29	Std Err of Coef.		0.007432	0.165211			

FIGURE 22.28. Using two independent variables yields a higher r^2 in this case.

The regression output looks similar to the earlier one except that there are two sets of values for the x coefficient and its corresponding standard error. These values let you create a new equation for predicting job performance. That equation takes the following form:

$$y = \text{constant} + (\text{x coefficient}_1 * x_1) + (\text{x coefficient}_2 * x_2)$$

Now you can create an even more accurate formula for predicting job performance. Just enter *+$D$22+$C$28*B3+$D$28*C3* into cell F3, and copy it to range F4..F16 as shown in Figure 22.29.

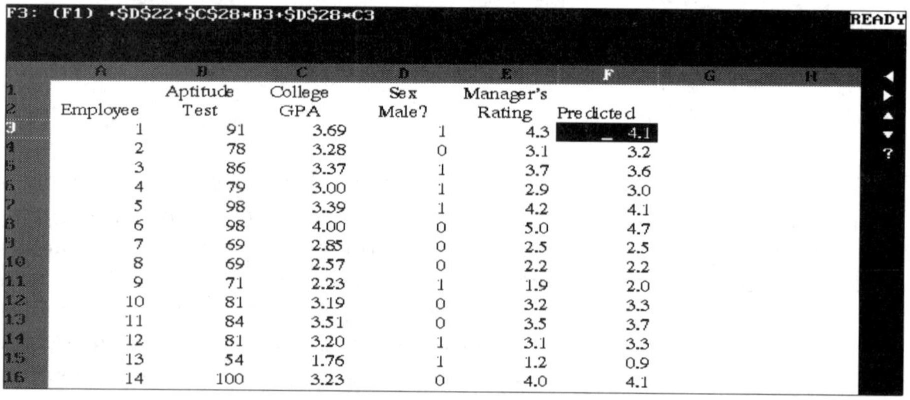
F3: (F1) +$D$22+$C$28*B3+$D$28*C3 READY

Employee	Aptitude Test	College GPA	Sex Male?	Manager's Rating	Predicted
1	91	3.69	1	4.3	4.1
2	78	3.28	0	3.1	3.2
3	86	3.37	1	3.7	3.6
4	79	3.00	1	2.9	3.0
5	98	3.39	1	4.2	4.1
6	98	4.00	0	5.0	4.7
7	69	2.85	0	2.5	2.5
8	69	2.57	0	2.2	2.2
9	71	2.23	1	1.9	2.0
10	81	3.19	0	3.2	3.3
11	84	3.51	0	3.5	3.7
12	81	3.20	1	3.1	3.3
13	54	1.76	1	1.2	0.9
14	100	3.23	0	4.0	4.1

FIGURE 22.29. Using multiple regression analysis, you can create a more accurate formula for predicting employee performance.

Plot a Regression Analysis

By combining 1-2-3's regression analysis tools with its graphing capability, you can create impressive presentations of sophisticated analyses. Such presentations are especially effective examining pricing policies and forecasting sales.

A Regression to Plot

Suppose your boss hands you data from a recent marketing study. Your company is trying to select a sales price for its new Comb Capper, and it is your job to come up with a recommendation. To see how you might handle such a problem, start with a blank worksheet and enter labels in row 1 and values in range A2..B6 as shown in Figure 22.30. Enter *+A2*B2* into cell C2. Enter *@ROUND(1.5*B2^1.01,0)* into D2, and enter *+C2–D2* in cell E2. Then copy range C2..E2 to range C3..C6.

The formula in cell D2 returns the approximate cost of shipping the Comb Cappers. Here, the cost per Comb Capper produced and shipped increases slightly as volume increases.

Determining r, t, and z in Simple Linear Regression

If you are a statistical sophisticate, you may want to know how to determine the values for *r, t,* and *z* in 1-2-3. You can ascertain these values based on the values given by 1-2-3's regression output. The general formulas for these measures follow. Replace the arguments with references to corresponding values from the regression output when entering the formulas.

To find *r*, use the general formula:

@SQRT(*r squared*)*@IF(*x coefficient*<0,–1,1)

To figure the value of *t*, use the general formula:

@SQRT(*r squared*)*@IF(*x coefficient*<0,–1,1)*
@SQRT(*degrees of freedom*/(1–*r squared*))

To determine *z*, if that measure is applicable, use the general formula:

@SQRT(*r squared*)*@IF(*x coefficient*<0,–1,1)*
@SQRT(*no. of observations*)

Use the Data Regression commands to generate the regression analysis shown in the figure. Use the *price* column as the independent variables and the *sold* column as the dependent variables. r^2 in the output tells you that there is a strong relationship between the dependent variables (sold) and the independent variables (price).

This isn't a very large sample, and that is something you might want to point out in a report. But you can still come up with a theoretical price that maximizes profit. To do that, start by copying the labels in range A1..E1 to cell A21. Then enter the label *Maximum* in cell F21.

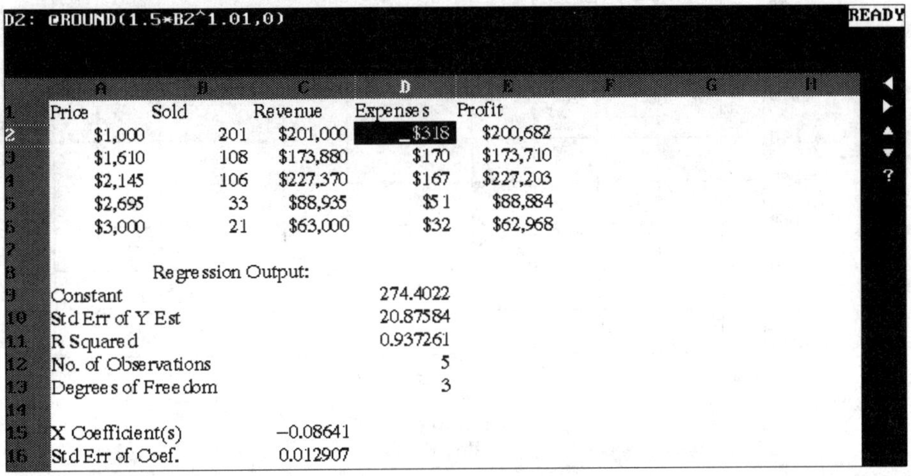

FIGURE 22.30. Analyze the results of a marketing test to find an appropriate pricing strategy.

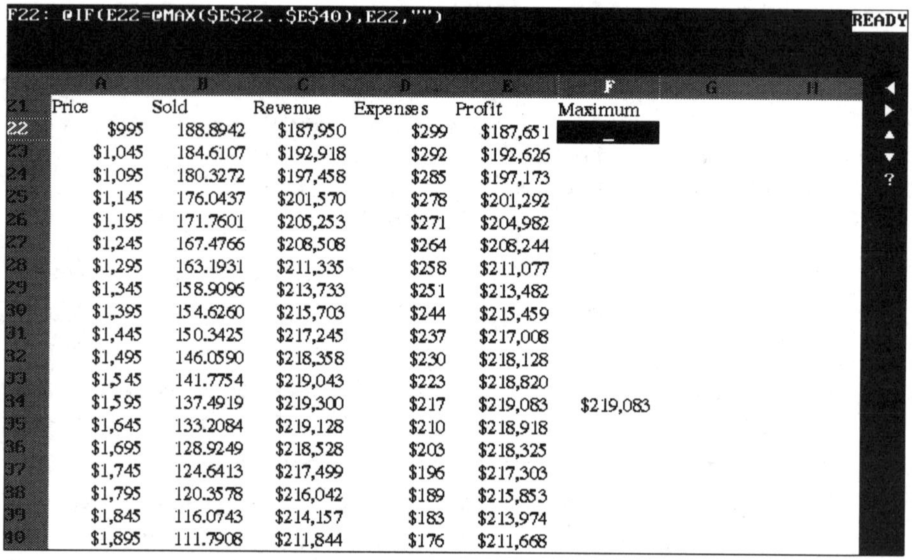

F22: @IF(E22=@MAX($E$22..$E$40),E22,"") READY

	A	B	C	D	E	F
21	Price	Sold	Revenue	Expenses	Profit	Maximum
22	$995	188.8942	$187,950	$299	$187,651	
23	$1,045	184.6107	$192,918	$292	$192,626	
24	$1,095	180.3272	$197,458	$285	$197,173	
25	$1,145	176.0437	$201,570	$278	$201,292	
26	$1,195	171.7601	$205,253	$271	$204,982	
27	$1,245	167.4766	$208,508	$264	$208,244	
28	$1,295	163.1931	$211,335	$258	$211,077	
29	$1,345	158.9096	$213,733	$251	$213,482	
30	$1,395	154.6260	$215,703	$244	$215,459	
31	$1,445	150.3425	$217,245	$237	$217,008	
32	$1,495	146.0590	$218,358	$230	$218,128	
33	$1,545	141.7754	$219,043	$223	$218,820	
34	$1,595	137.4919	$219,300	$217	$219,083	$219,083
35	$1,645	133.2084	$219,128	$210	$218,918	
36	$1,695	128.9249	$218,528	$203	$218,325	
37	$1,745	124.6413	$217,499	$196	$217,303	
38	$1,795	120.3578	$216,042	$189	$215,853	
39	$1,845	116.0743	$214,157	$183	$213,974	
40	$1,895	111.7908	$211,844	$176	$211,668	

FIGURE 22.31. After performing a regression analysis, you can set up a table of possible prices to see which one maximizes profit.

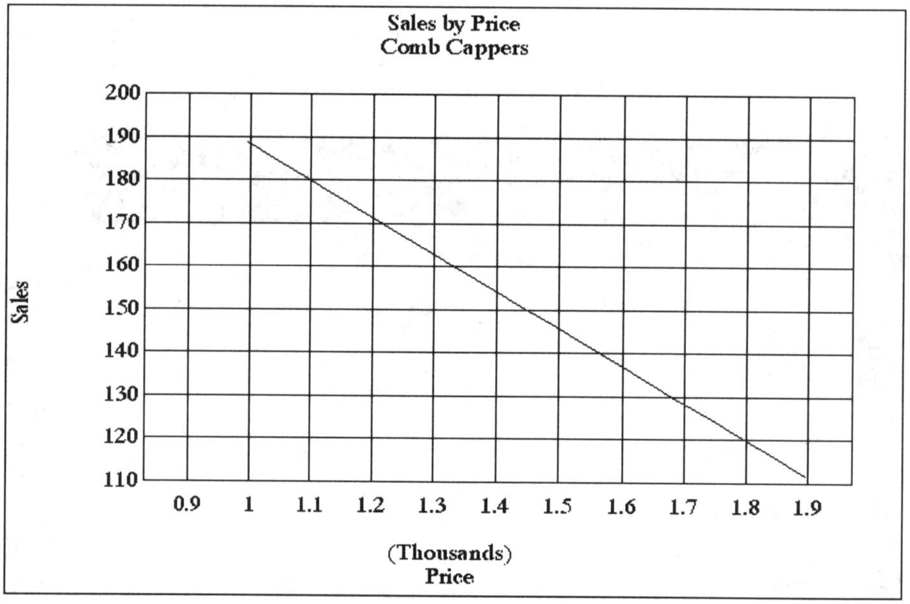

FIGURE 22.32. This XY graph shows the inverse, linear relationship between sales and price. This relationship is sometimes called the *demand curve.*

Calculate Projected Sales and Profits

You want to set up a table that shows predicted sales for a given sales price. For each price, the table should also reveal predicted revenue, expenses, and profit. The first step is to enter several possible prices for the Comb Capper. 1-2-3's Data Fill command makes that easy to do.

Move the cell pointer to cell A22. Select Data Fill, and indicate A22..A40 as the Fill range. Enter *995* as a starting price, and *50* as the Step value, and accept 8191 as the Stop value. 1-2-3 enters 19 price points in range A22..A40.

Next, use the regression output to predict the number of sales for each price point. Remember from the last chapter that the formula would be *+$D$9+$C$15*A22*. Enter it in cell B22, and copy to range B23..B40. The formula returns fractional amounts for the number sold. You will never sell just part of a Comb Capper, but rounding these values to integers makes a graphical representation of the regression results less attractive.

Enter *+A22*B22* in cell C22 to calculate revenues. Enter *@ROUND(1.5*B22^1.01,0)* in cell D22 to calculate shipping costs. Enter *+C22–D22* in cell E22 to calculate profits. And finally, enter *@IF(E22=*@MAX(*$E$22..$E$40),E22,""*) in cell F22. This locates the highest profit reported in column E.

Copy those formulas down their columns and format ranges as shown in Figure 22.31.

Now that you have this table of projections, you can create a variety of revealing graphs for presentation to management. Figures 22.32 through 22.35 show some of the graphs you can generate.

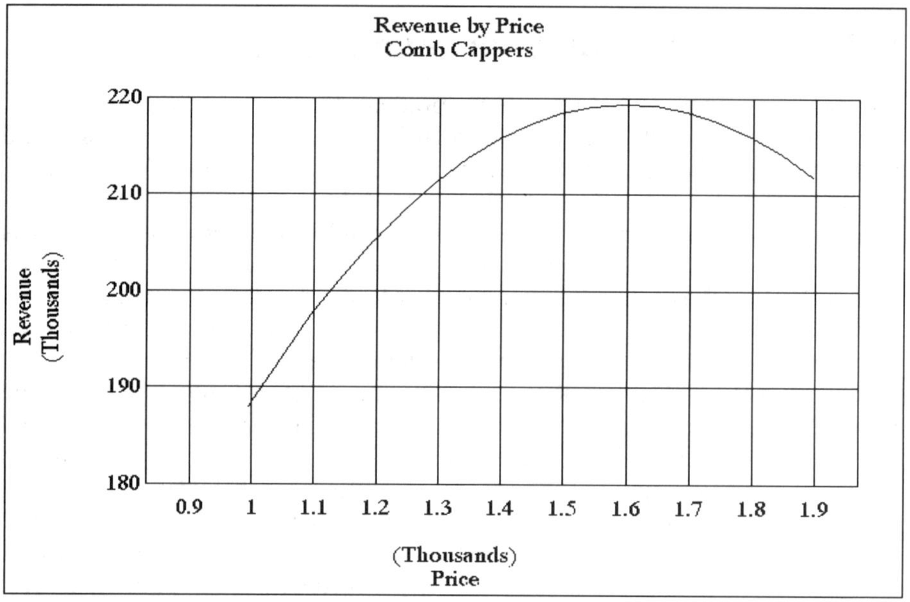

FIGURE 22.33. This XY graph shows how total revenue changes as price increases. Revenue is highest at a price somewhere around $1,600.

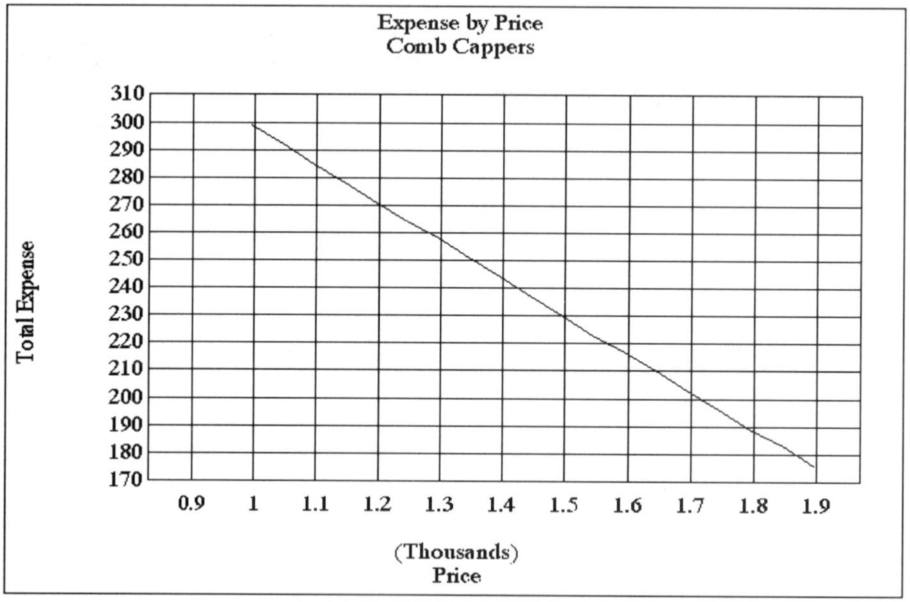

FIGURE 22.34. This XY graph shows the correlation between total expense and product price.

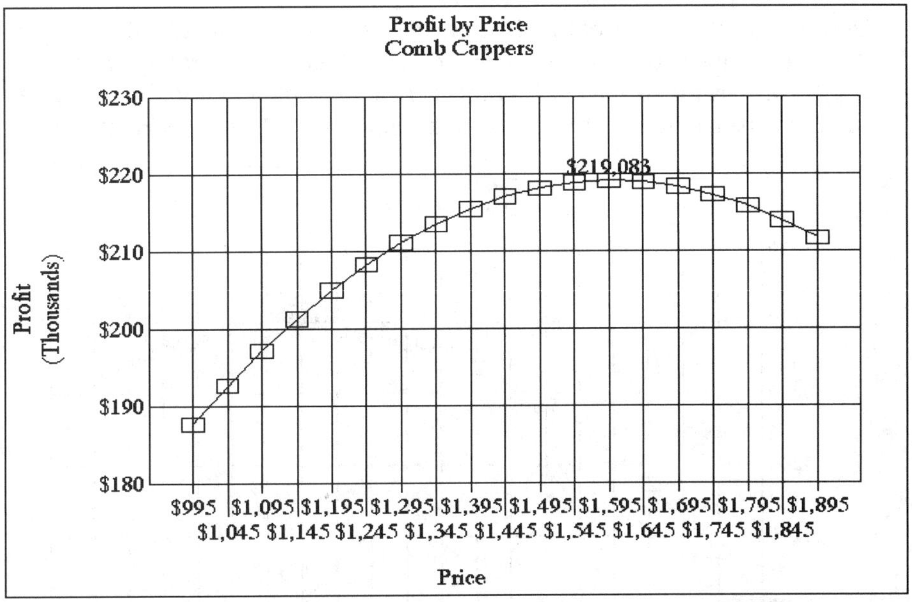

FIGURE 22.35. This Line graph presents management with the bottom line. The top of the curve is the maximum profit reached at a price of around $1,595. Note that the maximum profit and the maximum revenue don't always occur at the same price.

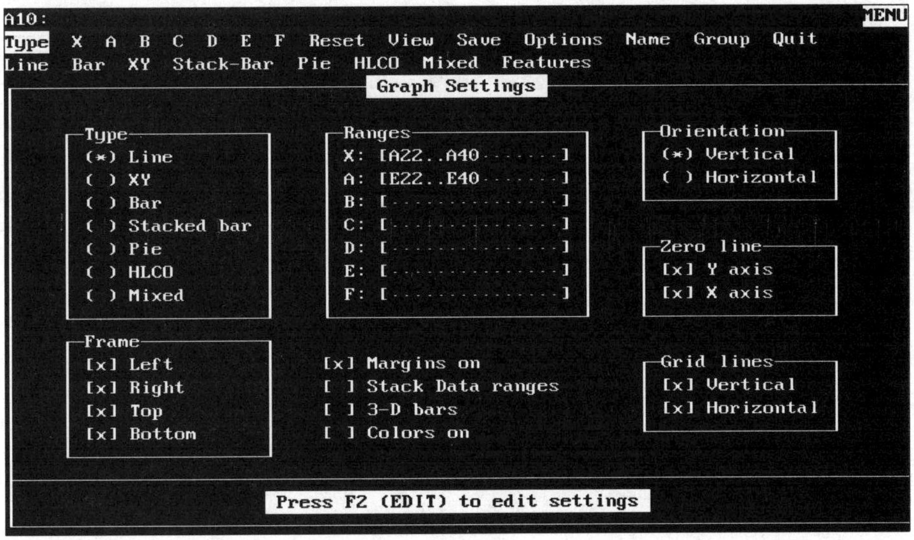

FIGURE 22.36. The Profit by Price graph has these main settings; adjust them from the Graph menu.

Of these graphs, the Profit by Price graph shown in Figure 22.36 is likely to be the most interesting to management. To create this graph, first select Graph Reset Graph to clear all graph settings. Then modify all settings to match the settings dialog boxes shown in Figures 22.36 through 22.38.

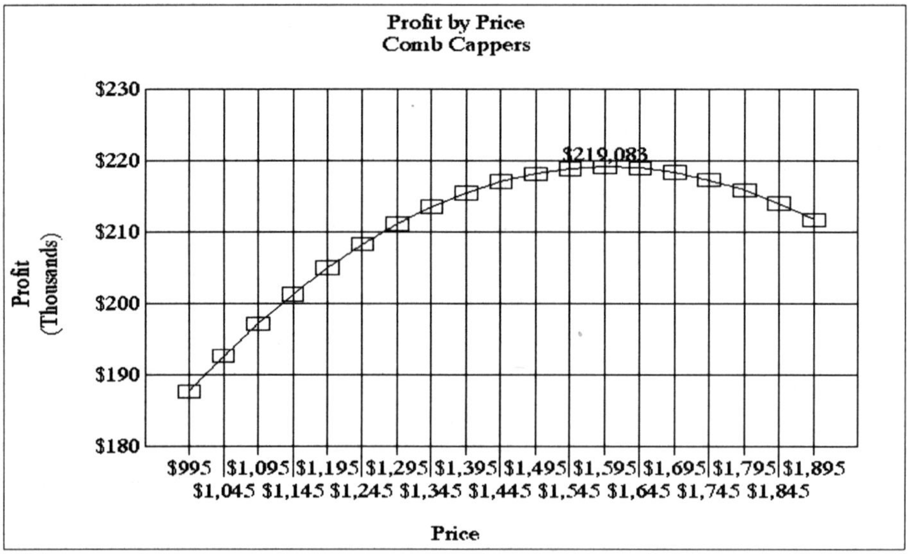

FIGURE 22.37. Select Graph Options to modify the Profit by Price graph's settings further.

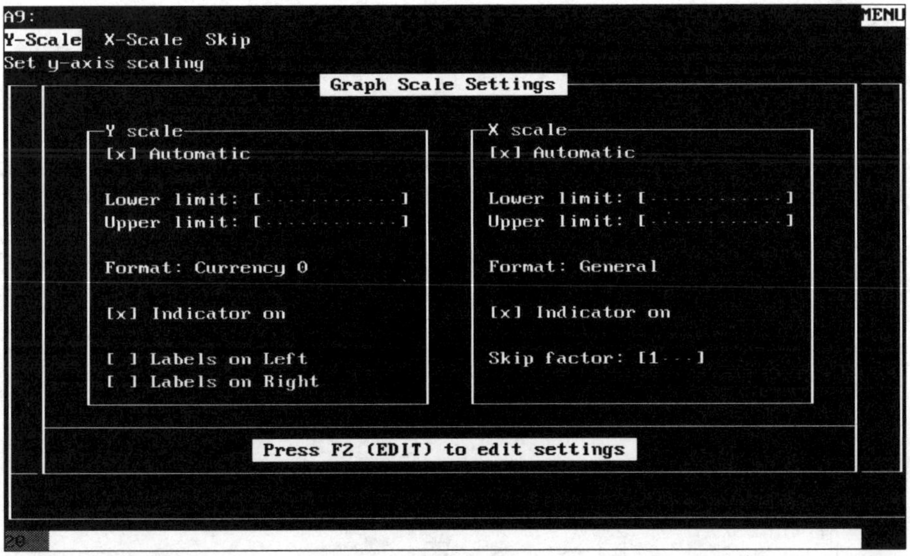

FIGURE 22.38. Select Graph Options Scale, and adjust the settings as shown.

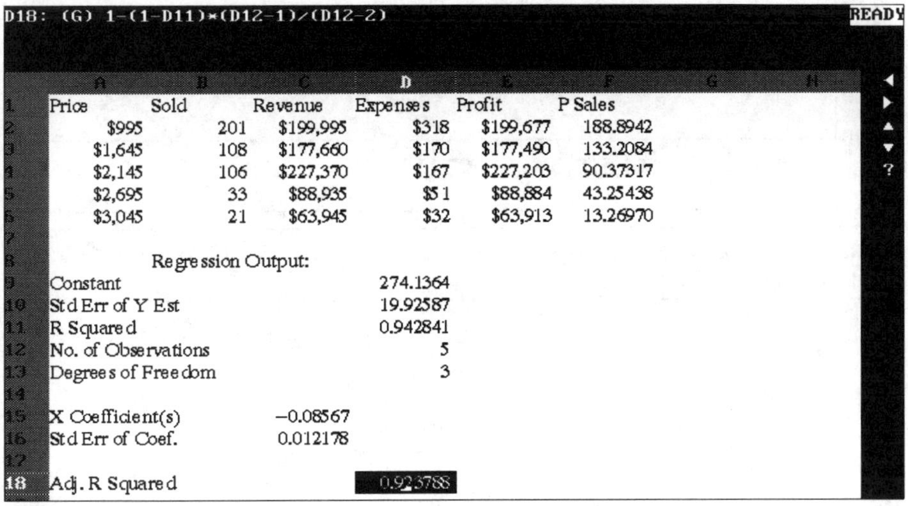

FIGURE 22.39. Check the regression analysis against the original data by creating a graph from the data.

Checking Results

Remember, you should always create a graph showing actual values against the regression line just to make sure that the regression line makes sense. Creating such a graph also lets you get a better idea of how reliable the regression predictions are. Enter the regression formula *+$D$9+$C$15*A2* in cell F2, and copy the formula down as shown in Figure 22.39.

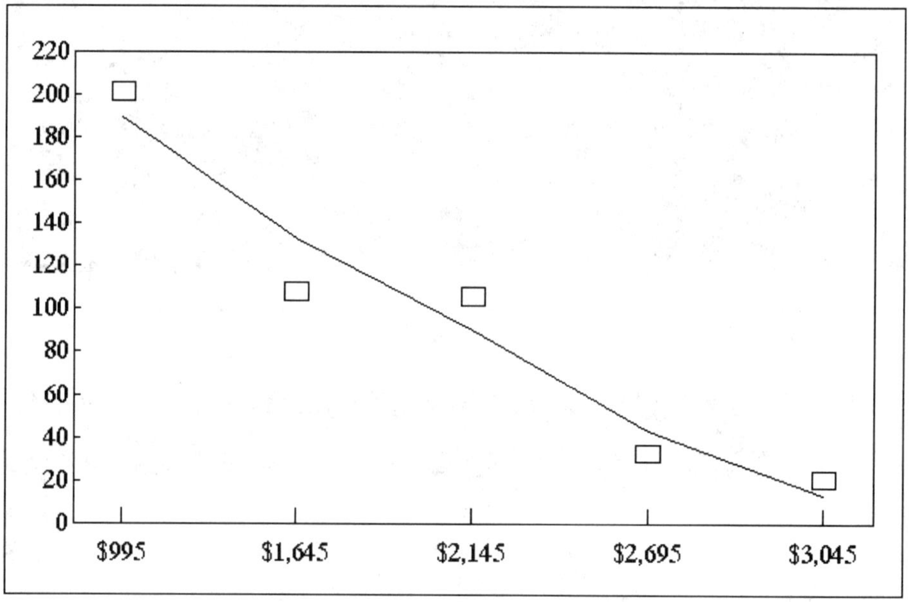

FIGURE 22.40. Always plot the regression line against the actual data points to see how well the predicted values match the actual data.

Clear the graph settings by selecting Graph Reset Graph. Use range A2..A6 as the X data range; use range B2..B6 as the A data range; and use range F2..F6 as the B data range. Select Options Format, and set the format of the A range to symbols. Set the format of the B range to lines. Select Quit Quit, and then view the graph. The graph, as shown in Figure 22.40, shows how closely the actual data points (squares) match the regression line (predicted values).

Having completed this chapter you should:

- *Be able to perform a sensitivity analysis to judge the risk of a capital investment*
- *Know how to create data tables to insert several values as variables into a collection of formulas*
- *Be able to cross-tabulate information stored in a database to generate totals and averages by department or other category*
- *Understand how to generate a frequency distribution and plot it as a histogram to reveal trends in your data*
- *Know how to use matrix math to evaluate the efficiency of several machines or processes*
- *Be able to perform regression analyses to determine how well a sample of data can predict further sampling of the data*
- *Have a firm sense of the methods by which you can predict the outcome of future events based on past outcomes of similar events*

Section 4 Present Your Data: Graphing, Enhancing, Printing

This section introduces you to the features of 1-2-3 that let you produce high-quality printed spreadsheets. It covers such topics as printing the basic spreadsheet, displaying spreadsheet data as graphs, selecting graph types appropriate to your data, dressing up text and numbers in the sheet, and creating near magazine-quality pages based on the entries in your worksheets.

It is one thing to lay out data, formulas, and labels into columns and rows of an electronic spreadsheet. It is quite another thing to make the information interesting to someone who may or may not have to read it. After all, when you've seen a few hundred spreadsheets, they all start to look pretty much the same. The same can be said of spreadsheet printouts.

Your job is to make your printouts interesting, or at least bearable, to the people who have to read them. If you are successful, you might also grab the attention of people who don't have to read your printouts but who could further your cause if they would.

Even if you fail to make your spreadsheets interesting, you should be able to make them clear. This probably means going beyond the standard numbers and letters and introducing a few graphs to help visually oriented readers. While you're at it, highlighting entries by putting them in boxes or boldfacing them could be just the emphasis you need to get across a point.

As you prepare a spreadsheet for printing, you may draw on 1-2-3's Print menus, on the Graph menus, and on the Wysiwyg add-in. This chapter explores all of these tools. It takes you first through the reporting features available in 1-2-3 without Wysiwyg. Then it explores the powerful spreadsheet publishing tools that Wysiwyg adds. By the time you complete this section, you will be able to produce dramatic reports directly from your spreadsheets —reports that will grab the attention of your co-workers, your managers, your customers, and your clients.

23

Vanilla Printing from 1-2-3

The people who suggested that computers were going to cut our reliance on paper and reduce the amount of clutter in our offices were writing science fiction. Recent history shows that the more we use computers, the more paper we handle. Perhaps what prognosticators overlooked is that computers make it much easier to put information onto paper.

Lotus 1-2-3 isn't a standout on this score. If you've installed 1-2-3 correctly and have a printer attached to the system, printing a spreadsheet is a lark. This chapter explores the printing-related features built into 1-2-3's main menus—without Wysiwyg. It explains how to print unadorned spreadsheets in a hurry and how to go about printing spreadsheets that are too large to fit in RAM along with the Wysiwyg add-in. The chapter finishes by suggesting that you might prefer always to print with Wysiwyg, but that there are times when printing without Wysiwyg is a good idea. The printing features that you learn about in this chapter will help you to grasp similar printing features when you study the Wysiwyg add-in in later chapters.

In this chapter you will:

- *Practice your model-building technique*
- *Follow seven steps to print a spreadsheet range*
- *Learn how to adjust print margins*
- *Set page headers and footers*
- *Establish print borders*
- *Learn the effects of unformatted printing*
- *See how to print listings of cell contents*
- *Establish default print settings*

Build a Model to Print

Learning how to print a spreadsheet is easiest when you have a spreadsheet to print. Of course, you can apply the techniques that we cover in this chapter to printing from any spreadsheet, but for the sake of

Please Build This Model
The model described in the setup box titled A Model for Practice Presentations will come in handy throughout this section on presenting data. Please build it now and save it on disk to retrieve for upcoming discussions.

consistency, we suggest that you create the simple model described in the setup box.

A Seven-Step Guide to No-Frills Printing

If all you are looking for is a quick printout of your worksheet, you have little to learn. Follow these seven steps to print Wickwork Apiary's production spreadsheet:

1. Make sure the printer is on and ready. If the printer has an On Line indicator light, it should be on. Also, make sure there is paper in the printer.
2. Align the printer. If you are using a tractor-fed printer or one that uses a platen to advance the paper, adjust the paper so that the printhead is about even with the top of a new page.
3. Set a Print range. Select Print Printer Range, and indicate range A1..F47 as the range to print.
4. Synchronize 1-2-3 with the printer. Although you have aligned the paper in the printer, 1-2-3 may not currently be prepared to print at the top of a page. Select Align to tell 1-2-3 that it is printing from the top of page 1. When you select Align, the menu doesn't change—but the Align command has an important effect.
5. Print the range. Select Go from the Print menu. 1-2-3 prints the entire Print range and then stops, leaving the Print menu on the display.
6. Eject paper (if needed). Depending on your printer, you may need to tell 1-2-3 to eject an extra page of paper before you can get to the entire printout. Do this by selecting Page from the menu.
7. Return to Ready mode by selecting Quit from the Print menu.

A Model for Practice Presentations

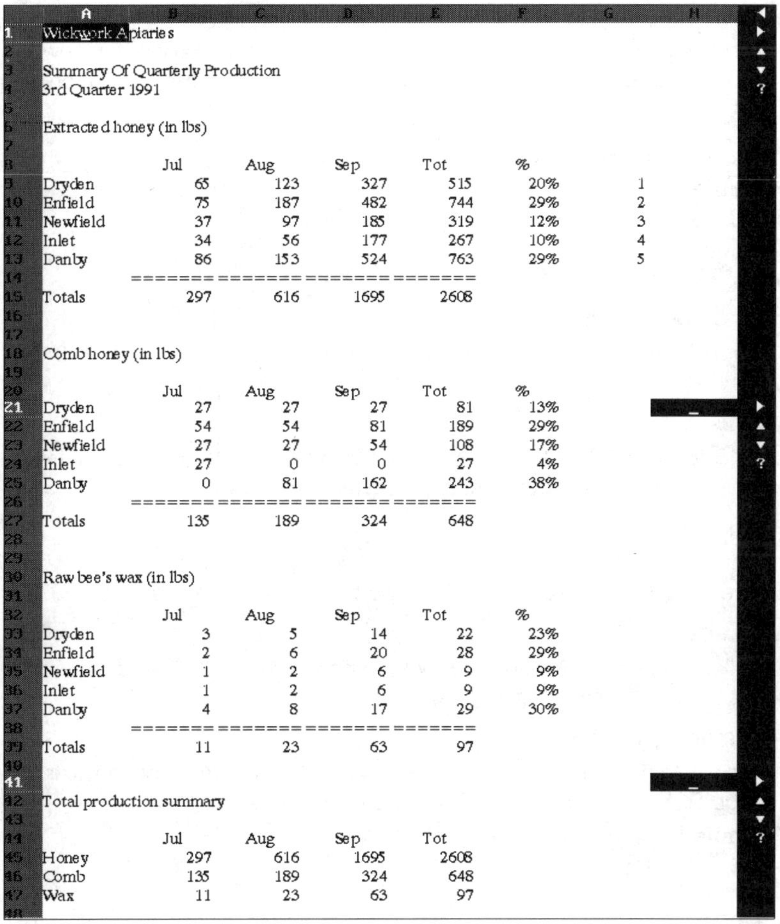

Wickwork Apiaries

Summary Of Quarterly Production
3rd Quarter 1991

Extracted honey (in lbs)

	Jul	Aug	Sep	Tot	%	
Dryden	65	123	327	515	20%	1
Enfield	75	187	482	744	29%	2
Newfield	37	97	185	319	12%	3
Inlet	34	56	177	267	10%	4
Danby	86	153	524	763	29%	5
	======	======	======	======		
Totals	297	616	1695	2608		

Comb honey (in lbs)

	Jul	Aug	Sep	Tot	%
Dryden	27	27	27	81	13%
Enfield	54	54	81	189	29%
Newfield	27	27	54	108	17%
Inlet	27	0	0	27	4%
Danby	0	81	162	243	38%
	======	======	======	======	
Totals	135	189	324	648	

Raw bee's wax (in lbs)

	Jul	Aug	Sep	Tot	%
Dryden	3	5	14	22	23%
Enfield	2	6	20	28	29%
Newfield	1	2	6	9	9%
Inlet	1	2	6	9	9%
Danby	4	8	17	29	30%
	======	======	======	======	
Totals	11	23	63	97	

Total production summary

	Jul	Aug	Sep	Tot
Honey	297	616	1695	2608
Comb	135	189	324	648
Wax	11	23	63	97

Follow the printed instructions to build this worksheet more quickly.

The instructions for setting up this worksheet don't follow in the progression that you might expect. If you follow the steps as listed, you will save many keystrokes and produce a model that matches ours exactly. Along the way you will apply many of the techniques that we have covered in earlier sections of this book.

1. Labels

Enter labels as they appear in rows 1 through 8 and in range A9..A15. The labels in row 8 are centered; either start each of them with caret (^) label prefixes or use the Range Labels Center command to realign them after you enter them. Create the dividing line in row 14 by entering \= into cell B14 and copying it to range C14..E14. Omit the other labels for now; you will use the Copy command to create some of them, and you will enter the remainder afterward.

2. Formulas

Enter formulas in the cells listed:

Cell	Formula
B15:	@SUM(B9..B13)
E9:	@SUM(B9..D9)
F9:	+E9/$E$15

3. Numeric Display Formats

Use the Range Format Percent command to assign a display format with 0 decimal places to cell F9.

4. Copy Cells

Copy cell B15 to range C15..E15. Copy Cell F9 to range F10..F13. Copy from range A6..F29 to cell A18 (it may sound weird, but trust us, it saves some time).

5. Edit Formulas

Edit the formula in cell F21 to read +E21/$E$27. Copy the new formula to range F22..F25. Edit the formula in cell F33 to read +E33/$E$39. Copy this formula to range F34..F37.

6. Replace Labels

Replace the label in cell A18 with the label *Comb honey* (*in lbs*), and replace the label in cell A30 with the label *Raw beeswax* (*in lbs*).

7. Create Summary Section

Enter the labels that appear in cells A42, A45, A46, and A47 of the illustration. Copy the labels from range B32..E32 to cell B44. Enter formulas in the cells listed:

Cell	Formula
B45:	+B15
B46:	+B27
B47:	+B39

Copy from range B45..B47 to range C45..E45.

8. Enter Data

Enter the values that appear in the illustration in ranges B9..D13, B21..D25, and B33..D37. The other values in the illustration are the results of formulas. They will appear in the appropriate cells as you work.

9. Save Your Work

Select File Save, and enter the file name BEESWAX. We'll come back to this worksheet several times in this section of the book, so it is useful to save a copy of it on your disk.

When You Print a Large Spreadsheet

Don't be fooled by our little demonstration. Printing this spreadsheet is easy because we created it to fit on a typical 8.5" by 11" page. Your spreadsheets won't always be of such a convenient size.

If your spreadsheet extends much farther down into the worksheet, 1-2-3 handles the added length without trouble. The software is aware of the standard page length. 1-2-3 fills a page, ejects paper to the top of the next page (leaving appropriate bottom and top margins for aesthetic reasons), fills the next page, and so on until the entire Print range is on paper.

If your Print range extends to the right beyond the width of a piece of paper, 1-2-3 prints each row across only to the right edge of the page and cuts off any extra text. After it completes one run through the print range, it restarts from the top, but this time it prints the text that was cut off on the first pass.

Practice Printing

Here is a little exercise to demonstrate printing behavior: Use the Copy command in your practice worksheet to copy from range B8..F39 to cell G8. The resulting worksheet doesn't make a lot of sense, but it will illustrate our point. By doubling the data across the sheet, you've made the data range too wide to print on a standard 8.5" by 11" page. (If you are using a wide form printer, this demonstration may not get the point across.)

Select Print Printer Range, and indicate A1..K39. Be sure you have aligned the paper in the printer, select Align, and select Go. Issue the Page command, if needed, and examine the resulting printout. With some transparent tape, you can align the rows of the printed pages and have a complete picture of the spreadsheet.

Control Your Print Options

When you print following the seven steps listed earlier, 1-2-3 makes all kinds of assumptions about how you want the finished page to look. By default, your software leaves a four-space margin on the left side of the page and another four-space margin on the right. 1-2-3 reserves three lines for a page header and another three lines for a footer. Added to that are a two line margin at the top of the page and two lines at the bottom, for a total of 10 lines of white space between the last line of printing on one page and the first line on the next. 1-2-3 also assumes that you are printing on pages that are exactly 66 lines, or 11 inches, long.

Margins

You can change these assumptions. For example, when you select Print Printer Options Margins, 1-2-3 lets you adjust any of the four margin settings. The higher the number for the left margin, the wider the margin. Conversely, the lower the number for the right margin, the wider the margin. 1-2-3 measures the left and right margins in terms of where they begin relative to the left edge of the page. It measures the top and bottom margins from the closest edge of the page, so a top margin of two begins two lines below the heading space, and a bottom margin of 2 begins two lines above the footer space.

If you set the right margin at a point beyond the width that your printer can handle, 1-2-3 prints as many characters per line as would fit out to the right margin setting. Any line that exceeds the printer's capacity wraps back to the beginning of the next line. For example, if you have an 80-column printer and you set the right margin at 100, any lines longer than 80 characters wrap to the next line on the printed page. This creates odd spacing throughout a document and makes for a poor presentation. Be sure that your print margins fit both your printer and the data you plan to print.

We will complete the remainder of this exercise with margins set at the defaults, so if you have worked your way into the margin setting menu, press Escape repeatedly until 1-2-3 returns to Ready mode.

Headers and Footers

We have mentioned the header and footer space that 1-2-3 reserves on each page, but we haven't explained how to use that space. You can enter a one-line header and a one-line footer that 1-2-3 will add to each page of a printout. Such headers and footers can contain any text, and they can contain page numbers that 1-2-3 generates automatically while printing.

To create a header, select Print Printer Options Header. Enter the text that you want at the top of each printed page. If you like, you can use alignment characters within your entry to control the way 1-2-3 positions the headers on the printed pages.

The alignment character is the vertical bar (¦) that appears on most keyboards on the same key as the backslash. Without an alignment character, your headers automatically align at the left edge of the page. So, for example, if you enter *My manuscript* as the header for this worksheet, the first few lines of printout will appear as shown in Figure 23.1

```
My manuscript

Wickwork Apiaries

Summary Of Quarterly Production
3rd Quarter 1991

Extracted honey (in lbs)

              Jul       Aug       Sep       Tot        %
Dryden         65       123       327       515       20%       1
Enfield        75       187       482       744       29%       2
Newfield       37        97       185       319       12%       3
Inlet          34        56       177       267       10%       4
Danby          86       153       524       763       29%       5
          ========================================
Totals        297       616      1695      2608
```

FIGURE 23.1. 1-2-3 assumes you want headers aligned at the left unless you specify otherwise.

To center a header, precede the header entry with a vertical bar. For example, the header entry ¦*My manuscript* produces a header centered on the page as shown in Figure 23.2.

```
                                  My manuscript

Wickwork Apiaries

Summary Of Quarterly Production
3rd Quarter 1991

Extracted honey (in lbs)

              Jul       Aug       Sep       Tot        %
Dryden         65       123       327       515       20%       1
Enfield        75       187       482       744       29%       2
Newfield       37        97       185       319       12%       3
Inlet          34        56       177       267       10%       4
Danby          86       153       524       763       29%       5
          ========================================
Totals        297       616      1695      2608
```

FIGURE 23.2. Using the ¦ symbol before your headers will center them.

Preceding the header text with two vertical bars slides the entire header over so it finishes flush with the right margin of the printed page.

But the header alignment characters are a bit more versatile than what we have just described. You can enter header text interspersed with alignment characters to control where specific pieces of the header will fall. For example, were you to enter *My manuscript|TITLE|June 27, 1991*, 1-2-3 would position the words *My manuscript* at the left of the heading space. It would center the word *TITLE* at the top of the page, and it would put the date, *June 27, 1991* flush with the right margin as shown in Figure 23.3.

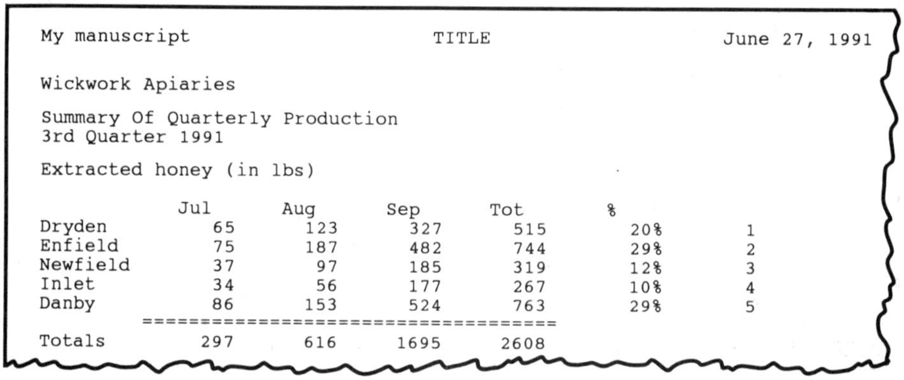

My manuscript TITLE June 27, 1991

Wickwork Apiaries

Summary Of Quarterly Production
3rd Quarter 1991

Extracted honey (in lbs)

	Jul	Aug	Sep	Tot	%	
Dryden	65	123	327	515	20%	1
Enfield	75	187	482	744	29%	2
Newfield	37	97	185	319	12%	3
Inlet	34	56	177	267	10%	4
Danby	86	153	524	763	29%	5
	=======	=======	=======	=======		
Totals	297	616	1695	2608		

FIGURE 23.3. You can align several text elements in the same header.

Do you want 1-2-3 to number pages automatically? Use the number sign (#) within the header line. For example, the header entry ||*page #* causes 1-2-3 to place a page number in the top-right corner of each printed page.

You can also include the day's date in a header by entering an @ sign. 1-2-3 replaces the @ sign with a date in the same format that appears in the bottom-left corner of the display.

It is possible to pull a page header out of a worksheet cell, rather than typing the whole thing in as a setting. To do this, under the Print Printer Options Header setting you enter a reference to the Target cell, preceded by a backslash. So, for example, the header setting \A1 in this practice worksheet would cause 1-2-3 to use the label *Wickwork Apiaries* as a left-aligned header on every page of the printout.

> ### Start with Align; Finish with Page
>
> It is a good habit to start your printing jobs by lining up the paper in your printer and selecting Align from the print menu. This tells 1-2-3 where the top of the page is. After selecting Align, don't eject paper manually; always finish a print job by selecting Page from the print menu.
>
> In almost all cases, 1-2-3 won't print a final page footer if you don't use the Print menu to eject the last page of paper. Of course, if you're not using a page footer, this isn't an issue. But 1-2-3 isn't aware when you manually eject paper from your printer. If you do so and then fail to realign the page before printing again, 1-2-3 may insert page breaks at unexpected intervals.

Create a Header and a Footer

In any case, if you haven't yet done so, select Print Printer Options Header. Enter *Wickwork*||@ as the header. It will be there later when we are ready to print. And, as long as you are at this point in the menus, select Footer. Enter |*page* - # as the footer. All the rules that apply to headers in 1-2-3 apply equally to footers, except that a footer appears at the bottom of the page rather than at the top. You will see the results of these entries in a bit.

Repeat Columns and Rows on Every Page

Just as 1-2-3 repeats headers and footers on every page, it can repeat selected columns or rows. For example, suppose that your spreadsheet contains a database like the one shown in Figure 23.4 that extends several hundred rows down the spreadsheet. If you were to print the entire database range, field headers on the first page would identify the contents of each column, but later pages would show only data.

	A	B	C	D	E	F
1		PHONE LIST				
2						
3	First	Last	Number			
4	Larry	Pierce	555-9988			
5	Shannon	McBride	555-3377			
6	Kelly	McBride	555-5758			

FIGURE 23.4. The first three records of a database that runs several hundred rows into the spreadsheet.

Undo Your Print Settings

Often you will establish print borders, headers, footers, margins, and the like for a special printing task. You need only a certain amount of information, delivered on paper in a certain way. After you get the printout, you might want 1-2-3 to revert back to whatever settings were established before you began your printing job.

To cancel your custom settings and return 1-2-3 to the existing default settings, select Print Printer Clear. You can reset all the print settings, clear only the print range setting, remove established print borders, or revert to a formatted printout after having printed the spreadsheet without page breaks.

By setting a print border, you can make the field headers appear on every page. To do this, select Print Printer Options Borders Rows, and indicate the row that contains the database field headers (range A3..C3 in our sample spreadsheet). Alternatively, you might include several rows in the border rows, so that the database title appears at the top of each page as well. In that case, you would set range A1..C3 as the print border.

Lotus 1-2-3 will print the border rows on any page, even if the print range you select isn't contiguous with the border rows. Moreover, 1-2-3 will print the border rows even if you have included them in your print range. In other words, if you set borders and include the border cells in your print ranges, 1-2-3 prints two copies of the border cells—one copy as a border and the other as part of the Print range. Of course, the same applies to border columns. Let's print using border columns so you can see how to use them.

Set Print Borders

If you haven't returned 1-2-3 to Ready mode, do so. Then select Print Printer Options Borders Columns. Indicate column A as the border column, and then select Quit. Select Range, and indicate range E8..F39 as the range to print. If necessary, make sure the paper is aligned in the printer, and then select Go. Select Page to make your printer eject a page.

Lotus 1-2-3 prints the border column immediately alongside the data from columns E and F. Be aware, that if you select a range too wide to fit within the established margins, 1-2-3 prints the border column on each page needed to fit the range.

Notice that 1-2-3 printed the page header and footer that you specified earlier; the word *Wickwork* appears at the top-left of the page, and the day's date appears at the top-right. If you selected Page to eject the paper from your printer, the page number appears centered at the bottom.

To remove established border row or column settings, select Clear Borders from the main printing menu—the menu that appears when you select Print Printer from Ready mode. Do this now before you continue with the printing exercises.

Alternative Output: Unformatted Text and Cell Listings

Sometimes it is more appropriate to print a spreadsheet without page breaks, headers, and footers. Printing this way is practical when you use continuous tractor-feed paper, but it is less reliable with printers that feed individual sheets of paper. In most cases they leave a space at the beginning and end of each page.

At any rate, to eliminate page breaks (and therefore headers from all but the first page and footers from all but the last page), select Print Printer Options Other Unformatted. To restore printing with automatic pagination, select Print Printer Options Other Formatted.

Print a Listing

Particularly useful for people who like to document their spreadsheets is the option that allows you to print listings of cells' contents. Such a listing contains a cell address followed by the label, value, or formula stored in the cell, for each entry in the print range.

See how this works. If you fiddled with the Formatted or Unformatted setting, make sure you return to the Formatted mode. The menu sequence from Ready mode is Print Printer Options Other Formatted. Selecting Quit Quit returns 1-2-3 to Ready mode. Now select Print Printer Range, and indicate range E8..F13 as the range to print. Then select Options Other Cell-Formulas Quit Align Go Page. The resulting page should contain the familiar headers and footers and the following cell listing:

```
E8:     ^Tot
F8:     ^%
E9:     @SUM(B9..D9)
F9:     (P0) +E9/$E$15
E10:    @SUM(B10..D10)
F10:    (P0) +E10/$E$15
```

> **When You Change Paper Size**
>
> Lotus 1-2-3 assumes that the paper in your printer is 8.5 by 11 inches. It also assumes that your printer prints six lines to an inch for a total of 66 lines to a page. For many printers, this is an incorrect assumption. Laser printers, as a rule, print 60 lines to a page. If you don't tell 1-2-3 about this, your printouts on a laser printer are likely to be disappointing.
>
> Tell 1-2-3 the page length your printer uses by selecting Print Printer Options Pg-Length and entering the number of lines that fit on a single page. If you are using 8.5 by 11 inch paper on a laser printer, the length should probably be 60. If you are using an odd size paper on a dot matrix printer, divide the page length in inches by six. The result is the page length that you should enter at the prompt.

```
E11:   @SUM(B11..D11)
F11:   (P0) +E11/$E$15
E12:   @SUM(B12..D12)
F12:   (P0) +E12/$E$15
E13:   @SUM(B13..D13)
F13:   (P0) +E13/$E$15
```

Select Options Other Formatted Quit Quit to reestablish standard printing mode and return to Ready.

What About Those Default Settings?

We have explored some of the printing options that 1-2-3 offers. In most cases, we looked at the commands that let you change settings from existing defaults. 1-2-3 comes from the factory with those defaults already set, but you can change them to suit your preferences and have custom defaults active at the beginning of every work session.

As we discussed in the first section of this book, you alter spreadsheet defaults by selecting Worksheet Global Default. Modify printer defaults by selecting Printer from the resulting menu. From the list of options that appears in the dialog box shown in Figure 23.5, you can see that only a few of the print settings we have already dealt with have modifiable defaults.

You can alter the number of lines that 1-2-3 prints on a page, and you can adjust the right, left, top, and bottom margins. Other settings that you control from the Global Default Printer menu determine how 1-2-3 communicates with your printer. If you installed more than one printer driver when you first

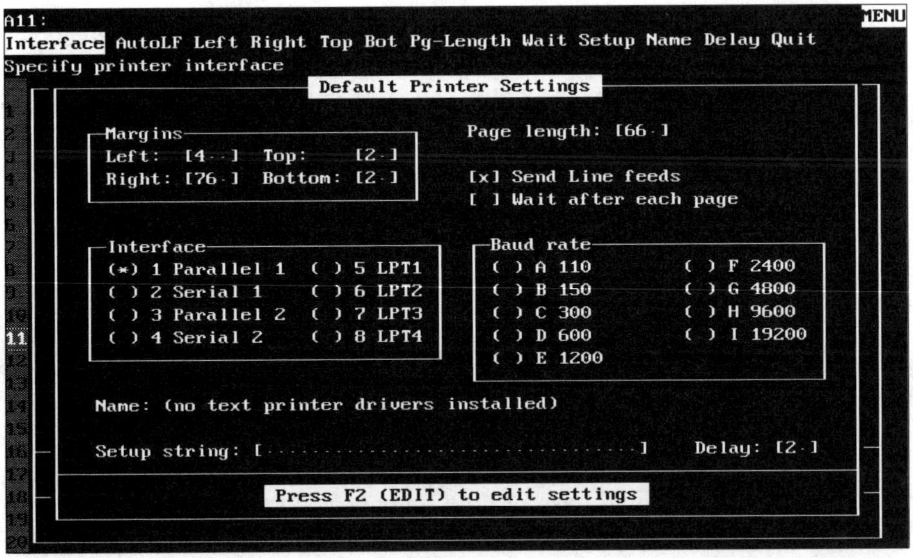

FIGURE 23.5. The Worksheet Global Default Printer dialog box revealing its original default settings.

set up the software, you can choose which printer to print with by selecting Name from the menu.

You also have control from the Default Printer menu over which printer port 1-2-3 uses to deliver its output. If you have gotten results from these printing exercises, then the port settings are correct. But if you add a second printer or decide to plug into a different port than the one you are currently using, this is the menu you will use to tell 1-2-3 about it.

If you do change margin or page length settings under the Default Printer menu, be sure you select Update from the Worksheet Global Default menu to record those changes in 1-2-3's configuration file. 1-2-3 reads that file at startup so your selected defaults will be established during a work session.

Print To Disk, Print Encoded, and Print in the Background

Sending the print range directly to paper isn't the only way to print in 1-2-3. When you select Print from the main menu, you must choose from four options to specify what happens to the printout after you select Go. You can send the print range to the printer, to a file on disk in one of two file formats, or to a print spooler that will print out the range in the background while you continue to work in the spreadsheet. Printing to disk lets you pass spreadsheet data easily into other programs, such as database managers and word processors. Printing in the background saves time by letting you continue in the worksheet no matter how long it takes your printer to complete a printout.

Print File

When you select Print File, 1-2-3 prompts you to enter a name for the file that will receive a printout. After you enter a file name, you have access to all of the commands we have discussed in this chapter for selecting a print range, setting headers and footers, and so on. However, when you select Go, 1-2-3 sends the desired output to disk. The result is a simple ASCII file that is an image of what would have printed on paper had you selected Printer as the print destination. The image is of characters that you can type at the keyboard only—it can't include underlining, special fonts, or other unusual attributes that you might use setup strings to create.

You might create an ASCII file if you want to move data from 1-2-3 into a stand-alone word processing document. ASCII files are also useful for passing data into some database management packages. 1-2-3 assigns the extension *PRN* to ASCII print files. Hence, if you enter *TEXT* as the name for a target print file, 1-2-3 saves the printout to a file named *TEXT.PRN*. When you use DOS to print a PRN file, no special print attributes appear in the printout.

Print Encoded

When you select Print Encoded, 1-2-3 again prompts you to enter a file name. You then have access to all of the commands described earlier in this chapter. However, when you select Go, 1-2-3 sends the printout to a file using a format that includes special printer control codes. The codes are specific to whatever printer you've installed to work with 1-2-3. An encoded file includes any setup strings that control the fonts, font styles, and other printing effects of the printer.

When you use DOS to print an encoded file, all of the special attributes that you established in 1-2-3 appear in the printout. You might use the Print Encoded option when you want to print several reports on a printer other than the one connected to your computer. You could print each report to disk, take the disk to another computer, and then use DOS's PRINT or COPY command to produce the final printout.

Print Background

When you use the Print Printer command to print a range, you must wait until 1-2-3 finishes printing before you can do further work in the sheet. The Print Background command lets you continue to work as the range prints. To use background printing, you must run a program in DOS called BPRINT before loading 1-2-3.

To run BPRINT, exit to DOS—use the Quit command, not System—and make the directory that holds 1-2-3's program files the current directory. In most cases, you need only to enter *BPRINT* at the DOS prompt and then restart 1-2-3. However, you can impart some instructions to the BPRINT command to tell it where to find your printer. For example, if your printer is on parallel port number one, enter the command *BPRINT -P=1*. If the printer is on serial port number two, enter *BPRINT -S=2*.

The BPRINT program is a *terminate and stay resident program* (TSR). This means that once you've run it by issuing the BPRINT command, it seems to disappear as if you hadn't run it at all. When you need the features of a TSR, they are available at the press of a key or at request of some other program. 1-2-3 calls on BPRINT's features when you issue the Print Background command.

To start background printing, select Print Background and enter a file name in which to store output on its way to the printer. Specify your print settings and select Go to send output to the interim file. You can alter the settings—change the print range, for example—and send further information to the file. When you have finished specifying the settings, select Quit from the print menu. The BPRINT TSR begins printing, and you can continue working in the spreadsheet. You can retrieve other spreadsheets and reissue the Print Background command again to do even more printing. Use a new name for the interim print file each time you exit and reenter the Print Background menus.

To stop printing one or all the files you've started printing in the background you must issue a command in DOS. To do this, use the System command to get into DOS. The 1-2-3 program directory should be current when the DOS prompt appears. Enter *BPRINT -T* to stop all printing. Enter *BPRINT -C C:\PATH\FILNAM*, where *FILNAM* is the name of the interim print file to stop from printing. When you've aborted printing of the appropriate files, type *EXIT* to return to 1-2-3.

Vanilla Printing Overdone

In the industry, an application that challenges your equipment very little while getting a job done is called a *vanilla* application. Most such applications run on any equipment, because they call upon none of the equipment's advanced features. At least the most basic tasks that a computer does are standardized from one machine to another; they are vanilla.

We have called this chapter Vanilla Printing because it covers only the basics of producing output from your spreadsheet. There are many subtleties to printing from 1-2-3, and mastering those subtleties lets you create some very dramatic effects. On the other hand, it requires a lot of work and experimentation to get fancy spreadsheet printouts directly from 1-2-3.

Rather than spend more time and space delving into the intricacies of creating polished reports from within 1-2-3, we opt instead to focus on the superior reporting capabilities of the Wysiwyg add-in.

Our counsel on printing directly from 1-2-3 boils down to two guidelines:

1. Use 1-2-3 without Wysiwyg when you need quick drafts in a hurry.
2. Use 1-2-3 without Wysiwyg when you don't have enough RAM to load Wysiwyg along with the spreadsheet you want to print.

We look closely at Wysiwyg in upcoming chapters. But before we do that, it will be useful for you to learn a bit about 1-2-3's ability to create graphs based on the data in a worksheet.

Having completed this chapter you should:

- *Understand how to print spreadsheet ranges using 1-2-3's Print menus*
- *Be able to customize a printout by changing margins, adding headers and footers, and establishing print borders*
- *Know how to print listings of cell contents to help document your spreadsheets on paper*
- *Be able to choose appropriately when to print without Wysiwyg*
- *Be prepared to apply your understanding of printing to produce output from Wysiwyg*

24

Go Visual: Graph Spreadsheet Data

Some members of your audience can get your message from lists of numbers and a few supporting labels. Others would rather skip the numbers and labels and jump directly to the pictures. The best way to reach the greatest possible audience is to incorporate pictures with the numbers and labels in your spreadsheets. The first step in doing that is to turn your data into graphs.

This chapter leads you through a series of exercises that will teach you how to create graphs in 1-2-3. We will examine the various types of graphs you can build and consider some of the situations in which to apply them. To make the whole adventure even more interesting, we will create a snazzy graph that looks like the product of hours of tedious work but requires only minutes of typing.

This chapter relies on hands-on interaction with 1-2-3 to get its points across. While you will be able to understand what is going on by reading only, we recommend that you work along at your computer. You will then be able to compare the results of your efforts with the illustrations throughout the chapter.

In this chapter you will learn how to:

- *Create simple graphs from spreadsheet data*
- *Enhance a graph with titles*
- *Apply the Graph Group command*
- *Add a legend to a graph*
- *Display a graph in two orientations*
- *Create the following graph types: Stacked-bar, bar with 3D effect, pie, line, mixed bar and line, area, HLCO, and XY*
- *Use a few of the available graph types*
- *Create an eye-catching XY graph*

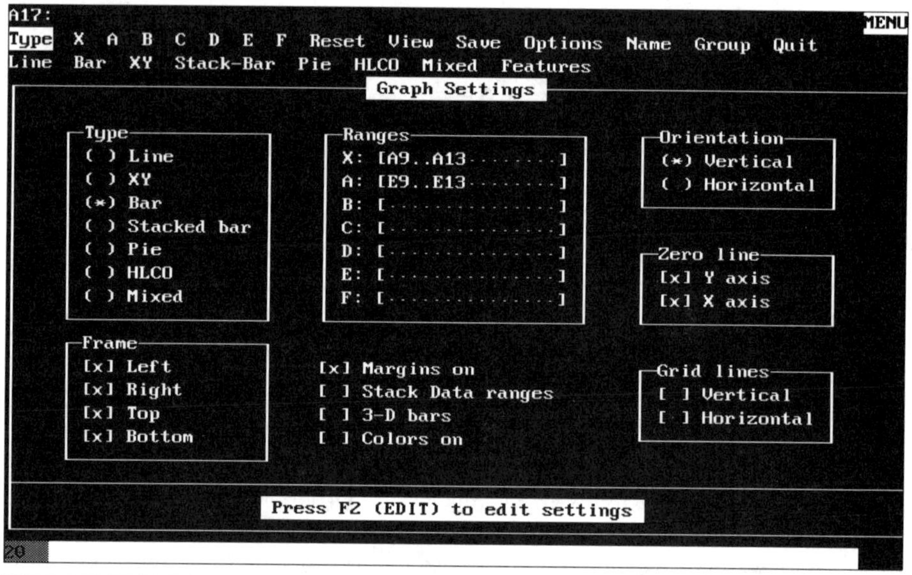

FIGURE 24.1. This graph dialog box reveals the settings used to create the graph of Wickwork Apiary's third quarter extracted honey production.

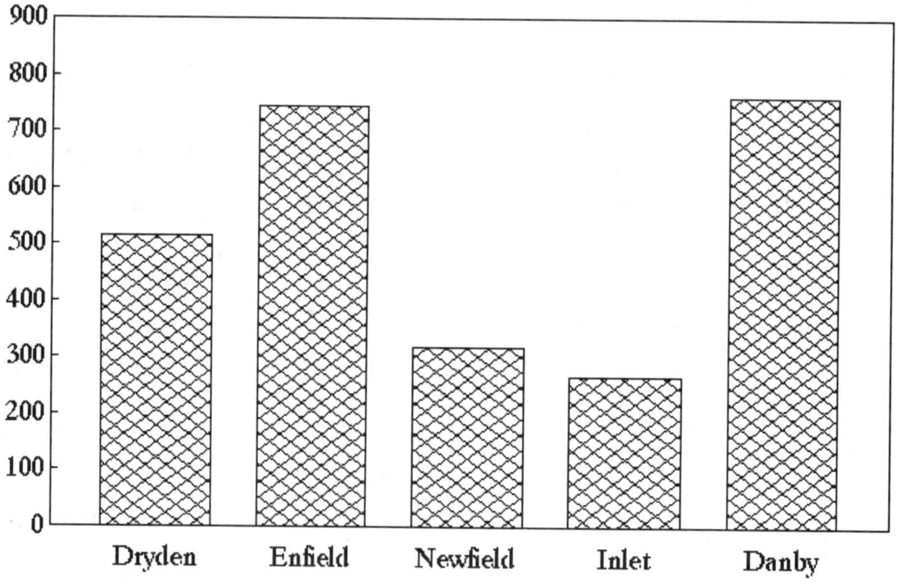

FIGURE 24.2. An unadorned bar chart shows Wickwork's third quarter extracted honey production.

Learn About Graphs by Building Them

By issuing the right commands in 1-2-3, you can create graphs that represent the data in your spreadsheets. The quickest route to understanding how this works is to build some graphs of your own. Retrieve the BEESWAX file that you created and saved in preparation for the discussion in the previous chapter. If you haven't created that file, do so now before you continue with this chapter. You will find instructions at the beginning of Chapter 23.

Your spreadsheet contains information on three products produced by Wickwork Apiaries, a small honey producer in upstate New York. Wickwork has several hive sites and records the honey and wax production from each of the sites.

Edwina, the operator of Wickwork, compares the monthly production from each of several hive locations.

You are Edwina's assistant. You don't particularly enjoy poking around in bee hives (it's a hypothetical scenario—at least pretend that you don't like to poke around in bee hives), so it is your job to log the honey and wax production and to produce reports. Edwina likes graphs.

The very simplest graph Edwina wants to see compares the total production of each site for a given product throughout the quarter. Let's create that graph for the extracted honey production.

Graph Wickwork's Honey Production

Start by selecting Graph from 1-2-3's main menu. You see right away that there is a dialog box associated with graph settings. Figure 24.1 shows that dialog box with the settings that you are about to establish. Use the dialog box, if you wish, to make the settings, or follow the menu instructions that we provide.

Select Type from the graph menu, and then select Bar. Select X, and indicate range A9..A13 as the X data range. Select A, and indicate range *E9..E13* as the A data range. Now select View. The spreadsheet vanishes, and a graph like the one in Figure 24.2 appears.

Lotus 1-2-3 has translated the graph ranges you established into a graphical image. The X data range has become labels for the X axis of the graph, and the A data range has become the bars of the graph. It is clear at a glance that Enfield and Dryden shared the highest honey production, while the Inlet site produced the least honey.

Add Titles

Actually, the only reason it is clear what the graph in Figure 24.2 represents is that we already know what it represents. If someone handed you a graph that looked like this without an explanation, you wouldn't have any idea what it portrayed. Adding a title or two will help to clarify the matter.

Press any key, and the graph vanishes, returning you to the main Graph menu and settings sheet. To create a graph title, select Options Titles First and enter *Wickwork: Extracted Honey*. Select Titles Second, and enter *3rd Quarter 1991*. Then select Quit and View to see the results of your handiwork.

While the added titles make it clear what the graph is supposed to represent, there is still something missing. Dryden's bar in the graph passes the 700 mark, but nothing answers the question, "700 of what?" Could it be 700 supers of honey? (Each box of a hive in which the bees store honey is called a super.) Perhaps the graph shows honey in units of volume?

Add a Y-axis title to further clarify the presentation. To do this, press a key to clear the graph, and return to the main graph menu. Select Options Titles Y-Axis, and enter *production in lbs*. Then press the GRAPH key (F10). Pressing GRAPH produces a display of the current graph, no matter where you are in the menus at the moment. The meaning of the graph in Figure 24.3 is now clear.

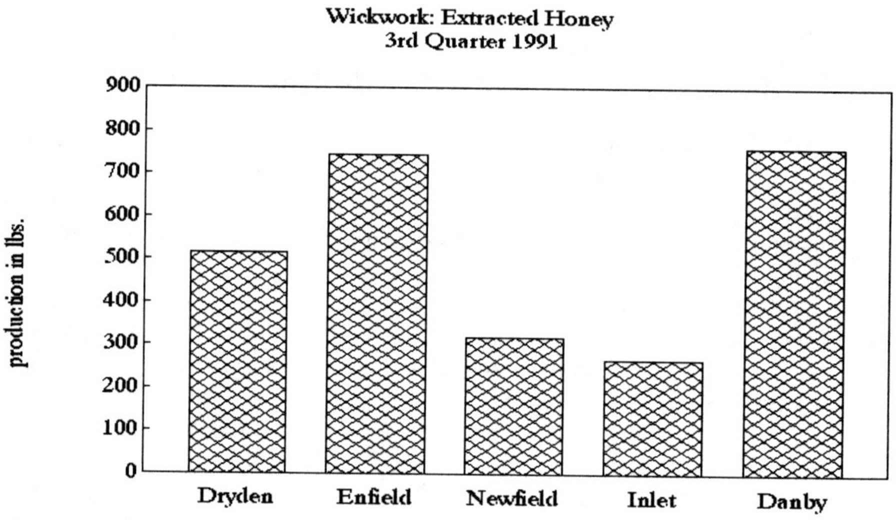

FIGURE 24.3. The titles applied to this bar chart reveal at a glance what the graph represents.

Graphs with Words: Label the Data

Clarity is important. If there is any doubt that your graph will convey its message, it needs more work. One way you can further enhance a graph is to label its data points. For example, with the simple bar graph shown in Figure 24.3, you can't tell exactly what value each bar represents. If precision is important, set a range of data labels to reveal the exact numbers.

To set the data labels, select Graph Options Data-Labels A. You are going to label each data point in the A graph range. Indicate E9..E13 as the worksheet range that contains the labels for each data point. Actually, the range contains numbers, but 1-2-3 will use those numbers to label the graph. Select Above, and then press the GRAPH key (F10). The resulting graph should match the one below.

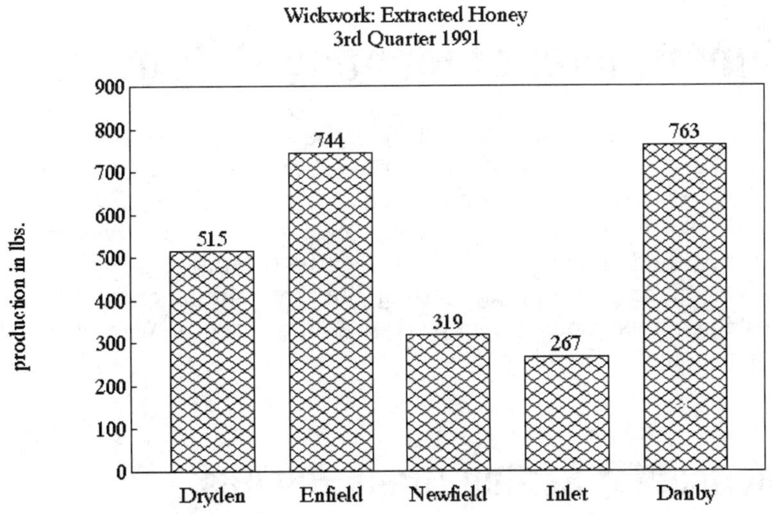

The data labels in this bar chart reveal the exact numbers on which the bars are based.

Preserve a Graph's Settings

Once you've created a graph in 1-2-3, you must give it a name if you want to go on and create other graphs. If you don't name a graph, any changes you make to the established settings affect that graph. This means that to create a new graph, you must abandon the settings of the current graph. By naming a graph, you make a record of its settings so you can alter the current settings with impunity. Try it to see how it works.

Press a key to eliminate the graph display. Then select Quit Name Create, and enter *exttot* as the name for the current graph. This makes a record of the current settings. Now erase the current settings by selecting Reset from the main Graph menu. There are options here for resetting any of the graph ranges, all of the ranges, all of the graph options, or all of the graph settings. Select Graph to eliminate all your established settings. The established graph ranges vanish from the dialog box, and the graph type setting reverts back to Line. Let's create a new graph to reinforce what you have just learned. We will use this second graph when we use Wysiwyg to lay out a spreadsheet report in a later chapter.

A Comparison of Monthly Output

This new graph will show the monthly output of extracted honey from each hive site. Again, select Type Bar from the Graph menu. Select X, and indicate range *B8..D8* as the X data range. Select A, and indicate *B9..D9* as the A data range. Set *B10..D10* as the B data range, *B11..D11* as the C data range, *B12..D12* as the D range, and *B13..D13* as the E range. Now select View.

It took a fair amount of range setting, but the resulting graph (Figure 24.4) is a striking comparison of honey production at each of Wickwork's sites in July, August, and September.

A Shortcut for Setting Graph Ranges

Press a key to clear the graph, and then select Reset Graph to dump its settings. We deliberately instructed you to create a bar chart the hard way. There is an easier way,

Select Type Bar, and then select Group. 1-2-3 prompts you to indicate a group range. To create the desired bar chart, you must include the headers and values in range B8..D13, so indicate that range. Now you must choose either the columns or the rows as data ranges. Just a moment ago you assigned each row as a data range, so select Rowwise. The data ranges appear instantly in the dialog box, just as they did after you entered them one-at-a-time. See Figure 24.5.

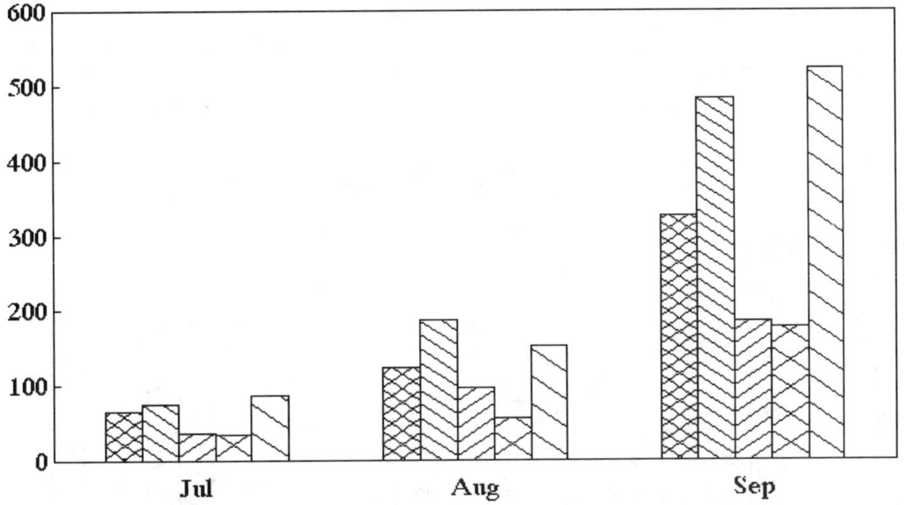

FIGURE 24.4. By assigning each row of data as a graph range, we have created a handy graph that compares extracted honey production in three months.

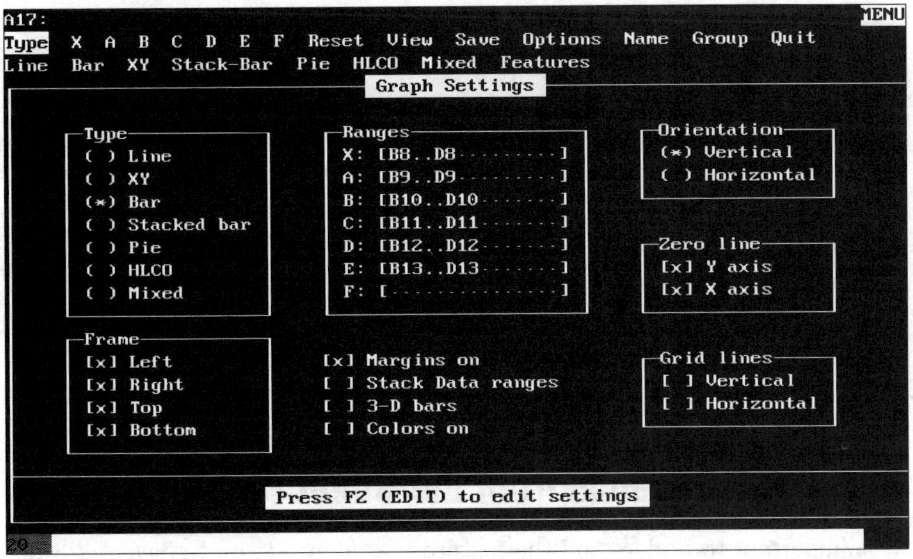

FIGURE 24.5. The Graph Group command established all of the data ranges in this dialog box in a single operation.

To clarify the graph, select Options Titles and enter *Wickwork: Extracted Honey* as the first title. Enter *3rd Quarter 1991* as the second graph title. Also, select Titles Y-Axis, and enter *production in lbs*. Press the GRAPH key (F10) to see the results of your handiwork, which should look like Figure 24.6.

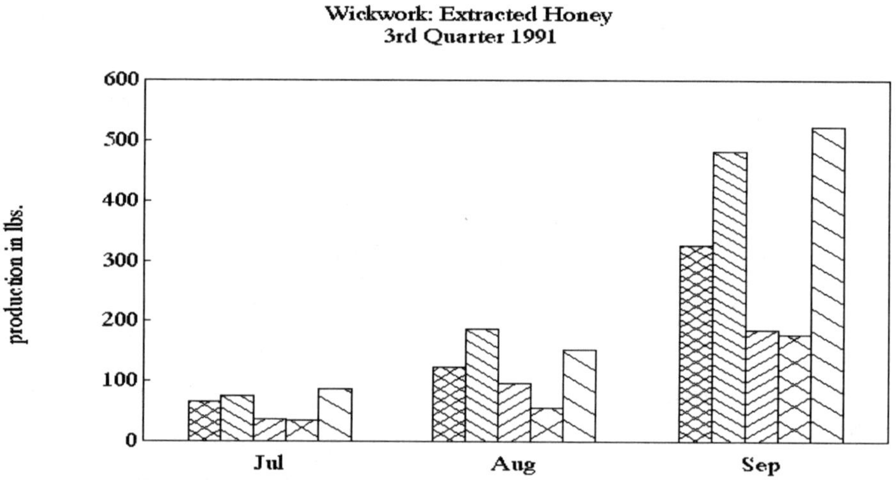

FIGURE 24.6. Even with the added titles, this graph is missing some important information. What does each of the bars represent?

As pretty as the graph is, you can't tell what it represents. It has something to do with honey production in July, August, and September, but what does each of the bars represent? This graph needs a legend.

Press a key to clear the graph from the display, and select Legend. The resulting menu lets you enter a specific descriptor for each data range or select a range in the worksheet that contains the descriptors. Select Range and indicate range *A9..A13*. Then press the GRAPH key. Figure 24.7 shows quite clearly what the bars in the graph represent.

Titles and Legends from the Sheet

It is important to understand the feature that allowed you to have 1-2-3 find legends in the worksheet. When you select Graph Options Titles or Graph Options Legend, 1-2-3 lets you type a label that will become a title or a legend. Press a key to clear the graph, and select Legend A to see how this works.

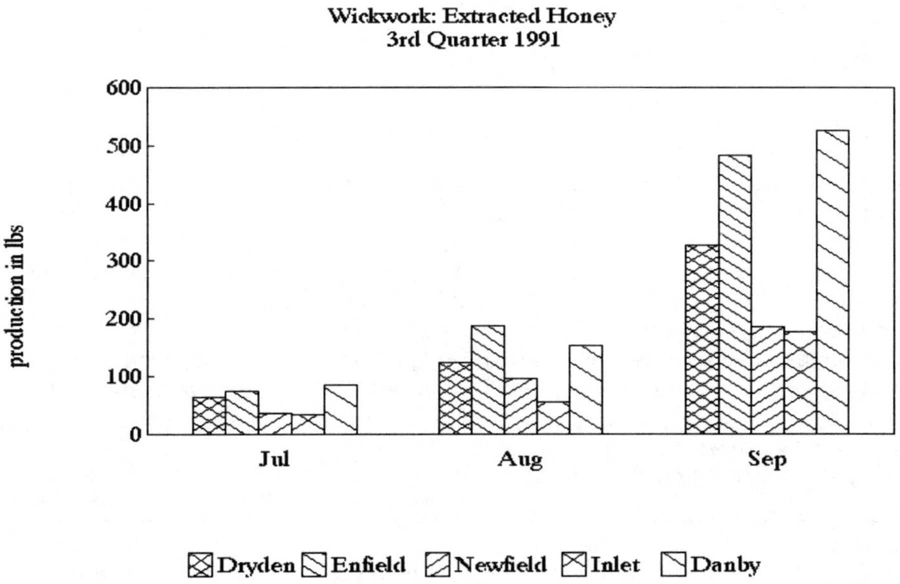

FIGURE 24.7. A legend added to the honey production comparison graph clarifies the meaning of the graph.

Lotus 1-2-3 shows that the current legend for the A data range is \A9. In fact, this is a reference to the spreadsheet. Press Backspace three times to erase the reference, and then enter *Stuff*. Press the GRAPH key, and see that *Stuff* has become the legend for the A data range.

You create a reference to the spreadsheet to establish graph titles or legends by entering a backslash followed by a cell reference or a range name. The Graph Options Legend Range command created a series of such references for you, but you can establish each individually to any cell in the worksheet.

Try it. Press a key to clear the graph display. Then select Legend A, and enter *\A9*. Select Quit and then View to see the result of your entry. Press a key to clear the graph when you finish your perusal.

Save the Settings

Do you remember how to save a graph's settings? Don't be fooled by the menu options. The Graph Save command has nothing to do with saving the settings. It is the Graph Name command that lets you maintain a collection of graphs in a sheet. Select Name Create, and enter the name *extsum*.

Save a Graph on Disk

In the past, you couldn't print a graph from within 1-2-3. If you wanted a graph on paper, you would create it as you've learned to do here. Then you would use the Graph Save command to create an image of the graph on disk. The graph image file that 1-2-3 creates has a .PIC file extension.

To print a PIC file, you exit 1-2-3 and run a program called Printgraph, which comes with 1-2-3. You can install it when you first install the software, but there is not much use for it when the Wysiwyg add-in is available because Wysiwyg lets you print graphs from within the worksheet.

Saving graph images in PIC files isn't a completely useless exercise. Many other programs, including graphics enhancers (like Lotus Freelance Plus) and desktop publishers (like Lotus Ami), can read PIC files and display the graphic images. Also, Wysiwyg itself can display images stored in PIC files. You might create graphs in several worksheets, save each to its own PIC file, and create a single consolidation worksheet that includes images from the PIC files.

Now there are two graphs established in the sheet. To view one and make its settings available, select Name Use and select a name from the menu list. In this case, select *extot*. 1-2-3 displays the first graph you created. Press a key to clear the graph, and once again select Name Use. This time choose *extsum* from the menu. The new graph appears.

Change a Graph's Orientation

Changing the orientation of a graph can add variety to a presentation. In all earlier releases of 1-2-3, you were stuck with graphs whose X-axis ran across the bottom of the display. With release 2.3, you can rotate any graph 90 degrees so that the X axis runs vertically along the left side of the display.

Try it with your graph. Press a key to clear the graph from the display. Then select Type Features Horizontal Quit View. This alternative perspective can come in handy when you are trying to fit graphs among data and text in a Wysiwyg presentation. A normal bar chart is difficult to interpret when it is squashed vertically. Rotate the graph 90 degrees as shown in Figure 24.8, and even a very low ceiling won't confuse the presentation.

Save the worksheet for use in future exercises.

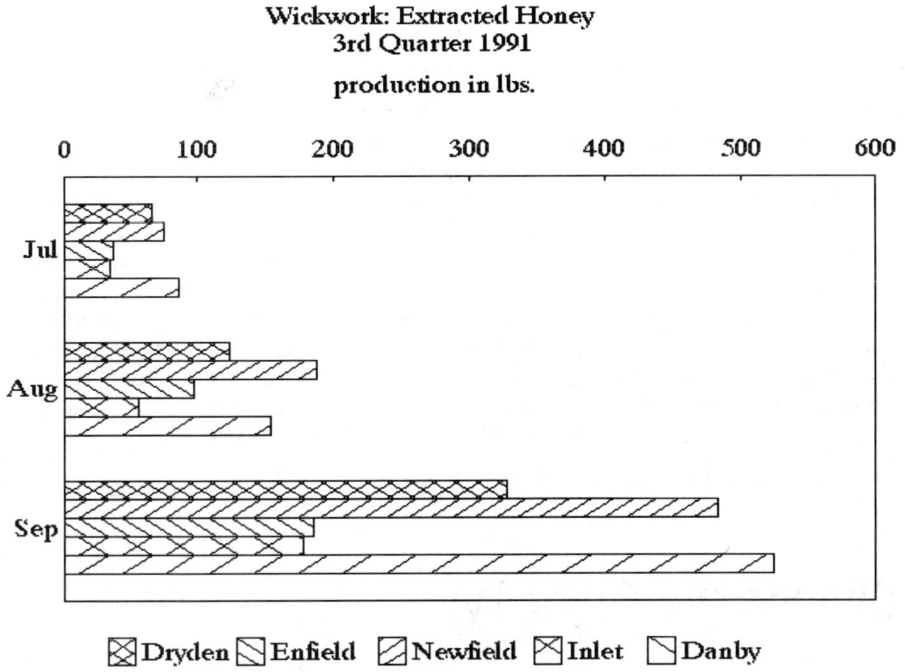

FIGURE 24.8. Display a bar graph horizontally if you need to compress it from top to bottom.

Control a Graph's Scaling

When you assign graph ranges and then view the resulting graph, 1-2-3 automatically displays the graph in a scale that handily accommodates the largest data elements. This automatic scaling eliminates a lot of thought from the plotting process, but it sometimes results in an unsatisfactory graph.

When this is the case, you can override the automatic scaling. From the main graph menu, select Options Scale and then Y-Axis or X-Axis. The resulting menu offers quite a few choices. You can set upper and lower limits for the selected axis, select a numeric display format for the numbers that appear on the selected axis, and even determine whether 1-2-3 should display the selected axis. The upper and lower limits that you set have no effect on the graph's display unless you also select Manual to override automatic scaling. Create a few graphs on your own or use the ones described in this chapter, and experiment with the graph scaling options.

On Your Own

We have looked at only a small part of the graphing power of 1-2-3. Explore the options available on 1-2-3's Graph menus further on your own. Scaling options let you alter the numeric display formats of the values along a graph's axes. The Graph Options Grid selections control whether 1-2-3 superimposes grid lines on a graph to help accentuate the limits of each data element. The Options Color selection lets you display graphs using colors to differentiate data ranges rather than the grid patterns that appear in our illustrations. Of course, you should probably eschew this option if you are using a monochrome monitor.

Whatever your needs, fiddle with the Graph menus until each of your graphs is easy to interpret. Use the Graph Name Create command to save the settings of each customized graph. If you need to alter some settings, use the Graph Name Use command to bring up the applicable settings. Make the desired changes, and then reissue the Graph Name Create command to save the new settings under the existing graph name.

Choose the Right Type

Even an average pool player can confirm that you must hit the cue ball a certain way to pocket the 8 ball and roll two rails so that you leave an easy shot on the 9 ball. If you don't stroke it just right, you don't get the reaction you want. This applies as well to creating meaningful graphs in 1-2-3; if you don't hit the right graph type, you won't impart the message you want to convey. You might end up with a long shot when you should have the presentation clinched.

It is hard to choose the right graph type if you don't know what types are available. Even when you do know, picking the graph type appropriate to your data requires some thought. The remainder of this chapter should give you a handle on the types of graphs 1-2-3 offers and when to apply them.

Variation on the Bar

Bar graphs quite handily describe many business scenarios. They are most appropriate when you want to compare a few variables at specified times. As you can see in the graph named extsum that you created earlier (make it

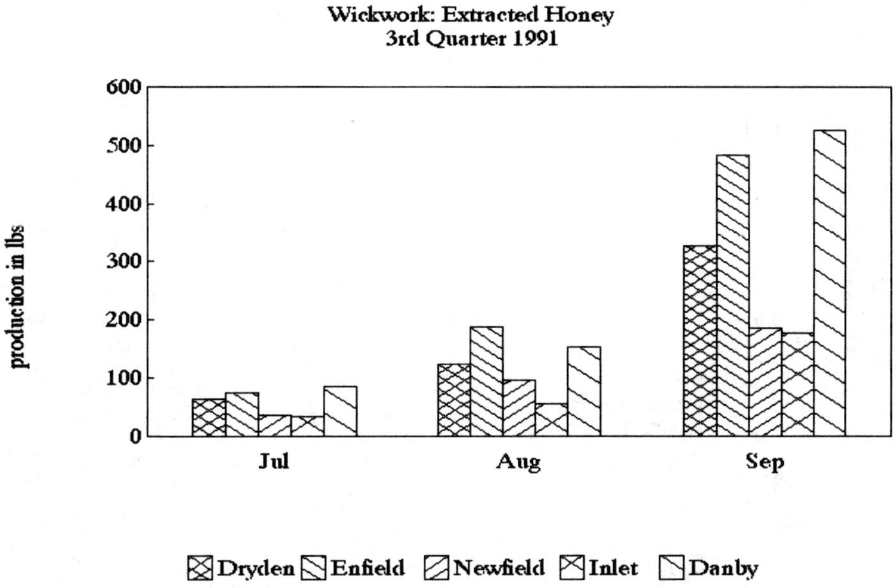

FIGURE 24.9. A bar chart provides clear comparisons of variables such as production, volume, and sales revenue.

visible by selecting Name Use from the Graph menu and entering *extsum*), the honey production of each site clearly stands out from the others when the production from each site appears as a bar.

Quite often, as is the case with the extsum graph, each cluster of bars in a bar graph represents a sum. The first cluster of bars in the extsum graph is the total amount of extracted honey produced in July. The second clump is total production for August, and the third is production for September.

The bar clusters don't highlight total honey production for each month. In fact, it is a bit of work to come up with a total for each cluster when you are faced with this type of bar chart. If you want the emphasis of the graph to be on total production per month and you still want it to reveal production from each site, use a stacked-bar graph.

Changing graph types is a snap. Press any key to clear the graph from the display, and then select Type Stack-Bar. Select View to see the results of the change. See Figure 24.10.

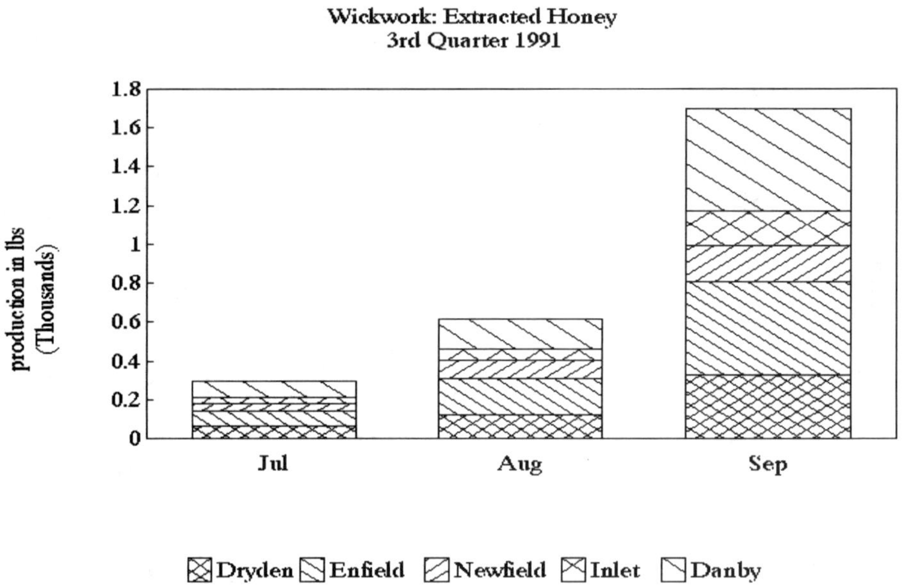

FIGURE 24.10. A stacked-bar graph reveals monthly honey production by site and emphasizes total production for each month.

The 3-D Effect Adds Pizzaz

Apparently, bar charts aren't interesting enough for some people. If you worry that your bar charts are, well, flat, then you might want to add a 3-D effect to give them a bit of depth.

Press a key to clear the graph display, and then select Type Features 3D-Effect Yes Quit. Select View to see the altered graph shown in Figure 24.11.

The three-dimensional effect is much more appealing on a color display with the color option selected than it is in black and white. If you have a color monitor, press a key to clear the graph, select Options Color Quit, and then select View.

As nice as the color graphs may look, keep in mind that your printouts are also limited by the available hardware. Most printers create black-on-white images, so a fancy color display may produce disappointing printouts. If, however, you are using graphs as part of a presentation given on the computer, you can take full advantage of the color option. Be aware of your graphing options, and apply them appropriately.

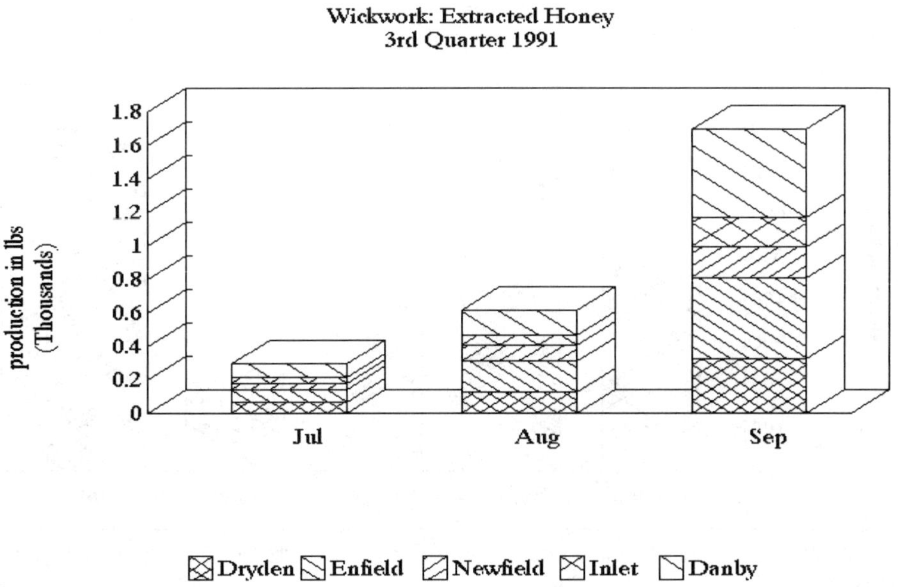

FIGURE 24.11. The 3D-Effect option adds some depth to a bar chart. The effect is more pleasing when your graph is in color.

In addition to showing both the site totals and the grand totals for Wickwork's extracted honey production, the stacked-bar graph gives you a handle on the percentage of production from each site. Because each bar is the total production for a month, a uniquely shaded section of the bar represents a percentage of the total. While the exact percentages aren't always apparent, a stacked-bar graph gives you a fair sense of them.

Pies Are Precise

If you're interested in reviewing the actual percentage of total production provided by each site, use a pie chart. In creating a pie graph, 1-2-3 sums the data points in the assigned data range and creates proportionately sized pie slices that together make up a whole pie. This is much clearer when you see it happen.

Clear the graph from the display. You might remember that the first graph you created in the BEESWAX worksheet showed total extracted honey production for each hive site. Select Name Use, and activate the graph named extot, which is shown in Figure 24.12.

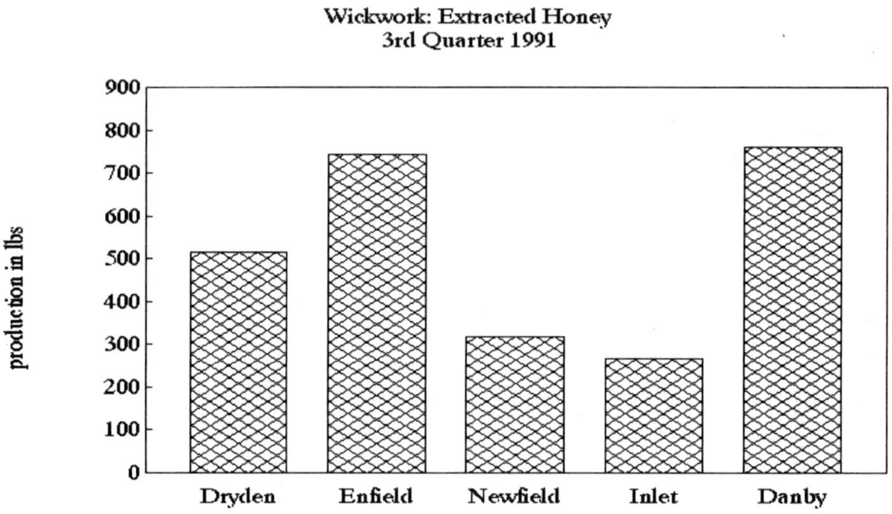

FIGURE 24.12. A bar chart that shows total extracted honey production in the third quarter for all of Wickwork's hive sites.

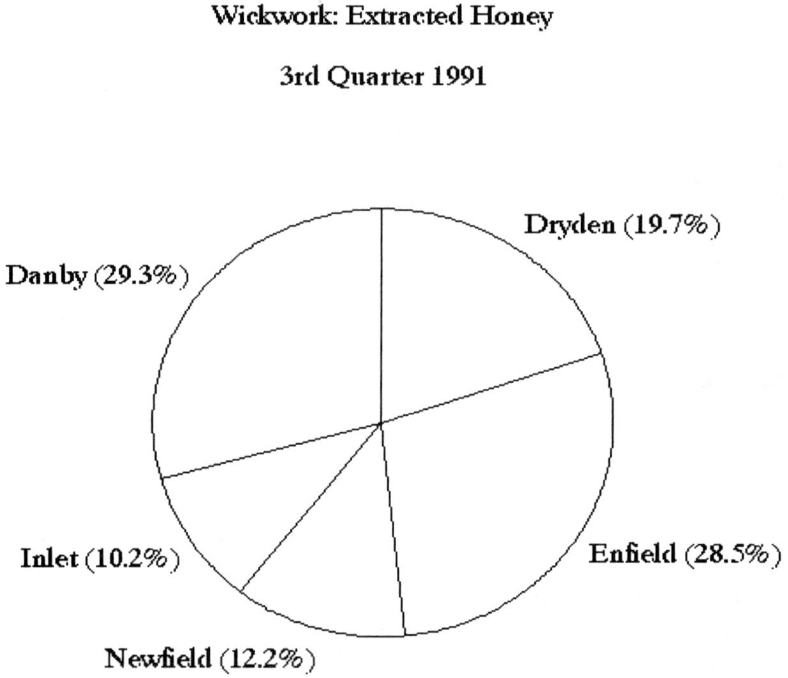

FIGURE 24.13. A simple pie chart shows the percentage of extracted honey produced by each hive site.

Using the same data ranges, plotting a pie graph will illuminate the percentages of total production from each hive site. Press a key to clear the display, and then select Type Pie. Select View again, and the pie chart appears as in Figure 24.13.

Notice that the Y-axis title, *production in lbs*, which appeared on the bar chart is absent from the display of the pie chart. The title is still stored in the graph settings dialog box, but 1-2-3 doesn't show it in the pie chart because there is no Y axis.

In truth, the pie chart isn't very interesting—just a circle with some lines in it. Let's look at the tools you can use to enhance it.

Lotus 1-2-3 uses the X data range in a pie chart as labels to identify what each slice of the pie represents. The A data range contains the values on which 1-2-3 bases the division of the pie. A third data range, the B range, controls the shadings (or colors) that 1-2-3 uses for each pie slice.

To see how this works, clear the Graph from the display, and select Quit from the Graph menu. There are five slices in the extracted honey pie, so enter the values 1 through 5 in range G9..G13 of the sheet. Select Graph B, and indicate range G9..G13 as the B data range, then select View. Your graph should match the one in Figure 24.14.

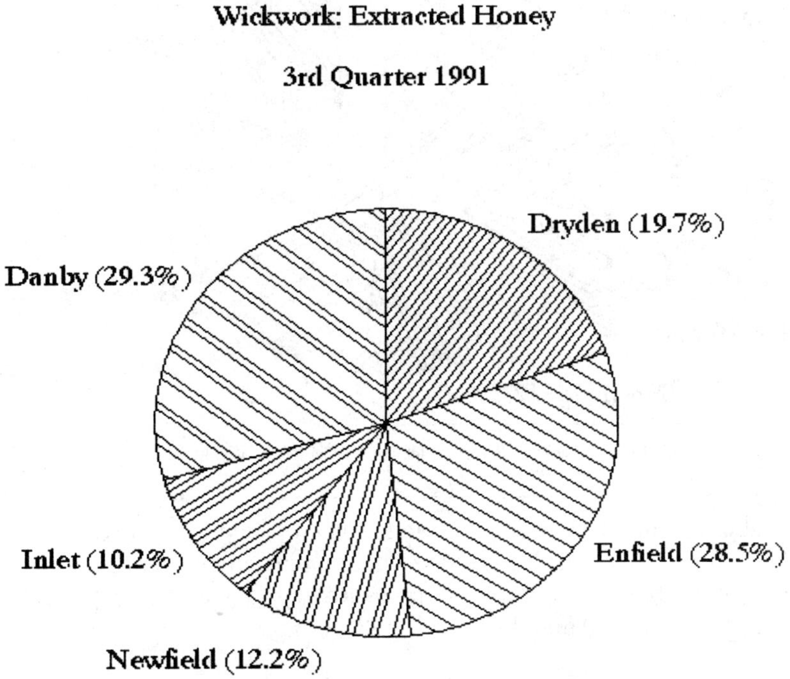

FIGURE 24.14. The B data range controls the hatch patterns (or colors) that 1-2-3 uses in each slice of a pie chart.

There are eight hatch patterns available for pie charts, numbered 1 through 8. But that's not all. The B-range data controls more than just which pattern appears in each pie slice; it also tells 1-2-3 whether to "explode" pie slices away from the main pie.

To make a slice explode (usually for added emphasis), you enter a B-range value that is a hatching pattern value plus 100. So, for example, to explode Dryden's slice and the slice for the Inlet hive site from the pie, you would enter the value 101 into cell G9 and 104 into cell G12. Try it. Clear the graph, and quit the Graph menu. Then replace the values in cells G9 and G12. Don't activate the Graph menu. Instead, press the GRAPH key (F10). 1-2-3 displays the graph with two slices exploded as shown in Figure 24.15.

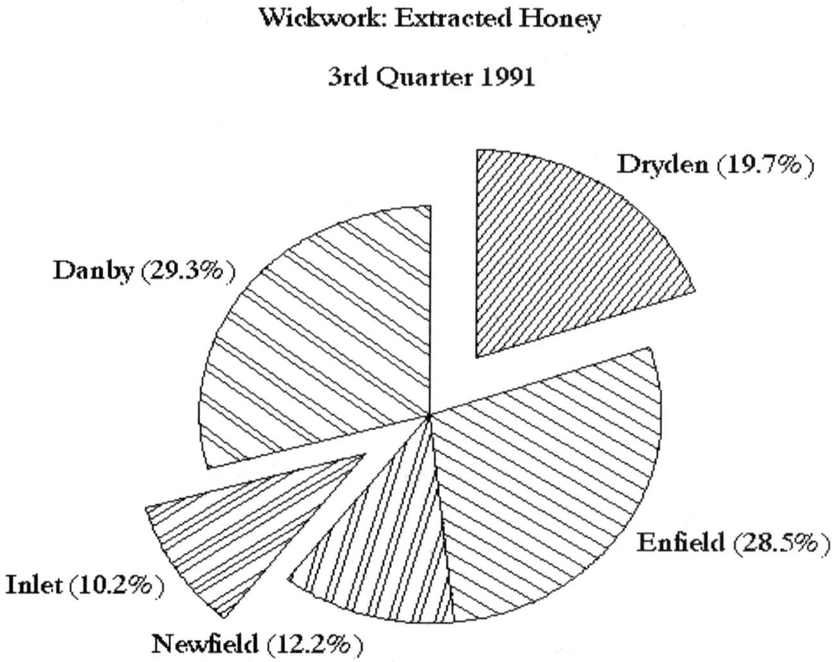

FIGURE 24.15. Adding 100 to a value in the B data range explodes the corresponding pie slice away from the rest of the pie.

Actually, you don't have to explode slices on this pie chart. Edwina (she's your boss, remember?) isn't interested in any particular site. She does prefer patterns over a flat white graph, so press a key to clear the graph and enter the value *1* into cell G9 and 4 into cell G12.

Quick Changes with the GRAPH Key

You can view the current graph any time from within the spreadsheet simply by pressing GRAPH (F10). This lets you alter values in the sheet, view the results in the graph, and return to the sheet to make further changes—without having to navigate the menus.

The GRAPH key also activates graphs from anywhere within 1-2-3's menus. If the urge grabs you, you can activate a graph from deep in the Worksheet Global Default menus. More practically, you can alter graph-related settings and press the GRAPH key to see the results instantly. This can eliminate a lot of navigation through menus when you are fine-tuning a graph's settings.

Select Graph Name Create, and enter *extperc* as the name for the pie chart.

Line Graphs Emphasize Change Over Time

Quite often in business you want to examine the change in a variable over time. The daily closing price of a stock, the weekly revenue of a company, the daily production of a manufacturing facility—these things generate so many data points that plotting them on a bar graph is impractical. A line graph serves best to illustrate such large quantities of data.

Unfortunately for this discussion, nothing in our worksheet deserves to be plotted as a line graph. We'll digress, for a while, from the BEESWAX worksheet so you can get a look at a few simple line graphs and a few other graph types as well. Quit the Graph menu, and save the worksheet, again under the name BEESWAX. Then issue the Worksheet Erase Yes command so you have a clean sheet in which to work.

Each morning when you get to work at Wickwork Apiaries, you open the newspaper to the business section and record the previous day's closing prices for the stocks in your portfolio. This way you have a running record of your portfolio's performance in a spreadsheet, so you can watch for fluctuations that might help you to make money over the long haul.

You have been recording stock prices for only a little while, so your spreadsheet looks like the one in Figure 24.16.

	A	B	C	D	E	F
1	Stock closings					
2						
3	Date	CombCap	Mythic			
4	03-Jul-91	17.375	16.375			
5	05-Jul-91	18.125	16.875			
6	08-Jul-91	18.125	16.75			
7	09-Jul-91	18.25	17			
8	10-Jul-91	18.375	17			
9	11-Jul-91	18	17.125			
10	12-Jul-91	18.875	17.5			
11	15-Jul-91	19.125	18.375			
12	16-Jul-91	18.125	18.125			
13	17-Jul-91	17.375	18.875			

FIGURE 24.16. Build this worksheet to help in your exploration of line graphs.

Create the worksheet so you will be able to follow the rest of this discussion. Set the width of column A to 10, and then enter the labels shown in cells A1, A3, B3, and C3. Use the @DATE function to enter the dates in column A, and assign the Date 1 format to range A4..A13. Finally, enter the values in columns B and C. Save the worksheet under the name STOCLOSE, so you will be able to retrieve it for future discussions if the need arises.

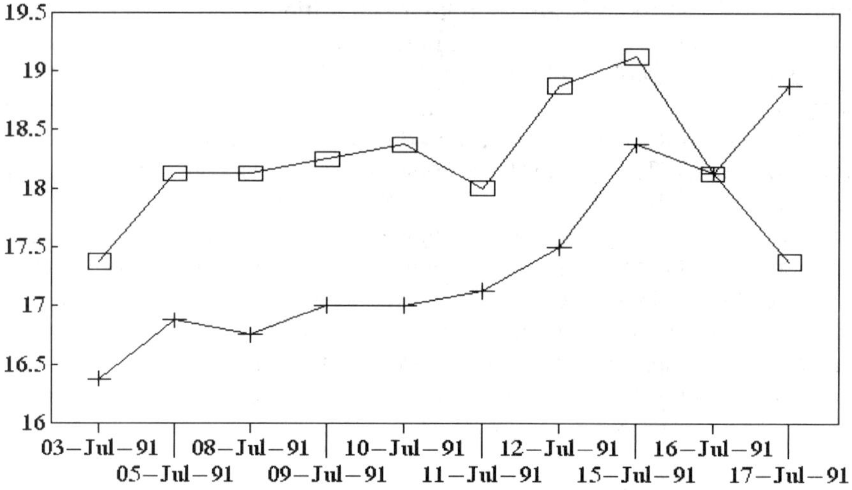

FIGURE 24.17. A line graph that shows closing stock prices is virtually meaningless without titles and a legend.

The data represent closing prices for the imaginary companies whose ticker symbols appear in cells B3 and C3. Let's create a simple line graph from these data to get a clear picture of how the stocks have performed.

Select Graph Group, and indicate range A4..C13 as the Group range. Select Columnwise so that column A becomes the X data range, column B becomes the A range, and column C becomes the B range. Then select View. The resulting graph, shown in Figure 24.17, is rather cryptic.

Still, there is something about the graph that is important to notice: The X-axis labels show the dates represented by each hash mark on the axis. Those hash marks are evenly spaced along the axis, even though the time from one date to another isn't constant. In other words, stocks don't trade on July 4, so there is a gap in the data for that date. Nor do, stocks trade on weekends, so July 6 and 7 and July 13 and 14 are missing from the sequence of dates.

Lotus 1-2-3 automatically spaces the data points in a line graph at equal intervals along the X axis. For many applications, this is exactly what you want. What is the sense, for example, of reserving points in the graph for data that could never exist? If you wanted weekends and holidays to show in the graph, you could enter their dates in sequence in the worksheet and leave the corresponding cells of columns B and C blank.

Try it. Clear the display, and select Quit to return to the worksheet. Move the cell pointer to cell A6, select Worksheet Insert Row, press DownArrow, and then press Return. This opens up two rows for the Saturday and Sunday dates that we omitted from the original data. There is no need to enter the missing dates, simply press the Graph key to see the result of the row insertion.

Mix Bars and Lines

Sometimes it is useful to mix bars and lines in a single graph. To do this in 1-2-3, select Graph Type Mixed. Data ranges A, B, and C become bars in the graph, and data ranges D, E, and F become lines. You might plot the specific sales of a division, for example, as bars, and add emphasis by plotting lines that reveal overall trends in your sales data.

It is not pretty. Clear the graph, and use the Worksheet Delete Row command to remove the extraneous rows. The point of the exercise is that you can omit data points from a line graph if you wish; 1-2-3 leaves a gap in the graph when there is no information to plot.

Enhance the Line Graph

Now let's add some information to clarify the meaning of your line graph. Making these enhancements will give you more practice with the commands on the graph menus.

Select Graph Options Titles First, and enter *Daily Stock Closings*. Select Scale Y-Scale Format Currency, and enter *2*. Select Quit Legend Range, and indicate range B3..C3. Finally, select Quit View. It is now clear what the lines and symbols in the resulting graph (Figure 24.18) represent.

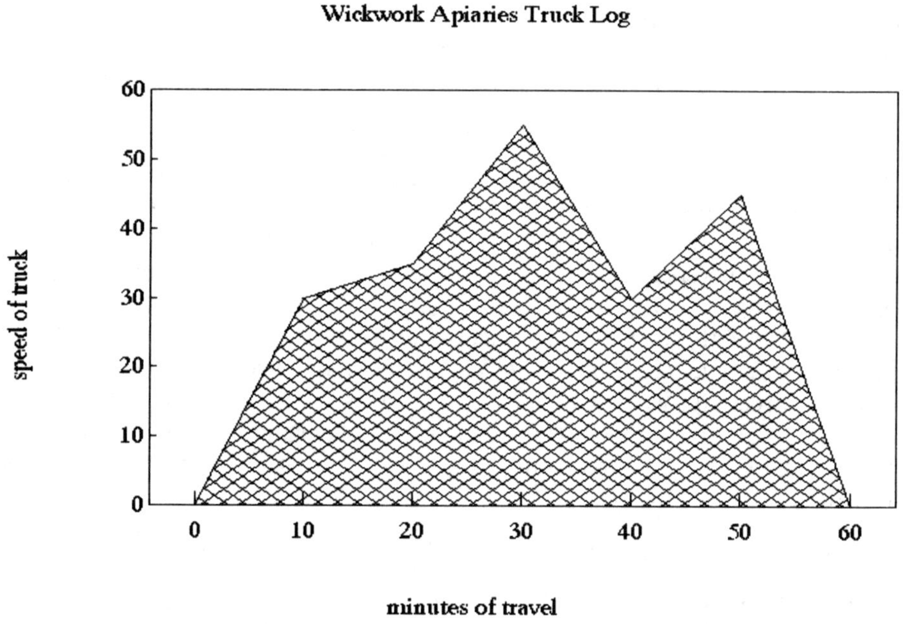

FIGURE 24.18. Titles, a legend, and a currency format applied to numbers on the Y axis clarify the lines and symbols of this graph.

There are other options that you can select to further alter the appearance of a line graph. For example, the labels along the X axis of this graph are a little crowded. Were you to add more data to the graph, the X-axis labels might become difficult to read. The scaling options can alleviate such crowding.

Clear the graph, and select Options Scale Skip. The default entry is 1; replace it by typing *2* and pressing Return. Then select Quit View. Now a label appears on every other point along the X axis. As the amount of graphed data increases, you can increase the skip factor to show fewer and fewer of the X-axis labels.

Create an Area Graph

As is the case with graphs of data that represent ongoing processes, the area under a line might be meaningful to the message that you are trying to impart. For example, the area under a line that shows a truck's speed versus its travel time is the distance that the truck travels:

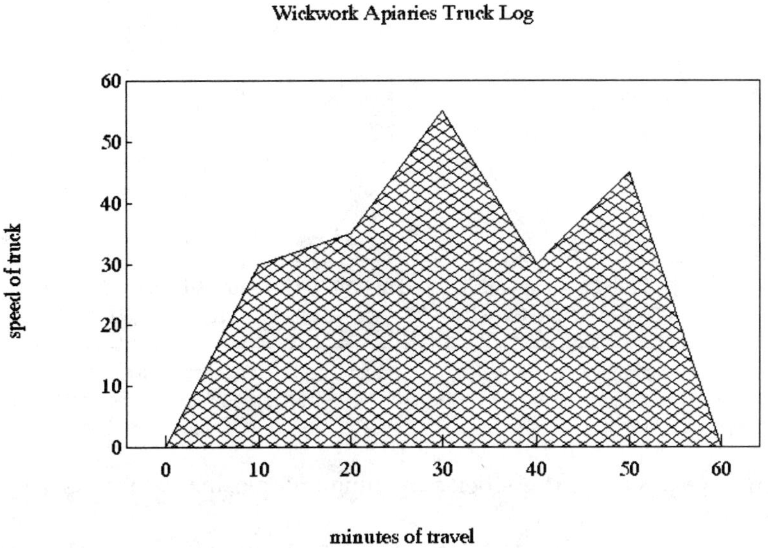

The area under the line on this graph of a truck's speed versus time reveals approximately how far the truck traveled.

To have 1-2-3 fill the area under a line, first create the line graph. Then, starting from the main Graph menu, select Options Format Graph Area Quit Quit. 1-2-3 fills the area with a hatch pattern unless you've selected the color option, in which case the area fills with a color.

A Better Graph for Stock Portfolios: The High-Low-Close-Open Chart

Tracking stock prices graphically with a 1-2-3 line graph is easy enough, but another graph type is more appropriate to the task—the High-Low-Close-Open (HLCO) chart. An HLCO chart shows a stock's high and low values for

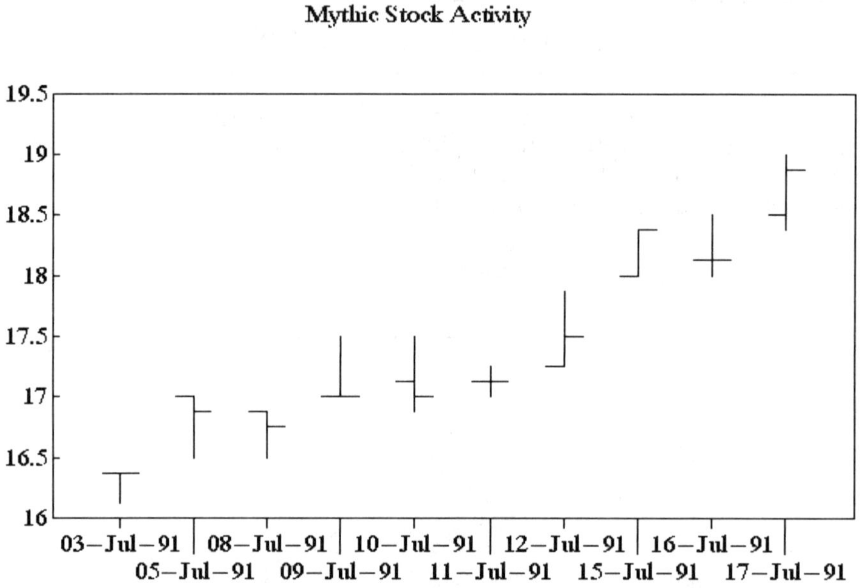

FIGURE 24.19. This graph reveals a stock's high and low for a day as prices at opposite ends of a vertical line. The day's opening and closing values appear as tick marks on the line—the opening value on the left side of the line, and the closing value on the right side.

a given day as well as the stock's opening and closing values, as you see in Figure 24.19.

To create this HLCO graph, you will have to modify the stock worksheet that you used to explore line graphs to fit Figure 24.20. Return to Ready mode in that sheet, and erase the data from range B3..B13. Use the Worksheet Insert Column command to insert one column to the left of column C. Then enter values and labels so that your worksheet matches the one in Figure 24.20. The values in column D are the closing values that you entered under Mythic in the previous exercise.

Select Graph Reset Graph to clear the way for new graph settings. Then select Group, indicate range A4..E13, and select Columnwise. Select Type HLCO. Then select Options Titles First, enter *Mythic Stock Activity*, select Quit, and select View.

The arrangement of data in the practice worksheet represents the order in which you must specify graph data ranges to establish an HCLO chart. While the data don't have to be in adjacent spreadsheet columns, the high values must be in the A data range, and the low values must be in the B range. The C range must contain the closing values, and the D range must contain the opening values. Each range must contain the same number of entries, and

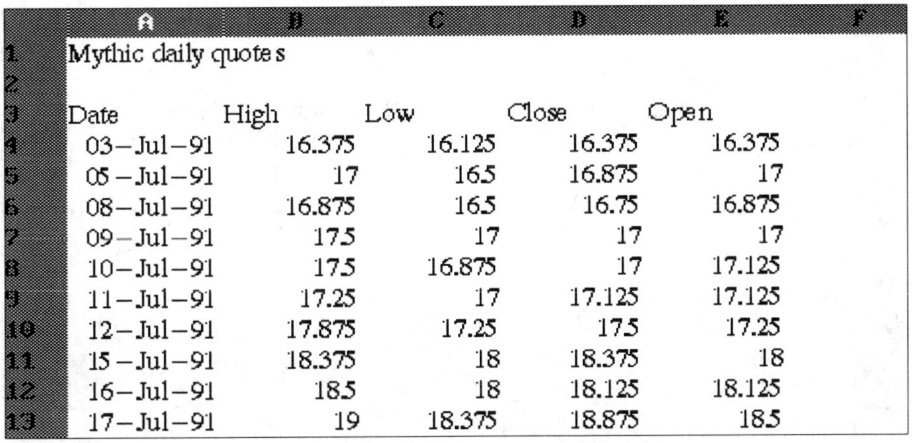

	A	B	C	D	E	F
1	Mythic daily quotes					
2						
3	Date	High	Low	Close	Open	
4	03-Jul-91	16.375	16.125	16.375	16.375	
5	05-Jul-91	17	16.5	16.875	17	
6	08-Jul-91	16.875	16.5	16.75	16.875	
7	09-Jul-91	17.5	17	17	17	
8	10-Jul-91	17.5	16.875	17	17.125	
9	11-Jul-91	17.25	17	17.125	17.125	
10	12-Jul-91	17.875	17.25	17.5	17.25	
11	15-Jul-91	18.375	18	18.375	18	
12	16-Jul-91	18.5	18	18.125	18.125	
13	17-Jul-91	19	18.375	18.875	18.5	

FIGURE 24.20. To examine HLCO graph types, you must add more data to your stock spreadsheet.

there should be a one-to-one correspondence between the entries in the ranges. If you leave out either a high or a low value for a stock on a given day, 1-2-3 won't draw a line to represent the stock's activity.

Practice a bit more with the graphing options, if you wish, by adding other enhancements to the HLCO graph.

Complete Graphics Control: The XY Graph

So far we have relied a lot on 1-2-3 to handle the details in the graphs we have created. The position of data within a graph data range has determined where 1-2-3 plots the data point along the X axis. A lot of data describe their positions along the X axis just as they do their positions along the Y axis. For example, you might plot the revenue generated per sale as a function of time; sales fall at unpredictable intervals, so a standard line graph would distort the data. In a market research study, you might plot the reported salaries of your subjects against their reported weekly spending. Data of this type are called Cartesian coordinates.

Cartesian coordinates are ordered pairs: the first piece of data represents a distance along the X axis, and the second represents a distance along the Y axis. You might have graphed such ordered pairs as scatter plots or scatter diagrams. In 1-2-3 these are called XY graphs.

XY graphs are appropriate for just about any data you have to plot. They are, however, unnecessary in many cases, as we have already seen. You should use XY graphs when your worksheet contains ordered pairs that

	A	B	C	D	E	F
1	Shrub W			A square		
2						
3	Date	Height		X–length	Y–length	
4	04–Apr–91	0		1	1	
5	05–Apr–91	0.25		1	2	
6	07–Apr–91	0.6		2	2	
7	08–Apr–91	0.8		2	1	
8	10–Apr–91	1.4		1	1	
9	11–Apr–91	1.9				
10	12–Apr–91	2.3				
11	15–Apr–91	3.1				
12	16–Apr–91	3.5				
13	17–Apr–91	4				

FIGURE 24.21. The data in columns A and B are Cartesian coordinates that show the growth of a shrub grown from a seed in a breeding experiment. The data in columns D and E are Cartesian coordinates that identify the corners of a square.

identify data in a non-linear fashion. You also should use XY graphs when your data fall at irregular intervals which are critical to understanding the data. Consider the listings in Figure 24.21.

The data for Shrub W were collected over a 13-day period. They show the heights for each of the days listed of a shrub grown in a plant breeding experiment. The data are supposed to show the plant's rate of growth, but because measurements are missing for some of the days, plotting the growth as a line graph may give an incorrect impression. If you plot the data in an XY graph, 1-2-3 will interpolate the missing points and draw an appropriate line, as shown in the comparison Figure 24.22.

The data under the label *A square* in columns D and E describe the corners of a square whose bottom-left corner is at the coordinate (1,1). If you set range D4..D8 as the X data range and E4..E8 as the A range, the resulting line graph in 1-2-3 would have the labels *1, 1, 2, 2,* and *1* along the X axis, and it would describe a weird bump. See Figure 24.23.

Plotted as an XY graph as in Figure 24.24, the same data produce the square that they represent. Trust us, it is really a square. The box titled When a Square Is a Rectangle explains why the square isn't exactly square.

The automatic scaling feature of 1-2-3 drops the plotted data onto the X axis, confusing the presentation a bit. That is fairly easy to fix. Plot the ordered pairs that describe a square, and we will fiddle a little to improve the presentation.

Start in a blank worksheet and enter the values shown in Figure 24.25.

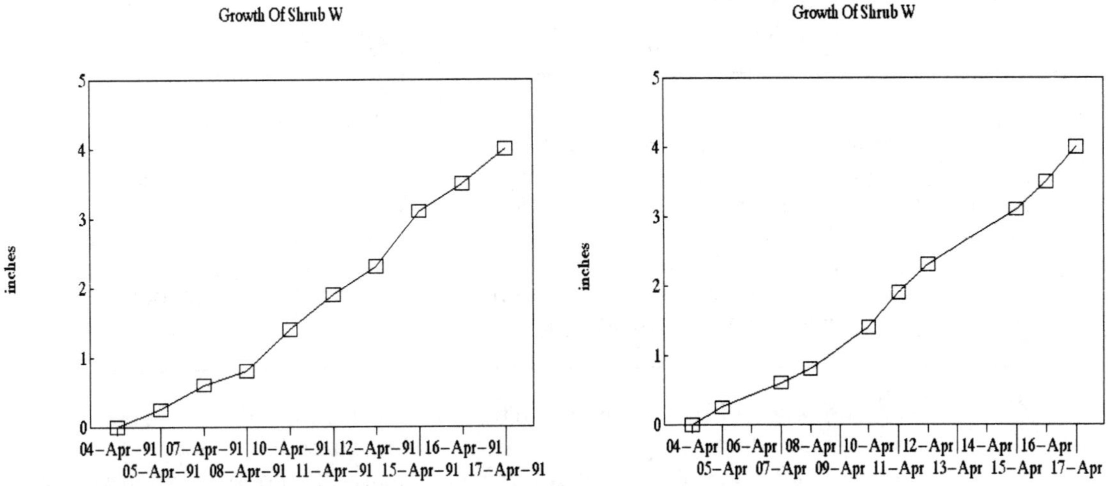

FIGURE 24.22. The line graph on the left fails to adjust for data points missing from the ordered pairs in columns A and B of the previous worksheet. The XY graph on the right automatically interpolates the missing points.

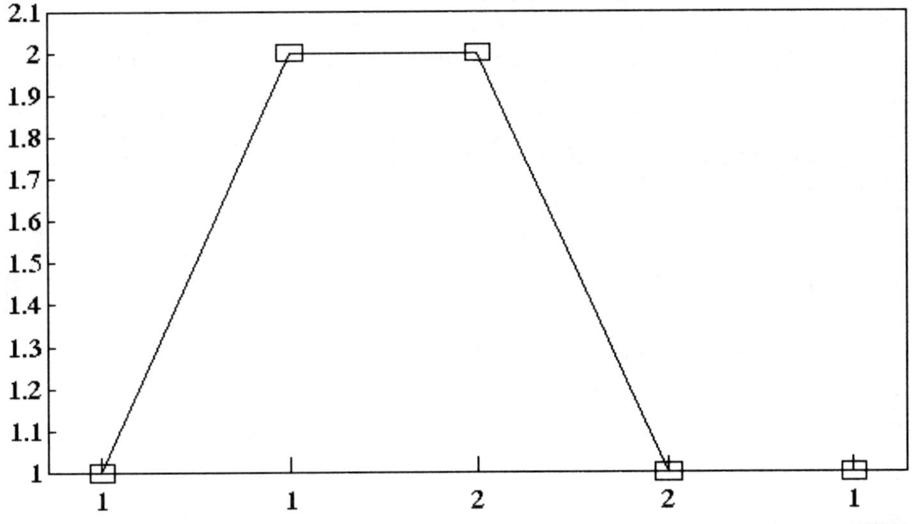

FIGURE 24.23. Ordered pairs plotted as a line graph paint a distorted picture.

Select Graph Type XY. Then select X and indicate range A1..A5 as the X data range. Select A, and indicate range B1..B5 as the A range. Select View to see the results so far. Your graph should match the one shown in Figure 24.24.

When a Square Is a Rectangle

Graphs in 1-2-3 suffer from distortion. They appear elongated along the X axis, perhaps because your computer's display is wider than it is high and Lotus programmers never adjusted for the difference when they wrote the graphics portion of the software. To be completely fair, few graphics programs fully account for the computer display's distorted aspect ratio—that is, the number of pixels that run horizontally versus the number of pixels that run vertically. While the distortion can be distracting, you can usually adjust for it when you place a graph in the worksheet. We will see how to put graphs in the sheet when we work with Wysiwyg in the next chapter.

The origin of the Y axis doesn't even appear on the display. This is somewhat misleading when you are expecting the square to fall above the axis. By using manual scaling, you can force the square off the axis. When you override automatic scaling, you force 1-2-3 to show a specific range of numbers on a particular axis—no matter what data you are graphing.

Press a key to clear the graph display. Then select Options Scale X-Scale Manual. If you look at the settings dialog box, you can see that the lower limit of the X axis is already set at 0, so you don't have to change that. However, the upper limit of the axis is also set at 0. Select Upper, and enter *3*. Select

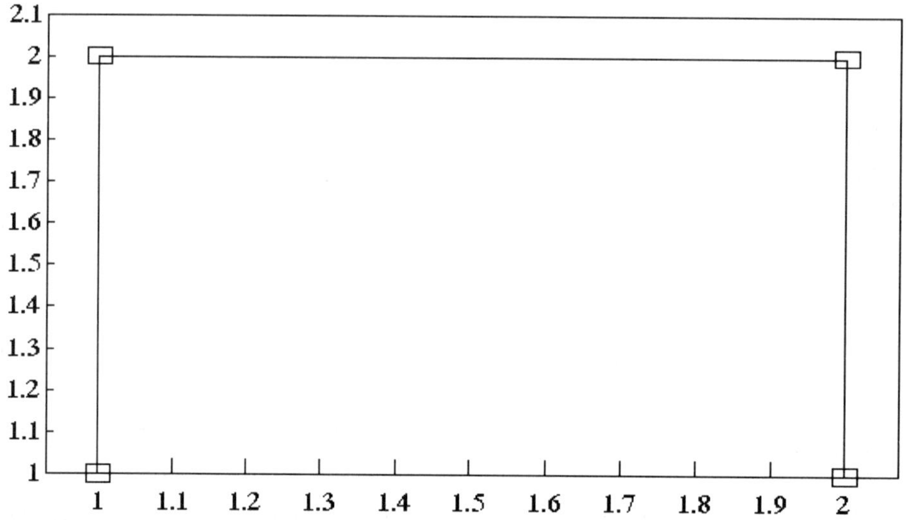

FIGURE 24.24. The ordered pairs (1,1), (1,2), (2,2), (2,1), and (1,1) describe the corners of a square when plotted as an XY graph.

FIGURE 24.25. We borrowed these ordered pairs from the earlier illustration. They represent a square whose bottom-left corner is at the coordinate (1,1).

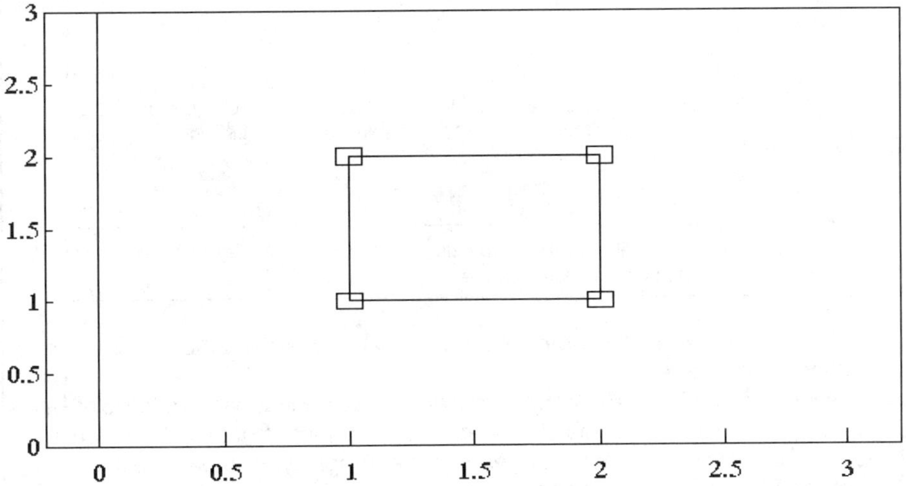

FIGURE 24.26. The XY graph of the square is clearer when you use manual scaling and force 1-2-3 to show the graph's origin—the Cartesian coordinate (0,0).

Quit, and then select Scale Y-Scale Manual. Here, too, select Upper and enter *3*. Finally, select Quit Quit and View. Now the square that you plotted hangs where it should relative to the graph's axes. See Figure 24.26.

XY graphs are versatile. As you saw in the Data Analysis and Statistics section of this book, XY graphs are particularly important in statistics; they can

A True Scatter Plot

A scatter plot gives you a visual assist in determining the profile of your data. It can help to answer such questions as, "Is there a relationship between the temperature and the distance bees fly from the hive in their search for nectar?" The following scatter diagram shows the relationship as Edwina measured it for one month of Wickwork Apiaries' honey production:

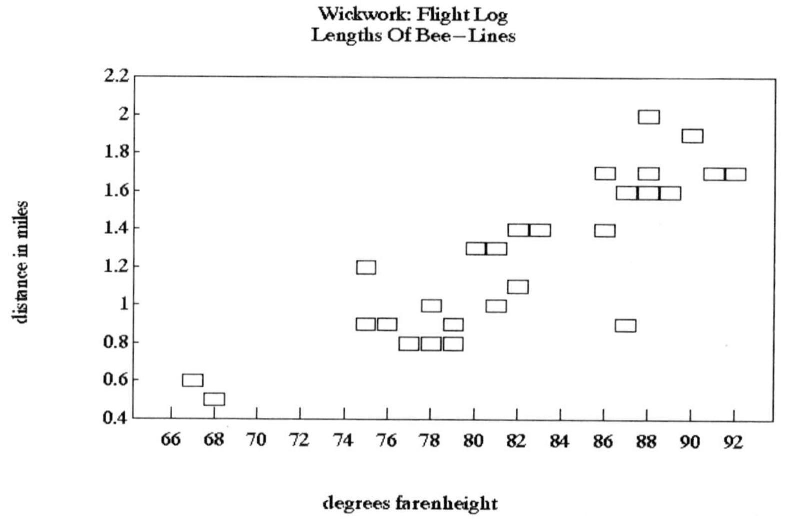

Edwina measured one beeline per day from a single hive to determine whether the temperature influences how far bees fly in their search for nectar.

A quick glance at the graph suggests that warmer weather drives bees farther from the hive.

A scatter plot is an XY graph that places a symbol at each data point but does not connect the points. To create a scatter plot of data in your own XY graph, first assign the data ranges and the graph type, then select Graph Options Format Graph Symbols Quit Quit.

Use a Simple XY Graph to Simulate Genius

Here is a graph that looks complex. People often think it takes special genius to calculate the data on which such a graph is based. But anyone can produce this graph in seconds by following the simple instructions below:

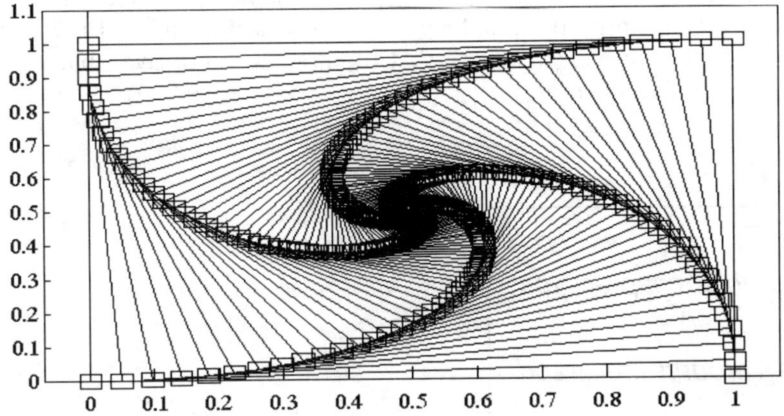

This XY graph looks complex, but with practice you can build it in less than a minute starting with a blank worksheet.

Enter data as follows:

	A	B	C	D	E	F	G	H
1	0	0	0.05					
2	0	1						
3	1	1						
4	1	0						
5	0	0						

In cell D1, enter the formula *+1–D1*. In cell A6, enter *+A1–(A1-A2)*$D$1*. Copy the formula from cell A6 to range A6..B300. Select Graph Type XY. Select X, and indicate A1..A300 as the X graph range. Select A, and indicate B1..B300 as the A data range. Select View to see the results of your handiwork.

reveal whether data points tend to fit specific profiles. If you can't think of a use for XY graphs in your own work, check out the box titled Use a Simple XY Graph to Simulate Genius for a diversionary look at this plotting option.

When you have built the graphs that best serve your reporting needs, you are ready to go to work in Wysiwyg. The add-in offers a second collection of graphing options that let you add emphasis to graphs you have already designed using 1-2-3's menus. Among other topics, the following chapter shows how to soup up the graphs you have created in the BEESWAX worksheet. Save the worksheet now so that the graphs will be available when you work through that chapter.

Having completed this chapter you should:

- *Know your way around the graph menus*
- *Understand the steps required to translate spreadsheet data into graphic images*
- *Be able to clarify a graph's meaning by adding titles and legends*
- *Have a grasp of how the GRAPH key (F10) saves time as you modify graph settings and spreadsheet entries to affect the graph's appearance*
- *Be able to select the graph type appropriate to the message you are trying to impart*
- *Be ready to apply your understanding of graphs as you work with Wysiwyg to produce a polished report*

25

Soup Up Your Spreadsheet with Wysiwyg

With 1-2-3 and the Wysiwyg add-in, you can turn almost any collection of data into an eye-catching presentation. Wysiwyg output from a laser printer can be magazine quality, rivaling output from full-featured desktop publishing software. Even a dot-matrix printer can produce a slick report if you spend some time enhancing your spreadsheet with Wysiwyg.

If you can afford the RAM, and you are not concerned about high-speed printing, you should probably have Wysiwyg active whenever you work in 1-2-3. In this chapter we explore ways to apply the add-in after you have created a spreadsheet using 1-2-3 without Wysiwyg. However, we don't mean to imply that that is the only way to fly. You can just as well create a spreadsheet with Wysiwyg active and use Wysiwyg's special formatting features as you go. Either way, you will be able to use Wysiwyg to produce reports, memos, letters, and notices that look as if they were prepared by a professional print shop.

Wysiwyg offers more than snazzy output. Some of its features let you customize the spreadsheet display in ways not offered by

In this chapter you will

- *Attach the Wysiwyg add-in*
- *Use Wysiwyg to align text and alter fonts and font styles*
- *Apply shading to worksheet ranges and put boxes around cells*
- *Place graphs into the worksheet*
- *Learn some of the theory of page layout and design*
- *Learn how to use Wysiwyg's graph editing tools*
- *Print a Wysiwyg spreadsheet*
- *Alter the resolution of the spreadsheet display*
- *Adjust the colors of the spreadsheet's display elements*
- *Change the characteristics of the worksheet frame*
- *Add a grid to the worksheet*

1-2-3. You can change the colors of the display, modify the appearance of the spreadsheet frame, superimpose grid lines on the sheet, and even zoom in and out on the sheet to gain different perspectives on your models.

To follow this discussion, you will need to retrieve the BEESWAX worksheet that you created in Chapter 23 from 1-2-3. It should include the named graph definitions that you established in the chapter titled Go Visual: Graph Spreadsheet Data. If you haven't yet created the BEESWAX worksheet, follow the instructions under the heading Get Some Data To Doctor at the beginning of the previous chapter.

Bring on the Publisher: Attach Wysiwyg

It's time to attach Wysiwyg. To do this, select Add-In Attach and choose WYSIWYG.ADN from the list of available add-ins. If WYSIWYG.ADN does not appear on the menu list, check to be sure that the directory path shown in the control panel is to the directory that holds your 1-2-3 program files. If you can't find the Wysiwyg add-in in your 1-2-3 program directory, you need to run the Install program to make the add-in available (see box).

Lotus 1-2-3 prompts you to select a function key to which it should attach Wysiwyg. Select No-Key. There is no need to select a function key because Wysiwyg's main menu appears when you type a colon in Ready mode. Select Quit to exit the Add-in menu.

The worksheet is transformed. The labels and numbers in the sheet appear in a new font—they are no longer monospaced, each occupying the same amount of space as the next. Rather, the font that Wysiwyg uses by default is proportionally spaced. Like the characters used in most books, magazines, and newspapers, each character in Wysiwyg occupies as much space as it needs. Letters like the lower case i occupy less room in a cell than do the capital W and M.

Run Install to Make Wysiwyg Available

If you didn't install Wysiwyg when you first put 1-2-3 on your hard disk, it is not too late. Exit to DOS, and find the disk that came with the software. Put disk 1, the install disk, into a floppy drive and make the drive current—if it is drive A, enter *A:*. Then type *INSTALL*, and press Return.

Follow the instructions that appear on your display. The install program's prompts and messages are easy to understand. Make the selections necessary to install Wysiwyg in the same directory as the 1-2-3 program files.

The worksheet frame looks a little different in Wysiwyg; lines appear between the column letters and the row numbers. If you are a mouse user, you'll notice that the mouse pointer has taken on a new shape; it has become an arrowhead.

Put the Publisher to Work: Change the Font

Wysiwyg lets you alter the spreadsheet in so many ways that it is hard to know where to begin. Any order of events is valid, so we'll ramble. By the time we've finished, the BEESWAX worksheet will contain a slick report and you'll be familiar with many of Wysiwyg's publishing features.

Start by changing the default font. The current font is more interesting than 1-2-3's normal one, but Edwina (the owner of Wickwork Apiaries) prefers more traditional text. To alter the font, you need to activate Wysiwyg's menu.

If you're working with the keyboard, get to Wysiwyg by typing a colon. If you're using a mouse, move the mouse pointer above the top frame of the spreadsheet as you do to access the main menu. Press the mouse button that normally doubles as the Escape key (the right button, in most cases) until the Wysiwyg menu appears. You can distinguish the Wysiwyg menu from the 1-2-3 menu by checking the mode indicator in the top-right corner of the display. It displays Menu while you are using the 1-2-3 menus and Wysiwyg while you are using Wysiwyg menus. On color monitors, Wysiwyg's menu pointer is a different color from that of 1-2-3. Of course, the selections on the two menus differ (see Figure 25.1), but you might not notice that at a glance.

The commands that control the fonts Wysiwyg uses are listed under the Format option on the main menu. Select Format, and then select Font. The resulting dialog box, as shown in Figure 25.2, lists eight fonts from which to choose as you alter the fonts in specific cells or ranges.

Font number 1 in the list is Wysiwyg's default—the font that all your entries assumed when you activated the add-in. By changing the font listed as number 1, you change the appearance of everything in the worksheet—much the way every unformatted cell in the sheet assumes a new format when you alter the global numeric display format. Select Replace from the Font menu.

Select 1 from the resulting menu then select Dutch. Wysiwyg prompts you to select a point size for the display characters. Accept the default of 12 by pressing Return. Select 2, and select Dutch for font number 2. This time enter a point size of 15. Select 3, and select Dutch for font number 3. Enter 24 as the point size. We have left five of the font selections unaltered. Those fonts

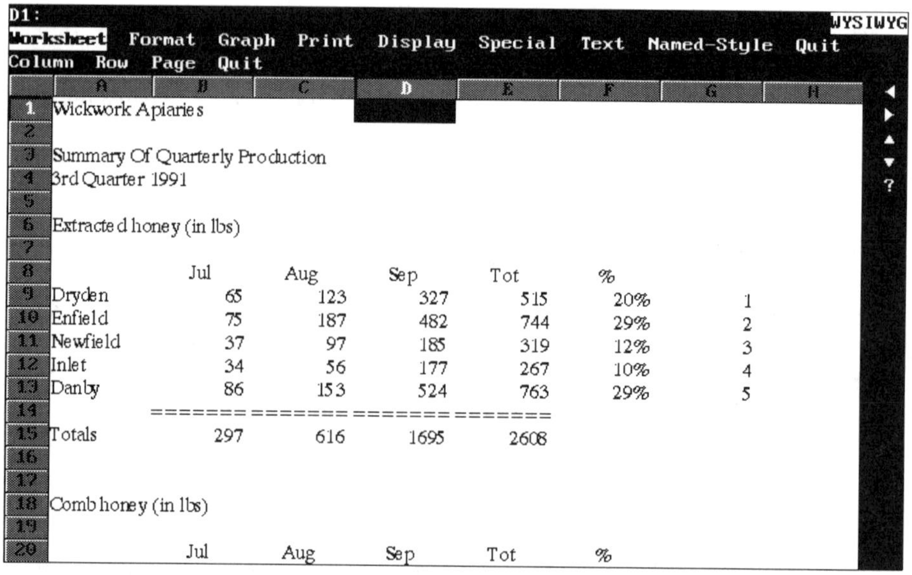

FIGURE 25.1. The selections on the Wysiwyg menu differ from those of 1-2-3. To further distinguish the menus, the mode indicator shows Menu while you use a 1-2-3 menu and Wysiwyg while you use Wysiwyg.

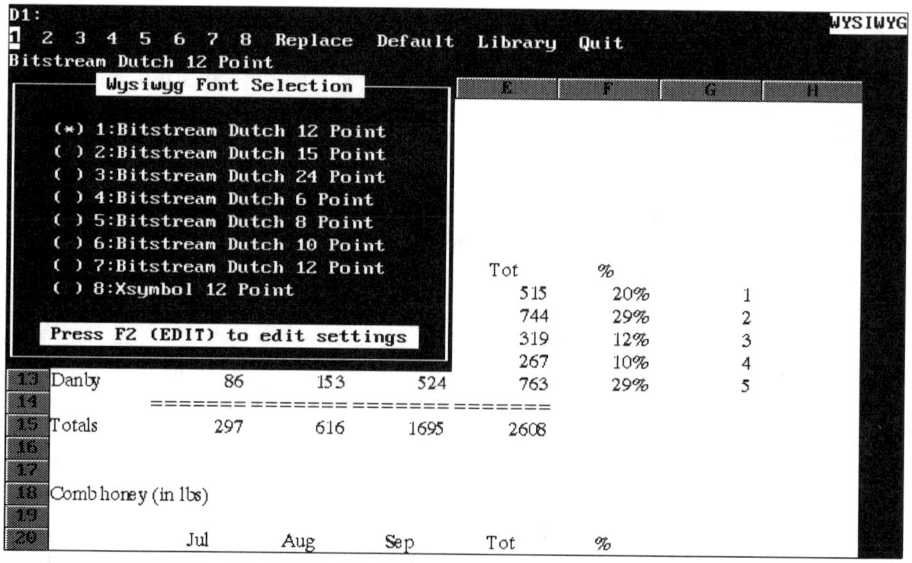

FIGURE 25.2. The Format Font dialog box lists eight fonts from which you can choose to alter the fonts of specific cells in the worksheet.

are probably already Dutch, and most of them are in point sizes other than the ones we selected. We will use only a few sizes anyway.

Select Quit Quit to return to ready mode. You will notice immediately that the characters in your worksheet have serifs; They are more formal than the Sans Serif characters of the Swiss font.

Make the Title Shine

There are a few things you can do to set the title of a page apart from the balance of the page. Often, the title is in a larger font than the other material. Sometimes the line weight of the title characters is heavier—the title is in boldface. Also, titles sometimes appear centered at the top of the page. We will apply all of those characteristics to the title of this report.

First, set the title in a larger font: activate the Wysiwyg menu, and select :Format Font. Select font number 3, and indicate cell A1 as the Target range. The title grows!

A Convention for Clarity

Throughout this book we have provided menu command sequences that you issue to perform the tasks at hand. We have begun each sequence with the command that you select from 1-2-3's main menu, assuming that you would activate the menu as appropriate either by pressing the slash key or by moving the mouse pointer into the menu area.

We can't predict how you will choose to activate Wysiwyg's menu, But to clearly distinguish Wysiwyg menu sequences from 1-2-3 menu sequences, from here on in, all Wysiwyg sequences begin with a colon. For example, the instruction to select Format Font from Wysiwyg's menu will read, select :Format Font. 1-2-3 menu sequences will continue to appear with the first selection you would make from 1-2-3's main menu. Hence, the instruction to select Worksheet Global from 1-2-3's menu would read, select Worksheet Global...

In fact, the row that contains the title has also grown. To make room for large fonts, Wysiwyg lets you vary the heights of rows just as 1-2-3 lets you vary the widths of columns.

Ok, let's make the title bold so it stands out a little more. Select :Format. You can see that three font styles are available on the: Format menu—Bold, Italic, and Underline. Select Bold and then Set, and indicate cell A1.

Center the title over the worksheet data. To do this, select :Text Align Center, and indicate range A1..H1. Wysiwyg centers the title within the range of specified columns.

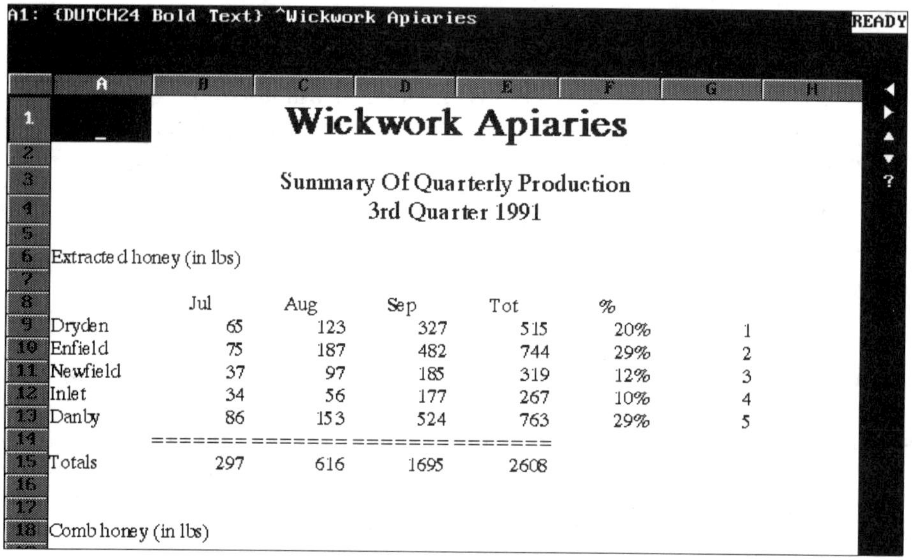

FIGURE 25.3. With only a little tweaking of the spreadsheet font and a few labels, the BEESWAX spreadsheet has become quite striking.

Come to think of it, this spreadsheet has a three-line title. It will look a little tidier with all three lines centered. Select :Text Align Center, and indicate range A1..H4 so that all the titles fall across the middle of the spreadsheet.

Select :Format Font 2, and indicate range A3..A4; even though the titles appear at columns C and D, they still reside in column A. Already the spreadsheet looks distinctive. See Figure 25.3.

Make Data Stand Out by Boxing and Shading Cells

While applying various fonts and font styles adds emphasis, you can draw attention more quickly to specific data by enclosing it in boxes. Wysiwyg excels at drawing boxes.

Draw boxes around each of the data cells that reports the monthly extracted honey production. Start by selecting :Format Lines. Plenty of options appear on the resulting menu. For starters, you can elect to place

Alter the Heights of Rows

Wysiwyg lets you change the heights of rows just as 1-2-3 lets you alter the widths of columns. To change row heights via the menus, select :Worksheet Row Set-Height. Indicate one or more rows whose heights you want to change, and then enter a row height in points (the standard row height is 14 points). Alternatively, press the UpArrow or DownArrow key to adjust the row height.

If you are using a mouse, you can set both row heights and column widths without accessing the menus. To set a row height, drag the line that is directly beneath the row's number in the spreadsheet frame. Likewise, to alter a column width, drag the line that is to the right of the column's letter in the spreadsheet frame.

Reset a row height by selecting :Worksheet Row Auto. This tells Wysiwyg to fit the height of the row to the size of the largest font set in the row.

lines around an entire range. You can also choose to place a line along the left side, right side, top, or bottom of every cell within a range. If you prefer, you can draw a box around every cell in a range.

If single lines don't do the trick, you can choose double lines or heavy lines in any or all of the positions available for standard-weight lines. There is even an option to add a drop-shadow effect to spreadsheet ranges, making it seem as though the ranges hover just a bit above the surface of the spreadsheet.

In this case, you are adding boxes around all the cells, so select All and indicate range B8..F13. For consistency, put the entries in column A into boxes as well; select :Format Lines All, and indicate range A9..A13.

A striking fact emerges: with Wysiwyg's line-drawing capabilities, there is really no need for the dividing lines that you created with repeating labels in 1-2-3. The equal signs in row 14 aren't really necessary. In fact, they look out of place. Let's clean things up a bit more.

Select Worksheet Delete Row, and indicate a cell in row 14. Now select :Format Lines All, and indicate range B14..E14. Finally, select :Format Lines Double Top, and indicate range B14..E14 a second time. The resulting worksheet appears in Figure 25.4.

The subtitle that identifies range A8..F14 as information about extracted honey is not doing its job; set it in boldface so you can tell more easily what the range represents. Select :Format Bold Set, and indicate cell A6. Then, use the Worksheet Insert Row command to insert a row above row 6. This further sets the titles apart from the rest of the worksheet.

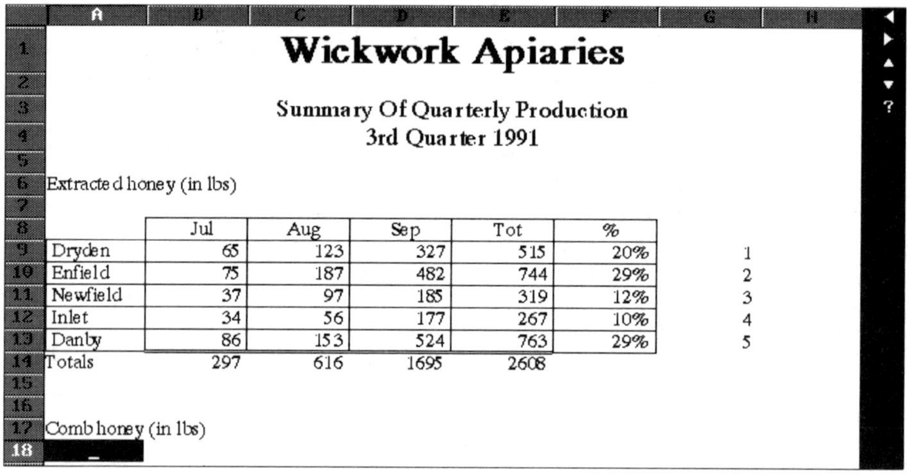

FIGURE 25.4. The BEESWAX worksheet with boxes added around the data for extracted honey production.

Finally, how about those totals? While the data itself is important, the totals in row 15 and column E are handy summaries. Setting them apart a bit more from the data will help draw the reader's eye. Select :Format Shade, and four shading options—Light, Dark, Solid, and Clear—appear. The Light option is dark enough for our purposes, so select Light and indicate range B15..E15. Select :Format Shade Light again, and indicate range E10..E14.

The top portion of your spreadsheet should match the one shown in Figure 25.5.

What if It Looks Bad?

Somedays you may apply a Wysiwyg format and then decide it was a mistake. A font size or style might not provide the emphasis you are trying to achieve. Or you might accidentally apply formatting options to the wrong cells. The formats you assign might simply clutter more than they clarify.

In any case, the command :Format Reset removes all applied formatting options from a specified range. Also, each of the formatting option menus has a selection to clear or reset the option. For example, the :Format Lines menu has a Clear option that lets you remove lines from around a range, from all the cells in a range, or from any side of each cell in a range. The :Format Shade menu also offers a Clear option that removes shading from select cells.

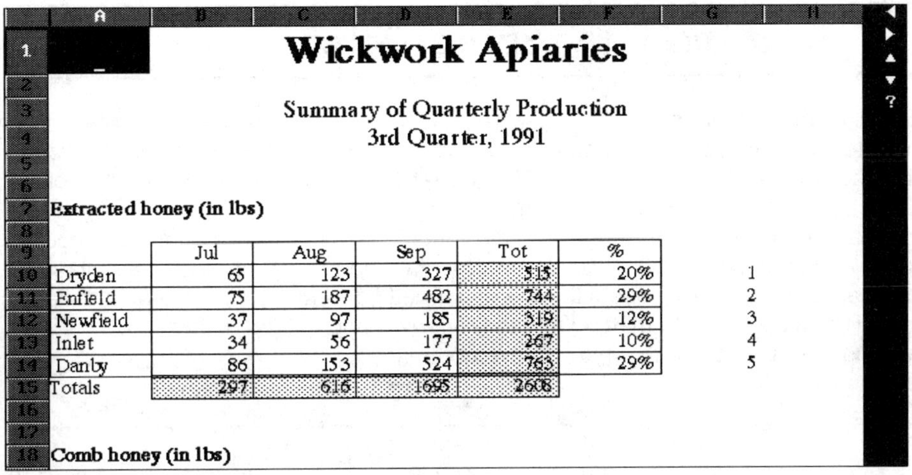

FIGURE 25.5. The Wysiwyg formatting options applied to the extracted honey data act as a model for formatting the remaining data blocks.

Copy Wysiwyg Formats from One Range to Another

Two blocks of data in the sheet are nearly identical in layout to the block that reports on extracted honey. The first block has the subtitle *Comb honey (in lbs)* and occupies range A18..F27. The second block is subtitled *Raw bee's wax (in lbs)* and occupies range A30..F39. It would be nice to apply boldface type to the subtitles and the lines around the cells without having to reissue the same commands repeatedly. Wysiwyg can do this easily.

Hold on a minute. Wysiwyg has a command that copies the special formatting from one range to another without copying cell contents. But before you use that command, you had better remove the repeating label dividing lines from rows 26 and 38 of the sheet. You removed the dividing lines a moment ago from the first range of formatted data. Failing to remove them from the remaining rows will result in improper juxtaposition of the lines in those ranges.

Select Worksheet Delete Rows, and indicate a cell in row 26. Then issue the command sequence a second time and indicate a cell in row 38. Now apply Wysiwyg's Copy command.

Do It Again: The Special Options

Wysiwyg's :Special option provides several ways to manipulate established formatting options without affecting the underlying cell contents. The :Special Copy command copies all Wysiwyg formatting options from one range to another, applying the options to whatever entries are in the Target range. The :Special Move command lifts Wysiwyg formatting options from a range and applies them to the cells in a Target range.

The :Special Export command copies only the established Wysiwyg cell formats to disk. This makes them available to the :Special Import command, which brings Wysiwyg cell formats from disk into the current worksheet. The :Special Import command can also bring in cell formatting from files you have modified with Wysiwyg and saved using 1-2-3's File Save command.

Select :Special Copy, and indicate range A7..F15 as the range to copy from. Indicate cell A18 as the range to copy to. Select :Special Copy a second time, indicate range A7..F15 as the range to copy from, and indicate cell A29 as the range to copy to. Wysiwyg repeats the formatting from the first range in each of the subsequent ranges, in each case leaving the underlying data intact.

Finish off the special effects by adding some shading and boxes to the summary section at the bottom of the sheet. To do this, drop on down to cell A40 and issue the :Format Bold Set command to boldface the label in that cell. Then issue the :Format Lines All command and indicate range B42..E45. Select :Format Lines All again, and indicate range A43..A45.

Shade in the summary values by selecting :Format Shade Light and indicating range B43..E45. Finally, make the summary data jump off of the page. Select :Format Lines Shadow Set, and indicate range A42..E45.

Add Pizzazz with Pictures

We have exercised several representative options under Wysiwyg's :Format menu. You can fiddle on your own to hone your skills and explore the remaining options. In the meantime, remember those graphs you created to illustrate the extracted honey data? Your quarterly report for Edwina won't be complete without the graphs.

To begin, recover some of the white space in the worksheet by narrowing some columns. Select Worksheet Column Column-Range, and indicate range B9..F9 (or any other range that spans columns B through F). Enter *5* as the width for these columns. Select Worksheet Column Set-Width, indicate a cell in column A, and enter *7*.

Color in Selected Ranges

If you are working with a color monitor and you are bored with the black-on-white or white-on-black of the standard spreadsheet display, Wysiwyg can change your life. The add-in provides many options for customizing the colors of the spreadsheet display. Some of those options are available on the :Format menu; others are available on the :Display menu. We look at the :Display options in depth later in this chapter, but you might have some fun right now with the :Format Color command.

The :Format Color menu lets you alter the colors of three display elements within a range—the background color, the color of cell entries, and the color of negative numbers. To change the background color of a range, you select :Format Color Background. Wysiwyg offers six colors from which to choose, in addition to the normal background color. You will find the same colors available for the contents of a range. Select one of the colors, and then indicate the range to color.

Here is an amusing thing to try: Select :Format Color Background, and assign a color to a range. Then select :Format Color Text and assign the same color to the same range. You won't get much work done within a range in which the background and text are the same color; you won't be able to see the cell entries.

Move range G10..G14 several columns to the right so that it won't interfere with the other display elements you will be adding to the sheet. The entries in this range determine what hatch patterns appear in the pie chart named extperc, so it is important to keep the range intact somewhere in the sheet. Select Move, indicate range G10..G14 as the range to move, and indicate cell M10 as the Target range.

Set the width of column G to 3 so that there is a space between the highlighted worksheet ranges on the left and any graphs or text that you establish on the right. By now you have noticed that changing all the column widths has skewed the titles that you so painstakingly centered a few minutes ago. Fix the titles by selecting :Text Align Center and indicating range A1..K4. The top-left corner of the worksheet should appear as shown in Figure 25.6.

The first graph to add is the one that shows total extracted honey production. Extracted honey is the main product of Wickwork, so Edwina prefers to see it as the leading element of a quarterly report. Select :Graph. There are quite a few selections on the :Graph menu. One of the commands lets you establish a graph in the sheet, and a second lets you remove an established graph.

Other :Graph options give you the ability to navigate easily among the graphs in the spreadsheet, move graph images, and change the display characteristics of a graph. You are about to put a graph into the sheet, so select Add.

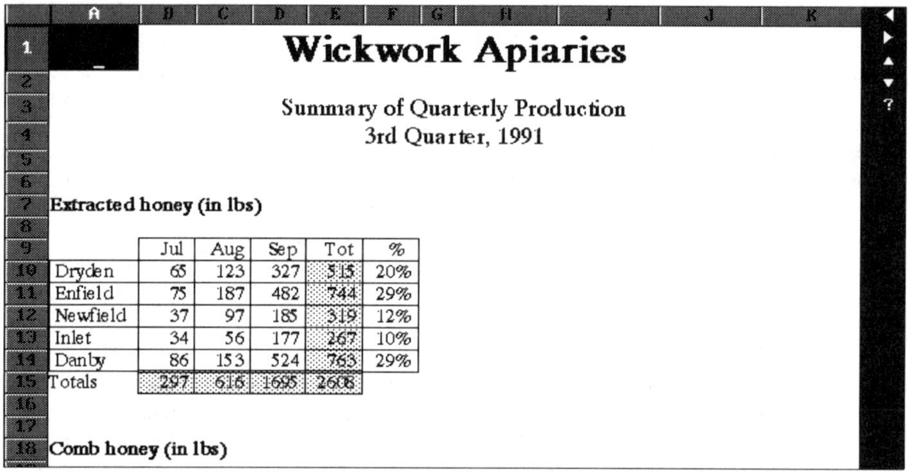

FIGURE 25.6. Squeezing some columns and moving the values out of column G make room for graphs and text that you will add to the Wickwork spreadsheet.

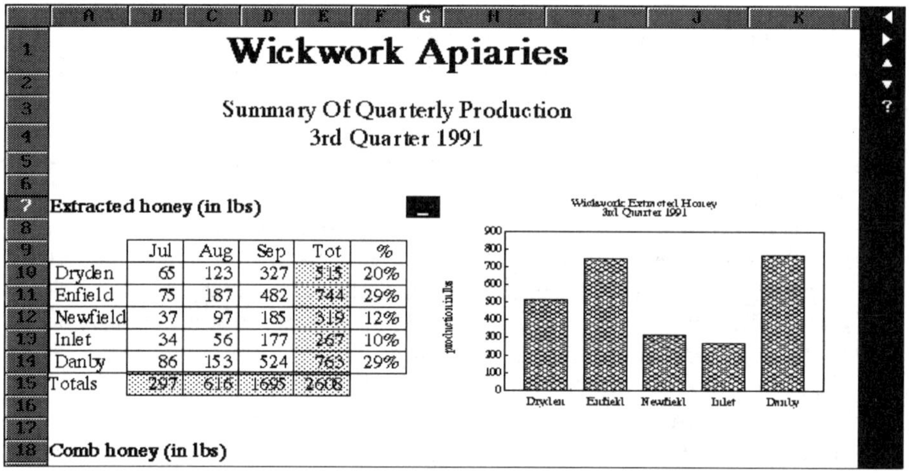

FIGURE 25.7. The top-left corner of the BEESWAX worksheet with a graph added is a dramatic change from the original 1-2-3 version of the sheet.

Wysiwyg can add graphs that originate from many sources. The first option on the :Graph Add menu is Current. This pastes an image of the graph whose settings currently appear in the graph settings dialog box. The second :Graph Add option is Named, which lets you add the image of any graph whose

Even Pictures are Possible: Metafile Images

Thank goodness for standardization. Many computer programs store data in unique file formats. The file format is the particular arrangement that a program uses when it records information on disk. Lotus 1-2-3 Release 2.3 uses a modified WK1 file format so similar to the Release 2, 2.01, and 2.2 formats that files created in any of these programs are interchangeable. 1-2-3 Releases 3 and 3.1 use the WK3 format and are not compatible with other releases of 1-2-3.

Computer Graphics Metafile format, or CGM, is an industry standard graphics format, but there are many other graphics formats. You know about the PIC file if you have read the preceding chapters in this book. Other formats include PCX, BMP, and DRW. Fortunately, some companies, while using proprietary graphic file formats for their own programs, give you the option of saving images as CGM files.

Because CGM is something of an industry standard, some software producers market *clip art* packages that feature CGM files. A clip art package is a collection of disk files that contain drawings you can load into your own programs. Several clip art images come with 1-2-3 and Wysiwyg and are available as CGM files in your 1-2-3 program directory.

settings you saved with the Graph Name Create command. Other options add graphs stored on disk as PIC files or in a file format called Computer Graphics Metafile (CGM) that is common to several commercial graphing packages.

You are adding a named graph to the spreadsheet, so choose Named, and select extot from the list of names that Wysiwyg presents. Indicate range H7..K17 as the target range; the range you select determines the size of the resultant graph. Your worksheet should match Figure 25.7.

If you've completed the earlier graphing exercise, you should have two more graphs named in the BEESWAX spreadsheet. While there is additional ungraphed data in the sheet, we will deal with only one of the remaining graphs and put a little more energy into polishing up the first third of the report.

To fit another graph of the extracted honey data into the sheet, you will have to open up some space beneath the first tier of information. Select Worksheet Insert Row, and indicate range A18..A34. This may open more rows than you need, but it is easy enough to remove the extra rows later.

Select :Graph Add Named, and choose the name extsum from the list of available graphs. Indicate range F18..K28 as the range to receive the graph image. This graph compares the production of extracted honey from Wickwork Apiaries' five hive sites. See Figure 25.8.

Give Readers a Break: Notes on Page Design

Is the Wickwork report starting to look busy to you? Most people prefer to cram as much information as possible into a small space without giving the reader claustrophobia. An effective presentation gets the point across with minimal involvement from the reader.

As you begin your own spreadsheet publishing, pay special attention to the overall design of each of your documents. Here is a short list of guidelines to use in preparing any single document:

- Use only a few fonts. In fact, use one font in a few carefully chosen sizes. Sometimes mixing fonts on a page works nicely, but in most of those cases the mixer is an experienced graphic designer.
- Use font styles sparingly. Boldface, italic, and underlining certainly add emphasis, but, when every sentence has an emphasized word or two, the page appears to be yelling. Your readers may want to cover their ears.
- Place only a few graphics on a page. One is probably enough. That is, unless you are writing a picture book.
- Use an outline structure. This applies especially to longer reports. Start with a title, include sections that focus on specific points, and try to break the sections into subtopics.
- Use titles and subtitles. Divisions and subdivisions are more accessible if each begins with a title that clearly identifies the material it covers.
- Use figure captions. Some people believe that the best articles can be read entirely as figure captions. You can have a long body of text to accompany the figures and captions, but we had better not have to read the text to fully understand the topic it covers.
- Use lists. The busy reader will scan large areas of grey text, pausing to read the bulleted and numbered lists. The list items might be all your audience remembers of your presentation.
- Summarize. The classic report begins with a one-page (or less) executive summary, which should tell all. Everything that follows is formality and only explores the points made in the summary in depth. It does not hurt to summarize after the fact, either.

Many of these guidelines won't apply to most of your spreadsheet publishing tasks. Throwing some boxes around data cells and adding some boldface type here and there may be all you do before printing the week's sales figures. When you stitch together lengthy reports, however, strive for directness and simplicity.

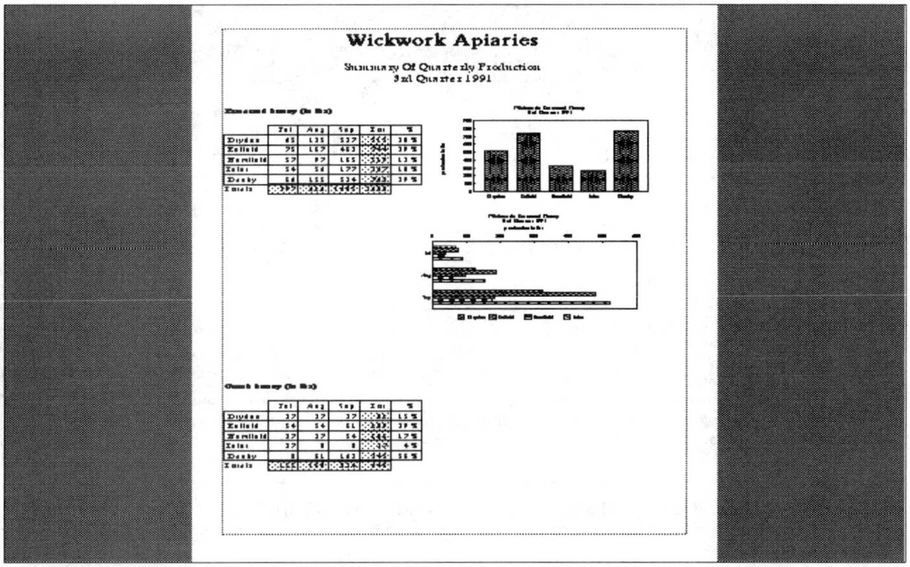

FIGURE 25.8. Using Wysiwyg's Print Preview, you can see how the first page of the report looks with two added graphs.

What is a Report Without a Report: Wysiwyg Text Processing

Most reports focas on the analysis of data and the conclusions drawn. So far, our report is deficient in these areas. Of course, Edwina can draw her own conclusions based on the data and the graphs, but she wants to hear what you have to say about activity during the quarter. We've prepared a little text that explains your analysis.

The purpose of entering this text is not to give you typing practice. Rather, it's to showcase Wysiwyg's text-processing capabilities. The :Text Edit command actually superimposes a rudimentary text processor on the spreadsheet. Try it.

See for Yourself

Select :Text Edit, and indicate range A18..K34. The graphs disappear, and a grey tint appears in their places. Also, a vertical bar appears at the top-left corner of range A18..K34. The vertical bar is a cursor that shows where characters will appear when you start typing.

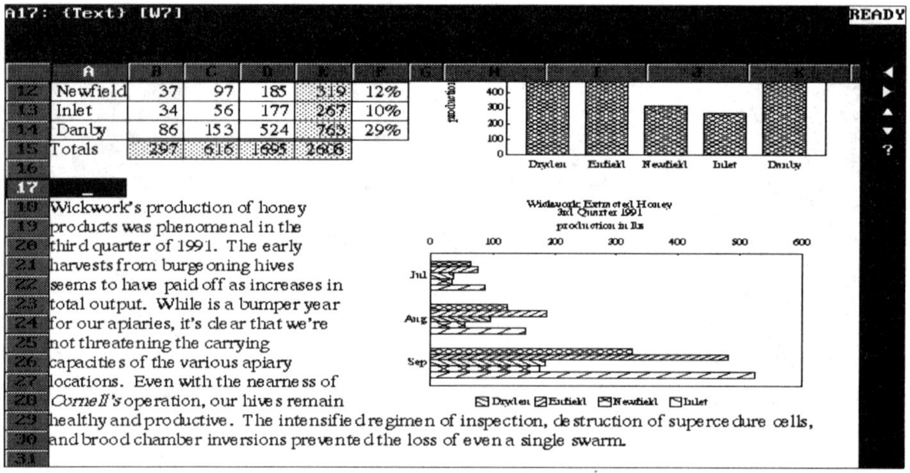

FIGURE 25.9. It is simple to wrap text around graphs for a dramatic presentation.

You have included the graph within the text editing range because Wysiwyg automatically wraps text around graphs added to the spreadsheet. Type the following text to see how this works. Type continuously without pressing Return at the end of a line. Wysiwyg takes care of word-wrap for you:

> Wickwork's production of honey products was phenomenal in the third quarter of 1991. The early harvest from burgeoning hives seems to have paid off as an increase in total output. While this is a bumper year for our apiaries, it is clear that we are not threatening the carrying capacities of the various apiary locations.

You are not finished yet, but we want to point out a text-editing feature that is easy to overlook. Continue to type the following sentence up to (but not including) the C in Cornell:

> Even with the nearness of Cornell's

Before you type the C, press the NAME key (F3). Wysiwyg presents a menu of font style options. You can alter the font for any number of characters; switch to boldface, italic, or underline; change the display color of characters; make characters superscript or subscript; and even apply a weird outline characteristic to the text. For this exercise, select Italic, and type *Cornell's*. Then press the NAME key again and select Normal. Continue typing with the following text:

Add Attributes Anywhere

Wysiwyg's Edit Text feature lets you apply special attributes to any character string within a worksheet label. For example, to apply the weird outline characteristic to the word *honey* in cell A7, move the cell pointer to that cell. Select :Text Edit, and indicate range A7..D7—the range must be as wide as the label is long.

Move the edit cursor to the space before the word *honey*. Press NAME (F3), and select Outline. Move the edit cursor to the space after the word *honey*, press NAME, and select Normal. Press Escape to complete the exercise.

Remove the outline attribute by re-entering the label *Extracted honey* (*in lbs*).

operation, our hives remain healthy and productive. The intensified regimen of inspection, destruction of supercedure cells, and brood chamber inversions prevented the loss of even a single swarm.

When you have finished entering the text, press the Escape key. The graphs reappear, and the spreadsheet returns to Wysiwyg's Ready mode as in Figure 25.9.

Wysiwyg's text processor is not powerful. While in :Text Edit mode, Wysiwyg lets you use the arrow keys to move the edit cursor within the Edit range. You can start typing anywhere in the range, and Wysiwyg will do its best to wrap the text at the ends of lines and around intervening graphs.

When you have finished entering text, you can alter the alignment of the text by selecting :Text Align and then Left, Right, Center, or Even. Try realigning the text you just entered. Select :Text Align Even, and indicate range A18..K34. Wysiwyg squares off the edges of the text alongside the graph.

A Bit More About Graphs

You may feel that this has been a grueling chapter. We've taken a plain 1-2-3 spreadsheet and souped it up on its way to becoming a publishing-quality report. But we're not yet finished. We've used many of Wysiwyg's features, but many more remain. Many of those help you to work with graphs in the spreadsheet. Another set of features lets you dramatically modify the spreadsheet display by changing the colors, the spreadsheet frame, and

When You Save With Wysiwyg

When you modify a spreadsheet with Wysiwyg, you create a set of formatting instructions that are not actually part of the spreadsheet. Wysiwyg keeps track of those instructions and applies them to the sheet in RAM. When you save a Wysiwygged spreadsheet, the add-in creates a disk file that records the specified formatting options. In other words, any sheet saved with Wysiwyg has two files.

For example, after you modify the BEESWAX spreadsheet with Wysiwyg and save it to disk, you have two BEESWAX files—BEESWAX.WK1 and BEESWAX.FMT. These files should always travel together (don't copy or back one up without copying or backing up the other.) Without the FMT file, Wysiwyg won't be able to recreate the formatting that you applied.

more. Let's look a little more closely at Wysiwyg's graph-related features and see how they help you to perfect the printouts from your spreadsheets.

Under the :Graph Settings menu is an option to replace one graph in the sheet with another. Another option lets you move a graph in the sheet or alter the size of the range it covers. The :Graph Settings Synch option lets you determine whether selected graphs will automatically be updated to reflect changes you make to data in the worksheet. By default, Wysiwyg does not update a graph based on changes to the sheet unless you specifically order it to do so.

The :Graph Settings Display option lets you "turn off" a graph. A marker appears where the graph resides in the sheet, but there is no graph image. Shutting off a graph display lets Wysiwyg update the spreadsheet quickly so your work won't drag when you have graphs in the sheet. The :Graph Settings Opaque command makes a graph transparent to data in underlying spreadsheet cells. This lets you enhance a graphic image by entering labels that show through the graph.

Of the other options on the main :Graph menu, two require more explanation—the :Graph View and :Graph Edit commands. You should be able to figure out the uses of the Move, Zoom, and Compute options.

The :Graph View command lets you look at images stored on disk without having to bring them into the spreadsheet. You may have used 1-2-3's Graph Save command to create PIC files on disk or you may have a collection of CGM images that you want to include in the sheet. To review PIC files, select :Graph View PIC, and edit the path name to whatever directory contains the PIC files. Likewise, review CGM files by selecting :Graph View Metafile and editing the path name. There is a small collection of CGM files that 1-2-3's install program copies into the 1-2-3 program directory. Examine a few of them if you want to practice with this menu option.

The :Graph Edit command is big—so big that it deserves an in-depth exercise of its own to provide a solid working knowledge of its components. We will explore the nature of working in a GUI environment. You will learn to deal with several graphical elements at once, and you will see how to apply Wysiwyg as you would a paint program. Before you go on, save this worksheet under the name BEESWAX.

Graphs in a GUI

Graphs are pictures of data that you can modify easily to suit your tastes. Any image that you can depict two-dimensionally can go into a graph; the trick is to master the tools that you use to create such images. In Wysiwyg, you can add geometric shapes, lines, arrows, text, and even freehand drawings to graphs that you have created in 1-2-3. You can also bring clip art into a Wysiwyg graphic and drop the image directly on the sheet.

Graphical Concepts

Working in a graphics editor isn't much like working in a text editor or a spreadsheet editor. Spreadsheets and documents are governed by rules that tell where certain elements must fall in relation to other elements. In a graphic, any element can fall anywhere in relation to any other; you can put things next to each other or on top of each other.

The "things" in a graph are called *objects*, and it is not always clear at a glance what is an object. A single bar of a bar graph might be an object, or the entire image of the graph might be a single object. You can manipulate graphical objects individually or in sets; moving them, resizing them, rotating them, copying them, and erasing them.

Once you have assembled a graphic image, individual objects don't matter a whole lot. The completed effort is a two-dimensional drawing that appears in the spreadsheet and that you can print on paper. However, as long as you are still customizing a graph, it is important to keep track of the objects you create, and to understand the many ways in which you can manipulate them.

To get the hang of working in a graphic, make sure that Wysiwyg is attached, and then retrieve the BEESWAX worksheet that you created earlier. Press the Home key so that your display matches Figure 25.10.

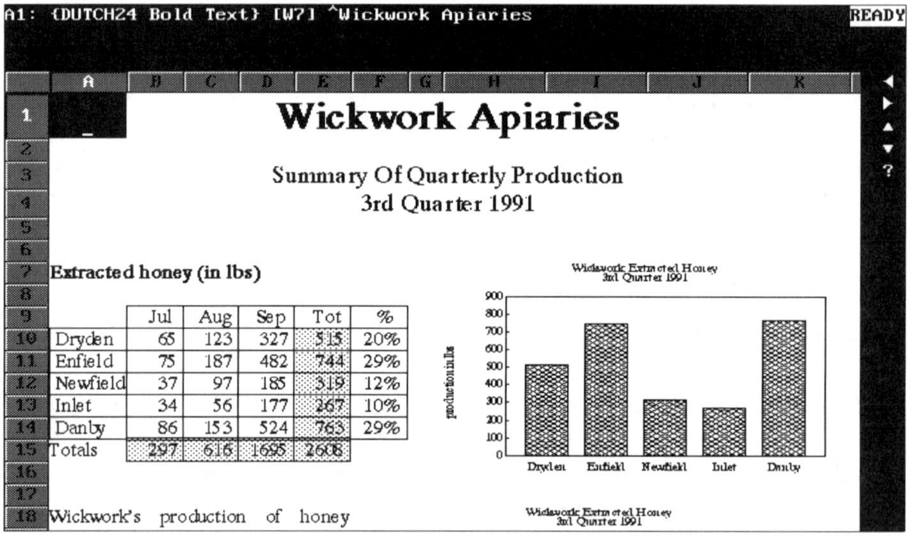

FIGURE 25.10. The quarterly report for Edwina is almost finished. This is the top-left corner of the BEESWAX spreadsheet as it appeared a few pages back.

Select :Graph Edit, and indicate cell H7 as the graph to edit. If you are using a mouse, double click anywhere within the graph that begins in cell H7. Wysiwyg expands the graph to fill more of the display, and the graph editing menu appears as in Figure 25.11.

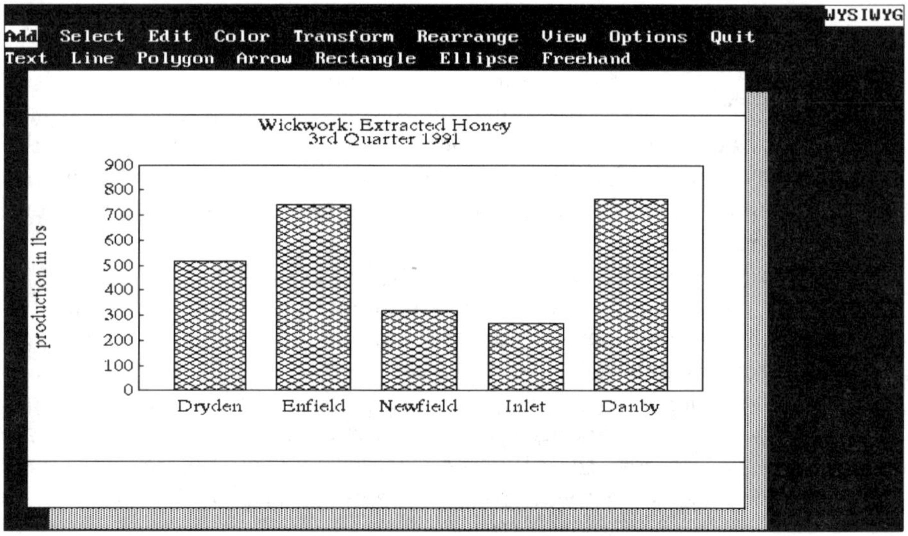

FIGURE 25.11. Selecting :Graph Edit activates the graph editing tools and transforms the spreadsheet display.

It's time to go to work. The :Graph Edit menu includes enough options to make the editor a program in and of itself. Fortunately, once you get the knack of working with graphical elements, you will be able to decipher the various menu options on your own. To help develop the knack, add some emphasis to the honey production data from the Inlet hive site. This was the first year of production for that location, and the output was exceptional.

Start by creating an oval that will contain a word by the time you finish this exercise. Creating the oval falls under the heading of adding a graphic element, so select Add from the :Graph Edit menu.

There are seven general categories of objects that you can add to the image. Select Ellipse, and expect things to get a little tricky.

Wysiwyg prompts you to establish the *box origin*, which is the top-left corner of a rectangle whose sides dictate the limits of the ellipse you are going to draw. In the top-left of the display, an X and a Y coordinate appear. These represent horizontal and vertical offsets of the graphics cursor from the top-left corner of the graphic. The graphics cursor itself is a set of cross hairs that is located somewhere on your display. Find it by repeatedly pressing one of the arrow keys or by moving the mouse on your desk.

In any case, Wysiwyg reports constantly on the coordinates of the cross hairs as you move them around in the graphic. If you are using the keyboard (mouse users, see the box titled The Mouse in Its Element; for that matter,

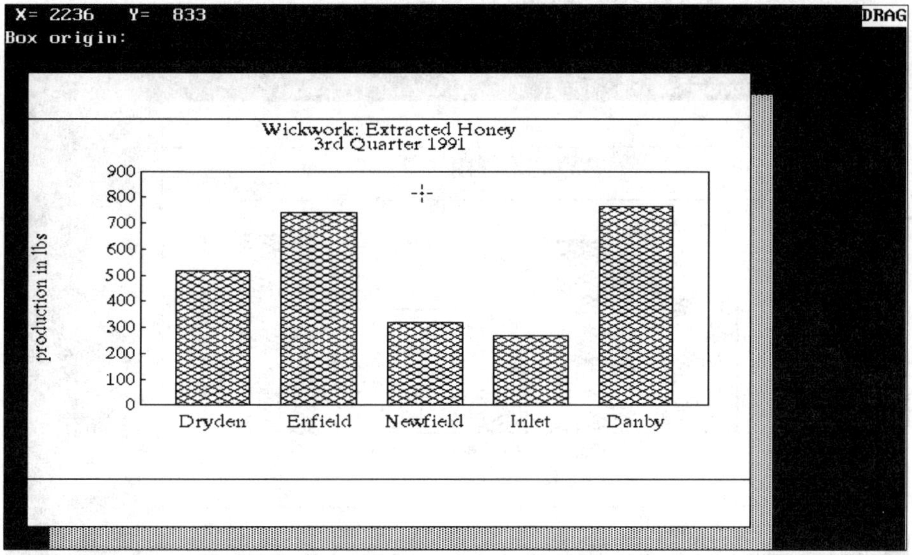

FIGURE 25.12. When you want to add an object to a graphic, Wysiwyg reports the location of the graphics cursor in terms of X and Y coordinates. The cursor itself is a set of cross hairs that you move by pressing the arrow keys or moving the mouse.

The Mouse in Its Element

Nowhere is a mouse more powerful than in a GUI graphics editor. Using the keyboard to add and modify graphic elements is painful when compared to working with a mouse.

For example, to add the ellipse in this graphic, select Add Ellipse from the graph editing menu. Then drag from coordinate X= 2108, Y= 1079, to coordinate X= 3134, Y= 1843. When you release the mouse button, the ellipse appears. We provide abbreviated mouse instructions through the remainder of this chapter to help out with the required mouse-moves.

read the box if you are still undecided about owning a mouse—working with graphics is the mouse's strong point), maneuver the cross hairs so they fall at coordinates X= 2108, Y= 1079, and press Return.

Wysiwyg prompts you to indicate the *box end*, which is the bottom-right corner of the rectangle that will define the ellipse. Press the RightArrow and DownArrow keys, and move the cross hairs to coordinates X= 3134, and Y= 1843. As you move the cross hairs, a rectangle stretches from the box origin point to the position of the cross hairs. This is exactly analogous to what happens in the spreadsheet when you use Point mode to establish a range reference. Press Return to finish the procedure.

The graph editor appears as in Figure 25.13.

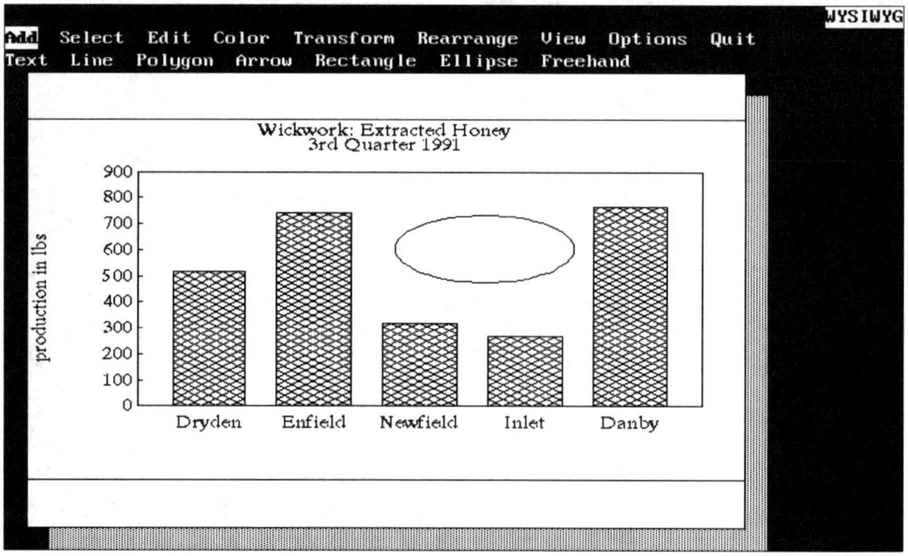

FIGURE 25.13. The extracted honey bar graph with an ellipse added.

Notice the tiny squares that appear at the top and bottom and at each end of the ellipse. These are called *handles*. Handles surrounding an object tell you that the object is currently selected. Right now, that is not important, but you will become more familiar with handles later in this chapter.

Make the Graph Yell

The oval in the graph makes little sense at this point. Soon, however, it will be a frame for the word *stellar*. To add the string, select Add Text. Wysiwyg prompts you to enter some text. Type *stellar*, and press Return. The text appears somewhere on the graph display, and the prompt *Place text* appears in the control panel.

If you are working with the keyboard, use the arrow keys to move the text object around until it is centered in the oval. Then press Return to park the text there. If you are using the mouse, the text object tracks the movements of the mouse. Move it into the oval, and click.

The array of handles around the text object shows that it remains selected. Take advantage of this to change the font of the text; the label is terribly small relative to the size of the frame. Choose Edit from the :Graph Edit menu, and then select Font. The fonts available on this menu are the same ones available on Wysiwyg's :Format Font menu. Select 3, and assign the Dutch 24-point font to the selected text object.

Fine Tune the Placement

It is unlikely that the first time you place and size a text object the object will fit exactly as you want. The word *stellar* is probably not perfectly centered in the oval. As long as the text is selected, you can fiddle with it to get just the right fit.

First, select Rearrange. Among the options on the resulting menu are Move, Copy, Delete, Front, and Back. Select Move. A box that represents the text object appears in place of the text, and an image of a hand appears in the box. Use the arrow keys (or the mouse) to reposition the box so that it is better centered in the oval. Press Return or click to place the text object. Select Rearrange Move, and reposition the object until it is as close to centered as you can manage.

You will probably find that you can't really center the word within the ellipse. One way to deal with that problem is to resize the text object. It is still selected, so choose Transform from the :Graph Edit menu.

Again, you have quite a group of options. You can rotate a selected object about its center, flip it horizontally or vertically, skew it vertically or horizontally, or resize it. Select size.

Use the arrow keys or mouse to stretch the text object a little bit vertically —and perhaps even a bit horizontally. Press Return or click to finish resizing, then use the Rearrange Move command to reposition the text once more. Alternate between resizing and moving until you have centered the text in the oval. When you have it just right, select Select None to clear the handles from the text object. Figure 25.14 shows how it should look.

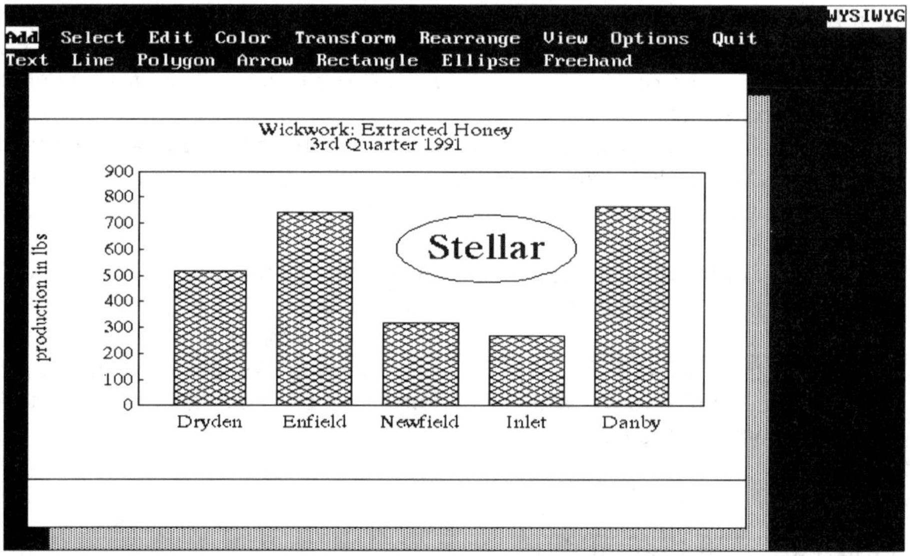

FIGURE 25.14. It might take a little juggling, but eventually you can center the word *stellar* inside the ellipse that you positioned earlier.

Arrows

You have established a flag to highlight something in the graph. As it stands, the flag could simply be pointing out that Wickwork's performance in the quarter was stellar. But, the point you want to make is that the Inlet hive site's performance was stellar. An arrow running from the oval to the bar for Inlet will focus attention at the proper place.

Select Add Arrow. Move the cross hairs to the center bottom of the oval, and press Return. Then move the cross hair to a point just above the top of the *Inlet* bar in the graph and press Return a second time.

Line Weight

It is quite clear now that production for the Inlet location was stellar. However, the lines that make up the ellipse and the arrow are rather thin. They don't stand up well next to the font of the word *stellar*. Make them a little heavier.

To alter the characteristics of more than one object at a time, select all the objects before issuing other commands. You are about to alter the line weights of two objects—the arrow and the oval. The arrow is already selected, so you just need to select the ellipse.

Choose Select, and then select More/Less. In this mode, pointing at a selected object and pressing Return deselects the object. Pointing at an object that isn't selected and pressing Return selects the object. Move the cross hairs to a point on the ellipse, and press Return. Handles appear on the ellipse and on the arrow.

Increase the weight of the selected objects by selecting Edit Width. The line weight in use now is Very Narrow. Select Narrow to increase the weight just a bit. Then select Select None to remove the handles from the graph objects. The image looks something like the one in Figure 25.15.

Select Quit from the :Graph Edit menu, and take a look at the worksheet.

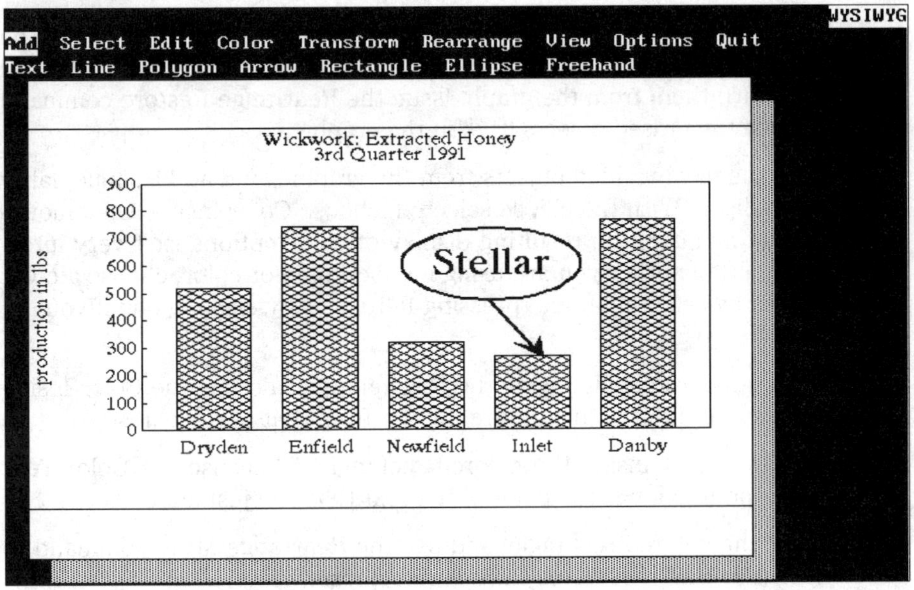

FIGURE 25.15. A word in an ellipse with an arrow emphasizes the honey production bar for the Inlet hive site.

Further Fiddling With Graphs

It would take far too long to walk you through all of the commands in Wysiwyg's graph editing facility. Besides, you'd get bored if we tried. You'll have a lot more fun, and learn more to boot, if you explore the menus on your own. Select :Graph Edit, and indicate cell F18 (or double click anywhere on the graph that begins in that cell). Use the white space in the top-right of the graph to experiment with the graph editing options.

Here are a few things to try:

1. Select Add, and place text, lines, boxes, ellipses, and arrows on the graphic. Also, select Add Freehand, and create your own line drawing on the graphic. A graphic has handles and therefore is selected immediately after you add it to the graph. This means that you can remove it quickly, if you wish, by selecting Rearrange Delete.
2. Add some text to the graph, and while it is selected, select Edit Font to apply a new font type.
3. With a text object selected, choose Transform Rotate. Then use the arrow keys or the mouse to spin the object around its center. Finish rotating the object by pressing Return or by clicking.
4. Use the Select One and the Select More/Less commands to select all the objects you have added, and then use the Rearrange Delete command to remove them from the graph. Issue the Rearrange Restore command to place the erased objects back in the graphic.
5. Clear the newly added objects from the graphic, and add a single, fairly large ellipse. With the ellipse selected, choose Color Inside. On a monochrome monitor, the resulting display of color options isn't very interesting, but whether you are using monochrome or color, choose a color pattern by selecting it and pressing Return or by clicking one if you are using a mouse.
6. Add a small rectangle inside the large ellipse, and use the Color Inside command to fill it with a different color from that of the ellipse.
7. Add some text inside the colored rectangle. Then use the Color Text command to change the color of the text that you just added.
8. Select the colored rectangle, and use the Rearrange Move command to place it so that it overlaps the colored ellipse.

9. Use the Rearrange Back command to move the rectangle behind the ellipse. Use the Rearrange Front command to bring the rectangle back to the foreground.
10. Choose Select All to place handles on the ellipse, the rectangle, and the text. Then select Transform Size and use the arrow keys or the mouse to enlarge all three objects.
11. Choose Transform Horizontal, and press the LeftArrow key a few times, or move the mouse to the left on your desk, until you've skewed the ellipse, the rectangle, and the text. Press Return or click to lock in the new shapes; then choose Select None to remove the handles from the objects.

Whatever fiddling you do, be sure to remove it from the graphic before you quit the graph editor. It wouldn't do to have superfluous symbols on the graph when you print out Edwina's quarterly report.

Print the Finished Report

You are there. It has been a long haul, but your report on Wickwork Apiaries' third quarter production is as finished as it will ever bee (pun intended). We've overlooked a lot of the data, and we've barely begun the written report itself, but we would start repeating ourselves if we went beyond this point. It's time to print a copy of the report to pass along to Edwina.

The procedures for printing from Wysiwyg are virtually the same as the ones for printing from 1-2-3. The trick is to remember to use Wysiwyg's Print

Don't Confuse the Print Menus

The first chapter in this section explained how to print using 1-2-3's menus. You find printing options in 1-2-3 by selecting Print from the main menu or by selecting Worksheet Global Default Printer. All of Wysiwyg's printing options are available when you select :Print.

None of the settings you make on either of 1-2-3's printing-related menus affects the printing you do using Wysiwyg's menus. Conversely, none of Wysiwyg's printing options affect the printing you do using 1-2-3's menus. This point causes users a lot of confusion, so we want to emphasize it.

If you want to print the special formatting and graphs you have established in Wysiwyg, you must use the :Print commands. If you select Print from 1-2-3's menus, you will end up with a vanilla printout.

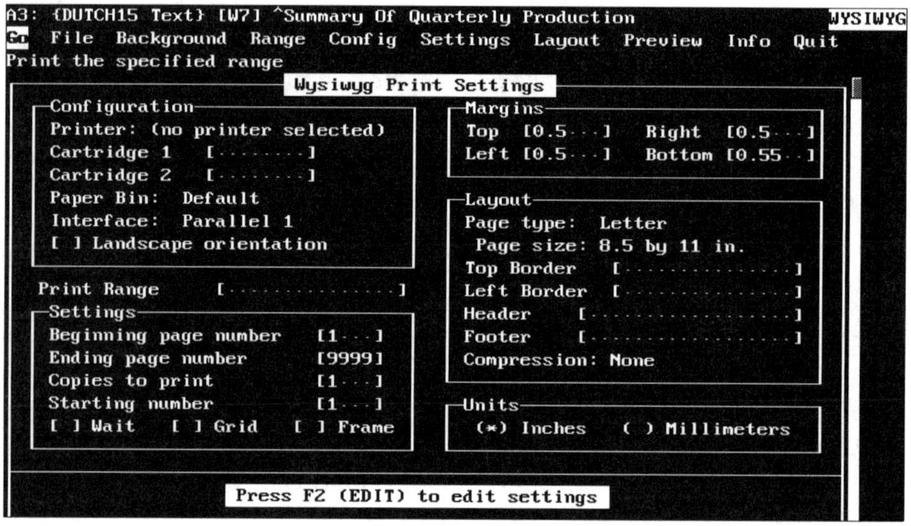

FIGURE 25.16. Wysiwyg's print settings dialog box reveals all of the options available under the :Print menus and their current settings.

menu, rather than that of 1-2-3. None of the settings you make under the 1-2-3 Print menus affect the printing that you do from Wysiwyg.

Select :Print. The settings dialog box that appears is quite complete. See Figure 25.16.

Poking around the menus and reading the options in the dialog box, you should easily recognize the features that we explored in Chapter 23 from 1-2-3. There are a few additions, such as a Page-Size option under the Layout menu, which allows you to select from among several popular pre-defined page sizes to match the one set in your printer. There is also a Compression option under the Layout menu. This lets you tell Wysiwyg to shrink the selected print range as needed to fit the width of a page.

Perhaps the most useful printing feature on the :Print menu is the Preview option. After setting a Wysiwyg print range, you can select Preview to see how the finished report will look on the printed page. Some of the detail might be missing from the screen preview, but you get a good sense of whether the enhancements you have added work well together.

If you don't want to add page headers and footers, to alter the print margins, change the orientation of the printout, or add print borders, follow these five steps to printing from Wysiwyg:

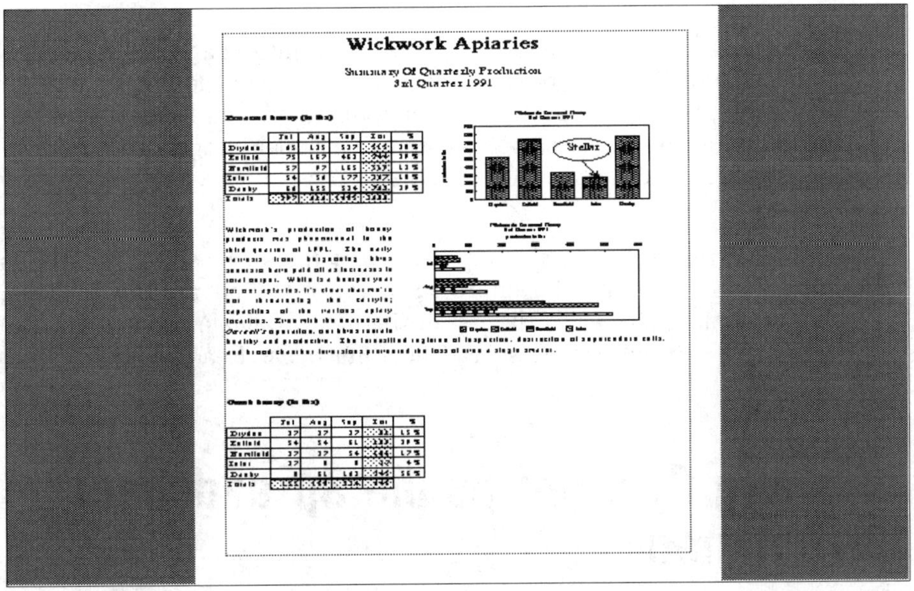

FIGURE 25.17. The Wickwork Apiaries report as it appears on the display when you select :Print Preview.

1. Make sure the printer is on and ready. If the printer has an On Line indicator light, it should be on. Also, make sure there is paper in the printer.
2. Align the printer. If you are using a tractor-feed printer or one that uses a platen to advance the paper, adjust the paper so that the printhead is about even with the top of a new page.
3. Set a Print range. For this exercise, select :Print Range Set and indicate range A1..K30 as the range to print.

Change the Print Orientation

Printing that runs from left to right across the width of an 8.5 by 11-inch page is in *portrait* mode. Rotated 90 degrees to run across the length of the page, the printing is in *landscape* mode. Lotus disabled Wysiwyg's landscape printing ability for most printers when they adapted the Wysiwyg technology from an add-in product called Impress. You can't use Wysiwyg to print in landscape mode on a dot-matrix printer.

You can, however, print in landscape mode on a laser printer. To do this, select :Print Config Orientation Landscape Quit before you follow the five steps to printing from Wysiwyg.

4. (Optional) Select Preview to see how the printed page will look. This warns you of any need to set print margins, place page breaks, or alter formatting before committing anything to paper. The habit of previewing before printing can save money in your paper budget—not to mention a small forest over the years. Press any key to clear the preview display.

5. Print the range. Select Go from the Print menu. Wysiwyg reports its progress as it prints the entire Print range. When printing is done, Wysiwyg ejects paper to the top of the next available blank page. The menu drops away, and the spreadsheet finishes in Ready mode.

Wysiwyg Customizes the Spreadsheet Environment

Are you ready for a diversion? We have explored the Wysiwyg features that are especially important to people who must produce reports from 1-2-3. But Wysiwyg offers additional options for customizing the display that give your spreadsheets in RAM a look all their own. Some of the options—altering colors, for example—are useful if you are using a color printer or plotter. Take a few minutes to learn about the remarkable assortment of display options that Wysiwyg offers.

The display options affect how the spreadsheet and its contents appear on your monitor. While there are practical applications for the commands on the :Display menu, simply fiddling with those commands and seeing how each one modifies the display can be quite entertaining. The ability to enlarge and decrease the overall size of the spreadsheet, alter the colors of the display elements, and change the look of the spreadsheet frame lets you customize the environment in occasionally outrageous ways. It is a huge step forward from the old blue and white on black that has characterized 1-2-3 since its birth.

It doesn't matter what data and text you have in the spreadsheet as you work through the rest of this chapter. For the sake of consistency, we will assume that you have a copy of the BEESWAX model modified with formatting options, graphs, and text as described in this and the previous chapter. Make sure that Wysiwyg is attached, and retrieve the BEESWAX worksheet. If you prefer, use a spreadsheet of your own. All that matters is that there are labels, values, and formulas in the sheet.

Black-And-White or Color? Set the Display Mode

As we pointed out several chapters back, Wysiwyg turns the spreadsheet into a GUI environment. There may, however, be times when you will want to switch back to the textual display—perhaps to see whether the changes you make in Wysiwyg will look acceptable to someone who will use your spreadsheet files without the add-in. Whatever the reason you can switch back to the textual display mode by selecting :Display Mode Text. Go ahead and do that, and then select Quit.

With Wysiwyg attached, all of its commands are available even in Text Display mode. The effects of those commands don't show until you switch back to the graphics mode, however, so you are better off doing Wysiwyg enhancements in Graphics mode. Get back to Graphics mode by selecting :Display Mode Graphics Quit.

The :Display Mode menu lets you shut off all color in the spreadsheet display. It works only when the spreadsheet is in Graphics mode, and it does have an important purpose. After you have altered display colors and applied various formatting options, you may want to know how the sheet would look to someone stuck with a monochrome monitor. For that matter, you may be the person with the monochrome monitor; the :Display Mode B&W option may make the display easier to read on a monochrome monitor than it is in the Color mode.

The Incredible Shrinking (Growing?) Sheet

Wysiwyg's :Display Zoom command can provide several minutes of entertainment pleasure. In Graphics mode, the :Display Zoom command enlarges or decreases the size of the spreadsheet image within the spreadsheet window. This zooming in and out has no effect on the size of a printed image. It does give you a way to examine a large spreadsheet area or to enlarge elements so you have a better sense of how they will appear when you print them out. If you are using a low-resolution monitor, such as a CGA adapter, zooming the spreadsheet up to 150% its normal size makes the fonts and graphs much easier to read.

Select :Display Zoom, choose Huge, and then select Quit. Move around in the spreadsheet to see the effect of enlarging the spreadsheet to 150% of its original size. Select :Display Zoom Tiny Quit, and view the worksheet at 63% of its normal size.

The most entertaining of the :Display Zoom options is the Manual selection. Try it. Select :Display Zoom Manual. You can adjust the size of the

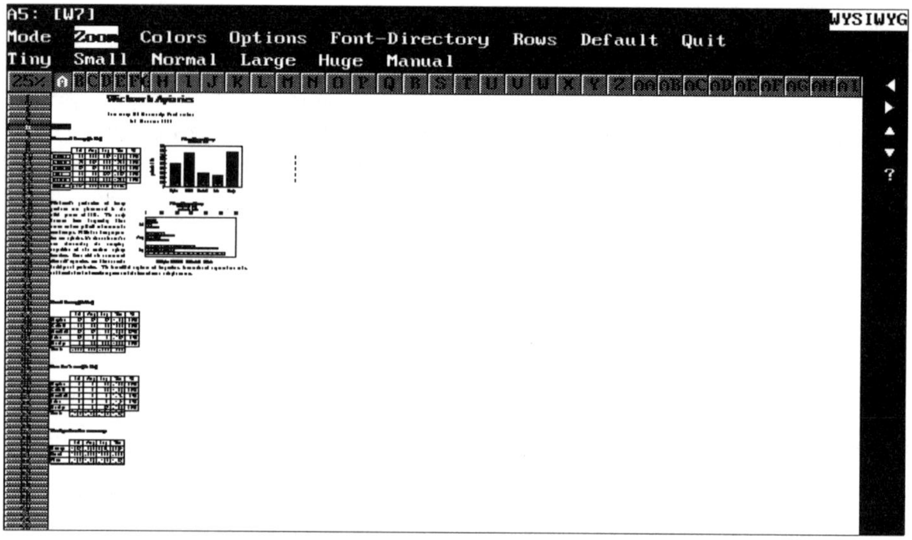

FIGURE 25.18. The BEESWAX worksheet displayed at 25% of its normal size.

spreadsheet from 25% of normal up to four times the normal (the relative sizes are approximations). Do this either by entering a value or by pressing arrow keys. Press the LeftArrow key repeatedly, and the worksheet shrinks before your eyes. Likewise, press RightArrow, and the spreadsheet grows.

The spreadsheet image won't always be pretty as you use the arrow keys to zoom in and out, but the image stabilizes properly when you press Return to lock in the new display size. When you are tired of fiddling, press Return. Then select Zoom Normal Quit.

A Splash in the Sheet—Of Color, of Course

If you don't have a color monitor, don't waste your time with this section. If you do have a color monitor, you can have several more minutes of fun changing the colors that make up the spreadsheet display.

Select :Display Colors. Here you find options for changing the background color of the spreadsheet, cell entries, entries in unprotected cells, the spreadsheet frame, and more. Rather than walk you through a specific exercise, we suggest that you experiment with these options on your own.

If you don't like the color that results when you change the setting of a display element, you might fiddle with the Replace option on the :Display Color menu. When you select :Display Color Replace, Wysiwyg lets you change the color assigned to a specific color option on the menus. For example, if you select :Display Color Replace Black, and enter *2*, the option Black on any color-related menu assigns a light green color rather than black to the selected display element.

Again, fiddle on your own until you understand how the color options work.

The Frame, the Grid, and the Pointer

The :Display Options menu lets you alter the appearance of the spreadsheet frame, superimpose a grid on the spreadsheet, change the character of the cell pointer, and increase the intensity of the display's colors. Select :Display Options Frame.

Try each of the options on this menu in turn. Under the Special option you will find several unusual ways to look at the spreadsheet. You can set the frame to reveal the spreadsheet's size in inches, centimeters, and even points.

Make Graph Paper
The :Display Options Grid command lets you superimpose grid lines on the spreadsheet display. The grid lines coincide with the boundaries between cells.

Visible Page Break Symbols

The command :Display Options Page-Breaks lets you activate and deactivate the display of page break symbols in the spreadsheet. You create page break symbols in the first place by moving the cell pointer to a cell beneath the point at which the page break should occur. Then you select :Worksheet Page Row. Alternatively, you can move the cell pointer to the right of that point and select :Worksheet Page Column. This applies particularly when you plan to print the spreadsheet in landscape mode.

Normally, Wysiwyg displays the page break as a dotted line across (or down) the spreadsheet. When you select :Display Options Page-Breaks No, Wysiwyg hides the page break symbols.

Inserting page breaks, by the way, is not necessary unless you want your reports to be paginated at specific places. While printing, Wysiwyg automatically fills a page, ejects to the next page, and so on, maintaining the same margins, heading space, and footing space that 1-2-3 uses when it prints. You might assert your own pagination when Wysiwyg's automatic pagination would split a table of related information.

A Box Or A Frame: Change The Cell Pointer
The commands :Display Options Cell-Pointer lets you select between having the pointer appear as a solid rectangle or as an outline around the current cell.

Change the Display Adapter

Here is an unlikely option to have within a program. When you first installed 1-2-3, you had to select from a menu the type of display adapter your computer uses. With the wrong adapter installed, 1-2-3 might not even run on your computer.

Here, within Wysiwyg, is a command that lets you change the display adapter setting as you work in the spreadsheet. Select :Display Options Adapter. Wysiwyg offers a menu of numbers. Use the arrow keys to navigate the menu and see what display adapter types are available. If you are running a VGA monitor, you should be able to select from most of the options on the menu. However, if the monitor that you selected when you first installed 1-2-3 can't handle a display type you try to select on this menu, Wysiwyg won't allow the selection.

The advantage of being able to alter the display adapter from within the spreadsheet is that you can see how your worksheets will appear when someone loads them on another computer. You can, that is, if your display adapter can mimic the other. A color VGA adapter, for example, can mimic EGA and CGA adapters.

Be Intense

Chances are you've never squinted to make out faint details on your computer's monitor. Most of the time, the image on the display is bright enough, and dousing nearby lights improves the relative intensity. The :Display Options Intensity command can also increase the display's brightness. Select :Display Options Intensity High, and the screen brightens up. Select :Display Options Intensity Normal, and the image softens.

What Is a Font Directory?

One of the options on Wysiwyg's :Display menu is Font-Directory. It seems out of place here, but to be able to draw a font, Wysiwyg needs to know where the font file is on disk. You may remember that when you first installed 1-2-3 and Wysiwyg, the installation program generated fonts. This procedure created information on disk that Wysiwyg uses both to print fonts and to display them.

The needed information is in a directory named \WYSIWYG in the 1-2-3 program file directory. Wysiwyg knows where those fonts are when you start up, so you may never have to use the :Display Font-Directory option.

You may want to change the font directory some day if you add more fonts to your system. You might, for example, obtain a commercial font disk and install it in its own directory. You would use the :Display Font-Directory command to make the new fonts available during a work session.

How Many Rows Can You See?
The :Display Rows command is a variation on the concept of zooming in and out on the spreadsheet display. This command lets you choose to display any number of rows from 16 up to 60. But when you scrunch 60 rows on a monitor, don't expect to be able to read their contents easily.

Back to Normal: How to Remove Custom Display Options

Was that enough play? You can learn a lot through fiddling, and it is certainly the best way to learn about the :Display options—except that you might have made some changes that you now regret. Fortunately, there is a simple way to reestablish the display settings that were in effect before you started this chapter. Select :Display Default Restore, and things return to normal.

Be cautious when visiting the :Display Default menu. There is an Update option there, and selecting it has far-reaching effects. When you select :Display Default Update, Wysiwyg stores any changes you have made to the display settings in a file on disk. The next time you start up Wysiwyg, those settings will be in effect.

But there is another feature of which you should be aware. After you set colors with Wysiwyg's :Display Colors menus, you can alter the colors that 1-2-3 uses even without Wysiwyg attached. To do this, you select Worksheet Global Default Update. Whatever colors you selected in Wysiwyg become the display colors for 1-2-3 as well.

Having completed this chapter you should:

- *Have a solid understanding of how to use Wysiwyg's features*
- *Know how to create eye-catching reports from your spreadsheets*
- *Understand some basic rules for designing effective documents*
- *Be able to incorporate graphs in your spreadsheets, and to add emphasis to those graphs*
- *Know how to use Wysiwyg's features to spruce up 1-2-3's display*
- *Be able to produce some of the snazziest memos, letters, and reports ever to originate from your company*

Section 5
Automate the Spreadsheet with Macros

Stop here unless you are ready to become a computer programmer. Computer programming is the process of automating tasks on the computer, and that's exactly what 1-2-3 macros do. They automate tasks that you can perform in the spreadsheet.

At their simplest, macros can help to format cells, enter data, set column widths, and more as you build your own spreadsheet models. Complex macros can act as software in and of themselves, managing customer databases, tracking inventory, balancing your company's accounts, and so on.

In truth, you can do a lot with macros without developing advanced computer programming skills. With very little understanding of 1-2-3, you can have simple macros running in minutes. It's easy to get started with macros, and if you do a lot of work in the spreadsheet, you can save time by building and applying some macros of your own.

Macros can also serve as a programming language; as your expertise increases, you can use macros to build complete systems of automated spreadsheets that lead other users by the hand through complex computing processes. Section 6 of this book presents some models that showcase macros used in this way.

The purpose of this section is to introduce you to macros and show how macros can help with your work. We start by learning what macros are and applying them to simple tasks in the sheet. Then we build on that knowledge as we explore topics in advanced programming. As you progress through the chapters, you'll develop a working understanding of key macro concepts, and you'll find yourself well on the way to becoming an advanced macro programmer.

It is difficult to suggest specific applications of the advanced macro topics that will be helpful to every reader. Instead, we suggest the types of problems that each of the concepts can help to solve. This section serves more as a primer on macro-related concepts and lays the groundwork for future forays into more advanced macro programming.

26

Instant Macros for Beginners

Macros let you automate spreadsheet tasks that you perform repeatedly. Do you enter a particular label time and again? Then use a macro. Do you often set and reset the widths of columns? Use a macro. Do you write a lot of @SUM formulas? Macros can write them for you. And in most cases, macros can perform their assigned tasks far more quickly than you could do them manually.

Macros are nothing more than labels stored in the spreadsheet. At their simplest, the characters in the labels represent keys that you press to perform spreadsheet tasks. Under the right circumstances, you can trigger 1-2-3 to read the labels and "press" the keys represented in the labels. If you record several dozen or even hundreds of keystrokes that you normally issue to complete a task, imagine how much effort you save by having 1-2-3 "replay" the keystrokes automatically.

In this chapter you will:

- *Learn what macros are*
- *Make 1-2-3 type your name automatically*
- *Discover macro key names*
- *Set column widths automatically*
- *Convert formulas to labels*
- *Convert labels to formulas*
- *Speed printing from 1-2-3 or Wysiwyg*
- *Date-stamp the worksheet*
- *Save the current file*
- *Establish a Learn range*
- *Activate 1-2-3 Learn mode*
- *Use Learn mode to create a simple macro*
- *Deactivate Learn mode*

Write Your First Macro

Let's get off to a quick start. The first macro you write will type your name for you automatically. Start in an otherwise blank worksheet, and enter your full name in cell B1. Enter the label *\m* in cell A1. Remember to begin by typing an apostrophe when you enter this label. If you were the authors of this book, your worksheet might look like the one in Figure 26.1.

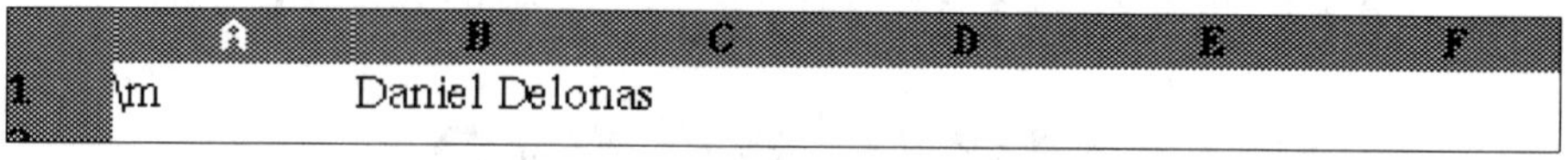

FIGURE 26.1. The label in cell B1 of this worksheet is a macro that types the name *Daniel Delonas.*

Assign the label in cell A1 as the name for cell B1. To do this, select Range Name Labels Right, and indicate cell A1 as the Label range. Alternatively, you can assign the name by selecting Range Name Create, entering *\m*, and then indicating cell B1.

You have just written a macro! The macro itself resides entirely in cell B1. The label in cell A1 identifies the macro when you look at the spreadsheet. Now put the macro to work. Move the cell pointer to cell B3, hold down the MACRO key (Alt), and press M. 1-2-3 types your name on the edit line in the control panel. Press Return to enter your name in cell B3, or press Escape to clear it from the edit line.

How the Macro Works

When you activate a macro, a part of 1-2-3 called the *macro processor* reads the labels in the macro cells and follows the instructions they contain. You can think of the macro processor as something that replaces you at the keyboard and follows your recorded macro instructions automatically.

In this case, the instructions for the macro are a series of recorded keystrokes. The character *D* in our version of the macro is the instruction that tells the macro processor to press the D key. The character *a* tells the macro processor to type the letter a.

There are two ways to activate macros; the method that you choose will depend in part on the nature of the names you give the macros. You have named your name-typing macro *\m*. This is a special type of name that lets you activate the macro quite simply by holding down the MACRO key and pressing M. You can start any macro whose name is a single letter following a backslash by holding down the MACRO key and pressing the appropriate letter.

The second way to activate a macro is to press the RUN key (hold down the Alt key and press F3) and then either enter the macro's name or select its

When You Name Macros

One of the conventions that we use for the macros presented in this book is the placement of labels to the left of named cells. Whenever a macro relies on a named cell (the first cell of each macro being a case in point), enter the cell's name as a label to the left of the cell.

Especially when you create very large macros, this technique can save some time. You will be able to use the Range Name Labels Right command to assign all the range names in one step, and you will know at a glance what names you have assigned.

name from the resulting menu listing. You can use this method to activate macros no matter what names you have assigned them.

Macros Do More Than Type Numbers and Letters

So far, your little macro isn't terribly impressive. Depending on the length of your name, the macro could save a lot of keystrokes if you need to enter your name often in a spreadsheet. But why should you have to press Return to place the typed name in the current cell? It seems that the macro ought to be able to enter the name for you.

Indeed the macro can enter your name. To prove it, move the cell pointer to cell B1 and press the EDIT key (F2). Type a tilde (~), and press Return. Again, if you were the authors of this book, the first two rows of your worksheet might appear as shown in Figure 26.2.

	A	B	C	D	E	F
1	\m	Daniel Delonas ~				

FIGURE 26.2. Our name-typing macro with a tilde added.

To try the macro, move the cell pointer to cell B4 and press MACRO-M. The macro processor types your name and enters it in cell B4.

The tilde is a *key name*—a symbol that identifies a *control key* to the macro processor. A control key is one that modifies the spreadsheet environment without necessarily adding a character or characters to the display. The function keys are control keys, as are the arrow keys on the cursor-control keypad. The Backspace, Insert, Delete, Escape, and Return keys are all control keys in 1-2-3.

Because Return is the most often-used control key, the Lotus programmers gave it a short macro key name. In most cases, when the macro processor encounters a tilde in a macro, the processor presses the Return key.

Most macro key names are more involved than the Return key name. They usually consist of a word enclosed in braces. For example, the key name for the DownArrow key is {DOWN}, and the one for Escape is {ESC}. Table 26.1 lists all of Release 2.3's macro key names:

Macro Key Names

Key	Key Name
Return	~
/ or <	/, <, or {MENU} (Pressing the < symbol is equivalent to pressing / when 1-2-3 is in Ready mode.)
UpArrow	{UP} or {U}
DownArrow	{DOWN} or {D}
LeftArrow	{LEFT} or {L}
RightArrow	{RIGHT} or {R}
Home	{HOME}
PageUp	{PGUP}
End	{END}
PageDown	{PGDN}
Backspace	{BACKSPACE} or {BS}
Insert	{INSERT} or {INS}
Delete	{DELETE} or {DEL}
Escape	{ESCAPE} or {ESC}
BigRight	{BIGRIGHT}

Macro Key Names (continued)

Key	Key Name
BigLeft	{BIGLEFT}
HELP (F1)	{HELP}
EDIT (F2)	{EDIT}
NAME (F3)	{NAME}
ABS (F4)	{ABS}
GOTO (F5)	{GOTO}
WINDOW (F6)	{WINDOW}
QUERY (F7)	{QUERY}
TABLE (F8)	{TABLE}
CALC (F9)	{CALC}
GRAPH (F10)	{GRAPH}
{	{{}
}	{}}
~	{~}
Alt-F7	{APP1}
Alt-F8	{APP2}
Alt-F9	{APP3}
Alt-F10	{APP4}

By applying the right macro key name, you can have the macro processor move the cell pointer down after it enters your name in the worksheet. Here's how: move the cell pointer to cell B3, and press the Delete key. This removes your name from that cell if you entered it there earlier. Now enter the label *{DOWN}* into cell B2.

Our spreadsheet looks like the one in Figure 26.3.

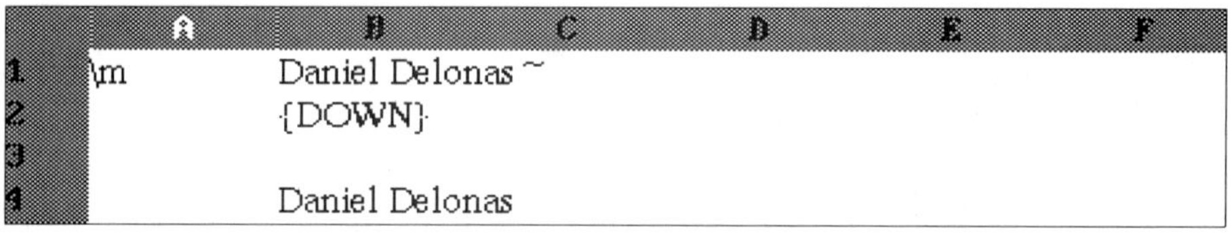

FIGURE 26.3. Our practice worksheet as it appeared after we entered the {DOWN} command into cell B2.

Move the cell pointer to cell B5, and press MACRO-M. The macro processor enters your name and moves the pointer down one row. Press MACRO-M again, and enter your name a second time. In fact, feel free to run the macro repeatedly and enter your name as far down the column as you want.

Flow of Control: The Fundamentals

The key name {DOWN} in cell B2 caused the macro processor to move the cell pointer down in the spreadsheet. This tells you something about the macro's *flow of control,* the order in which the macro processor reads commands.

When you activate a macro, the processor reads commands from left-to-right across a cell. When the processor exhausts the commands in the first cell, it looks for further commands in the next cell in the column. If that cell is blank or contains a numeric entry, the macro processor stops. If commands are there, processing continues from left to right across the cell.

We'll look at some of the commands that alter a macro's flow of control later in this section. Commands that let you alter the flow of control are what makes 1-2-3's macro facility a programming language.

Do It Again: Key Name Repeat Counts

Suppose that you want the macro processor to press the RightArrow key five times. You could enter the commands {RIGHT} {RIGHT} {RIGHT} {RIGHT} {RIGHT} or even the abbreviated commands {R}{R}{R}{R}{R}. But you could save some effort by using the most complete allowable abbreviation—the command {R 5}.

Each of the key names accepts a numeric argument that determines how many times the macro processor should press the named key. Using repeat count arguments can significantly reduce the length of some macros.

Macro Utilities Reduce Tedium

There is no easier way to learn about macros than to build a collection that you can use every time you work with 1-2-3. Macros that help to do basic spreadsheet operations such as setting column widths, entering data, date-stamping the worksheet, and so on are usually called utilities.

Utility macros are usually easy to create. Once you've built a few, you may come to rely on them. You may even wonder why some of the features you can create with macros are not already built into 1-2-3.

Set Column Widths

Almost everyone who writes macros has a width-setting macro in his past. Consider the number of keystrokes needed to set a column width: Press slash. Select Worksheet Column Set-Width. Widen or narrow the column, and then press Return. Of course, if you are using a mouse in Wysiwyg, you can simply drag to alter a column's width, so the macros we're about to present may not interest you.

We offer three width-setting macros. To try them out, start in a blank worksheet and make the entries shown in Figure 26.4.

	A	B	C	D	E	F
1	\e	/WCS{RIGHT}~				
2						
3	\n	/WCS{LEFT}~				
4						
5	\r	/WCR				

FIGURE 26.4. Three utility macros that help you to manage the widths of worksheet columns.

Remember to begin each of the entries by typing an apostrophe label prefix. After you have entered all the labels, select Range Name Labels Right, and indicate range A1..A7. This assigns the labels in Column A as names for the adjacent cells of column B. Cell B1 receives the name *\e*, cell B3 becomes *\n*, and so on.

Try out each of the macros. The macro named *\e* expands the width of the current column by one character. To see it in action, press MACRO-E. Press MACRO-E repeatedly to expand the current column to whatever width you desire. When you press MACRO-E, the macro processor takes control for a split second. It presses the slash key and selects Worksheet Column Set-Width from the menus. Then it presses RightArrow once to expand the column, and presses Return to lock in the new width.

To narrow a column, move the cell pointer into the column and run the macro named \n. It performs exactly like the macro named \e; however, the \n macro uses a {LEFT} command to make the column narrower each time you run it.

The macro named \r resets the width of a column to the worksheet default width. To use this macro, place the cell pointer in the target column and press MACRO-R.

You will notice a lot of flickering while these macros run. Stuff flashes around frenetically in the control panel. The flickering is the momentary display of menus that would appear if you were issuing width setting commands manually. Remember, the macro processor literally replaces you at the keyboard—it presses keys to perform tasks just as you must. 1-2-3 responds to the key presses in the same way, whether it is you making them or the macro processor.

Formula Editing Tools

Sometimes, after you type out a complex formula, you press Return only to have 1-2-3 beep and end up in Edit mode. Something about the formula is not acceptable. You may have to move to another cell in the spreadsheet before you can fix whatever is wrong—especially if what is wrong is that you have used a range name in the formula that you haven't yet assigned in the spreadsheet.

Rather than dump the formula, assign the range name, and then retype the entire formula. Store the formula by turning it into a label. Here is a little exercise to show you how this works:

Move the cell pointer to cell E1 and type *+test/8*. When you press Return, the Edit indicator appears, and the edit cursor jumps to the first t in the word *test*. There is no range named *test* in the spreadsheet.

Turn the incorrect formula into a label by pressing Home, typing an apostrophe, and then pressing Return. Now select Range Name Create, enter *test*, and indicate cell E2. You have fixed the problem with the formula, so convert the label back. To do this, with the cell pointer in E1, press EDIT (F2), Home, and Delete to remove the label prefix. When you press Return, 1-2-3 accepts the formula.

Where do the macros come in? Have a look at Figure 26.5.

	A	B	C	D	E	F
7	\l	{HOME}'~				
8						
9	\f	{EDIT}{HOME}{DEL}~				

FIGURE 26.5. These macros can help you recover from some formula errors.

In the same worksheet, create them as you did the previous ones. Enter the labels, beginning with an apostrophe when you type the entries for cells A7 and A9. Use the Range Name Labels Right command to assign the names \l and \f.

From here on in, if you get hung up when you try to enter a formula, press MACRO-L. It presses the Home key, types an apostrophe, and presses Return. After fixing the problem in the spreadsheet—whether by assigning a needed range name or adding a missing parenthesis—press MACRO-F. This macro presses the EDIT key and then presses Home to move the edit cursor to the beginning of the current cell. It presses the Delete key to remove the apostrophe and finally presses Return to store the formula.

Copy a Formula Absolutely

Sometimes you want to copy an established formula, but you don't want its relative references to adjust to its new location in the sheet. The quickest way to do this is to convert the formula to a label, copy the label, and then convert both copies of the label back into formulas. The macro named \f handles the final step of this procedure. Create the macro shown in Figure 26.6 to handle the first step.

	A	B	C	D	E	F
11	\a	{EDIT}{HOME}'~				

FIGURE 26.6. This simple macro lets you copy a formula without the formula's relative references adjusting at the copy's target location.

Remember, enter the labels and then assign the macro's range name. Try the macro on the formula in cell E1. Place the cell pointer in cell E1, and press MACRO-A. The macro presses the EDIT key, moves the edit cursor to the beginning of the formula, and types an apostrophe label prefix. Then it presses Return to store the new label.

Use the Copy command to copy the label from cell E1 to cell E4. Then run the \v macro twice—once with the pointer in cell E1 and again with the pointer in cell E4. Both of the resulting formulas refer to the cell named *test*—cell E2.

Date-Stamp the Worksheet

Do you ever need to know the date on which you last used a worksheet? In Chapter 16, we presented a macro you can use to record the serial number of today's date in a cell. A simple variation on that concept appears in Figure 26.7.

	A	B	C	D	E	F
13	\k	@NOW{CALC}~				
14		/RFD1~				

FIGURE 26.7. This macro enters today's serial number into the current cell and assigns the cell a date display format.

You must begin with an apostrophe label prefix when you enter each of the labels in this macro. Then assign the name \k to cell B13.

To use the macro, place the cell pointer in any cell in which you want to enter the date. Then press MACRO-K. The macro processor types an @NOW formula and presses the CALC key to convert the formula into its current value. Then it presses Return to store the date serial number in the current cell. Finally, the macro processor selects Range Format Date 1, and presses Return, thereby assigning a date format to the new entry.

If asterisks appear in the cell, run the macro named \e to widen the column until you see the date.

Quick Printing from 1-2-3 and Wysiwyg

Much of the printing you do from 1-2-3 and Wysiwyg requires you to do no more than indicate a Print range and say Go. If you don't have to adjust print settings, a simple macro can rocket you through the printing process. Actually, you'll need two macros—one for printing directly from 1-2-3 and one for printing when you're working with Wysiwyg. See Figure 26.8.

	A	B	C	D	E	F
16	\p	/PPR{?}~AGPQ				
17						
18	\w	:PRS{?}~G				

FIGURE 26.8. Each of these macros lets you set a Print range and then sends the range to the printer. The first macro prints from within 1-2-3; the second from Wysiwyg.

These macros introduce the advanced macro commands—a collection of special programming keywords that provide macros with capabilities beyond those of 1-2-3's menus and formulas. A few pages back, we mentioned flow of control; many of the advanced macro commands direct a macro's flow of control. Some of them substitute for familiar menu commands but operate more efficiently. Still others manipulate files, and a few "converse" with users. These concepts will make more sense in future chapters.

The advanced macro command in these macros is the {?} command. When the macro processor encounters a {?} command, it pauses and waits for you to press Return. During the pause, you can issue any number of keystrokes, and 1-2-3 will respond as if no macro were running. Then, when you press Return, the macro processor continues to follow the macro instructions immediately following the {?} command.

Enter and name the macros in Figure 26.8 to see the {?} command in action. To print in 1-2-3 press MACRO-P. The macro processor selects Print Printer Range and then pauses. Use this pause to indicate the range that you want to print. Again, any keystrokes are valid. Use the arrow keys to highlight a Print range, or type a range reference. (Sorry, mouse users, you lose mouse control while a macro is running.) When you press Return, the macro processor presses Return to complete the range designation and then selects Align Go Page-Advance Quit.

Press Return After the Pause

Quite often, you use the {?} command to make a macro pause where you must enter information in response to a menu prompt. Normally, you make such entries by typing something and then pressing Return.

While the {?} command is active, pressing Return simply tells the macro processor to resume processing. If you type an entry and press Return during the {?} command's pause, that Return is absorbed by the macro processor. The macro must contain a tilde to get the macro processor to press Return and complete whatever entry you have made. That is why a tilde appears after each of the {?} commands in the printing macros in Figure 26.8.

If you're printing from Wysiwyg, press MACRO-W. This causes the macro processor to select :Print Range Set. It pauses so you can indicate a range, and when you press Return it presses Return to complete the range designation. Then it selects Go.

Insta-Save

If you're a careful worker, you save the current worksheet every 5 to 15 minutes to avoid loss of large amounts of data. This can add up to a great many keystrokes in an average workday. The simple macro shown in Figure 26.9 lets you save with a quick flick of the fingers.

	A	B	C	D	E	F
20	\s	/FS~R				

FIGURE 26.9. This macro saves the current file in a jiffy. USE IT ONLY IF YOU HAVE ALREADY SAVED THE FILE AT LEAST ONCE.

This is a dangerous macro. Consider how it works: When you press MACRO-S, the macro processor selects File Save and presses Return. If you have saved the current file at least once before, 1-2-3 automatically tries to save under the old file name, but it displays a warning prompt. The macro processor selects Replace automatically.

If you haven't already saved the current worksheet and you run this macro, you'll wipe out an existing worksheet file. When the macro processor selects File Save, 1-2-3 offers a menu of existing files. By pressing Return, the processor accepts the first name in the list as the name of the file to save. It then replaces that disk file with the one in RAM.

Use this macro only after you have already saved the current file at least once! We offer a safer file-saving macro in Chapter 27.

To try the macro, select File Save, and enter *library*. 1-2-3 saves the spreadsheet in your default data directory. Now hold down the MACRO key and press S. The macro processor resaves the spreadsheet. Leave the new library file on disk so you can use it in later chapters.

Start a Macro Library

Maybe you weren't thrilled by the utility macros we presented in this chapter. That's OK. It is difficult to predict what tools you will need for a job. As you learn what your needs are, use some of these and create some of your own. Give each new macro a unique name, and store it in the LIBRARY worksheet.

When you begin to build your own models, retrieve the LIBRARY sheet and save it under a new name. Then work in the newly named sheet and all of the macros will be available to help with your work. Or you can use the add-in called Macro Library Manager, which lets you store collections of macros in a way that makes them available in all worksheets. We will see at the end of this section how to store the library worksheet macros in a Macro Library Manager macro library.

In the meantime, we will explore several more complex macros that also qualify as utilities. Add the ones you like to your collection, and pretty soon your worksheets will be able to create themselves. (Well, not really, but your work will be a lot easier.)

Macros That Write Themselves: Learn Mode

Writing macros is easy. You simply note what keystrokes are necessary to perform a task, enter the keystrokes as labels in the worksheet, and assign a range name. As simple as that is, there is a feature—macro Learn mode—that makes the job even easier.

While 1-2-3 is in Learn mode, you can work as you always would in the spreadsheet. As you work, however, 1-2-3 records your keystrokes as macro commands in a designated *Learn range*. You can assign a name to the Learn range and use the recorded keystrokes as a macro. Or you can copy labels from the Learn range into other macros. As long as you are creating simple macros—no more than recordings of keystrokes—macro Learn mode can save a lot of effort.

Set Up a Learn Range

The first step in using Learn mode is to set up a Learn range. Choose a range in an out-of-the-way area. The Learn range shouldn't be in the way of any changes you'll be making in the sheet. Be particularly aware of whether you'll be inserting or deleting rows, and be sure the selected range is located where the insertions and deletions won't affect it.

Aside from these considerations, setting the Learn range is a snap. Simply select Worksheet Learn. 1-2-3 offers a menu with three options—Range, Cancel, and Erase. Select Range, and indicate a range that falls within a single column. You can use a multi-columned range, but 1-2-3 automatically reduces the range definition to cover only the left-most column of the range that you indicate. Be sure the Learn range extends many rows down the sheet—several hundred is not too many. Setting a long Learn range lets you record a lot of keystrokes before you have to erase the contents of the range. It's important to understand that setting a Learn range is not the same as activating Learn mode. You'll activate Learn mode in a moment.

For this exercise, retrieve the library worksheet that you saved earlier. Then select Worksheet Learn Range and indicate range E1..E10—we've kept the Learn range small because you're going to record only a few keystrokes.

Activate Learn Mode

When you're ready to perform a task whose keystrokes you want to record, activate Learn mode. Try a simple one to see how this works. Enter the values shown in Figure 26.10.

	E	F	G	H	I	J
13	5			1		
14	8			6		
15	3					
16	9					

FIGURE 26.10. You'll use these entries first to create a macro with Learn mode and then to apply the macro.

Imagine that these entries are data you want to sum with formulas. The procedure for creating one summary formula works as well for creating almost any such formula when the values to sum fall in contiguous cells of a single column. Since this is the case, activate Learn mode before you create the first formula.

Start by moving the cell pointer to cell E18, the cell in which you'll create the first summary formula. Then activate Learn mode by holding down the Alt key and pressing F5. The Learn indicator appears at the bottom of the display.

Build the formula as follows: Type *@SUM(,* press UpArrow twice, and then press End UpArrow. Press the period key to anchor the cell pointer, and then press End DownArrow. Type *)* (a closing parenthesis), and press Return. Don't stop there. Press UpArrow once, and enter \= to create a dividing line label in cell E17.

That's the procedure. Now that you've finished, deactivate Learn mode. There's no sense in recording more keystrokes than are necessary to complete the specified task. To deactivate Learn mode, press the LEARN key a second time—hold down Alt and press F5. The Learn indicator vanishes.

Where is the recording? Even though it's the first cell of the Learn range, cell E1 seems to be blank. In fact, the recorded keystrokes are there. They haven't appeared because deactivating Learn mode doesn't cause 1-2-3 to redraw the spreadsheet. Press UpArrow, and the label appears, as shown in Figure 26.11.

FIGURE 26.11. Cell E1 contains a record of all of the commands that you issued while Learn mode was active. The keystroke recorder fills one cell of the Learn range with up to 40 characters and then continues recording in the next cell.

Apply the Learn Mode Macro

You can fire off the Learn mode macro quickly by using the RUN key. Create a new @SUM formula in cell H16 to see how this works.

Move the cell pointer to H16, and press RUN (hold down the Alt key and press F3). When 1-2-3 prompts for the name of the macro to run, enter *E1*. The macro processor follows the commands in cell E1 and creates an @SUM formula in cell H16.

The macro that you just recorded in Learn mode is a handy utility. Add it to the collection in the LIBRARY worksheet by copying it from the Learn range to cell B22. Then enter the label *t* (for total) into cell A22. Assign the name *t* to cell B22.

Clean up the macro library worksheet by erasing the entries in columns E and H, and then resave the worksheet under the name LIBRARY. We will retrieve the worksheet again later in this section.

In the meantime, experiment with Learn mode on your own. As we pointed out earlier, you don't need to use all the recorded macro commands as a single macro. You might record a much more involved task than the one you just did and then copy bits and pieces of the recorded code into a new range. There, you can combine the pieces into a new macro.

Having completed this chapter you should:

- *Know the advantages of automating worksheet tasks with macros*
- *Understand the basic mechanisms of building and running macros*
- *Know what utility macros are and have a small collection of such macros to use in your own spreadsheets*
- *Be able to use Learn mode to create simple keystroke recordings*
- *Be ready to explore macros in more depth and understand advanced macro programming concepts*

27

The Advanced Macro Commands

You're about to dive into the deep end. The macros we have explored so far are relatively simple keystroke recordings. As such, they can't do anything more than you do once you've decided which task to tackle. The emphasis here is on *once you decide*.

In this chapter you will:

- *Get a solid overview of the advanced macro commands*
- *Learn how to alter a macro's flow of control*
- *Apply macro commands that interact with users*
- *Write a macro that lets you enter dates naturally*
- *Create a macro that lets you jump around the spreadsheet*
- *Develop a formula-editing macro*
- *Write a safe file-saving macro*
- *Review the definition of a looping macro*
- *Explore the functionality of the {FOR} command*
- *Create a looping macro to print multiple copies of a range*

You see, you make decisions constantly as you work in the spreadsheet. What should you enter in this cell? Should you apply a currency or a fixed format? In which direction should you move the cell pointer? Advanced macro commands let your macros make the same types of decisions. But that's not all they do.

There are commands that control the appearance of the spreadsheet display; they can suppress the spreadsheet frame or prevent the control panel and screen from being redrawn each time the macro processor presses a key. Some commands cause the macro processor to prompt the user for information. When the user responds, the macro processor stores the information in the spreadsheet. Other commands let the macro processor read and write disk files, fix errors that arise during processing, and even sound an audible warning.

Combined with the options on 1-2-3's menus, the macro key words, and the calculating capabilities built into the spreadsheet, the advanced macro commands are an exceptionally powerful programming tool.

The advanced macro commands let you create powerful utility macros as well as sophisticated, automated applications that balance accounts, manage billing, analyze stocks, and more. This book is meant for intermediate-level spreadsheet users, so we won't be exploring the advanced macro commands and macro programming in depth. But it's important for even an intermediate 1-2-3 user to have a firm grasp of the advanced macro commands.

The Advanced Commands Revealed

You've already seen at least one of the advanced macro commands at work—the {?} command you used in the printing macros described in Chapter 26. All advanced macro commands have the same general format as the {?} command. That is, each consists of a command keyword enclosed in braces.

Unlike the {?} command, most advanced macro commands have arguments similar to the arguments that you use in @functions. An advanced macro command's arguments usually identify the cells or ranges on which the macro processor should act. They may also dictate particular behaviors of the macro processor relative to the command's general purpose. All of this should make sense by the time you've worked through this chapter.

What follows is a list of the advanced macro commands along with the arguments that each of the commands accepts. The command descriptions may seem cryptic at this point, but many of them will make sense by the time you complete this chapter.

{**?**} Pause until the user presses Return.

{**APPENDBELOW targ,source**} Copy from *source* to row directly beneath *targ* and extend *targ* (and any range names whose last row corresponds with that of *targ*) down one row.

{**APPENDRIGHT targ,source**} Copy from *source* to the column directly to the right of *targ* and extend appropriate range names to the right one column.

{**BEEP num**} Sound one of four audible tones.

{**BLANK rng**} Erase the contents of *rng*.

{**BORDERSOFF**} Suppress display of the worksheet frame.

{**BORDERSON**} Reactivate display of the worksheet frame.

{**BRANCH targ**} Transfer macro control to *targ*.

{BREAK} Clear menus and other commands in progress and return 1-2-3 to Ready mode under macro control.

{BREAKOFF} Disable the Break key.

{BREAKON} Enable the Break key.

{CLOSE} Close a file that was opened by the {OPEN} command.

{CONTENTS targ,source,width,format} Create a label in *targ* that looks like the contents of *source*—assuming a column width of *width* and a cell format defined by *format*.

{DEFINE targ1,targ2,...} Store values passed to a subroutine.

{DISPATCH targ} Transfer macro control to the cell named in *targ*.

{FILESIZE targ} Record in *targ* the total number of bytes in an open file.

{FOR cntr,start,stop,step,routine} Manage the progress of a FOR loop.

{FORBREAK} End processing of a FOR loop.

{FORM range,table,allow,exclude} Manage data entry into unprotected cells in *range*.

{FORMBREAK} End processing of a {FORM} command.

{FRAMEOFF} Same as {BORDERSOFF}.

{FRAMEON} Same as {BORDERSON}.

{GET targ} Cause the macro processor to pause until the user presses a key, and then store the keystroke in *targ*.

{GETLABEL "prompt",targ} Display *prompt* in the control panel, and store the user's response as a label in *targ*.

{GETNUMBER "prompt",targ} Display *prompt* in the control panel, and store the user's response as a number in *targ*.

{GETPOS targ} Record in *targ* the position of the byte pointer in an open file.

{GRAPHON name,nodisplay} Activate the graph settings for the graph named *name*. Without the *nodisplay* argument, the command both activates *name*'s settings and displays the graph.

{GRAPHOFF} Clear a graph displayed by the {GRAPHON} command.

{IF condition} Cause the macro processor to follow further commands in the same cell as this one if *condition* is true. Otherwise, the macro processor skips further commands in this cell.

{**INDICATE "prompt"**} Place *prompt* in the indicator at the top-right of the display.

{**LET targ,item**} Copy value of *item* to *targ*.

{**LOOK targ**} If a keystroke is pending in the keystroke buffer, store a copy of the keystroke as a label in *targ*.

{**MENUBRANCH targ**} Display a menu in the control panel based on menu instructions in the spreadsheet, and then transfer macro control to the routine associated with the menu item selected by the user.

{**MENUCALL targ**} Same as {MENUBRANCH}, but this command calls the associated routine as a subroutine rather than abdicating control to it.

{**ONERROR targ,message**} Transfer macro control to *targ* if an error arises that would normally stop the macro. The macro processor stores the resulting error message in *message*.

{**OPEN "file",access**} Open the file named *file* in one of three access modes.

{**PANELOFF clear**} Clear all information from the control panel, and suppress further display of changes there. Without the *clear* argument, simply freezes the control panel in its current state.

{**PANELON**} Reactivate the control panel display.

{**PUT range,column,row,item**} Copy the current value of *item* into *range* at the designated *column* and *row*.

{**QUIT**} Stop the macro processor, and return control to the user.

{**READ number,targ**} Read *number* characters from an open file, and store them as a string in *targ*.

{**READLN targ**} Read one line from an open file, and store it as a label in *targ*.

{**RECALC range,condition,iterations**} Recalculate the formulas in *range* row-by-row repeatedly until *condition* is true or until all *iterations* are completed. Without the *condition* and *iterations* arguments, the command recalculates *range* once.

{**RECALCCOL range,condition,iterations**} Same as {RECALC}, but calculation is column-by-column.

{**RESTART**} Terminate all active subroutines, and pass macro control to the following command.

{**RETURN**} End the most recent subroutine call.

{SETPOS position} Move the byte pointer to *position* in the open file.

{routine arg1,arg2...} Call a subroutine named *routine*, and pass along the listed arguments.

{SYSTEM command} Pass control to DOS without unloading 1-2-3 from RAM, and issue *command* as a DOS command. After DOS performs the command, control automatically returns to the macro in 1-2-3.

{WAIT serial} Cause the macro processor to pause until the time on the system clock matches *serial*.

{WINDOWSOFF} Disable updating of the display while the macro is running.

{WINDOWSON} Resume updating of the display while the macro runs.

{WRITE string} Record *string* in the open file starting at the location of the byte pointer.

{WRITELN string} Record *string* in the open file at the location of the byte pointer, and add a carriage-return and line-feed.

A Few Commands Up Close: The {LET} Command

That's a pretty terse list. Let's take a closer look at a few commands to get a sense of how they work.

The {LET} command is handy in many situations. You use it to assign values to spreadsheet cells—much as you'd use the Range Value command to copy the value of a formula from one cell to another. The {LET} command works more quickly than the Range Value command, so you can apply it in macros whenever you need to copy values in the sheet. The {LET} command has the following syntax:

{LET *targ,item*}

Targ is the cell that should receive the item, and *item* is a value, a string, a cell reference, a range name, or a formula.

The command {LET A1, "Sales"} causes the macro processor to place the label *Sales* into cell A1. The command

{LET target,sales+commission}

adds the values from cells named *sales* and *commission* and places the result in the cell named *target*.

The Subroutine Call

Subroutines are very important to good programming technique. They let you package a collection of commands under a range name and have a macro called on the collection as needed—as if you had created your own custom macro command. We use subroutines often, so here's a preview of the topic. We spend a lot more time exploring subroutine calls in the next chapter.

At its simplest, a subroutine call's syntax is {*name*} where *name* is the name of any cell that contains macro commands. When the macro processor encounters a subroutine call, control passes directly to the cell named in the command. The processor follows every command from the named cell onward until there are no more commands to follow or until it encounters a {RETURN} command. Then control passes back to the command immediately following the subroutine call. Figure 27.1 diagrams the flow of control directed by a subroutine call.

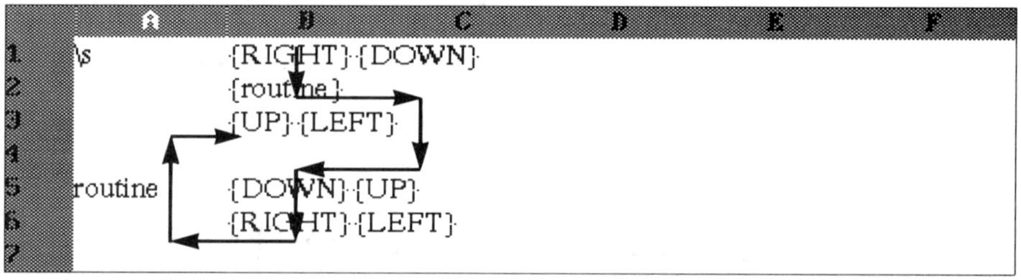

FIGURE 27.1. The arrows reveal the order in which the macro processor follows commands when a subroutine call is involved.

The {GETLABEL} Command

The {GETLABEL} command's syntax is {GETLABEL "Prompt",targ}. You use this command or the {GETNUMBER} command (whose syntax is identical) when your macros have to get information from the user. For example, your macro might prompt you to enter the date on which a transaction took place as you record that transaction in the spreadsheet.

When the macro processor encounters a {GETLABEL} command, it displays the command's prompt in the control panel and pauses until the user presses the Return key. The prompt can be any string or any formula that returns a string. You can type anything in response to the {GETLABEL} prompt, and when you press Return, the macro processor stores your entry as a label in *targ*. *Targ* can be a cell address or a named cell.

For example, when the macro processor encounters the command

{GETLABEL "Enter a date:",dcell}

it displays the prompt *Enter a date* in the control panel and waits for your entry. It stores your entry in the cell named *dcell*.

Advanced Macro Commands Applied

We have presented a few macros, scattered throughout this book, that apply these advanced macro commands. The worksheet in Figure 27.2 shows some of them.

	A	B	C	D	E	F
24	here					
25						
26	\g	{LET here,@CELLPOINTER("address")}				
27		{GOTO}{NAME}				
28						
29	\b	{GOTO}{here}~				
30						
31	dtmp					
32						
33	\d	{GETLABEL "Enter date:",dtmp}				
34		@DATEVALUE({dtmp})				
35		{CALC}~				
36		/WCS10~/RFD1~				

FIGURE 27.2. Three macros that capitalize on various advanced macro commands.

We've entered these macros in the LIBRARY worksheet. You can do the same if you created the worksheet in the previous chapter; if not, start in a blank worksheet and enter the labels exactly as shown in Figure 27.2. After entering the labels, select Range Name Labels Right and indicate range A24..A32. You must assign all the labels shown in Column A as names for the adjacent cells of column B.

The macros named *\g* and *\b* in the illustration work together. Suppose that you're working in a large worksheet and you want to examine entries in some other area without losing track of the cells in which you are working. These macros can help. The first macro records the address of the cell pointer and then presses the GOTO key, leaving you to enter a target address. The second

Auxiliary Cells Support Macro Processing

A macro sometimes needs to store information temporarily in a spreadsheet cell. For example, a macro might ask you a question such as *Do you want to save the file? (Y/N)* and await your response. The macro could store your answer in a cell and then use conditional statements to determine whether you answered Yes or No.

There are many circumstances under which macros rely on cells in this way. Figure 27.2 shows two such applications. A cell that a macro uses to keep track of information temporarily is called a *variable cell*. We use many of them throughout the remainder of this book. It's important that you label them as shown in the illustrations and assign the appropriate range names.

macro returns the cell pointer to the cell in which it resided before you ran the first macro.

Try the macros so that you better understand how they work. Press MACRO-G, and enter *Z45*. The cell pointer jumps to cell Z45. Now press MACRO-B. The cell pointer jumps back to where it started; the cell's position on the display has changed, but the cell pointer is in it nonetheless.

Here is how the macro works:

When you press MACRO-G, the macro processor encounters the {LET} command. As written, the {LET} command assigns the current result of the formula @CELLPOINTER("address") to the cell named *here*. The formula returns a label that represents the address of the current cell.

After making the assignment, the macro processor presses the GOTO key (F5) and then the NAME key. It stops and returns control to you. You then enter a target address and send the cell pointer off to some other part of the spreadsheet.

When you want to return to the starting cell, you press MACRO-B. The macro processor presses the GOTO key and then calls the cell named *here* as a subroutine. Because the earlier macro stored a cell address in *here*, the macro processor types that address as the target for the {GOTO} command. Finally, the macro processor encounters the tilde and completes the {GOTO} command; the cell pointer jumps back to its starting cell.

Use a Macro to Enter Dates

The macro named \d in Figure 41.1 helps you to enter dates in the spreadsheet. It lets you enter dates in the popular MM/DD/YY format rather than in 1-2-3's unconventional @DATE(YY,MM,DD) format. To use the macro, place the cell pointer in a blank cell in which you want to enter a date. When you press MACRO-D the macro processor encounters the {GETLABEL} command and prompts you to enter a date.

Enter the date using the standard MM/DD/YY format. The macro processor stores your entry in *dtmp*. Then it types the formula @DATEVALUE(*dtmp*) and presses the CALC key to convert the formula into its current value. Finally, the macro processor enters the newly calculated date serial number into the current cell, sets the width of the current column to 10, and assigns a date format.

The {BRANCH} Command

You know that a macro's flow of control is from cell-to-cell down a column. You also know about subroutine calls that let you temporarily divert a macro's flow from the main body of the macro to another macro routine. The {BRANCH} advanced macro command also changes the course of the macro processor. You use the {BRANCH] command in conjunction with conditional macro statements so that your macros can perform tasks appropriate to changing conditions in the worksheet. You can also use {BRANCH} statements to create looping macros. We explore these concepts a bit more later in this section.

The syntax of the command is simply {BRANCH *targ*} where *targ* is the cell to which macro control should transfer. When the macro processor encounters the command {BRANCH targ}, it immediately looks for commands to process in the cell named *targ* and continues from that cell onward until it finds no more commands to process.

One application of the {BRANCH} command is in a simple macro that can speed your data entry—especially if you prefer to enter values using the numeric keypad. The macro appears in Figure 27.3.

	A	B	C	D	E	F
38	ent	{?}~{DOWN}				
39		{BRANCH ent}				

FIGURE 27.3. A collection of four macro commands that can save enormous effort when you enter data in columns.

Enter and name this macro as you have the earlier ones, but notice that its name demands that you use the RUN key to activate it. Use the macro as follows:

Disable Cursor Movement for Data Entry

The arrow keys move the cell pointer around in the spreadsheet. But on many keyboards, the arrow keys double as a numeric keypad. If you want to type numbers rather than move the cell pointer, you must hold down the Shift key or press NumLock. As a skilled calculator operator, you know the value of the numeric keypad; you can work the keypad with one hand while reading numbers and holding your place in a list with the other hand. Unfortunately, it seems that you need a third hand to shift the cursor keys from cursor-movement to numeric-entry and back. Without it you might end up making all your entries into a single cell.

The macro shown in Figure 27.3 acts as the third hand. With the macro running, you can depress the NumLock key to activate the numeric keypad. Then use the keypad to type numbers, and press Return with your thumb or pinky finger, depending on the layout of your keyboard.

Place the cell pointer in the first cell of a column in which you must make a series of entries. For this discussion, move the pointer to cell E38. Then press the RUN key (hold down Alt and press F3) and select *ent* from the resulting list of range names. Nothing seems to happen, except that the Cmd indicator appears at the bottom of the display to tell you that the macro processor is in control.

Type an entry, and press Return. The entry appears in cell E38, and the cell pointer drops to cell E39. Type another entry, and press Return. The cell pointer moves down to the next cell.

Each time you press Return, the cell pointer drops down one cell in the sheet. This lets you take advantage of the numeric keypad for data entry.

When you've finished entering data in the current column, you can move the cell pointer to the first data entry cell in the next column without stopping the macro. If you are working with NumLock activated, hold down the Shift key and use the cursor keys to navigate. When you release the Shift key, you will once again disable normal cursor movement. If you're not working with the NumLock key activated, simply press the arrow keys to move the cell pointer to the next appropriate cell.

In either case, once the cell pointer has reached its target, resume entering data. Again, each time you press Return, the cell pointer moves down one row in the spreadsheet. When you've finished entering data, hold down the Control key and press Break. This should stop the macro and produce an error message. The error has no effect on the worksheet; clear it by pressing Escape or Return. If pressing Control-Break doesn't stop this macro, refer to the box titled Give Us a Break!

The data entry macro might seem a little odd. As simple as it is, it runs for a very long time. In fact, it runs until you do something intentionally to stop it

Give Us a Break!

What a bummer. If you're reading this box, it probably means that your data entry macro didn't stop running when you pressed Control-Break. This might mean that your computer isn't entirely IBM compatible (no matter what the manufacturer tells you). Pressing Control-Break is supposed to stop a macro, unless the macro processor has encountered a {BREAKOFF} command before you press the keys.

With some macros, you'll be trapped. The only way you'll be able to stop them is to restart your computer (either by turning it off and on or by simultaneously pressing the Alt, Control, and Delete keys).

Fortunately, this macro lets you use a trick to escape from it: Move the cell pointer to cell B39—the cell that contains the {BRANCH} command—and press the Delete key. This removes the {BRANCH} statement and prevents the macro from restarting itself the next time you press Return. Pressing Return now will stop the macro, and with a little repair work you'll have it up and running again for further data entry.

(or until a natural disaster intervenes and somehow shuts down your computer). This macro falls in the category of *looping* macros which we explore in depth later in the chapter. We'll also look at a version of this macro that includes a build-in stop mechanism. Here's how the macro works:

The macro processor encounters the {?} command and pauses until you press Return. You can type a cell entry or issue a simple command such as Range Format Currency. When you press Return to complete the entry or to finish the command sequence, the macro processor presses Return and moves the cell pointer down. Then it encounters the command {BRANCH ent}.

The {BRANCH} command transfers macro control to the cell named *ent*—the first cell of the macro. In other words, the macro restarts itself. You can make another entry, and the macro processor will move the pointer down and restart the macro once more. It should be quite clear why this is called a looping macro.

Record the Cell's Contents

One of the more extraordinary macro commands is the {CONTENTS} command. You use it in macros that have to convert values into labels, preserving in the labels images of any cell formats associated with the original values. In some regards {CONTENTS} is like the {LET} command. In other regards it is very different.

The {CONTENTS} command's syntax is

{CONTENTS *targ,source,width,format*}

with the *width* and *format* arguments being optional.

At its simplest, the {CONTENTS} command copies the value from the *source* cell to the *targ* cell. However, the result of the copy is a label that looks like the entry in the *source* cell. For example, the command {CONTENTS B1,A1} places the string "   8 " (seven leading spaces, the character 8, and one trailing space) into cell B1 if cell A1 contains the number 8.

The label that the {CONTENTS} command creates reflects whatever display format is in effect in *source*. So, if cell A1 has a Currency with two decimals format, the command {CONTENTS B1,A1} places the string " $8.00 " into cell B1.

Another way to express all of this is that the {CONTENTS} command creates a label in *targ* that is an exact image of the entry in *source*. But there is a twist.

The *width* argument lets you tell the {CONTENTS} command to pretend that the *source* cell has a width other than its true width. Consider what happens if column A has a width of 9, and contains an entry like the one shown in Figure 27.4.

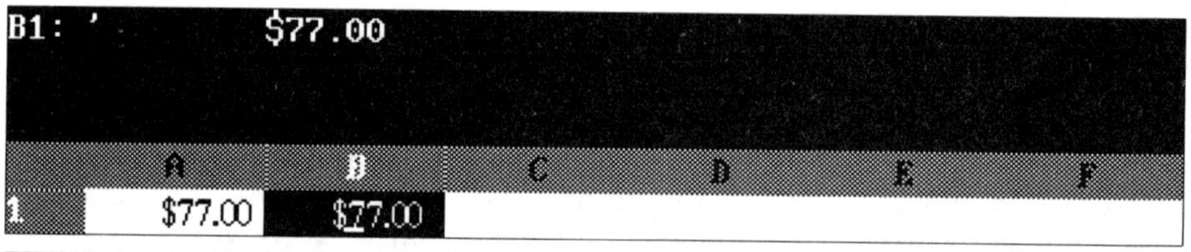

FIGURE 27.4. The label in cell B1 resulted from the macro command {CONTENTS B1,A1,15}.

The command {CONTENTS B1,A1,15} creates a label in cell B1 that is the image of cell A1 if column A's width were 15.

There is a second twist. The {CONTENTS} command's *format* option lets you control the display format represented in the finished label. Using a numeric code, you can tell the {CONTENTS} command to create a label that looks like the entry in *source* if it were formatted in a specific way. The *format* option overrides whatever display format exists in the *source* cell.

Consider the entry shown in cell A1 of Figure 27.5.

It is a value with a Currency display format. The entry in cell B1 is a string that resulted from the following macro command:

{CONTENTS B1,A1,9,17}

The command's *width* argument is *9*, so the label looks like a number formatted in a cell whose width is nine characters. The command's *format* argument is *17*—the code that means, "use the Scientific format with one decimal place."

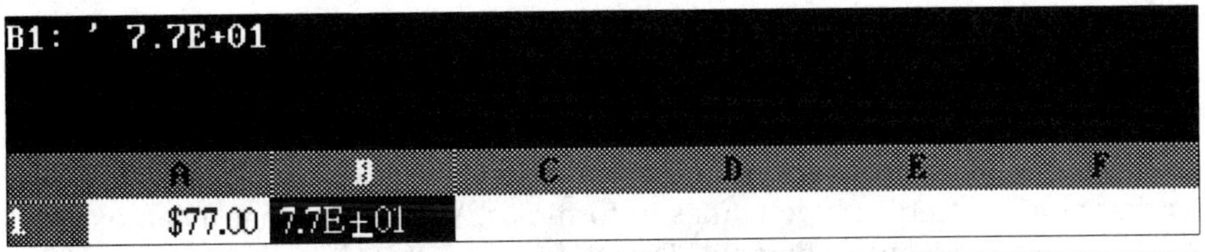

FIGURE 27.5. The {CONTENTS} *format* option lets you control the display format.

Table 27.1 lists the *format* codes along with the formats that they cause the {CONTENTS} command to simulate.

Code	Simulated Format
0–15	Fixed with 0 to 15 decimals
16–31	Scientific with 0 to 15 decimals
32–47	Currency with 0 to 15 decimals
48–63	Percent with 0 to 15 decimals
64–79	Comma (,) with 0 to 15 decimals
112	+/–
113	General
114–116	Dates 1 through 3
117	Text
118	Hidden
119–120	Dates 6 and 7 (time formats)
121–124	Dates 4, 5, 8, and 9
127	The current global format

TABLE 27.1. The {CONTENTS} command uses a format code from the left column of this table to produce a string that looks like a value with the display format shown on the right.

The {CONTENTS} Command Applied

If you use a lot of range names in your spreadsheets, the {CONTENTS} command wants to be your friend. Something that range name users learn early is that you can't edit range names in formulas. What does that mean exactly?

Try an experiment to find out. Drop down to cell B48, and enter the following formula—forgive us for its complexity, but it illustrates the point we are trying to make:

@LEFT(\e,3)&\r&@RIGHT(\f,4)&@LEFT(\a,6)&@LEFT(\f,6)

OK, the formula's result isn't at all meaningful. It's simply a conglomeration of meaningless chunks of strings. What is significant is that you wrote the formula using references to range names. Quite often you do that so you don't have to think about the addresses of the cells involved.

Now press the EDIT key (F2). The formula that appears on the edit line of the control panel includes no range names. Instead, 1-2-3 has substituted cell addresses. It is quite an effort to scan the formula for the @RIGHT function that derives its result from the entry in the cell named \f. The more involved a formula and the more range names it uses, the more confusing it is to edit.

The macro shown in Figure 27.6 eases the pain.

	A	B	C	D	E	F	G
41	hold						
42							
43	\c	{CONTENTS hold,@CELLPOINTER("address"),240,117}					
44		{LET hold,@TRIM(hold)}					
45		{hold}{EDIT}					

FIGURE 27.6. This macro lets you edit a formula with the formula's range names intact.

Press Escape to return the spreadsheet to Ready mode. Then enter the labels shown in Figure 27.6 and assign the ones in column A as names for adjacent cells of column B.

Try the new macro on the formula in cell B48. With the cell pointer in B48, press MACRO-C. The formula, with range names intact, appears on the edit line. Here's how the macro works:

When you press MACRO-C, the macro processor encounters a {CONTENTS} command. That command creates in *hold* a label that mimics the entry in the current cell as if the current cell had a width of 240 and the Text format. In other words, the {CONTENTS} command enters a label version of the formula followed by enough space characters to fill the cell.

The macro uses a width count of 240 to ensure that it can handle the longest possible formula. Suppose the width count you used in the macro was

How Does {CONTENTS} Get the Current Cell?

The macro shown in Figure 27.6 sneaks an advanced topic into this book for intermediate users. The topic is *dynamic macro code.* A dynamic macro command is one whose meaning changes depending on changes in the worksheet. One time, the macro processor encounters the command, and it means one thing. Another time the command might mean something else.

In this case, the dynamic quality is built into the {CONTENTS} statement. The source argument in that statement is an @function—@CELLPOINTER("address"). The macro processor resolves the formula to its current value before following the macro instruction. Hence, with the cell pointer in cell B48, the macro processor interprets the statement in cell B43 to read

{CONTENTS hold,B43,240,117}

Because the @CELLPOINTER function returns a different source cell address depending on the cell pointer's location, it gives the {CONTENTS} command a dynamic quality. You will encounter other dynamic macro commands in later chapters. Unfortunately, exploring them in depth is beyond the scope of this book.

50 and you ran the macro on a formula that contained 70 characters? The {CONTENTS} command would chop 20 characters off the formula label.

The second command that the macro processor encounters is a {LET} statement. The {LET} command replaces the entry in *hold* with the result of the formula @TRIM(hold). That formula strips from the formula label all the trailing spaces that the previous command created.

The macro's third command calls the cell named *hold* as a subroutine. This effectively types the contents of *hold* on the edit line in the control panel. *Hold* contains a label version of the original formula, complete with range names, so that is what appears on the edit line.

The macro's last command, {EDIT}, presses the EDIT key and puts 1-2-3 into Edit mode. You can make any needed changes to the formula—range names and all. When you're done, store the formula in the current cell by pressing Return.

Conditional Macro Statements

The macro processor can make decisions. Through the use of conditional statements, you can have a macro perform selected tasks based on a set of circumstances in the spreadsheet. You might create such instructions as, "If there is a label in the current cell, erase the cell," or "If the cell named *response* has a Y in it, print the Report range."

One of the keys to writing decision-making macros is the {IF} advanced macro command. This command has the syntax, {IF *condition*} where *condition* is an expression that resolves to zero or not zero—false or true. When *condition* is true, the macro processor looks for further commands to process within the cell that contains the {IF} statement. When *condition* is false, the macro processor skips further commands in the cell and control passes directly to the macro cell.

To better understand this, consider the macro commands shown in Figure 27.7.

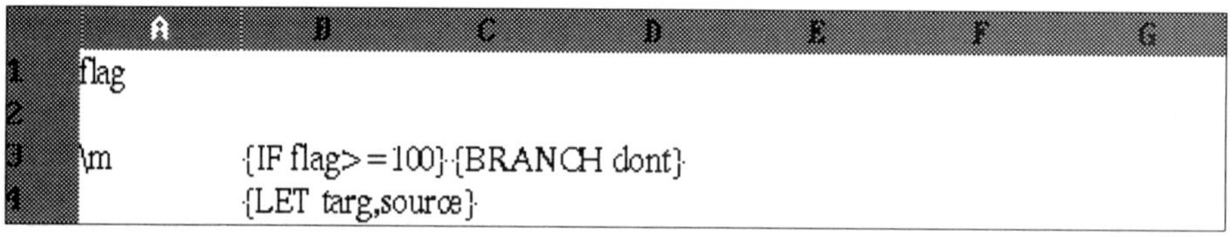

FIGURE 27.7. These macro commands reveal macro flow of control directed by an {IF} statement. When the value in *flag* is greater than or equal to 100, macro control branches to the cell named *dont*. When *flag* is less than 100, macro control passes to the {LET} command in cell B4.

The conditional statement of the {IF} command in cell B3 is *flag*>=100. When the condition is true, the macro processor reads and follows the {BRANCH} command that follows in that cell; macro control passes to commands in a cell named *dont*. When the condition is false, the macro processor ignores the {BRANCH} command in cell B3 and skips directly to the command in cell B4.

The {IF} Command Saves Files Safely

Uses for the {IF} command arise repeatedly when you write macro-driven spreadsheet applications. Even simple utility macros can put this command to work. That dangerous file-saving macro we presented in Chapter 26 becomes benign when you rewrite it to include an {IF} statement. The improved version appears in Figure 27.8.

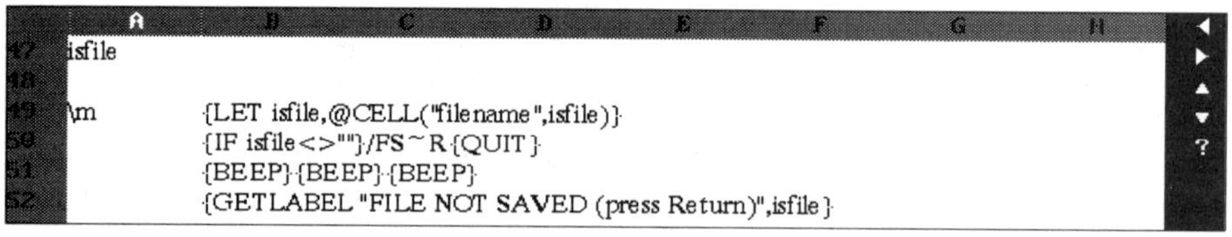

FIGURE 27.8. This file-saving macro won't accidentally overwrite an existing file if you haven't already saved the current one.

Before you create the macro, erase the formula that you entered a moment ago in cell B48. Then enter the macro's labels and name its associated cells. Use it to save the current file by holding down the MACRO key (Alt) and pressing M.

The macro processor first processes the {LET} command in cell B49. That command records the name of the current worksheet in the cell named *isfile*. If you haven't yet saved this worksheet, the {LET} command stores a null string in *isfile*. In either case, the macro processor encounters the {IF} command in cell B50.

The {IF} command's conditional statement is *isfile*<>"". This means, "the cell named *isfile* doesn't contain a null string." If *isfile* doesn't contain a null string, the statement is true. The macro processor then selects File Save, presses Return, and selects Replace to save the file. Then it encounters the {QUIT} command and stops.

If *isfile* contains a null string, the statement is false. The macro processor skips to the commands in cell B51. Those commands sound an audible tone three times to get your attention. Finally, the {GETLABEL} command in cell B52 causes the macro processor to display the message *FILE NOT SAVED (press Return)*. Press Return to stop the macro, and then use the File Save command to save the worksheet under a unique file name.

This file-save macro is universally useful. If you want a file-saving macro in your permanent macro library, this should be the one—especially if you create the library with the Macro Library Manager. For now, store the macro along with your other macros in the LIBRARY worksheet. We'll come back to this sheet once more in the last chapter in this section.

Coming Around Again... and Again, and Again: Looping Macros

Perhaps you have heard this tired old punchline: "The good news is, we're going in circles. The good news is, we're making great time." But wait! That's not the way you heard it. The going in circles part was supposed to be bad news. However, in many macro applications, going in circles is exactly what you want the macro processor to do.

A macro that goes in circles is called a *looping macro*. It is a sequence of commands written so that the macro processor follows those commands again and again and again. You can use looping macros to manage data entry procedures, report printing, and many other tasks. Looping of this type is so useful that virtually all programming languages contain at least one command expressly to control looping procedures. In 1-2-3, the command is {FOR}. As you develop your own macro-driven applications, you will find many opportunities to apply looping macros and the {FOR} command.

A Simple Loop Revisited

Earlier in this chapter we presented a simple looping macro to help you with data entry chores. That macro, shown again in Figure 27.9, contains only four commands, but it is a real work horse.

	A	B	C	D	E	F
1	\d	{?}~{DOWN}				
2		{BRANCH \d}				

FIGURE 27.9. This data entry macro appears with a different macro name in Figure 27.3 earlier in the chapter.

You use the macro to enter data by positioning the cell pointer at the top of a column that you want to fill with values or labels. Then you press MACRO-D. With the macro running, each time you press Return, the cell pointer moves down one row in the spreadsheet. This means that when you type a cell entry and press Return, the pointer moves down a row so you can make another entry.

We explained the data entry macro a bit earlier in the chapter. The point of reviewing it here is to examine its looping characteristics. When the macro processor finishes with the macro's first three commands, it encounters the command {BRANCH \d}. That causes the macro to restart. The macro accepts data, moves the cell pointer down, and restarts. It accepts data, moves the pointer down, and starts again.

Not only is this a looping macro, it is a special kind of looping macro called an *infinite loop*. It is an infinite loop because nowhere in the loop is there a command that tells the macro processor to stop.

In reality, there are few applications that require infinite loop macros. They can get you into trouble because you may have to restart your computer to get them to stop. A more prudently designed looping macro offers a way to stop the macro without restarting your computer. Depending on the application, you might want the loop to stop and return 1-2-3 to Ready mode. Or you might want the loop to end and pass macro control on to other commands. You might even want a loop to end and clear the current worksheet from RAM, leaving you face-to-face with a blank worksheet.

The Emergency Exit Is to Your Right

When you work with looping macros it is especially important to know how to stop the macro processor in mid-command. If you make a mistake in your macro code or the macro starts behaving strangely, you might want to shut it down without waiting for it to finish its assigned task. To stop a macro in an emergency, hold down the Control key and press Break. The Break key is near the top-right of most keyboards.

The advanced macro command {BREAKOFF} disables the Break key. In other words, if the macro processor is in control and it has already encountered a {BREAKOFF} command in the macro instructions, pressing Control-Break won't stop the macro. In that case, you must either wait for the macro to finish running or find another way to stop it—such as turning off the computer.

It is actually quite easy to modify the data entry macro so that it is no longer an infinite loop. The trick is to decide on a circumstance under which you want the macro to stop (aside from pressing the Break key).

A Finite Loop Data Entry Macro

What condition should cause the data entry macro to stop running? It should be something simple, but not so simple that it happens often by accident. How about, the macro should stop when you press Return without having entered data? Another way to express this is, the macro should stop when you press Return in an empty cell.

Check out Figure 27.10.

	A	B	C	D	E	F
1	\d	{?}~				
2		{IF @CELLPOINTER("type)="b"}{QUIT}				
3		{DOWN}{BRANCH \D}				

FIGURE 27.10. This data entry macro stops if the cell pointer is in a blank cell when you press Return.

We have added only two commands to the data entry macro, but it is no longer an infinite loop. Enter it in an otherwise blank worksheet, assign the range name *\d* to cell B1, and then take the macro for a spin.

Move the cell pointer to cell B6, and press MACRO-D. Type a number, and press Return. Type a number, and press Return. Type a number, and press Return—OK, it's still a looping macro. Now press Return without first typing a number. The macro stops, and the Cmd indicator at the bottom of the display vanishes.

You see, every time you press Return, the macro processor stores your entry in the current cell. Then it encounters an {IF} macro command. The {IF} statement's condition is @CELLPOINTER("type")="b". This condition is true when the current cell is blank. So, if you haven't typed anything before pressing Return, the macro processor gets to the {QUIT} command and the macro stops. If you have made an entry, the current cell isn't blank. The {IF} command's condition is false, so macro control passes to cell B2; the cell pointer moves down, and the macro restarts.

Ultra Loop Control: The {FOR} Command

Lotus 1-2-3 contains an advanced macro command whose sole purpose is to control the progress of a looping macro. That command, {FOR}, causes a macro to loop through a series of commands a specified number of times. In other words, you can use a {FOR} command when you know in advance that the macro processor should repeat a macro routine five times, or ten times, or some other set number of times.

The {FOR} command's syntax is {FOR *cntr,start,stop,step,routine*}. The *cntr* argument must be a reference to a cell in the worksheet, as must the *routine* argument. The {FOR} command uses *cntr* to keep track of the loop's progress. The *routine* argument identifies the instructions that constitute the macro's loop.

When the macro processor encounters the {FOR} command, it records the value of *start* in *cntr*. Then it compares the value of *start* with the value of *stop*. If *start* is greater than *stop*, the {FOR} loop stops and processing continues with the command following the {FOR} command.

If *cntr* is less than *stop*, the macro processes *routine*. After processing the commands in *routine*, the macro processor adds the value of *step* to the value in *cntr*, compares the result with *stop*, and either quits looping or performs *routine* another time.

My, that explanation is involved. The FOR loop isn't a simple concept, but, when you apply the {FOR} command to a few macro problems, it will make a lot more sense.

Just Erase Some Cells

Suppose that your spreadsheet contains a column with 100 rows of data (we use seven rows to keep our example simple). The data consists of values interspersed with labels, and you really don't want the labels to be there. You might write a looping macro that looks at each cell in the column. The macro would erase any label cells and leave the value cells intact. Figure 27.11 shows such a macro.

	A	B	C	D	E	F	G
1	cntr						
2							
3							
4	\b	{FOR cntr,1,7,1,rout}					
5		{BEEP}{BEEP}					
6							
7	rout	{IF @ISSTRING(@CELLPOINTER("contents"))}{DEL}					
8		{DOWN}{?}					
9		{RETURN}					

FIGURE 27.11. This macro illustrates the flow of control in a macro driven by a simple {FOR} command.

Create the macro by entering labels as shown. Assign all the labels in column A as names for the adjacent cells of column B. Then enter a column of values and labels as shown in Figure 27.12.

	A	B	C	D	E	F
11	8					
12	test					
13	4					
14	label					
15	5					
16	stuff					
17	5					

FIGURE 27.12. The FOR loop macro shown in Figure 27.11 will erase only the labels from the entries in this worksheet.

Now try the macro. Place the cell pointer in cell A11—the first of the seven data cells—and press MACRO-B. The number 1 appears in cell B1, and the cell pointer moves to cell A12. Then the macro pauses. Press Return, and the value in cell B1 becomes 2. The macro erases the label *test*, and the cell pointer moves down to cell A13.

Loops That Run Backward

It is easiest to explain how a FOR loop works if you stick to discussions of {FOR} commands that count upward toward the Stop value. However, a {FOR} command can count downward just as well.

If the {FOR} command's *step* argument is a negative value, the macro processor decreases the value of the counter cell with each cycle of the loop. The FOR loop ends when the counter value is less than the Stop value.

Each time you press Return, the value in cell B1 increases by 1 and the cell pointer moves down a row in the sheet. Eventually, the pointer moves into cell A18, the value in B1 becomes 8, and the macro beeps and stops running.

You would not normally include the {?} command in a macro of this type. We put it there so you'd be able to see the macro's progress after each loop. Re-enter the labels that the macro erased from column A. Then edit cell B8 and remove the {?} command. Finally, place the cell pointer back in B11 and run the macro a second time.

This time around, the cell pointer slides lickety-split down the column and the macro erases the labels without your intervention. How does the {FOR} command work in this macro? It is fairly straightforward.

The macro processor encounters the {FOR} command and places the value 1 (the *Start* value) into the cell named *cntr* (the *Cntr* cell). It compares *start* and *cntr*, and because *start* is the smaller number, the macro processor performs the commands in *routine*. Those commands erase the current cell, if it contains a label, and move the cell pointer down. The {RETURN} command does no more than mark the end of the routine; it is not needed, but some people will argue that you should include a {RETURN} command in all FOR loops to clarify the macro's purpose.

After the macro processor finishes *routine*, it adds 1 (the *Step* value) to the value in *cntr*. It compares *cntr* with *stop*, finds *cntr* to be the lower number, and again processes *routine*. Only when the macro processor has performed *routine* seven times does the value in *cntr* exceed the value of *stop*. Then macro control passes to the {BEEP} commands in cell B5, and the macro stops.

Print Several Copies

OK, the label-erasing macro isn't a thrilling example of macro utility. There are more versatile macros that can erase the labels from a column no matter how many entries the column contains. In fact, we encourage you to develop such a macro on your own for practice.

In the meantime, we hope we have explained the {FOR} command well enough that you can apply it in your own macros. Let's look at another example to prove that the command is truly useful.

The Wysiwyg add-in includes a settings option that controls the number of copies of a Print range that emerge from your printer when you select Go from the :Print menu. 1-2-3's Print menus don't include this option. If you print much from 1-2-3 without Wysiwyg, you might employ a macro to print multiple copies of a single print range. Figure 27.13 shows such a macro.

	A	B	C	D	E	F
1	copies					
2	cntr					
3						
4	\p	{GETNUMBER "Number of copies: ",copies}				
5		{BREAK}/PP				
6		{FOR cntr,1,copies,1,print}Q				
7						
8	print	AGP				

FIGURE 27.13. A macro can employ the {FOR} command to print a selected number of copies of an established Print range in 1-2-3 without Wysiwyg.

To try the macro, start in a blank worksheet and enter labels as shown. Assign the ones in Column A as names for the adjacent cells of column B.

Use the macro at any time after you have established the desired Print range. You can even trigger it while you're working within the Print menus (you can't start a macro running while a dialog box is active). Test the macro by printing three copies of the macro itself.

Select Print Printer Range, and indicate range A1..F8 as the range to print. Make sure your printer is on and ready to print, then press MACRO-P. If there is a dialog box, it vanishes when the macro starts. Macro processing proceeds as follows:

{GETNUMBER "Number of copies: ",copies} causes the macro processor to display the prompt *Number of copies*, and stores your response in the cell named *copies*. When the prompt appears on this test run, enter 3.

{BREAK}/PP clears the menus and returns 1-2-3 to Ready mode under macro control. Then the macro processor selects Print Printer.

{FOR cntr,1,copies,1,print}Q initiates processing of a FOR loop. The loop uses *cntr* as the counter cell. Counting starts with the number 1 and continues until the counter value exceeds the value in the cell named *copies*. Each cycle of the loop processes commands in the routine named *print*. Those commands are AGP—Align, Go, and Page—and they cause 1-2-3 to print one copy of the Print range and eject the printout from the printer. Three cycles of the loop produce three printed copies of the Print range. After completing the loops, the macro processor encounters the *Q* following the {FOR} command, and the processor selects Quit from the Print menu.

Advanced Means Another Book

Wow! This has been an exhausting chapter. We have tinkered with several of the advanced macro commands, yet we've hardly scratched the surface. This category of commands and the entire topic of macros deserve at least a book of their own. Our purpose is only to get you started in the right direction.

Experiment on your own with the advanced macro commands. The examples we have provided might spark some ideas for other applications you can create. In the meantime, work through the rest of this section. You'll dig deeper into specific advanced macro commands and find information that should help you to apply your understanding of macro commands intelligently. Finally, work through the applications in the last section of the book. They contain macros that apply the concepts we cover in this section, along with some very advanced macro techniques.

Having completed this chapter you should:

- *Understand how advanced macro commands provide programming power*
- *Have an idea of how to apply some of the advanced macro commands*
- *Understand the advanced programming topic of looping macros*
- *Be prepared to tackle even more advanced topics in macro programming*

28

Create Your Own Macro Commands

Lotus's programmers really blew it when they created 1-2-3. They left out all kinds of advanced macro commands that would be really useful in your macros. For example, they included the {WINDOWSOFF} command to suppress updating of the spreadsheet display while a macro runs, and they included the {PANELOFF} command to suppress activity in the control panel. But quite often you want to suppress the display of activity in both the spreadsheet and the control panel. Why isn't there a {WINPANOFF} command?

Maybe we should thank the programmers for leaving so much out of 1-2-3. Over the course of a year, macro enthusiasts could suggest so many commands that adding them all to the spreadsheet software would create serious logistical problems. Why carry the extra baggage of commands that only a few users will apply? Why not, instead, provide a method by which macro programmers can create their own macro commands? That's what Lotus did. Macro subroutines let you create custom macro commands.

Basics: The Subroutine Call

You create your own macro commands by building subroutines from existing commands. A subroutine can consist of any number of recorded keystrokes, key names, and advanced macro commands. When you assign a name to the macro routine, your macros can call the routine to perform the task it describes.

In this chapter you will:

- *Review the concept of subroutines*
- *Learn how subroutines lend structure to your macros*
- *Write a few simple subroutines*
- *Create subroutine calls that accept arguments*

A subroutine call looks a lot like an advanced macro command. At its simplest, it is the subroutine name enclosed in braces. So, for example, the expression {print} calls a subroutine named *print*.

The Case for Subroutine Calls
We present all of the subroutine calls in this book in lowercase characters. This isn't necessary; the macro processor understands a command whether it is presented in upper- or lowercase. We use lowercase to differentiate subroutine calls clearly from other macro commands, which we always show in uppercase characters. Chapter 30 explains the rationale for this convention.

When the macro processor encounters a subroutine call, control transfers directly to the first command in the subroutine. The macro processor follows the commands in the subroutine until it encounters a {RETURN} command or until no more instructions remain. Then control passes back to the command immediately following the subroutine call. The commands shown in Figure 28.1 illustrate a subroutine call's flow of control.

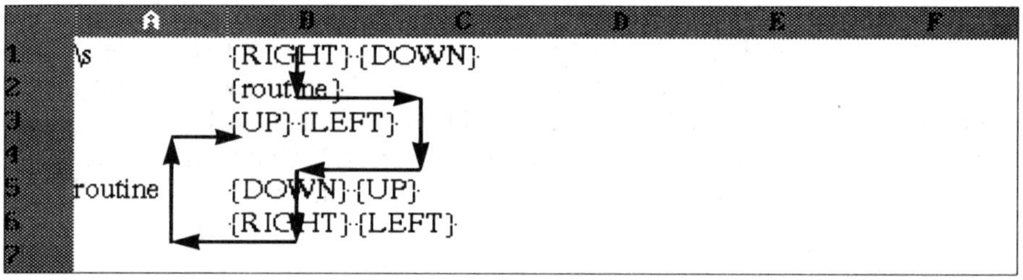

FIGURE 28.1. You might recognize this figure from Chapter 27. The arrows reveal the order in which the macro processor follows commands when a subroutine call is involved.

This macro moves the cell pointer to the right and then down. Then it calls the subroutine named *routine*. That routine moves the pointer down and up, right and left. Afterward, control passes back to the commands immediately following the subroutine call; the macro moves the cell pointer up and left.

Utilitarian Subroutines

Earlier we suggested a command to add to 1-2-3's list of advanced macro commands—the {WINPANOFF} command. When the macro processor encountered this command, the spreadsheet display and the control panel

> ## Why Stop the Flicker?
>
> When you issue commands in 1-2-3, menus appear in the control panel, highlights appear on the spreadsheet, the cell pointer moves, and so on. All of these things help to guide you in your work. When the macro processor issues commands, it doesn't need to see menu prompts and movements of the cell pointer. In fact, showing these things on the display slows a macro down.
>
> By suppressing the screen update, the macro processor achieves two things. First, it speeds processing; routines that access menus and move the cell pointer run more quickly with windows and the panel turned off. Second, it reduces the confusion that a macro can cause; watching 1-2-3 gallop about on its own might be intimidating to some users. In long macros, it is good practice to disable window and control panel updates when following the action on the display is not absolutely necessary.

would freeze. This way the activity of the macro wouldn't make the display flicker.

Actually, it is quite common in longer macros to want the display to remain static for a while, then to update the display and freeze it, update it and freeze it, and so on. This way you see only pertinent information on the display, and you don't have to sit through the fireworks of a macro accessing menus and moving things about in the spreadsheet.

Here is a perfect opportunity to create some subroutines. The command to freeze the worksheet display is {WINDOWSOFF}. The {PANELOFF} command freezes the control panel. Conversely, the {WINDOWSON} command reactivates the display, and the {PANELON} command activates the control panel. Pair up each set of commands, assign appropriate range names (as shown in Figure 28.2), and two subroutines are born.

	A	B	C	D	E	F
1	wof	{WINDOWSOFF}{PANELOFF}				
2						
3	won	{WINDOWSON}{PANELON}				

FIGURE 28.2. The {WINDOWSOFF} and {PANELOFF} commands together comprise one subroutine, and the {WINDOWSON} and {PANELON} commands comprise a second one.

Notice that we've named the subroutines *wof* and *won*. These names are short, so they are easy to type as you build a macro. The names are also fairly easy to remember; you might think of one as the "woff" routine, short for Windows Off, and the other as the "won" routine (pronounced as "on" with a W), short for Windows On.

To include the routines as you write a macro, simply enclose their names in braces wherever in the macro you need to apply them. The macro shown in Figure 28.3 uses the *wof* and *won* subroutines to manage activity on the monitor.

	A	B
1	wof	{WINDOWSOFF}{PANELOFF}
2		
3	won	{WINDOWSON}{PANELON}
4		
5	start	
6		
7	\m	{?}~
8		{IF @CELLPOINTER("contents")="t"}{titles}{?}~
9		{IF @CELLPOINTER("contents")="c"}{clear}{?}~
10		{R}{?}~{R}{?}~{R}{?}~{wof}{L 3}{D}
11		/RNCdbase~{D}~{won}{BRANCH \m}
12		
13	titles	{wof}{LET start,@CELLPOINTER("address")}
14		{HOME}{DOWN 3}/WTH
15		{GOTO}{start}~{DEL}{won}
16		
17	clear	{wof}/WTC{U 3}{D 3}{DEL}{won}

FIGURE 28.3. The data entry macro named *\m* in this worksheet calls on the *wof* and *won* subroutines to eliminate some of the flicker associated with macro processing.

Don't feel obligated to build the macro, it is intended as an illustration rather than as an exercise. It's designed to help with data entry in a four-field database as shown in Figure 28.4.

	A	B	C	D
1	Employee phone list			
2				
3	First	Last	Office	Ext
4	Herb	Torielli	7b	4345
5	Kadia	Maas	8b	0809

FIGURE 28.4. The macro shown in Figure 28.3 can help with data entry in this employee database.

If you were to enter the macro and create the database, you could use the macro to add new database records. You would start with the cell pointer in the first available cell of column A—cell A7 in our sample database.

Subroutines with Depth: Nesting Levels

When a subroutine contains a command to call a subroutine, the second subroutine is *nested* within the first. For example, in Figure 28.4, we have nested the subroutine calls {wof}, {start}, and {won} within the subroutine named *titles*.

Of course there is nothing to stop you from nesting a subroutine inside a nested subroutine inside a nested subroutine, but don't get carried away. 1-2-3 can keep track of 31 levels of nesting before it gets confused and causes your macro to fail.

Avoid nesting too many subroutine calls by being attentive to the current nesting level. Each time you create a call, be sure you know how many calls will be affected by the time the macro processor reaches the new one. Never have a macro branch from a subroutine to a point preceding the subroutine call that initiates the routine. Also be aware that the {FOR} command calls subroutines. An active FOR loop counts as one nesting level.

With each of the first three entries you make, the macro moves the cell pointer to the right. After you make a fourth entry, the macro calls {wof} and stops showing the action on the display. The cell pointer moves back to column A, and the macro extends the range name *dbase* (the database's Input range) down one row. Then the macro calls {won} to reactivate the display, and the sequence restarts.

If your first entry in a new record is a *t*, the macro calls a subroutine that locks the first three rows of the worksheet on the display. The subroutine's name is *titles*, and it begins with the {wof} command and ends with {won}.

You may not see much use for the {wof} and {won} commands early in your macro-writing career. However, as you build longer and more complex macros, you may find yourself using such routines in every one of your macro applications.

Subroutines with Arguments

A subroutine call can have arguments in the same way that an advanced macro command can. Such arguments might be values that the subroutine will modify or instructions that tell the subroutine what to do. You might want to include arguments in a column width setting subroutine call, for example, to tell the subroutine how wide to set a column; such a subroutine call might read {width 5} in one use and {width 10} in another.

When a subroutine call contains one or more arguments, it must pass the arguments to the subroutine. There is a special command that lets this happen.

	A	B	C	D	E	F
1	rng					
2						
3	print	{DEFINE rng:string}				
4		{BREAK}/PPR{rng}~AGPQ				

FIGURE 28.5. This subroutine, named *print*, stores an incoming argument as a label in the cell named *rng*. Then it prints the range named by the argument.

Consider the subroutine shown in Figure 28.5. It starts with a {DEFINE} statement that intercepts an argument from a subroutine call and stores the argument as a label in a cell named *rng*.

With the *print* subroutine available, the command {print report} will cause the macro processor to print the worksheet range named *report*—assuming that you are working in 1-2-3 without Wysiwyg. The command {print income} prints a range named *income*. Here is how the subroutine works:

> **{DEFINE rng:string}** accepts the incoming argument from the subroutine call and stores it as a label in the cell named *rng*. The incoming string identifies a range to print.
>
> **{BREAK}/PPR{rng}~AGPQ** clears any menus and selects Print Printer Range. Then the {rng} subroutine call types the label stored in *rng* as the range to print. The macro processor presses Return and selects Align Go Page Quit.

You might have a macro print several ranges in succession by lining up a series of subroutine calls, as shown in Figure 28.6. But lining up the subroutine calls this way isn't the only way you can use them. You might have your macro perform a series of tasks, print a range, perform some more tasks, print a range, and so on.

	A	B	C	D	E	F
7	\p	{print report1}				
8		{print report2}				
9		{print grdat}				

FIGURE 28.6. A series of subroutine calls to the *print* routine will print several worksheet ranges in succession.

If a subroutine call is going to pass arguments to the subroutine, the first command in the subroutine must be a {DEFINE} statement. Such a statement can receive variables as strings (as does the one shown in Figure 28.6) or as values. The syntax of the command is {DEFINE *targ1:type,targ2:type*,etc...}, up to 15 pairs of *targs* and *:types*.

Each *targ* argument identifies the target cell for the incoming argument. The *type* portion of each argument determines how 1-2-3 stores the incoming quantity. When *type* is *:string* (or *:s*), 1-2-3 stores the incoming argument as a label in the target cell—even if the argument in the subroutine call is a formula. When *type* is *:value* (or *:v*), 1-2-3 evaluates the incoming argument and stores its current value in the target cell.

If you omit the *:type* portion of an argument in a {DEFINE} statement, the macro processor uses the *:string* option by default. Omitting the *:type* portions lets a subroutine call pass as many as 31 arguments to a subroutine.

Subroutines Add Structure

The subroutine may be the most difficult concept you encounter in macro programming. It is important to understand how subroutines work because they are of paramount importance in serious macro development. We discuss this a bit in Chapter 30, but if you have stuck with the subroutine discussion to this point, you deserve a little more explanation.

It is possible to write a macro as a long sequence of commands, but such a sequence can be quite intimidating to a user who must read through the code and figure out what the macro does. In some cases, you might even repeat a sequence of commands several times to perform a set of operations on several ranges of cells. This is bad form.

Rather than present a giant blob of offensive macro code to illustrate the bad form we are describing, we have settled on the short blob of code shown in Figure 28.7.

	A	B	C	D	E	F
1	\m	/PPOML10~MR60~				
2		BC{?}~H{?}~S\015~				
3		QAGPR{?}~AGPR{?}AGP				
4		OML5~MR65~QR{?}AGPQ				

FIGURE 28.7. This short macro is a model for much larger macros that suffer from blobbiness. The macro performs several tasks and is difficult to decipher.

The macro selects several print options and then pauses to let you select a range to print. It prints the range and pauses so you can select a second range. It prints that range and pauses so you can select a third range.

	A	B	C	D	E	F
1	\m	{margins 10,60}				
2		{border}				
3		{head}				
4		{foot}				
5		{setup \015}				
6		{rngprn}{rngprn}				
7		{margins 5,65}				
8		{rngprn}				
9						
10	lft					
11	rght					
12						
13	margins	{DEFINE lft:s,right:s}				
14		/PPOML{lft}~MR{rght}~QQ				
15						
16	border	/PPOBC{?}~QQ				
17						
18	head	/PPOH{?}~QQ				
19						
20	foot	/PPOF{?}QQ				
21						
22	str					
23						
24	setup	{DEFINE str:s}				
25		/PPOS{str}~QQ				
26						
27	rngprn	/PPR{?}~AGPQ				
28						

FIGURE 28.8. This structured macro performs the same tasks as the macro shown in Figure 28.7, but it is much easier to decipher.

By breaking the blob up into subroutines as we have done in Figure 28.8, you clarify the operation of the macro. Creating such structure not only makes your macros easier to understand, it makes it easier to edit the macro later on. You can focus on discrete macro routines rather than on lines of code within the big blob.

The main body of the macro in Figure 28.8 is in cells B1 through B8. Reading down the column, you get a sense of the macro's function. The first command looks as though it sets left and right margins to 10 and 60, respectively. The second one has something to do with print borders. The third command must set a print header, and the fourth a print footer. The command in cell B5 apparently establishes *015* as the printer setup string. The two {rngprn} commands must have to do with setting print ranges, and they may even print the ranges. And there is that {margins} command again—this time setting margins to 5 and 65.

If you can't get the gist of a macro from the subroutine names that it comprises, then the subroutines are named poorly. Even when a subroutine's name is quite descriptive, its purpose can be hard to guess. If that's the case, press the GOTO key (F5), and enter the subroutine's name. Then examine the code that makes up the subroutine so you know its purpose.

Your Own Subroutines

We've gone a little overboard with our example. You might not apply subroutines until your macros are considerably more complex than the one we have shown. In fact, some subroutines might contain far more steps than we used for the entire macro in Figure 28.7.

Keep in mind the dramatic improvement in readability we achieved by going from small blobby macros to the longer structured one. When you create large macros, blobby just won't do. Break down the macro's functions into small tasks, and create subroutines that you can string together with subroutine calls.

Having completed this chapter you should:

- *Understand how macro subroutines work*
- *Know how subroutine calls can pass parameters to subroutines*
- *Be able to create subroutines that add features to the macro facility*
- *Be prepared to explore further advanced macro concepts that incorporate subroutines*

29

Make Your Own Macro Menus

Your macros can present users with the same type of menus that 1-2-3 offers. When the user makes a selection, the macro processor skips off to a routine that performs a task associated with the selection. You can use macro menus to organize collections of utility macros, or you can use them to guide users through large macro-driven applications. However you use them, macro menus make your macros as accessible as any of the commands on 1-2-3's menus.

Before 1-2-3's menus, the best software menus consisted of numbered lists of options. You selected an option by typing the number of the desired selection. The most advanced spreadsheet before 1-2-3 offered a list of letters on the display, and it was up to you to memorize what task each letter initiated.

Initially, 1-2-3's menus offered two ways to make menu selections: you could type the first letter of a menu option, or you could move a menu pointer to the option and press Return. Now you can also select menu options by clicking with a mouse, but that is only a slight improvement over using the cursor-movement keys.

The point is, these menus offer a tremendous amount of guidance, if you want it. As you move the menu pointer from one option to the next, a long prompt appears and explains the purpose of the associated menu item. Once you are familiar with the basics of 1-2-3, you can work your way through many new tasks if you watch the display while you work with the menus. Your macros will be just as easy to use when you create custom macro menus.

In this chapter you will:

- *Learn how to create customized macro menus*
- *Create menu trees that act like 1-2-3's moving-cursor menus*
- *Organize a collection of utility macros under macro menus*
- *Explore the difference between {MENUBRANCH} and {MENUCALL}*

To Build A Menu

The advanced macro commands that make the macro processor present menus to users are {MENUBRANCH} and {MENUCALL}. In all but one way, these commands behave identically. For now, pretend that the commands are identical, and we will explain how the {MENUBRANCH} command works. At the end of the discussion you will see how the two menu-creating commands differ.

The {MENUBRANCH} command tells the macro processor to display a menu based on a set of menu instructions that reside in the worksheet. The command's syntax is {MENUBRANCH *location*} where *location* identifies the top-left corner cell of the menu instructions.

Menu instructions are a collection of labels that describe how a menu should appear. The menu instructions take up two rows and from one to eight columns of the worksheet. Figure 29.1 shows a {MENUBRANCH} command and menu instructions for a three-item menu.

	A	B	C	D
1	\m	{MENUBRANCH menu1}		
2		{BEEP}{BEEP}		
3				
4	menu1	Down	Right	Stay
5		Move pointer down	Move pointer right	Don't move pointer
6		{DOWN 3}	{RIGHT 3}	{QUIT}

FIGURE 29.1. Range B4..D6 contains menu instructions for a three-item menu. We've widened columns B and C so you can read the labels in row 4.

The options built into our sample instructions aren't particularly exciting, but they provide a sense of how macro menus work. The first row of the menu instructions (range B4..D4) lists the menu items that the macro processor should offer in the control panel. The second row of the instructions (range B5..D5) includes the long prompts that the macro processor displays one-by-one as you move the menu pointer through the menu prompts. The entries in row 6 aren't part of the menu instructions; we will discuss those in a moment.

It's important to understand that the menu instructions are not the menu. The actual macro menu doesn't exist until the macro processor displays it in the control panel. The menu instructions serve only to map out how the finished menu will look and work. Understanding this is key to understanding the {MENUBRANCH} command.

The Menu, Please

Assemble the menu instructions as described above, so you can experiment with a macro menu. Start in a blank worksheet, and enter labels as shown in Figure 29.1. You don't have to change the column widths—leave them at 9 if you wish. Use the Range Name Labels Right command to assign the two labels in column A as names for the adjacent cells of column B.

Now try the macro. Hold down the MACRO key (Alt), and press M. The custom menu appears. If you're using a mouse with 1-2-3, you can not use it in a macro menu; there is no mouse control while a macro is running. So, use the arrow keys to manuever within the menu; highlight each selection in turn, and read the associated long prompts.

When you select Down, the cell pointer moves down three rows in the sheet. When you select Right, the pointer moves three columns to the right. If you select Stay, the macro stops without moving the cell pointer. The macro menu even responds when you press Escape; it sounds two tones. Run the macro several times, so you see that it works as described.

Menu Flow of Control

If you study the layout of the macro instructions and consider how the menu works, you can see that a macro menu provides a fairly sophisticated way to make a macro branch. Consider what happens when the macro processor encounters a {MENUBRANCH} command.

The {MENUBRANCH} command tells the macro processor to display a menu. Macro control stays with the {MENUBRANCH} command while the menu is visible. Only when you make a selection does the macro processor branch to further commands. In our example, if you select Down, the macro branches to the command beneath the associated prompts in the menu instructions. In other words, when you select Down, macro control passes from the {MENUBRANCH} command in cell B1 to the {DOWN} command in cell B6 and continues on down the column from there. If you select Right, control passes from the {MENUBRANCH} command to the {RIGHT} command in cell C6.

If you press Escape rather than making a menu selection, control passes from the {MENUBRANCH} command to whatever follows it. In this case, control passes to the {BEEP} commands in cell B2.

Remember, the macro processor doesn't branch until you make a selection or press Escape. And because menu instructions can have as many as eight items with associated long prompts, the {MENUBRANCH} command can send macro flow of control in any of nine directions—eight menu choices, plus Escape.

Don't Slop on the Menus

Menu instructions can lead to messy macros. Suppose that each of the options in the menu instructions leads to an involved macro routine. With standard column widths, the code that follows for each menu item will run into code into the adjacent column. Figure 29.2 shows a section of a macro whose menu instructions lead to some very confusing code.

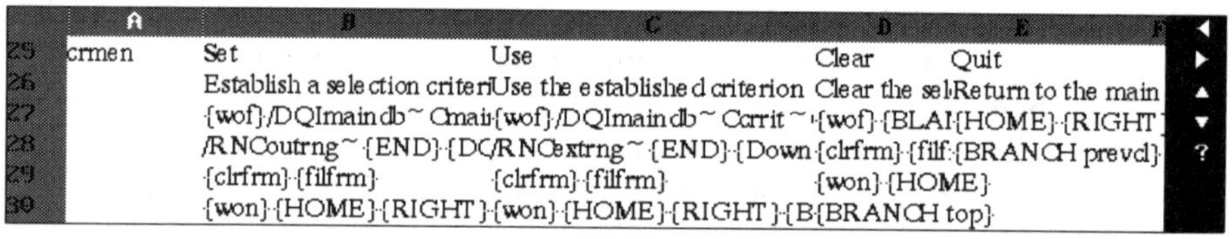

FIGURE 29.2. When you build macro routines directly beneath the menu instructions, your code is nearly undecipherable.

Rather than build a routine in each column, as we have done in Figure 29.2, use {BRANCH} commands directly after the menu instructions. When the user makes a selection from the macro menu, control will pass to a {BRANCH} command and then to the associated macro routine. A well-structured set of menu instructions appears in Figure 29.3.

Now only the menu prompts (and sometimes the {BRANCH} commands directly beneath them) overlap and confuse the display. When the user selects Set from the macro menu, the {BRANCH} command in cell B27 passes macro control to the *set* routine that begins in cell B29. Menu instructions are much clearer when you use this branching scheme.

Menus Within Menus Within Menus

Many of 1-2-3's menus lead to further menus, which in turn lead to further menus. A common question of macro designers is, "How do I get my macro menu trees to work like 1-2-3's menu trees?" It is not a difficult task.

Figure 29.4 shows two levels of an intricate menu tree.

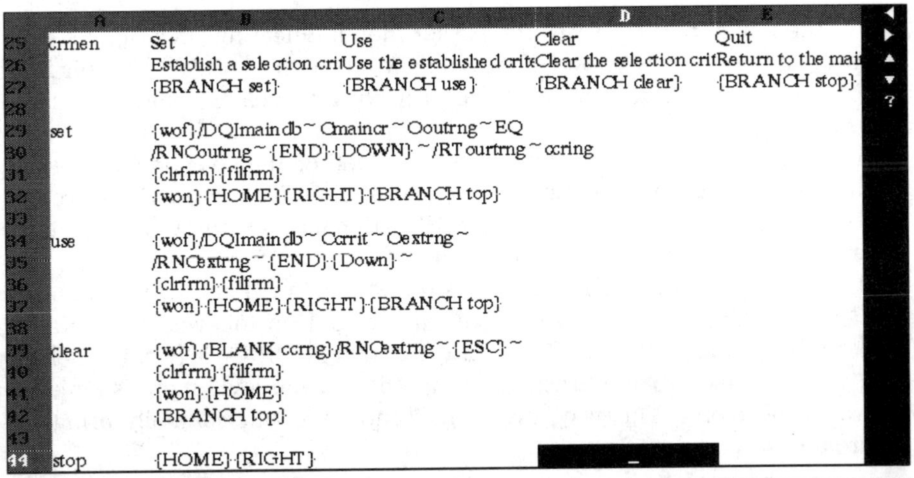

FIGURE 29.3. Breaking out the routine associated with each menu item clarifies the spreadsheet. The commands in cells B27, C27, D27, and E27 are {BRANCH set}, {BRANCH use}, {BRANCH clear}, and {BRANCH stop}, respectively.

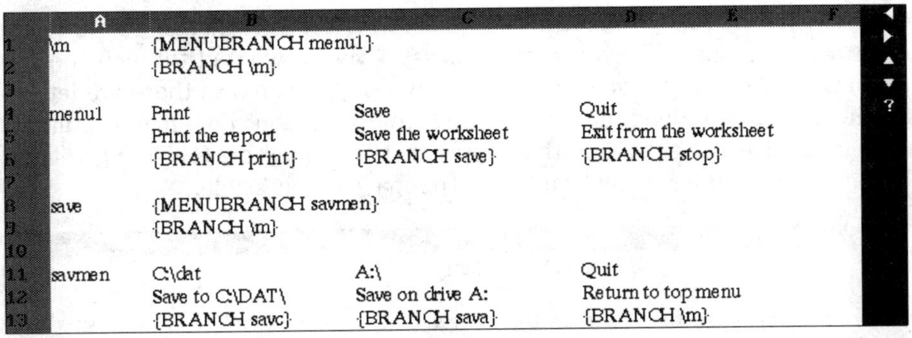

FIGURE 29.4. The two sets of menu instructions comprise part of a menu tree that works just like 1-2-3's menu trees.

The {MENUBRANCH} command in cell B1 activates the menu instructions that begin in cell B4. Pressing Escape in response to this menu leads to the {BRANCH} command in cell B2 which restarts the macro; the menu reappears. Selecting Print from the menu leads to a Print menu (not shown), and selecting Quit leads to a routine that ends the macro (also not shown). Selecting Save leads to the {MENUBRANCH} command in cell B8.

Cell B8's {MENUBRANCH} command activates a second menu whose instructions begin in cell B11. Pressing Escape in response to that menu leads to the {BRANCH} command in cell B9; it sends macro control back to the first cell of the macro and activates the earlier menu. Selecting C:\dat or A:\ from the second menu leads to one of two file-saving routines. Selecting Quit from the second menu transfers macro control back to cell B1, and the macro redisplays the first menu.

At each stage of the selection process—whether the selection is pressing Escape or choosing from a menu—the macro menu includes a way to return control to the previous {MENUBRANCH} command. This is what maintains the tree stucture of the interrelated menus.

If one of the options on the *savmen* menu led to yet another {MENUBRANCH} command, that command would be followed by a branch back to the cell named *save*. We used the command {BRANCH \m} in cell B2 to lock in the menu tree. Pressing Escape at the top-level menu simple reactivates the menu. This way, pressing Escape won't accidentally bring the macro to a stop.

Practice Building Your Own Menus

You may not be ready to create large macro-driven worksheets, but you may have a use for macro menus nevertheless. If you've worked through the entire macro section, you've created as many utility macros as there are letters in the alphabet. Indeed, if you've started to create your own macro utilities, you may have more macros than you can keep track of. Collecting related utility macros under menus can make the macros accessible.

	A	B	C	D	E
1	\b	{MENUBRANCH boxmen}			
2					
3	boxmen	Under	2_under	Box	D-box
4		Single under	Double und	Line around	2 lines around cell
5		{BRANCH u	{BRAND d	{BRANCH b	{BRANCH dbox}
6					
7	und	:FLB~			
8					
9	dund	:FLDB~			
10					
11	box	:FLA~			
12					
13	dbox	:FLDA~			

FIGURE 29.5. A single macro menu can provide access to as many as eight utility macros. This one has options for underlining and for putting boxes around cell contents.

Figure 29.5 shows a macro menu and four utility macros that work in Wysiwyg. You activate the menu by pressing MACRO-L, and then you select the line effect that you want to apply to the current cell.

Putting such simple command sequences on a macro menu like this doesn't save you many keystrokes when you use the macros. For example, it takes five keystrokes to underline a cell in Wysiwyg: press the colon key (this takes two keystrokes—hold down the Shift key and press the semicolon key), select Format Lines Below, and press Return. To issue the same command with our macro menu requires three keystrokes: hold down the Alt key and press L; then select Under. However, any procedure—no matter how complex—that you put on a menu like this takes only three keystrokes to perform.

When your macro library begins to get crowded or when you start to forget what utility macros it contains, group the routines under menus. As you do, keep in mind a few rules about menu instructions:

1. Put no more than eight items in the menu instructions.
2. Leave the cells to the right of the last menu item free of entries.
3. Start each menu item with a different letter. If you use the same letter to begin two or more items, typing the letter selects the left-most item only. You will have to use the menu pointer to select other items that begin with that letter.

What About {MENUCALL}?

With any luck, you now understand how the {MENUBRANCH} command works. We promised that once we had explained that, we would point out how {MENUCALL} differs from {MENUBRANCH}. Perhaps the simplest way to explain it is to point out the meanings of the command keywords.

Menubranch means "Display a menu, and then branch to the selected routine." Menucall means, "Display a menu, and then call the selected routine." In other words, {MENUCALL} is a subroutine call.

When you select an option from a {MENUCALL} menu, control passes to the associated macro routine. When the macro processor finishes the routine, control returns to whatever command immediately follows the original {MENUCALL} command. If you are not familiar with subroutines and subroutine calls, review Chapter 28, *Create Your Own Macro Commands.*

Work on your own to create some {MENUBRANCH} and {MENUCALL} menu instructions. Develop a sense of how to create menu trees, or at least learn to follow the flow of control through such trees when you examine other people's macros. Some of the applications in Section 6 use macro menus to interact with users. These models offer opportunities to see how carefully designed menus can guide users through advanced spreadsheet tasks.

Having completed this chapter you should:

- *Understand the benefits of moving-cursor menus*
- *Know how to create custom macro menus to manage your macros*
- *Understand the difference between a macro menu and macro menu instructions*
- *Be able to trace the flow of control through a {MENUBRANCH} or {MENUCALL} command*
- *Be prepared to understand further advanced macro concepts that might include customized menus*
- *Have a growing sense of how macro commands and techniques can combine to create sophisticated macro applications*

30

A Philosophy for Macro Programmers

There are almost no rules about how to assemble a spreadsheet. You can put whatever you want wherever you want and get the results you want as long as you understand the relationships between your data and your formulas. While this makes it very easy to knock together a working model, it can lead to some really sloppy worksheets.

In this chapter you will learn:

- *When and when not to write macros*
- *The importance of using range names in macros*
- *Ways to clarify the components of macros*
- *Strategies for structuring spreadsheet models*
- *Strategies for structuring macros*
- *Methods for documenting your work*
- *Ways that macros are likely to fail*
- *To notice macro error messages*
- *To use windows to track down macro errors*
- *How macro Step mode works*

The tidiness with which you develop a spreadsheet determines the ease with which you will be able to edit and modify it later on. This extends particularly into the realm of macro development. Being able to read a macro and understand how it works is important when you return to the macro in a week or a month to modify the code.

The guidelines we propose for laying out spreadsheets and macros have been accumulated during years of spreadsheet development experience. While these guidelines have proven invaluable over the years, they aren't rules. Build your spreadsheets any way you please, but if you please, you can use the philosophies presented in this chapter to help keep your models manageable.

To wrap up the guidelines, we consider the options available to you when your best efforts have resulted in macros that don't work properly. If you're familiar with the types of problems your macros can develop, and with the ways in which 1-2-3 can help you diagnose the problems, you will be well prepared to handle even the most perplexing macro programming errors.

Decide When Macros Matter

Don't use macros. Oh, yeah? What's the point of devoting a whole section to macros and then telling you not to use them? Well, the language is a little strong, but it is the single most important guideline to writing good macros.

Macros are considered the most difficult spreadsheet tools to master. Writing macros is, after all, computer programming. In spite of how difficult these things are to create, many users get in the habit of starting their questions with, "Is there a macro that does . . ." The question you should ask begins with, "Is there a way to . . ."

Exhaust all other possibilities before turning to macros. Is there a way to generate subtotals for salaries in each of 10 departments represented in an employee database? Check out the @D functions and the Data Table commands. Is there a macro to generate these subtotals? You could write several, but check out the @D functions and the Data Table commands first.

The point leads to a second guideline.

Learn 1-2-3 Cold Before Writing Significant Macros

If you're not familiar with all of 1-2-3's features, how can you know whether there is a command to do what you want to do? 1-2-3 might not be the most exciting thing you will ever study, but it certainly isn't dull.

Approach your study in small chunks. We've tried to take that approach with this book. Even the very long chapters are divided into sections that might engage you for 15 minutes to a half hour each. To learn more about a topic that we didn't cover, square off with the computer and work through examples in the 1-2-3 documentation. In 10 to 15 minutes of experimentation you can discover a lot about the spreadsheet.

Another useful strategy is to read all of the documentation that came with your software. There is no need to work through every example; just get the gist. When you face a new problem later on, something you have read might pop into mind.

When you're familiar with all of the features that 1-2-3 offers, your macros benefit. Knowing enough, you will discover ways in which macros can exploit one set of commands to achieve results that seem totally unrelated to the commands themselves.

If You Must Write a Macro

If you are convinced that you must write a macro, develop some standards. We have presented all of the examples in this book according to standards that we apply to all of our spreadsheet development. Try some on for size.

Use Range Names

Except on the rarest of occasions, never write a macro that uses cell and range addresses. Consider the macro shown in Figure 30.1. It contains a {LET} statement that squares the value from cell B1 and stores the result in cell B2.

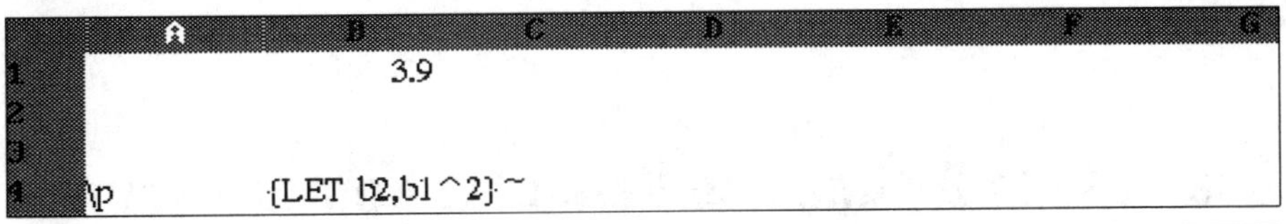

FIGURE 30.1. The {LET} command shown calculates the square of the value in cell B1 and places the result into cell B2.

Now that we've created the macro, we realize that we need to open up some rows for data at the top of the spreadsheet. We need room for a few variable cells above cell B1, so we use either the Move command or the Worksheet Insert Rows command to open up the space. The resulting worksheet appears in Figure 30.2.

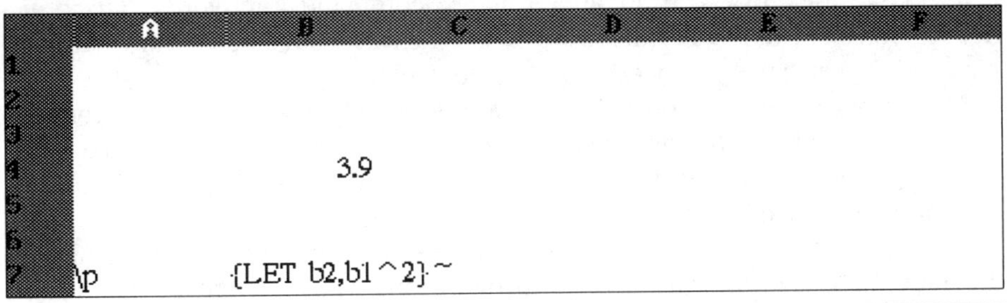

FIGURE 30.2. Inserting rows made way for more data, but suddenly the macro command in cell B7 doesn't know what it is doing.

The {LET} statement is supposed to square the value that is now stored in cell B4, but inserting the rows messed things up a bit. If we had assigned the original cells B1 and B2 range names and used those names in the macro, this problem would never have arisen.

Consider Figure 30.3. The {LET} statement there squares the value in *source* and puts the result in *targ*. Inserting and deleting rows or moving cells won't affect the macro's operation.

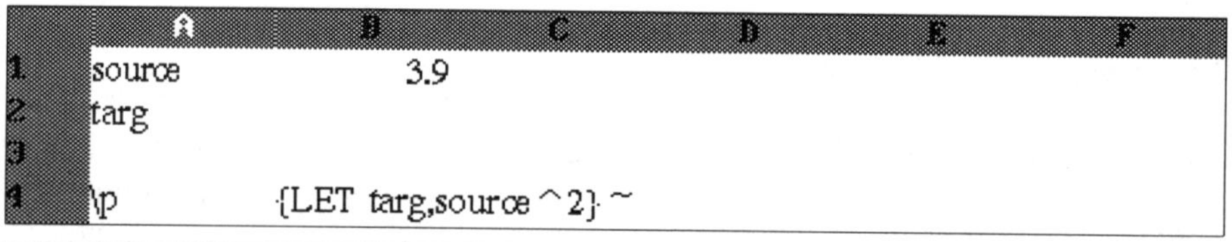

	A	B	C	D	E	F
1	source	3.9				
2	targ					
3						
4	\p	{LET targ,source^2}~				

FIGURE 30.3. Assigning range names and using them in macros gives you a lot of leeway when you need to rearrange the spreadsheet.

Use Case to Distinguish Variables from Constants

In this context we define variables more loosely than we might normally. Variables are those elements of a macro whose exact lettering or appearance isn't dictated by 1-2-3. Range names are variables because you can choose any range name you want to include in the macro. Cell and range addresses are variables because 1-2-3 doesn't force you to use specific ones to build your spreadsheets. File names and graph names also qualify as variables under this definition.

Things that are not variables include letters that make up menu sequences, macro key indicators, and advanced macro command key words. These are not variables because you must always use the same ones in the same ways to have 1-2-3 perform the procedures they control.

Use uppercase characters for nonvariables and lowercase characters for variables. Or, use lowercase characters for nonvariables and uppercase for variables. Whichever you do is OK with us. Just don't arbitrarily mix uppercase and lowercase between variables and nonvariables.

In Figure 30.4, we have done just that. The variables don't jump out at you, do they? You have to work a little to figure out what is what in that macro code.

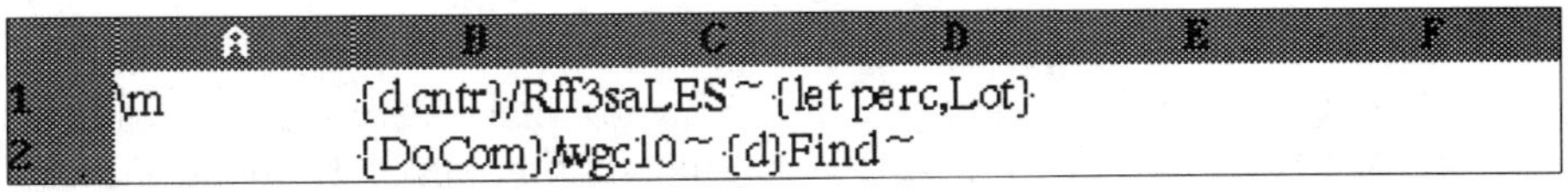

	A	B
1	\m	{d cntr}/Rff3saLES~{let perc,Lot}
2		{DoCom}/wgc10~{d}Find~

FIGURE 30.4. The variables in this macro blend right in with everything else the macro contains.

The worksheet shown in Figure 30.5 shows two copies of the same lines of code. The upper version shows lowercase variables, and the lower version shows uppercase variables. Many macro enthusiasts point out that uppercase variables among lowercase macro commands really stand out. If you are used to the opposite, the lowercase variables stand out well against uppercase commands. As we said, we don't care which way you do it; just pick one and stick with it. Your macros will be much easier to decipher when the need arises.

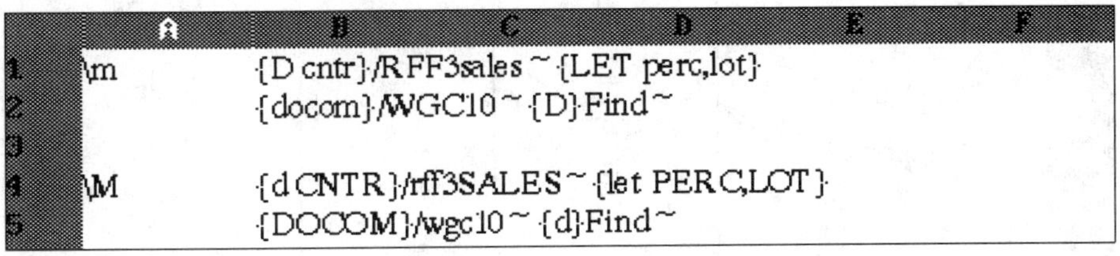

	A	B
1	\m	{D cntr}/RFF3sales~{LET perc,lot}
2		{docom}/WGC10~{D}Find~
3		
4	\M	{d CNTR}/rff3SALES~{let PERC,LOT}
5		{DOCOM}/wgc10~{d}Find~

FIGURE 30.5. Using upper- and lowercase consistently makes your macros easier to read.

Standardize Your Spreadsheets

Oh boy, does this sound dull. Dull, perhaps, but important. By standardizing the way you build spreadsheets, you speed development of all your models. If you have a plan before you start, you won't spend as much time tinkering around, figuring out where to put things.

Standardize your layout any way you want. There is no right or wrong way to standardize; just do it. One suggested layout puts the active area of the sheet at the top-left corner. This is the area with which users interact—usually to enter data or to examine data that has already been entered.

Place Criteria and Report ranges in the columns to the right of the active area, and put macros to the right of that. Reserve 10 columns for your macros.

The first column will contain labels that identify labeled cells. The second column should contain the main body of the macro, macro variable cells, and all the macro's routines. The remaining columns can hold macro menu instructions. Figure 30.6 diagrams this general structure.

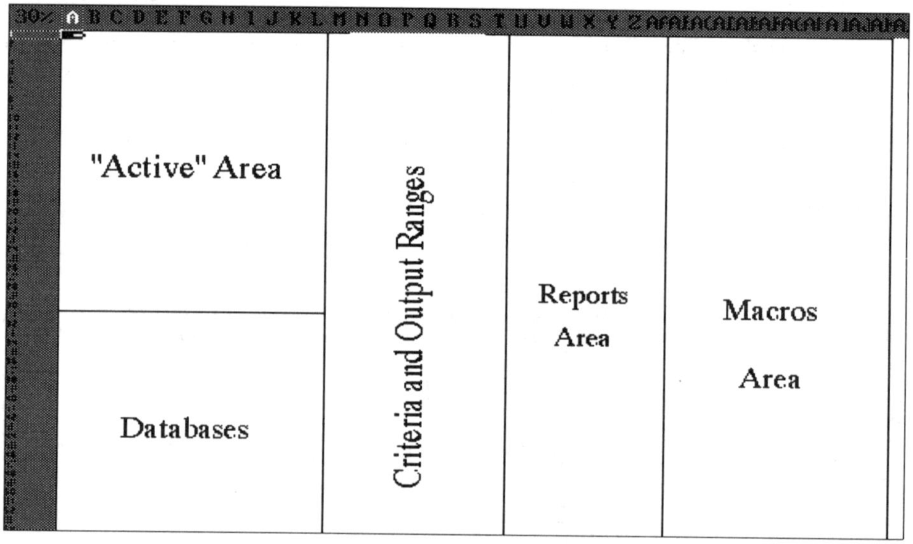

FIGURE 30.6. The boxes in this sheet roughly suggest a layout that you can use in all of your spreadsheets.

The macro area itself should have a little structure to help you decipher the purpose of a given macro. Place variable cells at the very top of the macro area and be sure to label each of them. Place tables on which the macro depends in the columns to the left of the variables. Group subroutines that the macro uses often beneath the variables, and place all of the macro menus directly beneath the subroutines. After all of these, begin the main body of the macro.

Ideally, a spreadsheet contains documentation that helps you and other users understand its contents. That is the point of entering labels to the left of named cells. Don't stop there. Enter labels to the right of each macro step. These labels should provide terse verbal descriptions of each step. You should be able to read down the extra column of labels and know exactly what the macro does.

Figure 30.7 shows some detail of a 10-column macro range, complete with documentation to the right of the macro cells.

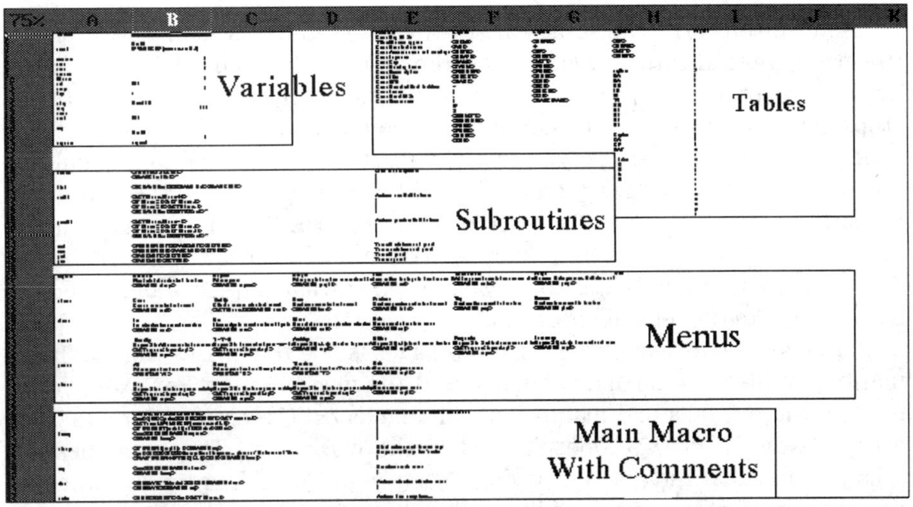

FIGURE 30.7. The macros area of a spreadsheet benefits from a standardized structure. The exact layout isn't important, but you should pick one and stick with it in all of your spreadsheets.

Swat Macro Bugs

Macros fail. It is an annoying truth about any type of computer programming that even when you write perfect computer code, things go wrong. Perhaps you left out a tilde or a closing parenthesis. Maybe your macro refers to a range name that you haven't yet assigned. Worst of all, your macro's logic may be poor—some part of it somehow changes the value of a variable that another part of it uses, rendering the variable invalid.

In most cases, macro errors expose themselves quite obviously while the macro is running. In some cases, you might not even be aware that something has gone wrong until you carefully examine the effect that the macro had on the worksheet. Whatever the case, you won't be able to remove the bugs from your macros if you don't know how to track them down.

Read The Error Messages

In many cases when a macro fails, 1-2-3 beeps and displays an error message. Read the message! It does its best to tell you what is wrong with the macro, even directing you to the offending line of macro code.

Useful macro error messages arise when something is wrong with one of the macro key indicators or an advanced macro command used in your macro. The macro processor processes commands up to the invalid one and then stops, pointing out which cell contains the command that failed.

If you read the message, you know what went wrong, and you should be able to repair it. Messages such as, *Invalid range in BRANCH (B1)* are particularly easy to fix (the Target range of the {BRANCH} command in B1 doesn't exist), while messages such as *Too many nesting levels in macro calls* are much trickier (it is not always obvious what sequence of subroutine calls has led to the legal limit of 31).

Perhaps the trickiest of the error messages is one that arises from an irregularity in a menu command sequence that the macro issues. For example, no matter where it falls in a macro, the commands /RFC2~crange~ produces an error message if *crange* doesn't exist in the worksheet. The error message tells you only that the macro is trying to use an invalid cell or range address—not very useful when you don't know what line of code produced the message.

Errors That Aren't Errors

Worse than a macro that fails with a tricky error message is one that fails with no error message at all. This happens when the commands that the macro issues could legitimately accomplish something in the spreadsheet, even if it is something you don't want to accomplish.

One example of this can arise when your macro performs database querying operations. The macro might issue commands to extract selected records from the database and then print the records. However, suppose that for some reason the criterion that the macro uses to perform the extract isn't the criterion that you intended to use? The extract will succeed and you will get a printout of the wrong records.

Through careless coding, your macros can end up erasing the wrong ranges, assigning formats to the wrong cells, recording the wrong values in variable cells, and worse. For the most part, 1-2-3 can't point out this type of error to you. You must recognize the errors when they arise and puzzle out what went wrong. Fortunately, there are tools and techniques to help.

Read the Macro Code

One very effective way to track down a bug is to read through the macro step-by-step. If simply reading the code doesn't reveal a problem, manually perform the commands that the macro processor would perform. Some things you can't do exactly as the macro processor does, but you can simulate all of it. For example, to walk through a FOR loop, manually enter the {FOR} command's Start value into the counter cell, issue the commands in the FOR loop's routine, increase the loop counter, and do the routine again.

With very large and complex macros, it is tough to both read the macro commands in the spreadsheet and issue the commands manually. One way to simplify the process is to print out the macro commands and read them from the printout as you issue them at the keyboard. A second way is to split the display into unsynchronized horizontal windows (Worksheet Windows Horizontal and then Worksheet Windows Unsynch).

Keep the cell pointer in the upper window as you issue the commands, and keep the macro visible in the lower window. When you need to scroll additional macro commands into the lower window, press the WINDOW key (F6) to get down there, move the cell pointer down a bit, and then press WINDOW again to return to the upper window.

You might need to hop back and forth a lot if your macros rely heavily on subroutines, but with a little practice you will be able to whip through a macro until you find the source of the error. Unfortunately, this debugging technique is not effective if your macro issues Worksheet Windows commands.

Step-By-Step Debugging

One of the most powerful of 1-2-3's macro debugging tools is Step mode. To activate Step mode, press the STEP key (hold down Alt and press F2). The Step indicator appears at the bottom of the display, but other than that, nothing seems to change.

When you run a macro, you'll find that a lot has changed. Try a little experiment. Enter two lines of macro code as shown in Figure 30.8, assign the associated range name, and activate Step mode. Then, with the cell pointer in cell A3, run the macro.

	A	B	C	D	E	F
1	\m	{DOWN}{RIGHT}8~				
2		/RFC2~~				

FIGURE 30.8. Create this simple macro so you can see the macro processor run in Step mode.

1-2-3 displays the first line of the macro code across the bottom of the display, and a highlight emphasizes the {DOWN} command. The highlight identifies the command that the macro processor is about to follow. You trigger the command by pressing any key. The spacebar is a good choice; press it.

The macro processor moves the cell pointer down and pauses. You can see on the display that the macro processor will next press the RightArrow key. Press the Spacebar, and it happens. Each time you press a key, the macro processor follows the next macro instruction in sequence. Since you know in advance what command 1-2-3 is about to perform, your chances of isolating an error in your macro are quite good.

When you have finished stepping through the macro, press the STEP key to deactivate Step mode.

Closing Thoughts on Macro Debugging

As you write longer and more complex macros, debugging them becomes an even greater challenge. The task is easiest if you've built the macros in modules, each activated by a subroutine call in the main body of the macro. This way, when a problem arises, you don't have to walk through every macro step to pinpoint it. In fact, the nature of a bug may incriminate a specific routine as its likely source.

Most important in creating bug-free macros is being prepared for the worst. Before you test-run any part of a macro, save the worksheet that contains it. If errors arise in the test run, figure out how to fix them, and then retrieve the file copy of the macro. Fix the error in this unused version of the model, save, and test-run it again.

When you are working in very large models, keep backups of different revisions as you go along. Adding a new module can sometimes mess up things that happen in other modules. Be sure additions to a working model also work before you commit earlier backups to the scrap heap.

Having completed this chapter you should:

- *Have a basic philosophy for approaching macro development*
- *Understand the advantages of standardizing your worksheet models*
- *Be able to lay out spreadsheets sensibly*
- *Understand the various ways that macros can fail*
- *Be able to track down and eliminate bugs that arise in your macro applications*
- *Be ready to tackle serious macro programming challenges*

31

The Jump into Hyperspace

So far, you have been creating macros in spreadsheets. This isn't going to change. But macros don't have to stay in the spreadsheets in which you create them. A macro in a spreadsheet can act only on that particular sheet. And, based on what we have told you so far, you must recreate each macro every time if you want to use it in other than its original sheet. Actually, that isn't the case if you use Hyperspace.

Hyperspace is the nickname of the Macro Library Manager add-in. (With a name like Macro Library Manager, you can see why it prefers its nickname.) The Hyperspace add-in lets you store spreadsheet ranges in RAM independent of any spreadsheet. You can't view a range stored in Hyperspace, but you know it is there because its macros run as though they were in the worksheet.

Better than that, a Hyperspace macro library stays in RAM even when you retrieve a new worksheet or erase the current one. You can use Hyperspace macros in any worksheet in any work session. This means that you can create a single macro to retrieve spreadsheets and print ranges or to add data to several sheets and update the graphs that rely on the added data.

In this chapter you will:

- *Learn the purpose of the Macro Library Manager add-in (Hyperspace)*
- *Attach the add-in*
- *Explore the rules for using Hyperspace*
- *Store some macros in a Hyperspace macro library*
- *Create an auto-load library*

Plot the Course into Hyperspace

To be able to store macros in Hyperspace, you must first attach the Hyperspace add-in. Chances are that the Install program copied the add-in onto your hard disk. Attach it by selecting Add-In Attach and then choosing MACROMGR.ADN from the resulting menu. Attach the add-in to a function key—use F10 for this discussion—and then select Quit to return to Ready mode.

With Hyperspace ready to roll, you need a few macros to store there. For now, enter the three simple macros shown in Figure 31.1.

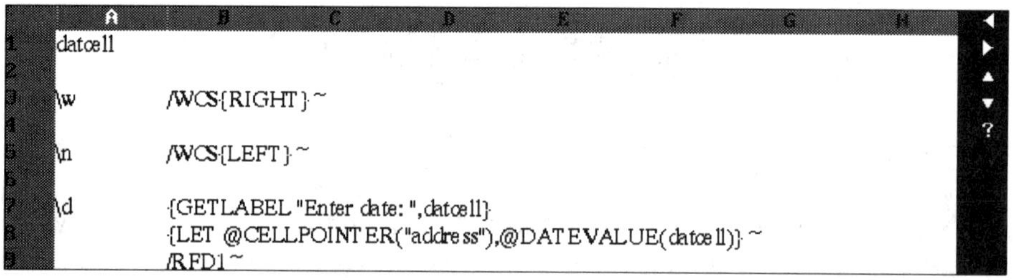

FIGURE 31.1. Use these three macros to help in your exploration of Hyperspace.

Be sure that you assign the labels shown in column A as names for the adjacent cells of column B. Then, if you wish, try the macros before you launch them into Hyperspace. The macro named *w* widens the current column by one character. The macro named *n* narrows the column, and the macro named *d* lets you enter a date using the standard MM/DD/YY format; it converts the date to a serial number, stores the number in the current cell, and assigns a date format. If asterisks appear in the cell, use the *w* macro to widen the cell.

Make the Jump

Having tested the macros, you are ready to send them into space. Press Alt-F10, and select Save. 1-2-3 prompts for the name of the library to save. Enter *TEST* as the name for this practice library. 1-2-3 prompts you to identify a range; indicate range A1..B9. Finally, 1-2-3 asks whether you want to lock the library with a password. Select No.

The macros vanish from the sheet. But they are not really gone. Hold down the MACRO key (Alt), and press W. The current column's width increases by one. Press MACRO-N, and the column narrows.

When you save a macro library, 1-2-3 creates a copy of the selected worksheet range both in RAM and on disk. The disk copy lets you reload the library in future sessions without first bringing the macros into the worksheet.

Test this by selecting Add-In Detach and indicating MACROMGR. Select Quit, and press MACRO-W to widen the column. 1-2-3 beeps because the Hyperspace library is no longer in RAM.

Now select Add-In Attach, and indicate MACROMGR.ADN. Once again attach the add-in to F10, and select Quit from the add-in menu. Press Alt-F10 to activate the Hyperspace add-in, and then select Load from the resulting menu.

1-2-3 offers a listing of the available macro libraries—there may be only one entry on the list at this point. Select TEST.MLB as the library to load, and then select Quit. Now press MACRO-W to alter the width of the current column.

Edit a Macro Library

When you send a range into Hyperspace, everything in the range goes along for the ride. Cell contents and range names within the range are stripped from the spreadsheet. Should you wish to add more macros to the library or edit existing macros, you must bring the library back from Hyperspace. Try it.

Press Alt-F10, and select Edit. 1-2-3 prompts you to select the library you want to edit; select TEST.MLB. 1-2-3 then asks whether to ignore incoming range names that conflict with those in the spreadsheet or to overwrite spreadsheet range names that conflict with names in the library. Select Overwrite for this exercise.

When 1-2-3 prompts for a Target range to receive the macro library, indicate cell A1. The macros return. After you edit the macros in the spreadsheet, you simply resave them to preserve them in the Hyperspace library.

When you use the Edit option to bring a library back from Hyperspace, 1-2-3 does not remove the Hyperspace macro library from RAM or from the hard disk. The old library remains in RAM until you issue a command to remove or replace it. See how this works by resaving the library you just brought out of Hyperspace—never mind that you didn't actually edit it.

Press Alt-F10, and select Save. 1-2-3 prompts for the name of the library to save. Select TEST as the name for the library. 1-2-3 warns you that the name is already in use; select Yes to erase the old version of the library and replace it with the new one. 1-2-3 prompts you to identify a range; indicate range A1..B9. Finally, 1-2-3 asks whether you want to lock the library with a password. Select No.

A Few Rules for Space Travelers

As powerful a tool as Hyperspace is, it must have rules for operation. Indeed it does, and understanding them can save you some confusion as you create and save your own macro libraries.

Order of Precedence

When you trigger the macro processor, it looks in the worksheet for any range names associated with a macro (including the macro's name). If it finds a name in the sheet, that is the name it uses in interpreting a macro command. If it doesn't find the name in the sheet, it looks in the macro library that you loaded earliest in the current work session. If the name isn't there, the macro processor looks in the second library loaded during the session, and so on.

Number of Macro Libraries

You can create as many macro libraries as you wish, but you can have no more than 10 in RAM at a time. Depending on the sizes of the libraries, the amount of RAM in your computer may further limit the number of allowable libraries.

Libraries Have No Cell Addresses

Macro libraries have no cell addresses. When a library range is in the sheet, you can refer to cells in terms of the spreadsheet addresses, but, once a worksheet range jumps into Hyperspace, you can identify its cells only if the cells have range names. Bracketed macro commands can act on any named cells in a Hyperspace library, but 1-2-3's menu sequences can act only on cells in the worksheet.

Formulas Can't Reach Into or Out of Hyperspace

A formula on the worksheet cannot refer to cells in Hyperspace. Conversely, a formula in Hyperspace can't refer to the worksheet. The only way that information can pass from a Hyperspace library to a worksheet and back is under the direction of bracketed macro commands. For example, if the cell named *targ* is in a library and *source* is in the worksheet, the formula +TARG entered in *source* is invalid. Nor will the macro command /Csource~targ~ work. The command {LET targ,source}, however, is valid.

Formulas Can Become Nonsensical

If you launch into Hyperspace a range that contains some of the cells involved in a spreadsheet formula, the spreadsheet formula doesn't notice that its data is missing. For example, the formula +A1 stored in cell B1 won't know that you have sent cell A1 into Hyperspace. The formula will continue to refer to cell A1 in the sheet and may return results that you would rather not see.

When you send formulas into Hyperspace, send along all the cells upon which the formulas depend. Likewise, if you send data cells into Hyperspace, be sure you don't leave behind any formulas that rely on those cells.

All Menu Sequences and Function Keys Act on the Sheet

Any menu command sequence or function key command that a Hyperspace macro issues affects the current worksheet. These commands cannot act on cells and ranges within a macro library.

Your Own Hyperspace Libraries

If you have worked through the entire macros section of this book, you have created a worksheet called LIBRARY that contains a collection of utility macros that you can apply in any spreadsheet. Retrieve that worksheet, if you like, and store it as a Hyperspace macro library. Then erase the original LIBRARY file from disk.

Perhaps you want your utility macros to be available every time you start up 1-2-3. It would become a chore to attach the add-in and load the macro library every single day. Instead, set up 1-2-3 to attach the add-in and load the library for you.

Start by creating the worksheet shown in Figure 31.2.

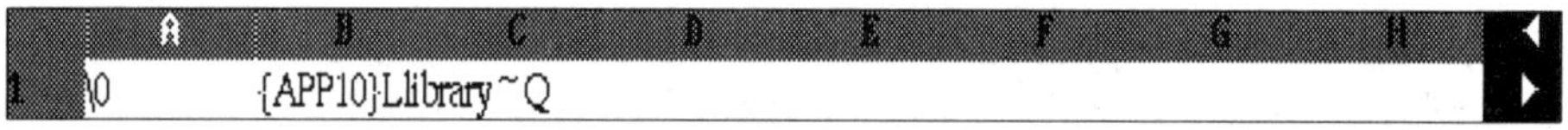

FIGURE 31.2. A macro named *\0* starts running automatically when 1-2-3 retrieves the worksheet that contains the macro.

The macro's name is *\0*, and 1-2-3 takes the name to mean, "Start running this macro automatically when you retrieve the worksheet that contains it." Saved under the file name AUTO123.WK1, it will automatically retrieve the worksheet at start-up, so select File Save, and enter AUTO123.

That takes care of automatically loading the macro library named LIBRARY. The macro you just created and saved presses F10, selects Load, and enters *library* as the name of the macro library to load. This won't work if the Macro Library Manager isn't already attached to 1-2-3. Here's how to make it attach automatically:

Select Worksheet Global Default Other Add-In Set, and choose F10; the autoexecuting macro you just created expects the add-in to be attached to F10. Select No from the resulting menu; the add-in should not start running automatically. Select Quit Update to preserve the new settings in 1-2-3's configuration file, and then select Quit to return to Ready mode. In all future work sessions, 1-2-3 will automatically attach the Macro Library Manager add-in and load the custom macro library named LIBRARY.

Closing Thoughts for Macro Enthusiasts

We have barely scratched the surface of this macro stuff. Even knowing all of the advanced macro commands and how they work won't turn you into a skilled macro programmer. If you want to become a "power user," consider taking a course or reading a book about structured programming techniques. At the same time, dig, dig, dig into the intricacies of 1-2-3's other capabilities.

Having completed this chapter you should:

- *Know what the Hyperspace add-in is*
- *Understand the advantages of storing macros in Hyperspace*
- *Be able to create your own Hyperspace macro library*
- *Be ready to experiment with a few completed macro applications*

Section 6 Advanced Applications

What is a section about advanced spreadsheet applications doing in a book for intermediate users? There are several answers to this question.

If you've worked through the material in this book, your knowledge of 1-2-3 is now more complete than that of the average user. Most users learn only as much about 1-2-3 as they need to do their jobs. Being grounded in so many of 1-2-3's features puts you ahead of the pack. Advanced applications reveal some of the ways in which you can apply the knowledge you have acquired.

With your current understanding of the spreadsheet, you should be able to build and apply models you find published in other books and in magazines. More important, you are ready to begin creating your own advanced applications. Building and using the applications in this section will get you started doing both of these things. It will also give you some tools—an address label printer and a loan schedule calculator—that you can use in your own work.

If you have only skimmed some of the material in the book, working through advanced applications may reveal topics that you should review. The book discusses most of the techniques used in these advanced applications.

32

Schedule Loan Payments, Print Mailing Labels, and Race Dogs

As you see the types of applications that you can build in 1-2-3 you might wonder, why? Why use the spreadsheet as a programming language? There are programs specifically designed to print mailing labels—why do it in 1-2-3? Calculating loan schedules? There is software to do it. In fact, any problem that can be solved with 1-2-3 can probably be solved with other software—in many cases more efficiently.

There are, however, several arguments for using 1-2-3 for applications development. The first is that you have 1-2-3. Obtaining additional software is usually expensive. If you have a little time and the inclination, you can knock together a spreadsheet model for much less than you would pay for similar commercial software.

> *In this chapter, you'll:*
>
> - *Learn why 1-2-3 is an excellent applications environment*
> - *Learn, step-by-step, how to create a load schedule*
> - *Learn an application to print perfect mailing labels from 1-2-3*
> - *Create a simulated race in the spreadsheet*

A second reason to use 1-2-3 as an applications tool is to be consistent. If you do 90% of your computing in 1-2-3, you are probably comfortable with the spreadsheet. When you buy a separate program, you have to learn new ways to use the computer, which is not a bad thing but can be time-consuming. You also start creating new types of data on your disk, because most programs create data files with unique formats. While many let you create files that you can exchange with other programs, this

What Is a High-Level Language?

A computer works by flicking switches on and off. When a switch is on, its value is 1; when it is off, its value is 0. There are millions of such switches in your computer, and the pattern of ones and zeros represents to the computer the information that you see as a spreadsheet and as the data and commands that you use in the sheet.

Computer programming has gone through several generations (or levels) of technology. In the first generation, programmers issued instructions to the computer using the same patterns of ones and zeros that the computer uses to keep track of its own processes. First generation program code is called *machine language*.

The second generation of code is called *assembly language*. Assembly language is a set of terse instructions that represent ways to move information around within the computer. While programming in assembly language isn't easy, it is much easier than programming in machine code.

The languages that you hear most about—C, BASIC, Pascal, COBOL, and so on—are third generation languages. These contain near English-language commands and are quite easy to learn. While the computer and its display start out as a sort of black box, you can use third generation languages to build any software you can imagine.

Macros within spreadsheets are fourth-generational. By the fourth generation, an enormous amount of programming has already been done—possibly in a second or third generation language. The programming you do fits within the context of an existing application (such as a spreadsheet), and the language simply manipulates that environment. As a macro programmer, you are developing software using a high-level language.

isn't as convenient as having all of your data in a single type of file.

A third reason to do applications development in 1-2-3 is the simplicity with which it can be done. If you want to develop an application, you will find few programming tools easier to use than 1-2-3. Lower-level programming languages, such as C and BASIC, simply are not as easy to comprehend as 1-2-3 macros. Not only that, but with 1-2-3, about 85% of the programming is already finished before you write any code. When you write a program in BASIC, you have to develop ways to store data, display information on the screen, save data in files, and so on. 1-2-3 already does these things—and you know how to make it do them. In most cases you can crank out a database management macro application in days using 1-2-3. Compare that to the months it would take to develop using BASIC or C.

Applications developed in 1-2-3 are not always as slick and responsive as those developed in lower-level languages, but they will probably fit better with the way that you work.

How to Work with Our Sample Applications

Don't think of the sample applications in this section as finished products. While you can apply them as is to your own work, you can also use them as the bases for creating your own more elaborate applications.

We have not provided step-by-step explanations of how the models work. Rather, each includes only the information you need to get it running and to use it properly. Once you get a model working, take the time to read through the macros. Try to decipher each macro's flow of control and to understand the logic the macro uses. Working through these examples should provide a good sense of what macros can do and help you to recognize situations in which to apply the various macro commands.

Generate a Loan Schedule

If you worked through Chapter 19, this model will be familiar. All we did was to superimpose two simple macros on the loan schedule worksheet that appeared in that chapter. The loan schedule we calculated there was for a 30-year mortgage. With very little effort, you can apply the same formulas to any loan calculation; you can use this loan analysis worksheet to calculate the principal and interest paid in any period of a loan. Start in a blank worksheet and proceed as follows:

Column Widths

Select Worksheet Column Column-Range Set-Width. Indicate range A1..F1, and set these columns to widths of 12 characters.

Labels And Values

Enter labels as shown in rows 1 through 9 of Figure 32.1. Use the quotation mark label prefix to align the labels in cells A3, A4, and A5 at the right of the column. To create the dividing lines, enter \- into cell A2, and copy it to cell B2. Copy it a second time to range A9..F9. Enter the value 1 into cell A10.

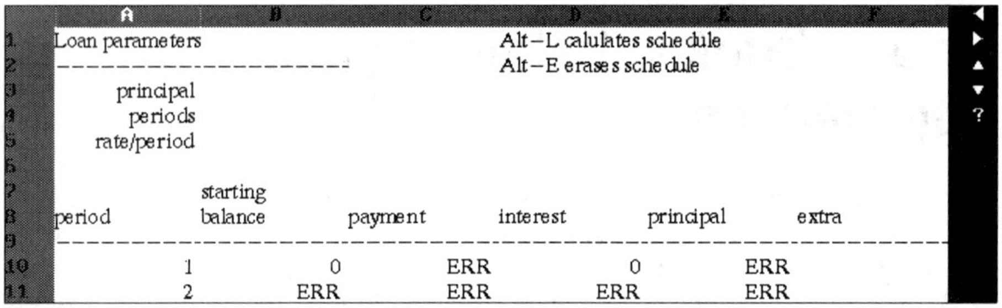

FIGURE 32.1. The labels and formulas in this worksheet form the basis of a loan schedule calculator.

Formulas

Enter formulas in the cells listed—never mind if some of the formulas return ERR.

Cell	Formula
B10	+B3
C10	+B3*B5/(1–(1*B5)^–B4)
D10	+$B$5*B10
E10	+C10–D10
A11	+A10+1
B11	+B10–E10–F10
C11	@IF(B11+B11*$B$5>C10,C10,B11+B11*$B$5)
D11	+$B$5*B11
E11	+C11–D11

Display Formats

Select Worksheet Global Format Currency, and enter *2*. Then assign range formats to the following cells and ranges:

Range	Format
B4	General
B5	Percent with two decimal places
A10..A11	General

For example, to assign the format to cell B4, select Range Format General and indicate cell B4.

The Macros

Enter labels as shown in Figure 32.2

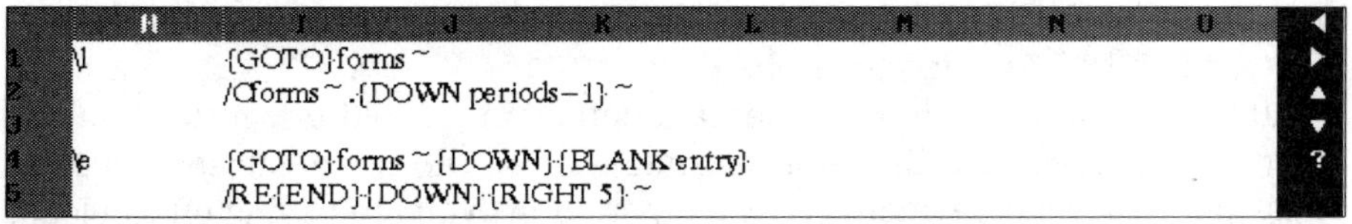

FIGURE 32.2. These macros actually generate the loan schedule and erase it if you so desire.

Range Names

Assign range names as listed:

Name	Range
\/	I1
\e	I4
forms	A11..E11
periods	B4
entry	B3..B5

Save the File

Select File Save, and enter a file name such as LOAN.

Use the Loan Schedule Worksheet

To create a loan schedule, enter values in cells B3, B4, and B5. The value in B3 should be the total amount of the loan—not the total purchase price of the item for which the loan is drawn. For example, if you are buying a car for $10,000 and put down $3,000, your loan is for $7,000.

The value in cell B4 should be the total number of regular payments you will make on the loan. If it is a three-year loan with monthly payments, for example, you will make 36 payments.

The value in cell B5 is the interest percentage for a single period of the loan. So, if the annual interest rate is 10.5% and you are making monthly payments, enter 10.5%/12 into cell B5.

After entering the values in the data entry range, hold down the MACRO key (Alt) and press L. 1-2-3 copies formulas down the spreadsheet as needed to calculate the loan payments for each period. As you are paying off the loan, you can enter any extra payments you make into the appropriate cells of column F; the formulas take those entries into account in determining the current balance of the outstanding principal on the loan.

To erase the loan schedule, press MACRO-E.

Print Mailing Labels

Addressing envelopes is the quintessential computer application. You can store people's addresses in a database on the computer, so why not print them from the computer? 1-2-3's database capabilities are good at dealing with this type of information, but printing mailing labels isn't the simplest task.

The trick to printing mailing labels lies in creating the right formulas. We recommend a set of very complex formulas—not to make things difficult but rather to generate the slickest possible labels.

Consider a typical assortment of computer-generated mailing labels. Some of the addresses include name, title, company name, street address, city, state, and zip code. Such an address occupies five lines on an envelope. Other addresses have only name, street address, city, state, and zip code. These occupy three lines. Our address formulas print 3-, 4-, or 5-line addresses without leaving gaps between the lines of the shorter addresses.

Before you can use this macro as-is, you must have access to a printer that handles tractor-feed one-up labels that measure 1 and 7/16 inches from the top of one label to the top of the next one. While you can easily adjust the size of the print range to handle deeper or shallower labels, it is quite another task to print on labels that are supplied two or three across or to print continuous lists of labels without a tractor-feed mechanism on your printer.

Here is how to build the worksheet:

Labels

Enter labels as shown in Figure 32.3. Don't make entries in row 4, in range A8..A12, or in cell B16—these are for formulas that you will enter in a moment. In this worksheet, it's important to enter the labels in exactly the cells shown; some of the macro's operations rely on the location of the labels in the spreadsheet.

Overlapping Labels

Several of the labels in the illustration overlap. Here is a list to help you get them right in your own worksheet:

Cell	Label
B21	Enter addresses into the database
C21	Alphabetize the database
D21	Print address labels
E21	Eject paper
B22	{BRANCH dent}
C22	{BRANCH sort}
D22	{BRANCH print}
E22	{BRANCH adv}

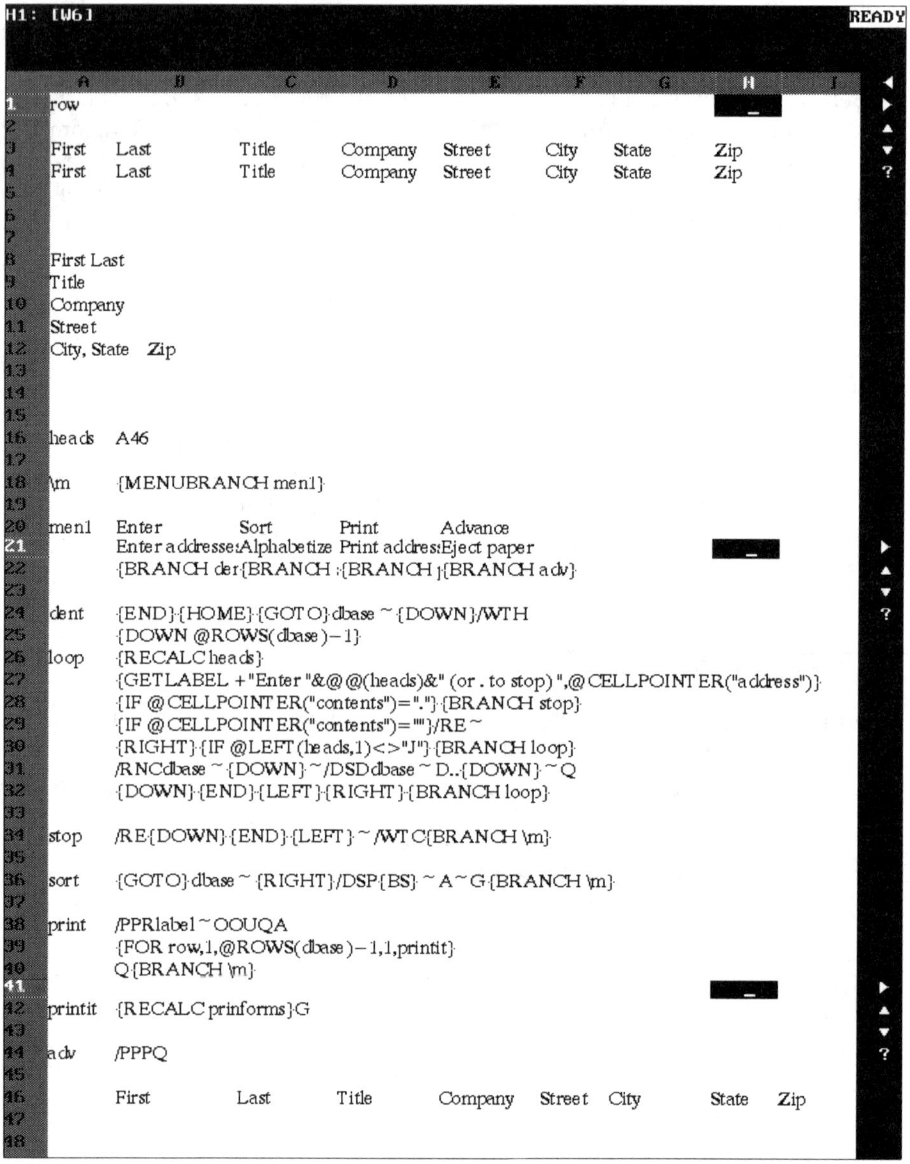

FIGURE 32.3. This figure shows all the labels necessary to create a simple mailing address database and a mailing list printing macro.

Range Names

Assign range names as listed:

Name	Range
first	A4
last	B4
title	C4
company	D4
street	E4
city	F4
state	G4
zip	H4
row	B1
heads	B16
\m	B18
men1	B20
dent	B24
loop	B26
stop	B34
sort	B36
print	B38
printit	B42
adv	B44

Name	Range
dbase	B46..I46
label	A6..E14
prinforms	A1..H12

To assign the first set of range names, select Range Name Labels Down, and indicate range A2..H3. Assign the second set of range names by selecting Range Name Labels Right and indicating range A16..A44. Also select Range Name Labels Right and indicate cell A1. Use the Range Name Create command to assign the final set of range names.

Formulas

Enter formulas in the cells indicated:

Cell	Formula
A4	@INDEX($dbase,0,$row)
B4	@INDEX($dbase,1,$row)
C4	@INDEX($dbase,2,$row)
D4	@INDEX($dbase,3,$row)
E4	@INDEX($dbase,4,$row)
F4	@INDEX($dbase,5,$row)
G4	@INDEX($dbase,6,$row)
H4	@INDEX($dbase,7,$row)
A8	@S(first)&" "&@S(last)
A9	@CHOOSE(@ISSTRING(title)+@ISSTRING(company),@S(street), @S(title)&@S(company),@S(title))

A10	@CHOOSE(@ISSTRING(title)+@ISSTRING(company),@S(city)&",”&@S(state)& " ”&@S(zip),@S(street),@s(company))
A11	@CHOOSE(@ISSTRING(title)+@ISSTRING(company),“”,@S(city)&",”& @S(state)&" ”&@S(zip),@S(street))
A12	@CHOOSE(@ISSTRING(title)+@ISSTRING(company),“”,“”,@S(city)&",”& @S(state)&" ”&@S(zip))
B16	@MID(@CELLPOINTER(“address”),1,(@MID(@CELLPOINTER(“address”),2,1)<> “$”)+1)&“46”

We had to break the last few formulas to make them fit across the page. When you enter those formulas, use space characters only where they appear between quotation marks. Don't leave spaces between the characters shown on one line and the characters that continue the formula on the next line.

Save the File

Select File Save, and enter a file name such as LABELS.

Use the Mailing Label Database

Start the mailing label macro by pressing MACRO-M (Alt-M). The menu offers four choices—Enter, Sort, Print, and Advance. When you select Enter, the macro leads you through a simple data entry routine. You enter addresses across a row, according to the headers in the row. 1-2-3 prompts for each of the entries.

When you have finished a row, the macro drops down to the next row and walks you through the entry of the next record. To stop entering data, type a period at any prompt and press Return. The macro erases any entries in the current row, and the menu reappears.

Alphabetize the database by selecting Sort from the menu. Print all of the addresses on continuous feed labels by aligning the top of a label with your printer's printhead and then selecting Print. Eject the last page of labels by selecting Advance.

Quite obviously this isn't a finished application. It is a bare bones approach to handling an address database for mass mailings. As you develop skill with 1-2-3 and the macro programming language, you may want to enhance our mailing label application, or borrow from it to create your own mail-handling tools.

Racing Dogs

All work and no play makes a spreadsheet a dull program. This short application gives you a taste of spreadsheeting on the wild side.

Racing dogs—that's what it is about. This application simulates a race involving five dogs. You act as the starter and tell the dogs to run by pressing MACRO-T. The dogs (or the vaguest representations of dogs) crawl across the display from the starting line to the finish, and if you've placed any side bets, you may be in the money.

Here's how to build the model:

Column Widths

Set the widths of columns as listed:

Column	Width
B	2
C	40

Labels

Enter labels as shown in Figure 32.4. Omit the values in cells B1 and B2—these are the results of formulas that you will create in a moment. Note that you must begin each of the entries in column D with an apostrophe label prefix.

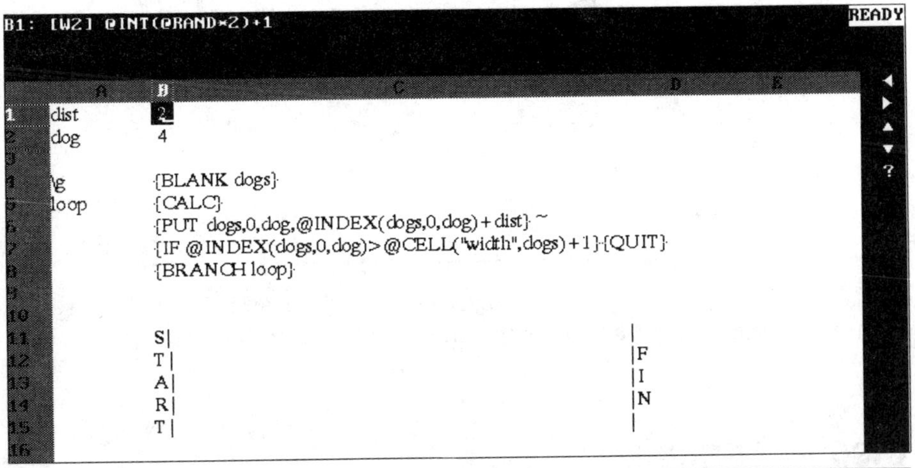

FIGURE 32.4. This spreadsheet lets you simulate a dog race.

Formulas

Enter formulas in the cells indicated:

Cell	Formula
B1	@INT(@RAND*2)+1
B2	@INT(@RAND*5)

Range Names

Assign range names as listed:

Name	Range
dist	B1
dog	B2

Name	Range
\g	B4
loop	B5
dogs	C11..C15

Use the Range Name Labels Right command to assign the first set of names. Use the Range Name Create command to assign the name *dogs*.

Display Formats

Select Range Format +/–, and enter *dogs* as the range to format.

Save the File

Select File Save, and enter a file name such as DOGS.

Running a Race

To run a dog race, press MACRO-G. The dogs charge out of the gates and burn up the track. The excitement builds as they approach the finish line, but even when one has a substantial lead, you can't predict which will come in first. A dog wins when its tracks turn to asterisks.

There is no need to reset the race track before you run another race. When you fire the starting gun, the tracks from the previous race vanish, and the dogs start fresh.

Appendix Drivers Make 1-2-3 Work with Your Hardware

With so many computer hardware manufacturers, it's a wonder that there is so much compatibility among the components that can make up a computer system. Depending on your setup, your software might need to control a keyboard, a monitor, disk drives, expanded and extended memory, math co-processors, printers, plotters, modems, networks, CD drives, tape drives, and so on. Because there are so many brands of hardware and so many different ways in which a computer can talk to a computer component, software manufacturers have developed *drivers* that act as interpreters between the software product and the computer's components.

Lotus 1-2-3's installation program leads you through a driver installation procedure when you first put 1-2-3 on your hard disk. You select the types of printers, plotters, and monitor that you want to be able to use with the software. The installation program places appropriate information in a driver file in the same directory as the 1-2-3 program files, and 1-2-3 reads the driver file each time you start up the spreadsheet.

If you ever want to change your installation options—perhaps because you have added a new printer to your system or bought a new monitor—you do so by reactivating the installation program. There are quite a few options that you can control with device drivers. Here is a list of the options that you will be most likely to want to change over the life of your computer:

- The computer's display in Graphics mode
- The computer's display in Text mode
- The make and model of the text printer on your system

- The make and model of the graphics printer on your system
- The order in which 1-2-3 arranges text and numbers during sorting procedures
- Which mouse button you press to click icons, cells, menu selections, and items in dialog boxes
- The fonts available to the Wysiwyg add-in

Display Drivers

The display driver determines the type of monitor 1-2-3 can use. Your computer might have a CGA, monochrome, EGA, or VGA monitor. The display driver also determines the number of rows and columns that appear on your monitor. While the available drivers allow as many as 50 lines on the display, we describe work in the spreadsheet assuming you have installed a 25-line driver.

Because a display typically can work in either Text mode or Graphics mode, the installation program lets you select a different driver for 1-2-3 to use in each of these modes. In almost any installation, you will use the same driver for both Graphics and Text mode.

Printer Drivers

The list of printers that 1-2-3 can handle is quite extensive. Some of the printers are capable of printing only text; most daisy-wheel printers fall into this category. Other printers can produce both text and graphics; dot-matrix printers, laser printers, ink-jet printers, and some plotters fall into this group. Finally, there are some very specialized plotters that you simply wouldn't use to do regular text printing but that do a superb job creating intricate graphic images. To install a printer, you simply scan the list until you find the make and model name of your printer.

Collating Drivers

The collating driver determines how 1-2-3 arranges spreadsheet entries when you issue the Data Sort command. Chapter 15 contains a short discussion on the way this works. With the "numbers first" driver, numbers sort above letters when you alphabetize a column of entries. The "numbers last" driver places numbers after letters when you sort a database. The ASCII driver causes 1-2-3 to arrange characters during a sort operation based on the numeric ASCII codes of the characters.

Change Mouse Button

Typically, your left mouse button controls the action in commercial software applications, though many programs let you decide which button to use. The installation program lets you activate either of the mouse buttons for use in the spreadsheet.

Change Wysiwyg Fonts

The Install program lets you increase the number of fonts available in Wysiwyg—unless you originally installed the maximum when you first put 1-2-3 on your hard disk. It also lets you tell 1-2-3 that you want to use Bitstream or Bitstream-compatible fonts beyond those supplied with the Wysiwyg software.

Alter Driver Options

When you want to change the installed driver options, first save your work. Then exit 1-2-3 by selecting Quit Yes. Use DOS's CD command to make current the directory that holds 1-2-3's program files. If that directory is named C:\LOTUS, enter *CD C:\LOTUS*.

Start the Install program by entering INSTALL at the DOS prompt. After a time, a screen full of instructions appears on your display. If you are not familiar with these instructions, read them, and then press Enter as the instructions indicate. Assume that you've already run the Setup program if you have been able to run 1-2-3 from your hard disk.

The directions that appear are self-explanatory. Use the UpArrow and DownArrow keys to scroll through the listed options. As you highlight each option, read the descriptive text in the box on the right of the display. The Install program makes choosing drivers as painless as possible. When you find the option that describes the function you want to perform, highlight that selection and press Enter.

When you finish selecting the new driver options, you must save the changes on disk if you want them to take effect when you run 1-2-3. Find the install screen titled Change Selected Equipment, and select Save the Current Driver Set from that menu. Read the resulting display. It explains how to name a driver set. If you like, you can create several sets, but each must have its own name.

A driver set that you name 123 is the one that 1-2-3 uses by default when you start the spreadsheet program by entering 123 at the DOS prompt. Should you create a second set with an alternate set of options, assign a name that describes the contents of the set. For example, you might name a set with an 80 by 50 display driver 80X50, 50ROWS or some similar mnemonic. To use the driver set named 80X50, when you start 1-2-3, enter *123 80X50* at the DOS prompt.

After you follow instructions to name your driver sets, the Install program lets you either return to DOS or work further with the installation options. The procedures to follow are clear from the on-screen instructions.

Index

A

B